Chicago. Ordinances, etc.

LAWS AND ORDINANCES

GOVERNING THE

CITY OF CHICAGO,

JANUARY 1, 1866,

WITH AN

APPENDIX,

CONTAINING THE

FORMER LEGISLATION

RELATING TO THE CITY,

AND NOTES OF

DECISIONS OF THE SUPREME COURT OF ILLINOIS,

RELATING TO CORPORATIONS.

PRINTED AND PUBLISHED BY AUTHORITY OF THE COMMON COUNCIL OF THE CITY.

COMPILED AND ARRANGED BY

JOSEPH E. GARY,

One of the Judges of the Superior Court of Chicago.

E. B. MYERS AND CHANDLER,
LAW BOOKSELLERS AND PUBLISHERS,
No. 111 Lake Street.
1866.

Nathan B. Hyde heirs
gt.

CHARTER OF THE CITY OF CHICAGO.

AN ACT to reduce the Charter of the City of Chicago, and the several Acts amendatory thereof, into one Act, and to revise the same.

CHAPTER I. City and Ward Boundaries.
" II. Officers: Their Election and Appointment.
" III. Powers and Duties of Officers.
" IV. The Common Council: Its General Powers and Duties.
" V. The Treasury Department.
" VI. The Board of Public Works.
" VII. Public Improvements and Special Assessments.
" VIII. Of Taxation.
" IX. Collection of Taxes and Assessments.
" X. The Police Department.
" XI. The Police Court.
" XII. The Fire Department.
" XIII. Schools and School Fund.
" XIV. The Reform School.
" XV. Chicago Water Works.
" XVI. Chicago Sewerage Works.
" XVII. Miscellaneous and Supplementary.

Be it enacted by the People of the State of Illinois, represented in the General Assembly:

CHAPTER I.

CITY AND WARD BOUNDARIES.

Section
1. Inhabitants incorporated; name and powers of the corporation.
2. Corporate limits established.

Section
3. Three divisions established; their boundaries.
4. Division into wards.

Section 1. The inhabitants of all that district of country in the county of Cook and State of Illinois, contained within Corporate powers.

the limits and boundaries hereinafter prescribed, shall be a body politic under the name and style of the City of Chicago; and by that name sue and be sued, complain and defend, in any court; make and use a common seal, and alter it at pleasure; and take and hold, purchase, lease and convey such real and personal or mixed estate as the purposes of the corporation may require, within or without the limits aforesaid.

Corporate limits.

SEC. 2. The corporate limits and jurisdiction of the city of Chicago shall embrace and include within the same all of township thirty-nine north, range fourteen east of the third principal meridian, and all of sections thirty-one, thirty-two, thirty-three, and fractional section thirty-four, in township forty north, range fourteen east of the third principal meridian; together with so much of the waters and bed of lake Michigan as lies within one mile of the shore thereof and east of the territory aforesaid.

North division. South division. West division.

SEC. 3. All that portion of the aforesaid territory lying north of the centre of the main Chicago river and east of the centre of the north branch of said river, shall constitute the *North Division* of said city; all that portion of the aforesaid territory lying south of the centre of the main Chicago river and south and east of the centre of the south branch of said river and of the Illinois and Michigan canal, shall constitute the *South Division* of said city; and all that portion of the aforesaid territory lying west of the centre of the north and south branches of said river and of the Illinois and Michigan canal, shall constitute the *West Division* of said city.

Division into sixteen wards.

SEC. 4. The city of Chicago shall be divided into sixteen wards, as follows:

First Ward. All that part of the South Division of said city which lies south of the centre of the main Chicago river and north of the centre of Monroe street, shall be denominated the first ward.

Second Ward. All that part of the South Division of said city which lies south of the centre of Monroe street, and north of the centre of Harrison street, shall be denominated the second ward.

Third Ward. All that part of the South Division of

said city which lies south of the centre of Harrison street, and north of the centre of Sixteenth street, shall be denominated the third ward.

Fourth Ward. All that part of the South Division of said city which lies south of the centre of Sixteenth street, and east of the centre of Clark street and a line corresponding with the centre of the last named street projected southerly to the city limits, shall be denominated the fourth ward.

Fifth Ward. All that part of the South Division of said city which lies south of the centre of Sixteenth street, and west of the centre of Clark street and a line corresponding to the centre of the last named street projected southerly to the city limits, shall be denominated the fifth ward.

Sixth Ward. All that part of the West Division of said city which lies south of the centre of Van Buren street, and east of the centre of Jefferson street continued to the south branch of the Chicago river, shall be denominated the sixth ward.

Seventh Ward. All that part of the West Division of said city which lies south of the centre of Van Buren street, west of the centre of Jefferson street continued to the south branch of the Chicago river, and east of the centre of Morgan street continued to the south branch of the Chicago river, shall be denominated the seventh ward.

Eighth Ward. All that part of the West Division of said city which lies south of the centre of Van Buren street, and west of the centre of Morgan street continued to the south branch of the Chicago river, shall be denominated the eighth ward.

Ninth Ward. All that part of the West Division of said city which lies south of the centre of Fourth street, west of the centre of Curtis street and Aberdeen street, and north of the centre of Van Buren street, shall be denominated the ninth ward.

Tenth Ward. All that part of the West Division of said city which lies south of the centre of Randolph street, east of the centre of Curtis street and Aberdeen street, and north of the centre of Van Buren street, shall be denominated the tenth ward.

Eleventh Ward. All that part of the West Division of said city which lies south of the centre of Fourth street, east of the centre of Curtis street, and north of the centre of Randolph street, shall be denominated the eleventh ward.

Twelfth Ward. All that part of the West Division of said city which lies north of the centre of Fourth street continued to the north branch of the Chicago river, shall be denominated the twelfth ward.

Thirteenth Ward. All that part of the North Division of said city which lies north of the centre of North avenue, shall be denominated the thirteenth ward.

Fourteenth Ward. All that part of the North Division of said city which lies south of the centre of North avenue, and north of the centre of Division street, shall be denominated the fourteenth ward.

Fifteenth Ward. All that part of the North Division of said city which lies south of the centre of Division street, and north of the centre of Huron street continued to lake Michigan and to the north branch of the Chicago river, shall be denominated the fifteenth ward.

Sixteenth Ward. All that part of the North Division of said city which lies south of the centre of Huron street continued to lake Michigan and to the north branch of the Chicago river, and north of the centre of the main Chicago river, shall be denominated the sixteenth ward.

CHAPTER II.

OFFICERS: THEIR ELECTION AND APPOINTMENT.

SECTION
1. Officers composing the city government.
2. Division of wards into election districts.
3. Time of municipal election; publication of notice.
4. Commencement of term of office.
5. Officers elected by the people; their term of office.
6. Election of aldermen and constables.

SECTION
7. Wards entitled to two aldermen; their term of office; divided into classes; vacancies, how created and filled.
8. A tie to be determined by lot.
9. Board of public works and board of police; election of commissioners; their term of office; vacancies, how supplied; qualification of commissioners.

SECTION
10. Removal of commissioners; mode of procedure.
11. Board of education, how constituted; election of inspectors and their term of office.
12. Guardians of reform school; their appointment and term of office.
13. Assessors; their qualification and appointment.
14. Inspectors of election, how appointed.
15. Bridge-tenders, bridewell keeper, and bellmen, how appointed.
16. Officers appointable by the mayor with the advice of the council; their term of office; appointments to fill vacancies.

SECTION
17. Officers removable by the council; charges to be preferred; mode of trial.
18. Vacancy in office of mayor; other vacancies.
19. Official bonds, when to be filed; no city officer to be taken as surety.
20. Who qualified to hold office; special disability.
21. Elections, how conducted; opening and closing of the polls; returns; clerk to notify persons elected.
22. Qualification of electors; challenge; oath to be taken.
23. Electors, when exempt from arrest; illegal voting punishable.

SECTION 1. The municipal government of the city shall consist of a common council, composed of the mayor, and two aldermen from each ward. The other officers of the corporation shall be as follows: *Officers of city government.*

A clerk, a comptroller, a board of public works, a city engineer, a board of police, a superintendent of police, a school agent, a board of education, a superintendent of schools, a board of guardians of the reform school, a commissioner of the reform school, a counsel to the corporation, a city attorney, a treasurer, a collector, a city physician, a board of assessors, two or more police justices, a clerk of the police court, one chief, and a first and second assistant engineers of the fire department, one or more harbor masters, one inspector of fish, three inspectors of elections for each ward or election precinct, and as many bridge-tenders, firemen, constables, policemen, sealers of weights and measures, inspectors, measurers, weighers, gaugers, keepers and assistants of work-houses, hospitals and bridewell or house of correction, bellmen, and such other officers and agents as may be provided for by this act, or the common council may, from time to time, direct.

(*Offices of chief and assistant engineers of fire department abolished*, Sec. 35, *post*, 199.)

SEC. 2. The common council may divide the wards of said city into so many and such convenient election districts as to the said common council shall seem proper. Each ward or district shall constitute an election precinct, and the inspectors of election and the places for holding elections therein, for city, town, county and state officers, shall be appointed by the common council. All elections for state, county and town officers in said wards and precincts *Election districts.* *Elections for state, county and town officers.*

shall be conducted, and returns thereof made to the county or town clerk, as provided by the law regulating state, county and town elections. And whenever at any election it shall appear that there have been more than six hundred votes polled in any election precinct, it is hereby made the duty of the common council, at least two months before the recurrence of another election, to divide such precinct into two or more districts, and appoint places for holding elections therein.

Municipal election.

SEC. 3. The municipal election in said city shall be held on the third Tuesday of April in each year, at which time there shall be elected by the qualified voters of said city, all officers to be elected at the general municipal election.

Notice of election.

Six days' previous public notice of said election shall be given by the city clerk, by publication in one or more newspapers published in said city, and no special election shall be hereafter held in said city, for the election of city officers, except as in this act provided.

Commencement of municipal year.

SEC. 4. The municipal officers to be chosen at the annual election, shall enter upon the duties of their respective offices on the first Monday of May succeeding their election.

Officers elected by the people.

SEC. 5. The mayor, city attorney, treasurer, collector, clerk of the police court, and chief and first and second assistant engineers of the fire department, shall be elected by the people, and shall hold their respective offices for the term of two years, and until their successors shall be elected and qualified. The person having the highest number of votes cast in the whole city for either of such offices, shall be declared elected.

(*Provision for election of engineers superseded,* Sec. 35, *post,* 199.)

Officers elected by wards.

SEC. 6. At the annual municipal election, the electors in their respective wards shall vote for one alderman and one constable, and the persons receiving the highest number of votes cast in the ward for such offices respectively, shall be declared elected.

Aldermen elected for two years.

SEC. 7. The several wards of the city shall be respectively represented in the common council by two aldermen, who shall be residents thereof, and who shall, except as herein otherwise provided, hold their offices respectively for two years from and after the first Monday in May next succeeding their election. They shall be divided into two classes, each class consisting of one alderman from each ward. The seats of the first class shall be vacated at the end of the first year, and of the second class at the expiration of the second year, so that one alderman from each ward may be annually elected. In all cases where two aldermen are to be chosen from the same ward at any annual election, the alderman having the highest number of votes shall be declared elected for two years, and the candidate having the next highest number of votes, for one year; and in case of the two successful candidates having an equal number of votes, the term of service to which they shall be respectively entitled, shall be determined by the casting of lots in the presence of the common council, and the result shall be entered upon their proceedings. If any alderman remove from the ward represented by him, or shall engage or continue in any service, business or employment causing a continuous absence from the city for more than four months, his office shall thereby become vacant; and whenever any vacancy shall occur in the office of any alderman, the common council shall, within ten days after the happening of such vacancy, order a new election, provided that more than six months of the term shall then remain unexpired.

Divided into classes.

Vacancies, how created and filled.

SEC. 8. Whenever there shall fail to be an election of any officer voted for by the people, in consequence of two or more candidates receiving the highest and an equal number of votes for the same office, the election shall be determined by the casting of lots in the presence of the common council, and the result shall be entered upon their proceedings.

A tie, how decided.

SEC. 9. The board of public works and the board of police shall each consist of three commissioners, in addition to the mayor, who shall be chosen by the people, one from the north, one from the south, and one from the west divisions of said city. The person having the highest number of votes in the whole city for either of such offices shall be declared elected. Said commissioners, when elected, shall

Board of public works and board of police, how constituted.

Term of office. hold their office, the commissioners of the board of public works for the term of six years, and the police commissioners for the term of three years, and until the election and qualification of their successors. The term of office of one commissioner of each board shall expire every year and every second year respectively, so that one commissioner shall be elected to the board of police every year and to the board of public works every second year from the division of the city in which the commissioner resides whose term of office expires. Vacancies, how filled. Should a vacancy occur, it shall be filled by appointment by the mayor, with the advice and consent of the common council of said city, until the next regular city election, when the qualified voters of said city may, as in other cases, fill such vacancy by an election of a successor, who shall hold his office for the unexpired term; said commissioners shall be elected in the same manner as is provided for the election of general city officers, by general ticket, by the qualified voters of the whole city; and no Qualification of commissioners. person shall be elected a commissioner of either of said boards, unless he has been a resident of said city at least three years, and a resident freeholder in the division of said city for which he is elected at least one year immediately preceding his election.

(*Mayor no longer member of either of said boards*, Sec. 19, *post*, 196. *Mode of election and term of office of police commissioners changed*, Secs. 11, 12, *post*, 193. *Mode of filling vacancy changed*, Sec. 17, *post*, 196.)

Removal of commissioners. SEC. 10. Any commissioner of the board of public works or of the board of police, may at any time be removed from office for any misdemeanor, malfeasance or delinquency in office, by the judge of the circuit court of Cook county, on charges in writing, to be presented against him by the mayor Mode of procedure. or the common council. On the hearing before said judge, witnesses may be produced and sworn, both in support of the allegations and against them. Five days' notice shall be given to such member, by service of a copy of such charges. The judge may proceed to hear such allegations, either in term time or in vacation, and may adjourn such hearing from time to time. No member of either of said boards shall perform any duties as such member, while such allegations are pending against him.

SEC. 11. The board of education shall consist of fifteen school inspectors, to be elected by the common council, on or before the first Monday of June next. The said board shall be divided into three classes, of five members each; those of the first class shall vacate their seats at the expiration of the first year, those of the second class at the expiration of the second, and those of the third class at the expiration of the third year; and the common council shall, annually, on or before the first Monday of June, elect five inspectors to succeed those whose term of office expires. The inspectors so elected shall hold their offices for three years from the said first Monday of June.

Board of education, how constituted.

Their election, and term of office.

(*Repealed, and new section enacted*, Sec. 8, *post*, 192, and Sec. 4, *post*, 191.)

SEC. 12. The board of guardians of the reform school shall consist of the comptroller and six guardians, to be appointed by the mayor, by and with the advice and consent of the common council. Said board shall be divided into three classes, of two members each; those of the first class shall vacate their seats at the expiration of the first year, those of the second class at the expiration of the second, and those of the third class at the expiration of the third year. There shall be appointed, annually, on or before the first Monday of June, two guardians to succeed those whose term of office expires. The guardians so appointed shall hold their offices for three years from the said first Monday of June, and until the appointment and qualification of their successors.

Guardians of reform school.

Their appointment, and term of office.

SEC. 13. The board of assessors shall consist of three assessors, who shall be freeholders in said city, one from each of the three divisions of the city, who shall be appointed on the second Monday of May in each year, or as soon thereafter as may be, and continue in office one year. The common council may increase the number of assessors so that said board shall consist of two members from each division of the city, if they think proper.

Assessors, their qualification and appointment.

(*Mode of appointment of assessors changed*, Sec. 28, *post*, 188, and Sec. 1, *post*, 191.)

Inspectors of election.

SEC. 14. The inspectors of election shall be appointed annually, by the common council, at least ten days before the annual municipal election.

Bridge-tenders and bridewell keeper.

SEC. 15. All bridge-tenders, keepers and assistants of work-houses, bridewell or house of correction, and bell-men, shall be appointed annually, by the mayor, and shall be removable at the pleasure of the mayor or common council.

(*Mode of appointment of bridge-tenders changed*, Sec. 27, *post*, 187, *and of bridewell keeper*, Sec. 1, *post*, 191.)

Other officers, their mode of appointment and term of office.

SEC. 16. All other officers mentioned in this act, and not otherwise specially provided for, shall be appointed by the mayor, by and with the advice and consent of the common council, biennially, on or before the second Monday of May, or as soon thereafter as may be, and shall respectively continue in office two years from the said second Monday of May, and until the appointment and qualification of their successors. Officers elected or appointed to fill vacancies, shall respectively hold for the unexpired term only, and until the election or appointment and qualification of their successors.

Officers to fill vacancies.

(*Mode of appointment of harbor master changed*, Sec. 27, *post*, 187; *and of clerk, city physician, fish inspector, sealer of weights and measures, inspectors, gaugers, and weighers*, Sec. 1, *post*, 191; *and of school agent*, Sec. 9, *post*, 192.)

Removals from office.

SEC. 17. Every person appointed to any office by the common council, or by the mayor with the advice and consent of the common council, and every person elected to any office by the people, for whose removal from office no other provision has been specially provided by this act, may be removed from such office by a vote of two-thirds of all the aldermen authorized by law to be elected. But no officer shall be removed except for cause, nor unless furnished with the charges and heard in his defense, and the common council shall have power to compel the attendance of witnesses and the production of papers when necessary for the purposes of such trial, and shall proceed, within ten days, to hear and determine upon the merits of the case, and if such officer neglect to appear and answer to such charges, then the common council may declare the office vacant; and any

Charges to be preferred.

Trial.

officer may be suspended until the disposition of charges, when preferred. Suspension.

SEC. 18. When any vacancy shall happen by death, resignation, removal or otherwise, in the office of mayor, such vacancy shall be filled by a new election, and the common council shall order a new election within ten days after the happening of such vacancy, provided more than six months of the term shall then remain unexpired. Any vacancy occasioned by the death, removal, resignation or refusal to serve, of any other city officer elected by the people, or appointed by the mayor with the advice and consent of the common council, may be filled by appointment by the mayor, with the advice and consent of the council, except in cases where a different provision is herein specially made for filling such vacancy. The common council, with the like exception, may fill any vacancy occurring in any office, to which, by this act, they have the power of election or appointment.

Vacancy in office of mayor, how filled.

Other vacancies.

(*Mode of filling vacancy in office of police commissioner*, Sec. 17, *post*, 196.)

SEC. 19. All city officers who are required, by the provisions of this act, or by any legal ordinance passed by the common council, to give bonds for the faithful performance of their official duty, shall file their bonds with the city clerk within fifteen days after their election or appointment, and he shall record the same, when approved, in a book kept for that purpose. When bonds are not filed with the city clerk within fifteen days after the votes shall have been officially canvassed, or after the appointment shall have been made, the person so in default shall be deemed to have refused said office, and the same shall be filled by appointment as in other cases. If, in any case, any official bond so filed, shall not be approved, the officer filing the same shall furnish a new and satisfactory bond within fifteen days after such disapproval, and in case of failure so to do, he shall be deemed to have refused said office, and the same shall be filled as above provided. No alderman or other city officer shall be taken as surety upon any bond, note or other obligation made to the city. No city officer, required to give bond as aforesaid, shall enter upon the

Official bonds, when to be filed.

No city officer to be taken as surety.

discharge of the duties of his office until such bond shall have been filed and approved as by this act provided.

Eligibility to office.

SEC. 20. All citizens of the United States, qualified to vote at any election held under this act, shall be qualified to hold any office created by this act, except in cases where a different provision has been herein especially made; but no person shall be eligible to any office or place under this or any other act in relation to said city, who is now or may hereafter be a defaulter to said city, or to the State of Illinois, or any county thereof; and any person shall be considered a defaulter who has refused or neglected, or may hereafter refuse or neglect, for thirty days after demand made, to account for and pay over to the party authorized to receive the same, any public money which may have come into his possession. And if any person holding any such office or place shall become a defaulter whilst in office, the office or place shall thereupon become vacant.

Public defaulter disqualified.

Elections, how conducted.

SEC. 21. The manner of conducting and voting at elections to be held under this act, and contesting the same, the keeping of the poll lists, canvassing of the votes and certifying the returns, shall be the same, as nearly as may be, as is now or may hereafter be provided by law at general state elections: *Provided*, The council shall have power to regulate elections. The voting shall be by ballot, and the inspectors of elections shall take the same oath and shall have the same power and authority as inspectors of general elections. The polls shall be opened by the inspectors at eight o'clock in the morning, and kept open until seven o'clock in the evening, and every violation of this provision shall subject the inspectors so offending to a penalty of one hundred dollars. After the closing of the polls, the ballots shall be counted in the manner required by law, and the returns shall be returned sealed to the city clerk within three days after the election, and thereupon the common council shall meet and canvass the same, and declare the result of the election. It shall be the duty of the clerk to notify all persons elected or appointed to office, of their election or appointment, and unless such persons shall respectively qualify within fifteen days thereafter, the offices shall become vacant.

Polls, when to be opened and closed.

Returns.

Notice to officers elected.

SEC. 22. No person shall be entitled to vote at any election under this act, who is not entitled to vote at state elections, and has not been a resident of said city at least six months next preceding the election; he shall moreover have been an actual resident of the ward or election precinct in which he votes, for thirty days previous to the election, and if required by any person qualified to vote thereat, shall take the following oath before he is permitted to vote: *Provided*, That the voter shall be deemed a resident of the ward in which he is accustomed to lodge: **Qualification of voters.**

"I swear, (*or* affirm,) that I am of the age of twenty-one years, that I am a citizen of the United States, (*or* was a resident of this State at the time of the adoption of the Constitution,) and have been a resident of this State one year, and a resident of this city six months immediately preceding this election, and am now, and have been for thirty days last past, a resident of this ward, (*or* election precinct,) and have not voted at this election." **Oath.**

And if required by any legal voter, such voter shall also swear or affirm to his place of residence, specifying the particular place and house in which he resides, and stating how long he has there resided, and his business or employment, and if he has not resided in such house for thirty days immediately preceding such election, he shall state where and in what house he has resided for the last thirty days. No further evidence of the right to vote shall be required in any case, at any municipal or other election. **Voter, if required, to specify his place of residence.**

SEC. 23. The persons entitled to vote at any election held under this act, shall not be arrested on civil process within said city upon the day on which said election is held, and all persons illegally voting at any election under this act, shall be punishable according to the laws of this State. **Exemption from arrest on election day.** **Illegal voting.**

CHAPTER III.

POWERS AND DUTIES OF OFFICERS.

SECTION
1. Officers to be sworn before entering upon their duties.
2. Duties of mayor; his salary; shall be a member *ex officio* of the boards of police and public works; may administer oaths.
3. Veto power of mayor.
4. Acting mayor, when and how appointed.

SECTION
5. Members of the council *ex officio* fire wardens and conservators of the peace; exempted from jury duty.
6. Clerk to keep seal and records; certified copies made evidence; may administer oaths.
7. Duties of counsel to the corporation, and city attorney.
8. Duties of assessors.
9. Duties of harbor master.
10. Duties of fish inspector.
11. Constables to give bond; their liabilities; powers.
12. Duties of city physician.
13. Other duties of officers may be prescribed by council; their compensation and bonds.

SECTION
14. Certain officers to give bond; conditions thereof.
15. Corporation newspaper; publication of ordinances and other proceedings.
16. Refusal to deliver official papers; penalty.
17. Officers to be commissioned by warrant.
18. Salaries to be established by council.
19. Fees received by salaried officers to be paid into the treasury.
20. Payment of salaries.
21. Recorder's salary.
22. Guardians of reform school and members of board of education to serve without compensation; not to be interested in contracts.

Oath of office.

SECTION 1. Every person chosen or appointed to an executive, judicial or administrative office under this act, shall, before he enters on the duties of his office, take and subscribe the oath of office prescribed in the constitution of this State, and file the same, duly certified by the officer before whom it was taken, with the city clerk.

Mayor's duties.

SEC. 2. The mayor shall preside over the meetings of the common council, and take care that the laws of the State and the ordinances of the city are duly enforced, respected and observed, and that all other executive officers of the city discharge their respective duties. He shall, from time to time, give the common council such information, and recommend such measures, as he may deem advantageous to the city. He shall have a salary of thirty-five hundred dollars per annum in full compensation of all official services devolved upon him by this or any subsequent act. He shall be a member *ex officio* of the board of police and of the board of public works, and shall be clothed with all the power and authority and be subject to all the general duties and responsibilities of a commissioner of each of said boards: *Provided, however*, That he shall not act as a commissioner of the board of public works in making any special assessment for any public work or improvement, nor shall he be required to give a bond to the city as a member of either of said boards. The mayor shall likewise have power, *ex officio*, to administer any oath authorized to be taken by the laws of this State.

Salary.

Ex officio member of boards of police and public works.

To administer oaths.

(*Mayor no longer member of the board of police or of the board of public works*, Sec. 19, *post*, 196.)

SEC. 3. Every act, ordinance or resolution, passed by the common council, before it shall take effect and within five days after its passage, shall be presented, duly certified by the city clerk, to the mayor for his approbation. If he approve, he shall sign it, if not, he shall return it with his objections in writing to the city clerk, and the clerk shall submit said objections to the common council at their next regular meeting, who shall enter said objections upon their record, and proceed to reconsider the matter, and if, after such reconsideration, two-thirds of all the members elected shall agree to pass the same, it shall take effect as an act or law of the corporation. If the mayor shall not return any act, ordinance or resolution so presented to him, within five days, it shall take effect in the same manner as if he had signed it. Mayor's veto.

SEC. 4. In case of a vacancy in the office of mayor, or of his being unable to perform the duties of his office, by reason of absence or sickness, the common council shall appoint by ballot one of their number to preside over their meetings, whose official designation shall be, acting mayor. And the alderman so appointed shall be vested with all the powers and perform all the duties of mayor until the mayor shall resume his office, or the vacancy be filled by a new election. Vacancy in office of mayor. Acting mayor.

SEC. 5. The members of the common council shall be fire wardens and conservators of the peace, and shall be exempted from jury duty during their term of office. Members of council to be fire wardens. Exemption.

SEC. 6. The clerk shall keep the corporate seal, and make a record of the proceedings of the common council, at whose meetings it shall be his duty to attend; and copies of all papers duly filed in his office, and transcripts from the records of the proceedings of the common council, certified by him under the corporate seal, shall be evidence in all courts, in like manner as if the originals were produced. He shall also have power to administer any oath authorized to be taken by the laws of this State. City clerk, his duties.

SEC. 7. The counsel to the corporation shall be the chief officer of the law department of the city. He shall, with the assistance of the city attorney, and subject to the directions of the comptroller, conduct all the law business Counsel to the corporation and city attorney, their duties.

of the corporation and of the departments thereof, and all other law business in which the city shall be interested, when so ordered by the corporation. Said officers shall hold their office in such place as the city may provide, and, when required, shall furnish written opinions upon subjects submitted to them by the mayor or common council, or any other department of the municipal government. The city attorney shall keep a docket of all the cases to which the city may be a party in any court of record, in which shall be briefly entered all steps taken in each cause, and which shall, at all times, be open to the inspection of the mayor, comptroller, or any committee of the common council. It shall also be the duty of said officers to draft all ordinances, bonds, contracts, leases, conveyances, and such other instruments of writing as may be required by the business of the city; to examine and inspect tax and assessment rolls, and all proceedings in reference to the levying and collection of taxes and assessments; and to perform such other duties as may be prescribed by the charter and ordinances of the city.

Attorney to keep a docket.

(*Further provision as to corporation counsel and city attorney*, Sec. 2, *post*, 191.)

Assessors, their powers and duties.

SEC. 8. The board of assessors shall perform all the duties in relation to the assessing of property, for the purpose of levying the taxes imposed by the common council. In the performance of their duties they shall have the same powers as are or may be given by law to county or town assessors, and be subject to the same liabilities.

Harbor-master, his duties.

SEC. 9. It shall be the duty of the harbor master to enforce all ordinances, and provisions of this act, in relation to the harbor.

Fish inspector, his duties.

SEC. 10. It shall be the duty of the fish inspector to inspect all pickled or salted fresh-water fish sold or received for sale, or on consignment, in the city of Chicago. Any person or persons bringing or causing to be brought to the city of Chicago, for the purpose of sale, any fresh-water fish, shall have the same duly inspected by the said inspector before such fish shall be sold or in any way disposed of; and it shall be the duty of every person having such fish in his possession, for the purpose of selling or of dealing in the same, and of every consignee having fish on consignment, before the said fish shall be sold or in anywise disposed of, to give notice to the inspector, and have such fish duly inspected and branded; and for this purpose, such person shall arrange the packages in a convenient manner, and have them in some suitable place. It shall be the duty of the inspector, on due application of any person or persons having such fish in possession, to repair to the place of deposit of such fish, if the same shall be within the limits of the city of Chicago, and inspect the same with as little delay as possible. The said inspector shall procure sealed weights, and carefully weigh all fish offered for inspection; and to entitle said inspector to grant a certificate of due inspection, or to brand the packages as duly inspected, he shall first find that the contents and weights of the several packages are as follows, viz.: **Weight of packages.** Each barrel shall contain 200 lbs.; each half barrel shall contain 100 lbs.; each quarter barrel shall contain 50 lbs.; and each eighth barrel shall contain 25 lbs. **Brand.** Such inspector shall, also, on branding any package of fish, plainly and distinctly mark on the head of each package, in some indelible manner, the kind, quantity and quality of fish contained in each package, respectively, together with his name and the year and month in which the same shall have been inspected. **Fees.** The inspector shall be entitled to the following fees for the performance of his duties, viz.: For unheading, heading, weighing, repacking, brining, and inspecting and branding each barrel, 20 cents; each half barrel, 10 cents; each quarter barrel, 5 cents; each extra hoop, 5 cents; each extra head, 20 cents. The inspector shall not put his brand upon any package of fish, as duly inspected, unless the same be well hooped and headed, and in all respects sufficient to retain brine, and also be in good shipping condition. **Record.** He shall keep a record of the number of packages and sizes, and of the kinds and qualities of fish, and for whom inspected, each year; and shall make a report of the same to the common council, on the first day of January in each year. **Office.** He shall keep an office at a convenient place, on or near the Chicago river, which shall be kept open during business hours, and in which the inspector shall at all times have some person, during his absence, to receive orders. No person holding the office of fish inspector for said city of Chicago, nor shall his employees or assistants, or either of them, buy or sell, or deal in, or in anywise be interested in, any fish sold or received for sale in the city of Chicago. He shall, before entering on the discharge of the duties of his said office, give bond, with two good and sufficient sureties, in the penal sum of five thousand dollars, and running to the People of the State of Illinois, and conditioned that he will well and faithfully perform the duties of said office, and satisfy all damages that may legally be demanded of him by virtue of the provisions hereof. Any fish inspector violating, refusing or failing to comply with any of the provisions of this section, so far as they are made incumbent upon him, shall, for every offense, be liable to a fine of not less than five dollars nor more than one hundred dollars; which said fine may be collected in the name and for the use of the city of Chicago; and shall also be subject to immediate removal from office. Said inspector shall have the right to appoint and remove at pleasure, one or more assistants, who shall have the same right to brand all packages inspected by either of them in the name of said inspector; but each assistant shall have some distinctive mark, with which he shall designate each package inspected by himself, so as to indicate by whom the inspection was actually made; and the said inspector shall have the right to take bond, with sufficient penalty and security, running to himself, from each of the assistants appointed by himself, and of the same tenor as the bond herein required to be executed by said inspector; and the said inspector shall be liable for the acts of his said assistants, and may sue on the bonds of any of them, to recover any damages that he may have suffered, by reason of their misfeasance or malfeasance. The said inspector shall have the right to sue, in any court having jurisdiction of the action, for his fees for services performed, either by himself or his assistants by virtue hereof.

Inspector prohibited from dealing in fish. Bond. Penalties. Power to appoint assistants. Bond of assistants.

Constables to give bonds.

SEC. 11. Every person appointed or elected to the office of constable, shall, before he enters upon the duties of his office, with two or more sureties to be approved by the common council, execute, in presence of the clerk of the city, an instrument in writing by which such constable and securities shall jointly and severally agree to pay to each and every person who may be entitled thereto, all such sums of money as the said constable may be liable to pay by reason or on account of any summons, execution, distress warrant, or other process which shall be delivered to him for collection. The clerk shall certify the approval of the common council on such instrument, and file the same; and a copy certified by the clerk, under the corporate seal, shall be presumptive evidence, in all courts, of the execution thereof by such constable and his sureties; and all actions thereon shall be prosecuted within two years after the expiration of the year for which the constable named therein shall have been appointed or elected, and may be brought in the name of the person or persons entitled to the money collected by virtue of such instruments. No constable appointed or elected under this act, shall have power to serve any civil process out of the city limits, except in cases of persons fleeing therefrom, and to commit on execution, where the defendant shall have been arrested within the city.

Actions thereon, how brought.

Powers of.

SEC. 12. The city physician shall attend and administer to all sick persons confined in any police station-house, bridewell, work-house, house of refuge or other city prison, and shall attend to such other duties as may be prescribed by the board of health or common council.

City physician, his duties.

SEC. 13. The common council shall have power, from time to time, to require further and other duties of all officers whose duties are herein prescribed, and prescribe the powers and duties of all officers appointed or elected to any office under this act, whose duties are not herein specifically mentioned, and fix their compensation. They may also require bonds to be given to the city of Chicago by all officers, for the faithful performance of their duties.

Council may impose other duties

May require bonds.

SEC. 14. The comptroller, treasurer, collector, and school agent, shall severally, before they enter on the duties of their respective offices, execute a bond to the city of Chicago, in such sum, and with such sureties, as the common council shall approve; conditioned that they shall faithfully execute the duties of their offices, and account for and pay over all

Certain officers to give bonds.

How conditioned.

moneys and other property received by them; which bonds, with the approval of the common council, certified thereon by the clerk, shall be filed with the clerk.

Corporation newspaper, how designated.

SEC. 15. The common council, at their annual meeting on the first Monday in May, in each year, or within not to exceed thirty days thereafter, shall designate one public newspaper printed in said city, in which shall be published all ordinances, and other proceedings and matters required in any case by this act, or by the by-laws and ordinances of the common council, to be published in the corporation newspaper. And if the proprietors of the newspaper so designated, shall at any time during the year suspend the publication thereof, or decline longer to publish said proceedings, another newspaper shall be designated in its stead. The common council may also, in its discretion, provide for the publication of said ordinances and other proceedings, or such portion of the same as it may think proper, in some newspaper printed in the German language.

(*Provisions as to job printing*, Sec. 35, *post*, 190. *Further provisions as to newspaper printed in the German language*, Sec. 37, *post*, 200.)

Officers to transfer official papers.

SEC. 16. If any person, having been an officer in said city, shall not, within ten days after notification and request, deliver to his successor in office all property, papers and effects of every description in his possession belonging to said city, or appertaining to the office he held, he shall forfeit and pay for the use of the city, one hundred dollars, besides all damages caused by his neglect or refusal so to deliver. And such successor shall and may recover possession of the books, papers and property appertaining to his office, in the manner prescribed by the laws of this State.

Penalty.

Successor may recover possession thereof.

Officers, how commissioned.

SEC. 17. All persons elected or appointed to any office under this act may be commissioned by warrant under the corporate seal, signed by the mayor or presiding officer of the common council, and clerk.

Salaries to be established by council.

SEC. 18. The common council may, by ordinance, establish salaries, as a fixed compensation for all officers of said city whose salaries are not named herein, and may provide for their removal from office, in case they receive or retain other or greater fees than so paid or fixed by the corporation for their services.

(*Further provisions as to salaries*, Sec. 26, *post*, 187.)

Fees received by salaried officers to be paid into treasury.

SEC. 19. All fees, perquisites and emoluments of office whatever, by way of compensation for the performance of any official duty or duties, are hereby expressly prohibited to be retained by any officer whose compensation is provided to be paid by a salary, to be fixed by the common council under this act; and all fees, perquisites and emoluments whatever, received or paid, or payable, to any officer, justice of the peace, mayor, clerk, attorney, collector, treasurer, commissioner of public works, comptroller, or other person, whose compensation is to be so paid by a fixed salary, shall belong to, and be paid by such person or persons, into the treasury of said city, the same as all other revenues belonging thereto; and any violation of this provision shall subject the offender to removal from his office, and the amount received by him shall be recoverable by action of debt or assumpsit, in favor of said city.

Salaries, how payable.

SEC. 20. All salaries shall be payable monthly or quarterly out of the appropriate fund, voted by the common council to pay the same, upon the warrant of the comptroller, as in other cases.

Recorder's salary.

SEC. 21. The common council shall have power to pay to the recorder of the city of Chicago, such compensation from time to time as said city council may deem proper, in addition to the salary prescribed by law.

Guardians of reform school and members of board of education to serve without compensation.

SEC. 22. No member of the board of guardians of the reform school, or of the board of education, shall receive any compensation for any services he may perform, nor shall any teacher, agent or employee of either board sell, dispose of or be interested in any articles purchased, or work done, for the school or schools. Nor shall he be interested in any contract, loan, or anything else whereby he may receive any commission, interest, or other profits from the fund appropriated to the reform school or public schools, under the penalty of having his office immediately declared vacant by the common council

CHAPTER IV.

THE COMMON COUNCIL — ITS GENERAL POWERS AND DUTIES.

SECTION
1. Mayor and aldermen constitute the common council; to determine time and place of meetings; mayor to preside; in his absence, any alderman; quorum.
2. No member to receive any compensation, hold any lucrative office, or be interested in any contract.
3. To hold stated meetings; special meetings, how called; to determine rules of proceedings; be the judge of the election of its members, and compel their attendance.
4. Ordinances, petitions and communications to be referred to committees; report of committees to be deferred and published on request of two aldermen.

SECTION
5. No vote to be reconsidered at special meetings unless as many are present as when such vote was taken.
6. Power to require reports from city officers.
7. On all ordinances to appropriate money, impose taxes or borrow money, the ayes and noes to be taken; the votes of a majority of the board requisite to their passage.
8. Council to have general control of finances and property; enumeration of powers.
9. Power to establish cemeteries, and make regulations therefor; the board of public works to superintend the grounds; sale of lots; penalty for violation of rules and regulations.

Common council, how constituted. SECTION 1. The mayor and aldermen shall constitute the common council of said city. The common council shall meet at such times and places as they shall by resolution direct. President. The mayor, when present, shall preside at all meetings of the common council, and shall have only a casting vote. In his absence any one of the aldermen may be appointed to preside. Quorum. A majority of the persons elected as aldermen shall constitute a quorum.

No member shall receive compensation, etc. SEC. 2. No member of the common council shall, during the period for which he was elected, receive any compensation for his services, or be appointed to, or be competent to hold, any office of which the emoluments are paid from the city treasury, or paid by fees directed to be paid by any act or ordinance of the common council, or be directly or indirectly interested in any contract, the expenses or consideration whereof are to be paid under any ordinance of the common council.

Council to hold stated meetings. SEC. 3. The common council shall hold stated meetings, and the mayor or any two aldermen may call special meetings, by notice to each of the members of said council, served personally, or left at his usual place of abode. Petitions and remonstrances may be presented to the common council, and the council shall determine the rules of its own proceedings, and be the judge of the election and qualifica-

To determine its own rules, and be judge of the election of members.

tions of its own members, and have power to compel the attendance of absent members.

SEC. 4. All ordinances, petitions and communications to the common council, shall, unless by unanimous consent, be referred to appropriate committees, and only acted on by the council at a subsequent meeting, on the report of the committee having the same in charge. Any report of a committee of the council may be deferred to the next regular meeting of the same, and the publication of said report in the corporation newspaper required, by request of any two aldermen present.

Ordinances to be referred to committees.

Report of committee to be deferred and published on request of two aldermen.

SEC. 5. No vote of the common council shall be reconsidered or rescinded at a special meeting, unless at such special meeting there be present as large a number of aldermen as were present when such vote was taken.

Reconsideration.

SEC. 6. The common council shall have power to require from any officer of said city, at any time, a report in detail of the transactions in his office, or of any other matter by said council deemed necessary.

Power to require reports from city officers.

SEC. 7. Upon the passage of all orders, ordinances or resolutions appropriating money, imposing taxes, or authorizing the borrowing of money, the yeas and nays shall be entered on the record of the common council, and a majority of the votes of all the aldermen entitled to seats in the board shall be necessary to their passage.

Yeas and nays required in certain cases.

SEC. 8. The common council shall have, subject to the provisions hereinafter contained, the general management and control of the finances, and all the property, real, personal and mixed, belonging to the corporation, and shall likewise have power within the jurisdiction of the city, by ordinance:

Council to control finances.

General powers.

First. To lease the wharfing privileges of the river, at the ends of streets, upon such terms and conditions as may be usual in the leasing of other real estate, reserving such rents as may be agreed upon, and employing such remedies in case of non-performance of any covenants in such lease, as are given by law in other cases. But no buildings shall be erected thereon; nor shall a lease for a longer period than three years at any time be executed; and the owner or owners of the adjoining lot or lots, shall, in all cases,

To lease wharfing privileges.

Restrictions.

have the preference in leasing such property; and a free passage over the same for all persons with their baggage shall be reserved in such lease: *Provided,* Nothing in this section shall be so construed as to impair or prejudice any rights which any person may have acquired by the acceptance of any proposition heretofore made by said city respecting the wharfing privileges.

Proviso.

River obstructions.

Second. To remove and prevent all obstructions in the waters which are public highways in said city, and to widen, straighten and deepen the same.

Forestalling, etc.

Third. To prevent and punish forestalling and regrating, and to prevent and restrain every kind of fraudulent device and practice.

Gaming.

Fourth. To restrain and prohibit all descriptions of gaming and fraudulent devices, and all playing of dice, cards and other games of chance, with or without betting.

Ardent spirits.

Fifth. To regulate the selling or giving away of any ardent spirits, by any shop-keeper, trader or grocer, to be drunk in any shop, store or grocery, outhouse, yard, garden, or other place within the city.

Furnishing to children, etc.

Sixth. To forbid the selling or giving away of ardent spirits or other intoxicating liquors, to any child, apprentice or servant, without the consent of his or her parent, guardian, master or mistress.

Sale of liquors, etc.

Seventh. To license, regulate and restrain tavern-keepers, grocers, and keepers of ordinaries or victualing or other houses or places, for the selling or giving away wines and other liquors, whether ardent, vinous or fermented.

Billiard tables, etc.

Eighth. To license, tax, regulate, suppress and prohibit billiard tables, pin alleys, nine or ten pin alleys, and ball alleys.

Hackmen, etc.

Ninth. To license, regulate and suppress hackmen, draymen, carters, porters, omnibus drivers, cabmen, carmen, and all others, whether in the permanent employment of any individual, firm, or corporation, or otherwise, who may pursue like occupations, with or without vehicles, and prescribe their compensation.

Auctioneers, etc.

Tenth. To tax, license and regulate auctioneers, distillers, brewers and pawn-brokers, and all keepers or proprietors of junk-shops and places for the sale or purchase of second-hand goods, wares or merchandise.

Eleventh. To license, tax, regulate and suppress hawkers and peddlers. **Peddlers.**

Twelfth. To regulate, license, suppress and prohibit all exhibitions of common showmen, shows of every kind, concerts or other musical entertainments, by itinerant persons or companies, exhibitions of natural or artificial curiosities, caravans, circuses, theatrical performances, and all other exhibitions and amusements. **Showmen, etc.** **Theaters.**

Thirteenth. To authorize the mayor, or other proper officer of the city, to grant and issue licenses, and direct the manner of issuing and registering thereof, and the fees to be paid therefor: *Provided*, That no license shall be granted for more than one year; and that not more than five hundred dollars shall be required to be paid for any license under this act, and the fee for issuing the same shall not exceed one dollar, but no license for the sale of wines or other liquors, ardent, vinous or fermented, at wholesale or retail, or by inn-keepers or others, as aforesaid, shall be less than fifty dollars. Bond may be taken on the granting of license, for the due observance of the ordinances or regulations of the common council. **Licenses.** **Proviso.** **Fee.** **Bond required.**

(*Further provisions as to licenses*, Sec. 34, *post*, 190.)

Fourteenth. To prevent any riot or noise, disturbance or disorderly assemblage. **Riots.**

Fifteenth. To suppress and restrain disorderly houses and groceries, and houses of ill-fame, and to authorize the destruction and demolition of all instruments and devices used for the purpose of gaming. **Disorderly houses.**

Sixteenth. To compel the owner or occupant of any grocery, cellar, tallow-chandler shop, soap factory, tannery, stable, barn, privy, sewer, or other unwholesome, nauseous house or place, to cleanse, remove or abate the same, from time to time, as often as may be necessary for the health, comfort and convenience of the inhabitants of said city. **Unwholesome and nauseous houses.**

Seventeenth. To direct the location and management of, and regulate and license breweries, tanneries and packing houses, and to direct the location, management and construction of, and regulate, license, restrain, abate, and pro- **Breweries, slaughter houses, etc.**

hibit, within the city and the distance of four miles therefrom, distilleries, slaughtering establishments, establishments for steaming or rendering lard, tallow, offal and such other substances as can or may be rendered; and all establishments or places where any nauseous, offensive or unwholesome business may be carried on: *Provided*, That for the purposes of this section, the Chicago river and its branches, to their respective sources, and the land adjacent thereto, or within one hundred rods thereof, shall be deemed to be within the jurisdiction of the city.

Proviso.

Chicago river within city.

Markets and public buildings.

Eighteenth. To establish and regulate markets and other public buildings, and provide for their erection and determine their location.

Butchers, etc.

Nineteenth. To regulate and license or prohibit butchers, and to revoke their licenses for malconduct in the course of trade, and to regulate, license and restrain the sale of fresh meats and vegetables in the city, and restrain and punish the forestalling of poultry, fruit and eggs.

Gunpowder.

Twentieth. To direct and prohibit the location and management of houses for the storing of gunpowder, or other combustible and dangerous materials, within the city.

Same.

Twenty-first. To regulate the keeping and conveying of gunpowder and other combustible and dangerous materials, and the use of candles and lights in barns, stables and outhouses.

Horse racing, etc.

Twenty-second. To prevent horse racing, immoderate riding or driving in the streets, and to authorize persons immoderately riding or driving as aforesaid to be stopped by any person; and punish or prohibit the abuse of animals; to compel persons to fasten their horses, oxen, or other animals, attached to vehicles or otherwise, while standing or remaining in the street.

Encumbering streets.

Twenty-third. To prevent the encumbering of the streets, sidewalks, lanes, alleys, public grounds, wharves and docks, with carriages, carts, sleighs, sleds, wheelbarrows, boxes, lumber, timber, firewood, posts, awnings, signs, or any substance or material whatever.

Bathing, indecent exposure, etc.

Twenty-fourth. To regulate and determine the times and places of bathing and swimming in the canals, rivers, harbors or other waters, in and adjoining said city, and to prevent any obscene or indecent exhibition, exposure or conduct.

Twenty-fifth. To restrain and punish vagrants, mendicants, street beggars and prostitutes. Vagrants.

Twenty-sixth. To restrain and regulate, or prohibit the running at large of cattle, horses, mules, swine, sheep, goats and geese, and to authorize the distraining, impounding and sale of the same for the penalty incurred, and the cost of the proceedings; and also to impose penalties on the owners of any such animals, for a violation of any ordinances in relation thereto. Impounding.

Twenty-seventh. To prevent and regulate the running at large of dogs, to tax, and to authorize the destruction of the same when at large contrary to the ordinance. Dogs.

Twenty-eighth. To prevent and regulate the rolling of hoops, playing of ball, flying of kites, or any other amusement or practice having a tendency to annoy persons passing in the streets, or on the sidewalks, or to frighten teams and horses. Kites, etc.

Twenty-ninth. To make regulations to prevent the introduction or spread of contagious diseases into the city; to make quarantine laws, and enforce the same within the city, and not to exceed fifteen miles beyond the city bounds. Quarantine.

Thirtieth. To control and regulate the streets and alleys, and to remove and abate any obstructions and encroachments therein. Streets and alleys.

Thirty-first. To compel all persons to keep the snow, ice and dirt from the sidewalks, in front of the premises owned or occupied by them. Snow, etc., on sidewalks.

Thirty-second. To prevent the ringing of bells, blowing of horns and bugles, crying of goods, and all other noises, performances and devices, tending to the collection of persons on the streets or sidewalks, by auctioneers or others, for the purposes of business, amusement or otherwise. Noises, etc.

Thirty-third. To abate and remove nuisances, and punish the authors thereof, by penalties, fine and imprisonment, and to define and declare what shall be deemed nuisances, and authorize and direct the summary abatement thereof; but nothing in this act shall be so construed as to oust any court of jurisdiction to abate and remove nuisances, in the Nuisances.

streets, or any other parts of said city, or within its jurisdiction, by indictment or otherwise.

Runners. *Thirty-fourth.* To license, regulate and restrain runners for boats and stages, cars and public houses.

Burials, bills of mortality. *Thirty-fifth.* To regulate the burial of the dead, and registration of births and deaths; to direct the returning and keeping of bills of mortality, and to impose penalties on physicians, sextons and others, for any default in the premises.

Lumber, wood, etc. *Thirty-sixth.* To regulate and prohibit the keeping of any lumber yard, and the placing, piling or selling lumber, timber, wood or other combustible material within the fire limits of said city.

Inspectors of lumber. *Thirty-seventh.* To regulate the measuring and inspecting of lumber, shingles, timber, posts, staves and heading, and all building materials, and appoint one or more inspectors.

Fish. *Thirty-eighth.* To regulate the place and manner of selling pickled and other fish.

Hay. *Thirty-ninth.* To regulate the weighing, and place and manner of selling, hay; and the cutting and sale of ice, and to restrain the sale of such ice as is impure.

Wood and coal. *Fortieth.* To regulate the measuring of wood and the weighing and selling of coal, and the place and manner of selling the same.

Inspection of flour, pork, etc. *Forty-first.* To regulate the inspection of flour, meal, pork, beef, and other provisions, and salt to be sold in barrels, hogsheads and other packages.

Inspection of liquors. *Forty-second.* To regulate the inspection of whisky and other liquors, to be sold in barrels, hogsheads and other vessels.

Inspectors. *Forty-third.* To appoint inspectors, weighers, gaugers, and regulate their duties and prescribe their fees.

Bread. *Forty-fourth.* To regulate the sale of bread within said city, and prescribe the weight of bread in the loaf, and the quality of the same.

Public pumps, wells, etc. *Forty-fifth.* To regulate public pumps, wells and cisterns, hydrants and reservoirs, and to prevent the unnecessary waste of water.

Pounds. *Forty-sixth.* To establish and regulate public pounds.

Forty-seventh. To erect lamps, and regulate the lighting thereof. **Lamps.**

Forty-eighth. To regulate and license ferries. **Ferries.**

Forty-ninth. To regulate and prohibit the use of locomotive engines within the city, and require railroad cars to be propelled by other power than that of steam; to direct and control the location of railroad tracks, and to require railroad companies to construct, at their own expense, such bridges, tunnels, or other conveniences, at public railroad crossings, as the common council may deem necessary; also to regulate the running of horse-railway cars, the laying down of tracks for the same, the transportation of passengers thereon, and the kind of rail to be used. **Steam cars.** **Railroad crossings.** **Horse railway cars.**

Fiftieth. To erect and establish, either within or without the corporate limits of the city, a bridewell or house of correction, and purchase grounds therefor, pass all necessary ordinances for the regulation thereof, and appoint a keeper and as many assistants as may be necessary. In the said bridewell or house of correction, shall be confined all vagrants, stragglers, idle or disorderly persons who may be committed thereto, by any criminal court or magistrate, in and for the city, and all persons sentenced to said bridewell or house of correction by any criminal court or magistrate, in and for the city, for any assault and battery, petit larceny or other misdemeanor punishable by imprisonment in any county jail; and all persons confined therein may be kept at labor or in solitary confinement. **Bridewell.** **Persons committed to bridewell.**

Fifty-first. To require every merchant, retailer, trader, and dealer in merchandise or property of any description which is sold by measure or weight, to cause their weights and measures to be sealed by the city sealer, and to be subject to his inspection; the standard of which weights and measures shall be conformable to those now established by law. **Weights and measures to be sealed.**

Fifty-second. Exclusively to erect and construct, or to permit or cause or procure to be erected and constructed, float, pivot, or draw bridges, over the navigable waters within the jurisdiction of said city, and keep the same in repair; said bridges to have draws of suitable width. **Bridges.**

Fifty-third. To preserve the harbor; to prevent any use **Harbor.**

of the same, or any act in relation thereto, inconsistent with, or detrimental to, the public health, or calculated to render the waters of the same, or any part thereof, impure or offensive, or tending in any degree to fill up or obstruct the same; to prevent and punish the casting or depositing therein any earth, ashes or other substance, filth, logs or floating matter; to prevent and remove all obstructions therein, and punish the authors thereof; to regulate and prescribe the mode and speed of entering and leaving the harbor, of passing the bridges, and of coming to, and departing from, the wharves and streets of the city, by steamboats, canal boats, and other crafts and vessels, and the disposition of the sails, yards, anchors and appurtenances thereof, while entering, leaving or abiding in the harbor, and to regulate and prescribe by such ordinances, or through their harbor master or other authorized officer, such location of every canal boat, steamboat, or other craft or vessel, or float, and such changes of station in, and use of, the harbor, as may be necessary to promote order therein, and the safety and equal convenience, as near as may be, of all such boats, vessels, crafts and floats; and to impose penalties not exceeding one hundred dollars for any offense against any such ordinance; and by such ordinance charge such penalties, together with such expenses as may be incurred by the city in enforcing this section, upon the steamboat, canal boat, or other vessel, craft or float. The harbor of the city shall include the piers and so much of lake Michigan as lies within the distance of one mile into the lake, and the Chicago river and its branches to their respective sources.

Speed of vessels.

Penalties.

What constitutes harbor.

Streets, alleys, bridges, walks, etc.

Fifty-fourth. To control, regulate, repair, amend and clear the streets and alleys, bridges, side and cross walks, and open, widen, straighten and vacate streets and alleys, and establish and alter the grade thereof, and prevent the encumbering of the streets in any manner, and protect the same from any encroachments and injury.

(*Further provisions as to vacating streets, alleys, etc.*, Sec. 10, *post*, 193, and Sec. 1, *post*, 206.)

Ornamental trees.

Fifty-fifth. To direct and regulate the planting and preserving ornamental trees in the streets and public grounds.

Fifty-sixth. To fill up, drain, cleanse, alter, relay, repair and regulate any grounds, yards, barns, slips, cellars, private drains, sinks and privies, direct and regulate their construction, and cause the expenses to be collected in the manner hereinafter provided. **Draining and cleansing of yards, etc.**

Fifty-seventh. To erect and establish one or more pest-houses, hospitals or dispensaries, and control and regulate the same. **Pest-houses, hospitals, etc.**

Fifty-eighth. To abate all nuisances which are or may be injurious to the public health, in any manner they may deem expedient. **Nuisances.**

Fifty-ninth. To do all acts and make all regulations which may be necessary or expedient, for the preservation of health, and the suppression of disease. **Health.**

Sixtieth. To prevent any person from bringing, depositing, or having within the limits of said city, any dead carcase, or any other unwholesome substance, and to require the removal or destruction by any person who shall have, place, or cause to be placed, upon or near his premises, any such substance, or any putrid or unsound beef, pork, or fish, hides or skins of any kind; and, on his default, to authorize the removal or destruction thereof by some officer of the city. **Putrid substances, removal of, etc.**

(*Further provisions as to health and nuisances*, Act of February 16, 1865, *post*, 200 *et seq.*)

Sixty first. To authorize the taking up and to provide for the safe keeping and education, for such periods of time as may be deemed expedient, of all children who are destitute of proper parental care, and growing up in mendicancy, ignorance, idleness and vice. **Mendicant children, education of, etc.**

Sixty-second. To lease or purchase, improve and maintain suitable grounds, either within or without the corporate limits of said city, for a house of refuge and correction, to erect buildings thereon, and adopt such rules and regulations for the government thereof, and the punishment of juvenile offenders therein, as may from time to time be deemed expedient. **House of refuge.**

Sixty-third. To authorize the arrest, fine and imprisonment in the city bridewell or house of correction, as vagrants, of all persons, who, not having visible means to maintain **Vagrants and idlers.**

themselves, are without employment, idly loitering or rambling about, or staying in groceries, drinking saloons, houses of ill-fame or houses of bad repute, gambling houses, railroad depots or fire-engine houses, or who shall be found trespassing in the night time upon the private premises of others, or begging, or placing themselves in the streets or other thoroughfares or public places to beg or receive alms; also keepers, exhibitors or visitors at any gaming table, gambling house, house for fortune-telling, places for cock-fighting, or other places of device; and all persons who go about for the purpose of gaming or watch-stuffing, or who shall have in their possession any article or thing used for obtaining money under false pretenses, or who shall disturb any place where public or private schools are held either on week day or Sabbath, or places where religious worship is held.

Trespassers, beggars, etc.

Gamesters.

Swindlers.

Other general powers.

Sixty-fourth. To make, publish, ordain, amend and repeal all such ordinances, by-laws and police regulations, not contrary to the constitution of this State, for the good government and order of the city, and the trade and commerce thereof, as may be necessary or expedient to carry into effect the powers vested in the common council, or any officer of said city, by this act; and enforce observance of all rules, ordinances, by-laws, and police and other regulations, made in pursuance of this act, by penalties not exceeding one hundred dollars for any offense against the same. The common council may also enforce such rules, ordinances, by-laws, and police and other regulations, as aforesaid, by punishment of fine or imprisonment in the county jail, bridewell, or house of correction, or both, in the discretion of the magistrate or court before which conviction may be had: *Provided,* Such fine shall not exceed five hundred dollars, nor the imprisonment six months.

Penalties.

Cemeteries.

SEC. 9. The common council is hereby authorized to purchase for said city such tracts of land without the city limits, for the purpose of establishing cemeteries for the interment of the dead therein, as they may think necessary, which shall be exempt from taxation under any law of this State; and they are also authorized and empowered to pass and enforce such ordinances, rules and regulations with

Regulation of.

regard to the improvement, preservation, laying out, and ornamenting the same, and the sale of burial places or lots for the interment of the dead therein, as they may deem proper. The ground or grounds so laid out shall be placed under the superintendence of the board of public works of said city, and the lots which may be laid out and sold shall, with the appurtenances, forever be exempt from execution and attachment. As soon as said grounds are regulated and laid out, a map or plat thereof shall be made out by the board of public works, and a copy thereof filed in the comptroller's office, who shall have charge of the sale and disposition of all lots therein, under the ordinances and regulations of the common council. The proceeds of such sales shall be paid into the city treasury, and be credited and charged on the books of the treasury department to a "cemetery fund," to be kept distinct from all other funds of said city. The said common council is also fully empowered and authorized to provide for the punishment, by ordinance, of all persons who shall, without said city limits, be guilty of any violation of the regulations, rules and ordinances, established by said city in relation to such cemeteries; and such violations may be punished by fine and imprisonment, as in other cases, by any court of competent jurisdiction within said city, and all process issued for the arrest of any person or persons guilty of such violation, may be executed without said city limits, by any officer or constable thereof, the same as if such offense had been committed within the boundaries of the corporation.

Superintendence of. **Sale of lots.** **Penalties.**

(*Further powers of council as to canals and tunnels*, Secs. 19, 20, *post*, 184, *and* Act of Feb. 16, 1865, *post*, 206 *et seq.*)

CHAPTER V.

THE TREASURY DEPARTMENT.

SECTION
1. Officers of the department.
2. General duties of the department.
3. Appointment of comptroller; his compensation and bond.
4. Comptroller to keep account of all appropriations, expenditures and receipts.
5. Comptroller to have supervision over all receiving and disbursing officers; his general powers and duties.
6. Accounts against the city to be audited by the comptroller.

SECTION
7. Warrants on the treasurer to be drawn by comptroller and countersigned by the mayor; doubtful claims to be submitted to decision of mayor and finance committee.
8. Receivers of city revenue to be charged with amount received; tax and assessment warrants to be countersigned by comptroller; comptroller to require reports of all receiving officers.
9. Annual statement of receipts and expenditures to be made by comptroller.
10. Annual estimate of city expenses to be furnished by comptroller.
11. Monthly statements of receipts and expenditures to be made by comptroller.
12. Duties of the treasurer.
13. Warrants on treasurer, how drawn.
14. Treasurer to keep separate accounts with each fund or appropriation.
15. Duplicate receipts to be given for money paid into the treasury; copy to be filed with the comptroller.
16. Treasurer to render monthly accounts to comptroller; warrants and other vouchers for moneys paid to be delivered to comptroller.
17. Custody of public moneys; treasurer prohibited from using them; penalty for violation.
18. Annual report of receipts and expenditures to be made by treasurer; register to be kept of all warrants paid by him.
19. Special assessment moneys to be kept as a special fund.
20. Bond of treasurer.
21. Duties of city collector.
22. Collector's books and papers placed under supervision of comptroller and finance committee; collector to pay over daily all moneys collected.
23. Collector to report weekly to comptroller; annual statement to be made in April.
24. Collector prohibited from retaining public moneys in his hands.
25. Bond of collector.
26. Penalty for selling land on which taxes have been paid.

SECTION
27. Annual reports of comptroller, treasurer and collector, to be examined and compared by finance committee.
28. Decision of finance committee binding in all controversies arising between comptroller, treasurer and collector.
29. Comptroller, treasurer and collector to appoint and be responsible for their own clerks.
30. Council may require of said officers other duties.
31. Special provisions respecting the custody of city moneys; penalty for embezzlement.
32. All accounts rendered by officers of treasury department to be verified by oath; form of oath.
33. Appropriations, how to be made, and when; fiscal year to commence the first of April.
34. City expenditures limited to amount provided for in annual appropriation bill; special exceptions.
35. Bonds authorized to be issued to pay floating debt of the city.
36. Certain other bonds authorized.
37. Bonds may be issued to purchase grounds and erect buildings for house of correction.
38. New bonds may be issued to satisfy and retire old bonds when due.
39. Comptroller to keep a register of outstanding bonds; all bonds sold or paid to be specified by comptroller in his annual report.
40. Provision for raising money to pay interest on the funded debt in case of necessity.
41. Comptroller authorized, in certain cases, to borrow of one fund to meet demands upon another.
42. No bonds or evidences of debt to be issued except those specially authorized.
43. No expense to be incurred, unless an appropriation has been made concerning it; all city officers prohibited from being interested in any sale or contract made to or by the city.
44. Common council authorized to provide for the appointment of a city auditor; his general duties defined.

Officers of the department.

SECTION 1. There is hereby established an executive department of the municipal government of said city, to be known as the "Treasury Department," which shall embrace the city comptroller, the city treasurer and the city collector, and all such clerks and assistants, including an auditor, as the common council may, by ordinance, see fit to prescribe and establish.

Its general duties.

SEC. 2. The said treasury department shall have control of all the fiscal concerns of the said corporation, except as herein otherwise provided, and shall prescribe the forms of keeping and rendering all city accounts whatever; and all accounts rendered to or kept in the several departments of the city government shall be subject to the revision and inspection of the officers of this department.

SEC. 3. There shall be appointed by the mayor, with the advice and consent of the common council, some discreet and able accountant, to be styled the city comptroller, who shall be chief of said treasury department, and hold his office until removed or a successor be appointed, who shall receive such compensation for his services as may be established by law, and who shall be removable at all times at the pleasure of the mayor with the concurrence of the common council, and he shall give bonds, with securities, to the amount of not less than one hundred thousand dollars, and the amount of his bond may be increased to such sum as may be fixed by the common council; said bond to be approved by the common council, and filed in the city clerk's office and entered on record. He shall also be sworn the same as other officers to the faithful discharge of the duties of his office.

Appointment of comptroller.

Bond required.

Oath of office.

SEC. 4. The comptroller shall open and keep in a neat, methodical manner, a complete set of books, under the direction of the mayor and finance committee of the common council, wherein shall be stated, among other things, the appropriations of the year for each distinct object and branch of expenditure, and also the receipts from each and every source of revenue so far as he can ascertain the same. Said books and all papers, vouchers, contracts, bonds, receipts, and other things kept in said office, shall be subject to the examination of the mayor, the members of the common council, or any committee or committees thereof.

Books to be kept by comptroller.

Subject to examination.

SEC. 5. The comptroller shall be charged with, and shall exercise a general supervision over, all the officers of the city charged in any manner with the receipt, collection or disbursement of the city revenues, and the collection and return of such revenues into the city treasury. He shall be the fiscal agent of said city, and, as such, shall have charge of all deeds, mortgages, contracts, judgments, notes, bonds, debts, choses in action, belonging to said city, except such as are confided by this act to the custody of the board of public works or city clerk, and shall possess and carefully preserve all assessment and tax warrants, except warrants

Comptroller's supervision over receiving and disbursing officers.

His general powers and duties.

for the collection of water rents or assessments, and the returns thereof made by any collector or receiver of taxes and assessments, and all leases of markets, wharfing privileges and other public property of said city. He shall also have supervision over the city debts, contracts, bonds, obligations, loans, and liabilities of the city, the payment of interest, and over all the property of the city, and the sale or the disposition thereof; over all legal or other proceedings in which the interests of the city are involved, and, with the approval of the mayor, to institute or discontinue such proceedings, and to employ additional counsel in special cases where he thinks the city interests require it, and generally, in subordination to the mayor and common council, to exercise supervision over all such interests of said city, as in any manner may concern or relate to the city finances, revenues and property.

Comptroller to examine and audit accounts.

SEC. 6. The comptroller shall have power to examine all accounts, claims and demands for or against the city; and no money shall be drawn from the treasury, or paid by the city to any person, except as herein otherwise provided, unless the balance due or payable be first settled and adjusted by the said comptroller; and for the purpose of ascertaining the true state of any balance or balances so due, he shall have and he is hereby clothed with full power and authority to administer an oath or oaths to the claimant or claimants, or any other person or persons whom he may think proper to examine as to any fact, matter or thing concerning the correctness of any account, claim or demand presented, and the person so sworn shall, if he swear falsely, be deemed guilty of willful and corrupt perjury, and be subject to punishment accordingly, the same as in other cases.

Power to administer oaths to claimants.

Warrants on the treasury, how drawn.

SEC. 7. All money found to be due and payable by the comptroller to any person, shall be drawn for by said comptroller by warrant on the treasurer, which shall be countersigned by the mayor, stating therein the particular fund or appropriation to which the same is chargeable, and the person to whom payable; but if said comptroller should, upon any examination of any account as aforesaid, still doubt as to its correctness, he shall submit the same to the mayor and finance committee for their decision thereon, which decision shall be binding upon the city and filed among his other vouchers in the comptroller's office; and no money shall be drawn from the treasury, except on the warrant of the comptroller drawn as aforesaid.

Doubtful claims to be submitted to mayor and finance committee.

SEC. 8. It shall be the duty of said comptroller, as nearly as may be, to charge all officers in the receipt of revenues or moneys of the city, with the whole amount, from time to time, of such receipts; and he shall countersign all tax and assessment warrants for the collection of revenue, issued under any ordinance or law of the city by virtue of which money is receivable or to be received or paid into the city treasury, except warrants for the collection of water rents or assessments, charging the proper officer the amount collectable thereon. He shall also require of all officers in receipt of city moneys that they shall submit reports thereof with vouchers and receipts of payment therefor, into the city treasury weekly or monthly, or as often as he shall see fit to require the same by any regulation which he may adopt; and if any such officer shall neglect to make an adjustment of his accounts when so required as aforesaid, and to pay over such moneys so received, it shall then be the duty of the said comptroller to issue a notice in writing, directed to such officer and his securities, requiring him or them within ten days to make settlement of his said accounts with the comptroller, and to pay over the balance of moneys found to be due and in his hands belonging to said city, according to the books of said comptroller; and in case of the refusal or neglect of such officer to adjust his said accounts, or pay over said balance to the treasury as required, it shall then be the duty of the said comptroller to make report of the delinquency of such officer to the mayor, who shall at once suspend him from office; and the mayor shall thereupon proceed forthwith to institute the necessary proceedings for the removal of such officer; and he is hereby authorized, in case of such suspension, to appoint, with the concurrence of the common council, some other person to exercise the functions of said office while such proceedings are pending.

Receiving officers to be charged with moneys collected.

Weekly or monthly reports required of them.

Notice to delinquent officers.

Removal of defaulters.

SEC. 9. The comptroller shall make out an annual

Comptroller's annual financial statement.

statement for publication, in the month of April in each year, before the annual election, giving a full and detailed statement of all the receipts and expenditures during the year ending the first day of said month. The said statement shall also detail the liabilities and resources of said city, the condition of all unexpended appropriations and contracts unfulfilled, and the balances of money then remaining in the treasury, with all sums due and outstanding; the names of all persons who may have become defaulters to the city, and the amount in their hands unaccounted for, and all other things necessary to exhibit the true financial condition of the city; which statement, when examined and approved by the finance committee, shall be published by him in the corporation newspaper.

Publication.

Comptroller's annual estimate of city expenses.

SEC. 10. The said comptroller shall, also, on or before the fifteenth day of May in each year, before the annual appropriations are made by the common council, submit to the same a report of the estimates necessary, as nearly as may be, to defray the expenses of the city government during the current fiscal year, commencing on the first day of April; he shall, in said report, class the different objects and branches of said city expenditure, giving, as nearly as may be, the amount required for each; and for this purpose he is authorized to require of all city officers and heads of departments, their statements of the condition and expense of their respective departments and offices, with any proposed improvement and the probable expense thereof, of contracts already made and unfinished, and the amount of any unexpended appropriations of the preceding year. He shall also, in such report, show the aggregate income of the preceding fiscal year from all sources; the amount of liabilities outstanding upon which interest is to be paid, and of bonds and city debts payable during the year, when due, and where payable, so that the common council may fully understand the money exigencies and demands of the city for the current year.

Monthly statement of receipts and expenditures.

SEC. 11. In addition to the other duties of the comptroller of said city, it is hereby made his duty, on or before the tenth day of each and every month, to make out a monthly statement, giving a full and detailed statement of all moneys received and from what sources, and on what account received, and of all moneys ordered to be paid, or drawn for by warrant by him, and on what account the same have been paid, for the month preceding that in which such statement is made, and the said comptroller shall cause the said monthly statement to be published in the corporation newspaper of said city, before the fifteenth day of each month, and shall deliver a true copy of such statement to the said common council at their next meeting. **Publication.**

DUTIES OF THE TREASURER.

SEC. 12. The city treasurer shall receive all moneys belonging to the city, and shall keep his office in some place to be designated by the common council, appropriated to the keeping of such office, in the treasury department. He shall keep his books and accounts in such manner as the city comptroller or common council may prescribe, and such books and accounts shall be always subject to the inspection of said comptroller and the finance committee. **Duties of treasurer.**

SEC. 13. All warrants drawn upon the treasurer must be signed by the comptroller and countersigned by the mayor, stating therein the particular fund or appropriation to which the same is chargeable, and the person to whom payable, and no money shall be otherwise paid than upon such warrants so drawn. **Warrants, how drawn.**

SEC. 14. He shall keep a separate account of each fund or appropriation, and the debits and credits belonging thereto. **Accounts.**

SEC. 15. He shall give every person paying money into the city treasury a duplicate receipt therefor, specifying the date of payment, upon what account paid; and he shall also file copies of such receipts with the city comptroller at the date of his monthly reports. **Receipts.**

SEC. 16. The treasurer shall, at the end of each and every month, and oftener if required, render an account to the comptroller, under oath, showing the state of the treasury at the date of such account, and the balance of moneys in the treasury. He shall also accompany such account with a statement of all moneys received into the treasury and on what account, together with all warrants redeemed **Monthly statement.**

Warrants to be returned.

and paid by him, which said warrants, with any and all other vouchers held by him, shall be delivered over to the comptroller, and filed with his said account in the comptroller's office upon every day of such settlement. He shall return all warrants paid by him stamped or marked "paid;" and shall give a list of said warrants, stating the number and amount of each.

Care and custody of city moneys

SEC. 17. The treasurer may be required to keep all moneys in his hands belonging to the city, in such place or places of deposit as the common council may by ordinance provide, order, establish or direct. Such moneys shall be kept distinct and separate from his own moneys; and he is hereby expressly prohibited from using, either directly or indirectly, the corporation money or warrants in his custody and keeping, for his own use and benefit, or that of any other person or persons whomsoever; and any violation of this provision shall subject him to immediate removal from office by the mayor, with the concurrence of the common council, who are hereby authorized to declare said office vacant; and the mayor, in case of said removal, shall nominate a successor, who shall be appointed to said office upon the confirmation of the said common council, and hold his office for the remainder of the unexpired term of such officer so removed.

Treasurer prohibited from using them.

Treasurer's annual report.

SEC. 18. The treasurer shall also report to the common council, annually, in the month of April, before the election, and oftener if required, a full and detailed account of all receipts and expenditures during the preceding fiscal year, and the state of the treasury. He shall also keep a register of all warrants redeemed and paid during the year, describing such warrants, their date, amount, number, the fund from which paid, and persons to whom paid, specifying also the time of payment; and all such warrants shall be examined at the time of the making such annual report to the common council, by the finance committee, who shall examine and compare the same with the books of the comptroller, and report discrepancies, if any, to the common council.

Special assessment funds.

SEC. 19. All moneys received on any special assessment shall be held by the treasurer as a special fund, to be applied to the payment of the improvement for which the assessment was made; and said money shall be used for no other purpose whatsoever.

Treasurer's bond.

SEC. 20. The treasurer shall give bond with sureties to the amount of not less than two hundred thousand dollars, and the amount of his bond may be increased to such sum as may be fixed by the common council; said bond to be approved by the common council, and filed in the clerk's office, and entered on record. He shall also be sworn the same as other officers, to the faithful discharge of the duties of his office.

CITY COLLECTOR.

Duties of collector.

SEC. 21. It shall be the duty of the city collector to collect all taxes and assessments which may be levied by said city, and perform such other duties as may be herein prescribed, or ordained by the common council. He shall keep his office in such place as may be designated and provided by the common council, appropriated to the keeping of such office in the treasury department, and shall keep in said office, besides his collection and revenue warrants, such other books, vouchers, records and accounts as the comptroller may, by regulation of the department, direct and prescribe, which books and records, with all other papers, shall remain in and pertain to said office, and be handed over to the successor or successors of said officer, or be deposited in the office of the comptroller.

Collector's books and papers.

SEC. 22. All the city collector's papers, books, warrants and vouchers, shall be examined by, and the same are hereby placed under the supervision of the comptroller, together with the finance committee; and the said collector shall, daily, on receipt of the same, pay over all moneys collected by him of any person or persons, to the city treasurer, taking his receipt therefor, which said collector shall immediately file in the comptroller's office.

To pay over daily all moneys received.

Weekly reports.

SEC. 23. The city collector shall make report, in writing under oath, to the comptroller, weekly, or oftener if required, of the amount of all moneys collected by him; the account upon which collected, and shall file with him the vouchers or receipts of the treasurer for the amount so collected. He shall also, in the month of April in each year, before

Annual statement.

the annual election, submit to the common council and finance committee, a statement of all moneys by him collected during the year, and the particular warrant, assessment or account upon which collected, and the balance of moneys uncollected on the warrants in his hands or returned to the comptroller, and a copy of such statement shall also be filed with the comptroller.

Collector not to retain the public money. SEC. 24. The city collector is hereby expressly prohibited from keeping the moneys of the city in his hands, or in the hands of any person or corporation to his use, beyond the time prescribed for the payment of the same to the city treasurer; and any violation of this provision shall subject him to immediate removal from office by the mayor, with the concurrence of the common council; and it is hereby declared to be the duty of the mayor, upon such removal being made, to nominate and appoint a successor, with the advice and consent of the common council.

Collector's bond. SEC. 25. The collector shall give bond with sureties, to the amount of not less than one hundred thousand dollars, and the amount of his bond may be increased to such sum as may be fixed by the common council, said bond to be approved by the common council and filed in the clerk's office and entered on record. He shall also be sworn the same as other officers to the faithful discharge of the duties of his office.

Liability for selling land when taxes have been paid. SEC. 26. If the collector shall receive any money for taxes or assessments, giving a receipt therefor for any land or parcel of land, and afterwards sell the same at any sale for taxes or assessments for the tax or assessment which has been so paid and receipted for by himself or his assistant, he and his bond shall be liable to the holder of the certificate given to the purchaser at the sale, for double the amount of the face of the certificate, to be demanded within three years from the date of sale, and recovered in any court having jurisdiction of the amount; and the city shall in no case be liable to the holder of such certificate.

GENERAL PROVISIONS.

Finance committee to examine all reports. SEC. 27. The finance committee and the comptroller shall, annually, meet in the month of April, and compare all such reports and statements as are made by the comptroller, treasurer and collector, and report thereon to the common council.

Finance committee to decide controversies between officers of treasury department.

SEC. 28. In the adjustment of the accounts of the treasurer and collector with the comptroller, there shall be an appeal to the finance committee, whose decision in all matters of controversy arising between said officers in the treasury department, shall be binding, unless the common council shall otherwise direct and provide.

Assistants and clerks.

SEC. 29. The comptroller, city treasurer and city collector, shall severally appoint such various assistants, clerks and subordinates, in their respective offices, as the common council may authorize; and shall be held severally responsible for the fidelity of the persons so appointed by them. Said subordinates shall in all cases be sworn to the faithful discharge of their duties, as other officers.

Other duties may be required.

SEC. 30. The said comptroller, collector and treasurer, shall perform such other duties, and be subject to such other rules and regulations, as the common council may from time to time by ordinance provide and establish.

City money not to be loaned or used by receiving officers.

SEC. 31. The treasurer and city collector, and all receivers of city money, are hereby required to keep safely, without loaning or using, all the city or public moneys collected by them, or otherwise at any time placed in their custody or disposal, till the same are paid over or directed by the proper officer, warrant, law, or order of the corporation, to be transferred or paid out, and to make all payments and transfers promptly when thereto required by any law or order of said corporation, or under any regulation of the comptroller. And if any one of said officers, or of those connected with them, in the collection, safe keeping, or disbursing of said city revenues, shall convert to his or their own use, in any way whatever, or shall use by way of investment in any kind of property or merchandise, or shall loan, with or without interest, any portion of said city moneys entrusted to him or them for safe keeping, disbursement, payment, transfer, or for any other purpose, every such act shall be deemed and adjudged to be an embezzlement of so much of the said moneys as shall be thus taken, converted, invested, used or loaned, which is hereby

Penalty for embezzlement.

declared a felony, and any officer or agent of said city, and all persons advising or participating in such act, or being a party thereto, shall, upon conviction before any court of competent jurisdiction in this State, be sentenced to imprisonment for a term of not less than six months nor more than ten years, in the penitentiary of this State; and also be fined in a sum equal to the amount of the money embezzled.

Officers' accounts to be verified by oath.

SEC. 32. All returns and accounts made or required to be rendered under this act, by any of the officers in said treasury department, shall be verified by the oath of the person rendering it; in which said oath it shall be declared that said statement, so far as he knows or has reason to believe, is a fair, accurate and full statement of the matters to which it relates, and of all moneys in his hands, or which he or any one for him has received since his last official account was rendered; and that he has not directly or indirectly used, loaned, invested or converted to his own use, or suffered any one to use, loan, invest, or convert to their or his use, any of the public moneys receivable or received by him, or subject to his warrant or control; but that he has acted diligently and without any collusion or fraud in the collection and disbursement of the public moneys of said city, and that he hath rendered a true and full account thereof in his said statement; which oath shall be attached to and filed with said accounts in the proper office of the comptroller or city clerk, as the case may be; and in case the said statements, or any of them, shall be false, the said person so making such statement shall be deemed guilty of willful and corrupt perjury, and shall be punished accordingly.

Appropriations, how and when to be made.

SEC. 33. All appropriations shall be based upon specific and detailed statements, made by some proper head of a department or officer of the city, and shall be made within the first quarter of the fiscal year; which fiscal year shall be held to commence on the first day of April in every year.

Fiscal year.

City expenditures limited.

SEC. 34. Neither the common council, nor any department or officer of the city, shall add to the city expenditures, in any one year, anything over and above the amount provided for in the annual appropriation bill of that year, except as is herein otherwise specially provided; and no expenditure for an improvement to be paid for out of the general fund of said city, shall exceed in any one year the amount provided for such improvement in the annual appropriation bill: *Provided, however*, That nothing herein contained shall prevent the common council from ordering any improvement, the necessity of which is caused by any casualty or accident happening after such annual appropriation is made. The common council may order the mayor and comptroller to borrow a sufficient amount to provide for the expense necessary to be incurred in making any improvement, the necessity for which has arisen as is last above mentioned, for a space of time not exceeding the close of the next municipal year; which sum and the interest shall be added to the amount authorized to be raised in the next general tax levy, and embraced therein. Should any judgment be obtained against the city, the comptroller, under the sanction of the mayor and committee of finance, may borrow a sufficient amount to pay the same, for a space of time not exceeding the close of the next municipal year; which sum and interest shall in like manner be added to the amount authorized to be raised in the general tax levy of the next year, and embraced therein. **Special exceptions.**

SEC. 35. The city comptroller is hereby authorized, under the sanction of the mayor and committee of finance, to issue and negotiate the bonds of said city, payable, principal and interest, in the city of New York, and bearing interest payable semi-annually at a rate not exceeding seven per cent. per annum, and becoming due and payable on the first day of April, 1881, to an amount sufficient to satisfy and retire all the floating debt now outstanding against said city, and which has not been heretofore provided for. Said bonds shall be in the ordinary form of bonds of said city, and shall be issued in denominations of five hundred or a thousand dollars each, as the said mayor and comptroller may deem proper; and it is hereby made the duty of the common council, at the time of levying the general tax in each year, to provide for the payment of the interest accruing on the whole funded debt of the city, which is not oth- **Issue of bonds to provide for floating debt** erwise provided for, in addition to the amount which they are authorized to levy for other purposes.

Certain other bonds authorized.

SEC. 36. In addition to the amount of bonds herein authorized to be issued, the common council may, in its discretion, provide by ordinance, for completing the issue of the bonds of said city to an amount not exceeding one hundred thousand dollars, authorized by the sixty-sixth section of the act amendatory of the city charter approved February 18th, 1861: *Provided*, That the whole amount of the bonds heretofore issued pursuant to said authority, and of the bonds hereafter issued by virtue of this section, shall not exceed the said sum of one hundred thousand dollars. The proceeds of said bonds, when sold, may be used in paying the general expenses of said city, and in payment of the expense, either in whole or in part, of such permanent improvements, chargeable to the general fund, as may be ordered by the common council, before the making of the next annual appropriation.

Bonds may be issued to establish house of correction.

SEC. 37. The common council may also, in its discretion, provide by ordinance for issuing and negotiating the bonds of said city, payable principal and interest in New York, in twenty years from date, and bearing interest at a rate not exceeding seven per cent. per annum, payable semi-annually, to an amount not exceeding one hundred thousand dollars, for the purpose of purchasing grounds, either within or without the corporate limits of said city, and erecting the necessary buildings thereon, for a city bridewell or house of correction. Such bonds shall be in the ordinary form of bonds of said city, and shall be issued in denominations of five hundred or one thousand dollars each, as the mayor and comptroller may deem for the best interest of said city.

New bonds may be issued, to satisfy old.

SEC. 38. Whenever any of the bonds of the city, which may have been heretofore, or may hereafter be, lawfully issued, shall become due, the common council may authorize the mayor and comptroller to issue new bonds to an amount sufficient to retire and satisfy the same, running either ten or twenty years, bearing interest at a rate not exceeding seven per cent. per annum, payable semi-annually, and payable, principal and interest, in the city of New York.

SEC. 39. The comptroller shall keep in his office, in a book or books kept separately for this purpose, a correct list of all the outstanding bonds of the city, showing the number and amount of each, and when and to whom the same were issued; and when any of said bonds are purchased or paid and canceled, said book or books shall show the same. In his annual report the comptroller shall describe particularly the bonds sold during the year, and the terms of the sale, with each and every item of the expense thereof. He shall also describe the bonds paid or purchased in order to be canceled, the person of whom purchased, and the amount paid, with each and every item of the expense thereof.

Register of bonds to be kept by comptroller.

Bonds sold or paid to be specified in annual report.

SEC. 40. In case there shall not be money enough in the treasury, applicable thereto, to pay any semi-annual installment of interest on the funded debt of the city, the comptroller shall present a statement, under oath, to the finance committee, of the amount of the deficiency, which shall be afterwards filed with the city clerk; and it shall then be lawful for the mayor and comptroller, under the sanction of said committee, to issue and negotiate drafts upon the treasurer, payable out of the first moneys that may come into the treasury applicable to the payment of said interest, to an amount sufficient to supply said deficiency. Said drafts shall not have more than ninety days to run; but they may be renewed, if necessary, ninety days successively, until there shall be revenue enough received into the treasury to pay the same.

Special provision respecting interest on funded debt.

SEC. 41. In case of a deficiency in any fund to meet any demand upon it, the comptroller may, with the sanction of the mayor and finance committee, use to meet such demand, any moneys standing to the credit of any other fund, either general or special, except the water fund, the school-tax fund, and special assessment funds: *Provided*, The consent of the officer or department more particularly charged with the disbursement of the fund so used, shall be first had and obtained thereto. A correct account of all moneys so transferred shall be kept by the comptroller, and said moneys shall be replaced by him, within not to exceed three months, out of the revenue subsequently received into the

Authority to borrow from one fund to meet demands upon another.

Proviso.

treasury to the credit of the fund thus supplied. No moneys shall be so used or transferred, unless adequate provision has been made which will permit their reimbursement within said period.

Issue of bonds restricted. SEC. 42. No bonds or other evidences of debt shall be issued by the city, except as is in this act provided.

(*Further provisions for issuing bonds and borrowing money*, Secs. 13, 14, 21, 25, 31, *post*, 181–189.)

Special provision as to contracts, etc. SEC. 43. No contracts shall be hereafter made by the common council, or any committee or member thereof, and no expense shall be incurred by any of the officers or departments of said city government, whether the object of expenditure shall have been ordered by the common council or not, unless an appropriation shall have been previously made concerning such expense. And no member of the common council, head of a department, clerk, city officer, assistant or employee in any department of said city, shall be directly or indirectly interested in any contract, work or business, or the sale of any article, the expense, price or consideration of which is paid from the city treasury, under the penalty of his immediate removal from office.

City auditor SEC. 44. The common council may hereafter, in their discretion, provide for the appointment of a city auditor, to hold his office for two years and until the appointment and qualification of his successor, whose duty it shall be to examine personally and certify to the correctness or incorrectness of all the accounts rendered for any money which may be collected or disbursed by any of the departments or officers of said city. The said common council may by ordinance prescribe his qualifications and more particularly define his duties; and he shall be removable from office at any time by the mayor with the concurrence of the common council.

(*Provision as to appointment and removal of auditor*, Sec. 1, *post*, 191.)

CHAPTER VI.

THE BOARD OF PUBLIC WORKS.

SECTION
1. Board of public works, how constituted.
2. Salary of commissioners; bond.
3. President and treasurer; by-laws.
4. Secretary of the board; city engineer.
5. Duties of city engineer.
6. Power to license land surveyors.
7. Plats of subdivisions to be approved by the board.
8. Board authorized to employ superintendents, surveyors and other subordinates.
9. Office and other expenses, how paid.
10. A majority of the board necessary for a quorum; record of proceedings; annual report; power to administer oaths.
11. General duties of the board.
12. Control over streets and alleys.
13. Permits for erection of wooden buildings within fire limits; fees for permits.
14. Board to act as commissioners to make special assessments.
15. Board to advertise for proposals for all work to be done by city; bidders to furnish bonds.
16. Contracts to be let to lowest reliable bidder.

SECTION
17. Reservations to be inserted in all contracts; estimates to be issued to contractors; liability of city to contractors.
18. Board authorized in certain cases to employ workmen to perform or complete any public work.
19. Materials, how purchased.
20. Advertising for bids may be dispensed with in certain cases.
21. Bonds and contracts to be made in the name of the city.
22. Commissioners forbidden to be interested in contracts.
23. Board to have exclusive charge of water and sewerage works.
24. Former contracts concerning water and sewerage works to be completed by the board; special provision relating to new contracts.
25. Annual estimate to be furnished by the board, of sums required for repairs and improvements; moneys raised for said board, how disbursed.
26. Oath of office; special requirement.
27. Members prohibited from deriving any profit from deposit of public moneys; custody of city funds; penalty for embezzlement.
28. Accounts to be kept of receipts and expenditures.

SECTION 1. There is hereby established an executive department of the municipal government of said city, to be known as the "Board of Public Works," to consist of the mayor, who shall be a member of the board *ex officio*, and three commissioners, to be chosen in the manner herein before prescribed. **Board, how constituted.**

(*Mayor no longer member of board of public works*, Sec. 19, *post*, 196. *Two members added, for special purpose*, Sec. 16, *post*, 182.)

SEC. 2. Said commissioners shall each receive an annual salary of twenty-five hundred dollars, and shall each, before entering upon the discharge of his duties, give bond to the city in the sum of one hundred thousand dollars, with sureties to the satisfaction of the common council, which bond shall be conditioned for the faithful discharge of his duties as such commissioner; and that he will well and truly pay over any and all moneys, and surrender any and all property, books and papers which may come into his **Salary.** **Bond.**

hands as such commissioner, on the expiration of his term of office, or when required to do so by the common council.

(*Salary fixed at three thousand dollars*, Sec. 16, *post*, 182.)

President and treasurer. SEC. 3. Said board shall elect from their number a president and a treasurer, who shall hold their offices for the term of one year, and until their successors are elected and qualified, and they shall establish by-laws for the regulation and conduct of their officers and employees. By-laws.

Secretary. SEC. 4. Said board shall appoint a secretary, and some competent and scientific person as civil engineer to said board, who shall be styled the city engineer. The officers so appointed shall be removable at any time, at the pleasure of the board of public works. City engineer.

Duties of city engineer. SEC. 5. It shall be the duty of the city engineer to perform all the civil engineering required by the board of public works in the prosecution of all public improvements committed to their charge, and to do such other surveying as may be directed by the board or by the common council. He shall receive for his services such annual salary as the common council shall direct; and shall devote his whole time to the duties of his office. He shall possess the same powers in making surveys and plats, within the city, as is given by law to county surveyors, and the like effect and validity shall be given to his acts, and to all plats and surveys made by such engineer, as are or may be given by law to the acts, plats and surveys of county surveyors.

Power to license land surveyors. SEC. 6. The said board of public works shall have power, upon application being made to them by any citizen, of whose character and qualifications satisfactory evidence shall be produced, to give such applicant a license, under the corporate seal, to act for two years as a land surveyor in said city, and for each license so granted said board shall require a fee of ten dollars to be paid into the city treasury. Oath of surveyors. Surveyors so licensed shall take the same oath required by law to be taken by the county surveyor, and shall give bond to the city of Chicago, with two sufficient sureties, to be approved by said board, in the penal sum of twenty-five hundred dollars, conditioned for the faithful performance of the duties of a land surveyor, and the payment of all damages that may be sustained by any individual for whom such services may be rendered, in consequence of the carelessness, misconduct or incompetency of such surveyor. Said bond shall be filed in the office of said board, and suits may be brought and recovery had thereon in the name of said city, by any party who may have sustained damages as above mentioned; but said city shall in no case be held liable for the costs of such action, nor for any delinquency, fault or misconduct of such surveyor. The license to be granted as above provided, with a certificate of the aforesaid oath subjoined thereto, shall be recorded in the office of the recorder of Cook county; and then, and not before, the person so licensed shall have full power and authority, for the term of two years from the date of such license, to make surveys within the city limits, and the like effect and validity shall be given to his acts, and to all plats and surveys made by him, as are or may be given by law to the acts, plats and surveys of county surveyors: *Provided*, That the surveyors so licensed shall be governed by such laws of the State of Illinois, and such ordinances of the city of Chicago, prescribing the mode of surveying, as are now or may hereafter be in force: *And Provided further*, That the said board of public works shall have power to revoke any license granted under the provisions of this section, upon satisfactory evidence being presented to them of the incompetency or official misconduct of the person so licensed.

License to be recorded.

Revocation of license.

SEC. 7. In all cases where lands in said city are hereafter subdivided and laid out into blocks or lots, sub-lots, streets and alleys, or new streets or public grounds are donated or granted to the public by any proprietor, in order to secure a uniform plan in the laying out of such streets and alleys, the map or plat thereof shall be submitted to the board of public works for their approval. If they approve the same, they shall certify upon it their approval; and no such map or plat shall be entitled to record or have any validity until so approved by said board.

Plats of subdivisions to be approved by the board.

SEC. 8. The board of public works is authorized to employ, from time to time, such superintendents, surveyors, clerks, assistants and workmen, in the discharge of their duties, as they may deem necessary, subject, however, to such regulations respecting the number of agents regularly

Superintendents, surveyors, clerks, etc.

or permanently employed, and their compensation and duties, as the common council may prescribe by ordinance.

Office expenses, etc.

SEC. 9. The office expenses, and the expenses for clerks, engineers and assistants, and the salaries of said commissioners of the board of public works and their officers, shall be a charge, and shall be paid, share and share alike, out of the funds pertaining to the general fund of said city, and the funds pertaining to the water and sewerage works of said city; each of said funds to bear one-third of said expense.

Quorum.

Record of proceedings.

Annual report.

Power to administer oaths.

SEC. 10. A majority of said board shall constitute a quorum to do business; they shall keep a record of all their acts and doings, and shall keep and preserve copies of all contracts, estimates, receipts, plans, profiles, and the papers of the board; and shall report their acts and doings in detail to the common council, on or before the tenth day of April in each year, and oftener when required so to do by the common council. Each of said commissioners shall have power to administer any oath authorized to be taken by the laws of this State.

Board to take special charge of streets, public buildings, river improvements, etc.

SEC. 11. It shall be the duty of said board to take the special charge and superintendence, subject to such general ordinances as may be lawfully established by the common council, of all streets, alleys, lanes or highways in said city, and of all walks and cross-walks in the same, and of all bridges, docks, wharves, public places, public landings, public grounds and parks in said city, and of all markets, market-places and market-houses, engine-houses, hospitals, armories and all other public buildings in said city, belonging to the city, except school-houses, and of the erection of all public buildings; of all lamps and lights for the lighting of the streets, alleys, lanes, highways, bridges, parks, public places and public buildings of the city, and of the erection and repair of such lamps and lights; of all works for the widening, deepening or dredging of the Chicago river, or either of its branches; of all sewers, and the works pertaining thereto; of the water works of said city; of all public improvements hereafter to be commenced by said city; and they shall perform all the duties by this act prescribed, and such other duties as the common council may prescribe by ordinance.

Permits for moving and raising buildings, etc.

SEC. 12. The said board shall have the exclusive privilege to grant permits, according to the ordinances of the city, for the moving of houses through the streets of the city, and the raising of buildings and sidewalks, and to regulate the building or placing of vaults under the streets, alleys and sidewalks, and require such compensation for the privilege as they shall deem reasonable and just, subject to the approval of the common council; also to regulate all open spaces for basement stories, and the use of the public streets in any legal and proper manner, except for railroad tracks; and no building material or obstruction of any kind shall be placed in the public streets, alleys, or on the public grounds, without the written permit of said board. Said board shall have full power to regulate and control the manner of using the streets, alleys, highways and public places of the city, for the laying down of gas or water pipes and sewers, and determine the location thereof, and to cause the prompt repair of the streets, alleys, highways and public places whenever the same may be taken up or altered; and they are hereby authorized and empowered to charge and collect, by suit or otherwise, in the name of the city of Chicago, the expense of such repairs to and from the person or persons by whom such street, alley, highway or public ground may have been taken up or altered.

Use of streets for gas and water pipes, etc.

Wooden buildings within fire limits.

SEC. 13. The said board shall have the exclusive privilege of granting permits for the erection of wooden buildings within the fire limits of said city, subject to such general regulations as the common council may by ordinance prescribe; and for all permits of every kind which said board is authorized to grant, it may make such reasonable charge as it may deem proper, or as the common council may by ordinance direct.

Fee for permits.

(*Further provision as to permits*, Sec. 19, *post*, 184.)

Commissioners of special assessments.

SEC. 14. The commissioners of the board of public works, with the exception of the mayor, shall in all cases, except as is in this act otherwise provided, act as commissioners to make special assessments, whenever the same may be ordered; for the making of which assessments they shall receive no fees.

(*Exception of the mayor superseded*, Sec. 19, *post*, 196.)

Board to advertise for proposals for doing public work. SEC. 15. Whenever any public improvement shall be ordered by the common council of said city, and the assessment for the same (where the same is to be paid for by special assessment,) shall have been confirmed, and one-half of such special assessment shall have been paid into the city treasury, the said board of public works shall advertise for proposals for doing said work; a plan or profile of the work to be done, accompanied with specifications for the doing of the same, being first placed on file in the office of said board; which said plan, profile and specifications shall at all times be open for public inspection; which advertisement shall be continued for at least ten days in the corporation newspaper, and shall state the work to be done. **Bids.** The bids for the doing of such work shall be *sealed bids*, directed to said board, and shall be accompanied with a bond to the city in the sum of two hundred dollars, signed by the bidder and two responsible sureties, conditioned that he shall execute the work for the price mentioned in his bid, and according to the plans and specifications, in case the contract shall be awarded to him; and in case of default on his part to execute a contract and perform the work, said bond may be sued and judgment recovered thereon by the city for the full amount thereof, in any court having jurisdiction of the amount. Said bids shall be opened at the hour and place mentioned in said notice. When the expense of any work or public improvement shall exceed the sum of five hundred dollars, and the same is to be paid out of the general fund, or the water or sewerage fund of said city, the doing of such work shall be let by contract, in the same manner as is provided in cases where the expense of the same is to be paid for by special assessment.

(*Improvement may be made, in some cases, before assessment*, Sec. 5, *post*, 179. *Work may be done by the board, in some cases, without contract*, Sec. 10, *post*, 180.)

Contracts to be let to lowest reliable bidder. SEC. 16. All contracts shall be awarded by said board to the lowest reliable and responsible bidder or bidders, who shall have complied with the abover equisition, and who will sufficiently guarantee, to the satisfaction of said board, the performance of said work, under the superintendence and to the satisfaction of said board: *Provided*, That the contract price does not exceed the estimate, or such other sum as shall be satisfactory to said board; copies of which contracts shall be filed in the office of the comptroller of said city.

Reservations to be inserted in contracts.

SEC. 17. The board of public works shall reserve the right, in their said contracts, to finally decide all questions arising as to the proper performance of said work; and in case of improper construction, to suspend said work at any time, and re-let the same; or to order the entire re-construction of said work, if improperly done; or re-let the same to some more capable and faithful contractor or contractors, with power hereby given to said board to adjust the difference of damages or price, (if any there be,) which the contractor or contractors failing to properly construct such work, in such cases of default, should, in their opinion, pay to the city, according to the just and reasonable interpretation of such contract; which difference or balance shall be recoverable at law in the name of said city, before any court having competent jurisdiction thereof, against such contractor or contractors. In all cases where the contractor or contractors shall proceed to properly perform and complete their said contracts, the said board may, in their discretion, from time to time, as the work progresses, grant to said contractor or contractors an estimate of the amount already earned, reserving fifteen per cent. therefrom, which shall entitle the holder or holders to receive the amount that may be due thereon when the money applicable to the payment of such work shall have been collected, and the conditions annexed to said estimate, if any, shall have been satisfied. Any persons taking any contracts with the city, and who agree to be paid from special assessments, shall have no claim or lien upon the city in any event, except from the collections of the special assessments made for the work contracted for; and no work to be paid for by a special assessment, shall be let except to a contractor or contractors who will so agree.

Estimates to be issued to contractors.

Liability of city to contractors.

SEC. 18. In case the prosecution of any public work

Board to employ workmen to complete an improvement in certain cases

should be suspended in consequence of the default of any contractor, or in case the bids for doing any such work should be deemed excessive, or the persons making proposals not responsible or proper persons to be entrusted with its performance, the board of public works may, with the written approval of the comptroller, where the urgency of the case and the interests of the city require, employ workmen to perform or complete any improvement ordered by the common council: *Provided*, That the cost and expense thereof shall in no case exceed the amount assessed or sum appropriated for completing the same.

Materials, how purchased.

SEC. 19. All supplies of materials, or necessaries of any kind, exceeding in amount the sum of five hundred dollars, shall be purchased by said board of public works, when practicable, by contract with the lowest responsible bidder, as is provided for the making of contracts for the doing of work.

Advertising for bids dispensed with in certain cases

SEC. 20. Whenever the said board of public works shall deem it necessary for the interests of the city, and to protect the same from great loss and damage, they shall report to the common council such necessity, and the reason for the same, asking from the council the power to enter into a contract (specifying such contract) without giving the notice in this act required to be given before letting a contract; and the common council, on being satisfied of such necessity, may, by resolution, grant such power: *Provided*, Three-fourths of all the aldermen elected shall vote in favor of such resolution.

Contracts to be made in name of city

SEC. 21. All contracts entered into by said board of public works, and all bonds taken by them, shall be entered into in the name of, and be made to, the city of Chicago.

Commissioners not to be interested in contracts, etc.

SEC. 22. No member of the board of public works, nor officer or clerk in their employ, shall be interested, directly or indirectly, in any contract made and entered into by said board of public works, for any work or for any materials to be furnished therefor; and all contracts made with said board in which any member or officer of said board shall be so interested, shall, at the option of the city, be declared utterly void and of no binding effect whatever; and any member or officer of said board interested in any contract shall thereby forfeit his office, and be removed therefrom on proof of such delinquency; and it is hereby made the duty of each member of said board of public works, and of the mayor, and of every officer of said city, to report to the common council any such delinquency when discovered.

Board to have exclusive charge of water and sewerage works.

SEC. 23. The board of public works shall have the exclusive charge and superintendence of the sewerage and water works of said city, and shall receive and collect all water rents, water taxes or assessments, and sewerage permits and licenses; and they shall report to the city treasurer once in each week all moneys so received by them, and at the same time pay over to said city treasurer all such moneys, with a statement of the same, to which account the same belong, and shall receive his receipt for all moneys so paid over.

Contracts for water and sewerage works.

SEC. 24. All bonds, contracts, agreements or obligations, of what kind or nature soever, heretofore executed by the board of sewerage commissioners, or water commissioners, shall be carried out and completed by said board of public works. All contracts entered into by said board on account of the sewerage or water works of said city, shall specify that they are for such works, and are to be paid out of the funds pertaining to such works.

Annual estimate of sums required for repairs, etc.

SEC. 25. The board of public works shall, on or before the first day of May in each year, submit a statement to the comptroller, to be by him laid before the common council, with his annual estimate, of the repairs and improvements to be paid for out of the general fund of the city, and necessary to be undertaken by said city during the current year, and of the sums by said board of public works required to make such repairs and improvements, as near as the same can be estimated, which report shall be in detail; and such estimate having been revised by the common council, the aggregate amount of the sums required after such revision shall be provided for in the general tax levy to be laid on said city. All moneys hereafter to be paid to any person or persons out of the moneys so raised and appropriated, or out of the sewerage or water funds, or any special assessment fund, shall be certified by the president

Mode of disbursement.

of the board of public works, or, in his absence, by the acting president of said board, to the comptroller, who shall draw his warrant on the treasurer therefor, stating therein the particular fund to which the same is chargeable, and the person to whom payable; and such warrant shall be countersigned by the president, or, in his absence, by the acting president, of the board of public works and the mayor.

Oath of office.

SEC. 26. The commissioners of the board of public works shall be sworn the same as other officers to the faithful discharge of the duties of their office; and no person hereafter elected shall act as a commissioner of said board until, in addition to the oath required of all city officers, he shall swear that he is then, and for the year immediately preceding has been, a resident freeholder in the division of the city from which he was elected, which oath shall be filed in the clerk's office.

Special requirement.

Members prohibited from deriving profit from public funds

SEC. 27. No member or officer of said board, or other officer of said city, and no member of the common council, shall either directly or indirectly receive any interest or profit whatever on account of the deposit of any of the funds belonging to the city; nor shall any member or officer of said board, or officer of said city, or any member of the common council, either directly or indirectly, make use of or borrow any of said funds for his own private benefit or advantage. The funds of said city in the hands of said board, shall, until deposited with the treasurer of said city, as herein before provided, be kept in such place or places of deposit as shall, by an order of said board, be directed, which order shall be entered upon the records of the said board. If either of the members or any of the officers of said board shall, either directly or indirectly, receive or appropriate for his own use or benefit any of the funds, money or property of the said city, or shall directly or indirectly take, pledge or borrow any of the said funds or property for his own use or benefit, such member or officer of said board shall be deemed guilty of embezzlement, and shall be liable to indictment, and on conviction thereof shall be sentenced to imprisonment for a term of not less than six months nor more than ten years, in the

Custody of city funds.

Penalty for embezzlement.

penitentiary of this State; and also be fined in a sum equal to the amount of the money embezzled. The members of said board shall be liable upon their bond for the loss of any or all moneys coming into the possession or control of said board.

SEC. 28. It shall be the duty of the said board to keep books of account, showing with entire accuracy the receipts and expenditures of the board, in such manner as to enable the same to be readily understood and investigated; and also to preserve on file in their office duplicate vouchers for all their expenditures, which books and duplicates shall at all times be open to the examination of the comptroller of said city, or to the finance committee of the common council, or to any other committee appointed by the common council. Account of receipts and expenditures, etc.

CHAPTER VII.

PUBLIC IMPROVEMENTS AND SPECIAL ASSESSMENTS.

SECTION
1. Power to lay out streets; to improve them; to widen and deepen the river; to construct sidewalks; and improve parks.
2. Expenses defrayed by special assessments.
3. Applications for public improvements to be made or referred to board of public works; board to report to council.
4. Plan or profile of improvements to be furnished in certain cases; facts to be specially reported; three-fourths vote of council required in certain cases.
5. Assessments for condemnation of real estate.
6. Commissioners to be sworn; notice of meeting; witnesses may be examined.
7. Damages to be appraised, deducting benefits.
8. Report to show amount to be paid or received for damage or benefit.
9. Value of land donated to be set off against benefits.
10. Valuation of buildings; owner to be notified thereof; refusing to take, buildings to be sold.
11. Each party in interest entitled to an award.
12. Damages and expenses to be assessed on real estate benefited.
13. Assessment roll to be filed; notice of application for confirmation; objections; proceedings thereupon.
14. Property owners may appeal; proceedings therein.
15. Condemnation effectual when assessment is confirmed; payment of damages.
16. Notice to be published of readiness to pay; city may then take possession.
17. When whole of lot taken, contracts to cease.
18. When part taken, to cease as to that part; to continue as to the residue.
19. Proceedings to be recorded.
20. Assessments for deepening the river.
21. Assessments for improving streets.
22. Assessments on railway companies.
23. Oath of commissioners; notice of meeting.
24. Return of assessment roll; notice; proceedings thereupon.
25. Owner to construct sidewalks and drains when ordered; assessment therefor.
26. Penalty for refusal.
27. If owner refuses to construct, board of public works may do the work and assess expense.
28. Repair of sidewalks and drains; expense, how collected.
29. Owners and occupants responsible for safe condition of sidewalk.
30. Erection of lamp posts; assessments therefor.
31. Removal of nuisances; expense, how collected.
32. Landlord to pay assessment when no agreement to the contrary; remedy when paid by tenant.
33. Guardians of infants, by whom to be appointed.

SECTION
34. Writ of *certiorari*, when to be issued.
35. New assessment when first insufficient; excess to be refunded.
36. On failure to collect, re-assessment may be made; assessments a lien for five years.
37. Commissioner interested disqualified from serving; vacancy, how filled.
38. Expense of river improvements may be defrayed by general tax.

SECTION
39. Improvements to be paid for out of general fund.
40. Construction of bridges by private enterprise.
41. Penalty for willful injury to city property.
42. Improvement of Michigan avenue.
43. Encroachment prohibited on public ground east of Michigan avenue.
44. Repealing clause.

Council empowered to lay out streets, etc.

SECTION 1. The common council shall have power, from time to time,

First. To lay out public streets, alleys, lanes and highways, and to make wharves and slips at the ends of streets, and extend, alter, widen, contract, straighten and discontinue the same; and to purchase and lay out public parks, squares or grounds.

(*Further provision as to vacating streets, alleys, etc.*, Sec. 10, *post*, 193, and Sec. 1, *post*, 206.)

To improve streets.

Second. To cause any street, alley, lane or highway, to be filled, graded, leveled, paved, curbed, walled, graveled, macadamized or planked; and keep the same in repair.

To widen and deepen river.

Third. To widen, deepen, or dredge out the Chicago river, or either of its branches, or any part or parts of the same.

Sidewalks and drains.

Fourth. To cause cross and sidewalks, area walls, lamp posts, and private drains, to be constructed and laid, relaid, erected, cleansed and repaired.

Public squares.

Fifth. To fill, grade, improve, protect and ornament, any public square, now or hereafter laid out.

Expenses, how defrayed.

SEC. 2. The expenses of any improvement mentioned in the foregoing section, shall be defrayed, save as is herein otherwise provided, by a special assessment upon the real estate benefited thereby, to be levied in the manner hereinafter prescribed.

Applications for improvements to be made or referred to board of public works.

SEC. 3. All applications or propositions for establishing the grade of streets or for a change of grade, the erection of bridges and lamp posts, the grading, re-grading, paving, re-paving, graveling and re-graveling, macadamizing, planking and re-planking of streets, alleys, highways, or lanes, the construction and repair of sidewalks and private drains, the improvement of public grounds or buildings belonging to the city, except school-houses, the widening, deepening or dredging of the Chicago river, or either of its branches, the opening, straightening, widening or closing of any street, alley, lane or highway, or for any other improvement, the doing of which is within the discretion and control of the municipal government of said city, shall hereafter be first made to the board of public works; or, if first made to the common council, shall be by them referred to said board. Upon receiving any such application, the said board shall proceed to investigate the same; and if they shall determine that such improvement is necessary and proper, they shall report the same to the common council, accompanied with an estimate of the expense thereof, and a proper ordinance or order directing the work. If they do not approve of such application, they shall report the reasons for their disapproval, and the common council may then, in either case, order the doing of such work, or the making of such public improvement, after having first obtained from said board an estimate of the expense thereof. The board of public works may also in like manner recommend, whenever they think proper, any improvement of the nature specified in this section, though no application may have been made therefor; and in all cases the common council, after having obtained from said board an estimate of the expense, may make such changes in the proposed plan as may be petitioned for by any of the owners of the property to be assessed.

Board to report to council.

Council may modify plans.

SEC. 4. Whenever the board of public works shall recommend the opening, straightening, widening, or extending, of any street, lane, alley or highway, in said city, or the widening of the Chicago river, or either of its branches, or any part or parts of the same, they shall furnish to the common council a plan or profile of the contemplated improvement, and shall also specially report whether, in their opinion, real estate to be assessed for said improvement can be found benefited to the extent of the damages, costs and expenses necessary to be incurred thereby; and whenever in any case they shall recommend to the common council the doing of any work, or the making of any public improvement, to be paid for by a special assessment, they shall, with such recommendation, certify to the

Plan or profile of improvement to be furnished.

Facts to be specially reported.

common council whether the contemplated improvement is asked for by the petition of the owners of a majority of the property to be assessed for such improvement, and if the owners of a majority of the property so to be assessed shall have failed to petition therefor, the same shall be ordered only by the votes of at least three-fourths of all the aldermen present, such vote to be entered by ayes and noes on the record of the common council. The certificate of said board of public works shall be *prima facie* evidence as to the number of said petitioners and of their interest in the property assessed.

Three-fourths vote.

CONDEMNATION PROCEEDINGS.

Assessment for condemnation of real estate.

SEC. 5. Whenever any order is passed by the common council, by virtue hereof, for the making of any public improvement mentioned in the first section of this chapter, which shall require the appropriation or condemnation of any land or real estate, the commissioners of the board of public works shall forthwith proceed to ascertain and assess the damages and recompense due the owners of such land respectively, and at the same time to determine what real estate will be benefited by such improvement, and assess the damages, together with the costs of the proceedings, on the real estate by them deemed benefited, in proportion, as nearly as may be, to the benefit resulting to each separate lot or parcel. If the proceeding be one for widening the Chicago river, or either of its branches, or any part or parts of the same, the assessment may, if so ordered by the common council, be made to include the estimated expense of excavation and completing the work, in addition to the value of the land condemned; but in all other cases shall cover only the damages awarded for the real estate appropriated and the costs of the proceedings.

Widening the river.

Oath of commissioners.

SEC. 6. Before proceeding to make said assessment, the commissioners shall be sworn, faithfully to execute their duties, according to the best of their ability. They shall then give six days' notice by publication in the corporation newspaper, of the time and place of their meeting for the purpose of making said assessment, in which notice they shall specify what such assessment is to be for, and shall

Notice.

describe the land to be condemned, as near as may be done by general description. The meeting of said commissioners when engaged in making such assessment, shall be held in a public place in said city, to be specified in said notice, and all persons interested in any such assessment, shall have the right to be present and be heard, either in person or by counsel. The commissioners shall view the premises to be condemned, and receive any legal evidence that may be offered, for the purpose of proving the true value thereof, or the damages that will be sustained, or benefit conferred by reason of the contemplated improvement; and the said commissioners, for this purpose, are hereby authorized to administer oaths to all witnesses produced before them. They shall permit the counsel to the corporation, or city attorney, to appear before them at such hearing, to represent the interests of the city, and may adjourn from time to time until said assessment is completed.

Evidence.

(*Several notices may be in one advertisement*, Sec. 8, *post*, 179.)

Appraisal of damage and benefit.

SEC. 7. The commissioners, in making said assessment, shall determine and appraise, to the owner or owners, the value of the real estate appropriated for the improvement, and the injury arising to them, respectively, from the condemnation thereof, which shall be awarded to such owners respectively, as damages, after making due allowance therefrom for any benefit which such owners may respectively derive from such improvement.

Report to show damage and benefit.

SEC. 8. If the damage to any person be greater than the benefit received, or if the benefit be greater than the damage, in either case the commissioners shall strike a balance, and carry the difference forward to another column, so that the assessment may show what amount is to be received or paid by such owners, respectively, and the difference only hall, in any case, be collectable of them, or paid to them.

Value of land donated may be set off against benefits.

SEC. 9. In the assessment of damages and benefits for the opening of any street or alley, it shall be lawful for the commissioners, in their discretion, in making such assessment, where part of the land to be laid out into such street or alley, has been theretofore donated by any person or persons for such street or alley, to appraise the value of the land so donated, and to apply the value thereof, as far as the amount so appraised shall go, as an offset to the benefits assessed against the person or persons making such donation, or those claiming under them; but nothing herein contained shall authorize any person or persons by whom such donation is made, to claim from the city the amount of such appraisal, except as an offset, as herein provided. And where the assessment is one for the widening of any street, which may have been theretofore, either in whole or in part, donated to the public by the proprietors of the adjoining land, it shall also be lawful for said commissioners, in their discretion, to make such allowance therefor, in their assessment of benefits, as shall to them seem equitable and just.

Valuation of buildings.

SEC. 10. If there should be any building standing in whole or in part upon the land to be taken, the commissioners shall add to their estimate of damages for the land, the damages also for the building or part of building necessary to be taken, if it be the property of the owner of the land. When owned by any other person, the damages for the building shall be assessed separately. The value of such building to the owner to remove, or of the part thereof necessary to be taken, shall also be determined by the commissioners, and notice of such determination shall be given by them to the owner when known, if a resident of the city, or left at his usual place of business or abode. If the owner is not known, or is a non-resident, notice to all persons interested shall be given by publication for ten days in the corporation newspaper. Such owner may, at any time within ten days after service, or the first publication of such notice, notify to said commissioners in writing his election to take such building or part of building at their appraisal; and in such case the amount of such appraisal shall be deducted by the commissioners from the estimated damages for the land and building, where they belong to the same owner, and from the estimated damages for the building where they belong to different owners; and the owner shall have such time for the removal of the building after the confirmation of the assessment, as the board of public works may allow. If the owner shall refuse to take the building at the appraisal, or fail to give notice of his

Notice to owner.

election as aforesaid, within the time prescribed, then no deduction shall be made from the estimated damages aforesaid, and the board of public works shall, after the confirmation of the assessment, and after the money is collected or otherwise provided and ready in the hands of the treasurer to be paid over to the owner for his damages, proceed to sell such building or part of building, at public auction, for cash, giving at least five days' public notice of the sale by publication in the corporation newspaper, and cause such building to be then forthwith removed. The proceeds of such sale shall be paid into the city treasury to the credit of the special assessment fund raised for the said improvement. **Sale of buildings.**

(*Several notices may be in one advertisement*, Sec. 8, *post*, 179.)

SEC. 11. If the lands and buildings belong to different persons, or if the land be subject to lease, the injury done to such persons, respectively, may be awarded to them by the commissioners, less the benefits resulting to them, respectively, from the improvement. **Each party in interest entitled to award.**

SEC. 12. Having ascertained the damages and expenses of such improvement, as aforesaid, the commissioners shall thereupon apportion and assess the same, together with costs of the proceedings, upon the real estate by them deemed benefited, in proportion to the benefits resulting thereto from the improvement, as nearly as may be, and shall briefly describe the real estate upon which their assessments may be made; and it shall constitute no legal objection to said assessment that the amount thereof either exceeds or falls short of the original estimate of the cost of the improvement submitted to the common council by the board of public works. **Damages to be assessed on real estate benefited.**

SEC. 13. When completed, the commissioners shall sign and file the assessment roll in the office of the city clerk, and a duplicate thereof in the office of the board of public works. Notice shall be given by said commissioners, by six days' publication in the corporation newspaper, of the filing of such assessment roll in the clerk's office; and that at the next regular meeting of the common council, to be held after the expiration of such publication, they will **Return of assessment roll.** **Notice** apply to the common council for a confirmation of said assessment. Objections to said assessment may be heard before the common council, but all parties objecting shall file their objections in writing, in the office of the city clerk, at least one day prior to such meeting of the council. Should no quorum be present at such meeting, the matter shall stand postponed to the next regular meeting of the council when there shall be a quorum. The council shall have power to adjourn such hearing from time to time, and shall have power, in their discretion, to revise and correct the assessment, and confirm or annul the same, and direct a new assessment to be made. Said assessment, when confirmed by the common council, shall be final and conclusive upon all parties interested therein, except as is hereinafter provided; and when said assessment is confirmed and no appeal is taken, as herein provided, a warrant shall issue for the collection of the same, signed by the mayor and city clerk. If said assessment shall be annulled by the common council or set aside by the court, the commissioners of the board of public works shall proceed to make a new assessment, and return the same in like manner, and give like notice as herein required in relation to the first; and all parties in interest shall have the like rights, and the common council shall perform like duties and have like powers in relation to any subsequent determination, as are hereby given in relation to the first.

Objections.

Action of council thereon.

(*Several notices may be given in one advertisement*, Sec. 8, *post*, 179.)

Appeal from confirmation.

SEC. 14. Any person whose property has been appropriated, and who has filed objections to said assessment, as herein before provided, shall have the right, at any time within ten days after the confirmation of the same by the common council, and not after that time, having first given notice of his or her intention so to do, to the counsel to the corporation, or city attorney, specifying in such notice the court to which the appeal is to be taken, to pray an appeal to any court of general jurisdiction in Cook county, from the order of the common council confirming such assessment, upon filing a bond to said city, approved by the judge or judges of the court to which the appeal is taken, conditioned to save the city harmless from all damages caused by the taking of such appeal. In case of appeal, a copy of the assessment roll, as confirmed by the common council, and of the objections to the final order confirming the same, shall be filed in the office of the clerk of the court to which such appeal shall be taken, and the cause shall be docketed by such clerk in the name of the person taking such appeal against the city of Chicago, as an "appeal from assessment." The said cause shall be then at issue, and shall have the preference in order of trial over all civil causes pending in said court. Such appeal shall be tried by the court, and on such trial the only questions to be passed upon, shall be, whether the common council had jurisdiction in the case, and whether the valuation of the property specified in the objection is a fair valuation, and the assessment, so far as it affects said property, is a fair and impartial assessment. The judgment of the court shall be either to confirm or annul the assessment, from which judgment no appeal or writ of error shall lie.

Condemnation effectual on confirmation.

SEC. 15. When any such assessment shall have been confirmed by the common council, and no appeal have been taken therefrom, or, if an appeal shall have been taken, when judgment to confirm the assessment shall have been rendered thereon, the same shall be a lawful and sufficient condemnation of the land or property ordered to be appropriated. The board of public works shall thereupon cause to be paid to the owner of such property, or to his agent, the amount of damages, over and above all benefits, which may have been awarded therefor, as soon as a sufficient amount of the assessment shall have been collected for that purpose; but the claimant shall in all cases furnish an abstract of title, showing himself entitled to such damages, before the same shall be paid. If, in any case, there shall be any doubt as to who is entitled to the damages for land taken, the city may require of the claimant a bond with good and sufficient sureties to hold said city harmless from all loss, costs and expenses, in case any other person should claim said damages. In all cases, the title to land taken and condemned in manner aforesaid, shall be vested absolutely in the city, in fee simple.

Payment of damages.

Notice of readiness to pay.

SEC. 16. As soon as the money is collected, and ready, in the hands of the treasurer, to be paid over to parties entitled to damages for property condemned, ten days' notice thereof shall be given by the board of public works in the corporation newspaper; and the city may then, and not before, enter upon, take possession of and appropriate the property condemned.

Possession, when to be taken.

(*Several notices may be in one advertisement*, Sec. 8, *post*, 179. *Further provisions as to when city may enter upon property condemned*, Sec. 7, *post*, 179.)

When whole lot taken, contracts to cease.

SEC. 17. When the whole of any lot or parcel of land or other premises under lease or other contract, shall be taken for any of the purposes aforesaid, by virtue of this act, all the covenants, contracts and engagements between landlords and tenants, or any other contracting parties touching the same or any part thereof, shall, upon publication of the notice required in the preceding section, respectively cease and be absolutely discharged.

When part taken, contracts to cease for such part.

SEC. 18. Where part only of any lot or parcel of land or other premises so under lease or other contract, shall be taken for any of the purposes aforesaid, by virtue of this act, all the covenants, contracts and agreements and engagements respecting the same, upon publication of the aforesaid notice, shall be absolutely discharged as to the part thereof so taken, but shall remain valid as to the residue thereof, and the rents, considerations and payments reserved, payable and to be paid for, or in respect to the same, shall be so proportioned as that the part thereof, justly and equitably payable for such residue thereof, and no more, shall be paid or recoverable for the same.

Proceedings to be recorded.

SEC. 19. All proceedings taken by said board of public works, in relation to the laying out of any street, alley, lane or highway, wharf, slip, public square or ground, or the widening, contracting, straightening or discontinuing the same, and all proceedings for the widening of the Chicago river, or either of its branches, shall be recorded by the said board, in a book or books kept for that purpose, describing particularly the said improvements, and the real estate to be taken therefor.

DEEPENING AND DREDGING THE RIVER.

SEC. 20. Whenever any order is passed by the common council, by virtue hereof, to deepen or dredge out the Chicago river, or either of its branches, or any part or parts of the same, the commissioners of the board of public works shall forthwith proceed to assess the amount directed to be assessed, on the real estate by them deemed benefited by any such improvement, in proportion, as nearly as may be, to the benefit resulting to each separate lot or parcel; and shall briefly describe in the assessment roll, to be made by them, the real estate assessed, and the amount of the assessment in each case.

Assessment for deepening river.

IMPROVEMENT OF STREETS.

SEC. 21. Whenever any order is passed by the common council, by virtue hereof, for the filling, grading, leveling, paving, curbing, walling, graveling, macadamizing, planking or repairing of any street, lane, alley or highway, the commissioners of the board of public works shall forthwith proceed to assess the amount directed by the common council to be assessed, on the real estate fronting or abutting on the contemplated improvement. Said assessment shall be made in such manner, as nearly as may be, that each separate block, lot, sub-lot, piece or parcel of land, on either side of the street or part of street to be improved, shall sustain the cost and expense of making or completing the improvement upon that half of the street directly adjacent to or in front of the same.

Assessment for improving streets, etc.

(*Repealed, and new section enacted*, Sec. 4, *post*, 179, and Sec. 1, *post*, 177.)

SEC. 22. Where, in any case, any portion of the cost and expense of making any improvement mentioned in the foregoing section, shall, by virtue of any valid law or ordinance of the corporation, or by virtue of any valid contract, be chargeable upon any railway company, the amount so chargeable may be assessed upon said railway company, and the balance only, upon the real estate fronting or abutting on such improvement; and the city may collect the amount so assessed upon the said railway company, by distress and sale of personal property, as in other

Assessment on railway companies.

cases, or by suit brought for that purpose: *Provided*, That any real estate belonging to such railway company and fronting or abutting upon the said improvement shall be assessed as in other cases.

(*Repealed, and new section enacted*, Sec. 4, *post*, 179, and Sec. 2, *post*, 178.)

Oath of commissioners. SEC. 23. Before proceeding to make an assessment, for any improvement mentioned in the three preceding sections, said commissioners shall be sworn as in other cases, **Notice of meeting.** and shall give six days' notice, by publication in the corporation newspaper, of the time and place of their meeting for the purpose of making said assessment, in which notice they shall specify what such assessment is to be for, and the amount to be assessed. All persons interested in any such assessment shall have the right to be present and be heard, either in person or by counsel, and the commissioners may, in their discretion, receive any legal evidence, and may adjourn, if necessary, from time to time.

(*Several notices may be in one advertisement*, Sec. 8, *post*, 179.)

Return of assessment roll. SEC. 24. When the commissioners shall have completed their assessment, they shall sign and return the same in like manner, and give like notice of the application to the common council for confirmation, as herein required in relation to assessments for the condemnation of real estate; and **Proceedings thereon.** all parties in interest shall have the like rights, and the common council shall perform like duties and have like powers in relation to such assessment, as are herein given in relation to assessments for the condemnation of real estate. When confirmed by the common council, said assessment shall be final and conclusive upon all parties interested therein, and shall be collected as in other cases; and no appeal shall lie in any case from the order of confirmation. If any assessment be annulled or set aside, the said commissioners shall proceed to make a new assessment, and shall return the same in like manner, and give like notices, as herein required in relation to the first.

(*Several notices may be in one advertisement*, Sec. 8, *post*, 179.)

SIDEWALKS AND DRAINS.

SEC. 25. All owners or occupants of real estate, in front of, adjacent to, or upon whose premises the common council shall order or direct any sidewalk or private drain to be constructed, shall construct such sidewalk or private drain at their own costs and charges, in the manner prescribed by said common council, and within such reasonable time, not exceeding twenty days, as the board of public works shall direct, of which time notice shall be given to such owner or occupant, by personal service, or leaving the same at his usual place of business or abode, or by three days' publication in the corporation newspaper. If the work be not done in the manner and within the time prescribed, the commissioners of the board of public works shall forthwith proceed to assess the amount necessary to be assessed therefor, together with all costs, upon the real estate aforesaid, which assessment shall be made and returned, and may be confirmed and collected in the same manner as in the case of filling, grading or paving streets, and when confirmed shall have the same force and effect; like powers, rights and duties being hereby conferred and imposed upon the said commissioners and common council and on all parties interested, in both cases.

Owners to construct sidewalks.

If delinquent, expense to be assessed.

(*Repealed, and new section enacted*, Sec. 4, *post*, 179, and Sec. 1, *post*, 177.)

SEC. 26. For any neglect or refusal to comply with any order of the common council in the preceding section referred to, the said common council may impose by ordinance such penalties upon the owners or occupants aforesaid, not exceeding twenty dollars for each day's neglect, as to the said common council shall seem proper.

Penalty for neglect.

(*Repealed*, Sec. 4, *post*, 179.)

SEC. 27. Upon the passage of any order in the two preceding sections referred to, the board of public works may, in their discretion, in case the said owners or occupants should fail to comply therewith, cause said improvement to be made and paid for out of any moneys in the treasury at their disposal, and afterwards cause the expense thereof, together with all costs, to be reimbursed by a special assessment to be levied and collected as in other cases, or the

On failure of owner to construct, board of public works may.

Expense to be assessed.

same may be recovered by suit from such owner or occupant, as for money paid and laid out for his use and at his request.

(*Repealed*, Sec. 4, *post*, 179.)

Repair of sidewalks and drains.

SEC. 28. When in any case, it shall be deemed necessary by the board of public works to cause any sidewalk to be raised, lowered, repaired or relaid, or any private drain to be raised, lowered, repaired or cleansed, it shall be lawful for said board to require the owner or occupant of the premises, in front of, adjacent to or upon which said improvement is to be made, to make the same forthwith, or within such reasonable time as the board of public works may prescribe, either upon written or verbal notice to that effect; and in case of neglect or refusal to comply with said requirement, as well as in all cases where the owner or occupant cannot be found, the board of public works may cause the work to be done and paid for out of any moneys in the treasury at their disposal. **Assessment therefor.** Said board shall then report to the common council the amount of said expenditure, giving a description of the lots or other premises liable therefor, and the amount for which each is chargeable. The common council shall thereupon assess the said expenses, by an order, ordinance or resolution, upon such lots respectively, and the same may be collected by warrant and sale of the premises, as in other cases. **Suit to recover expense.** A suit may also be maintained against the owner or occupant of such premises for recovery of such expenses, as for money paid and laid out for his use and at his request. The common council may also by ordinance impose such penalties upon the owners or occupants aforesaid for any neglect or refusal to comply with the aforesaid requirement, not exceeding twenty dollars for each day's neglect, as to the said common council shall seem proper.

Owners and occupants responsible for safe condition of sidewalk.

SEC. 29. Nothing in the preceding sections contained, shall be so construed as to relieve the owners or occupants of real estate from the duty of keeping the sidewalk in front of or adjacent to their respective premises, at all times in a safe condition and in a good and thorough state of repair; but such duty is hereby expressly enjoined and imposed upon all such owners and occupants; and if at any time any injury shall be sustained by any individual, or the city shall be subjected to any damages in consequence of any defect in any sidewalk, or its being out of repair, the owner and occupant of the adjacent premises, whose duty it is to make repairs, shall be jointly and severally liable therefor, and the same may be recovered by suit in any court of general jurisdiction. If the owner be a non-resident, proceedings may be commenced against the property by attachment, as in other cases of attachment under the laws of this State.

ERECTION OF LAMP POSTS.

SEC. 30. Whenever any order is passed by the common council, by virtue hereof, for the erection of lamp posts upon any of the streets in said city, the commissioners of the board of public works shall forthwith proceed to assess the amount directed by the common council to be assessed therefor, upon the several lots, pieces or parcels of land fronting or abutting on the street or part of street along which said posts are to be erected. Said assessment shall be made in such manner, as nearly as may be, that each separate lot, piece or parcel of land on either side of such street, for the whole distance proposed to be lighted, shall sustain its fair proportionate share of the expense, according to the number of lineal feet of each separate lot or parcel on such street; which assessment shall be made and returned, and may be confirmed and collected, in the same manner as in the case of filling, grading or paving streets, and when confirmed shall have the same force and effect; like powers, rights and duties being hereby conferred and imposed upon the said commissioners and common council, and on all parties interested, in both cases. Assessment for lamp posts.

(*Repealed, and new section enacted*, Sec. 4, *post*, 179, and Sec. 3, *post*, 178.)

REMOVAL OF NUISANCES.

SEC. 31. In all cases where expenses may be incurred in the removal of any nuisance, the common council may cause the same to be assessed against the real estate chargeable therewith, in the manner prescribed in the twenty-eighth section of this chapter. Such expense shall be like- Removal of nuisances; expense, how collected.

wise collectable of the owner or occupant of such premises in a suit for money expended to his or their use. Suit may, in like manner, be brought for such expenses against the author of such nuisance, when known, or any person whose duty it may be to remove or abate the same.

(*Assessment may be before expenses are incurred*, Sec. 6, *post*, 179.)

GENERAL PROVISIONS.

Landlord to pay assessments when no agreement to the contrary.

SEC. 32. In all cases where there is no agreement to the contrary, the owner or landlord, and not the occupant or tenant, shall be deemed the person who ought to bear and pay every charge or assessment made for the expense of any public improvement. Where any such charge or assessment shall be made upon or paid by any person, when, by agreement or by law, the same ought to be borne or paid by any other person, it shall be lawful for one so paying to sue for and recover of the person bound to pay the same, the amount so paid, with interest; or he may retain and deduct the same from any rent due or to become due to such person. Nothing herein contained shall impair or in any way affect any agreement between any landlord and tenant, or other persons, respecting the payment of such assessments.

Infant owners of real estate may have guardians.

SEC. 33. When any known owner residing in said city, or elsewhere, shall be an infant, and any proceedings had under this act shall render it necessary, the circuit court of the county of Cook, the judge thereof, or any judge of any court of general jurisdiction in said city, or the judge of the county court, may, upon the application of the board of public works, or such infant, or his next friend, appoint a guardian for such infant, taking security from such guardian for the faithful execution of such trust, and all personal notices and summons, required by this act, may be served on such guardian.

Certiorari, when to be issued.

SEC. 34. No writ of *certiorari* shall be allowed in the case of any special assessment proceedings commenced under the provisions of this act, unless applied for within thirty days after the confirmation of the assessment, and not then at the suit of any party who has neglected to file his objections to such confirmation as hereinbefore provided, unless the party applying for the writ shall satisfy the court by legal and satisfactory evidence, other than his own oath, that he has a sufficient legal excuse for such omission or neglect.

New assessment.

SEC. 35. If, in any case, the first assessment prove insufficient, the board of public works shall make a second in the same manner, and so on, until sufficient moneys shall have been realized to pay for such public improvement. If too large a sum shall at any time be raised, the excess shall be refunded rateably to those by whom it was paid.

Excess refunded.

On failure to collect, new assessment may be made.

SEC. 36. If, from any cause, the city shall fail to collect the whole or any portion of any special assessment which may be hereafter levied, and which shall not be canceled and set aside by the order of any court upon *certiorari* or appeal, for any public improvement required to be paid for by special assessment, the common council may, at any time within five years after the confirmation of the original assessment, direct a new assessment to be made upon the delinquent property, for the amount of such deficiency, and interest thereon from the date of such original assessment, which assessment shall be made, as near as may be, in the same manner as is herein prescribed for the first assessment. In all cases where partial payments shall have been made on such former assessment, they shall be credited or allowed on the new assessment to the property for which they were made, so that the assessment shall be equal and impartial in its results. If such new assessment prove ineffectual, either in whole or in part, the common council may, at any time within said period of five years, order a third, and so on, to be levied in the same manner and for the same purpose; and it shall constitute no legal objection to such re-assessments that the property may have changed hands or been encumbered subsequent to the date of the original assessment, it being the true intent and meaning of this section, to make the cost and expense of all public improvements to be paid for by a special assessment, a charge upon the property assessed therefor, for the full period of five years from the confirmation of the original assessment, and for such longer period as may be required to collect, in due

Assessment, a lien for five years.

course of law, any new assessment ordered by the common council within that period.

Interested commissioners disqualified.

SEC. 37. If, in any case, the commissioners of the board of public works, or either of them, are specially interested in any special assessment about to be levied, the commissioners or commissioner so interested shall be disqualified from serving in that particular case. Any vacancy occasioned in this manner, or by the absence, inability or refusal to serve of any commissioner, may be filled by appointment by the mayor. The special commissioner so appointed shall be allowed two dollars per day for his actual services, and shall be sworn in the same manner as the other commissioners.

Special commissioner.

River improvements may be paid for by general tax.

SEC. 38. Should the board of public works report to the common council, at any time, in favor of any proposed improvement of the Chicago river, or either of its branches, or any part or parts of the same, and at the same time recommend that the expense thereof be defrayed by a general tax upon all the taxable property in the city, it shall be lawful for the said common council to levy such a tax; and in such case, the amount required to be raised shall be assessed upon the whole taxable real and personal property in the city, and be included in the general tax levy of the succeeding year, under the head of "permanent improvement tax."

Improvements chargeable to general fund.

SEC. 39. The cost and expense of constructing or repairing wharves and slips at the ends of streets, of the cleaning of streets, alleys, lanes and highways, and of ordinary repairs upon the same, of purchasing public squares or parks, and improving the same, of all improvements at the intersections of streets or alleys, or of streets and alleys, (excepting sidewalks and area or street walls,) of the repair of public buildings belonging to the city, of the construction of cross walks, and of all bridges and other improvements not enumerated in the first section of this chapter, shall be chargeable upon, and paid out of, the general fund, or other appropriate fund of said city not raised by special assessment.

(*Lamp posts also excepted*, Sec. 1, *post*, 177.)

SEC. 40. Whenever any number of persons shall agree

to secure to the board of public works the full expense of constructing any bridge, the common council may, in their discretion, authorize the persons agreeing to bear the expense thereof, to contract for the building of such bridge. In such case, however, the board of public works shall have the entire charge and superintendence of such work, and the plans for the same shall be subject to their approval.

Construction of bridges by private enterprise.

SEC. 41. Any person or persons, who shall injure or destroy any bridge, the construction of which may have been heretofore or may be hereafter authorized or permitted to be built by the common council, or any public buildings or other property belonging to said city, or shall cause or procure the same to be injured or destroyed, or who shall wantonly spoil or damage any street, alley, sidewalk, public square or ground, shall be subject to a penalty not exceeding five hundred dollars for each offense, to be recovered by the city in an action of debt, and may be imprisoned for a term not exceeding six months, in the discretion of the court before whom such conviction may be had, and such person or persons shall also be liable in a civil action at the suit of the city for the damages occasioned by such injury or destruction.

Penalty for willful injury to public property.

SEC. 42. Upon the petition of a majority of the owners of lots upon Michigan avenue, lying between Washington street and the north line of a short street running from Michigan avenue to lake Michigan, on the north line of block twenty-three, in fractional section fifteen addition to Chicago, it shall be lawful for the common council to increase the width of said avenue thirty-six feet upon the east line thereof, from the north line of Randolph street to the north line of the short street running from Michigan avenue to lake Michigan, on the north line of block twenty-three, in fractional section fifteen addition to Chicago, and secure the east line of the proposed increase of width by a substantial stone wall, so far as the same is necessary for this purpose. Said council shall grade the increased width aforesaid, to a line of the present level of said street or avenue, and devote twenty feet of said width to the present road bed, graveling the same as the present road bed is graveled, and upon the remaining sixteen feet of said increased width,

Improvement of Michigan avenue.

construct and lay down a good and substantial stone sidewalk, and upon the wall aforesaid, so far as the same is constructed, and upon a proper stone foundation to be built, erect upon the same, a good and substantial iron fence, along the whole line aforesaid. The said common council, to defray the expense of said improvements, are hereby authorized to have the same assessed by the board of public works, two-thirds of which shall be assessed upon the blocks of land fronting upon Michigan avenue, and lying between Washington street and Twelfth street, and the remaining one-third shall be paid out of the treasury of the city.

Encroachments prohibited on grounds east of Michigan avenue.

SEC. 43. No encroachment shall be made upon the land or water, west of a line mentioned in the second section of an ordinance concerning the Illinois Central Railroad, (which line is "not less than four hundred feet east from the west line of Michigan avenue, and parallel thereto,") by any railroad company, nor shall any cars, locomotives, engines, machines or other things belonging to any railroad or transportation company be permitted to occupy the same, nor shall any cars or machinery be left standing upon said tract fronting any part of Michigan avenue south of Madison street, nor shall the city council ever allow any encroachments west of the line above described. And any person being the owner of, or interested in any lot or part of a lot fronting on Michigan avenue, shall have the right to enjoin said company and all other persons and corporations from any violations of the provisions of this section, or of said ordinance, and by bill or petition in chancery in his or their own name, or otherwise, enforce the provisions of said ordinance, and of this section, and recover such damages for any such encroachment or violation, as the court shall deem just; the State of Illinois, by its canal commissioners, having declared that the public ground east of said lots should forever remain open and vacant, neither the common council of the city of Chicago, nor any other authority, shall ever have the power to permit encroachments thereon, without the assent of all the persons owning lots or land on said street or avenue.

SEC. 44. All provisions of former acts relating to the

levying of special assessments in the city of Chicago are hereby repealed: *Provided, however*, That the city shall have the right to continue and complete all proceedings commenced under any former law or ordinance, and shall have and enjoy all the rights accrued or to accrue thereunder, the same as if said provisions remained in full force and effect. Repealing clause.

CHAPTER VIII.

OF TAXATION.

SECTION
1. Power to levy tax for general purposes; for schools; for police expenses; for reform school; for lighting streets; for sewerage purposes; for interest on funded debt; for permanent improvements; to pay temporary loans.
2. Sinking fund tax.
3. Street tax abolished.

SECTION
4. Improvements on school and canal lands and wharfing privileges, subject to taxation.
5. Insurance rates; how collected.
6. Insurance rates; how appropriated.
7. Repeal of sections 6, 7, 8 and 9, of act to incorporate Firemen's Benevolent Association.

SECTION 1. The common council shall have power, within the city, by ordinance: Council to levy taxes.

First. To annually levy and collect taxes, not exceeding four and a half mills on the dollar, on the assessed value of all real and personal estate, in the city, made taxable by the laws of this State, to defray the contingent and other expenses of the city, not herein otherwise specially provided for; which taxes shall constitute the general fund. Four and one-half mills for general expenses.

Second. To annually levy and collect a school tax, not exceeding two mills on the dollar, on all taxable real and personal estate, to meet the expenses of purchasing grounds for school-houses, and building and repairing school-houses, and supporting and maintaining schools. Two mills for schools.

(*Clause repealed, and new enactment*, Sec. 29, *post*, 188.)

Third. To annually levy and collect a tax, not exceeding two mills on the dollar, on all taxable real and personal estate, for the police expenses of said city. Two mills for police expenses.

(*Clause repealed, and new enactments*, Sec. 24, *post*, 186, and Sec. 22, *post*, 197.)

Fourth. To annually levy and collect a tax, not exceed- One mill for reform school. ing one mill on the dollar, on all taxable real and personal estate, for the support of the reform school.

Two mills for lighting streets. *Fifth.* To annually levy and collect a tax, not exceeding two mills on the dollar, on all taxable real and personal estate, to defray the expense of lighting the streets in said city.

Sewerage tax. *Sixth.* To annually levy and collect a tax of sufficient amount, on all taxable real and personal estate, to pay the interest accruing on the sewerage debt, and provide a sinking fund for the liquidation of said debt, and to maintain the sewerage works and keep the same in repair.

Interest tax. *Seventh.* To annually levy and collect a tax of sufficient amount, on all taxable real and personal estate, to meet the interest accruing on the general bonded debt of said city, and also to provide for the interest accruing upon the water-loan bonds, in case the revenue from the water works should be insufficient to pay the same.

Two and one-half mills for permanent improvements. *Eighth.* To annually levy and collect a tax, not exceeding two and a half mills on the dollar, on all taxable real and personal estate, when required, for the erection of a city hall, markets, bridewell or house of correction, or other public buildings, the purchase of grounds therefor, or for public squares or parks, the building of bridges, improvement of the river and harbor, or any other permanent improvement: *Provided,* That no tax shall be levied under this clause, unless a majority of all the aldermen elected shall vote in favor of the same.

Tax to pay temporary loans. *Ninth.* To annually levy and collect a tax of sufficient amount, on all taxable real and personal estate, when required, to pay any debt that may have been contracted for money borrowed, during the preceding year, to provide for the expense incurred in making any public improvement caused by any casualty or accident happening after the making of the annual appropriation for such year, or to pay any judgment that may have been recovered against the city and paid during such previous year.

(*Further power of taxation for other purposes,* Secs. 21, 22, *post,* 185.)

Sinking fund tax. SEC. 2. The common council shall also annually levy and collect a tax of one mill on the dollar on all real and personal estate in said city, made taxable by the laws of this State, to provide a sinking fund for the liquidation of the general bonded debt of said city, which amount shall be invested in the purchase of the bonds of said city, if they can be purchased upon satisfactory terms. All city bonds so purchased shall be immediately retired and canceled.

Street tax abolished. SEC. 3. The provision heretofore in force, requiring every male resident of the city, over the age of twenty-one years, and under the age of sixty years, to labor three days in each year upon the streets and alleys, or to commute therefor at the rate of fifty cents for each day's labor, is hereby abolished.

Improvements on school lands taxable. SEC. 4. All improvements on any school or canal lands or lots, and all improvements on the wharfing privileges in said city, together with the interest of the lessees or occupants in the premises, whether by lease, covenant or deed, shall be subject to taxation as real estate. And the personal property of the owner of such improvements, shall be liable for such taxes, and upon failure to pay the same, the collector may levy upon and sell the goods and chattels of such occupant or lessee, for the payment thereof and costs. And in case such lessee or occupant shall have no personal estate, and neglect to pay the taxes, the interest of such lessee or occupant in such premises, together with the improvements, may be sold as real estate: *Provided*, The purchaser shall acquire no greater rights in the land than the tenant or occupant thereof had, but shall take the same subject to all the covenants and agreements in relation thereto.

Personal property liable.

Insurance rates. SEC. 5. All corporations, companies or associations, not incorporated under the laws of this State, engaged in said city in effecting fire, marine or life insurance, shall pay to the city treasurer the sum of two dollars upon the hundred dollars, and at that rate upon the amount of all premiums, which, during the half year ending on every first day of July and January, shall have been received or have been agreed to be paid, for any insurance effected or agreed to be effected in said city, by or with such corporations, companies or associations respectively. Every person who shall act in said city as agent, or otherwise, for or on behalf of any such corporation, company or association, shall, on or before the fifteenth day of July and January in each year, render to the city comptroller a full, true and just account, verified by his oath, of all premiums which, during the half year ending on every first day of July and January preceding such report, shall have been received by him or any other person for him, or shall have been agreed to be paid, for or in behalf of any such corporation, company or association, and shall specify in said account, the amounts received for fire, marine and life insurance respectively. Said agents shall also pay over to the city treasurer at the time of rendering the aforesaid account, the amount of rates for which the company or companies represented by them are severally chargeable by virtue hereof. If such account be not rendered on or before the day hereinbefore designated for that purpose, or if the said rates shall remain unpaid after that day, it shall be unlawful for any corporation, company or association so in default, to transact any business of insurance in said city, until the said requisitions shall have been fully complied with; but this provision shall not relieve any company from the payment of any risk that may be taken in violation hereof. Any person or persons violating any of the provisions of this section shall be subject to indictment, and upon conviction thereof in any court of competent jurisdiction, shall be fined in any sum not exceeding one thousand dollars, or imprisoned not exceeding six months, or both, in the discretion of the court. Said rates may also be recovered of such corporation, company or association, or its agent, by action in the name and for the use of said city as for money had and received for its use.

Companies in default prohibited from doing business.

Penalty for violation.

Disposition of insurance rates.

SEC. 6. The comptroller shall keep three separate accounts of the moneys received from said insurance agents, one of which shall embrace all rates collected on premiums for fire insurance; the second, all rates collected on premiums for marine insurance, and the third, all rates collected on premiums for life insurance. The first insurance rates shall be used only for the purpose of promoting the efficiency of the fire department of said city, and providing a fund for the relief of disabled firemen; the marine insurance rates shall be exclusively appropriated to the improvement of the river and harbor; and the life insurance rates, to such sanitary measures as may be deemed necessary for the promotion of the public health.

SEC. 7. Sections six, seven, eight and nine, of an act approved June 21st, 1852, and entitled "An Act to incorporate the Firemen's Benevolent Association and for other purposes," and all other acts and parts of acts, so far as they require any individual, association or corporation engaged in the business of insurance, or any agent thereof, to pay any money to said firemen's benevolent association, upon their business profits or premiums, are hereby repealed. Repealing clause.

CHAPTER IX.

COLLECTION OF TAXES AND ASSESSMENTS.

SECTION
1. Valuation of taxable property by assessors; appraisal to be filed in clerk's office by first Monday in August; notice of meeting to hear objections.
2. Assessors to hear and consider objections; power to revise assessment.
3. Tax list of real estate to be made by clerk; form of the list; personal tax list.
4. Levy of annual taxes by common council.
5. Amount of taxes to be computed by city clerk and inserted in tax lists; collection warrants.
6. Delivery of warrants to collector.
7. Special assessment warrants, how and when to be issued.
8. Delivery thereof to collector.
9. Notices to be given by collector; duty of collector to levy; personal tax a lien on property.
10. Taxes made a lien on real estate from May first; on personal property from delivery of warrant to collector.
11. Five per cent. damages to be collected on taxes not paid on or before first of January; one per cent. a month on special assessments if not paid within sixty days after publication of notice.
12. Application for judgment against delinquent real estate; notice to be given.
13. Copy of advertisement to be filed in court.
14. Tax and assessment suits; mode of docketing.

SECTION
15. Judicial proceedings in such cases.
16. Order of sale.
17. Clerk to issue process for sale; collector empowered to sell; notice of sale.
18. Contents of advertisement.
19. Abbreviations may be used to describe property.
20. Mode of conducting sale; certificates of purchase.
21. Purchasers to make immediate payment; in case of default, property to be again offered; in the absence of bidders, property to be struck off to the city.
22. Return of precept by collector; record of sales to be kept by comptroller; certified copies made evidence.
23. Redemption from sale, when and by whom made; when deed to be executed to the purchaser; an abstract of deeds to be kept.
24. Certificates of purchase assignable.
25. Erroneous sales to be canceled.
26. Deeds *prima facie* evidence of certain facts; of what conclusive.
27. Successor of collector authorized to complete unfinished proceedings; comptroller to act in case of vacancy.
28. Assessment sales to be made at same time as tax sales, unless delayed by judicial proceedings.
29. Assessors and collector liable for neglect of duty.
30. Taxes and assessments valid, notwithstanding formal defects.
31. Redemption from sale when property is sold a second time within two years.

Valuation of taxable property.

SECTION 1. The assessors shall, immediately after their appointment in each year, proceed to examine and determine the valuation of the taxable real and personal estate in their respective divisions. Schedules of all the taxable real estate in the several divisions shall be furnished by the city clerk, to aid them in the performance of their duties, upon which they shall enter their valuations. Said appraisal, together with their appraisal of all the personal estate taxable in said city, shall be completed and filed in the office of the city clerk, on or before the first Monday of August in each year, unless further time shall be granted by the common council; and when so completed and filed, the said assessors shall fix upon a day for hearing objections thereto, and the city clerk shall give notice of the time and place of such hearing, by six days' publication thereof in the corporation newspaper. Any person feeling aggrieved by the assessment of his property, may appear at the time specified and make his objections.

When to be completed and filed.

Notice.

Power to revise.

SEC. 2. The said assessors shall meet at the time and place designated, to revise and correct their assessments. They shall hear and consider all objections which may be made, and shall have power to supply omissions in their assessment, and for the purpose of equalizing the same, to alter, add to, take from, and otherwise correct and revise the same. The said assessors may, if necessary, adjourn from time to time, until their revision shall have been completed.

Tax list of real estate.

SEC. 3. When said revision shall have been completed, the city clerk shall enter, under the direction of said assessors, in one or more books to be prepared for that purpose, a complete list of all the taxable real estate in said city, according to the schedules as returned and revised by the assessors, showing in a proper column, to be ruled for that purpose, the names of the different owners, so far as known to the said assessors, and in another column the amount of the valuation made in each case. Said books shall also have ruled therein an appropriate column for extending or inserting the amount of the taxes which may be levied upon said property. Said book or books shall together constitute the tax list of real estate for such year. The city clerk shall also enter, under the direction of said assessors, in

Personal tax list.

another book to be prepared for that purpose, a complete list of the taxable personal estate in said city, as returned and revised by said assessors, showing in the proper column the names of the different persons whose property has been assessed, and in other columns the valuations made by the assessors. Said book shall also have ruled therein an appropriate column for extending or inserting the amount of the taxes which may be levied thereon. Said book shall constitute the personal tax list for such year. The clerk shall add up the valuations in each list, and the aggregate amount thereof shall be entered by him at the foot of the appropriate column on the last page. When the said tax lists shall have been so completed, they shall be signed by the said assessors and left in the custody of the city clerk, and shall constitute the only record to be referred to in any case in which their said assessments may be drawn in question.

Tax levy.

SEC. 4. The common council shall thereupon, by an ordinance or resolution, levy such sum or sums of money as may be sufficient for the several purposes for which taxes are herein authorized to be levied (not exceeding the authorized percentage), particularly specifying the purpose for which the same are levied.

Taxes to be computed by clerk and inserted in tax lists.

SEC. 5. It shall be the duty of the city clerk to estimate the several taxes levied by the common council, computing them together as one tax, and to insert the total amount of such taxes in the appropriate column of the several tax lists, opposite to the person or property chargeable therewith. When completed, the city clerk shall attach to each of said tax lists, a warrant, under the corporate seal, to be signed by the mayor, comptroller, and city clerk, directed to the collector, commanding him to make, levy and collect, as the taxes for such year, the several sums of money set opposite to the real and personal estate or persons in said tax lists mentioned or described, of the goods and chattels of the respective owners of such real and personal estate; which warrants shall also designate the names and rates of the several taxes included therein.

Collection warrants.

Delivery of warrants to collector.

SEC. 6. Said tax lists, with the warrants attached, shall be delivered to the collector by the comptroller, on or before the last day of October in each year, and shall constitute the only process necessary to be issued for the collection of the annual taxes. The comptroller shall take a receipt from the collector for the said tax lists, specifying the amount of the taxes levied in each list.

Special assessment warrants.

SEC. 7. When any special assessment shall have been confirmed by the common council, and no right of appeal therefrom is given by this act, it shall be the duty of the city clerk to issue a warrant for the collection thereof, which shall be under the corporate seal and signed by the mayor, comptroller and city clerk, and shall contain a copy of the assessment roll as confirmed by the common council, or so much thereof as describes the real estate assessed and the amount of the assessment in each case. If the right of appeal from the order of confirmation should exist in any case, said warrant shall not be issued until the expiration of the time limited for the taking of such appeal; and if in any case an appeal should be actually taken, the issuing of the warrant shall be delayed until after the determination of such appeal.

Delivery to collector.

SEC. 8. All warrants issued for the collection of special assessments, shall be delivered by the comptroller to the collector, taking his receipt therefor in the manner prescribed in the case of warrants for the collection of the annual taxes.

Notices to be given by collector.

SEC. 9. Upon the receipt of any warrant for the collection of the annual taxes, or any special assessment, the collector shall forthwith give notice, by ten days' publication in the corporation newspaper, that such warrant is in his hands for collection, briefly describing its nature, and requesting all persons interested to make immediate payment at his office, and that in default thereof the same will be collected at the cost and expense of the persons liable for the payment of such taxes or assessments. Immediately after receiving the personal property tax list, he shall notify all persons through the post office of the amount of their personal property tax. In the notice to be published in the corporation newspaper, he shall notify all parties interested, that after the expiration of sixty days from the day of

Duty to levy

receiving said list, he will levy upon the personal property of all who shall have failed to pay; and, at the end of sixty days, he shall so levy, if property belonging to such delinquent persons can be found; and he shall be liable for the amount of their tax in case of neglecting to do so. Where persons cannot be found, or property belonging to them, out of which to make the tax, the collector shall advertise their names and call for information concerning them and their property, and state the amount of their tax in the corporation newspaper; and this tax shall be a lien upon any property they may have or may thereafter acquire, until paid; and the collector or his successor in office may at any time thereafter levy for the same. But nothing in this section contained shall be so construed, as to prevent the collector from levying at any time after the publication of the ten days' notice above required.

(*Several notices may be in one advertisement*, Sec. 8, *post*, 179; *provisions as to fees and proceedings of collector on levy and sale of goods and chattels*, Sec. 9, *post*, 180.)

Taxes a lien on real estate from first of May.

SEC. 10. All taxes levied by the common council under this act, shall be a lien upon the real estate on which the same may be imposed, and said lien shall continue until said taxes are paid. Every person owning real property on the first day of May, including all such property purchased on that day, shall be liable for the taxes thereon for that year. The city taxes shall also be a lien on the personal property of all persons owing taxes, from and after the delivery of the warrant for the collection thereof to the collector; and no sale or transfer of said property shall affect the lien, but the said property may be seized by the collector wherever found, and removed, if necessary, and sold to discharge the taxes of the person owing the same; and the same proceedings may be resorted to by the collector upon any warrant issued for the collection of a special assessment.

Lien on personal property.

(*Provisions as to fees and proceedings of collector on levy and sale of goods and chattels*, Sec. 9, *post*, 180.)

Damages, when collected.

SEC. 11. If, from any cause, the taxes charged in the real estate tax list shall not be collected or paid, on the lands or lots described therein, on or before the first day of January ensuing the date of the warrant, it shall be the duty of the collector to demand and collect, for the use of said city, in addition to the taxes remaining unpaid, five per cent. damages thereon in every case; and if the assessments charged in any special assessment warrant shall not be paid within sixty days after the first publication of notice by the collector that he has received such warrant for collection, the assessments then remaining unpaid shall be collected, with damages, at the rate of one per cent. thereon for each and every month thereafter until the same shall be paid.

Application for judgment against delinquent property.

SEC. 12. It shall be the duty of the collector, between the fifteenth day of January and the last day of February in each year, to make report to some court of general jurisdiction held in said city, at any special or general term thereof, of all the taxes and assessments then remaining unpaid upon the real estate tax list, and all special assessment warrants which were delivered to him on or before the last day of the preceding October, asking for judgment against the several lots and parcels of land, or other property described in such list or warrants, for the amount of taxes, assessments, damages and costs respectively due thereon.

Notice.

The collector shall give notice, by six days' publication thereof in the corporation newspaper, of his intended application for judgment, which shall briefly specify the nature of the respective warrants upon which such application is to be made, and request all persons interested to attend at such term. The advertisement, so published, shall be deemed and taken to be sufficient and legal notice of the aforesaid intended application by the collector to such court for judgment, and shall be held a sufficient demand and refusal to pay the said taxes and assessments.

(*Several notices may be in one advertisement*, Sec. 8, *post*, 179.)

Copy of notice to be filed.

SEC. 13. The collector shall obtain a copy of the advertisement or advertisements referred to in the preceding section, together with a certificate of the due publication thereof, from the printer or publisher of the newspaper in which the same was published, and shall file the same with the clerk of such court at the said term, with said reports.

SEC. 14. The clerk of said court, upon the filing of such reports, by the collector, shall receive and preserve the same, and shall record thereon all judgments, orders and other proceedings of said court in relation thereto. Each of said reports shall constitute a separate suit, and shall be docketed by the clerk in the following form as nearly as may be, to wit: **Tax and assessment suits.**

City of Chicago vs. ——— and others. — Suit for Taxes.

Or if it be an assessment for some specified improvement, in the manner following:

City of Chicago vs. ——— and others. —— Suit for Assessment on Warrant, for ———. Or in such other manner as will sufficiently indicate the nature of the improvement for which the assessment is due.

SEC. 15. It shall be the duty of the court, upon the filing of said reports, to proceed immediately to the hearing of the same, and they shall have priority over all other causes pending in said court. The said court shall pronounce judgment against the several lots and parcels of land or other property described in said reports, for which no objections shall be filed, for the amount of the tax or assessment, damages and costs due severally thereon. The owner of any property described in said reports, or any person beneficially interested therein, may appear at said court, at the time designated in the collector's notice, and file objections in writing to the recovery of judgment against such property; but no objection shall be sustained founded on any mere formal irregularity or defect. The court shall hear and determine all objections in a summary way, without pleadings; and shall dispose of the same with as little delay as possible consistently with the demands of public justice. But should justice require that for any cause the suit as to one or more owners should be delayed for more than twenty days, judgment shall then be rendered as to the other property and lands, and process shall issue for the sale thereof the same as in all other cases. **Judicial proceedings.**

SEC. 16. In all cases where judgment shall be rendered by default against the property described in said reports, the court shall thereupon direct said clerk to make out and **Order of sale.**

enter an order for the sale of the same, which said order shall be substantially in the following form:

WHEREAS, Due notice has been given of the intended application for a judgment against said lands and other property, and no owner hath appeared to make defense or show cause why judgment should not be entered against the said lands and other property for the taxes, (*or* assessment, *as the case may be*,) damages and costs due and unpaid thereon; therefore, it is considered by the court, that judgment be and is hereby entered against the aforesaid lots and parcels of land and other property, in favor of the city of Chicago, for the sum annexed to each lot or parcel of land or other property, being the amount of the taxes, (*or* assessment), damages and costs due severally thereon; and it is ordered by the court, that the said several lots and parcels of land or other property, or so much thereof as shall be sufficient, of each of them, to satisfy the amount of the taxes, (*or* assessment), damages and costs annexed to them severally, be sold as the law directs.

In all cases where a defense shall be interposed, and judgment shall be rendered against the property, a similar order, adapted to the circumstances of the case, shall be made out and entered of record. Ten cents costs shall be taxed to each lot against which judgment is rendered; five cents to be for clerk's and judge's fees, and five cents for advertising the notice of sale.

Process for sale. SEC. 17. It shall be the duty of the clerk of such court, within twenty days after such order is granted as aforesaid, to make out, under the seal of said court, a copy of so much of said collector's report in such case as gives a description of the land or other property against which judgment shall have been rendered, and the amount of such judgment, together with the order of the court thereon; which shall constitute the process on which all lands, lots, sub-lots, pieces and parcels of land or other property, shall be sold for the amount of any taxes, assessments, damages and costs so levied, assessed or charged upon them; and the said city collector is hereby expressly authorized and empowered to make sale of such lands, lots, pieces, or parcels of land or other property, upon ten days' notice, to be published at least three times in some newspaper printed in said city.

Notice of sale.

Contents of notice. SEC. 18. The said advertisement, so to be published in each case of a judgment upon any special or general collection warrant and report as aforesaid, shall contain a list of the delinquent lots and parcels of land or other property to be sold, the names of the owners, if known, the amount of the judgments rendered thereon respectively, and the warrant upon which the same was rendered, the court which pronounced the judgment, and a notice that the same will be exposed to public sale at a time and place to be named in said advertisement by said collector. The omission of the name of any owner, or any mistake respecting the same, shall not invalidate the sale, if the property be otherwise described with sufficient certainty. The proceedings may be stopped at any time upon payment of said judgment to the collector.

Abbreviations.

SEC. 19. In all proceedings and advertisements for the collection of such taxes and assessments, and the sale of lands therefor, letters and figures may be used to denote lots, sub-lots, lands and blocks, sections, townships, ranges, and parts thereof, the year and the amounts.

Mode of conducting sale.

SEC. 20. The sale shall be made for the smallest portion of ground, (to be taken from the east side of the premises), for which any person will take the same and pay the amount of the judgment thereon. Certificates of sale shall be made and subscribed by the collector, which shall be delivered to the purchaser, which certificates shall contain the name of the purchaser, a description of the premises sold, the amount of the tax or assessment, with the amount of the judgment for which the same was sold, and the time when the right to redeem will expire. The collector shall continue such sale from day to day, until all the lots or parcels of land or other property contained in his precept, on which judgment remains unpaid, shall be sold or offered for sale.

Certificates of purchase.

Purchasers to make immediate payment.

SEC. 21. The person purchasing any lot or parcel of land or other property, shall forthwith pay to the collector the amount of the judgment due thereon, and on failure so to do, the said property shall be again offered for sale in the same manner as if no such sale had been made; and in no case shall the sale be closed until payment shall have been made. If no bid shall be made for any parcel of land, or other property, the same shall be struck off to the city; and

If no bid, property to be struck off to the city.

thereupon the city shall receive, in the corporate name, a certificate of the sale thereof, and shall be vested with the same rights as other purchasers at such sales.

Return of precept. Record of sales.

SEC. 22. The collector shall make return of his precept to the court from which the same was issued. A record of all sales made by the collector shall be kept in the office of the comptroller, which shall be open to public inspection at all reasonable times; and said record, or copies thereof, certified by said comptroller, shall be deemed sufficient evidence to prove the sale of any land or other property for taxes or assessments, or any other fact authorized to be recorded therein.

Redemption

SEC. 23. The right of redemption in all cases of sales for taxes or assessments, shall exist to the owner, his heirs, creditors, or assigns, to the same extent as is allowed by law, in the case of sales of real estate for taxes, on the payment, in lawful money of the United States, of double the amount for which the same was sold, and all taxes accruing subsequent to the sale, with interest at the rate of ten per cent. per annum. If the real estate of any infant, *feme covert*, or lunatic, be sold under this act, the same may be redeemed, at any time within one year after such disability shall be removed. Redemption shall be made by the payment of the amount of redemption money to the treasurer, and taking his voucher therefor, and filing the same in the office of said comptroller, who shall thereupon note the fact of said redemption upon his record of sales; or, any person holding a certificate of sale may surrender the same to the comptroller to be canceled, and the fact shall in like manner be noted upon said record.

If not redeemed, a deed to be given.

Upon the return of the certificate, or proof of its loss, and the filing with the comptroller of the affidavit required by the constitution of this State, if the property shall not have been redeemed according to law, a deed shall be executed to the purchaser, or his assignee, under the corporate seal, signed by the mayor, comptroller and clerk, conveying to such purchaser or assignee the premises so sold and unredeemed as aforesaid. A memorandum of all deeds so made and delivered shall be entered by the comptroller in the book wherein tax sales are recorded; and a fee of one dollar may be charged by the comptroller for every deed so issued.

Certificates assignable. SEC. 24. Such certificate of purchase shall be assignable by indorsement, and an assignment thereof shall vest in the assignee, or his legal representatives, all the right and title of the original purchaser.

Erroneous sales to be canceled. SEC. 25. Whenever it shall appear to the satisfaction of the comptroller, before the execution of a deed for any property sold for taxes, that such property was not subject to taxation, or that the taxes had been paid previous to the sale, he shall make an entry opposite to such property on his record of sales, that the same was sold in error, and such entry shall be evidence of the fact therein stated; and this provision shall apply, so far as the same is applicable, to all sales for special assessments.

Tax deeds *prima facie* evidence of certain facts SEC. 26. All deeds made to purchasers, of lots, lands or other property, sold for taxes or assessments, shall be *prima facie* evidence, in all controversies, and suits, in relation to the right of the purchaser, his or her heirs or assigns, to the premises thereby conveyed, of the following facts:

First. That the land or lot conveyed, was subject to taxation, or assessment, at the time the same was advertised for sale, and had been listed and assessed, in the time and manner required by law.

Second. That the taxes or assessments were not paid at any time before the sale.

Third. That the land or lot conveyed, had not been redeemed from the sale at the date of the deed.

Conclusive evidence of certain facts And shall be conclusive evidence of the following facts:

First. That the land or lot was advertised for sale, in the manner and for the length of time required by law.

Second. That the land or lot was sold for taxes, or assessments, as stated in the deed.

Third. That the grantee, in the deed, was the purchaser.

Fourth. That the sale was conducted in the manner required by law.

Proof required to defeat tax title. And in all controversies and suits, involving the title to the lot or land claimed and held under and by virtue of such deed, the person or persons claiming title, adverse to the title conveyed by such deed, shall be required to prove, in order to defeat the said title, either that the land or lot was not subject to taxation at the date of the sale; that the taxes or assessments had been paid; that the land or lot had never been listed and assessed for taxation or assessment, or that the same had been redeemed according to the provisions of this act; and that such redemption was made for the use and benefit of the persons having the right of redemption, under the laws of this State; but no person shall be permitted to question the title acquired by the said deed, without first showing that he, she or they, or the person under whom he, she or they claim title, had title to the land or lot at the time of the sale, or that the title was obtained from the United States, or this State, after the sale, and that all taxes due upon the lot or land, have been paid by such person, or the person under whom he claims title as aforesaid; and no deed of land or other property sold for the non-payment of taxes or assessments, shall be questioned in any suit or controversy, unless the person wishing to contest the same, shall have tendered or deposited the amount of the redemption money and interest, as now provided by the laws of this State, in case of sales of real estate for taxes.

Successor of collector empowered to complete proceedings. SEC. 27. Any change made in the incumbent of the office of the collector during the pendency of any such proceedings, shall not operate to affect or delay the same, but the successor or successors in office of such collector shall be authorized to do all acts necessary to complete such proceedings, the same as if his predecessor had continued in office. **Comptroller to act when office vacant** In case of a vacancy occurring in any such office, the proceedings shall be prosecuted by the comptroller until such vacancy is filled by election or otherwise.

Assessment sales, when to be made. SEC. 28. All sales of property for the non-payment of taxes and assessments, for any improvement of what kind soever, shall be held at the same time with the general sale of property for non-payment of city taxes in each year, unless, in particular cases, said sale is stayed or delayed by examination or process of law; the intent hereof being that there shall be but one general collection by sale, of all taxes and assessments whatsoever in each and every year;

which sale shall take place in the manner hereinbefore provided, and at the same time in each year: *Provided*, That in all cases where judgment shall be delayed in consequence of any appeal, or the delay of any court in rendering its decision, such sales may be made at any time after final judgment shall have been rendered, upon notice to be given as in other cases.

Liability of assessors and collector for neglect of duty.

SEC. 29. Any assessor, collector, or other officer, who shall in any case refuse or knowingly neglect to perform any duty enjoined upon him by this chapter, or who shall consent to, or connive at, any evasion of its provisions, whereby any proceeding required by this chapter shall be prevented or hindered, shall, for every such neglect or refusal, be liable to said city, individually and upon his official bond, for double the amount of loss or damage caused by such neglect or refusal, to be recovered in an action of debt, in any court having jurisdiction of the amount thereof.

Formal defects not to defeat taxes or assessments.

SEC. 30. No assessment of property, or charge for taxes or assessments thereon, shall be considered illegal on account of any irregularity or informality in the tax lists or assessment rolls, or on account of the assessment rolls or tax list not being made, completed, or returned within the time required by law, or on account of the property having been charged or listed in the assessment or tax list without name, or in any other name than that of the rightful owner; and no error or informality in the proceedings of any of the officers entrusted with the levying and collection of taxes or special assessments, not affecting the substantial justice of the tax or assessment itself, shall vitiate or in any way affect the tax or assessment.

Redemption in case of second sale within two years.

SEC. 31. If any purchaser of lands, lots, or other property, sold for city taxes or assessments, shall suffer the same to be again sold for like taxes or assessments, before the expiration of two years from the date of his or her purchase, such purchaser shall not be entitled to a deed for the property until the expiration of two years from the date of the second sale; during which time the land, lot, or other property shall be subject to redemption, and the person redeeming shall only be required to pay, for the use of the purchaser at the first sale, the amount paid for the property, and double the amount paid by the second purchaser, for his use, as in other cases.

CHAPTER X.

THE POLICE DEPARTMENT.

SECTION
1. Board of police, how constituted; quorum.
2. Appointment of president and secretary; secretary's salary.
3. Commissioner's oath of office; bond.
4. Power and authority of the board; power to construct telegraph lines.
5. General duties of the board.
6. Authority to establish rules and regulations; organization of police force; appointments.
7. Qualifications and duties of police officers, their mode of trial and removal, to be prescribed by the rules of the board; appointment of superintendent; ineligibility; removals from office; promotions.
8. Salary of commissioners; salary of superintendent and other officers; members of the force prohibited from receiving gifts or fees for police service; not to aid in the defense of accused persons.
9. Complaints against police officers; trial; appeal.
10. Police life and health insurance fund.
11. Relief to be provided for disabled policemen.
12. Powers of police officers; certain officers authorized to enter buildings or vessels to prevent felonies, or arrest felons; power to serve process.
13. Detection and arrest of gamblers.
14. City to be divided into police precincts; police stations; superintendent to promulgate all regulations and orders.
15. Power to appoint special policemen.
16. Power to appoint patrolmen on request and at the expense of private persons; special patrolmen.
17. One week's notice required of intention to withdraw from police force; no person removed to be re-appointed.
18. Disposition of stolen property; books to be kept for entry of all complaints; registry of stolen property; record required to be kept.
19. Accommodations for the detention of persons arrested to be provided at each station; arrests to be reported; special provisions respecting the detention and examination of persons arrested; detention of witnesses; special bail.

SECTION
20. Police expenses made a city charge; power to appoint police officers for the county, and for village and town authorities.
21. Board to furnish comptroller with an annual estimate of police expenses; council authorized to revise the same; the police fund to be raised by general tax.
22. Police fund, how disbursed.
23. Authority of the board to incur expense limited; accounts subject to inspection.
24. Duty of the board to enforce city ordinances; power to issue subpœnas and administer oaths; may compel the attendance of witnesses.
25. Security to be taken from certain police officers; oath of office.
26. Superintendent to make quarterly reports; the board to make an annual report to common council.
27. Exemption from military and jury duty.
28. Penalty for assaulting electors on election day; and police officers when on duty; for neglecting to arrest offenders, and for fraudulently pretending to be a police officer.
29. The board to act as a board of health; power to abate nuisances.
30. Board empowered to take necessary measures to prevent the spread of infectious disease; reports of mortality.
31. Practicing physicians to report infected patients; penalty for neglect.
32. Visitation of vessels suspected of having disease on board.
33. All infected persons, not resident, may be removed to pest house; infected goods may be destroyed.
34. Vessels infected may be removed to quarantine; punishment for refusal to comply with orders.
35. Council may prescribe other powers and duties to be exercised for sanitary purposes; power to enter and examine houses, boats and vessels.
36. Repealing clause.

Board of police, how constituted. SECTION 1. There is hereby established an executive department of the municipal government of said city, to be known as the board of police. Said board shall consist of three commissioners, in addition to the mayor, who shall be *ex officio* a member thereof, to be chosen in the manner hereinbefore prescribed; and a majority of said board shall constitute a quorum for the transaction of business. Mayor a member *ex officio.* Quorum.

(*Mayor no longer member of board of police*, Sec. 19, *post*, 196.)

SEC. 2. The said board shall appoint one of their own number to act as president, and some other person to act as secretary; and the secretary shall receive such annual salary as may be determined upon by the board of police. President. Secretary, his salary.

SEC. 3. Before entering on the duties of their office, said commissioners shall take an oath to obey the constitution and laws of this State, and faithfully to perform the duties of their said office, the certificate of which oath shall be filed in the office of the city clerk. Each of said commissioners, before entering on the duties of his office, shall also give a bond to said city in the sum of twenty-five thousand dollars, with sureties to the satisfaction of the judge of the circuit court of Cook county, conditioned for the faithful discharge and performance of his duties as such commissioner; and that he will well and truly account for and pay over any and all moneys, and surrender any and all property, books and papers, which may come into his hands as such commissioner, on the expiration or other termination of his term of office. Oath of commissioners. Bond.

(*Further provision as to bond of present commissioners*, Sec. 18, *post*, 196.)

SEC. 4. Said board shall assume and exercise the entire control of the police force of said city, and shall possess full power and authority over the police organization, government, appointments, and discipline within said city. It shall have the custody and control of all public property, books, records and equipments belonging to the police department, and shall have power to erect and maintain, under the general laws of the State relating to telegraph lines, all such lines of telegraph in such places within the said city, as for purposes of police, the board shall deem necessary, whenever the common council shall authorize the establishment of such telegraph line or lines. General powers of the board. Power to construct telegraph lines.

General duties.

SEC. 5. It shall be the duty of the board of police hereby constituted, at all times of the day and night within the boundaries of the said city of Chicago, to preserve the public peace, to prevent crime and arrest offenders, to protect rights of person and property, to guard the public health, to preserve order, to remove nuisances existing in public streets, roads, places and highways, to provide a proper police force at every fire, in order that thereby the firemen and property may be protected, to protect strangers and travelers at steamboat and ship landings, and railway stations, and to obey and enforce all ordinances of the common council within the city which are applicable to police or health. Whenever any crime shall be committed in said city, or within the county of Cook, and the person or persons, accused or suspected of being guilty, shall flee from justice, the said board of police may, in their discretion, authorize any person or persons to pursue and arrest such accused or suspected person or persons, and return them to the proper criminal court, having jurisdiction of the offense, for trial.

Pursuit of fugitives from justice

Power to establish rules and regulations.

SEC. 6. The duties of the police force shall be executed under the direction and control of said board, and according to rules and regulations which it is hereby authorized to pass from time to time, for the more proper government and discipline of its subordinate officers and the police force of said city. The said police force shall consist of a superintendent of police, three captains of police, six sergeants, ninety police patrolmen, and as many more police patrolmen, sergeants, and deputy superintendents, as may be authorized by the common council on the application of the board. The said offices hereby created shall be severally filled by appointment in the mode prescribed by this act, and each person so appointed shall hold office only during such time as he shall faithfully observe and execute all the rules and regulations of the said board, the laws of the State, and the ordinances of the city.

Organization of police force.

Appointments.

(*Repealed, and new section enacted,* Sec. 20, *post*, 196, *and* Sec. 15, *post*, 195.)

Qualifications and duties, mode of trial and removal, to

SEC. 7. The qualifications, enumeration and distribution of duties, mode of trial and removal from office, of each officer of said police force, shall be particularly defined and prescribed by rules and regulations of the board of police: *Provided, however*, That no person shall be appointed to or hold the office of superintendent of police without the advice and consent of the common council to every such appointment; nor shall any person be appointed to or hold office in the police force aforesaid, who is not a citizen of the United States, or who shall not have resided within the State of Illinois two years next preceding his appointment, or who shall ever have been convicted of crime: *And provided*, That no person shall be removed therefrom, except upon written charges preferred against him to the board of police, and after an opportunity shall have been afforded him of being heard in his defense; but the board of police shall have power to suspend any member of the police department of the city, pending the hearing of the charges preferred against him: *And provided*, That whenever any vacancy shall occur in the office of captain of police, the same shall be filled by an appointment from among the persons then in office, as sergeants of police, and a like vacancy in the office of sergeant of police, shall be filled by appointment from among the persons then in office as police patrolmen.

be prescribed by rules of the board.

Appointment of superintendent.

Persons ineligible.

Removals not to be made, except for cause.

Promotions.

(*Repealed, and new section enacted*, Sec. 20, *post*, 196, *and* Sec. 16, *post*, 195.)

SEC. 8. The police commissioners shall receive such annual salaries as may be fixed upon and allowed by the common council, and no other compensation shall be paid or allowed. The superintendent of police shall receive a salary of fifteen hundred dollars per annum. Each captain shall receive a salary of seven hundred dollars per annum, and each sergeant a salary of six hundred and fifty dollars. The pay of each police patrolman shall be at the rate of not less than four hundred and eighty, nor more than six hundred dollars per annum. The salaries shall be paid monthly to each person entitled thereto. No member of the board of police, or of the police force, shall receive or share in, for his own benefit, under any pretense whatsoever, any present, fee, gift or emolument for police service, other than the regular salary and pay provided by this section, except by the unanimous consent of the board of police; nor shall any such member receive or share in any

Salary of commissioners.

Salary of superintendent and other officers.

Members of police force not to receive gifts or fees for service, without permission.

fee, gift or reward, from any person who may become bail for the appearance of any arrested, accused or convicted person, or who may become surety for any such person on appeal from the judgment or decision of any court or magistrate; or any fee, gift or reward, in any case, from any attorney at law, who may prosecute or defend any person arrested or prosecuted for any offense within the county of Cook; nor shall any such member either directly or indirectly interest himself, or interfere, in any manner whatever, in the employment or retainer of any attorney, to aid in the defense of persons arrested or accused; and for any violation of either of the foregoing provisions, the officer so offending shall be immediately removed from office.

(*Repealed, and new sections enacted*, Sec. 20, *post*, 196, *and* Secs. 13, 14, *post*, 194. *Before repeal, amended*, Sec. 23, *post*, 185.)

Any citizen may prefer charges against police officers.

SEC. 9. Any citizen of Chicago, with a view to the trial and suspension or removal from office of any officer or policeman of the police, may, on oath in writing, prefer or make, before the board, charges or complaint touching the character and competency, or affecting the acts, conduct or omissions of such officer or policeman, or for violation of, or misconduct as defined and prescribed by, the rules and regulations of the board; and said board, after reasonable notice, not exceeding ten days, to the person charged, shall proceed to the trial of said officer or policeman on such charges or complaint, and shall have power to, and shall issue subpœnas, tested in the name of the president of the board, to compel the attendance of witnesses, to administer oaths and affirmations, and generally shall, for the purposes of such trial, have and exercise the powers and duties of justices of the peace in civil cases, so far as the same are applicable, and may make an order of removal or suspension for some certain period. The party complaining, or person charged, feeling aggrieved by any such order, may at once, on giving bond to the president of the board, with security to be approved by him or the board, conditioned for the payment of accrued and accruing costs, appeal from the order or finding of the board to any court of record of Cook county (except the county court), which said court

Trial of charges.

Appeals.

shall proceed to the trial of said complaint as speedily as may be, and in preference to other cases, and make such final order in the case as equity and justice shall require; and said order shall be final and conclusive, without further appeal. If, on such trial, said charges or complaint shall be sustained, such officer or policeman shall pay the costs of such proceeding, and the same may be deducted and withheld from his pay, and, in case of his suspension, his pay shall also cease from the date of the charge and during the period of suspension. If such complaint shall be dismissed or not sustained, then the person making the same shall pay all costs. In trials under this section, the same costs shall be charged and taxed as in trials before justices, and be collected on execution, as the case may be, from the court, or on execution to be issued by any justice of the peace, on certificate of the same by the board and order for execution, said costs, when collected, to be paid to the treasurer of the board, for the benefit of those concerned. But the said board shall not tax or receive any fees for themselves, or for any member thereof.

Costs.

Police life and health insurance fund.

SEC. 10. All rewards, fees, proceeds of gifts and emoluments, that may be allowed by the board of police to be paid and given for or on account of extraordinary services of any member of the police force, and all moneys arising from the sale of unclaimed goods, shall be paid into the city treasury, and shall constitute a fund, to be called the "Police Life and Health Insurance Fund;" and the persons who shall, from time to time, fill the office of president of the board of police and that of the comptroller of the city of Chicago, are hereby declared the trustees of the said fund, and may invest the same as they shall see fit, either in whole or in part.

Disabled policemen to be relieved from the fund.

SEC. 11. Whenever any member of the police force, in actual performance of his duty, and in consequence of the performance of such duty, shall become bodily disabled, his necessary expenses during the time his disability as aforesaid continues, may become a charge upon the fund provided for in the preceding section, at the discretion of said board of police. The board shall inquire into the circumstances, and if satisfied the charge upon the said fund is correct, may order the same to be paid by the draft of the said trustees upon the said fund, each writing his signature thereto. But the provisions of this section shall not apply to special patrolmen appointed as hereinafter provided, at the request and expense of private parties.

Powers of police officers.

SEC. 12. The members of the police force of the said city of Chicago, shall possess in every part of the county of Cook, all the common law and statutory powers of constables, except for the service of civil process, and any warrant for search or arrest by any magistrate of the State of Illinois, may be executed in any part of the county of Cook, by any member of the police force of the said city of Chicago, without any backing or indorsement of the said warrant, and according to the terms thereof. The superintendent, deputy superintendent, or any captain of police, having just cause to suspect that any felony has been, or is being, or is about to be committed within any building, or on board of any ship, boat or vessel within the said city of Chicago or county of Cook, may enter the same at all hours of the day or night, to take all necessary measures for the effectual prevention or detection of all felonies, and may take then and there into custody, all persons suspected of being concerned in such felonies, and also may take charge of all property which he or they shall have then and there just cause to suspect has been stolen. The members of said police force may also serve or execute any process, civil or criminal, issued by the police court of said city, or either of the justices thereof.

Authority to enter buildings or vessels; to prevent felonies or arrest felons.

Power to serve process.

Detection and arrest of gamblers.

SEC. 13. If the superintendent of police shall report in writing to the board of police that there are good grounds for believing any house or room within the said city of Chicago, is kept or used as a common gaming house or cock-pit, and if two or more householders dwelling within the said city, and not belonging to the police force, shall make oath in writing before any one of the commissioners of police, to be annexed to said report, (which oath every commissioner of police is hereby empowered to administer, receive and subscribe,) that the premises complained of by the superintendent are commonly reported, and are believed by the deponents to be kept as a common gaming house or cock-pit, it shall be lawful for any commissioner of police, by order in writing, to authorize the superintendent, or the deputy superintendent of police, to enter upon such premises, taking with him or them, such members of the patrol force as shall be necessary, and, if necessary, to use force for the purpose of effecting such entry, whether by breaking open doors or otherwise, and the said superintendent shall be authorized to take into custody all persons who shall be found therein, and to destroy all implements of gaming found therein, and shall forthwith convey the person or persons found therein before one of the police justices in said city, who shall forthwith proceed to hear the proof, and if there be probable cause for believing that such person or persons have been guilty of any crime or misdemeanor, then the said magistrate shall forthwith order such person or persons to find good bail, with two householders of said city of Chicago, as his or their sureties, conditioned for his or their appearance at the proper criminal court, to answer any indictment which may be found; and in default thereof, such magistrate shall commit such person or persons to the county jail.

Destruction of gaming implements.

SEC. 14. It is hereby made the duty of the board of police, for more effectually distributing and enforcing its police government and discipline, to divide the said city of Chicago into precincts, without regard to ward boundaries, and to assign captains of police, and sergeants of police, to each of said precincts, as they shall deem for the best interest of said city. The board may, from time to time, establish a station or sub-station in each precinct or division, for the accommodation of the police force on duty therein. It shall promulgate all regulations and orders through the superintendent of police, and it shall be the duty of the police force to respect and obey the said superintendent as the head and chief of the same, subject to the rules and regulations and general orders of the board.

Police precincts.

Police stations.

Superintendent to be chief of police.

SEC. 15. The said board of police is hereby authorized to appoint persons of suitable character, who may be in the employment of the city in other branches or departments, special policemen: *Provided*, Such special policemen shall not be paid for their services as policemen out of the city

Special policemen.

treasury. Such policemen shall possess the same power as the regular police patrolmen, and shall obey the rules and regulations of the board, and conform to its general discipline.

Power to appoint special patrolmen for accommodation of private persons.

SEC. 16. The board of police, whenever it may see fit, shall, on the application of any person or persons showing the necessity thereof, appoint and swear any number of additional patrolmen to do duty at any place within the city of Chicago, at the charge and expense of the person or persons by whom the application shall be made, and the patrolmen so appointed shall be subject to the orders of the board of police, and shall obey the rules and regulations of the board, and conform to its general discipline and to such other special regulations as may be made, and shall wear such dress or emblem as the board may direct, and shall, during the term of their holding appointment, possess all the powers, privileges and duties of the patrol force herein prescribed. The persons so appointed may be removed at any time by the board of police, without assigning cause therefor. The board of police may also, upon any emergency or riot, pestilence, invasion, or during any day of public election or celebration, appoint as many special patrolmen from among the citizens of Chicago as it may deem advisable, and for a specified time, and during the term of service of any such special patrolmen, they shall possess all the powers and privileges and perform all the duties of patrolmen of the standing police force of the city.

Power to appoint additional patrolmen for special occasions.

Members of police force to give notice of intention to resign.

SEC. 17. No member of the police force, under penalty of forfeiting the pay which may be due to him, shall withdraw or resign from the police force, unless he shall have given one week's notice thereof, in writing, to the superintendent of police; and no person, who shall ever have been removed from the police force established by this act, for cause, shall be re-appointed by the board of police to any office in the said police force.

Persons removed not to be re-appointed.

Disposition of stolen property.

SEC. 18. All stolen or other property taken by the members of the police force, shall be deposited and kept in a place, and by a person to be designated by the board of police; and in case of the neglect or refusal of any officer to so deposit the property taken or found upon the possession of any person or persons arrested, he shall be subject to indictment, and be fined in a sum not exceeding three thousand dollars, and in no case less than the value of the property, and be imprisoned in the county jail not to exceed one year, and the sentence of the court, in such cases, *ipso facto*, shall vacate the office of the person so convicted. Every such article of property shall be entered in a book kept for the purpose, together with the name of the owner, if ascertained, and the name of the place where found, and of the person from whom taken, with the general circumstances and the date of its receipt, and the name of the officer recording the same. An inventory of all money or other property shall be given to the party from whom the same was taken; and in case the same shall not, within ten days after such arrest and seizure, be claimed by any other person or persons, it shall be delivered to the person from whom the same was taken, and to no other person, either attorney, agent, factor or clerk. In case said money or property shall, within said ten days, be claimed by any other person or persons, it shall be retained by said custodian, until after the discharge or conviction of the person from whom the same was taken; and if such claimant or claimants shall establish to the satisfaction of the committing magistrate, that he or they are the rightful owners, the same shall be restored to him or them, unless otherwise directed by the higher court; otherwise, it shall be returned to the accused personally, and not to any attorney, agent, factor or clerk of such accused person, after all liens or claims against the same have first been discharged and satisfied. The board of police shall also cause to be kept general complaint books, in which shall be entered every complaint, preferred upon personal knowledge of the circumstances thereof, with the name and residence of the complainant. It shall also cause to be kept books for the registry of lost, missing or stolen property, for the general convenience of the public, and of the police force of the city. It shall also cause to be kept books of records, wherein shall be entered the name of every member of the police force, with his time and place of nativity, the time and

Register to be kept.

Complaint books to be kept.

Registry of lost and stolen property.

Record to be kept of police force.

place when he became a citizen (if he was born out of the United States,) his age, his former occupation, number of family, and the residence thereof, the date of appointment or dismissal from office, with the cause of the latter, and in every such record, sufficient space shall be left against all such entries, wherein to make record of the number of arrests made by such members of the police force, or of any special services deemed meritorious by the captains of police. It shall also cause to be kept in proper books, the accounts of the board, and a record of their proceedings; and they shall preserve and file copies of all bills audited and allowed, and keep an accurate account of all the expenses of the police department. The board of police shall also cause to be kept and bound, all police returns and reports.

Record of proceedings.

Accommodations to be provided at police stations for detention of arrested persons.

SEC. 19. It shall be the duty of the board of police to provide at the expense of said city, all necessary accommodations, within such precincts as shall be contained within the boundaries of said city, for the station houses required by the board of police for the accommodation of the police force of such precincts, for the lodging of vagrants and disorderly persons, and for the temporary detention of persons arrested for offenses. It shall also be the duty of said board of police to furnish the same suitably, and to warm and light the same by day and night; and in every case of arrest, the same shall be made known to the captain upon duty in the precinct wherein such arrest was made, by the person making the same, and it shall be the duty of the said captain, as soon as practicable after such notice, to make written return thereof according to the rules and regulations of the board of police, together with the name of the party arrested, the offense, the place of arrest, and the place of detention. All persons arrested by the officers or members of the police force, shall be detained, while in their custody, only in the place or places provided for that purpose; and no trial or examination of any person arrested, shall be held in the office of the superintendent of the police or of the board. Necessary and usual articles of clothing or personal apparel on the person, or in the possession of persons arrested and detained, shall

Arrests to be reported.

Detention and examination of persons arrested.

not be taken or seized by the police, unless there be reason to suspect that the clothing has been stolen or obtained unlawfully. The board of police shall provide suitable accommodations within said city, for the detention of witnesses who are unable to furnish security for their appearance in criminal proceedings, and such accommodations shall be in premises other than those employed for the confinement of persons charged with crime, fraud or disorderly conduct; and it shall be the duty of all magistrates, in committing witnesses, to have regard to the rules and regulations of the board of police in respect to their detention. Every person arrested by the police, charged with the violation of any city ordinance, shall be entitled to give special bail for his appearance to answer to such charge; but no member of the police force shall become, or furnish bail for any person arrested.

Detention of witnesses.

Bail.

SEC. 20. The necessary expenses incurred in the execution of criminal process, and the maintenance of the police department, hereby created within the said city of Chicago, shall be a city charge. The board of supervisors of Cook county assembled, may call upon the board of police to appoint, for duty within the said county, as many men as it shall enumerate and describe, upon appropriating to the police fund the necessary expenses and salaries to be incurred thereby. Any of the village or town authorities within the said county, may also make such demand upon the board of police, upon making the like provisions of pay, and it shall be the duty of the board of police to appoint such officers, who shall thereafter become regular members of the police force of the city of Chicago, and subject to all the rules and regulations of the board, discharge the duties and possess powers and privileges as such members. The supervisors of the county of Cook are hereby authorized, from time to time, to levy and raise by tax upon the real and personal property taxable within said county, such sum or sums of money as may be required to carry into effect the provisions of this section, or the police purposes of this act.

Police expenses to be a city charge.

Power to appoint police officers for county, and village and town authorities.

SEC. 21. It shall be the duty of the board of police to prepare and submit to the comptroller, on or before the first

Annual estimate of police

expenses to be furnished by the board. day of May in every year, an estimate of the whole cost and expense of providing for and maintaining the police department of said city during the current fiscal year, which estimate shall be in detail, and shall be laid, by the comptroller, before the common council, with his annual estimate. To be raised by tax. The common council may revise said estimate, and the aggregate amount of the sums required after such revision, shall be provided for in the general tax levy to be laid on said city. Said money, when collected, shall be paid into the city treasury, and shall be styled the police fund, and shall be drawn out therefrom for police purposes, under the fiscal regulations established by this act.

Police fund, how disbursed. SEC. 22. All moneys hereafter to be paid to any person or persons out of the police fund, shall be certified by the president or acting president of the board of police, to the comptroller, who shall draw his warrant on the treasurer therefor, stating therein the fund to which the same is chargeable, and the person to whom payable; and such warrant shall be countersigned by the president, or, in his absence, by the acting president of the board of police and the mayor.

Power of board to incur expenses limited. SEC. 23. No expense, other than salaries and pay herein provided, shall be incurred by the board of police, except for rents, stationery, printing, advertising, fuel and light, unless the same shall be expressly authorized, and provision therefor made, as a separate county or city charge, by the board of supervisors for the county of Cook, or the common council of the city of Chicago, within which the expenditure becomes necessary. Books and accounts to be subject to inspection. The books and accounts kept by said board shall be at all times subject to the inspection of the mayor and comptroller; and the common council may, at any time, require any information respecting the same, the disclosure of which will not impair the usefulness and efficiency of the police department.

Board to enforce city ordinances. SEC. 24. The board of police shall at all times cause the ordinances of the city to be properly enforced; and it shall be the duty of said board, at all times, whenever consistent with the rules and regulations of the board and with the requirements of this chapter, to furnish all information desired, and comply with all the requests made by the common council of said city, or by the mayor thereof, to quell riots, suppress insurrections, protect the property and preserve the public tranquility. The board of police shall have the power to issue subpœnas, tested in the name of its president, to compel before it the attendance of witnesses upon any proceeding authorized by its rules and regulations. Each commissioner of police, the superintendent of police, and the secretary of the board of police, are hereby given power to administer, take, receive and subscribe all affirmations and oaths to any witnesses summoned and appearing in any matter or proceeding authorized as aforesaid, or to any depositions necessary by the rules and regulations of the board. Any willful and corrupt false swearing by any witness or person making deposition before any of the officers last mentioned, to any material fact, in any necessary proceedings under the said rules and regulations, shall be deemed perjury, and punished in the manner now prescribed by law for such offense. The provisions of law now existing in respect to attachment of witnesses before justices of the peace, and to the compulsory attendance of the said witnesses, to appear and testify before them, are hereby applied to the case of witnesses subpœnaed before the board of police.

Power to issue subpœnas for witnesses.

To administer oaths.

Power to compel attendance of witnesses.

SEC. 25. The board of police shall require and make suitable provisions respecting security to be entered into by the superintendent and deputy superintendent of police, and by the captains of police, and for the taking, by members of the police force, of an oath of office, and the registry of the certificate of the same in a book to be kept for that purpose by the board, which oath of office may be taken before any commissioner of police, who is hereby empowered to administer and receive the same.

Security to be taken from certain officers of police.

Oath of office.

SEC. 26. The superintendent of police shall make to the board, quarterly reports, in writing, of the state of the police force, with such statistics and suggestions as he may deem advisable for the improvement of the police government and discipline. The board of police shall, on or before the first Monday in April, in each year, report, in writing, the condition of the police within the said city, to the common council.

Superintendent to make quarterly reports.

Annual report to be made by board.

Exemption from military and jury duty, etc.

SEC. 27. No person holding office under this act shall be liable to military or jury duty, or to arrest on civil process, while actually on duty.

Penalty for assaulting electors, etc

SEC. 28. It shall be a misdemeanor, punishable by imprisonment in the county jail, not less than one year nor exceeding two years, for any person, without justifiable or excusable cause, to use personal violence upon any elector in said city of Chicago while attending the polls upon any election day, or upon any member of the police force thereof when in the discharge of his duty; or for any such member to neglect making any arrest for an offense against the law of the State, committed in his presence, or for any person, not a member of the police force, to falsely represent himself as being such member with a fraudulent design.

BOARD OF HEALTH.

Commissioners to act as a board of health.

Power to abate nuisances.

SEC. 29. In addition to their other powers and duties, said board of police shall also perform the duties of a board of health; and shall make diligent inquiry with respect to all matters affecting the health of said city, and cause all nuisances which may exist, which they may deem obnoxious to the health and lives of its inhabitants, to be abated or removed at their discretion, under a penalty of not less than five nor more than five hundred dollars, for every neglect or refusal of any person to comply with any order of said board.

Empowered to take measures to prevent the spread of disease.

Reports of mortality.

SEC. 30. It shall be lawful for said board to take such measures as they may from time to time deem necessary, to prevent the spread of any pestilential or infectious disease; to see that suitable provisions are made for the accommodation of such sick persons as properly come under the care of the city; and to make daily, weekly or monthly reports of the mortality of the city, as they may think proper and expedient.

Physicians to report infected patients.

SEC. 31. Every person practicing physic in the city, who shall have a patient laboring under any malignant or yellow fever, or other infectious or pestilential disease, shall forthwith make report thereof, in writing, to the secretary of said board; and for neglecting so to do, shall be considered guilty of a misdemeanor, and be liable to a fine of fifty dollars, to be sued for and recovered in an action of debt, in any court having cognizance thereof, with costs, for the use of said city.

SEC. 32. It shall be the duty of said board to detail some officer of the police force, to visit and inspect all boats or vessels coming, or lying and being within the harbor of the city, which are suspected of having on board any pestilential or infectious disease, and all stores and buildings which are suspected to contain unsound provisions or damaged hides or other articles, and to make report of the state of the same, with all convenient speed, to the president of said board. **Visitation of boats and vessels, etc.**

(*Board of police to appoint health officer, and his duties*, Sec. 5, *post*, 201.)

SEC. 33. All persons in said city, not resident thereof, who shall be infested with any pestilential or infectious disease, and all things which, in the opinion of said board, shall be infected by, or tainted with, pestilential matter, and which ought to be removed, so as not to endanger the health of the city, shall, by order of said board, be removed to some proper place, not exceeding fifteen miles beyond the city bounds, to be provided by the board at the expense of the person who may be removed, if able; and the board may order any furniture or wearing apparel to be destroyed, whenever they may judge it to be necessary for the health of the city, by making just compensation. **Non-resident infected persons may be removed.**

SEC. 34. In case any boat or vessel shall come or be within the harbor or jurisdiction of the city, and the said board shall believe that such boat or vessel is dangerous to the inhabitants of said city, in consequence of her bringing and spreading any pestilential or infectious disease among said inhabitants, or have just cause to suspect or believe, that if said boat or vessel is suffered to remain within the harbor or jurisdiction aforesaid, it will be the cause of spreading among the said inhabitants any pestilential or infectious disease, it shall and may be lawful for the said board, by an order in writing, signed by the president for the time being, to order such boat or vessel to be forthwith removed to any distance, not exceeding fifteen miles beyond the bounds of said city, after the delivery of such order to **Infected vessels may be removed to quarantine.**

the owner or consignee of said boat or vessel, to quarantine, under such regulations and for such time as the common council or said board may prescribe; and if the master, owner, or consignee, to whom such order shall be delivered, shall neglect or refuse to comply therewith, or if after such removal, such master, owner or consignee shall neglect or refuse to obey the regulation which may be prescribed, the said president may enforce such removal or other regulations, in such manner as the council may by ordinance direct; and such master, owner or consignee shall be considered guilty of a misdemeanor, and on conviction, shall be fined a sum not exceeding two hundred and fifty dollars, and imprisoned not exceeding six months in the jail of Cook county, or in the city bridewell or house of correction, by any court having cognizance thereof. The said fine shall be paid into the treasury.

Council may prescribe other powers and duties.

SEC. 35. The common council shall have power to prescribe other powers and duties to be exercised and performed by said board for sanitary purposes, and to punish by fine or imprisonment, or both, any refusal or neglect to observe the orders and regulations of the board upon this subject. The members of the police force shall be authorized, under the direction of said board, to enter all houses and other places, private or public, and boats or other vessels, at all times, in the discharge of any duty under the sanitary provisions of this act.

Repealing clause.

SEC. 36. All acts and parts of acts inconsistent with the provisions of this chapter, are hereby repealed, together with all modes and qualifications of appointment to office, as members of the police department, or of elections to office therein, inconsistent with the provisions hereof.

(*Board of police have control of fire department*, Sec. 23, *post*, 197.)

CHAPTER XI.

THE POLICE COURT.

SECTION
1. Justices of the peace to be designated by council to hold a police court.
2. Daily sessions to be held; power of justices to fine or imprison.
3. Execution to issue on rendition of judgment; when body of defendant may be taken; imprisonment for non-payment.
4. Appeals and changes of venue.
5. All suits in behalf of the city to be brought in corporate name.
6. The first process shall be a summons; when warrant may issue.
7. Penalties not to be remitted, unless by two-thirds vote of the council; mayor authorized to release prisoners committed to bridewell.
8. Salary of police justices; all fees to be paid into city treasury.
9. Election of police court clerk; oath of office and bond; salary; power to administer oaths and appoint deputies.

SECTION
10. When clerk's office vacant, the court may appoint *ad interim*.
11. Duties of clerk.
12. Witness fees, when to be taxed; how paid.
13. Clerk to prosecute in absence of city attorney; police officers prohibited from conducting prosecution.
14. Clerk to make daily reports to comptroller; moneys received to be paid over daily.
15. In case of failure to make report and pay over moneys, clerk to be removed.
16. Council authorized to provide for the appointment of prosecuting attorney; duties of said attorney.
17. Clerk and attorney to perform such other duties as council may prescribe.
18. Sessions of the court to be held only in one place; court room not to be changed without a vote of the council.

SECTION 1. The common council shall, in the month of May next after the commencement of the ensuing municipal year, and biennially thereafter, designate two or more justices of the peace in said city, who shall have exclusive jurisdiction as justices of the peace, for two years, or until their successors shall be appointed, in all actions for the recovery of any fine or penalty under the laws of said city, and all ordinances, by-laws or police regulations thereof. Should any vacancy occur, it shall be filled by the common council, but the person so appointed shall serve for the unexpired term only. **Justices of peace to be designated to hold a police court.**

SEC. 2. The said justices of the peace so designated, shall be styled police justices, and shall hold a police court in said city. One of them shall hold a session of said police court daily, (Sundays excepted,) in such place as the said common council may provide and appoint, until the business before them or him is disposed of. Said justices shall have power to fine or imprison, or both, in their discretion, where discretion may be vested in them by the ordinance or regulation, or by this act. **Sessions of the court to be held daily.**

(*Council may provide for police court in each division, etc.*, Sec. 3, *post*, 191.)

SEC. 3. Execution may be issued immediately on the **Execution, when issued** rendition of judgment. If the defendant in any such action have no goods or chattels, lands or tenements, whereof the judgment can be collected, the execution shall require the defendant to be imprisoned in close custody in the jail of Cook county, or bridewell, or house of correction, for a term not exceeding six months, in the discretion of the magistrate or court rendering judgment; and all persons who may be committed under this section, shall be confined one day for each fifty cents of such judgment and costs. All expenses incurred in prosecuting for the recovery of any penalty or forfeiture, when collected, shall be paid to the treasurer for the use of the city.

When defendant may be imprisoned.

Appeals and change of venue.

SEC. 4. Appeals and change of venue shall be allowed, and may be taken from police justices, in all cases, in the same manner as before other justices of the peace.

(*Change of venue to some other justice of a police court*, Sec. 3, *post*, 191.)

City suits to be brought in corporate name.

SEC. 5. All actions brought to recover any penalty or forfeiture incurred under this act, or the ordinances, by-laws, or police regulations made in pursuance of it, shall be brought in the corporate name. It shall be lawful to declare, generally, in *debt* for such penalty or forfeiture, stating the clause of this act, or the by-laws or ordinances under which the penalty or forfeiture is claimed, and to give the special matter in evidence under it.

"Declaration," debt.

First process shall be a summons, unless oath be made.

SEC. 6. In all prosecutions for any violation of any ordinance, by-law, police or other regulation, the first process shall be a summons, unless oath or affirmation be made for a warrant, as in other cases.

Penalties to be remitted only by two-thirds vote of council.

SEC. 7. Neither the mayor or common council shall remit any fine or penalty imposed upon any person for the violation of the laws or ordinances of said city, unless two-thirds of all the aldermen authorized to be elected, shall vote for such release or remission; but the mayor shall be authorized, in his discretion, to release from imprisonment, any person committed to the bridewell or house of correction, or county jail, for a violation of the ordinances of said city, by virtue of the judgment of said police court.

Mayor may release from the bridewell.

Salary of justices.

SEC. 8. The said justices shall be compensated by a

salary, to be fixed by the common council, for doing the business of said police court, in lieu of all other compensation or fees whatever accruing from the business to be disposed of; and the said justices, so designated, shall not enter upon their duties, nor be appointed to hold such court, as justices of the peace aforesaid, unless they first sign and execute an express relinquishment in writing in favor of the city, of all other fees, emoluments or compensation whatever, than what may be provided by a salary to be fixed as aforesaid by the common council; and such express relinquishment shall be filed in the comptroller's office; and all justices' fees and costs collected in all actions brought for said city, under the city charter, shall be paid into the city treasury as other revenue of the city.

Fees to be relinquished and paid into city treasury.

SEC. 9. There shall be elected by the people at the next municipal election, and biennially thereafter, one "police court clerk," who shall hold his office for two years, and until his successor is elected and qualified. He shall take an oath, the same as other officers elected under this act, and shall execute a bond with sufficient security to the city, to be approved by the common council. He shall receive a fixed salary for his services, the amount thereof to be determined by the common council. He shall have power to administer oaths, and appoint deputies, when in the opinion of the common council it may be necessary; in which case, said deputies shall be nominated by said clerk and approved by the common council, and the common council may prescribe the duties and fix the compensation of such deputies.

Election of police court clerk. **Salary.** **Powers.**

(*Further provision as to deputies*, Sec. 3, *post*, 191.)

SEC. 10. In case of the temporary inability or absence of the clerk, or in case of a vacancy in said office, and when there is no deputy, the police court may appoint some competent person to discharge the duties of the office, until the vacancy is filled or ceases.

Court may fill temporary vacancy.

SEC. 11. The duties of the police court clerk shall be to keep a full, detailed and complete account on his docket, of all cases and persons arrested and brought before the police court; how tried and disposed of; the number of cases disposed of; the cases in which moneys have been

Duties of clerk.

collected; and the cases in which money is to be collected; the amount of all forfeitures, penalties, and fines assessed, or the punishment fixed in each case, with the fees and costs accrued and accruing thereon; and to collect, prosecute and receive payment of all such fees, fines, penalties and forfeitures, and all judgments and executions, and all moneys whatever accruing or to be paid in, for the use of said city, from the enforcement of any of the laws thereof, and forthwith to pay over the same to the treasurer of said city.

Witness fees, when to be taxed.

SEC. 12. Witness fees in all cases in the police court, in which the city is a party, shall be taxed and collected only when demanded or claimed by the witness at the time of trial; and no witness shall be allowed more than one fee for any one day's attendance, nor shall any witness fee be taxed, in any case, in favor of any member of the police force. All witness fees, when collected, shall be paid into the city treasury for the benefit of such witnesses. It shall be the duty of the clerk to deliver to each witness who is entitled to receive from the city any witness fee, a certificate thereof, showing the name of such witness, the suit in which he testified, and the amount to which he is entitled. The comptroller shall draw his warrant on the treasurer, on presentation of said certificate, in favor of the party entitled to such fee, provided the same be presented within one week after the filing of the daily report, referring to said certificate, hereinafter required from the clerk of said court.

To be paid into city treasury.

Comptroller to pay witnesses.

Clerk to prosecute in absence of city attorney.

SEC. 13. It shall be the duty of the police court clerk, to see that all cases are properly prosecuted before said police court, in the absence of the city attorney, and no police officer shall conduct any prosecution. He shall take care that said fines, penalties, forfeitures, fees, judgments and executions are collected in all cases as speedily as may be, and the police justices shall, so far as is possible, aid said clerk in the collection thereof.

Clerk to make daily reports to comptroller.

SEC. 14. The said police court clerk shall, at the close of every day, make a written report to the comptroller, containing the name and number of each case disposed of during the day, in which the city is a party, and its final disposition; the names of all witnesses in each case, to whom certificates for witness fees have been issued, with the amount of each fee; and also the amount of all such fines, fees, penalties and forfeitures, as he may have collected during said day. He shall also specify in his said report, the number of cases pending; the number of cases in which any fine, forfeiture or penalty has been inflicted, and the amount thereof; and also the amount of moneys outstanding to be collected in such cases; and the state of each case respectively; and upon making each and every such statement, he shall verify the same by oath taken before some competent officer, that such statement is a full, fair and complete statement of the moneys received and collected by him during said day, and of all matters required by law to be embraced in said report. He shall also pay over to the city treasurer, at the close of every day, all moneys received and collected by him as such clerk, and shall file his receipt therefor with the said comptroller.

To pay over daily all moneys collected.

SEC. 15. In case of the failure of such clerk to make such report, and pay over said moneys daily, as herein required, a notice shall be served on him by the comptroller, that, within three days, he is required to make such returns, and pay over all moneys received, and, in case of the failure of said clerk to pay over said moneys and make such report to the satisfaction of said comptroller, he shall be suspended and removed from office, by the mayor, with the concurrence of the common council, and thereupon the mayor, by and with the advice and consent of the common council, shall appoint his successor to fill the vacancy during the unexpired term.

Clerk failing to report and pay over, to be removed.

SEC. 16. The common council, if it think proper, may, by ordinance, provide for the appointment of a prosecuting attorney for said police court, to manage all city cases before it, and, in such case, may provide for his compensation by a salary. In case of the appointment of such prosecuting attorney of the police court, he shall prosecute all cases before it, and also superintend the collection of fees, fines, forfeitures, judgments and executions, and keep a docket thereof, and file a monthly report of the number of

Council may provide for appointment of prosecuting attorney.

His duties.

all cases commenced, and all cases disposed of, with the names of parties sued, and the amount of fines, fees and forfeitures collected, with the number of cases where moneys are uncollected, and the amount thereof, and file such reports in the city comptroller's office.

Council may prescribe other duties

SEC. 17. The clerk of the police court and police prosecuting attorney (if any), shall perform such other duties as may be prescribed by ordinance of the common council.

Place of holding police court.

SEC. 18. The sessions of the police court shall be held in but one place, where all examinations upon criminal charges before the justices thereof shall be had; and where, also, all other business of every kind coming before the justices of said police court, shall be transacted; and the place of holding said court shall not be changed without a vote of the common council.

(*Council may provide for police court in each division, etc.*, Sec. 3, *post*, 191.)

CHAPTER XII.

FIRE DEPARTMENT.

SECTION
1. Power to prescribe fire limits; to prohibit the erection of wooden buildings.
2. Power to regulate construction of chimneys; deposit of ashes; dangerous manufactories; fire-works; to require scuttles in the roofs of houses; general powers relating to fires.
3. Common council to procure fire engines; to organize fire companies; to appoint firemen, and prescribe their duties.

SECTION
4. Engineers and firemen to take charge of fire engines and apparatus; council may define their duties.
5. Assistant engineers to act as fire wardens; their duties.
6. Council may authorize appointment of fire marshal; his duties and powers.
7. Members of the common council and firemen exempt from jury and military duty.
8. Fund to be set apart for relief of disabled firemen; fire telegraph fund.

Power to prescribe fire limits.

SECTION 1. The common council, for the purpose of guarding against the calamities of fire, shall have power to prescribe the limits within which wooden buildings shall not be erected or placed, or repaired, without permission, and to direct that all and any buildings, within the limits prescribed, shall be made or constructed of fire-proof materials, and to prohibit the repairing or rebuilding of wooden buildings, within the fire limits, when the same shall have been damaged to the extent of fifty per cent. of the value thereof, and to prescribe the manner of ascertaining such damage.

SEC. 2. The common council shall also have power:

First. To prevent the dangerous construction and condition of chimneys, fire-places, hearths, stoves, stove pipes, ovens, boilers and apparatus used in and about any building or manufactory, and to cause the same to be removed or placed in a safe and secure condition, when considered dangerous. **To regulate chimneys, etc.**

Second. To prevent the deposit of ashes in unsafe places, and to cause all such buildings and inclosures as may be in a dangerous state, to be put in safe condition. **Deposit of ashes.**

Third. To regulate and prevent the carrying on of manufactories dangerous in causing or promoting fire. **Dangerous manufactories.**

Fourth. To regulate and prevent the use of fire-works and fire-arms. **Fire-works.**

Fifth. To compel the owners or occupants of houses or other buildings, to have scuttles in the roofs, and stairs or ladders leading to the same. **Scuttles and ladders.**

Sixth. To authorize the mayor, aldermen, police, or other officers of said city, to keep away from the vicinity of any fire, all idle and suspicious persons, and to compel all officers of said city, and other persons, to aid in the extinguishment of fires, and in the preservation of property exposed to danger thereat. **To remove suspicious persons from the vicinity of any fire.**

Seventh. And generally, to establish such regulations for the prevention and extinguishment of fires, as the common council may deem expedient. **To establish regulations for prevention of fires.**

SEC. 3. The common council shall procure fire engines and other apparatus used for the extinguishment of fires, and have the charge and control of the same, and provide fit and secure engine-houses and other places, for keeping and preserving the same; and shall have power: **Fire engines and apparatus.**

First. To organize fire, hose, hook and ladder, and axe companies. **Fire companies.**

Second. To provide for the appointment of a competent number of able and reputable inhabitants of said city, firemen, to take the care and management of the engines and other apparatus and implements, used and provided for the extinguishment of fires. **Appointment of firemen.**

Duties and compensation of firemen.

Third. To prescribe the duties of firemen and their compensation, and to make rules and regulations for their government, and to impose reasonable fines and forfeitures upon them for a violation of the same; and for incapacity, neglect of duty or misconduct, to remove them.

(*Repealed*, Sec. 36, *post*, 200.)

Duties of chief engineer and assistants.

SEC. 4. The chief and assistant engineers of the fire department, with the other firemen, shall take the care and management of the engines and other apparatus and implements used and provided for the extinguishment of fires; and their duties and powers shall be defined by the common council.

(*Repealed*, Sec. 36, *post*, 200.)

Assistants to act as fire wardens.

SEC. 5. The assistant engineers of the fire department shall also act as fire wardens, and it shall be their duty to examine all buildings and inclosures, to discover whether the same are in a dangerous state, and to report to the chief engineer, all violations of the charter or ordinances of said city in relation to the prevention or extinguishment of fires.

(*Repealed*, Sec. 36, *post*, 200.)

Fire marshal

SEC. 6. The common council shall have power, in its discretion, to authorize the appointment of a fire marshal, whose duty it shall be to inquire into and investigate the cause of all fires which may occur in the city, as soon as may be after they occur, and to keep a record of his proceedings, and of the evidence in each case, and to file the same or a copy thereof in the office of the city clerk. He shall have power to compel the attendance of any person in said city to testify upon oath concerning any fire in said city, under such penalty as the common council may provide, and he is hereby authorized to administer oaths to all such witnesses. He shall be required to use his utmost exertions in the discovery, arrest and conviction of all incendiaries, and perform such other duties as the common council may prescribe. Any or all of the above mentioned duties may be devolved by the common council upon the chief engineer.

(*Repealed*, Sec. 36, *post*, 200.)

Aldermen and firemen

SEC. 7. The members of the common council and firemen shall, during their term of service as such, be exempt from serving on juries in all courts of this State, and in the militia. The name of each fireman shall be registered with the clerk of the city, and the evidence to entitle him to the exemption provided in this section, shall be the certificate of the clerk, made within the year in which the exemption is claimed. exempted from jury and military duty.

SEC. 8. One-eighth part of the amount of all fire insurance rates, which shall be annually paid into the city treasury, as hereinbefore provided, shall be reserved and set apart, to create a fund for the relief of distressed firemen, who may become disabled in the service of the city; and shall be used solely for that purpose. Said money shall be disbursed in such sums, and under such rules and regulations, as the common council shall prescribe. The remaining seven-eighths of the aforesaid revenue, shall be retained by the city and allowed to accumulate, until a sufficient sum shall have been realized to defray the expense of establishing a fire alarm or fire telegraph system in said city, and shall be then used for that purpose. After this purpose shall have been accomplished, this portion of the aforesaid revenue shall be applied to the purchase of fire engines and other apparatus used for the extinguishment of fires. Fund for disabled firemen. Fire telegraph fund.

(*Fire department placed under control of board of police, and reorganized*, Secs. 23 to 36, *post*, 197 to 200. *Sections 7 and 8 of this chapter, made applicable to new organization*, Sec. 30, *post*, 198.)

CHAPTER XIII.

SCHOOLS AND SCHOOL FUND.

SECTION
1. School fund of town. 39, range 14, vested in the city; power of council to manage; to lease and convey school property.
2. Principal of the fund not to be impaired; interest on, to be used only in paying teachers.
3. Powers of common council in reference to the management of schools.
4. School agent to have management of school fund.
5. Agent to give bond; compensation of, to be paid out of school fund; liabilities for misconduct.

SECTION
6. School fund to be kept loaned; securities required; rate of interest.
7. Securities to be taken in the name of the city.
8. Borrower to pay expenses attending loan.
9. Debts due school fund from deceased persons to be paid first.
10. Interest at 15 per cent. to be charged from default in payment; suits may be brought to recover interest.
11. Judgments to bear 12 per cent. interest; real estate sold on, may be bought in by the city; redemption.

SECTION
12. No judicial costs to be charged to school fund.
13. If any debt becomes insecure, further security may be required; if not given, suit may be brought.
14. School tax to be deposited with the city treasurer; to be kept a separate fund; mode of disbursement.
15. South Chicago school district abolished.
16. One or more schools to be established in each district; schools for negro and mulatto children.
17. Board of education to superintend and control the schools; general powers and duties of the board.
18. Board to establish by-laws and regulations for the government of schools; to employ teachers.
19. Board to have charge of school-houses and furniture; to provide fuel; bills for furniture and repairs to be paid out of the school tax fund.

SECTION
20. Teachers to make monthly reports; payment of teachers.
21. School agent to report quarterly to the common council the amount of interest on hand.
22. Board of education to appoint a president; to keep a record of proceedings.
23. Powers of the board to be exercised only at formal meetings; their proceedings to be published.
24. Duty of the board to recommend measures to the common council.
25. Board to prepare and publish an annual report.
26. Superintendent of schools to be appointed biennially.
27. Duties of the superintendent.
28. Members and officers of the board not to be interested in the sale of school books.

School fund of township 39, range 14, management of.

SECTION 1. The school lands and school fund of township thirty-nine north, range fourteen east of the third principal meridian, shall be, and the same are hereby vested in the city of Chicago. The common council shall, at all times, have power to do all acts and things in relation to said school lands and school fund, which they may think proper to their safe preservation and efficient management; and sell or lease said lands, and all canal or other lots or lands, or other property, which may have been, or may hereafter be donated to the school fund, on such terms, and at such times, as the common council shall deem most advantageous; and, on such sale or sales, lease or leasings, to make, execute and deliver all proper conveyances, which said conveyances shall be signed by the mayor and comptroller, and countersigned by the clerk, and sealed with the corporate seal: *Provided*, That the proceeds arising from such sales shall be added to, and constitute a part of the school fund.

Council may sell or lease school lands

Proceeds to be added to school fund.

Principal not to be impaired.

SEC. 2. Nothing shall be done to impair the principal of said fund, or to appropriate the interest accruing from the same, to any other purpose than the payment of teachers in the public schools in said township.

Powers of council.

SEC. 3. The common council shall have power:

Buildings.

First. To erect, hire or purchase buildings suitable for school-houses, and keep the same in repair.

Sites.

Second. To buy or lease sites for school-houses, with the necessary grounds.

Third. To furnish schools with the necessary fixtures, furniture and apparatus. **Fixtures, etc.**

Fourth. To establish, support and maintain schools, and supply the inadequacy of the school fund for the payment of the city teachers, from school taxes. **Maintenance.**

Fifth. To lay off and divide the city into school districts, and, from time to time, alter the same, or create new ones, as circumstances may require. **School districts.**

Sixth. And generally, have and possess all the rights, powers and authority necessary for the proper management of schools and the school lands and funds belonging to the township, with power to enact such ordinances as may be necessary to carry their powers and duties into effect. **General powers.**

SEC. 4. The school agent shall have the custody and management of the money, securities, and property belonging to the school fund, subject to the direction of the common council. **School agent, his powers.**

SEC. 5. The school agent, before entering upon his duties, shall give bond in such amount, and with such conditions and sureties, as the common council may require. His compensation shall be paid out of the school fund; and he shall be subject, for misconduct in office, to the same penalties and imprisonment, as school commissioners are or may be subject to, by law. **School agent to give bond. Compensation. Penalty for misconduct.**

SEC. 6. The school fund shall be kept loaned at interest, at the rate of twelve per cent. per annum, payable semi-annually, in advance. No loan shall be made, hereafter, for a longer period than ten years, and all loans shall be secured by unincumbered real estate of double the value of the sum loaned, exclusive of the value of perishable improvements thereon: *Provided,* The common council shall have power to reduce the rate of interest, by a vote of two-thirds of all the aldermen elected; and they may also, by a like vote, authorize the investment of said funds in the bonds of the city of Chicago. **School fund to be kept loaned. Security.**

SEC. 7. All notes and securities shall be taken, to the city of Chicago, for the use of the inhabitants of said township, for school purposes; and in that name, all suits, actions, and every description of legal proceedings, may be had. **Securities to be taken in name of the city.**

Borrower to pay expenses.

SEC. 8. All expenses of preparing or recording securities, shall be paid exclusively by the borrower.

School fund to have first claim on deceased persons' estate.

SEC. 9. In the payment of debts of deceased persons, those due the school fund shall be paid in preference to all others, except expenses attending the last illness and funeral of the deceased, not including the physician's bill.

Default in paying interest.

SEC. 10. If default be made in the payment of interest, or of the principal, when due, interest at the rate of fifteen per cent. upon the same, shall be charged from the default, and may be recovered by suit or otherwise. Suits may be brought for the recovery of interest only, when the principal is not due.

Suits to be brought.

Interest on judgments.

SEC. 11. All judgments recovered for interest or principal, or both, shall respectively bear interest at twelve per cent. per annum, from the rendition of judgment, until paid; and in case of the sale of real estate thereon, the city of Chicago may become the purchaser thereof, for the use of the school fund, and shall be entitled to the same rights given by law to other purchasers. On redemption, twelve per cent. interest shall be paid from the time of sale.

Judicial costs not chargeable to school fund.

SEC. 12. No costs made in the course of any judicial proceedings, in which the city of Chicago for the use of the school fund, may be a party, shall be chargeable to the school fund.

Insecure debts, proceedings, etc.

SEC. 13. If the security on any loan should at any time before the same is due, become, in the united judgment of the school agent and common council, insecure, the agent shall notify the person indebted, thereof; and unless further satisfactory security shall be forthwith given by the debtor, judgment may be recovered thereon, as in other cases, although no condition to that effect be inserted in the note or other security.

School tax fund.

SEC. 14. The school tax fund shall be paid into the city treasury and be kept a separate fund, for the building of school-houses and keeping the same in repair, and supporting and maintaining schools; and shall be drawn out only in payment of bills approved by the board of education, on the warrant of the comptroller, countersigned by the president of the board of education and the mayor.

SEC. 15. The act approved February 23rd, 1847, creating the South Chicago school district, and all other acts or parts of acts inconsistent with the provisions of this chapter, are hereby repealed.

South Chicago school district abolished.

SEC. 16. There shall be established in said city at least one common school in each school district, now or hereafter to be created; and free instruction, within their respective districts, shall be given in said schools, to all the children residing within the limits of the city, who are over the age of five years, and who may be sent to or attend such school, subject to such rules and regulations as may be established by the common council or board of education, pursuant to the provisions of this act. It shall be the duty of the common council to provide one or more schools for the instruction of negro and mulatto children, to be kept in a separate building to be provided for that purpose, at which colored pupils between the ages of five and twenty-one years, residing in any school district in said city, shall be allowed to attend; and hereafter, it shall not be lawful for such pupils to attend any public school in the city of Chicago at which white children are taught, after a school for the instruction of negro and mulatto children has been provided.

One free school to be established in every district.

Schools for negro and mulatto pupils.

(*Repealed, and new section enacted*, Sec. 8, *post*, 192, *and* Sec. 5, *post*, 192.)

SEC. 17. The board of education, subject to such general regulations as may be prescribed by the common council, shall have the entire superintendence and control of the schools; and it shall be their duty to examine all persons offering themselves as candidates for teachers, and when found well qualified, to give them certificates thereof gratuitously; to visit all the public schools as often as once a month; to inquire into the progress of the scholars and the government of the schools; to prescribe the courses and methods of discipline and instruction of the respective schools, and to see that they are maintained and pursued in a proper manner; to prescribe what studies shall be taught, and what books and apparatus shall be used. They shall have power to expel any pupil who may be guilty of gross disobedience or misconduct, and to dismiss and remove any teacher, whenever in their opinion he is unquali-

Board of education, its powers and duties.

To prescribe methods of discipline, etc.

Expulsion of pupils.

Removal of teachers.

fied to teach, or whenever, from any cause, the interests of the school may, in their opinion, require such removal or dismission. They shall have power to apportion the scholars to the several schools, but no scholar shall attend any school out of the district in which he or she resides, without the written permission of the board or the superintendent of public schools, except as herein otherwise provided.

To apportion scholars

(May admit children from adjoining towns of Cook county, Sec. 6, *post,* 192.)

To establish by-laws, etc.

SEC. 18. It shall be the duty of the board of education to establish all such by-laws, rules and regulations for their own government, and for the establishment and maintenance of a proper and uniform system of discipline in the several schools, as may in their opinion be necessary. They shall determine, from time to time, how many and what class of teachers may be employed in each of the public schools, and employ such teachers, and fix their compensation.

To oversee school property.

SEC. 19. It shall be the duty of said board to take charge of the school-houses, furniture, grounds and other property belonging to the school districts, and see that the same are kept in good condition, and not suffered to be unnecessarily injured or deteriorated; and also to provide fuel and such other conveniences for the schools, as in their opinion may be required. They shall also recommend to the common council such alterations, additions and improvements, as may be required in the school-houses or other property belonging to said districts. All bills for repairs, furniture, benches, desks, apparatus, fuel, *et cetera,* shall be audited by said board, and paid out of the school tax fund.

To provide fuel.

To recommend alterations, etc.

Teachers to report every month.

SEC. 20. The teachers in said district shall, at the end of each and every month, report to the superintendent of public schools, the number of days they have been employed in teaching school during the month, and the number of scholars in attendance on each day or half day; and at the close of each month, the board of education shall draw an order upon the agent of the school fund, in favor of said teacher, for the amount due to him or her. But no order shall be drawn upon the school fund for a greater

Payment of.

amount than the interest on hand at the time the same may be drawn, or than the amount raised and specially appropriated for the support of schools by the common council.

SEC. 21. It shall be the duty of the agent of the school fund to report at the end of each quarter, to the common council, the amount of interest on hand, and to give the board of education such information as they may, from time to time, request in reference thereto. School agent to report quarterly.

(*Further provisions for reports by agent*, Sec. 30, *post*, 188, *and* Sec. 9, *post*, 192.)

SEC. 22. The said board shall appoint from their own number, a president, and provide themselves with a well-bound book at the expense of the school tax fund, in which shall be kept a faithful record of all their proceedings. President of board. Record of proceedings.

SEC. 23. None of the powers herein conferred upon the board of education, shall be exercised by them, except at a regular or special meeting of the board. They shall have all their proceedings published immediately after their meetings, in some one or more of the newspapers published in the city, which will publish the same gratis, and also in the corporation newspaper, with such fullness as to inform the public, in every respect, of the business transacted by them; also, resolutions in regard to the adoption of new books to be used in the public schools, with the names of members who may introduce any proposition of interest to the public in regard to the schools, and the yeas and nays upon the same, if the question shall be thus taken. Powers, when exercised. Proceedings to be published.

(*Board, on some matters, to act only at regular meeting, and by majority of all, etc.*, Sec. 32, *post*, 189.)

SEC. 24. It shall be the duty of the board to report to the common council, from time to time, any suggestion that they may deem expedient or requisite in relation to the schools and the school fund, or the management thereof, and, generally, to recommend the establishing of such schools and districts, and the making such alterations or improvements therein, as they may deem beneficial and expedient. Board to recommend improvements to common council.

SEC. 25. The board of education shall annually prepare and publish, in the corporation newspaper, a report of the number of pupils instructed in the year preceding, the sev- Annual report to be published by the board.

eral branches of education pursued by them, and the receipts and expenditures of each school, specifying the sources of such receipts, and the objects of such expenditures. They shall also communicate to the common council, from time to time, all such information within their possession as may be required.

Superintendent of public schools. SEC. 26. For the more convenient discharge of the duties assigned by law to the board of education, and to aid them in the performance of the same, the office of superintendent of public schools is hereby created. How appointed. Said superintendent shall be appointed biennially by the board of education, by and with the advice and consent of the common council, Salary. and shall receive such annual salary as shall, from time to time, be fixed by the board of education, subject to the approval of the common council. Removal. The superintendent so appointed, may be removed at any time by a vote of the board.

To superintend schools SEC. 27. The said superintendent shall act under the advice and direction of the board, and shall have the superintendence of all the public schools, school-houses, books and apparatus. He shall devote himself exclusively to the duties of his office. He shall keep regular office hours, Other duties. other than school hours, at a place to be provided for that purpose, which place shall be the general depository of the books and papers belonging to the board, and at which the board shall hold their meetings. He shall acquaint himself with whatever principles and facts may concern the interests of popular education, and with all matters pertaining in any way to the organization, discipline and instruction of public schools, to the end that all the children in said city, who are instructed at the public schools, may obtain, within their respective districts, the best education which these schools are able to impart. To visit schools. He shall visit all the schools as often as his duties will permit, and shall pay particular attention to the classification of the pupils in the several schools, and to the apportionment among the classes, of the prescribed studies. He shall carefully observe the teaching and discipline of all the teachers employed in the public schools, To report to the board. and shall report to the board, whenever he shall find any teacher deficient or incompetent in the discharge of his or her duties. He shall attend all the meetings of the board, and shall act as secretary thereof. He shall keep the board constantly informed of the condition of the public schools, and the changes required in the same. He shall keep a record of all his proceedings, at all times open to the inspectors. A general report of the condition of the public schools, shall be prepared by him at the close of each school year, for publication. He shall moreover report to the board from time to time, such by-laws and regulations for the government, discipline and management of the public schools, as he may deem expedient; and shall also perform such other duties as the board of education shall from time to time direct.

To attend meetings of the board.

Shall make general report each year.

SEC. 28. It shall be unlawful for the superintendent, or any member of the board, to receive, either directly or indirectly, any fee, gift or reward from any book-publishing concern, book agent or book seller, or to act as agent or attorney for any book-publishing concern, book agent or book seller, or to be pecuniarily interested in the sale or publication of any book used in the public schools; and any violation of these provisions shall subject the offender to immediate removal from office by the common council.

Members and officers of the board not to be interested in sale of school books.

(*Provisions of the charter, relating to schools and board of education, to apply to same under amendment,* Sec. 7, *post,* 192.)

CHAPTER XIV.

REFORM SCHOOL.

SECTION
1. Reform school continued in existence; the common council may change its location; power to purchase grounds and erect buildings therefor.
2. Government of the school vested in the board of guardians; officers of the board; quorum.
3. General duties of the board; appointment of superintendent and other officers.
4. School to be visited by one or more guardians at least once every fortnight; annual report to be made to common council.

SECTION
5. Duties of superintendent.
6. Superintendent to have charge of the lands and buildings; to give bond; to keep accounts of receipts and expenditures; to keep a register of all inmates.
7. Appointment of commissioner; his duties and compensation.
8. Commitments to reform school by police magistrates and justices of the peace, when and how made; powers of commissioner.
9. Commitments by courts of record.

SECTION
10. Boys committed, to be detained until the age of 21, unless sooner discharged or bound out by the board; guardians clothed with sole authority to discharge; when found incorrigible, boys may be returned to committing court or magistrate.
11. Guardians authorized to bind out boys as apprentices or servants; tickets of leave.

SECTION
12. Guardians empowered, with concurrence of common council, to establish a reform school for girls.
13. Annual estimate to be furnished by the board, of amount required for maintaining the school; moneys raised, how disbursed.

Reform school continued in existence.

SECTION 1. The reform school, heretofore established by the city of Chicago, shall be continued in existence, as a school or place for the safe keeping, education, employment and reformation of all children in said city between the ages of six and sixteen years, who are destitute of proper parental care, and growing up in mendicancy, ignorance, idleness or vice. The common council may hereafter, in its discretion, change the location of said reform school, and purchase grounds and erect and maintain all necessary buildings therefor.

The council may change its location, etc.

Government of the school.

SEC. 2. The government of said school shall be vested in a board, consisting of the comptroller, and six guardians to be appointed in the manner herein before prescribed. The said board shall appoint a president, vice-president and secretary, from their own number; and a majority of the board shall constitute a quorum for the transaction of business.

Officers of board of guardians.

General duties of the board.

SEC. 3. It shall be the duty of the said board of guardians, to take charge of the general interests of said school; to see that its affairs are conducted in accordance with the requirements of this act; to see that strict discipline is maintained therein; to provide employment for its inmates; to appoint a superintendent and such other officers as the wants of the school may from time to time require, and to prescribe their duties; to exercise a vigilant supervision over said school, its officers and teachers, and to determine their salaries; such salaries to be subjected to the approval, regulation or alteration of the common council.

Superintendent.

Visits to the school.

SEC. 4. One or more of said guardians shall visit the school at least once in every two weeks, at which time the school, in all its departments, shall be examined. A record shall be regularly kept of such visits in the books of the superintendent. An annual report shall be made by the board of guardians to the common council, on or before the

Annual report.

tenth day of April, exhibiting the condition of the school, and giving a detailed account of its affairs for the preceding year.

SEC. 5. The superintendent, with such subordinate officers as the guardians shall appoint, shall have the charge and custody of the children; he shall himself be a constant resident at the institution, and shall discipline, govern, instruct, employ, and use his best endeavors to reform the inmates, in such manner as, while preserving their health, will secure the formation, as far as possible, of moral and industrious habits, and regular and thorough progress and improvement in their studies, trades, and various employments. Superintendent's duties.

SEC. 6. The superintendent shall, under the direction and control of the board, have charge of the lands, buildings, furniture, tools, implements, stock and provisions, and every other species of property pertaining to the institution, within the precincts thereof. He shall, before he enters upon the duties of his office, give a bond to the city of Chicago, with sureties to be approved by the common council, in the sum of one thousand dollars, conditioned that he shall faithfully perform all the duties incumbent on him as such superintendent. He shall keep in suitable books, regular and complete accounts of all his receipts and expenditures, and a complete enumeration of all property intrusted to him. He shall also exhibit in said books the income, from whatever source, of said institution and school land; he shall account to the treasurer of the city, in such manner as the guardians may require, for all moneys received by him from the proceeds of the land, the work and labor of the inmates, or otherwise. His books, and all documents relating to the school, shall at all times be open to the inspection of the guardians, who shall, at least once in every three months, carefully examine the said books and accounts, and the vouchers and documents connected therewith, and make a record of the result of such examination, in books to be kept by said guardians. He shall keep a register, containing the name and age of each child, and the circumstances connected with his early history; and he shall add such facts as may come to his knowledge, relating

Superintendent to have charge of lands, buildings, etc.

His bond.

To keep accounts.

Register

to the subsequent history of such children, while in the school, and after being discharged therefrom. He shall at all times be subject to removal by the board of guardians, and shall be governed by the rules and regulations they may establish.

Appointment of commissioner.

SEC. 7. It shall be the duty of the mayor of the city of Chicago, each year, on the application of the board of guardians of said reform school, to appoint some proper and discreet person, with the concurrence of said board, as commissioner, before whom all males within the ages prescribed by law, shall be sent, before any police magistrate or justice of the peace shall sentence or order such male to be committed to the reform school. Such commissioner shall keep a true and perfect record of his doings in relation to all persons brought before him, and shall retain the same during his term of office, and at the expiration thereof, shall deliver the same, with all preceding records, to the city clerk, who shall, upon the appointment of a new commissioner, deliver the same to him. There shall be paid to said commissioner such sum, from the reform school funds, as the board of guardians shall, from time to time, direct, and which shall not, in the aggregate, amount to more than one thousand dollars in any one year.

His duties.

Compensation.

Commitments by police magistrates and justices of the peace.

SEC. 8. Whenever any police magistrate or justice of the peace within the city of Chicago, shall have brought before him any male within the ages of six and sixteen years of age, who, he has reason to believe, is a vagrant, or destitute of proper parental care, or is growing up in mendicancy, ignorance, idleness or vice, he shall cause such person, together with the warrant on which he was arrested, and the list of witnesses which may be necessary to establish the situation and condition of such person, to be transmitted to said commissioner; and thereupon it shall be the duty of such commissioner to issue a summons or order in writing, addressed to the father of said person, if he be living and resident within the city, and if not, then to his mother, if she be living and so resident, and if not, then to his lawful guardian, if any there be, resident within said city, and if, on examination, it shall appear that such boy has neither father, mother nor guardian, so resident, then to

Examination by commissioner.

the person with whom, according to the examination and testimony, if any, received by such commissioner, the said boy shall reside; and if there be no person with whom he steadily resides, the commissioner may, at his discretion, appoint some suitable person to act in his behalf, requiring him or her, as the case may be, to appear before him, at such time and place as he shall in said summons or order appoint, and to show cause, if any there be, why the said boy shall not be committed to the reform school. And upon the appearance before him of the party named in said summons or order, or if, after due service had of the summons or order aforesaid, there shall be no such appearance, the said commissioner shall, upon the expiration of the time named in said summons or order for said appearance, proceed to examine said boy, and the party appearing in answer to said summons or order, if any such there be, and to take such testimony in relation to the case as may be produced before him; and in case it shall be proven to the satisfaction of the commissioner, by such examination, or by competent testimony, that said boy is a suitable subject for the reform school, and that his moral welfare and the good of society require that he should be sent to said school, for instruction, employment and reformation, he shall so decide, and shall thereupon certify his said opinion and decision to said magistrate or justice of the peace, as near as may be, in the following words:

Commissioner's report.

To A. B., Esq., a Justice of the Peace:

I hereby certify, that ———— has been examined by me agreeably to the statute, and, upon competent evidence, proved to be a suitable person for commitment to the Reform School.

C. D., Commissioner.

And thereupon, said magistrate or justice of the peace shall commit such person to the reform school; and such commitment shall be by warrant in substance as follows:

Warrant of commitment.

To any Sheriff, Constable or Police Officer within the City of Chicago:

You are hereby commanded, to take charge of ————, a boy above the age of six and under the age of sixteen years, who has been found by competent evidence to be a suitable subject for commitment to the Reform School, and a proper object for its care, discipline and instruction, and to deliver said boy, with this warrant, without delay, to the superintendent or other officer in charge of said school, at the place where the same is established; and for so doing, this shall be your sufficient warrant.

——— ———, J. P.

Dated at the city of Chicago, in the county of Cook, this —— day of ——, A. D. 18—.

But no variance from the preceding form shall be deemed material, provided it sufficiently appear, upon the face of the warrant, that the said boy is committed in exercise of the powers given by this act. And in case said commissioner shall be of opinion, and shall decide and certify that such boy is not a proper subject for commitment to the reform school, he shall order such boy, with the warrant, to be transmitted back to such police magistrate or justice of the peace, who shall thereupon deal with him in the same manner he would have done, had he not been transmitted to or examined by said commissioner. And said commissioner shall, in the performance of his duties under and by virtue of this act, be clothed with the powers of a justice of the peace, to compel the attendance of witnesses, and all other persons whose attendance and presence may be necessary to enable him to fully investigate the situation of all persons who may be brought before him; and the police officers of said city shall be subject to his direction, and shall serve, when called upon for that purpose, any summons, order or warrant, issued by him.

Powers of commissioner.

Commitments by courts of record.

SEC. 9. Whenever any male under the age of sixteen years and over the age of six years, shall be convicted in any court having criminal jurisdiction in the county of Cook, of any offense punishable by fine or imprisonment, who, in the opinion of the court, would be a fit and proper subject for commitment to said reform school, such court shall make an order committing such boy to said reform school; and thereupon, it shall be the duty of said court, by warrant in due form of law, to commit such boy to said reform school; and all warrants shall designate the offense or complaint for which such commitment is made, and the age of the boy; but no warrant shall be held invalid for want of form, and the same may be served by the sheriff or any constable of Cook county, who shall execute the same, and deliver the boy or boys named in such warrant to the superintendent of the reform school, with the warrant, and for such services shall be paid the same fees as are now provided in case of the commitment of a criminal to the county jail, for an offense punishable by imprisonment therein: *Provided, however*, That such boys only shall be committed to said reform school, as in the opinion of the court, are in need of and will be benefited by the reformatory influence of said school, the said school being intended as an educational and reformatory institution, rather than as a prison or place of punishment.

SEC. 10. Every boy above the age of six and under the age of sixteen, who shall be legally committed to said school, as herein before provided, shall be kept, disciplined, instructed, employed and governed, under the direction of the board of guardians of said school, until he be either reformed and discharged, or be bound out by said guardians, or until he shall have arrived at the age of twenty-one years; and said guardians are hereby clothed with the sole authority to discharge any boy or boys from said reform school, who have heretofore been or may hereafter be legally committed thereto; and such power shall rest solely with said board of guardians and with no other persons or body politic or corporate; but it shall be the duty of said board of guardians, and they shall have the power, to return any boy to the court, police justices or other authorities, ordering or directing said boy to be committed, when, in the judgment of said guardians, they may decree said boy an improper subject for their care and management, or who shall be found incorrigible, or whose continuance in the school they may deem prejudicial to the management and discipline thereof, or who, in their judgment, ought to be removed from such school for any cause; and in such case, said court, police justice or other authorities, shall have power, and are required, to proceed as they might have done, had they not ordered the commitment to such school.

Boys to be detained until the age of 21.

Guardians only shall have power to discharge

Boys found incorrigible, may be returned to committing court or magistrate.

SEC. 11. Said guardians shall have power to bind out all boys committed to their charge, for any term of time, until they shall have arrived at the age of twenty-one years, as apprentices or servants, to any inhabitant of this State; and the said guardians and master or mistress, ap-

Boys may be bound out as apprentices.

prentice or servant, shall respectively have all the rights and privileges, and be subject to all the duties set forth by the statute laws of this State, relative to apprentices and guardians and wards; and shall have the same power as overseers of the poor, or mayor and aldermen, and the same clauses and provisions required to be inserted in the indentures of apprentices, in such cases, shall be inserted in all indentures that may be executed by the said guardians. No person receiving such apprentice under the provisions of this act, shall transfer the indenture; and the said board of guardians shall have power in all cases, when, in their judgment, it shall be beneficial to the boy, to cancel such indentures of apprenticeship, for cruelty, negligence or other improper conduct, or for removal from the State, and recover possession of the child apprenticed. Said guardians shall also have power to permit such boys as they shall judge fit subjects for such treatment, to be placed out under the care of any proper person or persons in this State, on "tickets of leave," and such boys so placed out, may be kept and retained by such person or persons, during the pleasure of said board of guardians, and subject at all times to their control and regulation.

Tickets of leave.

Reform school for girls.

SEC. 12. The board of guardians of said reform school are hereby authorized, with the concurrence of the common council, to establish a branch reform school for girls under the age of sixteen years and over the age of six years; and for that purpose, to purchase such lands and erect such buildings thereon, as, in their judgment, are required; and such girls may, for the same causes, and by the same courts, and in the same manner, be committed to such branch reform school, as boys may be to the reform school, and all statutes and ordinances relative to the power, management and control of said reform school by the board of guardians, are hereby made applicable to said branch reform school, and the same powers are delegated to and vested in them in relation to the same; and all ordinances and statutes regulating the powers of police magistrates, justices of the peace and other courts, and of the commissioner, shall, in all respects, be made applicable to girls under the age of sixteen and over the age of six years, where they are found destitute of proper parental care, or leading a vicious life, or are found in streets, highways or public places, in circumstances of want, suffering, neglect or exposure.

SEC. 13. It shall be the duty of the board of guardians to prepare and submit to the comptroller, on or before the first day of May in every year, an estimate of the whole amount required to be raised by taxation, for providing for and maintaining the said reform school during the current fiscal year, which estimate shall be in detail, and shall be laid by said comptroller before the common council, with his annual estimate. The common council may revise said estimate; and the aggregate amount of the sums required after such revision, not exceeding the authorized per centage, shall be provided for in the general tax levy to be laid on said city. Said money, when collected, shall be paid into the city treasury, and shall be styled the reform school fund, and shall be drawn out only in payment of bills approved by the board of guardians, on the warrant of the comptroller, countersigned by the president, or, in his absence, by the vice-president of said board, and the mayor. But this section shall not be construed as repealing any of the provisions of the act to incorporate the Roman Catholic Asylum of the diocese of the Catholic Bishop of Chicago.

Annual estimate of expenses.

Moneys raised, how disbursed.

CHAPTER XV.

CHICAGO WATER WORKS.

SECTION
1. Board of public works to have charge of the water works.
2. Board to consider all matters relating to the sufficient supply of pure water.
3. Power to construct reservoirs and lay pipes.
4. Board required to construct hydrants for extinguishing fires.
5. Power to purchase and convey real estate.
6. Power to construct necessary buildings and machinery.
7. Power to purchase books and charts, and to make surveys.
8. Power to enter upon lands to make surveys and construct works; to agree with owners upon the compensation to be paid for land taken.
9. Mode of ascertaining damages in case of disagreement.
10. City authorized to construct aqueducts, pumping works and breakwaters.
11. Power to extend inlet pipes into the lake; to erect piers.
12. Board empowered to complete the issue of certain bonds heretofore authorized.
13. City authorized to borrow $500,000, for purposes pertaining to the supply of water; bonds to be issued; how issued, and by whom sold; water funds to be used exclusively for the water works.
14. Board desiring to issue bonds, shall make a report and estimate to the common council of the purposes for which the bonds are to be used; council to approve.

SECTION
15. Interest on bonds restricted to 7 per cent.; bonds not to be sold at less than par without consent of council.
16. Board to keep a register of all bonds issued.
17. Comptroller to keep a record of all bonds outstanding.
18. Interest on bonds to be paid by comptroller; also the principal when due; purchase of water loan bonds by the city; new bonds may be issued to pay those falling due.
19. Board to assess water rents on lots and buildings; assessment a lien.
20. Power to attach meters.
21. Record to be kept of all assessments.
22. Time of payment to be advertised; if not paid within 30 days, 10 per cent. may be added to assessments.
23. Collection of assessments; warrants to be issued; levy.
24. Commencing with 1864, assessment warrants shall be annually issued to city collector against lots assessed; proceedings thereon.
25. If assessments are omitted or not collected, they may be included in the next year's warrant.
26. Method provided for collecting all water rents unpaid May 1st, 1863.

SECTION
27. Board to make rules and regulations concerning the use of water; common council to provide penalties for their violation; where rules are violated, the water supply may be stopped.
28. Connections may be made between water pipes and sewers; board may use water for cleansing the sewers.
29. Surplus revenue from water works, how it may be used; annual report to show amount of bonds and debts outstanding, amounts due, and all expenditures on account of the works.
30. Board to report to comptroller on the 1st of May, the amount required during the year, over and above the ordinary revenue, to pay interest and principal on water loan bonds; common council to raise the same by a special tax.
31. Temporary loans authorized in certain cases.
32. Accounts pertaining to water works to be kept separate; moneys deposited with treasurer for said works to be kept as a special fund, and used for no other purpose.
33. Penalty for willful injury to water works property, or polluting the water.
34. Repealing clause.

Board of public works to have charge of water works.

SECTION 1. The board of public works of the city of Chicago, shall have charge and superintendence of the water works of said city.

Board to consider all matters relating to supply of water.

SEC. 2. It shall be the duty of said board to examine and consider all matters relative to supplying the city of Chicago with a sufficient quantity of pure and wholesome water, to be taken from lake Michigan, for the use of its inhabitants.

Power to construct reservoirs, to lay pipes, etc.

SEC. 3. Said board shall have power to construct reservoirs, jets, and public and private hydrants, and to lay pipes in and through all the streets and alleys of said city, and also across all rivers and streams in the said city, and in the county of Cook, not interfering with the navigation of the same, and, with the consent of the common council of said city, to construct fountains in the public squares or such other public grounds of said city, as they shall deem expedient.

Hydrants for extinguishing fires.

SEC. 4. It shall be the duty of said board to construct hydrants of sufficient size and capacity, and in such localities as they shall deem desirable, for the purpose of extinguishing fires.

Power to purchase and convey real estate.

SEC. 5. The said board shall have power to purchase, hold and convey any personal and real estate, which may be necessary and proper to carry out the intention and object of this chapter, but the title to all real estate purchased, shall be taken in the name of the city of Chicago; and no such purchase shall be made, without the approval of the common council being first had thereto.

SEC. 6. Said board shall have the power, and it is hereby made their duty, to purchase such lot or lots of land, subject to the approval of the common council, and to construct such buildings, machinery and fixtures, as shall be deemed necessary or desirable, to furnish a full supply of water for public and private use in said city.

To construct buildings and machinery.

SEC. 7. Said board shall have power to purchase such books, charts and other works, as may be found necessary or useful, and to cause such surveys to be made within said city and outside of its limits, as may be required for the objects of this chapter.

To purchase books and charts.

To make surveys.

SEC. 8. The said board are hereby authorized to enter upon any land or water, for the purpose of making surveys, or constructing any of the works authorized by this chapter, and to agree with the owners of any property which may be required for the purposes of this act, as to the amount of compensation to be paid to such owner, for the property so taken, or the amount of damages to be paid to such owner or owners, by reason of the construction of any of the works hereby authorized; but no such agreement shall be binding upon said city, until first approved by the common council thereof.

To enter upon lands to make surveys and construct works.

To agree with owners for land damages.

SEC. 9. In case of disagreement between the board and the owners of property, which may, in the judgment of said board, be required for any of the purposes specified in this chapter, as to the amount of compensation to be paid to such owners, or in case such owner shall be an infant, a married woman, or insane, or absent from this State, or in case of disagreement between the said board and any owner or owners of property, touching the amount of damages arising from the construction of any part of the work hereby authorized, the said board shall have the right to condemn said property, or to have the amount of such damages ascertained, or both; and the proceedings for the condemnation of such property, or the ascertainment of such damages,

Mode of ascertaining damages in case of disagreement.

or both, shall conform, as nearly as may be, to those specified and provided for in the act entitled "An Act to amend the law condemning the right of way for purposes of internal improvement," approved June 22, 1852, and the act or acts of which the same is an amendment.

Power to construct aqueducts, etc.

SEC. 10. The city of Chicago shall have the power to construct such aqueducts along the shore of lake Michigan, or in the highways, or elsewhere in said Cook county, and to construct such pumping works, breakwaters, subsiding basins, filter beds and reservoirs, and to lay such water mains, and to make all other constructions in said county, as shall be necessary in obtaining from lake Michigan a sufficient and abundant supply of pure water for said city.

To extend inlet pipes into the lake, to erect piers, etc.

SEC. 11. Said city shall have the power to extend aqueducts or inlet pipes into lake Michigan, so far as may be deemed necessary to insure a supply of pure water, and to erect a pier or piers in the navigable waters of said lake, for the making, preserving, and working of said pipes or aqueducts: *Provided*, That such piers shall be furnished with a beacon light, which shall be lighted at all such seasons and hours as the light on the pier at the entrance of Chicago river.

To complete the issue of certain bonds.

SEC. 12. The board of public works are hereby empowered to issue all bonds now authorized to be issued under the law of this State, incorporating the Chicago City Hydraulic Company, approved February 15th, 1851, or the acts amendatory thereof, or under any law authorizing the issue of bonds for the construction of the water works for the said city of Chicago.

City authorized to borrow $500,000 for water works.

SEC. 13. For such expenditures, pertaining to the supply of water to the said city as are hereby authorized, the said city shall have power to borrow, from time to time, as the board of public works and the common council of said city shall deem expedient, a sum of money not exceeding five hundred thousand dollars; and said board shall have power, by and with the approval of the common council, to issue bonds, pledging the faith and credit of said city, for the payment of the principal and interest of said bonds; but no bonds shall be issued, until the common council shall have approved of such issue, by a vote of a majority

Bonds may be issued.

of all the aldermen by law authorized to be elected; and all bonds issued by the said board, before they shall be binding upon said city, shall be marked "approved" by the mayor and clerk of said city, under the seal of said city, and such signature and seal shall be conclusive evidence to the holder of said bonds, of the fact of such approval: *Provided*, That all sales of water loan bonds which may be issued by said board, shall be made only by the comptroller of said city, who, on making such sales, shall deposit the proceeds thereof with the city treasurer, to the credit of the water fund, and shall file with the said board a duplicate receipt of the said treasurer, for the amount of such deposit: *Provided, also*, That all funds derived from the sale of said water loan bonds, or from water rents, or otherwise, for the water works of said city, shall be exclusively used and appropriated by said board, to the objects and purposes pertaining to the water supply of said city, herein specified, nor shall the same, or any part thereof, be used by the said board, or by the said city, for any other purpose.

Bonds to be sold by comptroller.

Water funds to be used only for water works.

SEC. 14. It shall be the duty of the said board, at any time when they shall desire to make an issue of bonds, as herein authorized, to make a report to the common council, setting forth the nature and amount of the work proposed to be executed, and the amount which will be required by them for such purpose, within a period to be stated in said report; which report shall be accompanied by an estimate of the cost of the things required to be purchased, and of the work to be done; and the common council may thereupon approve the issue of the whole amount of bonds called for by such report, or such part thereof as the said common council may deem expedient.

Board desiring to issue bonds, shall report the object to council.

Council to approve.

SEC. 15. The said bonds shall bear interest at a rate not exceeding seven per cent. per annum, and shall not be sold at a rate which will net to the said board less than their par value, unless the common council of said city shall, by a vote of a majority of all the aldermen elected, authorize the comptroller of said city to sell the same at a lower rate, and then only at such rate as shall be fixed by said council: *Provided, however*, That reasonable commis-

Interest on bonds limited to 7 per cent.

sions to brokers or agents employed in procuring the sale or negotiation of said bonds, may be paid by said comptroller.

Board to keep a register of all bonds issued

SEC. 16. It shall be the duty of the said board to keep an accurate register of all bonds, and all interest coupons, issued for the construction of said water works, showing the number, date and amount of each bond and coupon, and to whom issued or sold, and when and where payable, and the particular bonds at any time outstanding.

Comptroller to keep a record of outstanding bonds.

SEC. 17. It shall be the duty of the comptroller of the city of Chicago to keep such a record of all bonds, now or hereafter to be issued for the water supply of said city, as shall at all times exhibit the number and amount of such bonds outstanding, the rate of interest, and when and where the principal and interest are payable.

Payments of interest and principal to be made by comptroller.

SEC. 18. It shall be the duty of the comptroller of said city to pay the interest on said water loan bonds, and also the principal, as the bonds shall become due. The said comptroller, when there are funds for that purpose, may, with the approval of said board, purchase any such water loan bonds, whether the same have become due or not; and in case there are not sufficient water funds in the treasury of said city to meet all of the said bonds when the same shall become due, the said board shall have the right to issue new bonds, in the same manner as herein before provided, for such amount, and on such time, as the said board and the common council shall deem expedient, in the place of the bonds so becoming due as aforesaid; the said old bonds to be canceled in the registry thereof, and the said new bonds to be recorded in the manner herein before provided.

New bonds may be issued to pay those falling due.

Board to assess water rents on lots and buildings.

SEC. 19. The said board of public works shall, from time to time, assess as water rents or assessments, such amounts as they shall deem equitable, on any lots of land which shall abut or adjoin any street, avenue or alley in said city, through which the distributing pipes of the water works of said city are, or may hereafter be laid, which shall have a building or buildings thereon, which can be conveniently supplied with water from the said pipes; the said assessment shall be on the said lots and on the building or buildings thereon, whether the water from the water works of said city shall be used in such building or buildings, or on such lot, or not; and the said assessment shall be and become a continuing lien or charge upon all such lots, and the building or buildings situated thereon. **Assessment a lien.**

SEC. 20. The said board shall have power to attach meters to any premises using water, to enable them to determine the amount to be assessed against such premises; and assessments so from time to time made, shall be a charge and lien on the lot and building or buildings situated thereon, as in the case of assessments otherwise levied, and be collected in the same manner as herein provided for other water assessments. **Power to attach meters.**

SEC. 21. An accurate record of all water rents or assessments shall be kept by said board, which shall be subject to inspection. **Record of assessments**

SEC. 22. Ten days prior to the day designated by the board for the semi-annual or other periodical payment of the water assessment, they shall advertise in the corporation newspaper of said city, or if there be no corporation newspaper, then in some other newspaper in said city, that the said water assessments will at such time become due and payable; and if such assessments are not paid within thirty days from the day fixed as above for their payment, then the said board shall have power to add to such assessment an amount not exceeding ten per cent. thereof; and on premises assessed, but not supplied with water, the said board may make a discount on the assessment, if the same be paid within periods to be fixed by the board. **Time of payment to be advertised.** **If not paid within 30 days, 10 per cent. may be added.**

SEC. 23. It shall be the duty of the said board to collect the water rents and assessments so assessed; and in case the payment thereof shall be neglected or refused, for thirty days after the time fixed for the payment of the same, as herein before provided, then the said board may issue their warrants, under the corporate seal, and attested by the city clerk, directed to any constable of said city, commanding him to make the amount specified in such warrant, being the whole amount due at the date of the issue of such warrant, for water rents or assessments, as aforesaid, together with the costs of advertising the same, and such **Collection of assessments; warrants to be issued.**

fees as constables are entitled to, by the laws of this State, in the levy and sale of personal property upon execution, out of goods and chattels of the owner or owners of the lots and buildings so assessed, or of the owner or owners either of the lots, or of the building or buildings thereon, if the lot and building are not owned by the same person or persons; and the constable, in such case, shall levy under such warrant, upon any personal property of the person or persons against whom the same is issued, and shall sell the same at public auction, after giving ten days' notice of the time and place of sale, in some newspaper published in said city.

Levy.

Assessment warrants to be issued annually to city collector.

SEC. 24. Commencing with the year 1864, and annually thereafter, on or before the last day of October, the said board shall issue a warrant or warrants, under the corporate seal, and attested by the city clerk, directed to the city collector, (charging him with the amount collectible thereon, and taking his receipt therefor,) commanding him to make the amounts set against the several lots or parcels of land described in said warrant, being the amount of water rents or assessments which shall remain unpaid on said lots, for the year ending May first, next preceding the time of the issue of such warrants, out of the goods and chattels of the respective owners of said lots of land; and the same proceedings shall thereupon be taken with reference to said warrants, as with warrants issued by said city for the collection of assessments for the filling, grading or paving of streets; and they shall have the same force and effect, excepting, that the said collector shall pay over the amounts collected by him to the said board of public works; and and if any lots of land be struck off to the said city, at the sale for such water rents or assessments, as is provided in the case of other taxes or assessments, the certificates of the sale thereof shall be issued to the said board of public works, and shall be held by them, for the use and benefit of the water works of said city. Said board shall have the same rights, under such certificates, as other purchasers at tax or assessment sales, and said certificates shall be assignable, by the indorsement of the president of said board. Said warrants for the collection of water assess-

Proceedings thereon.

ments, when issued to the said city collector, shall have the same force and effect as warrants issued to the said collector by said city, for the assessments for filling, grading or paving streets; like powers, rights and duties being hereby conferred and imposed upon the said city collector, and on all parties interested, except as provided in this section: *Provided, however*, That nothing in this section contained shall be so construed as to prevent said board from resorting to any other method for the collection of water rents and assessments, which may be authorized in this chapter.

Assessments omitted or not collected, to be inserted in next year's warrant.

SEC. 25. If, in the issue of the said warrants to the said city collector for any one year, the assessments against any lot or lots should be omitted therefrom, or if, from any cause, the assessments on any lots should not be collected under such warrants, the said board may, in their warrants to be issued the next year to the city collector, include such back assessments; or the amounts with which such lots are chargeable, may be collected out of the personal property of the owners of the lots, or of the buildings, as is herein before provided, by the issue of the warrants of the board to any constable in said city.

Method of collecting water rents unpaid May 1st, 1863.

SEC. 26. For the collection of all water rents or assessments, remaining unpaid on the first day of May, A. D. 1863, the said board may issue their warrants, as is provided in section twenty-three of this chapter; and such warrants shall authorize the sale of any house or building on which any lien shall have attached, by reason of such water rent or assessment, if the building and lot on which the same is situated, are owned by different persons; or, if the building, and lot on which it is situated, against which such water rent is assessed, are owned by the same person, the said board may, as soon after the first day of May, A. D. 1863, as shall be practicable, report to the common council of said city, the lots on which there shall remain unpaid such water rents or assessments; and the common council shall, thereupon, take the same proceedings for the collection of such water rents or assessments, as are provided in this act for the collection of assessments for the repair of sidewalks; but any amount, collected under these proceedings, shall be paid over to said board; and certificates of sale of lots struck off to the city, shall be issued, as provided in the twenty-fourth section of this chapter.

Board to make regulations concerning use of water.

SEC. 27. It shall be the duty of the board to make all needful rules and regulations concerning the use of water supplied by the water works of said city, which regulations shall be printed in the water permits issued by said board, and, if rules and regulations are needed, other than what are now provided for in the ordinances of said city, it shall be the duty of the board to report to the common council the regulations which shall be adopted by them to provide for such necessity, and the common council shall, thereupon, pass an ordinance establishing such rules and regulations, and providing penalties for their violation, which penalties may be enforced in any court having jurisdiction of any offenses against any of the ordinances of said city. In all cases where said rules are not complied with, the said board shall have the right to stop or cut off the supply of water from premises where compliance with such rules is refused or neglected; and the shutting off of the water from such premises shall not make void the assessment thereon, but they shall be held for the assessment, as in the case of lots which are not supplied with water, but which abut upon a street or alley where the water pipe is laid.

Common council to provide penalties for their violation.

When rules are not complied with, water may be shut off.

Board may use the water to cleanse sewers.

SEC. 28. The said board are empowered to make connections between the water pipes and sewers of said city, and to furnish such amount of water, for the purpose of cleaning out such sewers, as shall be required, so far as the water can be conveniently supplied by the water works of said city, without lessening the supply needed for the use of its inhabitants.

Surplus revenue from water works, how to be used.

SEC. 29. If there shall be an annual income or revenue in any way, from the water works of said city, greater than is needed to pay the interest of the bonds issued for their construction, and to pay the current expenses of the works, and for maintaining them in thorough repair, then the said board shall have the power to direct such excess of revenue to be used in the purchase of the outstanding water loan bonds, or in making such additions to the water works of said city as shall have been approved by the common council, or to direct such surplus funds to be invested in the purchase of other bonds of the city of Chicago. The annual report of said board shall specify, in full, what amount of surplus funds shall have been invested, and the nature and amount of the respective securities held by them. The annual report of said board shall also show the amount of water loan bonds outstanding, and all debts outstanding on account of the water works, and the amounts due from parties to the city, for the water works, and shall accurately and clearly exhibit all the expenditures of the said board, on account of the same, which statement shall be certified by the commissioners of said board, under oath.

Annual report to show amount of bonds and debts outstanding, etc.

SEC. 30. It shall be the duty of the said board, on or before the first day of May, in each year, to report to the comptroller what, if any, sum will be needed by said board, over and above the revenue of said water works, to meet the payment of interest or principal of the said water loan bonds, which said report shall be laid, by the comptroller, before the common council, with his annual estimate; and it shall be the duty of the common council to raise said amount, if approved by them, by a special tax, in the same manner as general taxes, to be designated water tax, or in such other way as the said common council shall direct, and the said amount shall be paid over to the city treasurer, to be applied to the payment of the interest or principal of the water loan bonds.

Board to report to comptroller amount of tax necessary to be raised annually.

SEC. 31. The said board shall have power to authorize the comptroller of said city, to raise, by temporary loan, upon the credit of said city of Chicago, with the approval of the common council, such sums of money as may be needed for the payment of the interest on the said bonds, or the outstanding obligations of the said city, on account of the water works, and for which there shall be no funds in the hands of the treasurer of the said city; but, in all cases, such temporary loans shall be provided for out of the first revenue received from the water works into the city treasury.

Temporary loans authorized in certain cases.

SEC. 32. All accounts pertaining to the water works of said city, shall be kept separate and distinct from the accounts pertaining to other departments of said board; and all moneys deposited with the city treasurer on account of

Water works accounts to be kept separate.

Water funds to be used for no other purpose.

the water works, shall be by him kept separate and distinct from all other moneys, as the water fund, and shall only be applied for the uses and purposes for which the same were received; and such moneys shall be held by the treasurer of the city as a special fund, separate and distinct from other funds; and he shall be deemed guilty of embezzlement if he shall pay out such moneys for any account other than that belonging to such water fund, and shall be liable to indictment for so doing.

Penalty for willful injury to property of water works or polluting the water.

SEC. 33. If any person shall willfully do, or cause to be done, any act whereby any work, material or property whatever, constructed, provided or used within the city of Chicago, or elsewhere, by the said board, or by any person acting under their authority, for the purpose of procuring or keeping a supply of water, shall in any manner be injured, or if any person shall willfully pollute the water, such person shall be subject to indictment, and upon conviction thereof, shall be punished by fine not exceeding one thousand dollars, or imprisonment not exceeding six months, or both, in the discretion of the court.

Repealing clause.

SEC. 34. All acts or parts of acts, inconsistent with the provisions of this chapter, are hereby repealed.

CHAPTER XVI.

CHICAGO SEWERAGE WORKS.

SECTION
1. Board of public works to have charge of sewerage works.
2. Board to consider all matters in relation to drainage.
3. Power to purchase books and charts, and to make surveys.
4. Power to construct reservoirs and lay sewers.
5. Power to construct canals or sewers connecting the river and its branches with the lake; to construct dams and pumping works.
6. Power to purchase and convey real estate.
7. Power to enter upon land to make surveys and construct works; to agree with owners upon compensation to be paid for land taken.
8. Mode of ascertaining damages in case of disagreement.

SECTION
9. Board to report to common council what changes are necessary in the grade of streets; council may establish and alter grades; street gutters may be so laid as to remove the surface water.
10. Sewers may be so constructed as to furnish proper connections with private drains; the additional costs to be assessed on lots benefited.
11. Cost of private drains to be a special charge on lots benefited.
12. Board to prescribe location and construction of private drains which connect with the public sewers.
13. Board to cause private drains to be laid, communicating with the sewers, from every lot requiring it; may enter upon any lot for this purpose.

SECTION
14. Board may regulate the construction and cleansing of privies and cesspools.
15. Board empowered to complete the issue of certain bonds heretofore authorized.
16. City authorized to borrow $500,000, for sewerage purposes; bonds to be issued; how issued, and by whom sold; sewerage funds to be used exclusively for sewerage purposes.
17. Board desiring to issue bonds, shall make a report and estimate to the common council of the purposes for which the bonds are to be used; council may approve.
18. Interest on bonds restricted to 7 per cent.; bonds not to be sold at less than par without consent of council.
19. Board to keep a register of all bonds issued.
20. Comptroller to keep a record of all bonds outstanding.
21. Interest on bonds to be paid by comptroller; also the principal when due; purchase of sewerage bonds by the city; new bonds may be issued to pay those falling due.
22. Board to report to comptroller on the 1st of May the amount required to pay interest on outstanding bonds.
23. Board to report, at same time, the amount required for sinking fund.

SECTION
24. Board to report, at same time, the amount required for salaries, incidental expenses, and cleaning and repairing sewers.
25. The amount reported under last three sections to be raised by tax; treasurer to report monthly to board of public works the amount of sewerage tax collected.
26. Sinking fund to be invested in purchase of sewerage bonds or other bonds of the city; to be used for no other purpose than the liquidation of said bonds; annual report to specify the securities in which said fund is invested; also the progress and condition of sewerage works, amount of bonds and debts outstanding, amounts due, and all expenditures on account of the works.
27. Temporary loans authorized in certain cases.
28. Accounts pertaining to sewerage works to be kept separate; moneys deposited with treasurer on account of said works to be applied only for sewerage purposes.
29. Penalty for willful injury to sewers.
30. Board to make regulations concerning the public sewers; common council to provide penalties for their violation.
31. Provisions relating to sinking fund to be deemed as part of the contract with parties purchasing bonds.
32. Repealing clause.

SECTION 1. The board of public works of the city of Chicago, shall have charge and superintendence of the sewers of said city, and of all works pertaining thereto. *Board of public works to have charge of sewerage works.*

SEC. 2. It shall be the duty of the said board to examine and consider all matters relative to the thorough, systematic and effectual drainage of the city of Chicago, not only of surface water and filth, but also of the soil on which said city is situated, to a sufficient depth to secure dryness in cellars, and entire freedom from stagnant water, and in such manner as best to promote the healthfulness of said city. *Board to consider all matters in relation to drainage.*

SEC. 3. The said board shall have power to purchase such books, charts and other works, as may be found necessary or useful, and to cause such surveys to be made within said city, and outside of its limits, as may be required in carrying out the objects of this chapter. *Power to purchase books and charts. To make surveys.*

SEC. 4. The said board shall have power to construct reservoirs, and to lay sewers or drains in and through all the alleys and streets of the said city, and in any highway in Cook county, and also across all rivers and streams, not interfering with the navigation of the same, and through *To construct reservoirs and lay sewers.*

any or all breakwaters into lake Michigan, whether within the limits of said city or not.

To construct canals connecting river and its branches with the lake. To build dams, pumping works, etc.

SEC. 5. The said board are hereby empowered, with the approval of the common council of said city, to construct canals or sewers connecting lake Michigan with Chicago river or its branches, and such other canals, ditches, dams, sewers, embankments, reservoirs, pumping works or other works, and such buildings, machinery and fixtures, as they may find necessary or useful for the carrying out of the purpose of this chapter, whether the same are made within or without the limits of said city.

To purchase and convey real estate.

SEC. 6. The said board shall have power to purchase, hold and convey any personal and real estate, which may be necessary and proper to carry out the intention and objects of this chapter, but the title to all real estate purchased, shall be taken in the name of the city of Chicago, and no such purchase shall be made without the approval of the common council being first had thereto.

To enter upon land to make surveys and construct works. To agree with owners for land damages.

SEC. 7. The said board are hereby authorized to enter upon any land or water, for the purpose of making surveys, or constructing any of the works authorized by this act, and to agree with the owners of any property which may be required for the purpose of this act, as to the amount of compensation to be paid to such owners for the property so taken, or the amount of damages to be paid to such owner or owners, by reason of the construction of any of the works hereby authorized, but no such agreement shall be binding on said city, until first approved by the common council thereof.

Mode of ascertaining damages in case of disagreement.

SEC. 8. In case of disagreement between the board and the owners of the property, which may, in the judgment of said board, be required for any of the purposes specified in this chapter, as to the amount of compensation to be paid to such owners, or in case such owner shall be an infant, a married woman, or insane, or absent from this State, or in case of disagreement between the said board and any owner or owners of property, touching the amount of damages arising from the construction of any part of the work hereby authorized, the said board shall have the right to condemn said property, or to have the amount of such damages ascertained, or both; and the proceedings for the condemnation of such property, or the ascertainment of such damages, or both, shall conform, as nearly as may be, to those specified and provided in the act entitled "An Act to amend the law condemning right of way, for purposes of internal improvement," approved June 22, 1852, and the act or acts of which the same is an amendment.

(*Further provision for condemnation*, Sec. 18, *post*, 183.)

Board to report to common council necessary changes in grade of streets.

SEC. 9. It is hereby made the duty of the said board to report to the common council what grade or changes of grade, of the streets and alleys of said city, are necessary, to secure their thorough drainage and sewerage, as is contemplated by this chapter; and the common council may thereupon by ordinance establish or alter such grades. The said board may make such arrangements or alterations of the gutters along the streets and alleys, included in those parts of the city, the drainage from which can be conveniently introduced into the sewers, as shall be necessary to cause a rapid and effectual removal of the surface water from the same; and to this end, may enter upon, use and obstruct the said streets for such time as may be necessary to effect said object.

Street gutters may be so laid as to remove surface water.

Sewers may be so constructed as to furnish proper connections with private drains.

SEC. 10. The said board, while constructing the said drains or sewers, as herein provided, may construct such additions to the same as they shall deem expedient, to furnish the proper plans of connection with the private drains or sewers to be thereafter constructed; and the cost of such additions may be charged and assessed as a part of the expense of said private drains or sewers connecting therewith, when such private drains or sewers shall be constructed, and shall be chargeable to the lot or lots for the benefit of which the same are constructed, and collected in the same manner as herein before in this act provided for the collection of the costs of such private drains or sewers.

Additional costs, how defrayed.

Cost of private drains chargeable to lots benefited.

SEC. 11. The cost of the private drains and sewers, connecting the respective lots in said city with the public sewers, shall not be included in the cost of the general plan of sewerage, but the same shall be a special charge upon the lot or lots for whose benefit such private drain or sewer shall be constructed, and shall be collected as herein before in this act provided.

Board to prescribe location and construction of private drains.

SEC. 12. It shall be the duty of said board to prescribe the location, arrangement, form, material and construction of every private drain or sewer emptying into the said public drains or sewers, and to determine the manner and plan of such connection; and the work of constructing the same shall be, in all cases, subject to the superintendence and control of the said board, and shall be executed strictly in compliance with their orders.

Board to cause private drains to be laid from every lot, if needed.

SEC. 13. It shall be the duty of the said board to construct or provide for the construction of private drains or sewers, to communicate with the public drains or sewers, from every lot in the said city, which in their judgment requires it; and whenever the said board, by virtue of this act, are authorized to construct any such private drain or sewer, it shall be lawful for the said board, or their agents, to enter upon any of said lots and to construct thereon such drain or sewer, and for that purpose, to have free ingress and egress upon said lot or lots, with men and teams, and to deposit all the necessary building materials, and generally to do and perform all things necessary to a complete execution of the work.

To regulate construction of privies and cess-pools.

SEC. 14. The said board shall have power to regulate the construction of privies, and the manner of cleaning the same, and to construct and regulate the construction of cess-pools, and provide for the draining of privies and cess-pools; and like notices shall be served, so far as may be, and like proceedings had, and like measures taken for collecting the cost and expense, as is herein before in this act provided in the case of repairs of sidewalks.

To complete the issue of certain bonds.

SEC. 15. The said board of public works are hereby empowered to issue all bonds, now authorized to be issued under the law of this State, incorporating a board of sewerage commissioners for the city of Chicago, approved February 14th, 1855, and under an act in addition to the same, approved February 14th, 1859.

City authorized to borrow $500,000, for sewerage works.

SEC. 16. For the carrying out of the purposes and objects of this chapter, the said city shall have power to borrow, from time to time, as the board of public works and the common council of said city shall deem expedient, a sum of money not exceeding five hundred thousand dollars, upon the credit of said city of Chicago; and said board shall have power, by and with the approval of the common council, to issue bonds pledging the faith and credit of said city, for the payment of the principal and interest of the said bonds; but no bonds shall be issued until the common council shall have approved of such issue, by a vote of a majority of all the aldermen by law authorized to be elected; and all bonds issued by said board, before they shall be binding upon said city, shall be marked "approved," by the mayor and clerk of said city, under the seal of said city, and such signature and seal shall be conclusive evidence to the holder of said bonds, of the fact of such approval: *Provided*, That all sales of sewerage loan bonds, which may be issued by said board, shall be made only by the comptroller of said city, who, on making such sales, shall deposit the proceeds thereof with the city treasurer, to the credit of the sewerage fund, and shall file with the said board a duplicate receipt of the said treasurer for the amount of such deposit: *Provided, also*, That all funds derived from the sale of the sewerage loan bonds of said board, or otherwise, for the sewerage works of said city, shall be exclusively used and appropriated by said board, to the objects and purposes pertaining to the sewerage of said city, herein specified; nor shall the same, or any part thereof, be used by the said board for any other purpose.

Bonds may be issued.

Bonds to be sold by comptroller.

Sewerage funds to be used only for sewerage purposes.

(*Further provision for borrowing and issuing bonds*, Sec. 13, *post*, 181.)

SEC. 17. It shall be the duty of the said board, at any time when they shall desire to make an issue of bonds, as herein authorized, to make a report to the common council, setting forth the nature and amount of work proposed to be executed, and the amount which will be required by them for such purposes, within a period to be stated by them in said report; which report shall be accompanied by an estimate of the cost of the things required to be purchased, and of the work to be done; and the common council may thereupon approve the issue of the whole amount of bonds

Board desiring to issue bonds shall report the object to council.

Council to approve.

called for by such report, or such part thereof as the common council may deem expedient.

Interest on bonds limited to 7 per cent.

SEC. 18. The said bonds shall bear interest not exceeding seven per cent. per annum, and shall not be sold at a rate which will net to the said board less than their par value, unless the common council of said city shall, by a vote of a majority of all the aldermen elected, authorize the comptroller of said city to sell the same at a lower rate, and then only at such rate as shall be fixed by said council: *Provided, however*, That reasonable commissions to brokers or agents employed in procuring the sale or negotiation of said bonds, may be paid by said comptroller.

Board to keep a register of all bonds issued

SEC. 19. It shall be the duty of the said board to keep an accurate register of all bonds and all interest coupons, issued for the construction of said sewerage works, showing the number, date and amount of each bond and coupon, and to whom issued or sold, and when and where payable, and the particular bonds at any time outstanding.

Comptroller to keep a record of outstanding bonds.

SEC. 20. It shall be the duty of the comptroller of the city of Chicago to keep such a record of all bonds, now or hereafter to be issued for the sewerage of said city, as shall at all times exhibit the number and amount of such bonds outstanding, the rate of interest, and when and where the principal and interest are payable.

Payments of interest and principal to be made by comptroller.

SEC. 21. It shall be the duty of the comptroller of said city to pay the interest on said sewerage loan bonds, and also the principal, as the bonds shall become due. The said comptroller, when there are funds for that purpose, may, with the approval of the said board, purchase any such sewerage loan bonds, whether the same have become due or not; and in case there are not sufficient sewerage funds in the treasury of said city to meet all of the said bonds, when the same shall become due, the said board shall have the right to issue new bonds, in the same manner as herein before provided, for such amount and on such time as the said board and the common council of said city shall deem expedient, in the place of bonds so becoming due as aforesaid; the said old bonds to be canceled in the registry thereof, and the said new bonds to be recorded in the manner herein before provided.

New bonds may be issued to pay those falling due.

SEC. 22. It shall be the duty of the board to report to the comptroller, on or before the first day of May in each year, the amount which will be required to be raised for the municipal year next ensuing, to meet the payment of interest to accrue during said year on all the bonds theretofore issued, or which are, during said year, to be issued, for the sewerage of the said city. Board to report to comptroller amount required annually to pay interest

SEC. 23. It shall be the duty of the said board, further to report to the comptroller, at the time named in said last section, such amount as they shall, upon calculation, find necessary, in order to provide a sinking fund for the liquidation of the bonds, so issued as aforesaid, at the maturity thereof: *Provided*, That the amount to be raised for such sinking fund shall not exceed two per cent. of the amount of bonds theretofore issued, and which are, during said year, to be issued for the sewerage of said city. To report amount necessary to be raised for sinking fund

SEC. 24. The said board shall, at the same time, also report to the comptroller, the sum which will be by them required to pay salaries and incidental expenses, and for the cleaning and repairing, and for the proper maintenance of the sewers of said city. The reports required in this and the two preceding sections, shall be laid by said comptroller before the common council, with his annual estimate. To report amount required for salaries and maintaining sewers, etc.

SEC. 25. The amount which shall be so reported to the common council, as provided in said last three sections, shall be raised by the said common council, by a special tax on the property of the city, to be designated sewerage tax, which shall be collected in like manner with the other taxes of said city; and the amounts so collected shall be paid over by the collector of said city to the city treasurer, who, at the end of each month, shall report to the board of public works the amount of the sewerage tax paid over to him during such month. Amount required, to be raised by tax. Treasurer to report monthly to board, amount of sewerage tax collected.

SEC. 26. It shall be the duty of the said board to direct the comptroller of said city to invest the amount heretofore raised, or hereafter to be raised, to provide a sinking fund for the liquidation of said bonds, and such investment shall be by the purchase of said bonds, or other bonds of the city of Chicago; and in like manner to invest the interest received on such last mentioned bonds, and to invest Sinking fund, how invested.

and re-invest said sinking fund, and all proceeds thereof, in such manner as to make the same available for the liquidation of the said bonds. All such investments shall be made in the name of the said city, and shall be designated as the sewerage sinking fund, and shall in no case be used or appropriated for any other purpose whatsoever, than the liquidation of the said bonds. The annual report of said board shall specify in full the nature and amount of the respective securities in which the said sinking fund is invested. The annual report of said board shall state the progress and condition of the sewerage works, shall also show the amount of sewerage loan bonds outstanding, and all debts outstanding on account of the sewerage works, and the amount due from parties to the city for the sewerage works, and shall accurately and clearly exhibit all the expenditures of the said board on account of the same; which financial statement shall be certified by the commissioners of said board, under oath.

Annual report.

Temporary loans authorized in certain cases.

SEC. 27. The said board shall have power to authorize the comptroller of said city to raise, by temporary loan, upon the credit of said city of Chicago, with the approval of the common council, such sums of money as may be needed for the payment of the interest on the said bonds, or the outstanding obligations of the said city on account of the sewerage works, and for which there shall be no funds in the hands of the treasurer of the said city; but in all cases, such temporary loans shall be provided for out of the first sewerage tax, or other revenues on account of the sewerage works, received into the city treasury.

Sewerage accounts to be kept separate.

SEC. 28. All accounts pertaining to the sewerage works of said city, shall be kept separate and distinct from the accounts pertaining to other departments of said board; and all moneys deposited with the city treasurer, on account of the sewerage works, shall be by him kept separate and distinct from all other moneys, as the sewerage fund, and shall only be applied for the uses and purposes for which the same were received.

Sewerage funds to be used for no other purposes.

Penalty for willful injury to sewers.

SEC. 29. If any person shall willfully or maliciously obstruct, damage or injure any public or private sewer or drain in said city, or willfully injure any of the materials employed, provided or used in said city for the purposes specified in this act, he shall be subject to indictment, and upon conviction thereof, shall be punished by fine not exceeding one thousand dollars, or imprisonment not exceeding six months, or both, in the discretion of the court.

SEC. 30. It shall be the duty of the board to make all necessary rules, regulations and restrictions concerning the public and private sewers or drains of said city, and to report to the common council the regulations which shall be adopted by them; and the common council shall, thereupon, pass an ordinance, establishing such rules and regulations, and providing penalties for their violation; which penalties may be enforced in any court having jurisdiction of any offenses against any of the ordinances of said city.

Board to make regulations concerning sewers.

Common council to provide penalties for their violation.

SEC. 31. The provisions herein before contained, for the establishment of a sinking fund, shall be deemed and taken as a part of the contract with the parties purchasing said bonds, and shall not be repealed or modified, so as in any manner to impair the security thereby afforded to the said bond holders.

Sinking fund provisions deemed part of contract with purchasers of bonds.

SEC. 32. All acts or parts of acts, inconsistent with the provisions of this chapter, are hereby repealed.

Repealing clause.

(*Further provisions for cleansing river*, Secs. 11 to 18, *post*, 180 to 184, *and Act of February* 16, 1865, *post*, 206 to 208.)

CHAPTER XVII.

MISCELLANEOUS AND SUPPLEMENTARY.

SECTION
1. Ordinances imposing penalties to be published six days, before taking effect.
2. Ordinances to continue in force.
3. All actions and rights preserved.
4. Rights of property vested in the corporation; officers to continue until superseded.
5. No act invalidated or right divested by reason of this act.
6. No person incompetent to act as judge, witness or juror because an inhabitant of the city.
7. Powers of conservators of the peace.
8. Cemetery lots exempt from levy and attachment.
9. Criminals convicted in recorder's court may be sentenced to bridewell, instead of county jail.

SECTION
10. City not liable for board or jail fees of persons committed to county jail.
11. City not required to furnish an appeal bond or affidavit of merits in any suit; execution not to be issued against the city.
12. Ordinances, when published by authority, shall be evidence without proof.
13. This act a public act; courts to take judicial notice of it.
14. Certain acts respecting wharfing privileges in Chicago, continued in force.
15. Board of claims commissioners abolished.
16. Special provision concerning first election of aldermen under this act.

SECTION
17. Special provision concerning present commissioners of board of public works and board of police; election of their successors.
18. Police justices may be appointed after first Monday of May, 1863, to succeed those then in office.
19. Special provision concerning present guardians of reform school; appointment of their successors.
20. Ward supervisors now in office shall continue to serve until their present term expires; one supervisor to be elected in each ward at future elections for town officers.

SECTION
21. Certain officers in and for the towns of North, South and West Chicago abolished; compensation of town clerk for each of said towns not to exceed $100 a year; annual tax for town purposes restricted therein to $1000; school and other property, belonging to said towns, to be transferred to the city.
22. First election of city officers, under this act, to be held on the third Tuesday of April, 1863.
23. This act shall not be construed to extend to any railroad company any new rights or privileges.
24. Special provisions respecting the use of the railway tracks of any company, in the streets and alleys, by other companies.
25. This act to take effect from its passage.

Ordinances imposing penalty, to be published six times.

SECTION 1. Every ordinance, regulation or by-law, imposing any penalty, fine, imprisonment or forfeiture, for a violation of its provisions, shall, after the passage thereof, be published six times in the corporation newspaper, and proof of such publication, by the affidavit of the printer or publisher of said newspaper, taken before any officer authorized to administer oaths, and filed with the city clerk, or any other competent proof of such publication, shall be conclusive evidence of the legal publication and promulgation of such ordinance or by-law, in all courts and places.

Ordinances now in force, to remain in force.

SEC. 2. All ordinances, regulations and resolutions, now in force in the city of Chicago, and not inconsistent with this act, shall remain in force, under this act, until altered, modified or repealed by the common council, after this act shall take effect.

Existing actions and rights vested in corporation.

SEC. 3. All actions, rights, fines, penalties and forfeitures, in suit or otherwise, which have accrued under the several acts consolidated herein, shall be vested in, and prosecuted by the corporation hereby created.

Property vested in corporation.

SEC. 4. All property, real, personal or mixed, belonging to the city of Chicago, is hereby vested in the corporation created by this act; and the officers of said corporation, now in office, shall respectively continue in the same, until superseded in conformity to the provisions hereof; but shall be governed by this act, which shall take effect from and after its passage.

This act not to invalidate

SEC. 5. This act shall not invalidate any legal act done

by the common council of the city of Chicago, or by its officers; nor divest their successors, under this act, of any rights of property or otherwise, or liability, which may have accrued to, or been created by said corporation, prior to the passage of this act.

prior acts or rights.

SEC. 6. No person shall be an incompetent judge, justice, witness or juror, by reason of his being an inhabitant or freeholder in the city of Chicago, in any action or proceeding, in which the said city shall be a party in interest.

Citizens competent as witnesses or jurors.

SEC. 7. All officers of the city, created conservators of the peace, by this act, shall have power to arrest, or cause to be arrested, with or without process, all persons who shall break, or threaten to break the peace, and, if necessary, detain such persons in custody over night, in the watch-house, or other safe place; and shall have and exercise such other powers, as conservators of the peace, as the common council may prescribe.

Powers of officers created conservators of the peace.

SEC. 8. The cemetery lots which have been or may hereafter be laid out and sold, by said city, for private places of burial, shall, with the appurtenances, forever be exempt from execution and attachment.

Cemetery lots exempt from execution.

SEC. 9. It shall be lawful for the recorder's court to sentence criminals convicted of offenses committed in the city of Chicago, punishable by imprisonment in the county jail, to imprisonment in the city bridewell, to be there kept at labor.

Recorder may sentence criminals to bridewell.

SEC. 10. The city of Chicago shall not be liable, in any case, for the board or jail fees of any person who may be committed by any officer of the city, or by any court or magistrate, to the jail of Cook county, for any offense punishable under the statutes of this State.

City not liable for board of prisoners in jail.

SEC. 11. When, in any suit, the city of Chicago prays an appeal from the judgment of any court in this State, to a higher court, it shall not be required to furnish an appeal bond; nor shall any affidavit of merits be required of said city, in any suit to which it is a party defendant, to entitle it to defend the same. No suit shall be brought against the city, except in a court of record; nor shall any writ of

City not required to furnish an appeal bond, etc.

execution be issued for the collection of any judgment recovered against said city.

Printed ordinances to be received in evidence.

SEC. 12. All ordinances of the city, when printed and published by authority of the common council, shall be received in all courts and places, without further proof.

This act public.

SEC. 13. This act shall be deemed a public act, and may be read in evidence, without proof; and judicial notice shall be taken thereof, in all courts and places.

Wharfing privileges.

SEC. 14. Nothing in this act contained, shall be held to repeal either of the following acts, to wit: "An Act to adjust and settle the title to the wharfing privileges in Chicago, and for other purposes," approved February 27th, 1847, and "An Act to amend an act entitled 'An Act to adjust and settle the title to the wharfing privileges in Chicago, and for other purposes,' approved February 27, 1847, and in relation to wharves and docks in said city," approved February 11th, 1853; but both of said acts, with the exception of the fifth section of the first mentioned act, are hereby ratified and continued in force.

Claims commissioners.

SEC. 15. Section sixty-six and a half of the act amendatory of the city charter, approved February 18th, 1861, constituting a board of claims commissioners in and for said city, is hereby repealed.

First election of aldermen.

SEC. 16. All aldermen now in office, and whose terms, by virtue of previously existing laws, will not expire until the year 1864, shall represent in the common council the respective wards in which they reside, as the same are hereby established, to the end of the term for which they were chosen; but if, in any case, more than two such aldermen may happen to reside in the same ward, two of them, to be designated by lot, shall retain their seats as above provided, and the other or others shall retire from office on the first Monday of May next. Two aldermen shall be chosen, at the next annual election, in each of said wards which would not otherwise be fully represented in the common council; but no alderman shall be then chosen in any ward, which, by virtue of the provisions of this section, will be fully represented in the common council during the ensuing municipal year.

Present commission-

SEC. 17. One commissioner of the board of public

works shall be elected, at the next annual election, to succeed the commissioner whose term of office will expire on the first Monday of May next. That one of the other two commissioners now in office, having the shortest term to serve, shall continue in office until the first Monday of May, 1865, and the one having the longest term to serve, shall continue in office until the first Monday of May, 1867, at which several times their respective terms of office shall expire. The provisions of this section shall also extend to and include the commissioners of the board of police, except as to the time of their continuance in office, which shall be until the first Monday of May, 1864, for the one having the shortest term to serve, and until the first Monday in May, 1865, for the one having the longest term to serve.

ers of boards of public works and of police, continued in office; election of their successors.

(*Further provisions as to commissioners of board of police,* Secs. 11, 12, *post,* 193.)

SEC. 18. Any vacancy now existing in the office of police justice, or which may occur before the first Monday of May next, may be filled in the manner prescribed by present laws; but the police justices then in office, shall hold only until the election and qualification of their successors.

Police justices to be elected in May, to succeed those then in office

SEC. 19. The two guardians of the reform school, now in office, having the longest term to serve, shall continue in office until the first Monday of June, 1865; the two guardians having the next longest term to serve, shall continue in office until the first Monday of June, 1864; the other three guardians shall continue in office until the first Monday of June next; at which several times, their respective terms of office shall expire.

Guardians of reform school continued in office.

SEC. 20. The supervisors now in office, who were elected from the different wards of the city of Chicago, as they were heretofore constituted, shall continue in office until the expiration of the term for which they were chosen. At all future elections for town officers, one supervisor shall be elected in each of the wards of said city, as the same are hereby established.

Ward supervisors.

SEC. 21. The offices of overseer of the poor, commissioner of highways, overseer of highways and pound master, in and for the towns of North Chicago, South Chicago and

Certain town offices abolished in North, South and West Chicago.

West Chicago, respectively, are hereby abolished; and hereafter the town clerk of neither of the said towns shall receive for his official services, a compensation exceeding one hundred dollars a year; nor shall it hereafter be lawful to raise a tax for town purposes, in either of said towns, exceeding one thousand dollars a year, in any one year. All school property, and all other public property of every description, in the towns of North Chicago, South Chicago and West Chicago, shall belong, and be forthwith transferred to the city of Chicago. All moneys in the hands of the treasurer of Cook county, or in the hands of any town officer or agent, collected or raised for school purposes, or for the construction or repair of highways or bridges, in either of said towns, including money received for licenses, and all such moneys as shall hereafter come into the hands of said treasurer, or other officer, shall be paid over to the treasurer of the city of Chicago; and said moneys shall be applied by said city to the purposes for which the same were collected or raised.

Tax for town purposes.

Transfer of town property to city.

(*Further provision as to amount of tax for town purposes*, Sec. 22, *post*, 197.)

First election of city officers by the people.

SEC. 22. The first election of all city officers to be chosen by the people, shall be held, except as is herein otherwise provided, on the third Tuesday of April next.

Railroad companies to derive no new rights from this act

SEC. 23. This act shall not operate or be construed, to extend to any railroad company any rights, privileges or benefits, which they do not now possess under their respective acts of incorporation or existing laws.

Use of the railway tracks of any company in the streets and alleys, by other companies.

SEC. 24. Whenever any railroad or railway company, which has been heretofore or may hereafter be authorized to extend its railway tracks along the streets and alleys and across the waters controlled by the city, within the limits of said city, shall desire to use the track or tracks of any other railroad or railway company, in said streets and alleys and across the waters controlled by said city, within said limits, for the passage of their cars and engines, and the transaction of their business, or either, it shall be lawful for such company to apply, by petition, to the judge of the circuit court of Cook county for such leave; and the owner or owners of such track or tracks, so desired to be used, having been first notified to appear and answer to such petition, it shall be the duty of said court to appoint three commissioners, to determine the time or times, mode, manner, extent and rates at which such track or tracks may be used as aforesaid; and the said commissioners shall grant a certificate to the party or parties so applying, setting forth in such certificate their decision; and the party applying as aforesaid, acting in pursuance of said certificate, shall be authorized to use such track or tracks in compliance with such certificate. An appeal may be taken, by either party, to the circuit court of Cook county, from such decision. All proceedings in said court and before said commissioners, when so appointed, shall be conducted in the manner provided for the condemnation of rights of way, in an act to amend an act entitled "An Act to amend the law condemning right of way for purposes of internal improvement," approved June 22nd, A. D. 1852, and the amendments thereto. The provisions of this section shall not authorize the use of the railway track of any party, for the running of the regular trains of another party, or in such manner as in any way to interfere with the running of the regular trains, or materially with the general business of the party owning such railway track; and such use of such railway track, and the cars and engines passing over the same, shall be under the exclusive direction and control of the superintendent of the railway, the track of which is so used, and shall be limited to the railway tracks laid down in, along and over the streets, alleys and waters of said city, as herein before stated. Whenever, by the use of any such track, under any decision made as above specified, either party shall deem the terms of said use unjust or inequitable, or to require revision, he or they may have a re-adjustment of the same, upon application and hearing in the manner herein above provided.

SEC. 25. This act shall take effect from and after its passage. Act to take effect from its passage.

Approved February 13, 1863.

PRIOR LAWS AFFECTING THE CITY.

CEMETERY.

AN ACT granting a Lot of Land to the Town of Chicago for the Burial of the Dead.

SECTION
1. Town of Chicago permitted to use a lot of canal land for a burial ground, on terms, etc.

SECTION
2. To be used forever as a burial ground; subdivisions.

Use of lot for burial ground.

SECTION 1. *Be it enacted by the People of the State of Illinois, represented in the General Assembly*, That the inhabitants of the town of Chicago, under the direction of the president and trustees of said town, are hereby authorized and permitted to use a lot of canal land, situated near the said town, for a burial ground, being the east half of the south-east quarter of section number thirty-three, in township number forty, range fourteen east of the third principal meridian: *Provided*, The president and trustees of said town will, by an order to be entered upon the records of their proceedings, engage and agree to pay to the State of Illinois whatever sum the said land may be valued at by the agents of the State, whenever the State shall authorize a sale of the canal lands in the vicinity of the town of Chicago; the said land to be valued at the same price of other canal lands of a like quality and situation, and without regard to the use to which it is applied.

Purchase thereof.

Title vested.

SEC. 2. When the land described in the foregoing section shall be paid for as therein provided, the title to the same shall be vested in the president and trustees of the town of Chicago and their successors forever; but the said trustees shall not thereby acquire the right to sell, dispose of or lease the said land, or any part thereof, but the same shall forever remain for a public burying ground, and shall never be used for any other purpose: *Provided*, That the

Forever to remain a burial ground.

trustees may lay off a part thereof for the burial of the citizens of Chicago, and a part for the burial of strangers and transient persons, and make such other subdivision thereof as may be deemed necessary to the public convenience. Subdivisions.

Approved February 10, 1837.

COUNTY SEAT.

AN ACT to create and organize the Counties therein named.

SECTION 1. Cook county constituted, and county seat established at Chicago.

SECTION 1. *Be it enacted by the People of the State of Illinois, represented in the General Assembly,* That all that tract of country, to wit: Commencing at the boundary line between the States of Indiana and Illinois, at the dividing line between towns thirty-three and thirty-four north; thence west to the south-west corner of town thirty-four north, of range nine east; thence due north to the northern boundary line of the State; thence east with said line to the north-east corner of the State; thence southwardly with the line of the State to the place of beginning; shall constitute a county to be called Cook; and the county seat thereof is hereby declared to be permanently established at the town of Chicago, as the same has been laid out and defined by the canal commissioners. Cook county constituted. Chicago the county seat.

* * * * * * *

Approved January 15, 1831.

FIREMEN'S BENEVOLENT ASSOCIATION.

AN ACT to amend an Act entitled "An Act to incorporate the Firemen's Benevolent Association," and for other purposes.

SECTION 4. Trustees to make a permanent fund; interest to be applied, *first*, for relief of persons described, and *second*, for fire alarm telegraph and benevolent institutions.

* * * * * * *

SEC. 4. The board of trustees shall make the sum of forty thousand dollars ($40,000), if there be that amount in Permanent fund.

the hands of said association; if not, then they shall make the sum of thirty-six thousand dollars, a permanent fund, the annual interest of which shall be applied —

Relief of members, etc.

First. To the relief of distressed, sick, injured or disabled members, and their immediate families, and the clothing and the education of the orphans or half orphans of indigent deceased members of said association, also to provide a suitable burial and burial place for indigent members and their immediate families.

Surplus to city for telegraph and to benevolent institutions.

Second. Any surplus interest as aforesaid, after providing for the objects aforenamed, and paying the necessary expenses of the said trust, shall be annually equally divided and paid, one equal one-quarter to the city of Chicago when the said city, by its authorities, shall have erected a good and sufficient fire-alarm telegraph, costing not less than twenty-five thousand dollars ($25,000), to be paid so long and no longer than the said fire-alarm telegraph shall be kept in good order and operated by said city; one equal one-quarter of said surplus interest to the Chicago orphan asylum (Protestant); one equal one-quarter of said surplus interest to the Catholic orphan asylum; one equal one-quarter of said surplus interest to the Home of the friendless, all of Chicago. The orphan asylums and home of the friendless herein named shall have and receive each one equal one-third part of said surplus interest until the aforesaid city of Chicago shall complete said fire-alarm telegraph.

* * * * * * *

Approved February 13, 1863.

FISH INSPECTOR.

Sec. 10, Chap. 3, of Charter.

This Act was not known to be in existence until too late to refer to it under the section above cited, or to place it with the amendments of the Charter.

AN ACT in relation to the Fish Inspector of the City of Chicago.

SECTION
1. Council have power to fix pay of inspectors.

SECTION
2. This act public, and in force from its passage.

SECTION 1. *Be it enacted by the People of the State of Illinois, represented in the General Assembly,* That the common council of the city of Chicago shall have power to fix and regulate the pay of fish inspectors. Power of council to fix pay.

SEC. 2. This act shall be deemed a public act, and have effect from and after its passage. Act public and in force.

Approved February 16, 1865.

STATE'S ATTORNEY.

AN ACT to amend an Act entitled "An Act in relation to the Attorney General and State's Attorney," approved February 28th, 1847.

SECTION
1. State's attorney to be allowed same fees in recorder's court as in circuit court, to be paid by the city of Chicago.

SECTION
2. Act in force from its passage.

SECTION 1. *Be it enacted by the People of the State of Illinois, represented in the General Assembly,* That the State's attorney of the seventh judicial circuit shall be allowed the same commissions and fees for his services in the recorder's court of the city of Chicago, that he is now entitled to receive by law for like services in the said circuit court, to be paid by the city of Chicago. State's attorney's fees to be paid by city.

SEC. 2. This act to take effect and be in force from and after its passage. Act in force.

Approved February 24, 1859.

STREETS.

AN ACT authorizing Incorporated Cities to change, alter and vacate Streets or parts of Streets.

SECTION
1. Vacation of streets upon petition; conveyance of interest of city.

SECTION
2. Assessment of benefits and damages.

SECTION 1. *Be it enacted by the People of the State of Illinois, represented in the General Assembly,* That when the corporate authorities of any city may deem it for the best Vacation of streets on petition.

interest of their respective cities that any street or part of street shall be changed, altered or vacated, said authorities shall have the power, upon the petition of the property holders owning property on such street or part of street, to change, alter or vacate the same, and to convey by quit-claim deed all interest which said city may have had in the street or part of street so vacated, to the owner or owners of lots and lands next to and adjoining the same, upon the payment by such owner or owners of all assessments which may be made against their lots or lands for and on account of benefits to the same arising from such change, alteration or vacation of any street or part of street, as aforesaid.

Convenance of interest of city.

Benefits and damages.

SEC. 2. The benefits and damages caused by changing, altering or vacating any street or part of street, as aforesaid, shall be assessed and determined in the manner pointed out by the act incorporating such city, or by the ordinances thereof in other cases.

Approved February 15, 1851.

AN ACT to authorize the Common Council of the City of Chicago to vacate Streets and Alleys.

SECTION
1. Vacation of streets and alleys; assessments for damages.

SECTION
2. Act in force from its passage.

Vacation of streets and alleys.

SECTION 1. *Be it enacted by the People of the State of Illinois, represented in the General Assembly,* That the common council of the city of Chicago be and is hereby empowered and authorized to vacate any street or alley within said city, and if any person shall be entitled to damages, such damages shall be assessed and paid in the same manner as they would be in the opening of a street in said city.

Assessments for damages.

Act in force.

SEC. 2. This act shall be in force from its passage.

Approved February 12, 1859.

SUPERVISORS.

Sec. 20, Chap. 17, of Charter.

AN ACT to reduce the Act to provide for Township Organization, and the several Acts amendatory thereof, into one act, and to amend the same.

SECTION 3. Each Ward in Chicago and Peoria to elect a supervisor.

* * * * * * *

ARTICLE EIGHTEENTH.

* * * * * * *

SECTION 3. The cities of Chicago and Peoria shall be entitled to elect one supervisor in each ward, in addition to the township supervisors, and the several supervisors so elected shall be members of the board of supervisors of the county, and shall have, possess and enjoy all the rights, powers and privileges that are now or hereafter shall be possessed and enjoyed by the several township supervisors, as members of the board of supervisors of the county. The election for such supervisor to be held at the same time and in the same manner as the election for township supervisors in the counties in which said cities are situated. Each ward to elect a supervisor.

* * * * * * *

Approved February 20, 1861.

WHARFING PRIVILEGES.

The two Acts upon this subject, here following, except the fifth section of the first Act, are continued in force by Sec. 14, Chap. 17, of Charter.

AN ACT to adjust and settle the Title to the Wharfing Privileges in Chicago, and for other purposes.

PREAMBLE. Reciting the necessity for a determination of the questions as to title to wharfing privileges.

SECTION

1. Power of council to vacate certain streets; compromise conflicting claims; make ordinances, deeds, agreements, etc.; saving of rights of individuals, corporations and State; two-thirds vote necessary.

SECTION

2. Bill in chancery may be filed to determine rights of parties; process, and proceedings thereon.
3. Proceedings on appeal.
4. Power of council to alter, etc., or discontinue certain streets; saving of rights of canal trustees and the State.
5. Power of council to widen the Chicago river and branches; proceedings for that purpose.

Preamble. WHEREAS, Those portions of land, or parts of South Water, North Water, West Water and East Water streets, in the original town of Chicago, (on the sides of said streets nearest the river,) which lie eighty feet distant from the lines of the lots laid out on the sides of said streets furthest from the river, sometimes known as the "wharfing privileges," are now, and have been for a long time past, made the subject of much controversy between different persons and corporations claiming the title to the same; and whereas, as they are now situated, neither the city of Chicago, nor any person or body corporate, derive any benefit from the same, except the persons who are occupying them, but they are a fruitful source of discord, dissatisfaction and illegal violence; and whereas, it is for the benefit of all parties claiming an interest therein, that the questions arising as to the title to the same shall be settled and determined as speedily as possible; now, therefore,

Power of common council to discontinue certain streets, etc. SECTION 1. *Be it enacted by the People of the State of Illinois, represented in the General Assembly*, That the common council of the city of Chicago shall have full power and authority to discontinue and vacate any part or portion of South Water, North Water, West Water and East Water streets, which lies beyond a line eighty feet distant from the line of the lots laid out on the sides of said streets furthest from the river, (sometimes known as "wharfing privileges,") or any such parts or portions as lie between the line first aforesaid and the river, and to compromise, adjust and determine all conflicting rights or claims arising between the city and any or all persons and corporations who are or may be claimants of such portion of said streets or wharfing privileges; and, for this purpose, the said common council is authorized to make and establish all necessary ordinances, rules and regulations, and to make, execute and deliver all such deeds, agreements, leases and conveyances, and to enter into, take or receive any and all such agreements as the said common council shall deem proper and expedient touching said premises: *Provided*, That nothing in this section contained shall authorize said city to do any act which shall deprive any private individuals or corpora-

To adjust and compromise conflicting rights, etc.

To pass ordinances, and make deeds.

Shall not deprive citizens, body corporate, etc., of

tions, the trustees of the Illinois and Michigan canal, or the State, of any right, title, interest or claim he, she, they or it may have in and to said wharfing privileges, or portion of streets, as property, without his, her, their or its consent; and all the rights, if any, of said State, and trustees of said canal, are hereby expressly reserved: *Provided*, That upon all questions arising in said council under this section, a vote of two-thirds of all the aldermen authorized by law to be elected, shall be necessary.

Wharfing privilege without consent.

All rights reserved.

Two-thirds vote necessary.

SEC. 2. For the purpose of adjudicating, settling and determining all the rights of the various parties, including the State, trustees of the Illinois and Michigan canal, and the city of Chicago, and all and every person and corporation who claims or may claim any portion of said streets or said wharfing privileges, or any interest therein, of whatever name or description, the said city, or any person or corporation, claiming an interest in said portions of said streets or land, or wharfing privileges, is hereby authorized to file a bill in chancery in either the circuit court of Cook county or the Cook county court, and to make said State, the trustees of the Illinois and Michigan canal, the city of Chicago, and every person and corporation claiming any interest in said premises, a party thereto; and said court in which such bill shall be filed, is hereby authorized to hear and determine the same, and to adjudicate, decree and determine the respective rights of the several parties to said bill or proceedings, respectively, fully and particularly; and said court is hereby clothed with full power and jurisdiction to carry into effect all its decrees and determinations in the premises; and in case of the failure of any party to execute any deed, conveyance or other instrument required by said court, to empower the master in chancery of Cook county, or any commissioner appointed by said court, to make, execute and deliver such deed, conveyance or instrument, and the decision of such court shall be final and conclusive in the premises, unless the same shall be appealed from within ninety days from the entering of the final decree: *Provided*, That in case of appeal it shall not be necessary that the party appealing should enter into bond, but the filing a notice in writing in the clerk's office of said court, signed

City to file bill of interested parties in chancery.

In courts of record.

Court authorized.

In case of failure, master in chancery to make and deliver deed.

Appeal allowed within ninety days.

No bond required on appeal.

Notice, sufficient evidence of appeal. Notice to be served on certain parties.

by such party's attorney or solicitor, shall be deemed sufficient evidence of the taking of the appeal: *And provided further*, That notice of the filing of said bill shall be served on the governor, the secretary of said trustees, and a notice thereof published in three of the newspapers published in Chicago, for sixty days before the day of hearing of said bill: *And provided further*, That the ordinary process of summons in chancery shall issue, and be directed to the proper officer or officers, to be executed as in other cases in chancery: *And provided further*, That the judge of said court shall have full power and authority to make all necessary orders for the entering of the appearance of any party to said suit.

Summons shall issue. Judge empowered to make orders for entering appearance, etc.

Supreme court, powers of, on appeal.

SEC. 3. In case of appeal, the supreme court shall possess as full powers in the premises as in other cases of appeal; but the appeal of any party shall not require the said supreme court to adjudicate any question which shall not arise between said appellant and some other party to such bill or proceeding.

Council empowered to alter river streets. Certain rights not to be affected, etc.

SEC. 4. The common council of said city shall have as full power to alter, widen, contract, straighten and discontinue North Water, South Water, East Water and West Water streets in said city, as any other streets: *Provided*, That the rights of the State and the trustees of the Illinois and Michigan canal, if any, shall not be affected, or invalidated, or prejudiced, by any such act of the said common council.

To widen Chicago river by cutting away, or otherwise. Proceedings, how regulated.

SEC. 5. The said common council are hereby fully empowered to widen the Chicago river and the branches thereof, within the city, from time to time, as they may deem proper and necessary for the commercial business of said city, by cutting away the whole or any part of the streets or lots on the bank of said river or its branches. And in case said common council shall determine thus to widen said river, or either of its branches, by cutting away any lot, lots or part of a lot, such proceedings shall be had, for the condemnation and appropriation of such lot or lots, or part of a lot, and the assessment of damages and benefits, as are authorized and directed by the act to incorporate the city of Chicago, and the acts amending the same, for the opening of streets and alleys; and the provisions of said acts shall apply to the widening of said river or its branches, so far as they are applicable; but nothing in this section contained shall authorize the taking of private property for any such purpose, without making adequate compensation to the owner thereof. Private property not to be taken without compensation.

Approved February 27, 1847.

AN ACT to amend an Act entitled "An Act to adjust and settle the Title to the Wharfing Privileges in Chicago, and for other purposes," approved February 27, 1847, and in relation to Wharves and Docks in said City.

SECTION
1. Power of council to vacate certain streets; compromise conflicting claims; convey portions of streets vacated; deeds to be approved by court; proceedings therefor; provisions of former extended to matters done under this act.
2. Appeals, when and how taken.
3. Wharves and docks, and the use of, and compensation therefor.
4. Wharves and docks erected without authority of the city to be removed; penalty for neglect to remove.
5. Parties to, and subject-matter of, bills in chancery, under this and the former act.
6. Proceedings upon such bills in chancery; partial decrees.
7. Proceedings may be had in vacation, but as of next succeeding term of the court.
8. Act in force from its passage.

SECTION 1. *Be it enacted by the People of the State of Illinois, represented in the General Assembly,* That the common council of the city of Chicago shall have power and authority to discontinue and vacate the whole or any part or portion of North Water, East Water, and West Water streets, and so much of any other street in said city as immediately fronts Chicago river, or either of its branches, and to compromise, adjust and determine all conflicting rights or claims arising between the city and any or all persons and corporations who are or may be claimants of the fee of any part or portion of said streets, or of any right or interest therein; and upon such compromise and adjustments said city may convey, by deed or otherwise, the fee in such parts or portions of said streets as may be thus vacated or discontinued to such person or persons as said council may deem entitled to the same under the provisions of this act, or the act to which this is an amendment; and all deeds or other conveyances which have been made and delivered, or which may hereafter be made and delivered by

Council empowered to vacate certain streets, adjust claims, etc.

To convey by deeds to parties entitled, etc.

said city under the provisions of this act, or the act to which this is an amendment, shall be deemed valid and effectual to the conveying the title in fee of the premises therein described, to the person or persons to whom the same are or shall be respectively made, their heirs and assigns: *Provided*, That before any such deeds or conveyances shall bar or preclude the rights of any other person or persons claiming an estate in such portions of said streets thus vacated or discontinued, such deeds or conveyances shall be approved by the court under the provisions of this act, or the act to which this is an amendment; or an order of the circuit court shall be made upon petition filed by said city or any person or party claiming title under such deeds or conveyances respectively, approving and confirming such deeds or conveyances, upon notice given by publication in at least three of the daily papers published in said city of Chicago, for the space of time required in said act to which this is an amendment, directed to all persons claiming any right or interest in the premises described in said deeds or conveyances, to appear and show cause, if any they have, why such deeds or conveyances should not be approved and confirmed. The provisions of said act to which this is an amendment, shall apply to such parts or portions of the above named streets as may be discontinued by virtue of this act, as far as the same may be applicable.

Deeds valid to convey fee. Proviso, that such deeds shall be approved, etc. Circuit court may make order approving, etc., how. Notice required. Former act extended to this, etc.

Appeals, how to be taken.

SEC. 2. Appeals from any order of approval or confirmation under this act, may be taken within the time and in the manner and as is provided in said act to which this is an amendment, and not otherwise.

To authorize wharves, etc., and collect dockage.

SEC. 3. The city of Chicago may authorize and empower any person or persons to whom any portion of said streets thus discontinued or vacated has been or may be conveyed under the provisions of this act, or the one to which this is an amendment, to erect wharves or docks, extending into the Chicago river, in front of the premises thus conveyed, for the purpose of facilitating the trade and commerce of said river, and to receive and collect reasonable wharfage or dockage for the use of the same; and no person, except the owner of the same, or the person entitled under such owner, shall use or occupy any wharf or dock erected

No person except owner to occupy, etc.,

in said city under the permission of the common council thereof, without making reasonable compensation for such use to the owner thereof, or to the party entitled to the use thereof under such owner.

without compensation.

SEC. 4. Every wharf or dock which shall be extended or erected in any portion of the Chicago river or either of its branches, without the express permission or authority of said city, shall be forthwith removed; and if any person or persons shall continue or occupy any such wharf or dock not authorized by said city, after having been notified in writing to remove the same, such person or persons shall forfeit and pay to said city twenty dollars for each day they shall thus occupy such wharf or dock, or suffer the same to remain in said river after the expiration of ten days from the date of said notice, to be recovered by action of debt as other penalties under the charter or ordinances of said city may be recovered.

Wharves built without permission to be removed.

Penalty.

How recovered.

SEC. 5. Neither this act, nor the act to which this is an amendment, shall be so construed as to make it necessary to make any other person or corporation a party to any bill authorized to be filed by the last named act, except such persons or corporations as shall have an interest in the fee or private use of so much of the premises, lot or wharfing privilege or street, to settle the title of which such bill may be filed; and the bills which have been or may be filed under said acts may include such parts and so much of the streets, wharfing lots or wharfing privileges as the complainants may see fit to include therein: *Provided*, That the court may require such other premises to be included therein as may be deemed necessary by said court.

This act how construed.

Proviso.

SEC. 6. The court in which any suit may be pending under the provisions of the act to which this is an amendment, or of this act, is hereby authorized and empowered, from time to time, to adjudicate and determine the rights of the respective parties to any wharfing lot or wharfing privilege, or part thereof, and to enter a final decree touching such lot or part of lot, without deferring such final decree until the rights to other lots or premises shall be determined, so that the title to each wharfing lot or part of lot may be adjusted at the earliest possible day, and not be

Court authorized to adjudicate claims.

delayed on account of any conflicting claims or litigation respecting other lots or premises.

Circuit court or judge may hear and determine in vacation.

SEC. 7. The circuit court, or the judges thereof, may hear and determine all matters arising under this act, or the one to which it is an amendment, in vacation, but all final decrees or final orders made therein shall be considered as made and entered at the next succeeding term of said court, in case such final order or decree shall be made in vacation, so far as the right to except to or appeal from the same, and the computation of time in which such appeal must be taken, is concerned.

When act to take effect.

SEC. 8. This act shall take effect and be in force from and after its passage.

Approved February 11, 1853.

AMENDMENTS TO CITY CHARTER.

AN ACT to amend an Act, entitled "An Act to reduce the Charter of the City of Chicago, and the several Acts amendatory thereof, into one Act, and to revise the same," approved February 13, 1863.

SECTION
1. Improvement of streets, etc.; sidewalks and drains; assessments therefor.
2. Railway companies; how assessed.
3. Lamp posts; assessments therefor.
4. Certain sections of charter repealed.
5. Work may be done before assessment.
6. Power of assessment for removal of nuisances extended.
7. When condemned property appropriated.
8. Several similar notices as to taxes and assessments may be in one advertisement.
9. Fees and proceedings of collector.
10. River and harbor improvements may be made without contract.
11. Plan for cleansing river.
12. Further as to such plan.
13. Power to borrow money and issue bonds.
14. City may contribute to enlarge canal.
15. Consulting board of engineers.
16. Additional members of board of public works appointed for purposes of this act.

SECTION
17. Plan and estimates to be reported to common council.
18. Canal between river and lake; power to condemn lands.
19. Council may pass ordinances necessary for purposes of this act; drainage.
20. Tunnels under river may be built.
21. Funds therefor; how to be raised.
22. Street tax.
23. Salaries of police force.
24. Police tax.
25. Divers acts of common council confirmed.
26. Salaries of city officers.
27. Harbor masters and bridge tenders.
28. Assessors.
29. School tax.
30. School agent to report.
31. School construction bonds.
32. Board of education; exercise of powers limited.
33. City bonds; registry and endorsement thereof.
34. Liquor licenses.
35. Job printing.
36. This act public, and to take effect from passage.

SECTION 1. *Be it enacted by the People of the State of Illinois, represented in the General Assembly*, That whenever any order shall be passed by the common council of said city, pursuant to the authority conferred by chapter seven, of the act of which this is an amendment, for the filling, grading, leveling, paving, curbing, walling, graveling, macadamizing, planking or repairing of any street, lane, alley or highway, or for the construction, re-construction, laying or re-laying of any sidewalk, or any private drain, the commissioners of the board of public works shall forthwith proceed to assess the amount directed by the common council to be assessed for that purpose, with the costs of the proceedings therein, upon the real estate by them deemed benefited by any such improvement, in proportion, as nearly as may be, to the benefit resulting thereto. The assessment in such cases

Improvements of streets, etc.

Assessments.

shall be made and returned, and may be confirmed and collected in the manner provided by sections twenty-three and twenty-four of chapter seven, of the act above mentioned, and the provisions of said two last named sections shall in all respects apply to the assessments hereby authorized. The expense of constructing and relaying sidewalks and area or street walls, at the intersection of streets or alleys, or of streets and alleys, when required to be constructed by any such order of the common council, shall be included in their said assessment, but all other improvements made at such intersections, excepting lamp posts, shall be, as heretofore, chargeable upon and paid out of the general fund, or other appropriate fund, not raised by special assessment.

Include what expenses.

Railway company; how assessed.

SEC. 2. Where, in any case, any portion of the costs and expense of making any improvement mentioned in the foregoing section, shall, by virtue of any valid law or ordinance of the corporation, or by virtue of any valid contract, be chargeable upon any railway company, the amount so chargeable may be assessed upon said railway company, and the balance only upon the real estate benefited thereby, and the city may collect the amount so assessed upon the said railway company, by distress and sale of personal property, as in other cases, or by suit brought for that purpose: *Provided*, That any real estate belonging to such railway company, and deemed benefited by the said improvement, shall be assessed as in other cases.

Lamp post assessments.

SEC. 3. Whenever any order shall be passed by said common council, for the erection of lamp posts upon any of the streets in said city, the commissioners of the board of public works shall forthwith proceed to assess the amount directed to be assessed therefor, with the costs of the proceedings therein, upon the several lots, pieces or parcels of land fronting or abutting on the street or part of street along which said posts are to be erected. Said assessment shall be made in such a manner, as nearly as may be, that each separate lot, piece or parcel of land, on either side of such street, for the whole distance proposed to be lighted, shall sustain its fair proportionate share of the expense and costs, according to the benefit resulting thereto, which assessment shall be made and returned, and may be confirmed and collected in the same manner as assessments for filling, grading or paving streets, and, when confirmed, shall have the same force and effect, like powers, rights and duties being hereby conferred upon the said commissioners and common council, and on all parties interested, in both cases.

SEC. 4. Sections twenty-one, twenty-two, twenty-five, twenty-six, twenty-seven and thirty, of chapter seven of the above mentioned act, are hereby repealed, but all other provisions in the said chapter contained, not inconsistent with the provisions of this act, shall be and remain in full force. **Repealing.**

SEC. 5. Upon the passage of any order referred to in the first and third sections of this act, the board of public works may, in their discretion, cause said improvement to be made, and paid for out of any moneys in the treasury at their disposal, and afterwards cause the expense thereof, together with all costs, to be reimbursed by a special assessment, to be levied and collected as in other cases. **Work may be done before assessment.**

SEC. 6. The power of assessment conferred by section thirty-one, of chapter seven of the above mentioned act, shall extend to all cases where it shall have become necessary to incur expenses for the removal of any nuisance, as well as to those cases where expenses shall have been actually incurred. **Nuisance assessment.**

SEC. 7. Whenever the damages awarded to the owner, for any property condemned by said city for public use, shall have been paid to such owner or his agent, or when sufficient money for that purpose shall be in the hands of the city treasurer, ready to be paid over to such owner, and ten days' notice thereof shall have been given in the corporation newspaper, the city may enter upon and appropriate such property to the use for which the same was condemned. **When condemned, property appropriated.**

SEC. 8. Two or more of the notices required or authorized to be given by the board of public works, or the commissioners of said board, by publication in the cor- **Several similar notices in one advertisement.**

poration newspaper, in any special assessment proceedings, may be comprised in one advertisement: *Provided*, Such notices are of the same general character, or for like objects, and provided that, in other respects, the notice so published shall sufficiently comply with the essential statutory requirements. And the provisions of this section shall extend to and embrace all notices required to be given in the corporation newspaper by the city collector, of the delivery to him of all tax and special assessment warrants for collection, and of his intended application to some court of general jurisdiction for judgment thereon.

Fees and proceedings of collector.

SEC. 9. The city collector shall be allowed, for the use of said city, one-half the same fees and charges for making distress and sale of goods and chattels for the payment of city taxes and special assessments, as may be allowed by law to constables for making levy and sale of personal property on execution, and his proceedings in such cases shall conform, as nearly as may be, to those prescribed for town collectors by the general laws relative to the collection of the revenue.

River or harbor improvements without contract.

SEC. 10. Whenever, in the prosecution of any river or harbor improvement by said city, the board of public works shall be of opinion that the proposed work can be better or more cheaply done by the board itself, without the intervention of a contractor, they shall report their said opinion to the common council, and the reason for the same, and the common council may, thereupon, by resolution, authorize said board to procure the necessary machinery and material, and to employ workmen to make the said improvement, without letting the work by contract: *Provided*, Three-fourths of all the aldermen elected shall vote in favor of such resolution.

Plan for cleansing river.

SEC. 11. That the board of public works of the city of Chicago be, and they are hereby authorized, required and empowered to devise, and, with the approval of the common council of said city, or otherwise, as hereinafter provided, to adopt and execute a plan for cleansing the Chicago river and its branches, and keeping the same in a pure and healthy condition, and also by contract with the trustees of the Illinois and Michigan canal, or otherwise, for changing the water in said river and branches; but if the consent of said trustees can be had, and in the judgment of said board it is expedient, the experiment of cleansing said river by using the pumping works of said canal, shall be first thoroughly tried, before any expenditure for constructing any other canal or conduit shall be incurred.

SEC. 12. If, in the judgment of said board, it shall be found that permanent and complete drainage of said river and branches can be best effected by constructing a channel from some point on the Chicago river or its branches, southwardly towards or near Lockport, or by widening and deepening the Illinois and Michigan canal, the said board are hereby authorized and empowered to devise a plan for that purpose, with the consent of the common council, or otherwise as hereinafter provided, to make any contract necessary to carry into effect such purpose, in conformity with and subject to the general provisions of the city charter, with the trustees of the Illinois and Michigan canal, or with the United States, or the State of Illinois, or with any party or parties, and to construct a canal, or to widen or deepen the Illinois and Michigan canal, or otherwise to remove and change the waters of the Chicago river and its branches; and the said trustees of the Illinois and Michigan canal are hereby authorized and empowered to make such contract as they may deem just and proper, with the said board or the city of Chicago, for said purposes or any of them. Same.

(*Further provisions for cleansing river*, Act of February 16, 1865, *post*, 206 *et seq.*)

SEC. 13. For the purpose of carrying out the improvements contemplated by the eleventh, twelfth, fourteenth and eighteenth sections of this act, and sections five, six, seven and eight, of chapter sixteen, of the act of which this is an amendment, the said city shall have power to borrow, from time to time, as the board of public works and common council shall deem expedient, an additional sum of money, not exceeding two million dollars, upon the credit of said city of Chicago, and to issue bonds Borrow money. Issue bonds.

therefor, in the manner authorized by section sixteen of said chapter; and all the provisions in said chapter contained respecting the issue and sale of sewerage-loan bonds, the custody and expenditure of the proceeds thereof, and the payment of the principal and the interest to become due thereon, and providing for a sinking fund for the liquidation of the same, shall in like manner apply to the bonds hereby authorized; and the said fund so raised shall constitute a special fund to be held and used for the purposes of such improvement, and for no other purpose whatsoever.

Contribution to canal improvement.

SEC. 14. Should the work of enlarging and deepening the said canal, for a ship or steamboat canal, be prosecuted by the United States, or by the State of Illinois, or the trustees of the Illinois and Michigan canal, the common council of the city of Chicago are hereby authorized and empowered to make a contribution towards such improvement, of such sum of money or bonds, or part of the bonds in the preceding section of this act provided for, or their proceeds, not exceeding $2,000,000, as they shall deem proper.

Consulting board of engineers.

SEC. 15. Upon application of the board of public works, the mayor, by advice and consent of the common council, may appoint a consulting board, of not less than three nor more than five competent engineers, to aid in devising the plans and arranging details rendered necessary by this act.

Additional members of board of public works.

SEC. 16. For the purpose of cleansing the Chicago river and its branches, as in this act provided, Roswell B. Mason and William Gooding are hereby appointed additional members of the board of public works, who shall each receive the same salary as the other members of said board, which is hereby fixed at three thousand dollars per annum for each, and when the work herein contemplated shall be completed, they shall cease to be members of the said board: *Provided*, That the said additional members shall have no power or authority in the said board, save and except in reference to the said work: *And Provided also*, that in no event shall their term of office extend longer than six years from and after May 1st, 1865. In case of the death, resignation or removal from this State of either of said additional members of said board, the vacancy caused thereby shall be filled by the governor of the State of Illinois.

Plan and estimates.

SEC. 17. The said board of public works, after they shall have agreed upon a plan for cleansing the Chicago river, shall forthwith report the said plan to the common council, with a statement of its probable cost, and the said council shall examine the said plan, and if they shall approve the same, it shall be and continue the plan of said work, except so far as it may be changed by the board of public works, in matters of detail, or be otherwise changed or abandoned, as hereinafter provided. If the common council shall disapprove the said plan, they shall refer the same back to said board of public works, with a statement of the reasons for such disapproval. If the said board of public works shall, after considering such objections, adhere to the said plan, by a vote of the majority of all the members of said board, they shall report the same back to the common council, and, after the expiration of thirty days, the said plan, unless withdrawn by said board, shall be and continue the plan of said work, with the exception as to details aforesaid, and the contracts entered into in reference to the same by said board shall be in accordance with and subject to the general provisions of the city charter: *Provided, however*, That said plan may be afterwards abandoned or changed for a different plan, if the said board and the common council, by a majority of all the members of each of said boards, consent hereto: *Provided also*, That the appropriation of money and the issuing and sale of bonds for said work shall be and remain under the control of the common council; and the general provisions of the city charter relating to appropriations, to the custody and sale of city bonds, and the custody and disbursement of the city moneys, shall, and they are hereby intended to apply to the appropriations, the custody and sale of the bonds, and the custody and disbursements of the moneys, for the prosecution of said work.

Control of council.

Canal between river and lake.

SEC. 18. If the said board and the common council shall, in their judgment, deem it desirable, to effect the object of this act, by the construction of one or more canals, to or from the Chicago river or either of its branches to Lake Michigan or elsewhere, it shall be lawful for the said commissioners to condemn such land as shall be necessary for the bed of such canal or canals, and the deposit of the material thereon out of the same, and the proper use and control thereof, not exceeding three hundred feet on each side of said canal or canals: *Provided*, That in case said board shall widen or deepen the Illinois and Michigan canal, then, and in that case, only so much land shall be taken as is necessary for that purpose; and when, in the opinion of said board and the common council, it shall be needful for the interest of said works hereby authorized, that the fee in any real estate acquired for right of way or for other purposes by said board, shall be vested in said city, such real estate shall, upon payment for the same as aforesaid, become the property of said city in fee simple absolute.

Ordinances. SEC. 19. The common council is hereby authorized and empowered to pass all such ordinances as they may deem necessary for the protection, preservation and use of the work hereby authorized, and the property which may be obtained or possessed under this act, and provide such penalties for the infraction thereof as they may deem expedient, not to exceed the penalties now provided by law for the protection of the Illinois and Michigan canal, or other public works or property of the State; and it shall not be lawful for any person to drain from any point within the limits of Chicago, into the Chicago river or either of its branches, or into any canal or canals constructed under the authority of this act, without first obtaining a permit for such drainage from the board of public works, and the said board are hereby authorized to grant such permits, and to exact license fees for the same, proportioned to the amount and kind of drainage.

Drainage.

Tunnels. SEC. 20. The common council shall have power to cause or authorize the building of one or more tunnels under the Chicago river and its branches, at the intersection of any street, or at such other points, as, in their opinion, the public good may require, and the said city shall have power to purchase and hold all such real estate as may be necessary for constructing said tunnels and the approaches thereto; and in case of disagreement between the said city and the owners of any property which may be required for the purposes aforesaid, as to the amount of compensation to be paid such owners, or in case such owner shall be an infant, a married woman, or insane, or absent from the State, the said city shall have the right to condemn said property; and the proceedings for the condemnation of such property, shall conform to those specified or provided by the act above mentioned, in the case of the condemnation of land for a public street in said city, as far as the same are applicable.

SEC. 21. To defray any expense that may be incurred pursuant to the power and authority granted by the preceding section, the common council shall have power annually to levy and collect a tax not exceeding two mills on the dollar, on the assessed value of all real and personal estate in the city, made taxable by the laws of this State; and in case the entire revenue derivable from said two mill tax shall be insufficient to cover the expense of constructing any tunnel that may be ordered by the common council, the deficiency may be supplied by a temporary loan, to be made for a space of time not exceeding the close of the next municipal year, and said loan shall be provided for in the tax levy of that year, by a tax levied pursuant to the authority conferred by this section. And said city shall also have power and authority to issue and sell bonds for said purposes, not exceeding $100,000, in any one year. Said bonds to be issued and to become due, at such times as the common council may by ordinance determine.

Funds for.

Taxes.

Loan.

Bonds.

SEC. 22. The common council shall have power annually to levy and collect a tax, not exceeding two mills on the dollar, on all taxable real and personal estate in said city, to defray the expense of cleaning and repairing the streets and alleys in said city, and the moneys thus raised shall be held by the treasurer as a special fund, and shall be used for no other purpose whatsoever.

Street tax.

SEC. 23. The common council are hereby authorized to establish, from time to time, the salaries to be paid to the police force of said city: *Provided*, That such salaries shall

Police salaries.

never be reduced below the amounts now authorized by the act of which this is an amendment, nor shall the same be increased so as to exceed the amounts thus authorized, more than fifty per cent.

(*Further provision as to salaries*, Sec. 13, *post*, 194.)

Police tax. SEC. 24. The common council shall have power to annually levy and collect a tax, not exceeding two and a half mills on the dollar, on all taxable real and personal estate in said city, for the police expenses of said city, and the third clause of section one, chapter eight, of the act of which this is an amendment, is hereby repealed. **Repealing.**

(*Further provision as to tax for police expenses*, Sec. 22, *post*, 197.)

Divers acts of council confirmed. SEC. 25. So much of the resolution passed by the common council on the 12th day of December, A. D. 1864, as authorized an increase of pay for the police force of said city, during the present municipal year, is hereby ratified and confirmed. And to provide for the increased expenditure thereby authorized, as well as to raise a perpetual fund that shall be hereafter available for the prompt payment of police expenses incurred during the first six months of every succeeding fiscal year, before the tax annually levied for that purpose shall have been received into the city treasury, the city comptroller is hereby authorized, under the sanction of the mayor and finance committee, to issue and negotiate the bonds of said city to an amount not exceeding fifty thousand dollars, payable, principal and interest, in the city of New York, and bearing interest, payable semi-annually, at a rate not exceeding seven per cent. per annum, and becoming due and payable on the first day of April, 1885. All moneys expended from the fund last mentioned, shall be reimbursed annually, from the proceeds of the aforesaid tax, so that the said fund shall be perpetually preserved without diminution, to meet the yearly recurring exigency above referred to. The several other orders, ordinances and resolutions of the common council, increasing compensation and rates of payment, passed since the passage of the general appropriation ordinance for the municipal year 1864, are hereby ratified and confirmed, and any money in the city treasury not otherwise appropriated, may be applied in payment of the same. Any estimates now or hereafter to be issued by the board of public works for dredging the harbor, under a contract with Messrs. Fox and Howard, entered into July 17th, 1863, are hereby legalized. In case the unappropriated moneys in the treasury should prove to be insufficient to pay said estimates and said increased compensation and rates of payment, the city comptroller is hereby authorized, under the sanction of the mayor and finance committee, to issue and negotiate the bonds of said city to an additional amount, not exceeding thirty thousand dollars, payable, principal and interest, in the city of New York, and bearing interest, payable semi-annually, at a rate not exceeding seven per cent. per annum, and becoming due and payable on the first day of April, 1885, and from the proceeds of said bonds, to pay such deficiency, including any deficiency which may exist in the proceeds of the lamp tax, for the said year 1864. To provide for monthly, or any other payments which shall have been authorized by the common council, and required to be made at any time before the collection of the taxes of any year, the comptroller may, with the sanction of the mayor and finance committee, borrow the necessary money for a time, not longer than the first day of February next thereafter.

SEC. 26. The salaries of all city officers, who receive a fixed compensation for their services, and whose salaries are not definitely prescribed by the city charter, including all officers and employees in the police force and fire department of said city, shall be established by the common council in the annual appropriation bill, or by some ordinance passed prior to the passage of such annual appropriation bill, and the salaries or compensation thus established, shall neither be increased nor diminished by the said common council after the passage of said annual appropriation bill, during the then current municipal year, and no extra compensation shall ever be allowed to any such officer or employee in any department of the city government, over and above that provided in manner aforesaid. Salaries.

SEC. 27. All harbor-masters and bridge-tenders in the service of said city, shall be hereafter appointed by the Harbor-masters and bridge-tenders.

board of public works, and shall be required to give such bonds for the faithful discharge of their duties, as said board may prescribe, and shall be removable at the pleasure of the board.

Assessors. SEC. 28. The assessors of said city shall be appointed annually by the mayor, by and with the advice and consent of the common council, on the first Monday in March, or within thirty days thereafter. Any provision in the act to which this is an amendment, conflicting with this section, is hereby repealed.

(*Further provision as to appointment of assessors*, Sec. 1, *post*, 191.)

School tax. SEC. 29. The common council shall have power annually to levy and collect a school tax, not exceeding three mills on the dollar, on the assessed value of all real and personal estate in the city, made taxable by the laws of this State, to meet the expenses of purchasing grounds for school-houses, and building and repairing school-houses, and supporting and maintaining schools; and the second clause of the first section, of chapter eight, of the act of which this is an amendment, is hereby repealed. The board of education are hereby authorized, unless prohibited by the common council, to continue the public schools during the remainder of the present fiscal year, notwithstanding any deficiency in the appropriation heretofore made, and taxes levied for that purpose; and, to provide for the expense thereby incurred, the comptroller may, with the sanction of the mayor and finance committee, borrow the necessary money, which shall be repaid out of the school tax for the year 1865.

School agent report. SEC. 30. It shall be the duty of the school agent to report to the president of the board of education, on the first day of each month, the condition of the school fund derivable from all sources, specifying the amount of money on hand, and the amount received and expended during the month just terminated. This report shall be presented to the board at its next regular meeting, and be entered upon its minutes.

School construction bonds. SEC. 31. The common council may, upon the application of the board of education, provide by ordinance for the issue and sale, within four years from the first day of January, 1865, of not to exceed one hundred bonds of said city, of the denomination of one thousand dollars each, payable, principal and interest, in the city of New York, and bearing interest payable semi-annually at a rate not exceeding seven per cent. per annum, and becoming due and payable in twenty years from date. Not more than twenty-five of said bonds shall be issued in any single year, and their proceeds shall be used for no other purpose than the construction of school-houses in said city. Said bonds shall be countersigned by the president of the board of education, and shall be known as "school construction bonds." And it shall be the duty of the comptroller to purchase and retire five of said bonds each year, so long as any of said bonds shall remain outstanding. And when they cannot be purchased at less than ten per cent. premium, he shall select five by lot, in the presence of the president of the board of education, for purchase at that price, and the interest on all bonds so selected, shall thereafter cease. All necessary provisions to give effect to the foregoing condition may be inserted in said bonds, and as fast as said bonds shall be purchased and retired, the comptroller shall report the numbers of the same to the board of education, and the same shall be entered upon their regular minutes.

Board of education.

SEC. 32. No expenditure of money or increase of liabilities, and no new text books shall be ordered or authorized by the board of education, except at a regular meeting, and with the concurrence of a majority of the members of the entire board, upon a call of the yeas and nays.

Registered bonds.

SEC. 33. The common council may provide by ordinance for the substitution of registered bonds, payable to the order of the owner, and assignable only by transfer on the books of the comptroller, for bonds payable to bearer, upon application and request of the owner of any of the bonds of the city; and the common council may provide that by indorsement of the comptroller on any bond payable to bearer, when presented for that purpose by the owner, such bond shall become payable only to the party named in such indorsement, his assignees or legal representatives, anything on the face of such bond to the contrary notwithstanding.

Speciai indorsement

Liquor licenses.

SEC. 34. Licenses to sell liquor shall not be granted to any person but the party in actual possession of the premises in which liquor shall be sold; and no license shall be granted to females, except upon the recommendation of a majority of the members of the committee on licenses of said city; and the mayor of said city may, in his discretion, revoke all licenses held in violation of this section, and all licenses held or granted to any person who may be convicted of gambling, immorality, or keeping a disorderly house. And no license shall hereafter be issued or granted to any person convicted as aforesaid, except upon the recommendation of not less than six reputable householders, living in the neighborhood of the applicant, and the board of police.

Job printing.

SEC. 35. The board of public works, the board of education, and the board of police commissioners, shall have exclusive control and direction of all job printing required in their several departments, respectively, for which appropriations shall have been made by the common council, and shall, in all cases, procure the same to be done by contract with the lowest responsible bidder.

This act public, and to take effect.

SEC. 36. This act shall be deemed a public act, and shall be favorably construed for all the purposes herein expressed in all courts and places, and shall be in full force from and after its passage.

Approved February 15, 1865.

AN ACT to amend an Act, entitled "An Act to reduce the Charter of the City of Chicago, and the several Acts amendatory thereof, into one Act, and to revise the same," approved February 13th, 1863.

SECTION
1. Divers officers; how appointed.
2. Corporation council and city attorney; duties.
3. Police court.
4. Board of education.
5. Common schools.
6. Children of adjacent towns may attend.
7. Provisions of charter extended.
8. Certain sections repealed.
9. School agent.
10. Vacating streets and alleys.
11. Police commissioners; term of office.
12. Police commissioners; election.
13. Salaries of police department.
14. Police department; salaries paid monthly; not to receive gifts, etc.

SECTION
15. Police force; control and organization.
16. Police force; regulations, qualifications and removal; vacancies filled by promotion.
17. Vacancy in board of police.
18. Commissioners of police to give bonds.
19. Mayor no longer member of boards of police and public works.
20. Certain sections repealed.
21. Military equipments under control of board of police.
22. Police tax; town taxes.
23. Board of police to have control of fire department.
24. Fire department; organization.

25. Fire department; regulations.
26. Board of police to furnish equipments and instructions.
27. Board of police to furnish estimates of expenses.
28. Assistant marshals to act as fire wardens.
29. Marshal to investigate cause of fires.
30. Provisions of charter extended.
31. Salaries of fire department.
32. Fire engines, houses, etc.
33. Bills of fire department.
34. Records of fire department.
35. Offices of chief and assistant engineers abolished.
36. Certain sections repealed.
37. Publication in German.
38. Former acts not invalidated.
39. Ordinances, etc., to remain in force.
40. This act public, and to take effect from passage.

SECTION 1. *Be it enacted by the People of the State of Illinois, represented in the General Assembly*, That the following officers of said city, to wit, the clerk, city physician, fish inspector, sealer of weights and measures, inspectors, gaugers, and weighers, shall be appointed by the common council by ballot, biennially, on the second Monday of May, or as soon thereafter as may be. The bridewell-keeper of said city shall be elected by ballot, by the common council, annually. The assessors of said city shall be appointed annually by ballot by the common council, on the first Monday in March, or within thirty days thereafter. Any provision in the acts to which this is an amendment, conflicting with this section, is hereby repealed. In case the common council of said city shall provide for the appointment of a city auditor, he shall be appointed by ballot of the common council, and may be removed at any time, by a vote of two-thirds of all the aldermen authorized by law to be elected. **Appointment of divers officers.**

SEC. 2. The corporation counsel of said city, and the city attorney, shall devote themselves exclusively to the duties of their respective offices, and shall have their office in such place as shall be provided by the common council. Neither of said officers shall be employed in any other business than that which relates to the duties of their offices respectively, during the terms for which they were chosen. **Duties and office of corporation counsel and city attorney.**

SEC. 3. The common council shall have power to provide for the holding of a police court in each division of said city; to designate a justice of the peace to hold each of said courts; to fix places for holding them, and to provide for the appointment of a sufficient number of deputy police court clerks for the same. Changes of venue from a justice of a police court, shall be taken to some other justice of a police court. **Police court.**

SEC. 4. The terms of office of the present members of **Board of education.**

the board of education shall expire on the second Monday of May next, and the board of education of said city shall consist of sixteen school inspectors, one to be selected from each ward in said city, to be elected by the common council on the second Monday of May next, or at its next regular meeting thereafter. The said board shall be divided by lot, in the presence of the common council, into four classes: those of the first class shall vacate their seats at the expiration of the first year; those of the second class at the expiration of the second year; those of the third class at the expiration of the third year; and those of the fourth class at the expiration of the fourth year; and the common council shall, annually, in the month of May, after the first Monday thereof, elect four inspectors to succeed those whose term of office expires.

Schools. SEC. 5. There shall be established in said city, at least one common school in each school district, now or hereafter to be created, and free instruction within their respective districts shall be given in said schools, to all children residing within the limits of the city who are over the age of six years, and who may be sent to or attend such school, subject to such rules and regulations as may be established by the common council, or board of education, pursuant to the provisions of this act, and the act to which this is an amendment.

Children of adjacent towns. SEC. 6. The board of education shall have power to admit to the public schools of said city, children residing within those towns of Cook county which immediately adjoin the said city, upon such terms and conditions as said board may prescribe.

Charter extended. SEC. 7. All the provisions of the act to which this is an amendment, so far as they relate to schools and the board of education, shall apply with equal force and effect to schools and to the board of education herein provided for, except as modified or changed by the terms of this act.

Repealing. SEC. 8. Section eleven of chapter two, and section sixteen of chapter thirteen, of the act to which this is an amendment, are hereby repealed.

School agent. SEC. 9. The school agent of said city shall be appointed biennially, by the board of education, by and with the advice and consent of the common council, and shall receive such annual salary as shall, from time to time, be fixed by the board of education, subject to the approval of the common council, and before he shall enter upon the duties of his office, he shall execute a bond to the city of Chicago, in such sum and with such securities as the common council shall approve. The school agent so appointed may be removed at any time by the common council, upon the recommendation of said board, and he shall make such reports, from time to time, to the said board and the common council, concerning the condition of the school funds, as they, or either of them, may require. The first appointment of school agent under the provisions of this section, shall be made on the second Monday of May next, or as soon thereafter as may be.

Vacating streets, etc.

SEC. 10. The vacating or closing of any street or alley, or portion of the same, in said city, shall be ordered only by the vote of at least three-fourths of all the aldermen authorized by law to be elected; such vote shall be taken by ayes and noes, and entered on the record of the common council.

(*Further provisions as to vacating streets, alleys, etc.*, Sec. 1, *post*, 206.)

Police commissioners; term of office.

SEC. 11. The commissioner of the board of police of said city, now having the longest term to serve, shall continue in office until the next general election for county officers in the year one thousand eight hundred and sixty-seven, and until his successor shall be elected and qualified. The other two commissioners of the board of police of said city shall continue in office until the day of the general election for county officers, in the year one thousand eight hundred and sixty-five, and until their successors shall be elected and qualified.

Election.

SEC. 12. At the general election, in the year one thousand eight hundred and sixty-five, for county officers, there shall be elected by the qualified voters of Cook county, two commissioners of the board of police, as successors to those whose term of office will then expire by the provisions of the foregoing section; and the commissioner so elected from the north division of said city, shall continue in office for six years, and the commissioner so elected from the south division of said city, shall continue in office for four years, and until their successors shall be elected and qualified; and at the general election for county officers in the year one thousand eight hundred and sixty-seven, and biennially thereafter, there shall be elected by the qualified voters of said county, one commissioner of said board of police, as successor to the commissioner whose term of office will then expire by the provisions of this act, who shall hold his office for the term of six years. The residence and qualifications of the said commissioners of the board of police, shall be the same as are now provided by law.

Salaries.

SEC. 13. The said commissioners shall receive an annual salary of twelve hundred dollars each, and the president of the board shall receive an additional sum of three hundred dollars per annum. The superintendent of police shall receive an annual salary of not less than eighteen hundred dollars, nor more than twenty-five hundred dollars. The deputy superintendent shall receive an annual salary of not less than fifteen hundred dollars, nor more than two thousand dollars. Each captain of police shall receive an annual salary of twelve hundred dollars. Each sergeant shall receive an annual salary of nine hundred dollars. Each patrolman shall receive an annual salary of not less than six hundred dollars and not more than eight hundred dollars. Within the limits prescribed, the board of police commissioners, with the concurrence of the common council, shall have power to establish the salaries of the officers enumerated in this section.

Paid monthly.

SEC. 14. The salaries shall be paid out of the city treasury, monthly, to each person entitled thereto. No member of the board of police, or of the police force, shall receive or share in, for his own benefit, under any pretense whatever, any present, fee, gift or emolument for police service, other than the regular salary and pay provided by this section, except by the unanimous consent of the board of police; nor shall any such member receive or share in any fee, gift or reward, from any person who may become bail for the

Not to receive gifts, etc.

appearance of any arrested, accused or convicted person, or who may become surety for any such person on appeal from the judgment or decision of any court or magistrate; or any fee, gift or reward, in any case, from any attorney at law, who may prosecute or defend any person arrested or prosecuted for any offense within the county of Cook; nor shall any such member directly or indirectly interest himself, or interfere, in any manner whatever, in the employment or retainer of any attorney to aid in the defense of persons arrested or accused; and for any violation of either of the foregoing provisions, the officer so offending shall be immediately removed from office.

SEC. 15. The duties of the police force shall be executed under the direction and control of said board, and according to rules and regulations which it is hereby authorized to pass from time to time, for the more proper government and discipline of its subordinate officers, and the police force of said city. The said force shall consist of a general superintendent of police, one deputy superintendent of police, three captains of police, sergeants of police not exceeding twelve, and as many police patrolmen, not exceeding two hundred, as may be authorized by the common council, on the application of the board of police commissioners, and each patrolman so appointed shall hold office only during such time as he shall faithfully observe and execute all the rules and regulations of said board, the laws of the State, and the ordinances of the city: *Provided*, That for incompetency, neglect of duty, or other sufficient cause, the said board may at any time remove the superintendent and deputy superintendent of police, or the fire marshal and assistant marshals. **Police; control and organization**

SEC. 16. The qualifications, enumeration and distribution of duties, mode of trial and removal from office, of each officer of said police force, shall be particularly defined and prescribed by rules and regulations of the board of police; nor shall any person be appointed to, or hold office on the police force aforesaid, who is not a citizen of the United States, or who shall not have resided within the State of Illinois two years next preceding his appointment, or who shall ever have been convicted of crime; and pro- **Regulations** **Qualifications.**

Removal. vided that no person shall be removed therefrom except upon written charges preferred against him to the board of police, and after an opportunity shall have been afforded him of being heard in his defense; but the board of police shall have power to suspend any member of the police department of the city, pending the hearing of the charges preferred against him; and provided that whenever any vacancy shall occur in the office of captain of police, the same shall be filled by an appointment from among the persons then in office as sergeants of police, and a like vacancy in the office of sergeant of police, shall be filled by appointment from among persons then in office as police patrolmen.

Vacancies filled by promotion.

Vacancy in board of police.

SEC. 17. Should a vacancy occur at any time in the said board of police commissioners, it shall be filled by the appointment of the board of supervisors of said county, until the next annual election for county officers, when the qualified voters of said county may, as in other cases, fill such vacancy by an election of a successor, who shall hold his office for the unexpired term.

Commissioners to give bond.

SEC. 18. Each of the commissioners of police of said city shall, on or before the first Monday of May next, give bonds to said city in the sum of twenty-five thousand dollars, conditioned for the faithful performance of their duties as commissioners, under the provisions of this act; said bonds to be filed and approved as now required by law; and in case of the failure of any commissioner to comply with the requirements of this section within the time above provided, his office of commissioner shall be deemed vacant, and shall be filled as in this act provided.

Mayor not member of boards, etc.

SEC. 19. From and after the passage of this act, the mayor of said city shall cease to be in any manner a member of the board of police, and of the board of public works of said city.

Repealing.

SEC. 20. Sections six, seven and eight, of chapter ten, of the act to which this is an amendment, are hereby repealed.

Military equipments.

SEC. 21. All fire-arms and military equipments belonging to said city, shall be under the custody and control of the said board of police.

SEC. 22. The common council shall have power to annually levy and collect a tax not exceeding three and one-half mills on the dollar, on all the taxable real and personal estate in said city, for the police expenses of said city; and the third clause of section one, of chapter eight, of the act to which this is an amendment, is hereby repealed. It shall be lawful to levy a tax for town purposes, in any year, in the towns of West Chicago, North Chicago and South Chicago, for any amount not exceeding the sum of fifteen hundred dollars.

Police tax.

Town tax.

SEC. 23. The board of police of said city shall assume and exercise the entire control of the fire department of said city, and shall possess full power and authority over its organization, government, appointments and discipline, within said city. It shall have the custody and control of the engine-houses, engines, hose carts, trucks, ladders, horses, telegraph lines, and all other public property and equipments belonging to the fire department.

Fire department.

SEC. 24. The fire department of said city shall consist of a fire marshal, and assistant marshals not exceeding three, and as many competent, able and respectable citizens of said city as shall be appointed by the board, to be known as the fire police, who shall, under the direction of said board, have the care and management of the engines, apparatus, equipments, engine-houses, and other property used and provided for the extinguishment of fires: *Provided*, That the common council may limit the number of the fire police. The said offices of marshal and fire police, hereby created, shall be severally filled by the appointment of said board. It shall promulgate all regulations and orders relating to the fire department, through the fire marshal, and it shall be the duty of the subordinate officers and the fire police, to respect and obey the said marshal as the head and chief of the department, subject to the rules, regulations and general orders of the board.

Organization.

SEC. 25. The duties of the respective members of the fire department shall be defined by said board, and executed under its direction and control, and according to rules and regulations which it is hereby authorized to pass from time to time, for the more proper government and discipline of the

Regulations.

members of the fire department; and the said board may impose reasonable forfeitures upon them for a violation of the same, and, for incapacity, neglect of duty or misconduct, may remove them, or either of them.

Equipments and instructions. SEC. 26. The board shall furnish the fire police with necessary equipments, and give them requisite instruction, so that in case of risk or sudden emergency, or whenever the board may deem it necessary, they may be called to the assistance of the regular police, and when so employed, they shall possess all the powers and privileges of the patrol police.

Estimates of expenses. SEC. 27. It shall be the duty of the board of police to prepare and submit to the comptroller, on or before the first day of May, in every year, an estimate of the whole cost and expenses of providing for and maintaining the fire department of said city during the current fiscal year, which estimate shall be in detail, and shall be laid by said comptroller before the common council, with his annual estimate.

Fire wardens. SEC. 28. The said board may require the assistant marshals of the fire department to act as fire wardens, and while so acting, it shall be their duty to examine all buildings and enclosures, to discover whether the same are in a dangerous state, and to report to the board all violations of the charter or ordinances of said city in relation to the prevention or extinguishment of fires.

Fire marshal to investigate cause of fires. SEC. 29. The board shall have power, in its discretion, to direct the fire marshal to inquire into and investigate the cause of all fires which may occur in the city, as soon as may be after they occur, and to keep a record of his proceedings, and of the evidence in each case, and to file the same, or a copy thereof, in the office of the board. He shall have power to compel the attendance of any person in said city, to testify upon oath concerning any fire in said city, under such penalty as the common council may provide, and he is hereby authorized to administer oaths to all such witnesses. He shall be required to use his utmost exertions in the discovery, arrest and conviction of all incendiaries, and perform such other duties as the board may prescribe.

Charter extended. SEC. 30. The provisions of sections seven and eight, of chapter twelve, of the act to which this is an amendment, are hereby extended to and made applicable to the fire police, to the same extent that they are now applicable to firemen.

SEC. 31. The said fire marshal shall receive an annual salary not exceeding twenty-five hundred dollars, nor less than eighteen hundred dollars. The assistant fire marshal shall receive an annual salary not exceeding twelve hundred dollars, and each member of the fire police shall receive an annual salary not exceeding seven hundred and twenty dollars: *Provided*, That such members of the fire police who may act as engineers of steam fire engines, may be paid an annual salary not exceeding one thousand dollars. Within the limits prescribed by this section, the said board, with the concurrence of the common council, shall have the power to fix the salaries provided for by this section. **Salaries.**

SEC. 32. The said board shall, from time to time, as it may be authorized by the common council, procure fire engines and other apparatus used for the extinguishment of fires, and the common council shall procure fit and secure engine-houses, for keeping and preserving the same. And the said board shall, at the cost of the city, furnish all necessaries and supplies for the engines, houses and apparatus, and cause all necessary repairs to be made, so that the fire department may at all times be in an efficient condition. **Apparatus.**

SEC. 33. All bills of the fire department shall be approved by the board, and shall be paid only upon the warrant of the comptroller, countersigned by the mayor and president of the board. **Bills, how paid.**

SEC. 34. A full and complete record of the proceedings of the board, so far as the same relates to the fire department, shall be kept in a book expressly for that purpose, and the said board shall, on or before the first Monday in April, in each year, make a full report in writing, to the common council, of the condition of the fire department. **Record and report.**

SEC. 35. The office of the chief engineer and assistant engineers of the fire department of said city are hereby abolished, and the present chief engineer and assistants shall act as fire marshal and assistant fire marshals, respec- **Offices abolished.**

tively, under the direction of the board, as herein provided, for the term for which they were elected.

Repealing. SEC. 36. Sections three (3), four (4), five (5), and six (6), of chapter twelve, of the act to which this is an amendment, and all other acts or parts of acts inconsistent herewith, are hereby repealed.

German newspaper. SEC. 37. The proceedings, notices and ordinances of said city, and the departments thereof, may be published in the newspaper printed in the German language, having the largest daily circulation in said city, as fully as they are now required to be published in the corporation newspaper: *Provided*, That in no judicial or other proceeding shall the publication in such German paper be called in question, either as to the fact of its publication or the correctness thereof.

Effect of this act. SEC. 38. This act shall not invalidate any legal act done by the common council of the city of Chicago or by its officers, nor divest their successors, under this act, of any rights of property or otherwise, or liability, which may have accrued to, or been created by said corporation, prior to the passage of this act.

Same. SEC. 39. All ordinances, regulations and resolutions now in force in the city of Chicago, and not inconsistent with this act, shall remain in full force, under this act, until altered, modified or repealed by the common council, or other competent authority, after this act shall take effect.

Public act, and take effect. SEC. 40. This act shall be deemed a public act, and shall take effect and be in force from and after its passage.

Approved February 16, 1865.

AN ACT to provide Sanitary Measures and Health Regulations for the City of Chicago, and to provide for the appointment of a Health Officer for the City of Chicago.

SECTION
1. Dead hogs to be removed four miles from the city.
2. Rendering offensive matter not to be within four miles of the city.
3. Rendering machinery.
4. Drains and privies.
5. Health officer.
6. Penalty for violating first section.
7. Penalty for violating fourth section.
8. Penalty for violating third section.

SECTION
9. Penalties; how recovered.
10. State's attorney to prosecute.
11. Penalty and proceedings for violating second section.
12. Penalty and proceedings in other cases of nuisance.
13. Ordinances as to nuisances to remain in force.
14. This act public, and in force from passage.

SECTION 1. *Be it enacted by the People of the State of Illinois, represented in the General Assembly,* That it shall be the duty of all person or persons, corporation or corporations, having the ownership or control of dead, undressed, unslaughtered hogs, cattle, or other animals or animal matter, within the city of Chicago, or within four miles of the limits of said city, to remove the same within twenty-four hours of their arrival within the above described locality, to some point not only out of the city of Chicago, but beyond the distance of four miles from the limits of said city; and in case the person or persons having ownership, control or possession of such dead animals shall fail so to remove them within the time specified, it shall be the duty of the health officer of Chicago to take immediate possession of and remove the same.

Dead hogs, etc.

Removal.

SEC. 2. No person or persons, corporation or corporations, shall render or try out any dead, undressed hogs, cattle or other animals, or any decayed, putrid or unsound animal matter, either in the city of Chicago, or within four miles of the limits of the same; nor shall it be lawful for the common council of the city of Chicago, or any other board or body, to license, authorize or permit establishments for the above described business within the limits aforesaid.

Rendering, etc.

SEC. 3. No person or persons, corporation or corporations, shall render or manufacture any lard, tallow or soap-grease within the limits of the city of Chicago, without adopting such measures, in the way of condensers and other machinery, "to the end" of preventing unwholesome and disagreeable odors, as the health officer of the city of Chicago may direct.

Machinery.

SEC. 4. The owner, agent or occupant having the charge of any tenement used as a dwelling, or for lodging purposes, within the city of Chicago, shall furnish the same with a sufficient drain, under ground, to carry off waste water, and also with a suitable privy, sufficient for the accommodation of all who may use it; nor shall the contents of any vault be allowed to accumulate within twelve inches of the even surface of the ground, or otherwise being offensive.

Drains and privies.

SEC. 5. It shall be the duty of the board of police commissioners of the city of Chicago, to appoint some person

Health officer.

who shall be known as health officer of the city of Chicago, and whose duty it shall be to see that all ordinances and laws affecting the health of the city, are enforced, and who shall be liable to be removed from office by a majority of said board, and who shall be paid out of the police fund such salary as the said board may direct; and it shall be the duty of the police commissioners at all times to detail a sufficient police force to enable the said health officer to enforce the provisions of this act, as well as all health ordinances of the city of Chicago. It shall be the duty of the common council of Chicago to provide sufficient funds to enforce the provisions of this act.

Penalty. SEC. 6. Any person or corporation violating the provisions of the first section of this act, shall be liable to a fine of one hundred dollars for each offense.

Penalty. SEC. 7. Any person or persons neglecting to comply with the provisions of section four of this act, shall be liable to a fine of twenty-five dollars for failing to comply with the same within a reasonable time (not to exceed thirty days) after notice from the health officer of the city of Chicago, and a fine of five dollars for every day's neglect and failure thereafter to comply with the provisions of said section four.

Penalty. SEC. 8. Any person or persons, corporation or corporations, neglecting or refusing to comply with the provisions of section three of this act within a reasonable time (not to exceed thirty days) after being notified by the health officer of the city of Chicago to comply with the same, shall be liable to a fine of one hundred dollars, and fifty dollars per day for every day thereafter that he or they shall so refuse or neglect to comply with the provisions of said section third.

How recovered. SEC. 9. The penalties provided for in this act shall be recovered in an action of debt, to be brought in the name of the People of the State of Illinois, against the party offending, in any justice court or court of record in the county of Cook; one-half of the penalty or penalties shall go to the informer who may institute and prosecute such action, and the other half of such penalty shall go to the city of Chicago.

SEC. 10. It shall be the duty of the State's attorney for.

the county of Cook to institute and prosecute actions for all offenses under the act which shall come or be brought to his knowledge, and when so instituted and prosecuted by him, he shall be entitled to one-half of such penalty as his fees, the other half going to the city of Chicago. **State's attorney to prosecute, etc.**

SEC. 11. Any person or persons violating the second section of this act, shall be liable to a fine not less than one hundred dollars per day for every day they shall continue in violation of the same; and it shall be the duty of the health officer of said city of Chicago to at once enter upon and take possession of the premises and fixtures of said person so violating, and when said prohibited business is being conducted, and immediately thereafter file with the State's attorney for Cook county a sworn statement or complaint, setting forth facts of such seizure, and describing the premises seized, together with the name or names of the owner or owners thereof, and thereupon the State's attorney shall at once file an information in any court of record for the city of Chicago or county of Cook, in the name of the People of Illinois, and against the person or persons owning said establishment, and said information shall be tried and determined in the court where the same has been filed, with all convenient speed, giving the same precedence of all but criminal business in said court; and if the person or persons so charged in said information shall be adjudged guilty, then, in addition to the fine herein provided for, the costs shall be taxed against the defendant or defendants in said information, and the court shall issue a writ of injunction perpetually enjoining said establishment, and the owner or owners thereof, from renewing or continuing the said prohibited business. And it shall be the duty of the State's attorney to file an information against any person or persons owning or running any such establishment, upon the sworn complaint of any three citizens and freeholders of Chicago, and immediately upon the filing of the same, the court where the same may be filed shall issue process directed to the health officer of Chicago, or to the sheriff of Cook county, authorizing and requiring them, or either of them, to enter upon and seize the premises and fixtures where such business is being done, and retain pos- **Penalty and proceedings.**

session of the same until a trial upon said information shall be had, as in this act before provided; and if the parties so charged shall be adjudged to be guilty, a writ of injunction shall issue from said court, perpetually enjoining said parties from renewing or continuing said business, but if adjudged not guilty, the premises and fixtures shall be restored to the owner or owners thereof.

Further provisions as to proceedings in case of nuisance.

SEC. 12. If any person or persons, corporation or corporations, shall be engaged in rendering any dead animals, or grease of any description whatever, or in the manufacture, preparation or storage of any offal, blood or any other animal matter, or in the slaughtering or feeding of any animals, or in any other business tending to produce noxious or unwholesome matter, within the city of Chicago, or within four miles of the limits thereof, in such a manner as to create unwholesome or offensive odors, it shall be the duty of the State's attorney for Cook county, upon a complaint in writing, and under oath, filed with him, made by the health officer of said city, and whose duty it shall be, having knowledge of the fact, to make such complaint, upon like complaint made by any three residents and freeholders of Chicago, said complaint to set forth the fact of the carrying on of a business producing unwholesome, noxious or offensive odors, together with a description of the premises where the same is conducted, and the name or names, if the same can be ascertained, of the person or persons conducting such business, to file an information, in the name of the People of Illinois, in any court of record in and for the city of Chicago or county of Cook, against said establishment, or the persons carrying on the same; and immediately upon the filing of such information, process shall issue from the court whence such information shall be filed, directed to the health officer of the city of Chicago, or to the sheriff of Cook county, authorizing and requiring them, or either of them, to take possession of the premises and fixtures where such business is being conducted, and retain possession of the same until a trial of said information shall be had, and to summon the person or parties in said information named, so to appear and answer the same forthwith. And it shall be the duty of the court in which such information may be filed, to proceed to the hearing of said information as soon as may be, giving the same precedence of all other causes, except criminal business; and if, upon the hearing of said cause, the person or persons against whom said information shall be filed, shall be found guilty as in said information charged, they shall be adjudged to pay the costs and fine of not less than one hundred dollars, nor more than five hundred dollars, and the court shall issue a writ of injunction, perpetually enjoining him or them from continuing such business in any offensive or injurious manner. In case the parties so charged shall not be found guilty, the property seized shall be at once restored to them. If in any case prosecuted under the eleventh and twelfth sections of this act, there existed probable cause for the complaint or seizure, it shall be the duty of the court to so certify, and no action shall then lie against the party or parties making such complaint or seiznre, and in that case the costs shall be paid by the city.

Ordinances remain in force.

SEC. 13. All ordinances heretofore passed by the common council of said city, and now in force in relation to the abatement of nuisance, shall continue in full force and effect until altered, amended or repealed by the said common council, except so far as the provisions thereof may be inconsistent with the provisions of this act; and it shall be the duty of the common council to pass, from time to time, all such additional ordinances and regulations as may be found necessary or expedient for the carrying out of the objects of this act.

Public act, and take effect.

SEC. 14. This act shall be deemed a public act and be in force from and after its passage.

Approved February 16, 1865.

AN ACT in relation to the Vacation of Streets, Squares, Lanes, Alleys, and Highways.

SECTION
1. Street, etc., how vacated, and effect thereof.

SECTION
2. This act to take effect from passage.

Street, etc., vacated. SECTION 1. *Be it enacted by the People of the State of Illinois, represented in the General Assembly,* That when any street, square, lane, alley, highway, or part thereof, shall have been or may hereafter be vacated, under or by virtue of any act or acts of this State, the lot or tract immediately adjoining shall extend to the central line of any such street, square, lane, alley, highway, or part thereof, so vacated, unless otherwise specially provided in the act vacating the same: *Provided,* That the common council of any city in this State shall not have power to vacate or order closed any street or alley, or portion of the same, unless such vacation shall be ordered upon the vote of at least three-fourths of all the aldermen of said city, authorized by law to be elected; such vote to be taken by ayes and noes, and entered on the records of the common council.

How vacated.

When act to take effect. SEC. 2. This act shall be in force and take effect from and after its passage.

Approved February 16, 1865.

AN ACT to provide for the Completion of the Illinois and Michigan Canal upon the plan adopted by the State in 1836.

SECTION
1. Deepening canal.
2. Capacity of; navigation not to be obstructed.
3. Power of condemnation.

SECTION
4. Amount expended to be a lien on canal.
5. State may pay off lien.

Preamble. *Whereas,* It has been represented that the city of Chicago, in order to purify or cleanse the Chicago river, by drawing a sufficient quantity of water from lake Michigan directly through it and through the summit division of the Illinois and Michigan canal, would advance a sufficient amount of funds to accomplish this desirable object; and

Whereas, The original plan of the said canal was to cut down the summit so as to draw a supply of water for navigation directly from lake Michigan, which plan was abandoned for the time being, after a large part of the work had been executed, only in consequence of the inability of the State to procure funds for its further prosecution; and

Whereas, Under the law creating the trust, the plan of the summit division of the canal was changed, the level being raised so as to require the principal supply of water to be obtained through the Calumet feeder, subject to serious contingencies, and by pumping on to the summit with the hydraulic works at Bridgeport; now, therefore,

SECTION 1. *Be it enacted by the People of the State of Illinois, represented in the General Assembly*, That to secure the completion of the summit division of the Illinois and Michigan canal upon the original "deep cut" plan, with such modifications and change of line, if necessary, as will most effectually secure the thorough cleansing or purification of the Chicago river, and facilitate the execution of the work, the city of Chicago, through its constituted authorities, may at once enter into an arrangement with the board of trustees of said canal with a view to the speedy accomplishment of the work. **Canal to be deepened.**

SEC. 2. The canal shall not be constructed of a less capacity than the plan adopted by the canal commissioners in 1863, nor shall the work of deepening it be prosecuted so as to materially interfere with the navigation. By consent of the board of trustees, however, the navigation may be opened later and closed earlier than usual in former years, but it shall never be diminished to a less time than six months. **Capacity of; navigation not to be obstructed.**

SEC. 3. It shall be lawful for the city of Chicago to enter upon and use any lands which may be necessary for the right of way for said canal, if the route should in any part vary from the present line of canal, and to take and use any materials of any description necessary for the prosecution of the work contemplated along the line thereof, the **Power of condemnation.**

value of the same to be determined in the mode provided by the general laws of this State.

Amount expended lien on.

SEC. 4. The amount expended by the city of Chicago in deepening the summit division of the canal, according to the plan adopted by the canal commissioners in 1836, shall be a vested lien upon the Illinois and Michigan canal and its revenues, after the payment of the present canal debt, and the next revenue of the canal shall all thereafter be applied to the payment of the principal and interest of the sum expended in accomplishing the object of this act, until the whole amount is reimbursed to the city: *Provided*, The cost shall not exceed two and a half millions of dollars.

How relieved.

SEC. 5. The State of Illinois may at any time relieve this lien upon the canal and revenue, by refunding to the city of Chicago the amount expended in making the contemplated improvement and the interest thereon.

Approved February 16, 1865.

AN ORDINANCE

FOR REVISING AND CONSOLIDATING THE GENERAL ORDINANCES OF THE CITY OF CHICAGO.

WHEREAS, It is expedient that the general ordinances of this city should be consolidated, and arranged in appropriate chapters and sections; that omissions should be supplied, and defects amended; and that the whole should be rendered plain, concise and intelligible; therefore,

Be it ordained by the Common Council of the City of Chicago, in manner following, *that is to say:*

CHAPTER I.

ATTORNEY.

SECTION 1. City attorney to report to common council.

SECTION 1. In addition to the other duties of the city attorney, it shall be his duty, in the months of January and July, in each and every year, to report in writing to the common council a list of all suits instituted and pending in courts of record in which the city of Chicago is plaintiff or defendant, in which report shall be stated the names of all defendants and plaintiffs, the nature of the actions, the date of the commencement, and the several steps that may have been taken in court during his term of office to bring such suits to final issue, to be accompanied with such explanatory remarks as said attorney may see fit to append — to the end that the common council may be kept more fully advised as to the legal affairs of the city. He shall also attach to his said report a list of all such cases as may have been disposed of during his term of office and subsequent **Report to council.**

to his last report, together with their results: said reports shall be made up to the first days of January and July in each year.

CHAPTER II.

AUCTIONS.

SECTION
1. Auction sales of goods, etc., by licensed auctioneers; license; charge; bond.
2. License, application for, and transfer.
3. Penalty for selling without license.

SECTION
4. Duties on sales; accounts; penalty.
5. Accounts to be on oath.
6. Exemption from duties.
7. Fee and duty of comptroller.
8. Sales in streets, etc.; penalty.

Licensed auctioneer. SECTION 1. All sales of goods, chattels, or personal property, at public auction, except such as are made under and by virtue of legal process, within said city, shall be made by an auctioneer, his copartner or clerk, who shall first have obtained a license, under the hand of the mayor and seal of the city, and shall also have paid therefor, to Charge. the collector, at the rate of fifty-two dollars per year, and no other fees, and shall have executed a bond to said city, with security to the satisfaction of the mayor, in the penal Bond. sum of one thousand dollars, conditioned for the payment of all duties that are or may be imposed, by this chapter or any subsequent ordinance, on sales made by him, or by any person for or under him; said license to be in force until the first day of May next after the date thereof.

Application. SEC. 2. Every person who may wish to obtain a license as above mentioned, shall apply in writing for the same to the mayor, setting forth therein the proposed place of business, and the name or names of his security or securities; and in Transfer. no case shall the said license be transferable, or the place of business changed, except by leave of the council.

Penalty. SEC. 3. Any person or persons who shall sell, or attempt to sell, at public auction, in said city, any goods, chattels or personal property whatever, except under and by virtue of legal process, without first having obtained a license therefor as above required, shall forfeit and pay for each offense the sum of fifty dollars.

Duties. SEC. 4. A duty of one per cent. shall be assessed and paid to the collector on the first days of August, November, February and May, upon all sales of goods, chattels, and personal property, made by an auctioneer as aforesaid, during the preceding quarter year; and each auctioneer shall at the same times render an account to the comptroller, of such sales, and the duties that accrued thereon, accompanied by the receipt of the collector for such duties, and for a failure to do so, for the space of ten days after the expiration of the quarter, his license may be declared forfeited, and he shall be subject to a further penalty of five dollars for each and every day such duties and accounts shall be withheld. Accounts. Penalty.

SEC. 5. Every account rendered shall have an oath or affirmation attached thereto, signed by the said auctioneer, his copartner or clerk, setting forth, in substance, that the same contains a true and accurate statement of the amount of all sales at public auction, made by said auctioneer, or by any one for his benefit, with the duties thereon imposed by the city of Chicago, and that no misrepresentations, subterfuges or deceits have been used by them, whereby to defraud the said city, either in the sales made, or the accounts so rendered. Oath.

SEC. 6. The following described articles shall be exempt from duty, and shall be so marked in the accounts rendered by auctioneers, viz.: Exemption.

First. Ships and vessels, utensils of husbandry, and neat cattle and horses.

Second. Articles that belong to the United States.

Third. The effects of a deceased person, when sold by order of the executor or administrator or any court, and the effects of any bankrupt or insolvent, when sold by order of the assignee.

Fourth. All goods damaged by water transportation, if sold within twenty days after they have been landed, and sold for the benefit of the owners alone, and not insured, which shall appear by affidavit.

SEC. 7. The comptroller shall receive for the use of the city twenty-five cents for filing and examining each quarterly return, and shall report the same to the council at the next meeting after such return, and furnish the names of the delinquents, for each quarter, to the city attorney for prosecution. Fee. Report.

Sales in street. SEC. 8. Any auctioneer, or other person, who shall sell, attempt to sell, or cry for sale at public auction within any of the streets, alleys or commons of the city of Chicago, (unless by the written permission of the mayor,) any horses, mules or cattle, or any wagon, carriage, or other vehicle drawn by any or either of the animals aforesaid, shall be deemed guilty of a nuisance, and of obstructing the streets of said city; and upon conviction shall be subject to a fine of not less than five nor more than twenty dollars for each offense. Penalty.

CHAPTER III.

BOOT BLACKS.

SECTION
1. Boot blacks to be licensed.
2. Mayor to license; charge.
3. License to expire, when; badge.

SECTION
4. Clerk to keep register.
5. Penalty for violating this chapter.

License required. SECTION 1. No person shall follow the calling of a boot or shoe black in any of the streets, alleys or public places in the city of Chicago, without first having obtained a license so to do.

License. SEC. 2. The mayor is authorized in his discretion, to license under his hand, attested by the clerk and city seal, any person who may apply to him therefor, to black boots and shoes in the streets, alleys, or other public places, upon the payment of fifty cents, and no other fees, for each and every license so granted. Charge.

License expire. SEC. 3. Every license granted under the provisions hereof, shall expire on the first day of October after the date thereof, and every person licensed as aforesaid, shall wear, while exercising his vocation, conspicuously on the left breast, a metallic badge with the words "Boot Black No. —." Badge.

Register. SEC. 4. It shall be the duty of the clerk to keep a register of the name, residence, and number of the license, of every person so licensed.

Penalty. SEC. 5. Any person who shall violate, or fail to comply with any of the provisions of this chapter, upon conviction thereof, shall be subject to a fine of not less than one dollar, nor more than five dollars, for each and every offense, and in the discretion of the mayor, shall have his license revoked.

CHAPTER IV.

BRIDEWELL.

SECTION
1. Bridewell established.
2. Keeper to have custody, rule, etc.
3. To receive, and keep at labor, persons committed.
4. To keep record and copy of commitments.
5. Further duties of keeper.
6. To adopt, read and enforce rules of discipline.
7. Penalties to persons committed, for various offenses.
8. To arrest persons interfering with discharge of his duties; penalty.
9. Mayor and committee on bridewell to visit.
10. Police to return mittimus to comptroller.
11. Comptroller to keep record.
12. Treasurer to receive fines; comptroller to certify for discharge.
13. Persons released only on certificate.
14. Keeper to report to comptroller monthly.

SECTION 1. The buildings and enclosures erected and now standing, or that may be erected on the south half of block numbered eighty-seven, in the school section addition to the original town of Chicago, together with the said south half of block eighty-seven, situate and lying within the city of Chicago, are constituted and established a bridewell for the said city; and any buildings and enclosures that may hereafter be erected on any lot or lands, purchased, owned or leased by the city of Chicago for the purposes of a bridewell, whether within or without the limits of said city, shall be subject to the conditions and provisions of this chapter. *Bridewell established.*

SEC. 2. The keeper of the bridewell shall have the custody, rule, charge and keeping of the bridewell, and of all persons committed thereto, under the supervision and direction of the mayor and common council. *Keeper to have custody, etc.*

SEC. 3. It shall be the duty of the keeper of the bridewell to receive into the said bridewell such persons as may be committed thereto by any criminal court or magistrate, in and for the city, and none others; and he shall keep such persons at labor, or otherwise, according to the respective sentences or commitments of such persons, in such manner as the mayor and committee on bridewell or the common council shall from time to time direct. *Persons committed.* *Labor.*

SEC. 4. The keeper of the bridewell shall keep a record, in which he shall enter the name of every person *Record.*

committed to said bridewell, the nature of the offense, by whom and when committed, and the date when and how, and by what authority discharged; and he shall carefully preserve a copy of every order or warrant of commitment.

Clean. SEC. 5. The bridewell shall at all times be kept clean and in good order, and in a healthy condition, and the prisoners confined therein shall be furnished with a sufficient supply of good and wholesome food, three times each day; and it shall be the duty of the keeper of the bridewell to see that this section is strictly complied with, and be present at the bridewell during the business hours of each and every day, actively supervising the same, except when the legitimate duties of his office require his absence.

Food.

Discipline. SEC. 6. The keeper of the bridewell may adopt rules of discipline, to be approved by the mayor and committee on bridewell. He shall read said rules to each person committed, at the time of his or her reception, and it shall be the duty of said keeper to enforce rigidly such rules, and to maintain toward persons under his charge a uniformly humane and dignified deportment.

Escape. SEC. 7. Every person committed to the bridewell shall obey the keeper thereof in all his lawful commands, and shall not molest or hinder him in the discharge of his duty, and shall not escape nor attempt to escape, or assist others to escape or attempt to escape therefrom, or destroy or injure any property appertaining to the bridewell; and shall not transgress or violate the rules of discipline or any of them. Any person violating this section shall be fined not exceeding one hundred dollars, and imprisoned not exceeding ninety days, or either, in the discretion of the magistrate or court convicting.

Penalty.

Interference. SEC. 8. It shall be lawful for the keeper of the bridewell, and it is hereby made his duty, to arrest or cause to be arrested and taken before a police justice of the city, every person who shall molest or in any manner interfere with the said keeper, or with any person in his custody or charge as a prisoner, while in the discharge of his duty, either in the bridewell or elsewhere; and any person who shall so molest or interfere with the keeper of the bridewell, or person in his custody or charge, shall be fined in a sum not exceeding fifty dollars. Penalty.

SEC. 9. The mayor and committee on bridewell shall visit the bridewell as often as once in each month, and see that the same is kept in good order and condition, and that the rules and regulations thereof are strictly observed. Visitation.

SEC. 10. It shall be the duty of all members of the police force of the city of Chicago committing any person to the bridewell, to return immediately to the comptroller the mittimus or execution, or a duplicate thereof, by virtue of which said person was committed. Duty of police.

SEC. 11. It shall be the duty of the comptroller to keep a record of the names of all persons committed to the bridewell in a book or books to be provided for that purpose, showing the date of committal, days of imprisonment, amount of fine, etc. Record.

SEC. 12. It shall be the duty of the treasurer to receive all fines of persons who may have been committed to the bridewell, and to make a duplicate receipt of the payment thereof to the comptroller; and when it shall appear by the books of the comptroller that the term of imprisonment of any person is ended by virtue of such payment, or the expiration of his term of sentence, or both, the comptroller shall certify the fact to the bridewell keeper, who shall carefully preserve said certificate, and thereupon discharge the prisoner named. Fines. Discharge.

SEC. 13. No person shall be released from the bridewell by the bridewell keeper, except on the certificate of the comptroller, as provided in section twelve of this chapter, or by an order of the mayor or common council or some court of competent jurisdiction. Discharge.

SEC. 14. It shall be the duty of the bridewell keeper to make out and deliver to the comptroller on the first day of each month, a statement, duly sworn to, showing the names of all persons who have been confined in the bridewell during the month past, the number of days of their several confinements during said month, the date of Keeper to report.

their committal, and the names of all persons discharged or released during said month, and by what authority they were discharged or released.

CHAPTER V.

BRIDGES.

SECTION
1. Not to cross, when, etc.; penalty.
2. Crossing fast; penalty.
3. Overloading with cattle; penalty.
4. Stopping upon; penalty.
5. Teams to keep to the right.
6. Teams from streets; order.

SECTION
7. Breaking lines; resisting officer; penalty for violating this and last two sections.
8. Crowds, assemblies, etc.; penalty.
9. Bands of music; penalty.
10. Bridges to be shut, for fire engines, etc., to cross; penalty.

When not to cross. SECTION 1. Any person or persons who shall drive or attempt to drive any team, wagon, dray, or other carriage on or across the draw of any bridge in the city of Chicago, while the same is opening or shutting, or after the signal is given by the bridge tender for the opening thereof, and before the opening is begun, or who shall disobey or resist the tender thereof in his efforts to keep and promote order and equal convenience among those crossing the same, shall, for every offense, be fined in a sum not less than five dollars nor exceeding twenty-five dollars. Penalty.

Crossing too fast. SEC. 2. No person shall ride, lead, or drive any wagon, carriage, dray, cart, or other vehicle or conveyance, nor any horse, mare, ox, or other animal, over or across any of the bridges within the limits of Chicago, at a faster gait or pace than a common walk; and any person or persons who shall be guilty of a violation of this section, shall, for each and every offense, forfeit and pay to said city the sum of five dollars, to be recovered before any court having jurisdiction. Penalty

Droves. SEC. 3. No person or persons shall drive or assist in driving on or across any one of the bridges within the city, to exceed eight head of cattle or horses, at any one time, in a drove; and any person violating the provisions of this section shall forfeit and pay for each offense a penalty of not less than two dollars, nor exceeding twenty-five dollars, in the discretion of the magistrate convicting. Penalty.

Stopping on. SEC. 4. If any person or persons shall unnecessarily or willfully remain or stop with any team or teams, horses, oxen, wagon, sleigh, sled, or any other vehicle whatever, upon any of the bridges within the city of Chicago, or in and upon the approaches to any such bridge, such person or persons shall, on conviction thereof, be fined in the sum of five dollars for each offense. **Penalty.**

SEC. 5. It shall be the duty of all drivers or persons in charge of any wagon, dray, carriage, or vehicle of any kind, to keep to the right, when crossing the bridges upon the Chicago river and its branches. **Keep to right.**

SEC. 6. When a bridge has been opened and closed, the teams and vehicles shall cross in the following order, to wit: Those occupying the street upon which the bridge is situated, shall cross first; those occupying the cross streets, and upon the right hand side of the bridge, shall cross next, and those occupying the cross streets, and upon the left hand side of the bridge, shall cross next. **Order of crossing.**

SEC. 7. No person shall cross or attempt to cross, or break into, the line of teams or vehicles, while crossing or attempting to cross any bridge, nor shall any person disobey or resist any officer in charge of any bridge or crossing within said city; and whoever shall be guilty of violating any of the provisions of this or the two foregoing sections, shall be liable to a penalty of not less than five, nor more than twenty-five dollars; and also for all damages that may result to the bridge or any individual, or property of any person, by reason of such violation, to be recovered before any court having competent jurisdiction. **Breaking lines.** **Resisting officer.** **Penalty.**

SEC. 8. No person or persons shall gather in assemblies or crowds on any of the bridges of this city, or the approaches leading to the same, so as to obstruct in any manner the passage of foot passengers, teams, carriages or persons across the same, or be and remain upon any of the sidewalks or main passages of any of the bridges of this city, nor upon the railings of the said bridges, longer than will be necessary to pass over the same, under a penalty of five dollars for every such offense. **Crowds.** **Penalty.**

SEC. 9. No band of musicians shall play, or beat time, or keep step with each other, while they, or any procession or body of persons marching with them, or any portion **Band of Music.**

thereof, are upon or crossing any bridge in this city, under a penalty, upon the leader or director of such band, of not less than five dollars, nor more than twenty-five dollars.

Penalty.

Close for fire engine, etc.

SEC. 10. Whenever at any alarm of fire, any fire engine, hose cart or other fire apparatus, shall approach any bridge, for the purpose of crossing the same toward such fire, the bridge tender shall, if said bridge is open, close the same as soon as practicable, or if closed, and after the same is closed, keep it closed, until such engine, hose cart, or other fire apparatus, shall have had an opportunity to pass over said bridge, notwithstanding vessels may thereby be delayed, under a penalty for a failure to comply with this section of not less than ten dollars, nor more than one hundred dollars.

Penalty.

CHAPTER VI.

CEMETERY.

SECTION
1. Interments prohibited in cemetery; exception; Lincoln Park set apart.
2. Cemetery fund; how used.
3. Board of public works to keep record of lots; treasurer to keep cemetery account.
4. Offenses relating to cemetery; penalty.

Interments prohibited.

SECTION 1. Hereafter no body shall be buried in all that part of the south-east quarter of the south-east quarter of section thirty-three, township forty north, range fourteen east of the third principal meridian, (excepting therefrom four acres, not the property of the city,) and blocks numbered 50, 49, 48, 36, 35, 34, 33, 18 and 17, in said section, as the same are numbered on the plat of the survey of the canal trustees, heretofore set apart for the burial of the dead, and known and distinguished as the "Chicago Cemetery," except in the lots which have been sold by the city. All of the north part of said tract which has not been surveyed and divided into cemetery lots, consisting of blocks 17, 18, 33 and 34, and the north part of blocks 35 and 36, is hereby set apart for and declared to be a public park, and shall be known by the name of "Lincoln Park."

Exception.

Lincoln Park.

Fund.

SEC. 2. All moneys hitherto arising from the sale of lots therein, shall be kept a distinct fund, and be exclusively expended in adding to or ornamenting and improving

How used.

the cemetery grounds not set apart above as a park, and the board of public works are hereby authorized and empowered to take such steps as they may deem proper for the improvement of the cemetery grounds, and to improve the walks and drains, or ditches, connected therewith, in such manner as they may deem most conducive to public convenience, and the proper preservation of the same; and for the payment of all such expenses, they shall certify their approval of the same to the comptroller, who shall pay the same by draft on the treasurer, payable out of the cemetery fund.

SEC. 3. The Board of Public Works shall keep a record, in which shall be recorded the number of every lot heretofore sold in the cemetery, beginning with number one, with columns ruled therein for the name of the purchaser, the appraisal, price sold for, and date of sale; and the treasurer shall keep a cemetery account, in which all moneys received or paid on account of the cemetery, shall be entered.

Record of lots.

Cemetery account.

SEC. 4. If any person shall bury or attempt to bury any dead body in any unsold lot, or in any lot belonging to another, without permission in writing; or be found discharging firearms, hunting or trespassing in any other manner in the cemetery; or shall injure, deface or destroy any tree, shrub, stone, stake, post, fence, monument, vault or other fixture, building or thing of value or ornament in the cemetery, or trespass on any grave in the cemetery, he or they shall severally be subjected to a fine of not less than ten dollars nor exceeding five hundred dollars; and the court or magistrate may, in any aggravated case, cause the offender to be imprisoned for a period not exceeding six months, in addition to the fine.

Offenses in cemetery.

Penalty.

CHAPTER VII.

DOGS.

SECTION
1. Dog pound; appointment and compensation of keeper.
2. Unmuzzled dogs impounded, when; penalty; costs; reward.
3. Keeper to receive and take care of dogs in pound; to report to comptroller.
4. Unclaimed dogs destroyed; penalty for resisting.

SECTION
5. Slut in heat running at large; penalty.
6. Proclamation of Mayor forbidding dogs running at large.
7. Dogs running at large unmuzzled; penalty.
8. Dog having bitten a person; proceedings.
9. Further proceedings; penalty.
10. Construction of words.

Pound Keeper. Appointment. Compensation.

SECTION 1. The board of public works shall construct a good and suitable dog pound, at such place in the city as the mayor shall direct, to be placed under the care and direction of a pound keeper, to be appointed in accordance with the provisions of section 16, of chapter 2, of the Revised Charter of 1863, who shall receive as his whole compensation all the penalties and costs accruing on account of dogs impounded in his pound; and he shall pay all the expenses of his pound, other than the cost of the building, and the rewards paid by him under the next section, for which he shall be reimbursed by the city.

Dogs impounded. Penalty. Costs. Reward.

SEC. 2. Each and every dog that shall be found running at large within the limits of said city between the first days of June and October, in each and every year, unless they shall be securely muzzled with a wire muzzle, to be fastened on with a leather strap or chain, or that shall be found running at large within said limits at any time, without a collar or strap around the neck with the name of the owner marked or engraved thereon, may be impounded by any person in the dog pound, from which they shall not be released until the owner shall pay to the pound keeper a penalty of two dollars and fifty cents per head, and the further sum of twenty cents costs per head for every day or part of day they shall have remained in such pound; and said pound keeper shall be authorized and required to pay a reward of fifty cents for each and every dog over three months old delivered alive at said pound by any person fifteen or more years old, according to the provisions of this section.

SEC. 3. It shall be the duty of the pound keeper to keep

in a suitable book a record of all dogs received into the pound, the names of the persons who bring them, and the names of the owners, if the same can be ascertained. He shall take proper care of the dogs while in his custody, shall deliver them to the owners upon said owners paying to him the penalties and costs as herein fixed, and shall take upon said book or record, from all persons claiming and redeeming as owners, receipts for all dogs delivered. At the end of each month he shall render to the comptroller a full and complete statement on oath of the dogs received, of the dogs delivered to owners receipting for them, and of the number destroyed, as hereinafter provided, and also of all the sums of money received as penalties and costs, and the sums paid as rewards to those who have delivered the dogs to him to be impounded.

Keeper to receive and take care of dogs.

Report.

SEC. 4. All dogs not claimed and redeemed as herein provided within four days of the time of impounding of the same, shall be destroyed by the pound keeper, and any person resisting his so doing shall be liable to a fine of twenty-five dollars for so resisting such officer.

Dogs destroyed.

SEC. 5. Every person who shall suffer or permit any slut to run or be at large while in heat, shall, in addition to the penalties herein otherwise provided, be liable to pay a further fine of three dollars and costs.

Slut in heat.

Penalty.

SEC. 6. It shall be lawful for the mayor at any season or time whenever in his opinion there are mad or rabid dogs within or near the city, and the public health is thereby in danger, to issue his proclamation forbidding the running at large of any dog not muzzled as hereinbefore specified, and offering such premium for their destruction as to him shall seem proper. He or the board of police may also, in his or their discretion, require any and all policemen to destroy any dog at largo in violation of this section.

Proclamation by Mayor.

Dogs destroyed.

SEC. 7. In addition to the foregoing provisions, every owner or keeper of any dog, who shall permit the same to run or be at large between the first days of June and October without being muzzled as provided in the second section, shall pay a penalty of five dollars for each offense; and the informer thereof shall be entitled to one-half of said penalty when collected.

Dogs at large.

Penalty.

Dog biting. SEC. 8. Whenever affidavit shall be made before either of the justices of the police court of the city of Chicago, that any dog has bitten a person in said city, and that the person so bitten was not at the time trespassing upon the person or property of the owner or possessor of said dog, Proceedings the said justice shall issue an order directing the owner or possessor of said dog to kill him within forty-eight hours after having received such order.

Penalty. SEC. 9. The owner or possessor of any such dog who shall refuse or neglect to kill him within forty-eight hours after having received such order, shall be fined in any sum not exceeding twenty-five dollars, and the further sum of two dollars for every twenty-four hours thereafter, until such dog shall be killed. And it shall be the duty of any police officer to destroy said dog whenever he shall be found at large in said city, forty-eight hours after the service of said order.

Construction of words. SEC. 10. The words "dog" and "dogs" wherever used in this chapter, shall be construed and taken in their general sense, embracing alike both sexes and all ages.

CHAPTER VIII.

FEES.

SECTION 1. Fees of city officers.

Fees. SECTION 1. Any city officer upon whom the duty devolves is hereby authorized to demand and receive as fees for the use of the city—

For issuing each license, one dollar.

For transferring each license, one dollar.

For taking bond on such transfer, one dollar.

For each deed for real estate issued by the city, two dollars.

For the use of the corporate seal on any attestation, acknowledgment or other certificate, fifty cents.

For each certificate not under the corporate seal, twenty-five cents.

Administering oath and attesting the same, twenty five cents.

For canceling each tax or other certificate of sale, twenty-five cents.

For certified copies of any record, each seventy-two words, twenty-five cents.

CHAPTER IX.

FIRE DEPARTMENT.

SECTION
1. South division fire limits.
2. West division fire limits.
3. North division fire limits.
4. Buildings in fire limits; how constructed.
5. Buildings on wharfing privileges.
6. Sheds; privies; ashes.
7. Raising, repairing, enlarging or removing buildings in fire limits.
8. How damages to buildings ascertained.
9. Penalties for violating preceding sections.
10. Wooden buildings; nuisances; abated; expenses.
11. Stove pipes.
12. Using open candle and lamp.
13. Keeping shavings, etc., in shop; stoves; candles.
14. Scattering shavings, etc.
15. Carrying fire.
16. Keeping ashes.
17. Chimneys; how constructed.
18. Same.
19. Same.
20. Stove pipes; protection.
21. Chimneys for steam works.
22. Hay stacks, etc.
23. Burning hay, etc.
24. Lumber yards in fire limits.
25. Hatchways, etc., when closed.
26. Misusing fire apparatus.
27. Power to fire marshal, etc., at fire.
28. Limits at fires.
29. Persons at fires to obey orders.
30. Fire marshal may require aid at fires.
31. Hindering firemen, etc.
32. Power of fire marshal, etc., to arrest.
33. Fire apparatus, how drawn.
34. Protection of hose when laid at fires.
35. Power to remove property at fires.

SECTION 1. All that part of the south division of said city embraced within the following limits, shall be known as the fire limits of the south division, to wit: Beginning at the centre of the Chicago river, at its junction with the lake; thence south-westerly along the lake shore to the centre of Harrison street; thence west, on the centre of Harrison street, to the centre of the Chicago river; thence down the centre of Chicago river, to the place of beginning. *South division fire limits.*

SEC. 2. All that part of the west division of said city embraced within the following limits, shall be known as the fire limits of the west division, to wit: Beginning at the centre of West Madison street, at its intersection with the centre of the south branch of the Chicago river; thence west, on the centre of West Madison street, to the centre of Jefferson street; thence north, on the centre of Jefferson street,, to the centre of West Lake street; thence east, on the centre of West Lake street, to the centre of said south branch; and thence up the centre of said south branch to the place of beginning. *West division fire limits.*

North division fire limits.

SEC. 3. All that part of the north division of said city embraced within the following limits, shall be known as the fire limits of the north division, to wit: Beginning at the centre of North Franklin street, at its intersection with the river; thence north, on the centre of North Franklin street, to the centre of Michigan street; thence east, on the centre of Michigan street, to the centre of North Wells street; thence north, on the centre of North Wells street, to the centre of Ohio street; thence east, on the centre of Ohio street, to the centre of Pine street; thence south, on the centre of Pine street, to the centre of North Water street; thence southerly, on the east line of water lot No. 22, Kinzie's addition, to the centre of the river; thence up the centre of the river to the place of beginning.

Buildings in fire limits.

SEC. 4. No building shall be erected within the fire limits, (except as hereinafter excepted,) unless the same shall be constructed in conformity with the following provisions:

Construction.

First. All outside and party walls shall be made of stone, brick or other fire-proof material.

Thickness of walls.

Second. Outside and party walls not exceeding twenty-four feet in height from the top of the sidewalk to the under side of the roof joists or rafters, (except for stores, mills, breweries and warehouses,) shall not be less than eight inches in thickness, if of brick, nor less than sixteen inches in thickness, if of stone; but stores, mills, breweries and warehouses, exceeding twenty-four feet in height as aforesaid, shall not be less than twelve inches in thickness, if of brick, nor less than eighteen inches in thickness, if of stone, and if exceeding three stories in height, the two lower stories shall not be less than sixteen inches in thickness, if of brick, nor less than twenty-four inches in thickness, if of stone.

Timbers and cornices.

Third. All joists, beams and other timbers in outside and party walls shall be separated at least four inches from each other with stone or brick laid in mortar, and all wooden lintels or plate pieces in the front or rear walls shall recede from the outside of the wall at least four inches, except that lintels of timber may be used in rear of cast-iron fronts, and plates of wood may be used in cornices. But all such cornices shall be securely fastened to the walls of the building with iron rods, in such manner as that in case of fire they will not fall until burned into pieces.

Fourth. There shall not be more than thirty feet space between the party or outside walls of any building, unless such building shall be supported by iron or other columns or supports of fire-proof material. **Supports.**

Fifth. All end and party walls shall extend above the sheeting of the roof at least seven inches or three courses of brick, and in no case shall the planking or sheeting of the roof extend across any party or end wall. **Fire walls.**

SEC. 5. Buildings which may have been heretofore erected of wood on the wharfing privileges within the fire limits, for warehouse and storage purposes only, shall not be used for any other than warehouse or storage purposes; and if they shall be so used, they shall be subject to be removed by the board of public works, after thirty days' notice to the owner or occupant thereof to remove the same, to be given by said board. **Buildings on wharfing privileges.**

SEC. 6. Sheds not exceeding twelve feet in height at the peak or highest part thereof, and privies not exceeding ten feet square and twelve feet in height at the peak, may be constructed of wood, and shall not be subject to the provisions of this chapter: *Provided*, That the term "shed" be so construed as to mean a structure with a roof sloping one way, with one or more sides of said structure entirely open. But all depositories for ashes within or without the fire limits shall be built of brick or other fire-proof material, without wood in any part thereof. **Sheds and privies.** **Proviso.** **Ashes.**

SEC. 7. Permission is given to all owners and occupants of buildings in the fire limits, to raise wooden buildings to the established grade, and to build basements or cellars of brick or stone under the buildings so raised. But otherwise no wooden building or part of building within the fire limits shall be raised, repaired or enlarged, nor shall the same be removed to any other lot within the same; nor shall any such building be removed into the fire limits: *Provided*, That when the sidewalk may be raised above the threshold of any building, said building may be so raised and so far raised as to keep the first floor a reason- **Raising, repairing or removing wooden buildings in fire limits.** **Proviso.**

able distance, not to exceed six inches, above the sidewalk, without brick or stone foundation. Nor shall any wooden building within said limits, which may hereafter be damaged to the extent of fifty per cent. of the value thereof, be repaired or rebuilt; nor shall such building, where the damage is less than fifty per cent. of its value, be so repaired as to be raised higher than the highest point left standing after such damage shall have occurred; or so as to occupy a greater space than before the injury thereto.

Damage, how found. SEC. 8. The amount or extent of damage that may be done to any building may be determined by three disinterested persons, residents of the city, one of whom shall be selected by the owner of the building, the second by the mayor or any two members of the committee on fire and water, and the two so chosen shall select a third; and the decision of the persons so appointed shall be final and conclusive; and it shall be the duty of the owner of any building, before said reference is made, to deposit with the city clerk the sum of six dollars, which sum shall be applied to the payment of reference expenses; the remainder, if any, shall be returned to such owner.

Penalties for violating foregoing provisions. SEC. 9. Any owner, builder or other person who shall own, build or aid in the erection of any building or part of building within the said limits, contrary to, or in any other manner than authorized by the provisions of this chapter, or who shall own, remove or assist in removing any wooden building within said limits from one lot to another therein; or who shall own, remove or assist in removing any such building from without said limits into the same, or own, repair or assist in repairing any damaged wooden building, contrary in either case to any provision of this chapter, shall be subject to a fine of not less than twenty-five dollars and not exceeding five hundred dollars, in the discretion of the court, for the first offense, and to like fine for every forty-eight hours such person shall fail to comply with the provisions of this chapter, or continue in the violation thereof.

Wooden building, nuisance. SEC. 10. Any wooden building which may be erected, enlarged, removed or repaired, or in process of erection, enlargement, removal or repair, contrary to this chapter, shall be deemed a nuisance; and upon information it shall be the duty of the board of public works, after twenty-four hours' notice to the owner, occupant, person in charge, or builder thereof, to abate the same, to raze such building to the ground. The expenses thereof shall be reported by the said board to the common council for assessment, or may be collected of the owner of such building by suit. **Abated.** **Expense.**

SEC. 11. No pipe of any stove or Franklin shall be put up, unless it be conducted into a chimney made of brick or stone. And any person putting up the pipe of any stove or Franklin contrary to this section, shall, for every such offense, forfeit five dollars, and the further sum of one dollar for every twenty-four hours the same shall remain so put up after notice given by the fire marshal or any assistant marshal to remove the same. **Stove pipe.** **Penalty.**

SEC. 12. No lighted candle or lamp shall be used in any stable, or other place or building, where hay, straw or other combustible materials shall be kept, unless the same shall be well secured in a lantern, under the penalty of two dollars for each offense; and no fire shall be kept in any stove, or otherwise, in any such building, or any room where such combustible material is kept, under a penalty of ten dollars, and an additional penalty of five dollars for each and every twelve hours that said fire shall so remain. **Using open candle or lamp.** **Fire.** **Penalty.**

SEC. 13. Every person keeping or occupying a shop or other building, wherein shavings or other combustible materials are made, accumulated, or may be contained, shall forfeit the sum of two dollars for every neglect to clear or remove the same out of such buildings and the yards belonging thereto, at least three times in each week, provided such buildings are situated within two hundred feet of any other building; and no stove shall be used in any such shop or building, unless the same shall be set in a box surrounded with fire-proof material, with the pipe carefully set up according to the provisions hereof; and no lighted candles shall be used in any such shop or building, except they be placed in a candlestick made of a material not liable to take fire, under the penalty of two dollars for each offense. **Shavings, etc.** **Shop stoves.** **Candles.** **Penalty.**

Scattering shavings, etc. SEC. 14. No person, in removing any chips, or shavings, or other combustible materials, shall scatter or strew them in any street, or shall at any time direct, permit or suffer any chips, shavings, or other combustible matter, to be taken, or thrown, or scattered on any street or alley, under the Penalty. penalty of two dollars for every offense.

Carrying fire. SEC. 15. No person shall carry fire in or through any street, or lot, or other public or private place, except the same be placed or covered in some close or secure pan Penalty. or other vessel, under the penalty of one dollar for each offense.

Ashes. SEC. 16. No ashes (except at manufactories where ashes are used,) shall be kept or deposited in any part of the city except the same be in a close and secure vessel, or brick Penalty. or stone ash room, under the penalty of three dollars for each offense, and a further penalty of one dollar for every twenty-four hours the same shall thereafter remain so kept or deposited.

Chimneys; construction. SEC. 17. No chimney shall be built with less than four inches thickness of brick or stone, completely imbedded in lime morter and plastered on the inside with a smooth coat of the same. No flue shall in any case be less than eight by eight inches; and if intended for two full stories, not less than eight by twelve inches; and for three stories or more, not less than eight by sixteen inches. Holes for stove pipes shall have a sheet iron thimble, or other fire-proof material, inserted into the chimney, imbedded in mortar, and a tin or sheet iron stopper, with a flange at least one inch wide, Penalty. outside of the brick. Every person who shall build or cause to be built a chimney contrary to this section, shall, for every such offense, forfeit and pay the sum of ten dollars; and every owner of any chimney that shall be built con- Altering. trary to this section, shall cause the same to be altered within ten days after notice shall be given by the fire marshal or any assistant marshal so to do, or forfeit the Penalty. sum of ten dollars, and also ten dollars for every month thereafter, so long as said chimney shall remain unaltered.

Same. SEC. 18. No person shall build or cause to be built a chimney resting upon any part of a building liable to settle, unless such foundation is permanently connected with the rafters where the chimney passes through the roof, so that the whole may settle together, under a penalty of ten dollars for every such offense, and a further sum of ten dollars for every week it shall remain after notice given by the fire marshal or any assistant marshal, to alter the same. **Penalty.**

SEC. 19. No chimney shall be commenced in any loft, unless there are fixed stairs leading to the same, easy of access at all times; and no stove pipe shall pass through more than one ceiling before entering a chimney, under a penalty of ten dollars for each offense, and a further sum of two dollars for every week either shall remain after notice shall be given by the fire marshal or any assistant marshal, to alter the same. **Same.** **Penalty.**

SEC. 20. Stove pipes shall not be less than four inches from any wood or other combustible materials, unless there is a double circle of tin connected together, and air holes through the connecting tin between said pipe and the combustible substance, under the penalty of three dollars, and the sum of one dollar for every three days it shall remain after notice from the fire marshal or any assistant marshal, to alter the same. **Stove pipes.** **Penalty.**

SEC. 21. All chimneys erected in any building or place within the city for manufacturing purposes appertaining to, used or to be used for conveying off the smoke of, any steam boiler or steam engine, shall be firmly and substantially built of brick or stone, and shall be erected to the height of not less than fifty-five feet. Any person or persons, who shall build or construct, or use or occupy any chimney heretofore or hereafter built, for the purpose above specified, of any other material or in any other manner than above specified, shall forfeit and pay the sum of fifty dollars. **Chimneys for steam works.** **Penalty.**

SEC. 22. No person or persons shall deposit or stack any hay, straw, or other combustible substance, within one hundred feet of any dwelling-house, barn, stable, out-house, or building of any description, within the limits of the city of Chicago, without first having obtained a written permission from the mayor and both the aldermen of the ward in which the same may be located, under a penalty of twenty- **Stacking hay, etc.** **Penalty.**

five dollars for each offense, and a like penalty for every week the same may remain after notice.

Burning hay, etc. SEC. 23. No hay, straw, shavings or other combustible matter shall be set fire to or burned within any street, alley, public or private ground, within the fire limits of the city. Nor shall any straw, hay, shavings or other combustible matter be set fire to, or burned without the fire limits and within the city, nearer than one hundred feet to any house, fence, barn, shed, or wooden buildings, unless by the direct permission in writing, or superintendence, of the fire marshal or of one of the assistant marshals, under a penalty of Penalty. not less than five dollars nor more than twenty dollars for each offense.

Lumber yard in fire limits. SEC. 24. No lumber yard for the sale of lumber shall be kept upon any premises within the fire limits, which are Penalty. not now occupied for that purpose, under a penalty upon the person or persons keeping the same, of ten dollars for every offense, and a like penalty for every week the same shall be allowed to remain.

Hatchways, etc. SEC. 25. All buildings within the city having hatchways, hoistways, cellar openings or other openings leading from floor to floor, (except properly protected skylights,) of whatever name or description, shall be provided with good and substantial shutters or doors for all of such hatchways, hoistways, cellar doors or other openings. And the said shutters or doors shall be kept closed except when in actual When closed. use, from the hour of six o'clock P. M. to six o'clock A. M. of each day. All persons violating any or either of the provisions of this section shall, on conviction, pay a fine of Penalty. not less than ten dollars nor more than one hundred dollars, and shall also, in addition, be personally liable to all firemen or persons, in damages, for all injuries by reason of such violation or neglect.

Misuse of fire apparatus. SEC. 26. If any person having charge of an engine or other fire apparatus shall suffer or permit the same to be applied to private uses, or taken beyond the limits of the city, without the consent of the fire marshal, or, in his absence, the acting fire marshal, he shall forfeit a penalty of Penalty. not less than five dollars nor more than twenty-five dollars for each and every such offense, besides being personally liable for all damages.

SEC. 27. The fire marshal or assistant marshal in command, or, in the absence of the fire marshal and of all the assistant marshals, the mayor or two aldermen, may direct the hook-and-ladder men to cut down and remove any building, erection or fence, for the purpose of checking the progress of any fire; and the fire marshal or the assistant marshal in command, with the advice and concurrence of two members of the common council, shall have power to blow up or cause to be blown up, with powder or otherwise, any building or erection during the progress of the fire, for the purpose of extinguishing or checking the same.

Power to fire marshal, etc.

To remove building, etc., at fires.

SEC. 28. The fire marshal or the assistant marshal in command, may prescribe limits in the vicinity of any fire, within which no person excepting those who reside therein, members of the fire department, and those admitted by order of the officers of the fire department or of the city, shall be permitted to come.

Limits at fires.

SEC. 29. Every person not a fireman, who shall be present at a fire, shall be subject and obedient to the orders of the fire marshal and the assistant marshals, in extinguishing the fire and the removal and protection of property; and in case such person shall refuse to obey such orders, he shall forfeit and pay for every offense the sum of five dollars: *Provided*, That no such person shall be bound to obey any of said officers, unless such officers shall bear their respective badges of office, or their official character shall be known or made known to them; and all such officers shall have power to arrest any person or persons so refusing to obey such lawful orders as aforesaid, and hold them in custody until after the fire is extinguished, when he or they shall be taken before a magistrate to be dealt with according to law.

Persons at fires to obey orders.

Penalty.

Proviso.

SEC. 30. It shall be lawful for the fire marshal and the assistant marshals to require the aid of any drayman with his horse and dray, driver of a licensed wagon with his team and wagon, or any citizen, inhabitant or bystander, in drawing or conveying any engine or other fire apparatus

Fire marshal may require aid.

to the fire, and in working and using the same, while at a fire; and on the refusal or neglect of any person to comply with such requisition, the offender shall for every default forfeit and pay a penalty of not less than one dollar nor more than five dollars.

Penalty.

Hindering firemen, etc.

SEC. 31. Any person who shall willfully offer any hindrance to any officer or fireman in the performance of his duty at a fire, or shall willfully in any manner injure, deface or destroy any engine or fire apparatus belonging to the city of Chicago, shall for every such offense forfeit and pay a penalty of twenty-five dollars, and shall furthermore be liable for all damage or injury done.

Penalty.

Power of fire marshal and assistants to arrest, etc.

SEC. 32. During the time of a fire, and for and during the period of thirty-six hours after its extinction, it shall be lawful for the fire marshal and the assistant marshals, in any part of the city, to arrest any suspected person, or any person hindering, resisting, conducting in a noisy and disorderly manner, or refusing to obey any such officer while acting in the discharge of his duty, and, as soon as their duties in relation to the extinguishment of the fire will permit, take such person before a magistrate to be dealt with according to law. Said officers shall be severally vested with the usual powers and authority of police officers to command all persons to assist them in the performance of such duty.

Fire apparatus, how drawn.

SEC. 33. No hose carriage, hook-and-ladder carriage, or engine, shall be drawn faster than a walk on its return from a fire or an alarm of fire; nor shall any such carriage or engine be drawn on any sidewalk opposite a paved or planked street; nor shall any such carriage or engine be drawn to a fire or alarm of fire in a manner calculated to endanger the safety of persons or property in the streets or alleys of said city, under the penalty of not less than five dollars nor more than twenty-five dollars, to be paid by the person or persons committing the offense.

Penalty.

Crossing hose.

SEC. 34. No person shall go over any unprotected hose of the fire department of the city of Chicago, when laid down to be used at any fire or alarm of fire, with any vehicle, without first obtaining the consent of the marshal or assistant marshal in command, under a penalty of not

Penalty.

less than five dollars nor more than one hundred dollars. And the fire marshal shall procure and cause to be carried with each hose cart at every alarm of fire, efficient protectors of said hose, and cause the same to be laid down with said hose, when said hose is laid on any street, in such manner as to protect said hose from injury, when vehicles go over the same; and he shall also cause all such hose to be taken up from the streets, as soon as it is no longer needed to be so laid for use. **Hose protectors.** **Hose to be taken up.**

SEC. 35. Whenever it shall become necessary for the preservation of property from fire, or to remove property to prevent the spreading of fire, or to protect adjoining property from fire, the fire marshal is hereby authorized to cause the removal of such property as may be necessary. **Power to remove property.**

CHAPTER X.

GRADES.

SECTION
1. Base for city levels.
2. Grades fixed; tables.
3. Grades straight lines; exceptions.
4. Sidewalks.
5. Construction of this chapter.

SECTION 1. The grades hereinafter fixed are referred to the plane of low water in the year 1847, as established by the trustees of the Illinois and Michigan Canal, and adopted by the late sewerage commissioners and by the board of public works of the city of Chicago as the base or datum for the city levels, and was eight and twenty-three hundredths ($8\frac{23}{100}$) feet below the then water table of Loomis' store, on the south-west corner of Clark and South Water streets, and is eleven and seventy-one hundredths ($11\frac{71}{100}$) feet below the water table on the south-west corner of the main or central building of the court-house, in the city of Chicago. **Base.**

SEC. 2. The grades of the top of the sidewalk, at the edge next to the street, on the streets of the city of Chicago, mentioned in the tables in this chapter contained, shall be, at the intersections of said streets with each other, or with other objects, or at the points at which if they were extended **Grades fixed.**

they would so intersect, fixed at the heights shown by the figures (which indicate feet and decimal fractions thereof,) set in the places where the spaces between the lines containing the names of such streets, or other objects, at the left hand sides of said tables, intersect the spaces between the lines containing the names of such streets or other objects at the tops of said tables respectively.

I. TABLE OF SOUTH DIVISION.

	Calumet Avenue.	Prairie Avenue.	Indiana Avenue.	Michigan Avenue.	Wabash Avenue.	State Street.	Third Avenue.	Dearborn Street.	Fourth Avenue.	Clark Street.	Griswold Street.	LaSalle Street.	Sherman Street.	Wells Street.	Franklin Street.	Market Street.	South Branch of Chicago River.
South Water Street	...	...	...	14.	12.*	11.*	...	11.	...	11.	...	11.	...	11.	11.	...	...
North side of Lake Street	...	...	...	14.	12.25*	11.5*	...	11.5	...	11.5	...	11.5	...	11.5	11.5	11.5	...
South side of Lake Street	...	...	...	14.42	12.25*	11.5*	...	11.5	...	11.5	...	11.5	...	11.5	11.5	11.5	...
North side of Randolph Street	...	...	...	14.42	12.5	12.	...	12.	...	12.	...	12.	...	12.	12.	12.	...
South side of Randolph Street	...	...	...	13.6	12.5	12.	...	12.	...	12.	...	12.	...	12.	12.	12.	...
Washington Street	...	...	...	13.6	12.75	12.5	...	12.5	...	12.5	...	12.5	...	12.5	12.5	12.5	12.5
Madison Street	...	...	...	13.6	13.	13.	...	13.	...	13.	...	13.	...	13.	13.	13.	...
Monroe Street	...	...	...	13.6	13.66	13.22	...	12.95	...	12.64	...	12.36	...	12.07	...	11.5	*
Adams Street	...	...	...	13.6	13.66	13.22	...	...	...	12.64	...	12.36	...	12.07	11.78	11.5	*
Jackson Street	...	...	...	13.6	13.66	13.22	13.02	...	12.88	12.64	12.45	12.36	12.26	12.07	11.78	11.5	*
North side of Van Buren Street	...	...	...	13.6	13.66	13.22	13.02	...	12.88	12.64	12.45	...	12.26	12.07	11.78	11.5	*
South side of Van Buren Street	...	...	...	14.	13.66	13.22	13.02	...	12.88	12.64	12.45	...	12.26	12.07	11.78	11.5	*
North side of Congress Street	...	...	...	14.	13.66	13.22	13.02	...	...	...	...	...	...	...	...	...	...
South side of Congress Street	...	...	...	14.42	13.66	13.22	13.02	...	...	...	...	...	...	...	...	...	*
North side of Harrison Street	...	...	...	14.42	13.66	13.22	13.02	...	12.88	12.64	12.45	...	12.26	12.07	11.78	...	*
South side of Harrison Street	...	...	...	13.	13.66	13.22	13.02	...	12.88	12.64	12.45	...	12.26	12.07	...	...	*
Polk Street	...	...	...	13.	13.66	13.22	13.02	...	12.88	12.64	12.45	...	12.26	12.07	...	...	*
North side of Peck Court	...	...	...	13.	13.66	13.22	13.02	...	...	...	...	...	...	...	...	...	*
South side of Peck Court	...	...	...	12.75	13.66	13.22	13.02	...	...	...	...	...	...	...	...	...	*
Taylor Street	...	...	...	...	...	13.22	13.02	...	...	12.64	12.45	...	...	12.07	...	...	*
North side of Twelfth Street	...	...	...	12.75	13.66	13.22	13.02	...	12.88	12.64	...	...	...	...	...	...	*
South side of Twelfth Street	...	...	...	14.	13.66	13.22	13.02	...	12.88	12.64	...	...	...	...	...	...	*
Thirteenth Street	...	...	...	14.	13.66	13.22	13.02	...	...	...	...	...	...	...	...	...	...
Fourteenth Street	...	...	14.	14.	13.66	13.22	13.02	...	12.88	...	...	...	...	...	...	...	...
South side of Sixteenth Street	...	...	14.	14.	13.66	13.22	...	...	...	...	...	...	...	...	...	...	...
Seventeenth Street	...	14.	...	...	...	...	...	...	...	...	...	...	...	...	...	...	...
Eighteenth Street	...	15.	15.	14.	13.66	13.22	...	...	...	...	...	...	...	...	...	...	...
Nineteenth Street	...	16.	...	...	13.66	13.22	...	...	...	...	...	...	...	...	...	...	...
Twentieth Street	15.	16.	16.	14.	13.66	13.22	...	...	...	...	...	...	...	...	...	...	...
Twenty-first Street	15.	16.	15.	14.	13.66	13.22	...	...	...	...	...	...	...	...	...	...	...
Twenty-second Street	15.	16.	14.	14.	13.66	13.22	...	...	...	...	...	...	...	...	...	...	...

* See Section 3 as to grades on South Water and Lake Streets, between State Street and Wabash Avenue, and as to grades near the river south of Madison Street.

II. TABLE OF WEST DIVISION.

	West line of West Water Street.	Canal Street.	Clinton Street.	Jefferson Street.	Desplaines Street.	Union Street.	Halsted Street.	Green Street.	Peoria Street.	Sangamon Street.	Morgan Street.
Kinzie Street......	....	....	11.	11.	11.	11.	11.	11.	11.	11.	11.
Carroll Street......	....	11.5	11.5	11.5	11.5	11.5	11.5	11.5	11.5	11.5	11.5
Fulton Street.....	....	12.	12.	12.	12.	12.	12.	12.	12.	12.	12.
Lake Street.......	....	13.	13.	13.	13.	13.	13.	13.	13.	13.	13.
Randolph Street...	21.*	18.7	16.2	14.	14.	14.	14.	14.	14.	14.	14.
Washington Street.	....	14.	13.5	13.	12.5	12.	11.5	11.86	12.22	12.58	12.94
Madison Street....	....	14.	13.6	13.2	12.8	12.4	12.	12.31	12.62	12.92	13.23
Monroe Street.....	....	14.	13.6	13.2	12.8	12.4	12.	12.5	13.	13.5	14.
Adams Street......	....	14.	13.7	13.4	13.1	12.8	12.5	12.92	13.34	13.75	14.17
Jackson Street....	....	14.	13.8	13.6	13.4	13.2	13.	13.33	13.67	14.	14.33
Van Buren Street..	....	14.	14.	14.	14.	14.	14.	14.	14.	14.	14.
Tyler Street.......	....	....	....	....	....	....	14.	13.87	13.75	13.62	13.5
Harrison Street....	....	14.	14.	14.	14.	14.	14.	.....	.....	.....	.....

	Carpenter Street.	Curtiss Street.	Aberdeen Street.	May Street.	Ann Street.	Rucker Street.	Elizabeth Street.	Throop Street.	East line of Union Park.	Loomis Street.	Loflin Street.	Reuben Street.
Kinzie Street......	11.	11.5	.....	12.	12.5	....	13.	.....	....	.....	.....	15.5
Carroll Street......	11.5	11.75	.....	12.5	12.8	....	13.4	.....	....	.....	.....	15.5
Fulton Street.....	12.	12.	.....	12.2	12.4	....	13.3	.....	....	.....	.....	16.
Lake Street.......	13.	13.	.....	13.5	13.62	....	14.2	.....	....	.....	.....	16.5
Randolph Street...	14.	14.	.....	14.	14.	....	14.6	.....	15.5	.....	....	....
Washington Street.	13.30	13.66	.....	14.02	14.38	....	15.	.....	15.5	.....	.....	....
Madison Street....	13.54	13.85	15.	14.15	14.46	15.5	15.	16.	....	15.67	15.33	15.
Monroe Street.....	.....	.....	15.	.....	.....	15.	....	15.	....	15.	15.	15.
Adams Street......	.....	.....	15.	.....	.....	14.8	....	14.6	....	14.4	14.2	14.
Jackson Street....	.....	.....	15.	.....	.....	14.6	....	14.2	....	13.8	13.4	13.
Van Buren Street..	.....	.....	14.	.....	.....	13.6	....	13.2	....	12.8	12.4	12.
Tyler Street.......	.....	.....	13.25	.....	.....	13.	....	12.75	....	12.5	12.25	12.
Harrison Street....	.....	.....	13.25	.....	.....	13.	....	12.75	....	12.5	12.25	12.

* See Section 3 as to grade of Randolph street, descending from West Water street to fourteen feet at a line forty feet east of Jefferson street.

III. TABLE OF NORTH DIVISION.

	Sedgwick Street.	Market Street	Franklin Street.	Wells Street.	La Salle Street.	Clark Street.	Dearborn Street.	Wolcott Street.	Cass Street.	Green Bay Street.	Astor Street.	Rush Street.	Pine Street.	St. Clair Street.
South side of North Water Street	......	9.	9.	11.	9.	11.	9.	7.*	11.	......	......	11.	10.9	10.9
North side of North Water Street	......	10.5	10.5	11.	10.5	11.	9.	7.*	11.	......	......	11.	10.9	10.9
Kinzie Street	......	11.	11.	11.	11.	11.	11.	11.	......	......	......	......	......	......
Michigan Street	......	11.5	11.5	11.5	11.5	11.5	11.5	11.5	11.5	......	......	11.5	11.5	11.5
Illinois Street	......	11.62	11.62	11.62	11.62	11.62	11.62	11.62	11.62	......	......	11.62	11.62	11.62
Indiana Street	......	11.74	11.74	11.74	11.74	11.74	11.74	11.74	11.74	......	......	11.74	11.74	11.74
Ohio Street	......	11.86	11.86	11.86	11.86	11.86	11.86	11.86	11.86	......	......	11.86	11.86	11.86
Ontario Street	......	11.98	11.98	11.98	11.98	11.98	11.98	11.98	11.98	......	......	11.98	11.98	11.98
Erie Street	......	12.1	12.1	12.1	12.1	12.1	12.1	12.1	12.1	......	......	12.1	12.1	12.1
Huron Street	......	12.22	12.22	12.22	12.22	12.22	12.22	12.22	12.22	......	......	12.22	12.22	12.22
Superior Street	......	12.34	12.34	12.34	12.34	12.34	12.34	12.34	12.34	......	......	12.34	12.34	12.34
Chicago Avenue	......	12.5	12.5	12.5	12.5	12.5	12.5	12.5	12.5	12.5	......	......	12.5	......
Pearson Street	......	12.62	12.62	12.62	......	......	......	12.62	12.62	12.62	......	......	12.62	......
Chestnut Street	......	......	......	......	12.67	12.67	12.67	......	......	......	......	......	......	......
Hinsdale Street	......	12.72	12.72	12.72	......	......	......	12.72	12.72	12.72	......	......	12.72	......
Washington Place	......	......	......	......	......	12.8	12.8	......	......	......	......	......	......	......
White Street	......	12.83	12.83	12.83	12.83	......	12.83	12.83	12.83	13.3	......	......	13.3	......
McCagg Place	......	......	......	......	12.87	12.87	......	......	......	......	......	......	......	......
Whiting Street	......	12.94	12.94	......	......	......	......	......	......	......	......	......	......	......
La Fayette Place	......	......	......	13.26	......	12.94	12.94	......	......	......	......	......	......	......
Whitney Street	......	......	......	......	......	......	12.95	12.95	......	13.9	......	......	......	......
Oak Street	......	13.04	13.04	13.04	13.04	13.04	13.04	13.06	......	14.1	......	......	......	......
Wendell Street	......	13.15	13.15	13.15	......	......	......	......	......	......	......	......	......	......
Oakwood Street	......	......	......	......	......	......	......	14.	......	14.3	......	......	......	......
Maple Street	......	......	......	......	13.22	13.6	13.6	......	......	......	......	......	......	......
Hills Street	......	13.26	13.26	13.26	......	......	......	......	......	......	......	......	......	......
Cedar Street	......	......	......	......	......	......	......	14.5	......	14.5	......	......	......	......
Elm Street	......	13.87	13.87	13.4	13.4	13.8	14.2	......	......	14.8	......	......	......	......
Division Street	13.5	13.5	13.6	14.	14.	14.5	14.7	15.1	......	......	......	......	......	......
Scott Street	......	......	......	......	......	......	......	15.4	......	......	15.	......	......	......
Granger Street	13.55	......	......	14.	......	......	......	......	......	......	......	......	......	......
Gœthe Street	13.76	......	......	14.	......	16.	......	......	......	......	......	......	......	......
Grand Haven Street	......	......	......	......	......	......	......	15.7	......	......	15.	......	......	......
Banks Street	......	......	......	......	......	......	......	16.	......	......	15.	......	......	......
Sigel Street	13.89	......	13.89	14.5	......	......	......	......	......	......	......	......	......	......
Schiller Street	13.91	......	13.89	15.	......	17.	16.5	16.5	......	......	15.	......	......	......
Carl Street	......	......	......	16.5	16.5	......	......	......	......	......	......	......	......	......
Grand Street	......	......	......	......	17.	17.5	......	......	......	......	......	......	......	......
North Avenue	14.5	......	15.5	17.	17.5	18.5	......	......	......	......	......	......	......	......

* See Section 3, as to grade of North Water Street east and west from Wolcott Street.

Grades straight lines. SEC. 3. All grades between the points mentioned in said tables shall be straight lines, drawn from one fixed point to the next nearest fixed point. Except, that the grade of South Water street shall proceed on a level eastwardly from State street, until it intersects the former established grade of ten feet on State street and twelve feet on Wabash avenue, and thence rise to the grade now established; and the grade of Lake street shall proceed on a level eastwardly from State street, until it intersects the former established grade of ten and five-tenths feet on State street, and twelve and twenty-five hundredths feet on Wabash avenue, and thence rise to the grade now established; and from the north and south streets in the south division south of Madison street, to and including Twelfth street, next to the south branch of the Chicago river, the grades of the east and west streets shall descend towards the river at the rate of one inch in each one hundred feet. And except, also that the grade of West Randolph street shall descend uniformly from the west line of West Water street to a grade of fourteen feet at a line forty feet east of Jefferson street, and thence proceed on a level to Jefferson street. And except also, that the grade of North Water street shall rise each way from Wolcott street at the rate of one foot in each one hundred feet, until it meets the grade which corresponds with a grade of nine feet at Wolcott street, as provided by a contract with the Galena and Chicago Union Railroad Company, of May 30, 1864, ratified by an ordinance of July 11, 1864.

Exception.

Exception.

Sidewalks. SEC. 4. All sidewalks shall incline upwards from the outer edge, towards the line of buildings or lots at the rate of one inch in three feet.

Construction of this chapter. SEC. 5. Nothing herein contained shall be construed to confer any power on any party, person or firm, to fill streets or raise the grade of sidewalks in front of their own or any other premises until such streets have, by the common council, been ordered filled to grade; the true intent and meaning of this chapter being to fix and determine the grade for streets or portions of streets to which it refers, but not to order them or any of them filled up to that grade.

CHAPTER XI.

GUNPOWDER AND GUN-COTTON.

SECTION
1. Dealers in gunpowder and gun-cotton to have permits; proviso.
2. Application for permit; register; quantity and how kept; sale at night; sign; penalty.
3. Carrying through streets; penalty.
4. Vessels laden with, not to land or discharge within certain limits; penalty.

SECTION
5. Mayor may cause removal of vessel; penalty.
6. When permits expire; persons to whom not granted; charge for.
7. Officers to report violations.
8. Appropriation of penalties.

SECTION 1. No person shall keep, sell or give away gunpowder or gun-cotton, in any quantity, without permission in writing, signed by the mayor and clerk, and sealed with the corporate seal, under a penalty of twenty-five dollars for every offense: *Provided*, Any person may keep for his own use not exceeding one pound of gunpowder or gun-cotton at one and the same time. **Permit required.** **Proviso.**

SEC. 2. All applications for permits shall be made to the mayor. Not exceeding four permits shall be granted in any block. When the number of applications in any block shall at any time exceed the number to be granted, the requisite number shall be chosen by ballot by the common council. When issued, the clerk shall make an entry thereof in a register to be provided for the purpose, which entry shall state the name and place of business, and date of permit. Persons to whom permits may be issued shall not have or keep at their place of business, or elsewhere within the city, a greater quantity of gunpowder or gun-cotton than fifty pounds at one time, and the same shall be kept in tin canisters or cases containing not to exceed thirteen pounds each, and in a situation remote from fires or lighted lamps, candles or gas, from which they may be easily removed in case of fire. Nor shall any person sell or weigh any gunpowder or gun-cotton after the lighting of lamps in the evening, unless in sealed canisters or cases. It shall be the duty of every person to whom a permit shall be given, to keep a sign at the front door of his place of business, with the words "gunpowder" painted or printed thereon in large letters. A violation of any clause of this **Application for permit.** **Register.** **Quantity.** **How kept.** **Sale at night.** **Sign.**

Penalty. section shall subject the offender to a fine of not less than ten dollars nor exceeding one hundred dollars.

Carrying through streets. SEC. 3. No person shall convey or carry any gunpowder or gun-cotton, (exceeding one pound in quantity,) through any street or alley in the city, in any cart, carriage, wagon, dray, wheelbarrow or otherwise, unless the said gunpowder or gun-cotton be secured in tight cases or kegs, well headed and hooped, and put into and entirely covered with a leather bag or case, sufficient to prevent such gunpowder or gun-cotton from being spilled or scattered, under a penalty of one hundred dollars. Penalty.

Restriction on vessels. SEC. 4. No vessel laden in whole or in part with gunpowder or gun-cotton shall land at or make fast to any dock or wharf upon the Chicago river, or either branch thereof, between the south line of the school section and Chicago avenue, or discharge such gunpowder or gun-cotton within said limits. Penalty. If any master or owner of any vessel, or other person, shall violate any provision of this section, he shall be subject to a fine of not less than twenty dollars and not exceeding one hundred dollars.

Mayor may remove vessel. SEC. 5. The mayor shall have power to cause any vessel to be removed from the limits mentioned in the previous section to any place beyond the same, by a written order, which shall be executed by the harbor master or any member of the police. If any person shall neglect or refuse to obey such order, or shall resist any officer in the execution of the same, he shall be subject to a penalty of one hundred dollars. Penalty.

Expire. SEC. 6. All permissions granted under this chapter shall expire on the tenth day of June in each year. And no permit shall be granted to any retailer of intoxicating liquors or to any intemperate person. No permit to whom. The collector shall receive, for the use of the city, five dollars for every permit which may be issued. Charge.

Officers to report violations. SEC. 7. It shall be the duty of the officers of the police and fire departments to report all violations of this chapter which may come to their knowledge, to the city attorney for prosecution.

Appropriation of penalties. SEC. 8. One-half of the moneys collected for fines or penalties under the provisions of this chapter shall be paid to the firemen's relief fund, and constitute a part of said fund, and the remaining half shall be expended by the fire marshal in the embellishment or improvement of the instruments of the fire department.

CHAPTER XII.

HARBOR.

SECTION
1. Harbor master to keep office; pass along river; carry trumpet; keep accounts, record, and report to council; have charge of life-boat, and perform other duties.
2. To give orders as to vessels in harbor; penalty for disobeying.
3. Vessels adrift, etc., owner notified; penalty to owner not securing.
4. Harbor master may secure; expenses a lien; penalty for resisting.
5. Penalties, etc., a lien; how enforced; to be paid into treasury; penalty.
6. Vessels not to remain at south pier; penalty; proviso.
7. Obstructing passage; injuring bridges; penalty.
8. Speed at bridges; obstructing same; penalty.

SECTION
9. Vessels to be towed at bridges; penalty.
10. Injuring bridges; penalty.
11. Cargo left projecting over wharf; penalty.
12. Smoke-pipes to prevent sparks; joints in; speed; vessels not to be left alone; laden with gunpowder and gun-cotton not to land in certain limits; harbor master to prevent; rules as to anchors and yards; lights; fires; fastening; penalty.
13. Penalties, etc., a lien; how enforced.
14. Depositing obstructions in harbor; penalty.
15. Harbor master to be policeman.
16. Construction of words.
17. Tug boats injuring dredges or other machines; penalty.

SECTION 1. The harbor master shall keep an office in such place as the common council shall designate or provide, where, at all times during the season of navigation, he can be found, or where orders can be left that shall receive prompt attention. He shall pass along so as to see the entire harbor, as far up as Lake street bridge, at least three times each day; and as far up the south branch as Twelfth street, and as far up the north branch as Chicago avenue, at least twice each day during the time the harbor is navigable. He shall, at all times while on duty, carry a speaking trumpet, which shall be his badge of office, and through which his orders can be heard at a distance. He shall keep an accurate account and record of each case of damages to bridges, docks and all other city property pertaining to the harbor, accruing by any and every breach of the provisions of any ordinance, by any person, vessel, craft or float, the name of such vessel, craft or float, the owner, master, or consignee thereof, and shall gather all evidence and information in his power, concerning any such breach or breaches,

Harbor master. Office.

To pass along the river.

Trumpet.

Keep accounts.

forthwith after the occurrence of such breach; keep an accurate record of the amount of such damage, when, to whom, and how paid, and an account of all claims against the city made by vessel owners, or persons navigating the harbor, for damages sustained in said harbor, to vessels or other crafts, and make a detailed report of all such record, semi-annually, (or oftener if required by the council,) and submit the same to the common council. He shall have charge of and be responsible for the safe-keeping of the city life-boats and any other property that may be placed in his charge by the common council, or the board of public works. He shall perform all the duties required of him by this chapter or any ordinance, or resolution of the common council, or order of the board of public works.

Record and report.

Life-boats.

Other duties.

Give orders.

SEC. 2. The harbor master shall give such orders and directions relative to the location, change of place or station, manner of moving or use of the harbor, of every vessel, craft or float, lying, moving or laid up in the harbor not in use, as may be necessary to promote good order therein, and the safety and equal convenience of such vessels, crafts or floats; and any owner, master, or other person having charge of the same, who shall refuse or neglect to obey any such order or direction, shall be subject to a penalty of twenty-five dollars for every such neglect or refusal; which penalty shall constitute a lien upon such vessel, craft or float, until fully paid.

Penalty.

Vessels adrift.

SEC. 3. Whenever there shall be in the harbor any vessel, craft or float insecurely fastened, adrift, sunken or laid up, not in use, which may require to be fastened, raised, removed, or its location changed, the harbor master shall notify the owner, master or other person, who may be in charge thereof, to secure, raise or remove such vessel, craft or float without delay. But if the harbor master shall be unable to find the master, owner or person in charge of such vessel, craft or float as aforesaid, or if no person answering such description can be found by him, such notice shall not be required. And any person who shall refuse or neglect to comply with such order or direction, shall be subject to a penalty of twenty-five dollars,

Notice.

Penalty.

and the further penalty of ten dollars for every day he or they shall refuse or neglect to observe the same, which penalty shall constitute a lien upon such vessel, caft or float until fully paid.

SEC. 4. If any vessel, craft or float shall not be secured, raised, removed, or its location changed, in compliance with the direction of the harbor master after notice, or if the harbor master shall be unable to serve such notice as aforesaid, in either case he shall cause such vessels, craft or float, to be secured, raised, removed, or its location changed as aforesaid, employing such assistance as may be necessary for the purpose. All expenses which may be incurred in any case, shall be recoverable of the owner, consignee, master, or other person having charge of such vessel, craft or float; and the same expenses are hereby declared to be a lien upon such vessel, craft or float until fully paid. And if any person shall resist the harbor master, or any person acting under him, in the execution of such duty, or of any duty imposed upon him by this chapter, such person so resisting shall be subject to a fine of not less than ten dollars and not exceeding one hundred dollars, and may be imprisoned not exceeding thirty days.

Harbor master to secure vessels. **Expenses a lien.** **Penalty.**

SEC. 5. All penalties, fines, damages, and expenses, which may be made, or become a lien upon any vessel, craft or float, by the provisions hereof, shall attach from the time the right of action may accrue, and the harbor master shall detain any vessel, craft or float, subject to such lien, or such parts of her, or of her rigging, anchors or apparel as shall be sufficient to discharge the same. Such lien, if not otherwise discharged, may be enforced against the vessel, craft, or float, or other property so detained, by an attachment against such vessel, craft or float, by her or its name, or against the owner or owners thereof, if known, in the manner provided by the laws of this State for the enforcement of maritime claims against boats and vessels. All suits which may be brought under this chapter, whether *in rem* or *in personam*, shall be brought in the name of the city of Chicago, and all the expenses which may be incurred in such detention, shall likewise be a lien upon such vessel, craft, or float, and recoverable as a part of the original cause of action. All

Penalties, etc., a lien. **How enforced.**

Paid into treasury. moneys which may be paid to or collected by the harbor master, or which shall be collected in any suit instituted as aforesaid, shall be paid by the officer collecting the same into the city treasury. If any person or persons shall resist the harbor master, or any person acting under him, in the detention of any vessel, craft or float, for the purposes Penalty. aforesaid, he and they shall be subject to a fine of not less than ten dollars and not exceeding one hundred dollars.

Vessels at south pier. SEC. 6. No master, owner, or any person in charge of any vessel, craft or float, shall cause or suffer the same to remain at or within one hundred feet of the south pier for a longer period than is actually necessary to furl sail on Penalty. coming in, or make sail on departing, under a penalty of ten Proviso. dollars: *Provided*, That rafts or vessels necessarily used in the construction or repair of the piers, shall not be deemed to be within this provision.

Passage not to be obstructed. SEC. 7. No vessel, craft or float shall be so moored or anchored within the harbor, or in any slip or dock, as to prevent the passage of any other vessel, craft or float; nor Injuring bridge. shall any vessel, craft or float be so moved as to run against or injure any bridge across the river, or any branch thereof, Penalty. under a penalty of not less than ten dollars nor exceeding one hundred dollars, to the master, owner or person in charge thereof.

Speed at bridge or ferry. SEC. 8. All vessels, crafts or floats navigating the harbor, when passing any bridge or ferry, shall be moved past the same as expeditiously as is consistent with a proper movement in the harbor, but in no case shall any vessel, craft or float, while passing any bridge or ferry and obstructing the passage across such bridge or ferry, move at a rate of speed Obstructing same. less than two miles per hour; and no vessel, craft or float shall be so anchored or fastened as to prevent any bridge from a free and speedy opening, or any ferry-boat from a free and direct passage; nor shall any line or fastening be so thrown, laid or made fast as to cross the track of any Penalty. bridge or ferry, under a penalty of twenty-five dollars for each offense, to the master or other person having charge of such vessel, craft or float.

To be towed at bridges. SEC. 9. All vessels, crafts or floats, not propelled by steam, navigating the harbor, for which the opening of any bridge may be necessary, shall, while approaching and passing such bridge, be towed by a steam tug, under a penalty, upon the master, owner or person in charge thereof, of not less than twenty-five dollars nor exceeding one hundred dollars. **Penalty.**

Injuring bridge. SEC. 10. Whenever any person having charge of any vessel, craft or float shall wish to move the same past any ferry or bridge, reasonable time shall be allowed for the opening of the same; and any person who shall move any vessel, craft or float against any bridge or ferry, or the draw of any bridge, before the same shall be opened, to the injury thereof, shall be subject to a fine not exceeding five hundred dollars, and be likewise answerable to the city for damages. **Penalty.**

Cargo left projecting. SEC. 11. No person discharging the cargo of any vessel, craft or float shall suffer any part of such cargo to remain projecting over the front of any wharf after such vessel, craft or float shall remove from the wharf, under a penalty, to the master, owner or other person having charge of such vessel, craft or float occupying such wharf, of ten dollars for every hour such projection shall continue. **Penalty.**

Rules. SEC. 12. All vessels, crafts or floats lying in or navigating the harbor, shall be respectively governed by the following further provisions:

Smoke-pipes. *First.* All vessels using steam shall have their smoke-pipes so constructed and managed as to prevent sparks or coals of fire escaping therefrom, and shall be moved slowly at a speed not exceeding three miles per hour, and under a low head of steam. **Speed.** All tug boats or steam vessels used chiefly for towing, shall have a joint in their smoke-pipes, and shall be constructed in all respects in such a manner as to be able to pass under any bridge which is not less than thirteen feet above the surface of the water. **Joint in smoke-pipe.**

Speed. *Second.* All sail vessels shall likewise be moved slowly and under short sail, so as not in any case to endanger or injure other vessels.

Person in charge. *Third.* No master or other person owning or having charge of any vessel, craft or float, shall leave the same in the harbor without having on board or in charge thereof some competent person to control, manage and secure the same, without first obtaining permission of the harbor master.

Gunpowder and gun-cotton.

Fourth. No vessel laden in whole or in part with gunpowder or gun-cotton shall land at or make fast to any dock or wharf upon the Chicago river, or either branch thereof, between the south line of the school section and Chicago avenue, or discharge such gunpowder or gun-cotton within said limits. The harbor master shall prevent any vessel with gunpowder or gun-cotton on board from making fast to any wharf or dock, or unloading within the limits aforesaid.

Anchors.

Fifth. All vessels, crafts or floats, whether using steam or otherwise, while in the harbor, shall have and keep their anchors inboard or suspended from the hawse-pipe by the ring or shackle, and said ring and shackle shall be below the surface of the water, and their lower yards cock-billed and their upper yards braced up sharp.

Yards.

Lights.

Sixth. They shall likewise have and keep outboard during the night time a conspicuous light, and shall have extinguished or safely secured at dark all fires which may be kept on board.

Fires.

Insecure.

Seventh. No vessel, craft or float shall be suffered to lie in the harbor adrift or insecurely fastened.

Penalty.

Eighth. Any master, owner or other person having charge of any such vessel, craft or float, shall be subject to a fine of not less than twenty dollars nor exceeding one hundred dollars, for every violation of any of the foregoing provisions, and to like fine for every refusal to conform thereto when directed by the harbor master.

Penalties a lien.

SEC. 13. All penalties, fines and damages which may be incurred by the owner, consignee, master or other person having charge of any vessel, craft or float, under any provision of this chapter, are hereby declared to be recoverable of and a charge and lien on the vessel, craft or float of which he may be owner, consignee, master or in charge; and such lien may be enforced in the same manner as other liens against the same.

Obstructing harbor.

SEC. 14. No person shall cast or deposit, or suffer to be cast or deposited, in the harbor or slips within the limits of the city, any earth, ashes or other heavy substance or substances, filth, logs or floating matter, or any obstructions, under a fine of not more than one hundred dollars for each and every offense, and not more than twenty-five dollars for every day the same shall be suffered to remain there. Penalty.

SEC. 15. The harbor master shall be appointed a special policeman for the purpose of carrying more readily into effect the police regulations of the city concerning the harbor under his charge, and to preserve the public peace and quiet in and about said harbor. Harbor master a policeman.

SEC. 16. The words "vessels, crafts and floats" shall be deemed to include every species of steam and other vessels or boats lying or floating in or navigating the harbor, and also all rafts of logs, timber, wood, lumber or other floating matter; and the "harbor" shall be deemed to include the Chicago river and its branches to their respective sources, the piers, and so much of lake Michigan as lies within the distance of one mile of the shores of the city. Construction of words.

SEC. 17. If any owner, or master or other person in charge of, or command of, or sailing any tug boat or towing boat in and upon the Chicago river, or any of the branches of said river, or upon lake Michigan within said city limits, shall run, sail, or cause to be run or sailed, such tug boat, or towing boat or anything that they may have in tow, upon, against or over any rope, chain or other fastening mooring any dredge in said river, or any branch thereof or lake within said city, or other machines used by said city in either of said river branches or lake, for deepening, widening and improving the same, or either of them, or any part thereof, so that the said dredge or other machine shall be displaced, hindered or delayed in the working thereof, such persons so offending shall forfeit and pay to said city any sum not less than ten dollars nor more than one hundred dollars for each offense. Tug boats injuring dredges. Penalty.

CHAPTER XIII.

HAY.

SECTION
1. City weighers; how appointed.
2. To give bonds and take oath.
3. To provide scales; weigh hay; make deduction and give certificate; fees.
4. To have scales inspected every three months, or oftener if required; proviso as to expense thereof.
5. To keep book; manner of weighing and giving certificate; expense of re-weighing; duty to detect offenders.

SECTION
6. Hay stands; hay sold by the load to be weighed by city weigher; alteration or misuse of certificate; diminishing quantity after weighing.
7. Bales of hay to be weighed and marked; if of less weight than marked, offense.
8. Hay stands designated.
9. Penalty for violation.

Appointment of city weighers. SECTION 1. There shall be appointed by the common council by ballot, biennially, on the second Monday of May, or as soon thereafter as may be, such number of competent persons in each division of said city as may be deemed necessary, who shall be denominated "City Weighers."

Bonds SEC. 2. The said city weighers, before they or any of them shall enter upon the duties of their respective offices, shall respectively give bonds in the penal sum of five hundred dollars, with sureties to be approved by the mayor, conditioned for the faithful discharge of their duties, and Oath. they shall also severally take and subscribe to the usual oath of office.

Scales. SEC. 3. It shall be the duty of the said city weighers severally to provide themselves with proper scales, and well and Weighing. truly to weigh any cart, wagon or sled load of hay, when applied to by any person desiring the same, and to make such Deduction. reduction from the weight of such hay as to them may seem reasonable and just by reason of said hay being damp, wet or not well cured, and deliver to the person so applying, a Certificate. certificate thereof, for which the said weighers may demand Fees. and receive the sum of ten cents from the person having the same weighed.

Testing of scales. SEC. 4. The said city weighers shall severally have their said hay scales inspected and tested as often as once in three months by the city sealer of weights and measures, and oftener if required by any person desiring to use the Proviso. same: *Provided*, if any person shall require the same to be tested as aforesaid oftener than once in three months, and they are so tested and found correct, the person so requiring the same to be tested shall pay the expenses of such testing.

SEC. 5. The said city weighers shall severally provide themselves with, and each shall keep, a book in which he shall enter the amount of each load, and the name of each person for whom, and the date when the same was weighed; and when the vehicle and load shall be weighed together, the city weigher's certificate shall state the gross weight thereof, and upon the sale or delivery of said load, the vehicle shall again be weighed, without charge, by the city weigher who weighed the original load, and thus the net weight of the load ascertained; and in no case shall any city weigher state in his said certificate the weight of any vehicle which may have been weighed with any load until such city weigher shall have ascertained the weight of such vehicle by actually personally weighing the same on his said scales. And on request of any purchaser, every load or bale of hay so offered for sale shall be re-weighed, and the expense of re-weighing shall be paid by the purchaser, if the weight be found correct, but if found incorrect, the expense of weighing such load or bale of hay shall be paid by the seller. And it is hereby made the express duty of the city weighers to use great diligence in detecting and bringing to punishment any person or persons who shall offend against any of the provisions of this chapter.

Book.

Manner of weighing and certificate.

Re-weighing.

Expense.

Detecting offenders.

SEC. 6. All hay which shall be offered for sale by the load in the city of Chicago, shall stand at one of the hay stands hereinafter designated, in such order and manner as the mayor shall direct, and no person shall offer for sale or sell any load of hay within the limits of the city of Chicago, without the same having first been weighed by a city weigher, and if offered for sale at the West Randolph street hay stand, by the city weigher at said stand, and a certificate thereof, in conformity herewith, given. No person shall alter any certificate of any city weigher, or use or attempt to use the same for any other load or parcel than the one for which the same was given, nor, after the weighing and before the sale and delivery of any load or parcel, diminish the quantity thereof.

Loads of hay; stands, and weighing.

Frauds.

Bales of hay weighed and marked. SEC. 7. All hay sold or offered for sale by the bale, shall first be weighed on some proper scales by the person offering the same for sale, and the amount of the weight of said bale shall be stamped or marked, with the name of the person so selling the same, on such bale; and if said bale of hay so sold or offered for sale shall weigh less than the amount so stamped or marked thereon, the person so selling or offering the same for sale, shall be deemed guilty of violating this chapter. Offense.

Hay stands. SEC. 8. West Randolph street, from the middle of the block between Desplaines and Union streets, to the east line of Halsted street, and Illinois street, from the east line of North Clark street to the west line of North Dearborn street, leaving a space of at least twenty feet open in the centre of the street for the passage of teams, are hereby designated hay stands.

Penalty. SEC. 9. Any person who shall offend against any of the provisions of this chapter shall be fined, on conviction, in any sum not exceeding one hundred dollars, in the discretion of the court.

CHAPTER XIV.

HEALTH DEPARTMENT.

SECTION
1. Precautions; penalty; proviso.
2. Health officer; duties and powers.
3. Duty as to nuisances; penalty and expense.
4. To visit sick; remove them to hospital; provide nurses and attendance.
5. Notices of small pox; penalty for removal; occupant responsible.
6. Duty of health officer as to hospitals; proviso.
7. Offensive matter in streets, etc.; or premises; penalty.
8. Same in lake, river or grounds; penalty.
9. Physicians to report contagious diseases; penalty.

SECTION
10. Removing into public place sick persons; penalty.
11. City physician; duties and powers.
12. Quarantine regulations.
13. Police force at quarantine.
14. Power to stop vessels, etc., at, or bring back to, quarantine.
15. Board of police to make quarantine and health regulations.
16. Quarantine physicians, agents, nurses, etc.; pay; proviso.
17. Quarantine regulations to be obeyed.
18. Quarantine fund.
19. Penalty for violating, etc.

Precautions. SECTION 1. The board of police may take such measures as they may from time to time deem necessary to prevent the spread of the small pox, (or other pestilential diseases,) by issuing an order requiring all persons in the city, or any part thereof, to be vaccinated within such time as they shall prescribe; and all persons refusing or neglecting to obey such order shall be liable to a fine of not less than three dollars nor more than twenty-five dollars: *Provided*, That it shall be the duty of the board to provide for the vaccination of such persons as are unable to pay for the same, at the expense of the city. **Penalty.** **Proviso.**

SEC. 2. It shall be the duty of the health officer to carry out all the orders of the board of police and the laws of the State and ordinances of the city in relation to the sanitary regulations of the city; to proceed immediately, and from time to time, to make a thorough and systematic examination of the city, and cause all nuisances to be abated with all reasonable promptness. And for the purpose of carrying out the foregoing requirements, he shall be permitted at all times, from the rising to the setting of the sun, to enter into any house, store, stable, or other building, and to cause the floors to be raised, if he shall deem it necessary, in order to a thorough examination of cellars, vaults, sinks or drains; to enter upon all lots or grounds, and to cause all stagnant waters to be drained off, and pools, sinks, vaults, drains or low ground to be cleansed, filled up, or otherwise improved or amended; to cause all privies to be cleansed and kept in a good condition; and to cause all dead animals or other nauseous or unwholesome things or substances to be buried or removed beyond the limits of the city. **Health officer. Duties.** **Powers.**

SEC. 3. In order to the carrying out of the provisions of the foregoing section, it shall be the duty of the health officer to serve a notice in writing upon the owner, occupant or agent of any lot, building, or premises in or upon which any nuisance may be found, or who may be the owner or cause of any such nuisance, requiring them to abate the same in such manner as he shall prescribe, within reasonable time: *Provided*, That it shall not be necessary in any case for the health officer to specify in his notice the manner in which any nuisance shall be abated, unless he shall deem it advisable so to do; and such notice may be given or served by any officer who may be directed or deputed to give or make the same; and if such owner, occupant or agent shall neglect or refuse to comply with the requirements of such order within the time specified, they shall be subject to a fine of not not less than three dollars nor more than fifty dollars for **Notice to abate nuisance.** **Proviso.** **Penalty.**

every such violation. And it shall be the duty of the said officer to proceed at once, upon the expiration of the time specified in said notice, to cause such nuisance to be abated: *Provided*, That whenever the owner, occupant or agent of any premises in or upon which any nuisance may be found, is unknown or cannot be found, the said health officer shall proceed to abate the same without notice; and in either case the expense of such abatement shall be collected in the manner provided by the city charter and amendments thereto.

Proviso.

Health officer to abate.

Expense.

Removal to hospital.

SEC. 4. It shall be the further duty of the health officer to visit and examine all sick persons who shall be reported to him as laboring, or supposed to be laboring under any yellow or ship fever, small pox, cholera, or any infectious or pestilential disease, and under the advice of the city physician, cause all such infected persons to be removed to the cholera, small pox, or other hospitals, or to such other safe and proper place as he may think proper, or as he shall be directed by the said city physician, not exceeding three miles from said city, and cause them to be provided with suitable nurses and medical attendance, at their own expense, if they are able to pay for the same, but if not, at the expense of the city.

Nurses and attendance.

Notice of small pox.

SEC. 5. It shall be the further duty of the health officer, when directed by the city physician, or by the board of police, to cause a notice, printed or written in large letters, to be placed upon or near any house in which any person may be affected or sick with small pox, upon which shall be written, *small pox here;* and if any person or persons shall deface, alter, mutilate, destroy, or tear down such notice, without permission of the board of police, or of the health officer, such person or persons shall be liable for each offense to pay a fine of not less than twenty-five dollars nor more than fifty dollars. The occupant of any house upon which such notice shall be placed or posted as aforesaid, shall be held responsible for the removal of the same, and if the same shall be removed without the permission of the board of police, or of the health officer, such occupant shall be subject to the like fine of not less than twenty-five dollars nor more than fifty dollars, unless he shall notify the board

Penalty.

Occupant of house responsible.

of police or the health officer within twenty-four hours after the removal of the said notice.

SEC. 6. It shall be the duty of the health officer to see that the hospitals of the city are supplied with suitable nurses, furniture, nourishment, fuel and medicines, under the direction of the board of police or city physician, and that persons dying therein, or in other places under the charge of the city, are decently and promptly buried at the expense of the city: *Provided*, Such deceased persons have not the means to defray their own expenses of sickness or burial.

Duty of health officer as to hospital.

Proviso.

SEC. 7. No person shall throw, place or conduct, or suffer his or her servant, child or family to throw, place or conduct into any street, alley or lot, any putrid or unsound beef, pork, fish, hides or skins of any kind, or any filth, offal, dung, dead animal, vegetables, oyster shells, or other unsound or offensive matter whatever, or anything likely to become offensive. Nor shall any person allow such filth, offal, dung, or other offensive matter as aforesaid, to be or remain upon their premises, or in any out-house, stable, privy or other place owned or occupied by them, or in any alley or street in front of such premises, in such manner as to be offensive to the neighborhood. And every person who shall violate any of the provisions of this section, shall be fined in a sum not exceeding twenty-five dollars.

Offensive matter in streets, etc.

Premises.

Penalty.

SEC. 8. No person or persons shall throw, place or deposit, or cause to be thrown, placed or deposited, any dung, carrion, dead animal, offal or other putrid or unwholesome substance, or the contents of any privy, upon the margin or banks or into the waters of lake Michigan within the limits of said city of Chicago, or upon the margin or banks or into the waters of the Chicago river or either of its branches, or upon any public grounds, or upon any lot within the limits of said city, under the penalty of twenty-five dollars for each and every offense, and a further penalty of five dollars for each and every day the same shall be allowed to remain after a conviction for the first offense.

Offensive matter in lake, river, etc.

Penalty.

SEC. 9. Every practicing physician in the city, who shall have a patient laboring under any malignant or yellow fever, small pox, or other infectious or pestilential disease,

Physician to report.

shall forthwith make report thereof in writing to the secretary of the board of police, describing the street, number and locality of the house or place where the said patient may be located, so that it may be easily found, and for neglecting so to do, shall be liable to a fine of fifty dollars.

Penalty.

Infectious diseases.

SEC. 10. No person shall put out, remove, or allow to be put out or removed, from the premises or place occupied or owned by him, into any street, alley or other public place, in said city, any person having the small pox or any other infectious or pestilential disease, but such owner or occupant shall immediately report such case to the health officer, or secretary of the board of police. Any person who shall violate any clause of, or neglect to perform any duty required in this section, shall pay a penalty of not less than ten dollars, nor more than one hundred dollars, and may be confined in the city bridewell, not exceeding sixty days.

Penalty.

City physician.

SEC. 11. It shall be the duty of the city physician:

Duties.

First. To have and exercise a general supervision over the sanitary condition of the city, and to report to the board of police all nuisances, the prevalence of any epidemic, contagious or infectious disease, or other causes, which in his opinion are likely to be detrimental to the general health.

Vaccine.

Second. To keep on hand, at all times, a sufficient supply of genuine vaccine matter, and see that all persons, so far as he may have it in his power, are properly vaccinated, especially those in the vicinity of any person attacked by small pox.

Contagious or infectious diseases.

Third. Upon being informed of the existence or introduction of any contagious or infectious disease within the city, to inquire immediately into the facts, and report the same to the board of police, and see that the orders of the board of police are obeyed, so far as practicable.

Hospitals.

Fourth. To superintend the small pox, cholera and other city hospitals, and administer to all persons conveyed there, who have no other physician, or who are unable to employ one; to attend and administer to such other indigent persons as he may be directed to by the board of police or the health officer; and to visit and administer to prison-

Poor persons.

ers, sick in the city work-house, calaboose, watch-house, or house of correction. Prisoners.

Fifth. To attend the meetings of the board of police, and report to it all cases where any sick person has not been properly attended to, and all other matters which he may deem important, and give such information as the said board may desire, in relation to the sanitary condition or regulations of the city, so far as he may be able so to do. Reports to board of police.

Sixth. To examine, at the request of the board of police or the health officer, boats and vessels coming into port, the officers, crew or passengers of which may be supposed to be affected by any contagious or infectious disease, and advise the health officer what disposition shall be made of the same; and to perform such other duties as the common council shall hereafter prescribe, including the vaccination of the children in the public schools, or of others requesting him to do so; and to make a monthly report of his transactions to the common council, together with such sugestions as experience may point out as calculated to promote the general sanitary condition of the city. Boats and vessels. Schools. Report to council.

SEC. 12. The board of police, by and with the approval of the common council, may select, purchase, lease and establish such sites, places and boundaries for quarantine stations and purposes, and with the approval of said council may erect from time to time such buildings and hospitals upon such sites and places, and so keep the same in repair as in their judgment shall be deemed necessary. And the said board, whenever and at such times as by them it shall be deemed necessary, may, by proclamation (the approval of the common council being first had and obtained,) require all boats, vessels, railroad cars or other public conveyances bound for this city, before the same shall land or stop at any wharf, depot, or landing or stopping place therein, to touch or stop at any or either of the sites, places or boundaries so selected and established for quarantine purposes, and leave all such emigrants, travelers or persons recently from seaboard, and all such sick, diseased or unclean persons, with their stores and baggage, as in the opinion of the officers stationed at such quarantine sites, places or boundaries, shall be deemed proper, on account of Quarantine regulations.

the existence or general report of cholera, ship fever or any contagious disease, or disease apprehended to endanger the health of the city; and whenever it shall be deemed necessary to issue the said proclamation, it shall be the duty of the said board to send the same, together with the substance of the regulations for quarantine, and the period for which the same shall be in force, unless sooner revoked, to New York, Buffalo, Detroit, Toledo, La Salle, Saint Louis, Galena, Dubuque, Burlington, and such other cities and places as by them shall be deemed proper; and shall also cause to be stationed at such quarantine sites, places and boundaries as said board may deem advisable, one or more physicians or health officers, whose duty it shall be to go on board and examine all boats, vessels, cars or other public conveyance, so as aforesaid required to touch or stop at said quarantines respectively, and then and there determine what emigrants, passengers or persons (if any) shall be permitted to come to the city, and what emigrants, passengers or persons, (if any) shall stop at such quarantine; and it shall be the duty of all persons conducting or in charge of any such vessel, boat, car or public conveyance, to aid and assist any physician or health officer so as aforesaid stationed, in the exercise of his duties; and the said physicians or health officers shall attend to all sick persons who may be landed or placed in quarantine, and provide medicines and necessaries for their use, and shall have general supervision of such quarantines and compel persons therein to purify their bodies, clothes and baggage, and do all such acts and things as shall be proper in the premises, keeping correct accounts of all expenditures and wages, which shall be allowed and paid by order of the said board. And whenever the physician or officer in charge of any quarantine station or place, as aforesaid, shall, upon examination, be satisfied that there is no longer occasion for the detention of any boat, vessel, car or conveyance at such quarantine or place, and such boat, vessel, car or conveyance shall have been thoroughly cleansed, and such persons as aforesaid landed and placed in the care of such physician or officer such physician or officer shall give such vessel, boat, car or conveyance a permit, signed by him, to enter the city which shall be ample authority for the entry of said boat, vessel, car or conveyance. And the said officers respectively shall discharge all persons in quarantine by their certificate for that purpose, whenever they are satisfied that such persons are free of disease, and their baggage and effects properly purified: *Provided, however*, That the board in their discretion, by proclamation for that purpose, may, during the prevalence of cholera, ship fever or other contagious or fatal disease, forbid the admission of emigrants or others peculiarly liable thereto, into any or all of said quarantines or stations, until, in their opinion, the health of the city will justify the same. **Proviso.**

SEC. 13. It shall be the duty of the said board, whenever by them it shall be deemed necessary, to keep at the quarantine station or stations a sufficient police force, whose duty it shall be to enforce all regulations by this chapter required, or by said board to be established, and to arrest all persons violating said regulations, or committing any breaches of the peace, and bring such persons before any court having jurisdiction, for trial, and to arrest and commit for trial all persons disobeying, or interfering with, or resisting any physician, health officer, or other person in authority at such quarantine site, place or station. **Police at quarantine.**

SEC. 14. In case any boat, vessel, car or public conveyance shall leave any quarantine station, place or boundary without a permit as aforesaid, or shall fail to stop at the same, when so as aforesaid required by the issuing of the said proclamation, or whenever the person in charge thereof, or any person under his command, shall fail or refuse to obey any regulation or command of the said board, health officer, physician or person in charge of any quarantine station or place, or any provision or requirement of this chapter, the said board shall have power, and it is hereby made their duty, if in their opinion the health of the city requires it, to send sufficient police force to such boat, vessel, car or public conveyance, and cause the same, with the crew and passengers on board, to be landed, or stopped, or conveyed to the quarantine station or place, and there to remain until properly discharged by the permit as aforesaid; **Power to stop at quarantine.**

and the owner, master or the person in charge of any such boat, vessel, car or public conveyance, shall be liable to the city for all expenses and costs incurred by reason thereof, and if any emigrant, traveler or person, so placed in quarantine as aforesaid, shall leave the same without permission as aforesaid, he may be arrested and taken back to said quarantine, and there retained until such permission shall be given.

Power to make rules and regulations.

SEC. 15. The said board shall make such rules and regulations for the government of the quarantine or health of the city, as from time to time they shall deem necessary; and the physicians or health officers in charge of any quarantine station or place, shall have power to make and enforce such regulations as may be necessary for the proper conducting and management thereof; and it shall be the duty of all persons in quarantine, and all agents, officers, policemen or others employed by the city in and about said quarantine stations or places, to carry out and obey the same.

Quarantine physicians.

SEC. 16. The said board, by and with the approval of the common council, may appoint one or more competent physicians as quarantine physicians, who shall be present at such quarantine stations as the said board shall designate, and at such times as said board shall direct, and attend to all the duties imposed by this chapter or by the regulations of said board, who shall receive, each, for actual services rendered, and for such time as such services shall be actually required, not less than five dollars nor more than ten dollars per day, to be allowed by the said board; also the said board may employ such agents, servants, nurses or temporary medical assistance, for the purpose of carrying into effect the objects and intent of this chapter, or of any regulation of the board, as in their judgment shall, from time to time, be necessary, or authorize the employment thereof by the physicians or health officers in charge of any quarantine or station. All the salaries, wages and expenses in this section contemplated are to be audited and allowed by the said board, and when so allowed, are to be paid out of the fund set apart for quarantine purposes, or, in case of necessity, out of the contingent fund of the city: *Provided*, That,

Pay.

Agents, nurses, etc.

Expenses.

Proviso.

when practicable, the persons taken in such quarantine or stations, and receiving the aid and care afforded thereby, shall each pay a sum of money sufficient to meet all expenses, labor and care incurred in his behalf, which said amounts shall be faithfully kept, reported and accounted for by the physician, health officer or other person in charge of said quarantine or station, to the said board; and all other expenses incurred or to be incurred by reason of this chapter, or of any regulation of said board, shall be paid out of the fund set apart for quarantine purposes, or, when necessary, out of the contingent fund of the city.

Quarantine regulations to be obeyed.

SEC. 17. No person, master, captain, conductor in charge of any boat, vessel, railroad car or public conveyance, shall knowingly bring into this city any person or persons diseased of cholera, small pox, ship fever or contagious or communicable disease whatsoever; and no vessel, boat, railroad car or public conveyance, at any time covered by the said proclamation, shall pass by any quarantine station or place without stopping, nor shall leave the same without the permit aforesaid; and no person stopping in said quarantine, or so as aforesaid received therein, shall leave the same without first obtaining permission as aforesaid; nor shall any person aid or abet any master, conductor or person in charge of any boat, vessel, railroad car or public conveyance, in violating, neglecting or evading any provision or requirement of this chapter; nor shall any person interfere with, resist, or neglect, or refuse to obey the orders of any physician, health officer, policeman or other person in authority at any quarantine station or place of quarantine so as aforesaid established, nor do any act or thing in violation of, or in disobedience to any of the provisions, clauses or sections of this chapter; nor shall commit any breach of the peace, or do any act calculated in any way to defeat or interfere with the provisions or requirements of this chapter, or of any regulation of the said board, physician or officer in charge of any quarantine.

Quarantine fund.

SEC. 18. The moneys appropriated to the quarantine fund shall be faithfully applied by the said board to the true objects and purposes of its appropriation, and the said board shall make reports of their doings and expenditures to the common council, whenever requested so to do.

Penalty. SEC. 19. Any master of a vessel, conductor, captain or person whatsoever, who shall violate any clause, provision, requirement, duty or regulation of this chapter, or of any rule or regulation of the said board, or physician, or health officer in charge of any quarantine, or who shall fail or neglect to comply with any such clause, provision, requirement, duty or orders, or who shall interfere with, or in any manner resist any officer or agent of the city in the discharge of his duty as herein contemplated, or who shall commit any breach of the peace, or be guilty of any act or thing calculated to defeat or interrupt the carrying into effect any part of this chapter, or any regulation of the said board, shall, in cases where no other penalty is provided, on conviction, pay a fine of not less than two dollars nor more than one hundred dollars.

CHAPTER XV.

HORSE RAILROADS.

SECTION
1. Gauge.
2. Kind of rail, and how laid.
3. When other kinds displaced.
4. Companies to sprinkle streets, when and what.
5. To keep tracks and streets in repair.

SECTION
6. Board of public works to see to compliance; reports, and book for complaints.
7. To notify companies to repair, when and how.
8. Penalty for not repairing; report and prosecution.

Gauge. SECTION 1. The gauge of all horse or other city railroads in the city of Chicago, now laid, or hereafter to be laid, is hereby fixed at four feet eight and one-half inches.

Rail. SEC. 2. All rails which shall hereafter be laid on any horse railroad track, or other city railroad track, on the streets, alleys, or other public grounds of the city of Chicago, shall be a tram rail, having a profile, taken crosswise of the rail, such as is shown on the sketch following, marked "A profile of rail to be used in the streets of the city of Chicago."

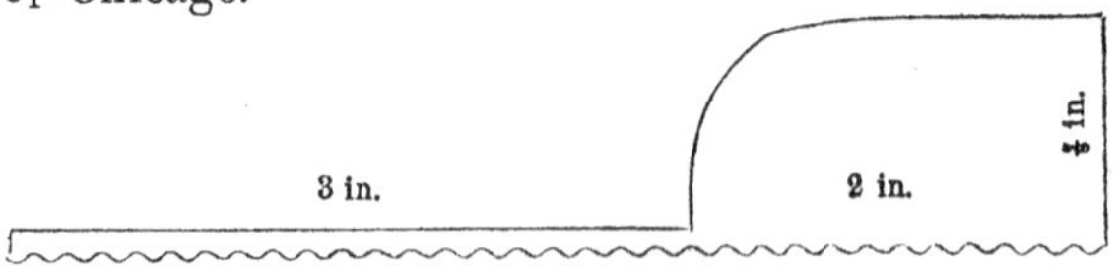

The width of said rail from outside to outside shall be five (5) inches. The width of the tram shall be three (3) inches, horizontal. The height along the wagon edge, or the height from the tram to the highest part of the rail, shall not be more than seven-eighths ($\frac{7}{8}$) of an inch. The upper part of the rail shall be laid below the level of the surface of the street, and the whole manner of constructing said railways, so as to carry out the provisions of this chapter, shall be under the direction of the board of public works.

How laid.

SEC. 3. In all streets where a railway is now laid with rails of a different form from that hereby prescribed for use, such rails shall be displaced by rails of the form herein prescribed whenever the common council shall order the streets in which such railways are laid, to be paved, graded, macadamized, planked, or otherwise improved.

When displaced.

SEC. 4. The several horse railroad companies having their railway tracks located in and along the different streets within the city of Chicago, shall, from and after the first day of May, and during and until the first day of November, in each and every year, keep moistened and well sprinkled with water the several streets within the city of Chicago upon and along which they, or either of them, may use or operate their respective railway tracks.

Sprinkling.

SEC. 5. Said companies shall keep the tracks of their respective roads in such condition, that said tracks shall not at any time be elevated above the surface of the streets on which they are laid; so that vehicles can easily and freely, at all times, cross said tracks at all points, in any direction, without obstruction. They shall also keep in good repair, such portions of the streets as they severally have agreed, or may agree, with said city, so to do.

Tracks and streets to be kept in repair.

SEC. 6. The board of public works shall see that the provisions of the last section are complied with, and shall require inspectors of sidewalks and foremen of street labor, to report to said board all cases that come to their knowledge of any neglect or failure of any of said companies so to comply. Said board shall also keep a book, accessible to the public, in which any resident in said city may enter com-

Duty of board of public works.

Reports.

Book for complaints.

plaint of the condition of said tracks or the streets in which the same are laid.

To notify companies to repair.

SEC. 7. Whenever said companies or either of them shall neglect or fail to comply with the provisions of section five, the board of public works shall cause a notice to be served upon such company or companies, requiring the track or tracks, or part of track or tracks, or the portions of the streets required to be kept in repair by such company or companies, mentioned in such notice, to be put in the condition required by section five, within five days after the service of such notice.

Penalty for not repairing.

SEC. 8. Either of said companies who shall neglect or fail to put their track or tracks, or part of track or tracks, or any portion of the streets, mentioned in such notice, in the condition required by section five within five days after the service of such notice, shall forfeit and pay not less than one hundred dollars and not more than five hundred dollars for every day such neglect or failure shall continue after the expiration of said five days; and the said board shall report every such case to the city attorney, who shall immediately prosecute the offending company to judgment and execution before any court of competent jurisdiction.

Report and prosecution.

Cars and omnibuses obstructing crossings.

SEC. 9. All proprietors, conductors, or drivers of horse railroad cars or omnibuses, are prohibited from stopping their cars or omnibuses at any street crossing, so as to interfere with, or interrupt the travel of the several streets which they in their respective routes are required to cross. In stopping their cars or omnibuses for the accommodation of passengers, they shall in all cases pass over the respective cross streets and not stop until the rear of the car or omnibus, as the case may be, shall arrive at the last sidewalk crossing in the direction in which the car or omnibus shall be moving. All persons violating the provisions of this section shall be liable to a fine of not less than three dollars, nor more than twenty-five dollars for each and every offense.

Penalty.

Obstructing street cars.

SEC. 10. In all cases where any team or vehicle shall meet a car upon either of the horse railways upon the streets of said city, such team or vehicle shall give way to said car. Nor shall any person willfully or maliciously obstruct, hinder, or interfere with any of said railway cars, by placing, driving, or stopping, or causing to be placed, or driven in a slow pace, or stopped, any team, vehicle, or other obstacle, in, upon, across, along or near to the track of said railways, or either of them, in said city, after being notified by the ringing of the car bell. Whoever shall willfully violate any of the provisions of this section, shall forfeit the sum of not less than five dollars nor more than twenty-five dollars for every such offense. **Penalty.**

CHAPTER XVI.

INSPECTION OF FISH.

SECTION
1. No person to act as inspector but the inspector under charter.
2. Obstructing or interfering with inspector.
3. Penalties for violating, etc.
4. Compensation for cooperage and salt.
5. Fresh water fish in packages to be inspected; penalty.

SECTION 1. It shall not be lawful for any person not duly appointed and qualified as fish inspector, or assistant, under the revised charter of 1863, to act or assume to act as inspector of fish, or hold himself out to the public to be such inspector, in and for the city of Chicago. **No person to inspect but inspector.**

SEC. 2. No person shall directly or indirectly obstruct or willfully interfere with the fish inspector of the city of Chicago, lawfully appointed as aforesaid, or any of his assistants or employees, in the legitimate exercise of any of the rights, or the performance of any of the duties given, imposed, or prescribed in and by section ten, of chapter three, of said charter. **Obstructing or interfering with inspector.**

SEC. 3. Any person who shall violate either of the provisions of the first section of this chapter, shall forfeit the sum of twenty-five dollars for each and every offense of unlawfully acting or assuming to act as such inspector, and the like sum for every day he shall unlawfully hold himself out to the public to be such inspector; and any person who shall violate either of the provisions of the second section hereof, shall forfeit the sum of twenty-five dollars for each and every offense. **Penalties.**

SEC. 4. Whenever the said fish inspector shall, in the

Compensation for cooperage and salt. course of his employment as such, furnish any cask, barrel, or other cooperage, or supply salt, it shall and may be lawful for him to charge therefor a just compensation.

Fish to be inspected. SEC. 5. Any and all persons bringing, or causing to be brought, to the city of Chicago, or receiving on consignment or otherwise, for the purpose of sale, any fresh water fish in packages, shall have the same duly inspected by the fish inspector of the city of Chicago before such fish shall be sold or in any way disposed of; and it shall be the duty of every person having such fish in possession for the purpose of selling or dealing in the same, and of every consignee having fish on consignment, before the said fish shall be sold or in any way disposed of, to give notice to the inspector and have such fish duly inspected and branded; and for this purpose such person shall arrange the packages in a convenient manner, and have them in a suitable place. Any person or persons violating any of the provisions of this section, shall be fined in a sum not to exceed twenty-five dollars for every barrel or other package of fish so sold without such inspection. Penalty.

CHAPTER XVII.

INSPECTION OF FLOUR.

SECTION
1. Appointment of inspector.
2. Deputies; bond; remedy on.
3. Flour to be inspected; inspection defined; penalty; proviso as to flour in bags; taking sample.
4. Office, and duty to inspect.
5. Weights and scales; weighing; branding.
6. Grades; proviso as to flour sold by sample.

SECTION
7. Liability for damages; proviso.
8. Fees and sample.
9. Inspector and deputies not to deal in flour.
10. To keep record and report to council.
11. Penalty to inspector and deputies.
12. Bond and oath of inspector.
13. This chapter not to affect inspection of board of trade.

Appointment of inspector. SECTION 1. There may be appointed by the common council, by ballot, biennially, on the second Monday of May, or as soon thereafter as may be, an inspector of flour for the city of Chicago, who shall be known as "The City Flour Inspector."

Deputies. SEC. 2. Said inspector may appoint and remove at pleasure one or more deputy inspectors, who shall have the right to brand all barrels or bags of flour inspected by any or either of them in the name of the said inspector, and the said inspector shall have the right to take bond with sufficient penalty and security necessary to himself, from each of said deputies, and of the same tenor as the bond hereinafter required to be executed by the said inspector, and the said inspector may sue on the bond of any or either of his said deputies, to recover any damages that he may have suffered by reason of the misfeasance or malfeasance of any or either of them, while acting in the capacity of such deputy flour inspector.

Bond.

Remedy on.

SEC. 3. It shall be the duty of every person or business firm bringing flour to this market, and every person or business firm receiving flour on consignment, or in any way dealing in flour, at wholesale or retail, before selling said flour, if its inspection be desired by the buyer or seller thereof, to procure the same to be inspected by the said city flour inspector or his deputy, and such person, business firm or dealer shall have the same properly arranged so as to be accessible to such inspection; and the term inspection, as employed in this chapter, shall be held to embrace any examination, by an expert or other person, of flour by sample or otherwise, in order to ascertain the quality thereof. Every person, business firm or dealer in flour, violating any of the provisions of this section, shall be fined in the sum of five dollars for each and every barrel so sold without such inspection: *Provided*, It shall not be deemed necessary to inspect flour in bags, except by mutual agreement of buyer and seller, and any flour taken from bags for the purpose of inspection shall be replaced when inspected, with the exception that the said inspector may take not to exceed eight ounces of flour as a sample of any one lot of not less than twenty bags.

Flour to be inspected.

Inspection defined.

Penalty.

Proviso as to flour in bags.

Sample.

SEC. 4. The inspector shall provide and keep an office in some convenient place in the city of Chicago, which shall be kept open from 7 A. M. to 6 P. M. every day, Sundays excepted, and in which the said inspector shall at all times have some person during his absence, to receive orders, and, on due application, either himself or his deputy shall proceed with as little delay as possible to any point

Office.

Duty to inspect.

within said city, where the inspection of flour is required, and inspect the same.

Weights and scales. SEC. 5. It shall be the duty of the said inspector to procure sealed weights and scales, and weigh or cause to be weighed, so much of each lot or number of barrels of flour offered for inspection, as shall be sufficient to satisfy the said inspector of the whole lot or number of barrels offered and so inspected by him, or by any or either of his deputies, and shall see whether each barrel contains one hundred and ninety-six pounds of flour; and he shall brand or cause to be branded on the head of each and every barrel of flour so inspected and weighed, by plainly and distinctly marking in some indelible manner upon the head of the barrel, the quantity and grade of the flour contained therein, together with his name, and the month and year the same was inspected.

Weighing.

Branding.

Grades. SEC. 6. The following grades of flour are hereby established, and the inspection of the same shall conform to, and each barrel inspected shall be branded in accordance with, the following standard, to wit:

First Grade—All flour which is sound, made from select winter wheat, free from impurities, properly milled, and thoroughly cleaned in every respect, shall be denominated "double extra."

Second—All flour which is sound, made from select spring wheat, and such sound flour as may be made from winter wheat, which may approach but not equal in quality "double extra," the same having been thoroughly cleaned and prepared in every respect, shall be denominated "extra."

Third—All sound flour which is not equal in color or quality to "extra," shall be denominated "extra superfine."

Fourth—All sound flour not equal in color or quality to "extra superfine," but free from bran, shorts or other refuse, shall be denominated "superfine." All the above grades of flour shall be put up in good, tight, well-coopered barrels. All flour inferior to "superfine" shall be rejected: *Provided*, That nothing in this section or in section five shall apply to flour bought and sold by sample. But it shall be

Proviso as to flour sold by sample.

the duty of such inspector to brand each barrel so bought and sold by sample with the word "inspected," together with his name, and the month and year the same was inspected.

SEC. 7. The said inspector shall be liable for all damages that may occur to any person, for want of a just and faithful inspection of such flour as may be by him inspected, or inspected by any or either of his deputies, and any person thus damaged may have right of suit in all courts having jurisdiction of the same: *Provided*, Said flour shall not be exposed to inclement or damp weather or stored in damp places after such inspection shall have been made, without making void any claims for damages against said inspector.

Liability of inspector.

Proviso.

SEC. 8. The said inspector shall be entitled to two cents for inspecting each barrel and bag of flour when no other price shall be agreed upon, and shall be entitled to take from each barrel not to exceed four ounces of flour as a sample of the same.

Fees.

SEC. 9. Neither the said inspector, nor any or either of his deputies, shall be allowed to buy or sell or deal directly or indirectly in flour, or act as the agent or agents of any person or persons for the purchase or sale of flour, while he or they or any of them holds the office of flour inspector or deputy flour inspector.

Inspectors not to deal.

SEC. 10. The said inspector shall keep a record of all flour inspected by him and his deputies, and shall report in writing to the common council, on the first Monday in May in each year, the number of barrels and bags of flour of each grade so inspected, and such other information with regard to the inspection of flour as the common council may by order or resolution require.

Record and report.

SEC. 11. Any inspector or deputy inspector willfully violating, refusing, or failing to comply with any of the provisions of this chapter, so far as they are made incumbent upon any or either of them, shall, for every such offense, be subject to a fine of not less than five dollars nor more than one hundred dollars, and shall also be subject to immediate removal from office.

Penalty to inspectors.

SEC. 12. Any inspector appointed under this chapter, shall, before entering upon the duties of said office, give

Bond.

bond, with two or more good and sufficient sureties, to be approved by the common council, in the penal sum of five thousand dollars, payable to the city of Chicago, and conditioned that he will faithfully perform the duties of said office, and satisfy all damages that may legally accrue against him as city flour inspector under this chapter; and he shall also take an oath of office.

Oath.

Not to affect inspection by board of trade.

SEC. 13. Nothing in this chapter contained shall affect, interfere with, or relate to any flour inspected under the authority of the Chicago board of trade.

CHAPTER XVIII.

INSPECTION OF GAS METERS.

SECTION
1. Appointment of inspector; oath.
2. To examine and test meters.
3. To provide standards and provers, at expense of city.
4. Notice to company and consumer, of testing.

SECTION
5. Inspection conclusive.
6. Arrearages to be paid before inspection.
7. Fees, and how paid.
8. Certificate.

Appointment of inspector.

SECTION 1. There shall be appointed by the common council, by ballot, biennially, on the second Monday of May, or as soon thereafter as may be, some suitable person or persons, to be styled "The Inspector or Inspectors of Gas Meters." Before entering upon the duties of his or their office or offices, the said inspector or inspectors shall be sworn to the faithful performance of his or their duties, as the same may, by ordinance, be assigned or prescribed.

Oath.

Test meters.

SEC. 2. It shall be the duty of such inspector or inspectors to examine and test any gas meters furnished to the consumer by any gas company furnishing gas in this city, whenever requested so to do by such consumer.

Standards and provers.

SEC. 3. The said inspector or inspectors shall procure and keep at some convenient place or places within the city, one or more good and sufficient standard meters and provers, the expense of procuring and keeping the same to be paid by the said city of Chicago.

Notice of testing.

SEC. 4. The said inspector or inspectors shall always give notice to the consumer and the gas company who furnish the meter, at their office, of the time and place when and where he or they intends or intend to test such meter.

SEC. 5. The inspection herein provided for shall be conclusive, both upon the company and the consumer, as to the amount of gas consumed three months before the close of the month in which any meter shall be inspected, and until a new inspection shall be had—a new inspection relating back, as herein provided. Inspection conclusive.

SEC. 6. Before any meter complained of by a consumer shall be examined, the consumer shall pay to the gas company all arrearages for gas consumed, which are then due and payable, and such gas company shall refund or receive, as the case may be, according to the result of the examination. Payment of arrearages.

SEC. 7. The said inspector or inspectors shall be entitled to receive in advance, from any consumer requiring his or their services, the sum of one dollar and his or their reasonable expenses, not exceeding two dollars for each meter by him or them inspected; such sum, however, to be refunded by the gas company, upon presentation to their treasurer, of the inspector's certificate, that the meter has been found by him or them to measure more gas than was actually consumed. Fees. How paid.

SEC. 8. The inspector or inspectors shall, when so requested by either party, furnish to the consumer or to the gas company, free of charge, a certificate of the result of the examination made by him or them, of any meter. Certificate.

CHAPTER XIX.

INSPECTION OF LIQUORS.

SECTION
1. When liquors to be inspected.
2. Appointment of inspector.
3. Provide instruments; gauge and mark quantity and proof.
4. Altering, defacing or changing marks; penalty.
5. Deputy, when inspector may appoint.
6. Oath of deputy; inspector accountable for him.

SECTION
7. Neglect or extortion by inspector; penalty.
8. Fees.
9. Oath.
10. Assuming office; penalty.
11. Council may appoint one other inspector under this chapter; inspection not compulsory.

SECTION 1. Where the parties cannot agree, all foreign and domestic liquors that shall be sold by the barrel, hogs- Inspection, when.

head or cask in the city of Chicago, shall be inspected, and gauged and branded, as hereinafter provided.

Appointment of inspector. SEC. 2. There shall be appointed by the common council, by ballot, biennially, on the second Monday of May, or as soon thereafter as may be, a competent person, who shall be called "Inspector and Gauger of Liquors."

To provide instruments. SEC. 3. It shall be the duty of the inspector and gauger so appointed, to provide himself with the most approved instruments for ascertaining the capacity of a barrel, hogshead, cask or other vessel, and the quality or proof of spirituous liquors, and when called upon for that purpose shall immediately attend with the same in any part of the city, Gauge. and there gauge and ascertain the contents of any barrel, hogshead, cask or other vessel, and examine the quality and Mark quantity and proof. proof thereof, and mark on such barrel, hogshead, cask or other vessel, the true quantity contained therein in wine gallons, and the proof of such spirits, together with the name of such inspector, in legible and durable figures and characters, upon the same.

Alter, deface or change marks. SEC. 4. If any person shall alter, deface or change any of the marks or characters made by the inspector aforesaid, on any barrel, hogshead or other vessel by said inspector so inspected, each and every person so offending shall, for Penalty. each and every offense, on conviction thereof, forfeit and pay to the city of Chicago, a sum not exceeding twenty-five dollars, together with cost of prosecution.

Deputy. SEC. 5. If the said inspector of liquors aforesaid shall be unable, in consequence of sickness, absence from the city, or otherwise, to attend to the duties of his office, he may appoint, with the approbation of the mayor, one other person to attend to the duties of his office during such inability.

Oath of deputy. SEC. 6. The person appointed in place of such inspector, by virtue of the last preceding section, shall take an oath faithfully to perform his trust, and the inspector in whose stead such person is deputed, shall be accountable for the official conduct of such person.

Neglect or extortion by inspector. SEC. 7. If the inspector aforesaid shall neglect to attend in person to the duties of his office (except in case of sickness or other disability), or shall ask, demand or receive any greater compensation for his services than is allowed by section eight, next herein following, he shall forfeit and pay to the city of Chicago, for every offense, the sum of twenty-five dollars. Penalty.

SEC. 8. The said inspector shall, for his services, be entitled to demand and receive from the person or persons employing him as aforesaid, compensation as follows: for gauging and inspecting every barrel, hogshead, cask, or other vessel, the sum of eight cents. Fees.

SEC. 9. The person so appointed inspector of liquors shall, before entering upon the duties of his office, take and subscribe an oath or affirmation, faithfully and impartially to execute the office of inspector and gauger of liquors. Oath.

SEC. 10. If any person shall exercise the office of inspector of liquors or gauger in the city of Chicago, without the authority of the common council as aforesaid, every person so offending shall, for each and every day or part of a day he shall so exercise, or attempt to exercise, such office aforesaid, forfeit and pay to the city of Chicago, on conviction, a sum not less than ten dollars nor more than thirty dollars. Assuming office. Penalty.

SEC. 11. The common council of the city of Chicago shall have power, at any time hereafter, to appoint one other inspector of liquors, if it shall by said council be deemed necessary, who shall be subject in all respects to the provisions of this chapter: *Provided*, Inspection or gauging under this chapter, shall in no case be compulsory upon the buyers or sellers of any liquors herein mentioned, unless the same has been agreed to by mutual consent of the parties. Other inspector. Proviso. Inspection not compulsory.

CHAPTER XX.

INTELLIGENCE OFFICES.

SECTION
1. Keepers to be licensed; penalty.
2. License; charge; expiration; revocation.

SECTION
3. Frauds; penalty.

SECTION 1. No person shall establish or keep any intelligence office within the city of Chicago, for the purpose of obtaining places or employment for male or female family do- Keepers to be licensed.

mestics, servants or other laborers, or for procuring or giving information concerning such places for or to such domestics, servants or laborers, or for procuring or giving information concerning such domestics, servants or laborers for or to employers, without a license as hereinafter provided, under Penalty. a penalty of not less than ten dollars nor more than one hundred dollars for every day such office shall be so kept, to be recovered before any magistrate or court having jurisdiction.

License. SEC. 2. The mayor of said city is hereby authorized to license any person or persons, being a resident or residents of said city, over twenty-one years of age, to keep an in- Bond. telligence office as aforesaid, upon such persons giving bonds to the city, to be approved by the mayor, in the penal sum of five hundred dollars, conditioned for the faithful observance of all ordinances of the city, and upon payment of Charge. the sum of fifty-two dollars for the use of the city, and no Proviso. other fees: *Provided*, All licenses so issued shall expire on Expire. Revocation. the first day of July of each year, and may be revoked, in the discretion of the mayor.

Frauds. SEC. 3. Any person keeping an intelligence office as aforesaid, with or without license, who shall violate any of the provisions of this chapter, or directly or indirectly, or through any agent or other person or persons, make use of any improper device, deceit, false representation, false pretense or any imposition whatsoever, for any improper purpose, or for the purpose of obtaining a fee, money, gratuity or other thing of value from any customer, person or persons, or patron or patrons, shall, on conviction, be fined in Penalty. a sum not less than five dollars nor more than one hundred dollars.

CHAPTER XXI.

JUNK DEALERS, AND DEALERS IN SECOND-HAND GOODS.

SECTION
1. Dealers defined
2. To be licensed; penalty.
3. License; character; charge; bonds.
4. Expiration of license
5. To keep book of purchases; if using boat, same to be painted, how; penalty.

SECTION
6. Book to be submitted to police, etc.; penalty.
7. Pawnbrokers not affected by this chapter.

SECTION 1. Any person who keeps a store, boat, office or place of business for the purchase or sale of old metal, rags, old rope, old canvas, iron and the like, is hereby defined to be a junk dealer; and any person who keeps a store, office, or place of business, for the purchase or sale of second-hand clothing, or garments of any kind, or second-hand goods, wares or merchandise, is hereby defined to be a dealer in second-hand goods. Dealers defined.

SEC. 2. No person or persons shall carry on or conduct the business or calling, either of a junk dealer or dealer in second-hand goods, within the city of Chicago, without having first obtained a license so to do, in accordance with the provisions of this chapter, under a penalty of twenty-five dollars for each and every offense. To be licensed. Penalty.

SEC. 3. The mayor is hereby authorized to grant a license to junk dealers or dealers in second-hand goods, on the following conditions: License.

First. The person so applying for such license shall, to the satisfaction of the mayor, be a person of good character, and shall pay to the collector the sum of twenty-seven dollars, and no other fees. Character. Charge.

Second. The person so applying shall execute a bond to the city of Chicago, in the sum of three hundred dollars, conditioned that the said applicant will in every particular conform to the requirements of this chapter, and with the requirements or provisions of any ordinance hereafter to be passed concerning junk dealers or dealers in second-hand goods, as the case may be, and thereupon the clerk shall issue a license under the corporate seal, signed by the mayor and countersigned by the clerk. Bond.

SEC. 4. All licenses issued under this chapter shall expire on the first day of August next after the issuing of the same. Expire.

SEC. 5. Every person licensed as aforesaid shall keep at his or her place of business a substantial and well-bound book, in which he or she shall enter a minute description of all personal property purchased by him or her, the date of purchase, the name and residence or place of business of the person or persons from whom such purchase was made, and particularly mentioning any prominent or descriptive marks Book.

that may be on such property, which said book shall be kept clean and legible, and all the entries therein shall be made with ink, and no entry therein shall be erased, obliterated or defaced; and every person so licensed, carrying on his business upon a boat, shall have his name, and the number of his license, plainly painted in letters and figures at least one and a half inches in size, in a conspicuous place, on the outside of each side of such boat; and every person so licensed failing to comply with any of the provisions of this section, shall, upon conviction, be fined in a sum not less than twenty-five dollars nor more than one hundred dollars for each and every offense.

Boat to be painted, how.

Penalty.

Police to inspect book.

SEC. 6. Every person so licensed as aforesaid, shall, during the ordinary hours of business, when requested by the mayor, general superintendent of police, or any police officer of the city, submit and exhibit said book, in the fifth section provided for, to the inspection of any of the above named officers, and shall also exhibit any such goods or personal property to any of the aforesaid officers; and every such licensed person refusing to submit said book, goods or property as aforesaid, upon the request of any of the aforesaid officers, shall, upon conviction, be fined in a sum not less than twenty-five dollars for each and every offense, and shall be subject, in the discretion of the mayor, to have his or her license revoked.

Penalty.

Pawnbrokers not affected.

SEC. 7. Nothing contained in this chapter shall affect the sale of second-hand goods by any person or persons now or hereafter licensed as pawnbrokers, and who shall in the course of their business as pawnbrokers sell any goods, wares or merchandise which have been pledged to them and remain unredeemed.

CHAPTER XXII.

LAMPS.

SECTION
1. Post-office boxes on lamp posts; penalty for injuring.

SECTION
2. Injuring or meddling with public lamps or posts; penalty.

Post-office boxes on.

SECTION 1. The postoffice department hereby have permission, under the direction of the board of public works, to attach and fasten postoffice boxes to the public lamp posts in said city; and any person or persons who shall deface or in any way injure such postoffice boxes, shall, for such offense, be liable to a fine of not less than twenty-five dollars nor more than one hundred dollars for each and every offense. Penalty for injuring.

SEC. 2. Any person who shall carelessly or maliciously break, deface or in any way injure or destroy any public lamp or lamp post of this city, or climb upon or hitch any horse or other animal to any public lamp post, or hang or place any goods or merchandise thereon, or place any goods, boxes, wood, or any other heavy material upon or against the same, or who shall extinguish or cause to be extinguished, or light or cause to be lighted, any of said lamps, unless duly authorized so to do by the board of public works, shall forfeit the penalty of ten dollars for each offense. Injuring or meddling with. Penalty.

CHAPTER XXIII.

LICENSES.

SECTION
1. Licenses subject to existing and subsequent ordinances, and for violation thereof may be revoked.
2. Not assignable or transferable, and no one but licensee to act under.
3. Term, and how issued; mayor to hear and grant applications in his discretion.

SECTION
4. Collector to receive moneys for, and penalties on ball-alleys, billiard tables, etc.; when party is licensed.
5. Persons in default on payments, clerk and collector to report to mayor, etc.

SECTION 1. All licenses which may be issued under any ordinance of the common council, shall be subject to the ordinances and regulations which may be in force at the time of issuing thereof, or which may subsequently be made by the common council. And if any person so licensed shall violate any of the provisions thereof, he shall be liable to be proceeded against for any fine or penalty imposed thereby, and his license shall be subject to be revoked in the discretion of the mayor or of the court or magistrate before whom he shall be convicted of such violation. Subject to existing and subsequent ordinances. Penalty. Revocation.

SEC. 2. No license granted under any ordinance shall be assignable or transferable, without permission of the Assignment or transfer.

mayor or common council, nor shall any such license authorize any person to do business or act under it but the person named therein, unless such ordinance shall otherwise provide.

Term. How issued. SEC. 3. No license shall be granted at any one time for a longer period than one year, and all licenses shall be signed by the mayor and countersigned by the clerk, under the corporate seal. And in all cases where it is not otherwise expressly provided, the mayor shall have power to hear and grant applications therefor, upon the terms specified by the ordinances of the city, and all licenses shall be issued to such person or persons as shall comply in all respects with the different provisions of the ordinances of the city, and as the mayor, in his discretion, shall deem suitable and proper persons to exercise the occupation for which he, she or they apply to be licensed, and to no others.

Application to mayor.

Discretion.

Collector to receive money for, and penalties on ball alleys, etc. SEC. 4. The collector shall receipt for all moneys for any licenses that may be applied for or granted under the authority of said city upon any account whatever. He shall also receipt for all auction dues, and all penalties incurred by the keeping of ball alleys and billiard tables within said city, also receipt for all moneys paid in from the licenses of theatres, shows, museums, and other entertainments of like character. His receipt for the same shall be a discharge to the person to whom given, to the extent and purport thereof, but no person shall be deemed to be licensed in any case until the issuing of the license in due form as required by the ordinances of the city.

Clerk and collector. SEC. 5. Whenever it shall appear from the license register kept by the clerk, or the books of the collector, that any person holding any license or permit of any kind, or privilege granted by the city, has failed to pay the amount due thereon, whether for a penalty for billiard tables (reckoning five dollars for every table per month), or other kind of penalty, license, fine, debt or liability whatever, the clerk or collector (as the case may be) shall report the fact to the mayor, whose duty it shall be to promptly revoke said license, permit or privilege.

Duties.

CHAPTER XXIV.

MARKETS.

SECTION
1. License to sell fresh meat; exception; penalty; proviso.
2. Selling unwholesome provisions; penalty.
3. Heads, shanks, skin, fat, etc.; restrictions and penalty.
4. Meats to be weighed; frauds; penalty.
5. Rent of stalls and obligations of lessees; forfeiture.
6. Mayor to issue butchers' licenses.
7. Expiration of, and charge for.
8. Cleanliness, want of; penalty.
9. Filth in streets, alleys, etc.; penalty.
10. Stalls to be cleaned; expense; penalty.
11. Market regulations; penalty.
12. Space occupied; penalty.
13. Cleanliness, want of; penalty.
14. Lease, when forfeited.
15. Market, stalls, etc., closed Sunday; penalty.
16. Butcher defined.
17. Comptroller to have charge of market; lease, and collect rents.

SECTION 1. No person shall, by himself, agent or servant, sell, or cut in pieces for the purpose of selling, any fresh meat, excepting fresh venison, poultry, fish or wild game, in any quantity in the said city, at any other place than the market-house, without having first obtained a license as hereinafter provided, under a penalty of ten dollars for each offense: *Provided*, That nothing herein shall prohibit any person from selling beef or other fresh meat by the quarter, or any greater quantity, at any time or place in the said city, the same being the produce of their own farm or raising.

License to sell fresh meat. **Exception.** **Penalty.** **Proviso.**

SEC. 2. If any person shall expose for sale in any market-house or elsewhere in said city, any emaciated, tainted or putrid meat or provisions, which from these or other causes may be deemed unwholesome, such person shall forfeit the penalty of five dollars for each offense, and the unwholesome meat or other provisions, so exposed for sale, shall, without delay, upon view of the mayor or comptroller, be seized and destroyed.

Selling unwholesome provisions. **Penalty.**

SEC. 3. No person shall, between the first day of May and the first day of November, in any year, bring into, or place, or suffer or permit to be brought into or placed, in any market or licensed stall, any untried fat, commonly called gut fat, nor at any time or season the heads, shanks or feet of any animal, unless the same be skinned or properly cleansed, nor any hides or skins of any kind, except the hides of calves, (these shall be removed from the market

Heads, shanks, fat, etc.

Penalty. as soon as taken from the veal,) under the penalty of five dollars for each offense.

Weighing. SEC. 4. All meats sold at the markets or licensed stalls, excepting shanks, offal, heads and plucks, poultry or wild game, shall be previously weighed in a scale, by weights or a beam, properly sealed; and in case any fraud shall be committed in the weight of any meat, and in case any meat, excepting as aforesaid, shall be sold without being weighed as herein directed, the person selling the same shall forfeit the sum of five dollars for each offense.

Fraud.

Penalty.

Rents, how payable. SEC. 5. All rents for stalls or rooms in the public market-house shall be paid monthly in advance, and the lessees shall observe the ordinances regulating the city market, or their leases shall be forfeited.

Butchers' license. SEC. 6. The mayor of the city of Chicago shall, from time to time, issue licenses under his hand and the seal of said city, to exercise and carry on the business of butchers, in such places other than the market, as may be designated in such licenses, but not elsewhere.

Expire. SEC. 7. All licenses, so issued, shall expire and cease on the first Monday of April after the granting thereof, unless sooner revoked, and shall be renewable by the mayor on application. For license issued as aforesaid, the sum of one dollar shall be paid on the granting of the same, and a like sum for every renewal of such license.

Charge.

Cleanliness. SEC. 8. Every butcher or other person shall keep his cellar and stall in the market, or elsewhere in the city, neat, and free from filth of all kinds; and the comptroller, or any person by him authorized, shall at all times have free access thereto, under the penalty of five dollars, to be paid by the butcher or other person who shall refuse or prevent such access.

Penalty.

Filth in ways and streets, etc. SEC. 9. No butcher or other person shall sweep or deposit any dirt or filth of any description in or upon the public passage way or ways in said market or cellars, or in or upon the market-grounds or streets adjacent to said market. Any person violating the provisions hereof, shall, upon conviction, be subject to a fine of not less than ten dollars nor more than fifty dollars.

Penalty.

Stalls to be cleaned. SEC. 10. In case the lessee, occupant, or person in charge of any stall, shall not clean the same, it shall be the duty of the comptroller, if, after giving due notice to such occupant, such stall shall not be cleansed as directed, to cause the same to be done at the expense of the lessee or occupant of such stall; and each one refusing or neglecting to pay, when required, any sum which the comptroller, in his discretion, is authorized to charge, not exceeding one dollar and fifty cents, shall forfeit a penalty of ten dollars for each offense. **Expense.** **Penalty.**

SEC. 11. The comptroller shall have power, from time to time, to establish regulations for the opening and closing of the market and stalls; and also in regard to the keeping of fowls or other birds or animals, in coops or otherwise, in the market. And if any person, who shall use or occupy any stall or place in said market, shall keep or attempt to keep therein any fowls, birds or animals in coops or otherwise, or shall open his stall or place, or attempt to keep the same open, or sell, or attempt to sell therein, contrary in either case to any regulation of the comptroller as aforesaid, after due notice thereof, to be given by posting such regulations in the market in at least four public places, he shall be subject to a fine of not less than five dollars nor exceeding twenty dollars in every case. **Market rules.** **Penalty.**

SEC. 12. No person renting or leasing a stall in the market-house, shall use or occupy, for any purpose whatever, more than three feet in front of his said stall, under the penalty of five dollars. **Space occupied.**

SEC. 13. Any person who shall kill or dress any animal in or near any market, or who shall throw or permit any brine, bones, filth, slops, offal, water or other liquid or other substances, to be thrown out of the doors or windows, or around or near any market-house or any licensed stall, except in places which may be provided for the purpose, shall be subject to a fine of not less than five dollars nor exceeding twenty dollars. **Uncleanliness.** **Penalty.**

SEC. 14. If any lessee of any stand or stall shall be twice convicted of violating any provision or ordinance of this city in relation to markets, his lease shall, on said second conviction, be adjudged to be forfeited. **Lease, when forfeit.**

SEC. 15. All public markets, and all stalls or places in this city, licensed under any ordinance of this city, shall **Sunday.**

be closed before twelve o'clock on Saturday night of each week, and so be kept and continued closed until Monday morning following. Any person who shall open any such market, or stall, or place in said city upon *Sunday*, and within the hours above named, or shall sell, offer or attempt to sell in said city, any meat, fish, vegetables or other article or thing kept in such market, place or stall, upon *Sunday*, (except by written permission of the mayor,) within said hours, shall, on conviction, pay a fine of not less than ten dollars nor more than fifty dollars.

Penalty.

Butcher defined.

SEC. 16. The word "butcher," in the sense used in this chapter, is hereby defined to mean a vendor of meats.

Comptroller to have charge of market.

SEC. 17. The comptroller, with the concurrence of the mayor, shall lease at auction or otherwise, from time to time, the stalls and stands in the public market. He shall have in charge the halls and other rooms in the market-house, leasing them at proper times for such sums as shall, by the mayor and himself, be deemed just and equitable. He shall also collect all rents for stalls, stands, halls or rooms, and deposit the amount collected immediately in the city treasury, taking a receipt therefor.

CHAPTER XXV.

MISDEMEANORS.

SECTION
1. Vagrancy; penalty.
2. Bathing out of certain limits; penalty.
3. Indecent exhibition of stud horse or bull; penalty.
4. Tippling house open on Sunday; disorderly house; penalty.
5. Keepers, inmates, supporters, landlords of brothels; penalty.
6. Indecency; lewdness; penalty.
7. Cruelty to animals; penalty.
8. Intoxication; begging; penalty.
9. Billiard table, ball alley, shooting gallery; penalty.
10. Certificate of commutation of penalties; posting; revocation.
11. Gaming devices; penalty.
12. Disorderly or gaming house; penalty.
13. Police may seize gaming devices; penalty for resisting; may enter by force.
14. Gamblers; penalty; revocation of licenses.
15. Discharging fire-arms, etc.; penalty.
16. Fast driving; penalty; duty of police and power of citizens to stop offender.

SECTION
17. Selling poison without marking; penalty.
18. Scaffolds; penalty.
19. Flying kites in frequented streets; penalty.
20. Throwing stones; penalty.
21. Same; penalty.
22. Cutting ice in river; proviso; penalty.
23. Teams left unfastened; penalty.
24. Drays, etc., left unchained; penalty.
25. Dangerous sports; penalty.
26. Vehicles to keep to the right; penalty.
27. Open cellar doors and gratings, broken sidewalks; penalty.
28. Selling impure milk; penalty.
29. Disorderly conduct; penalty.
30. Disturbing worship; penalty.
31. False alarms, collecting crowds in streets; penalty.
32. Killing birds; penalty; reform school.
33. Misdemeanors, imprisonment as well as fine.

SECTION 1. All persons who, not having visible means to maintain themselves, are without employment, idly loitering or rambling about, or staying in groceries, drinking saloons, houses of ill-fame or houses of bad repute, gambling houses, railroad depots or fire-engine houses, or who shall be found trespassing in the night time upon the private premises of others, or begging, or placing themselves in the street or other thoroughfares or public places to beg or receive alms; also, keepers, exhibitors or visitors at any gaming table, gambling house, house for fortune-telling, places for cock-fighting, or other places of device, and all persons who go about for the purpose of gaming or watch-stuffing, or who shall have in their possession any article or thing used for obtaining money under false pretenses, or who shall disturb any place where public or private schools are held, either on week day or Sabbath, or place where religious worship is held, shall be deemed vagrants, and upon conviction shall be fined in a sum not less than two dollars nor exceeding one hundred dollars, or imprisoned in the city bridewell for a term not exceeding three months, or both. **Vagrancy.** **Penalty.**

SEC. 2. No person shall swim or bathe in the river or its branches, or in the lake within one mile of the shore thereof, except as follows, to wit: at any place in the south division of the city of Chicago, between the south pier and the north line of Randolph street, and at any place south of the south line of Twenty-fifth street produced. Also, at any place in the north division, from a point two hundred feet north of the north pier and south of Indiana street, and at any place north of the south line of the Catholic cemetery. Any violation hereof shall subject the offender to a fine of not less than two dollars and not exceeding twenty dollars. **Bathing.** **Penalty.**

SEC. 3. No person or persons shall indecently exhibit any stud horse, or bull, or let any such horse to any mare or mares, or any bull to any cow or cows, within the limits of this city, unless in some inclosed place out of public view, under a penalty of not less than five dollars nor more than one hundred dollars for each and every such offense. **Indecent exhibition of stud-horse or bull.** **Penalty.**

Disorderly house.

SEC. 4. If any person shall keep open any tippling house on the Sabbath day or night, or shall keep open any bar or place where intoxicating drinks are or may be kept, or shall sell or retail any intoxicating drinks on the Sabbath day or night, or shall keep a common ill-governed or disorderly house, or suffer any person to play at cards or other game of chance on his premises, with or without betting, every such person, on conviction, shall be fined in a sum not less than ten dollars nor exceeding one hundred dollars.

Penalty.

Brothel.

SEC. 5. Any person who shall be guilty of keeping or maintaining, or be an inmate of or in any way connected with, or in any way contribute to the support of any disorderly house, or house of ill-fame, or place for the practice of fornication, or knowingly own or be interested as proprietor or landlord of any such house, shall, on conviction, be fined in a sum not exceeding one hundred dollars, and in the further sum of one hundred dollars for every twenty-four hours the said house shall be continued after the first conviction, or after any such person shall be ordered by any member of the common council or police to suppress, restrain or discontinue the same.

Penalty.

Indecency and lewdness.

SEC. 6. If any person shall appear in a public place in a state of nudity, or in a dress not belonging to his or her sex, or in an indecent or lewd dress, or shall make any indecent exposure of his or her person, or be guilty of any lewd or indecent act or behavior, or shall exhibit, sell or offer to sell any indecent or lewd book, picture or other thing, or shall exhibit or perform any indecent, immoral or lewd play or other representation, he shall be subject to a fine of not less than twenty dollars nor exceeding one hundred dollars.

Penalty.

Cruelty to animals.

SEC. 7. If any person shall inhumanly, unnecessarily or cruelly beat, injure or otherwise abuse any dumb animal, or overload any team, or expose any calves or sheep upon the streets or sidewalks, with their legs tied, he shall be subject to a fine of not less than five dollars nor exceeding twenty dollars in any case.

Penalty.

Intoxica-on

SEC. 8. If any person shall be drunk or shall be in a state of intoxication in any highway, street, thoroughfare or public place within the city; or in any private house or place, to the annoyance of any citizen or person; or shall solicit alms from any person without written permission from the mayor or some officer of the city, he shall be deemed guilty of a misdemeanor, and, on conviction, pay a fine not exceeding one hundred dollars. **Begging.** **Penalty.**

SEC. 9. No person shall have or keep for his or their gain within said city, any billiard table, pin alley, nine or ten pin alley, ball alley or shooting gallery, under a penalty of five dollars for each and every month each and every billiard table and each and every alley in any pin or ball alley and shooting gallery shall be so kept and used by him or them. And the owner or owners of any building in which any such billiard table, ball alley or shooting gallery shall be so had and kept, shall be liable to the like penalties as above prescribed. **Billiard table, ball alley, etc.** **Penalty.**

SEC. 10. Whenever any person shall pay to the collector the sum of twenty-five dollars, upon or before the first day of July of any year, for each billiard table, nine or ten or other pin alley, or shooting gallery that he shall own, keep, or in any way have in his possession, the comptroller shall give such persons a commutation certificate, stating the number of such tables, alleys or galleries, upon which such payment shall be made, which shall be in full discharge of any and all penalties or fines or other dues under any ordinance of said city, for owning, or keeping, or in any way having in possession the number of tables, alleys, or galleries, specified, until the first day of the next succeeding July: *Provided*, That any person who shall not procure a certificate of commutation for each and every such table, alley, and gallery, or who shall not voluntarily call at the collector's office and pay the full twenty-five dollars for each additional one that he may own, keep, or in any way have in his possession, by subsequent purchase or otherwise, during any fraction of a year, or in any other way attempt to deceive the city authorities, his certificate of commutation shall be revoked by the mayor, and he be liable to the same fines and penalties as if this section had not passed. All persons must elect, before the first day of July in each year, whether they will avail themselves of the provisions of **Certificate of commutation of penalties.** **Proviso.**

this section. Said certificate of commutation shall be conspicuously posted in the room of such tables, alleys, or galleries; and whenever any person shall play thereon for money, liquor, or any other article or thing, the mayor shall promptly revoke said certificate of commutation.

Posting. Revocation.

Gaming device.

SEC. 11. No person shall have, keep or permit to be used in any building or place within this city, used, occupied or controlled by such person, any E. O. table, keeno table, faro bank, shuffle board, bagatelle, playing-cards or any other instrument, device or thing used for gambling, whereon or with which money, liquor or other articles shall in any manner be played for, under a fine not exceeding fifty dollars.

Penalty.

Disorderly or gaming house.

SEC. 12. If any person or persons shall keep a disorderly or gaming house, such person or persons shall, for each and every offense, forfeit and pay a penalty of twenty-five dollars, and also the further penalty of twenty-five dollars for every forty-eight hours during which such person or persons shall continue to keep the same after the first conviction for any violation of this section.

Penalty.

Police to seize gaming device.

SEC. 13. Any member of the police of this city may seize any instrument, device or thing used for the purpose of gaming, or by, on, or with which money or other articles of value may be lost or won, and all such instruments, devices or things may be demolished or destroyed. Any person obstructing or resisting any member of the police in the performance of any act authorized by this section, shall be fined in a sum not exceeding one hundred dollars. If the owner or keeper of, or any person within any gambling house or room, any disorderly house or any house of ill-fame within this city, shall refuse to permit any member of the police to enter the same, it shall be lawful for such member or members of the police to enter or cause the same to be entered by force, by breaking the doors or otherwise, and to arrest, with or without warrant, all suspicious persons found therein.

Penalty for resisting.

May use force.

Gamblers.

SEC. 14. Any person who is a frequenter, visitor, inmate, door-keeper, solicitor, runner, agent, abettor or pimp, of or for any house, store, grocery, hall, room, or any other place where are kept any E. O. tables, keeno table, faro bank, shuffle board, bagatelle, playing cards, pigeon holes, or any other instrument, device or thing, used for gambling, whereon or with which money, liquor or other articles, shall be played for, shall, upon conviction, be fined in a sum not Penalty. less than five dollars and not exceeding one hundred dollars, or imprisoned in the bridewell for a term not more than ninety days, or both, in the discretion of the court before whom such conviction shall be had. It shall be the duty of the mayor forthwith to revoke any license given to any Revocation of license. person or persons who shall violate any provision of the fourth, ninth, eleventh, twelfth, and fourteenth sections of this chapter.

SEC. 15. No person shall fire or discharge any cannon, Fire-arms, etc. gun, fowling piece, pistol or fire arms of any description, or fire, explode or set off any squib, cracker or other thing containing powder or other combustible or explosive material, without permission from the common council or written permission from the mayor, which permission shall limit the time of such firing, and shall be subject to be revoked by the mayor or common council at any time after it has been granted. Any violation hereof shall subject the party to a Penalty. fine of not less than two dollars nor exceeding ten dollars.

SEC. 16. No person shall immoderately ride or drive Fast driving. any horse in any avenue, street, alley or lane within the limits of this city, under a penalty of not less than two Penalty. dollars nor more than ten dollars. And it is hereby made the duty of every officer, and it shall be lawful for any citizen, to stop any person who may be immoderately riding Power to stop. or driving as aforesaid.

SEC. 17. No person shall vend, give or deliver, within Poison. this city, any deadly poison, knowing the same to be such, without marking the same, in legible characters, "poison," Penalty. under a penalty of five dollars for each offense.

SEC. 18. All scaffolds erected in this city for use in the Scaffolds. erection of stone, brick or other buildings, shall be well and safely supported, and of sufficient width and properly secured so as to insure the safety of persons working thereon, or passing under or by the same, against the falling thereof, or of such materials as may be used, placed or deposited thereon. Any scaffold which may be otherwise erected shall be deemed a nuisance; and any person who shall erect or use, or cause to be erected or used, any scaffold contrary to the provisions hereof, shall be subject to a fine of not less than five dollars and not exceeding one hundred dollars, and to like fine for every day the same shall remain after notice to remove.

Penalty.

Flying kites.

SEC. 19. No person shall raise or fly a kite in any part of any street, avenue or lane of this city devoted to business, or in which there shall be much traveling, under a penalty of one dollar for every offense.

Penalty.

Throwing stones, etc.

SEC. 20. No person shall throw or cast any stone or any other missile upon or at any building, tree or other public or private property, or upon or at any person in any street, avenue, alley, lane, public place, or inclosed or uninclosed ground in this city, or aid or abet in the same, under a fine for each offense of not less than five dollars nor more than twenty-five dollars.

Penalty.

Same.

SEC. 21. No person shall throw or cast any stones or other missiles in, from or into any street, avenue, alley or lane, public place or uninclosed grounds in this city, under a penalty of five dollars for each and every offense.

Penalty.

Cutting ice.

SEC. 22. No person shall cut any ice or any holes therein in the Chicago river, and its branches, within this city, without a written permission from the mayor, and without first inclosing that portion of the ice intended to be cut with a good and sufficient fence: *Provided*, That in no case shall permission be given to cut any ice at the end of any street which extends to the river or its branches, or between the lines of any street which cross the same. Any person violating the provisions of this section shall forfeit a penalty of twenty-five dollars, and a further penalty of twenty-five dollars for every day any hole so cut in ice shall so remain uninclosed.

Proviso.

Penalty.

Teams unfastened.

SEC. 23. No person shall leave any horse, horses or other animals attached to any carriage, wagon, cart, sleigh, sled or other vehicle, in any of the streets, avenues, alleys or lanes of this city, without securely fastening such horse, horses or other animals, under a penalty, for each offense, of not less than two dollars nor less than ten dollars.

Penalty.

Chain on dray wheels.

SEC. 24. Every truckman, drayman or cartman shall

have a strong chain attached to the body of his truck, dray or cart, which shall be made fast to one of the wheels when ever the horse in such dray, truck or cart shall be left standing alone in any of the streets, avenues, alleys or lanes of this city, under a penalty of two dollars for each neglect so to do. **Penalty.**

SEC. 25. Any person who shall use any sport or exercise likely to scare horses, injure passengers, or embarrass the passage of vehicles, shall be subject to a fine not exceeding fifty dollars. **Dangerous sports.** **Penalty.**

SEC. 26. In all cases of persons meeting each other in vehicles in any highway or thoroughfare, or upon or near any bridge, each person so meeting shall in all cases turn off and go to the right side. Whoever shall violate this section shall be subject to a fine of not less than two dollars nor exceeding fifty dollars; he shall likewise be subject to the payment of all damages which may arise from collision, unless he shall be able to prove that the collision was wholly owing to the fault or misconduct of the other party. **Law of the road.** **Penalty.**

SEC. 27. Any person who shall keep or leave open any cellar door, or grating of any vault on any highway or sidewalk, or suffer the same to be left or kept open, or who shall suffer any sidewalk in front of his premises to become or continue so broken as to endanger life or limb, shall be subject to a fine of not exceeding fifty dollars in every case. **Open cellar doors, etc.** **Penalty.**

SEC. 28. No person shall sell, offer to sell or dispose of any impure, unwholesome, adulterated or diluted milk in said city, under a penalty of not less than twenty-five dollars nor more than one hundred dollars, for each offense. **Impure milk.** **Penalty.**

SEC. 29. Any person who shall make, aid, countenance or assist in making any improper noise, riot, disturbance, breach of the peace, or diversion, or shall use threatening or abusive language towards any other person tending to a breach of the peace, in the streets or elsewhere within the city, and all persons who shall collect in bodies or crowds for unlawful purposes, or for any purpose, to the annoyance or disturbance of citizens or travelers, shall be severally subject to a fine of not less than one dollar nor exceeding one hundred dollars. **Disorderly conduct.** **Penalty.**

Disturbing worship. SEC. 30. Any person who shall disquiet or disturb any congregation or assembly met for religious worship, by making a noise, or by rude and indecent behavior or profane discourse within their place of worship, or so near the same as to disturb the order and solemnity of the meeting, shall be subject to a fine of not exceeding fifty dollars. Penalty.

False alarm. SEC. 31. Any person who shall willfully give or make a false alarm of fire or watch; or who shall employ any bell-man, or use or cause to be used any bell, horn, or bugle, or other sounding instrument; or who shall employ any device, noise or performance tending in either case to the collection of persons on the streets, sidewalks or other public places, to the obstruction of the same, for any purpose whatsoever, without permission of the mayor, in writing, shall be subject to a fine not exceeding twenty-five dollars. Penalty.

Killing birds. SEC. 32. Every person who shall kill or wound, or attempt to kill or wound, by the use of fire-arms, bow and arrow, pelting with stones, or otherwise, any bird within the city limits, or shoot an arrow, or throw a stone or club, or other missile, at any bird within any private grounds, or public parks, squares or grounds, (such bird not being the property of the person so offending,) or enter upon any private inclosure or public ground belonging to the city, for the purpose of doing any act prohibited in this section, shall forfeit and pay not less than five dollars nor more than ten dollars for each offense. Penalty. Reform school. Every person who shall be convicted for a second time of any offense in this section mentioned, who is under the age of sixteen years, may, in the discretion of the court, be sentenced to the reform school.

Imprisonment. SEC. 33. In all cases arising under this chapter, punishable as misdemeanors by the laws of this State, the court or magistrate before whom conviction may be had, shall have power, in addition to the penalty or fine, to cause the offender to be imprisoned for a period not exceeding three months, in their discretion.

CHAPTER XXVI.

NEWSBOYS.

SECTION
1. License required.
2. How issued; charge for.
3. Expiration of; badges.

SECTION
4. Register of licenses.
5. Penalty for violation.

SECTION 1. No person shall sell or offer for sale any newspaper, at any place in, upon, along or through any of the streets, avenues, alleys, or other public places within the city of Chicago, without a license so to do. **License.**

SEC. 2. The mayor is hereby authorized to license under his hand, attested by the clerk and city seal, any person or persons, in his discretion, who may apply to him therefor, to peddle newspapers in the streets and other public places in said city, upon the payment of fifty cents and no other fees for each license so granted; to be paid to the collector. **How issued.** **Charge.**

SEC. 3. Every license granted under the provisions hereof, shall expire on the fifth day of January, after the date of such license, and every person so licensed, and not belonging to the "newsboys' association" of the city of Chicago, shall wear a black leather badge upon his hat or cap, with the word "licensed" and the number of his license plainly painted thereon, with white letters and figures at least one-half inch in size. And every person belonging to the "newsboys' association" of the said city, shall wear a white metal badge upon the left lappel of his coat, with the words "newsboys' association" and the number of his license plainly raised or engraved thereon, in letters and figures. **Expire.** **Badge.**

SEC. 4. It shall be the duty of the clerk to issue the licenses herein provided for, when requested so to do by the mayor, and keep a register of the name of every person so licensed, his residence or place of business, and the number of his license. **Register.**

SEC. 5. Any person who shall violate any provision of this chapter, or who shall neglect or fail to comply with the provisions hereof, shall pay a fine of not less than one dollar nor more than five dollars for each offense; and the mayor is hereby authorized to revoke any license granted under this chapter, in his discretion. **Penalty.**

CHAPTER XXVII.

NUISANCES.

SECTION
1. Keeping more than ten cattle or swine, or less number so as to be offensive; penalty.
2. Carrying on distillery, slaughtering, or rendering establishment, without permit; penalty.
3. Applications for permit; bond; license.
4. Offal, etc., how disposed of; cleanliness; penalty.
5. Permitting offal, filth, etc., to be discharged from premises, etc.; penalty.
6. Permitting same to remain on premises exceeding certain times; penalty.
7. Rendering offensive matter; penalty.
8. Suffering shops, factories, distilleries and other establishments, to become foul or offensive; penalty.

SECTION
9. Premises becoming offensive; penalty.
10. Privies offensive; penalty.
11. Cellars, vaults, drains, sinks, etc., becoming offensive; penalty.
12. Suffering swine to run at large; penalty.
13. Posting bills; penalty.
14. Duty of police to ascertain and report violations of foregoing provisions.
15. Board of police to abate nuisances.
16. Notice to owner or occupant of premises to abate nuisance; in case of neglect or refusal, to be chargeable with expense.
17. Informers to have half of fines.
18. Obstructions in river; penalty.

Keeping more than ten cattle or swine, or less, so as to be offensive.

SECTION 1. Any person or persons who shall own, keep or use any yard, pen, place or premises within the city of Chicago, in or upon which more than ten cattle or swine shall be confined or kept at any one time, and any person or persons who shall own, keep or use any yard, pen, place or premises, in or upon which a less number of cattle or swine than ten shall be so kept as to be offensive to those residing in the vicinity, or an annoyance to the public, shall be deemed the author of a nuisance, and, on conviction, shall be subject to a fine of not less than twenty-five dollars and not exceeding one hundred dollars in every case, and to a like fine for every day he or they shall neglect or refuse to abate such nuisance, when notified by the mayor or board of police to abate the same.

Penalty.

Distillery, slaughtering or rendering establishment, without permit.

SEC. 2. Any person or persons who shall carry on, occupy, or use any distillery, slaughtering establishment, or establishment for steaming or rendering lard, tallow, offal, dead animals, or other substances of like nature, within the limits of the city of Chicago, or within the distance of four miles therefrom, without permission of the common council, to be granted in the manner hereinafter provided, shall be deemed the author of a nuisance, and, on conviction, shall be subject to a fine of not less than fifty dollars nor more than one hundred dollars in every case, and to a like fine for every day he or they shall neglect or refuse to abate

Penalty.

such nuisance, when notified by the mayor or board of police to abate the same.

SEC. 3. Any person desirous of obtaining a permit, under the provisions of this chapter, shall make application therefor to the common council in writing, stating the business he is desirous of pursuing, and specifying the premises whereon the same is to be conducted. If such application shall be granted, the applicant shall thereupon be required to enter into a bond, with one or more sureties, to be approved by the mayor, in the penal sum of not less than one hundred dollars nor more than five thousand dollars, conditioned that the said applicant will faithfully comply with all the requisitions of this chapter, and such other ordinance or ordinances as may be hereafter passed by the common council upon this subject. And upon the execution and delivery of said bond, it shall be the duty of the mayor and clerk to issue a license to the applicant, under the corporate seal, which license shall continue in force for the period of one year from and after the date thereof, and no longer, and the clerk shall keep a register of all licenses which shall be issued.

Application for permit.

Bond.

License.

SEC. 4. No person who shall obtain a license for any business, employment, or purpose mentioned in the preceding sections, or who shall conduct or carry on any such business or employment within the limits of the city, or within the distance of four miles therefrom, or upon the Chicago river or either of its branches, or within one hundred rods thereof, shall allow or suffer any blood, bones, offal, still slops, or other offensive matter, to run, fall, or get into the Chicago river, or into either of the branches thereof, or any of the canals or slips connected therewith; or place, cause, or permit to be placed, or permit or suffer to remain on his premises, as aforesaid, any blood, bones, offal, filth, still slops, or other offensive matter, for a longer period than twenty-four hours at any one time, from the first day of March to the first day of November in any year, or exceeding forty-eight hours during any other part of the year; but the same shall be collected in tubs or vats, constructed as the health officer may direct, and removed within the time above prescribed, to a distance of at least forty rods from

Offal, etc.

How disposed of

said river and its branches, and from lake Michigan, and a like distance from any dwelling or public street or highway, in covered and tight boxes as the health officer may direct, and shall be then buried in the ground and covered with a layer of earth at least twelve inches in depth, so as not to become a nuisance or matter of offense. And every such person shall at all times keep his premises in a clean, healthy and inoffensive condition. Any person who shall violate any of the provisions of this section shall be subject to a fine of not less than twenty-five dollars and not exceeding one hundred dollars for each and every offense, and the license so granted to him, if any license shall have been granted, may be revoked, at the pleasure of the common council.

Cleanliness.

Penalty.

Offal, filth, etc., discharged from premises.

SEC. 5. Any distiller, tanner, brewer, butcher, pork and beef packer, soap boiler, tallow chandler, dyer, livery-stable keeper, or other person whatsoever, who shall cause or suffer any offal, manure, rubbish, filth, still slops, or any refuse animal or vegetable matter, or any foul or nauseous liquor, to be discharged out of or flow from any premises owned or occupied by him, or to be thrown into, deposited or left in the Chicago river, or either of its branches, or any of the slips or canals connected therewith, or into lake Michigan, or into any slough within the jurisdiction of the city, or in or upon any street, alley, public square, vacant lot, wharf or dock, river bank or lake shore, shall be subject to a fine of not less than twenty-five dollars and not exceeding one hundred dollars for every offense.

Penalty.

Offal, filth, etc., remaining on premises.

SEC. 6. No person shall permit or suffer any substance of the nature mentioned in the preceding section which is liable to become putrid or offensive, or injurious to the public health, to remain on any premises owned or occupied by him for a longer period than twenty-four hours at any one time, from the first day of March to the first day of November in any year, or exceeding forty-eight hours during any other part of the year, but the same shall be removed and buried within the time above designated, in the manner and according to the requisitions prescribed in like cases in the fourth section of this chapter. Any person who shall violate any provision of this section, shall be subject to a fine of not less than twenty-five dollars and not exceeding one hundred dollars for every offense, and a further penalty of twenty-five dollars for each day the same shall be allowed to remain after a conviction for the first offense. Penalty.

SEC. 7. No person shall steam, or boil, or in any way render any offal, tainted or damaged lard or tallow, or steam or render any animal substance in such a manner as to occasion any offensive smell, or which will, by undergoing such process, so taint the air as to render it unwholesome or offensive to the smell, within the limits of the city, or within the distance of two miles therefrom. Any person who shall violate any provision of this section, shall be subject, for each offense, to a fine of not less than twenty-five dollars and not exceeding one hundred dollars, in the discretion of the court. Rendering offensively. Penalty.

SEC. 8. Any owner or occupant of any tallow chandler's shop, soap factory, tannery, distillery, livery stable, cattle yard or shed, barn, packing house, slaughter house or rendering establishment, who shall suffer the same to become nauseous, foul or offensive, shall be fined in a sum not less than twenty-five dollars and not exceeding one hundred dollars in every case. Foul or offensive premises. Penalty.

SEC. 9. If any person shall own, occupy or keep any grounds or other premises in such condition as to be offensive and a nuisance to the neighborhood, he shall be subject to a fine of not less than twenty-five dollars and not exceeding one hundred dollars, and to a like fine for every day such nuisance shall continue after the first conviction. Same. Penalty.

SEC. 10. If any person shall erect or continue any privy within forty feet from any street, or the dwelling, shop or well of any other person, unless the same be furnished with a substantial vault, six feet deep, and made tight, so that the contents cannot escape therefrom, and sufficiently secured and inclosed, he shall incur a penalty of ten dollars, and a like penalty for every week he shall continue the same after the first conviction. Offensive privy. Penalty.

SEC. 11. If any person shall suffer, or permit any cellar, vault, private drain, pool, privy, sewer, or sink, upon any premises belonging to or occupied by him, to become nauseous, foul, offensive or injurious to the public health, he shall Offensive cellar, drain, etc.

Penalty. be subject to a fine of not less than five dollars and not exceeding fifty dollars in every case, and to a like fine for every day the same shall continue, after notice to remove and abate such nuisance.

Swine at large. SEC. 12. If any person, being the owner of any hog, shoat or pig, shall suffer the same to run or be at large, or be found at large, he shall be subject to a penalty of two dollars in every case. Penalty.

Posting bills. SEC. 13. Any person who shall stick or post any hand-bill, or placard of any description, upon any public or private house, store or other building, or upon any fence, without the permission of the owner or occupant of the same, shall be subject to a fine of not less than three dollars and not exceeding twenty-five dollars in every case. Penalty.

Duty of police to ascertain and report violations of foregoing. SEC. 14. For the purpose of carrying the foregoing provisions into effect, it shall be the duty of the board of police to detail a sufficient number of the police force, not less than two from each division of the city, and said force to be under control of the health officer, to make, from time to time, and as often as may be requisite, a thorough and systematic examination of the city, and to ascertain and report to the proper authority, for prosecution, all violations of this chapter, and for this purpose they shall be permitted at all times to visit or enter into or upon any building, lot or grounds, within the jurisdiction of the city, and make examination thereof.

Board of police to abate nuisances. SEC. 15. Whenever any nuisance shall be found on any premises within the city, contrary to any ordinance, the board of police are hereby authorized, in their discretion, to cause the same to be summarily abated, in such manner as they may direct.

Notice to owner or occupant to abate. SEC. 16. In all cases where a nuisance shall be found in any building, or upon any ground or other premises within the jurisdiction of the city, twenty-four hours' notice may be given in writing, signed by the board of police, or by some officer of said board, or by the general or deputy superintendent of police, or by the acting health officer, to the owner or occupant of such building or other premises, where he is known and can be found, to remove such nuisance; and in case of his neglect or refusal to abate the same in accordance with such notice, he shall be chargeable with the expenses which may be incurred in the removal thereof, to be collected by suit or otherwise, in addition to the fine or penalty. Expense in case of neglect or refusal.

SEC. 17. Any person or persons, other than members of the police force, who may hereafter give information that shall lead to the conviction of any person or persons guilty of a violation of this chapter, shall be entitled to one-half the fine imposed for such violation, to be paid when the same shall be collected, upon the certificate of the clerk of the police court, stating the person who gave such information, and the time when it was given. Informers have half the fine.

SEC. 18. Every pile, timber or stone which may have been or shall be driven, placed or laid, or projected in, along, or across the Chicago river or its branches, below low water mark or any water line which may be established by the common council, for the purposes of a wharf or otherwise, shall be deemed a nuisance. And every person who shall drive or place any pile, timber, or stone, as aforesaid, or be the owner of any premises on which the same shall be so driven, placed or erected, shall be subject to a fine of not less than twenty dollars and not exceeding one hundred dollars for every violation hereof, and to a like fine for every three days such nuisance shall continue after notice to abate the same. Obstructions in river. Penalty.

CHAPTER XXVIII.

ORDINANCES.

SECTION
1. Recording, and proof of publication.
2. When to take effect.
3. Effect of repeal or modification; saving clause.
4. Election under which to proceed, where more than one applicable to offense.
5. Not revived by repeal of repealing ordinance.
6. Rules of construction; proviso.

SECTION
7. Penalty for breach of, where none declared.
8. Powers and duties of mayor, who to exercise in his absence; construction of words "reasonable time," "reasonable notice."
9. Liability for damages resulting from breach of, besides penalty.
10. Repeal of former ordinances; saving clause.

SECTION 1. All ordinances passed by the common council shall be recorded by the clerk in the book of ordinances. The originals shall be filed in the clerk's office; Record, and proof of publication.

and due proof of the publication of all ordinances requiring publication, by the affidavit of the printer or publisher, shall be procured by the clerk and attached thereto, or written and attested upon the face of the record of such ordinances.

When to take effect.

SEC. 2. All ordinances passed by the common council, requiring publication, shall take effect from and after the due publication thereof in the corporation paper, unless therein otherwise expressly provided; ordinances not requiring publication shall take effect from their passage, unless therein otherwise expressly provided.

Effect of repeal or modification.

SEC. 3. Whenever an ordinance, or part of an ordinance, shall be repealed or modified by a subsequent ordinance, the ordinance or part of ordinance thus repealed or modified shall continue in force until the due publication of the ordinance repealing or modifying the same, when such publication shall be required to give effect thereto, unless therein otherwise expressly provided. But no suit, proceeding, right, fine or penalty, instituted, created, given, secured or accrued under any ordinance previous to its repeal, shall in anywise be affected, released or discharged, but may be prosecuted, enjoyed and recovered as fully as if such ordinance had continued in force, unless it shall be therein otherwise expressly provided.

Saving clause.

Election under which to proceed.

SEC. 4. In all cases where the same offense may be made punishable, or shall be created by different clauses or sections of the ordinances of the city, the prosecuting officer may elect under which to proceed; but not more than one recovery shall be had against the same person for the same offense.

Revival by repeal.

SEC. 5. When any ordinance repealing a former ordinance, clause or provision, shall be itself repealed, such repeal shall not be construed to revive such former ordinance, clause or provision, unless it shall be therein so expressly provided.

Construction.

SEC. 6. Whenever any words in any ordinance importing the plural number shall be used in describing or referring to any matters, parties or persons, any single matter, party or person shall be deemed to be included, although distributive words may not be used. And when any subject matter, party or person shall be referred to in any ordinance by words importing the singular number only, or the masculine gender, several matters, parties or persons, and females as well as males, and bodies corporate, shall be deemed to be included: *Provided*, That these rules of construction shall not be applied to any ordinance which shall contain any express provision excluding such construction, or where the subject matter or context of such ordinance may be repugnant thereto. **Proviso.**

SEC. 7. Whenever in any ordinance the doing of any act, or the omission to do any act or duty, is declared to be a breach thereof, and there shall be no fine or penalty declared for such breach, any person who shall be convicted of any such breach, shall be adjudged to pay a fine of not less than three dollars nor more than one hundred dollars. **Penalty where none declared.**

SEC. 8. Whenever any power shall be vested in the mayor, or he shall be required to do any act or perform any executive function, in his absence it shall be the duty of the acting mayor or presiding officer of the common council, for the time being, to exercise such power and perform such act or executive function as fully as if expressly named in the ordinance, unless it shall be therein otherwise expressly provided, or such act would be in derogation of the charter. In all cases where any ordinance shall require any act to be done in a "reasonable time," or "reasonable notice" to be given to any person, such reasonable time or notice shall be deemed to mean such time only as may be necessary in the prompt execution of such duty or compliance with such notice. **Who to act in place of mayor in his absence.** **Construction.**

SEC. 9. Whenever in any ordinance the doing of any act, or the omission to do any act or duty, is declared to be a breach thereof, and damage, loss, expense or injury to the city, or to any person, is a result or consequence of such doing or omission, compensation for such damage, loss, expense or injury may be recovered from the offender by the party aggrieved. **Damages, etc., result of breach of ordinance.**

SEC. 10. All ordinances of the city of Chicago heretofore passed in relation to the subject matter of, or inconsistent with, any of the provisions of this ordinance, be and the same are hereby severally repealed: *Provided*, That such **Repeal of former ordinances.**

Saving clause. repeal shall not affect any act done or any right accruing or accrued, or established, or any suit, action or proceeding had or commenced in any civil case before the time when said repeal shall take effect, nor any offense committed, nor any penalty or forfeiture incurred, nor any suit or prosecution pending at the time of such repeal, for any offense committed, or for the recovery of any penalty or forfeiture incurred under any of the ordinances so repealed.

CHAPTER XXIX.

PARKS AND PUBLIC GROUNDS.

1. Names.
2. Games and plays on; penalty.
3. Trespassing upon or injuring; penalty.
4. Duty of board of public works to superintend and improve.
5. Police to arrest offenders.
6. Hay on, to be cut for fire department.

Names. SECTION 1. The several public parks, squares and grounds in the city of Chicago, shall be known and designated by the names applied thereto respectively on the map of the city of Chicago published by Mr. J. Van Vechten in the year 1863, except that the park set apart from the north part of the cemetery, shall be known and designated as "Lincoln Park."

Games in. Penalty. SEC. 2. No person shall play at ball, cricket, or at any other game or play whatever, in any of the inclosed public parks or grounds in this city, under the penalty of five dollars for every offense.

Injury to. Penalty. SEC. 3. No person shall walk, stand or lie upon any part of any of the enclosed public parks or grounds laid out and appropriated for shrubbery or grass; or pull up, break down or injure any of the trees, grass, shrubbery, fences, or other fixtures or things in and about or pertaining to any inclosed public park or ground, or erect any booth or other structure therein, under a fine of not exceeding twenty dollars for every offense.

Duty of board of public works as to. SEC. 4. It shall be the duty of the board of public works to superintend all inclosed public grounds, and keep the fences thereof in repair, the walks in order, and the trees properly trimmed, and improve the same according to plans approved by the common council. They shall likewise cause printed or written copies of the second and third sections of this chapter to be posted in the said grounds or parks.

SEC. 5. Any member of the city police shall have power to arrest any person who shall not desist from any violation hereof, when directed, and cause him to be committed for examination. **Police to arrest offenders.**

SEC. 6. The fire marshal may cause any grass fit for hay, growing or grown upon any of the public parks or grounds, to be cut and cured, under the direction of the board of public works, and appropriated for the use of the teams used by the fire department. **Hay on, to be cut for fire department.**

CHAPTER XXX.

PAWNBROKERS.

1. License required; penalty.
2. Definition of pawnbroker.
3. Conditions of granting license; charge; bond; fee.
4. Expiration of licenses.
5. Register of licenses.
6. Book of pawns or pledges; how to be kept; penalty.
7. Mayor and police may inspect such book; penalty for refusal to permit.
8. Receiving pawns or pledges from minors; penalty; revocation of license.

SECTION 1. No person or persons shall carry on or conduct the business or calling of a pawnbroker, within the city of Chicago, without having first obtained a license so to do, under a penalty of not less than twenty dollars nor more than one hundred dollars for each offense. **License.** **Penalty.**

SEC. 2. Any person who loans money on deposit, or pledge of personal property, bonds, notes or other securities, or who deals in the purchasing of personal property or choses in action, on condition of selling the same back again at a stipulated pricc, is hereby defined and declared to be a pawnbroker. **Definition.**

SEC. 3. The mayor is hereby authorized to grant a pawnbroker's license to any person of good character who may apply therefor, on the following conditions: The person so applying shall first pay to the collector a sum of money in proportion to the sum of one hundred dollars per annum for the time such license shall be granted, and shall execute **License.** **Charge.**

Bond. a bond to the city of Chicago in the sum of five hundred dollars, conditioned that the said applicant will in every particular conform to the requirements of this chapter, and with the requirements or provisions of any ordinance hereafter to be passed concerning pawnbrokers, and thereupon the clerk shall issue a license in due form, under the corporate seal, signed by the mayor and countersigned by the clerk; said applicant shall, previously to the issuing Fee. of such license, pay to the clerk a fee of one dollar for such license.

Expire. SEC. 4. All such licenses issued under this chapter shall expire on the first day of April next after the time of such issuing.

Register. SEC. 5. The clerk shall keep a register of all licenses granted under this chapter, in which he shall record the name of the person licensed, the time of issuing the same, and the place of business of the person so licensed.

Book of pledges. SEC. 6. Every person so licensed as aforesaid shall keep at his place of business a substantial and well-bound book, in which he shall enter, in writing, a minute description of all personal property, bonds, notes or other securities received on deposit or purchase, as aforesaid, the time when they were so received, and particularly mentioning any prominent or descriptive marks that may be on such property, bonds, notes or other securities, together with the name and residence of the person or persons by whom they How to be kept. were left; which said book shall be kept clean and legible, and no entry therein shall be erased, obliterated or defaced, and all the entries therein shall be made with ink. Every Penalty. such licensed person failing to comply with any of the provisions of this section, shall forfeit to said city the sum of twenty-five dollars.

Mayor and police may inspect book. SEC. 7. Every person so licensed as aforesaid, shall, during the ordinary hours of business, when requested by the mayor, or any police officer of the city, submit and exhibit such book, in the sixth section provided for, to the inspection of said mayor, or police officer, and shall also exhibit any goods, personal property, bonds, notes or other securities that may be so left with said licensed person, to the inspection of said mayor, or police officer;

and every such licensed person refusing to submit said books, goods, personal property, bonds, notes or other securities as aforesaid, upon request of the mayor, or any police officer of said city, shall forfeit to the city of Chicago the sum of fifty dollars. Penalty.

SEC. 8. No person licensed as aforesaid, shall take or receive in pawn or pledge for money loaned, or shall take, receive or purchase, within the line of business of such pawnbroker, any article, property or thing of and from any minor, or any article, property or thing of and from any person, the ownership of which property, article or thing is in, or claimed by, any minor, the said pawnbroker knowing said article, property or thing to be owned or claimed by such minor. Any person violating any or either of the provisions of this section, shall, on conviction, be fined in a sum not exceeding one hundred dollars. Any person so licensed violating any of the provisions of this chapter, or of any ordinance hereafter passed, concerning pawnbrokers, shall be subject, in the discretion of the mayor, to have his license revoked. Receiving from minors. Penalty. Revocation.

CHAPTER XXXI.

PEDDLERS.

SECTION
1. Peddler defined.
2. License required; penalty.
3. License conditions; charge; bond; character; application; term; revocation; proviso as to books, fruit, etc.; fraud, imposition, etc.; penalty.

SECTION
4. This chapter not to apply to certain classes of peddlers.
5. Peddler using vehicle to have same painted, how.

SECTION 1. Every person who shall sell, or offer any goods, wares, merchandise, or other articles of value for sale, barter or exchange at any place in, upon, along or through the streets, avenues, alleys, or other public places, docks and wharves, shall be deemed a peddler. Peddler defined.

SEC. 2. It shall not be lawful for any peddler to exercise his calling within this city without a license; and any person violating this section shall be subject to a penalty of License required.

Penalty. not less than ten dollars nor more than one hundred dollars for every offense.

License. SEC. 3. The mayor is hereby authorized, in his discretion, to grant a peddler's license to any person applying in writing for the same, upon the payment of twenty-two dollars, and no other fees: *Provided*, Such person so applying shall execute to the city of Chicago a good and sufficient bond, with ample security, to be approved by the mayor, in the penal sum of three hundred dollars, conditioned for the faithful observance by him of all ordinances of the city, and for the payment of all sums of money he may become liable to pay on account of any debt, fine or penalty incurred by him at any time during the period of such license; and further, conditioned for the payment of all liabilities he may incur by reason of any deceit, fraud or misrepresentation to any person or persons with whom he may deal as such peddler: *And Provided, further*, That the mayor shall be satisfied that the person so applying is in all respects a suitable and proper person to be so licensed, and of good moral character. Every application for license shall specify the kind and aggregate value, as near as may be, of the goods, merchandise or articles desired to be peddled, and also the mode of conveyance of the same, whether by cart, trunk, hack or wagon, or otherwise; and the license issued shall also set forth such description and mode of conveyance. Such license shall be granted for one year, and shall be subject to be revoked by the mayor, in his discretion, for any improper conduct on the part of the person so licensed: *And Provided, further*, That the license to peddle books, fruit, nuts, cakes, refreshments or bread, may be granted on payment of two dollars only. Any person licensed as aforesaid, who shall be guilty of any fraud, cheat, misrepresentation or imposition while acting in such capacity, or who shall peddle any other kind of goods, merchandise or article, or use any other mode of conveyance than that specified in his license, without leave of the mayor, shall, on conviction thereof, be subject to a fine of not less than ten dollars nor more than one hundred dollars.

Charge. Bond. Character. Application. Term. Revocation. Proviso. Fraud, imposition, etc. Penalty.

Not to apply to country produce. SEC. 4. This chapter shall not be so construed as to apply to any person or persons coming into the city from the country with teams or otherwise, with any produce for market; or to any person selling any vegetables, berries, or the produce of their own farms or premises; nor shall the same be so construed as to make it a penal offense for children under the age of twelve years to peddle apples or other fruit, provided they do not occupy a stand; nor be construed to apply to the peddling of newspapers. Children peddling fruit, or newspapers.

SEC. 5. Any person who shall exercise the vocation of a peddler, by means of wagon, cart, or other vehicle, shall cause his name, together with the number of his license, to be painted on the outside of his vehicle, in letters and figures not less than one inch in length. Any violation of this section shall subject the offender to a fine of not less than five dollars and not more than fifty dollars. Peddler using vehicle, to have painted, how.

CHAPTER XXXII.

PETROLEUM, AND OTHER DANGEROUS LIQUIDS.

SECTION
1. Restrictions on storage of petroleum and other dangerous fluids.
2. Exemption from last section under certain conditions.
3. Appointment of inspector, and his duties.
4. Inspector, fees and deputies.
5. Oath of inspector and deputies, and bond of inspector.
6. Inspector and deputies not to deal, etc.
7. Account and book of inspector.
8. Frauds, evasions, etc.; penalty.

SECTION 1. It shall be unlawful for any person, persons, or corporation, to store or keep for sale within the corporate limits of the city of Chicago, any crude petroleum, gasoline, naphtha, benzine, camphene, spirit gas, burning fluid, or spirits of turpentine, exceeding a quantity of five barrels of forty-five gallons each; and it shall be unlawful to keep for sale, or on storage, any refined carbon oil, kerosene, or other products—for illuminating purposes—of coal, rock, or earth oils, excepting such refined oil as will stand a fire test of one hundred degrees of Fahrenheit, according to the method and directions of John Tagliabue; and it shall not be lawful to keep any quantity of said articles exceeding one barrel of forty-five gallons in any part of a building, excepting a cellar, the floor of which shall be five feet below the grade of the adjacent streets; and no crude petroleum, Restrictions on storage. Fire test.

On street, sidewalk, etc. gasoline, naphtha, benzine, carbon oil, camphene, spirit gas, burning fluid, or spirits of turpentine, shall be kept, or stored, in front of any building, or on any street, alley, wharf, lot or sidewalk, for a longer time than is sufficient to receive in store or in delivering the same: *Provided*, Such time shall not exceed six hours. Proviso.

Storage in fire-proof warehouse. SEC. 2. Any person, persons, or corporation, having within the city a fire-proof warehouse, detached and clear of other buildings, and at least fifty feet distant, and exclusively used for the storage of such articles as are named in this chapter, and properly ventilated for that purpose, having beneath its ground floor an open space or cellar, three feet or more in depth below the surface of the adjacent ground, on procuring the approval, in writing, of the fire marshal, may apply to the common council of this city for a permit to use said warehouse exclusively for said purpose; and if the common council, with the consent of the mayor, shall grant such permit, then while the same shall remain in force said parties using said warehouse shall not be subject to the foregoing section of this chapter. Permit.

Inspector. SEC. 3. There shall be appointed by the common council, by ballot, biennially, on the second Monday of May, or as soon thereafter as may be, an inspector of mineral oils. Said inspector shall be a suitable, qualified person, who is neither directly or indirectly interested in manufacturing, vending or selling, either as principal or agent, any of the articles mentioned in this chapter. He shall, at his own expense, provide himself with the necessary instruments and apparatus for testing the quality of said articles named in this chapter, and whose duty it shall be to examine and test the quality of all said oils and products that he shall be requested by any importer, dealer, or vendor, to examine; and if upon such testing and examination, the oils so tested and examined shall meet the requirements of this chapter, he shall brand the same with the date of examination, his name, and this device, "Approved: the fire test being ——," on each package, cask or barrel containing it; and it shall be lawful for any dealer to sell the same. But if the oil so tested shall not meet the requirements of this chapter, he shall mark upon each package, cask or barrel, his name, the Appointment. Duties. Branding.

date of examination, and this device, "Condemned, as dangerous for illuminating purposes: the fire test being ——," and it shall be unlawful for the owner thereof to offer the same for sale within the limits of this city, for illuminating purposes. **Condemned, not to be sold, etc.**

SEC. 4. The inspector provided in this chapter, may charge not to exceed six cents for inspecting or examining each package, cask or barrel, and collect the same of the party employing him. He may also, if necessary to the convenient dispatch of his duties, appoint a suitable number of deputies, for whom he shall be accountable, which deputies are empowered to perform the duties of inspector. **Fees.** **Deputies.**

SEC. 5. Every person appointed inspector or deputy inspector shall, before entering upon the duties of his office, take an oath, or affirmation, to perform the duties of his office with fidelity, and every inspector shall file a bond to the city of Chicago, with two sureties, in the sum of ten thousand dollars, conditional for the faithful performance of the duties imposed upon him, which bond shall be for the use of all parties aggrieved by the acts of such inspector. **Oath.** **Bond.**

SEC. 6. No inspector or deputy inspector, while in office, shall buy, sell, bargain, or otherwise trade in any article which they are appointed to inspect, and for any violation of this chapter he shall be liable to the forfeiture of his bond. **Dealing, etc.**

SEC. 7. Every inspector shall, within twenty-four hours after inspection of oils heretofore mentioned, return a true and accurate account thereof to the party employing him, and shall make an entry of all oils inspected, in an intelligible manner, in a book prepared for that purpose, which shall be open to inspection by all parties. **Account.** **Book.**

SEC. 8. Any person, persons or corporation who shall violate either of the provisions of this chapter, or who shall use or refill casks, barrels, or packages having the inspector's brands thereon, for the purpose of fraudulently evading the conditions of this chapter, or shall mark the inspector's device, or any marks purporting to be marks of inspection, on any cask, barrel or package of any of the articles named in this chapter, or shall offer for sale within the city any of said oil that has not been examined by said inspector or **Frauds, evasions, etc.**

Penalty. Informer. his deputy, shall be subject to a fine of not less than twenty-five dollars nor more than one hundred dollars for each offense, one-half of which shall go to the informer, and the penalties for a violation of this chapter may be recovered in any court of competent jurisdiction.

CHAPTER XXXIII.

POLICE DEPARTMENT.

SECTION
1. General duties and powers of police.
2. To enter buildings, if refused, with force, and arrest, etc.
3. Police neglecting duty; penalty.
4. Resistance to, or interference with; penalty.
5. Duty to aid police; penalty for neglect or refusal.
6. Falsely representing police, etc.; penalty.
7. Hackmen, etc., at depots, etc., to obey; penalty.
8. Mayor's police; appointment and duties.
9. May be dismissed by mayor; compensation.
10. Mayor to report appointments to police commissioners, who are to empower, etc.

Duties and powers. SECTION 1. The several members of the police force of the city of Chicago, when on duty, shall devote their time and attention to the discharge of the duties of their stations, according to the laws and ordinances of the city and the rules and regulations of the board of police; and it shall be their duty, to the best of their ability, to preserve order, peace and quiet, and enforce the laws and ordinances throughout the city. They shall have power to arrest all persons in the city found in the act of violating any law or ordinance, or aiding and abetting in any such violation, and shall arrest all persons found under suspicious circumstances, and shall take all such persons so arrested to the place designated by such rules and regulations. They shall have power and authority in the city to serve and execute warrants and other process for the apprehension and commitment of persons charged with or held for examination or trial, or taken in execution for the commission of any crime or misdemeanor, or violation of any law or ordinance of the city; and while executing or serving, or assisting in the execution or service of any such warrant or process, shall be vested with and have all the powers and authority conferred on constables at common law, and by the laws of this State.

SEC. 2. They shall have power and authority, in a peaceable manner, or if refused admittance after demand made, with force, to enter into a house, store, grocery, shop or other building whatever in the city, in which any person or persons may reasonably be expected to be for unlawful purposes, and if any person or persons shall be found therein, guilty of any crime or misdemeanor, or violation of any ordinance for the preservation of the peace and good order of the city, or who may reasonably be suspected thereof, or who shall be aiding or abetting such person or persons so found, they shall apprehend and keep in custody such person or persons as in cases of other arrests. To enter buildings, and arrest.

SEC. 3. Any member of the police force who shall neglect or refuse to perform any duty required of him by the ordinances of the city or the rules and regulations of the board of police, or who shall, in the discharge of his official duties, be guilty of any fraud, extortion, oppression, favoritism, partiality or willful wrong or injustice, shall forfeit and pay a penalty not exceeding one hundred dollars for each offense. Neglect of duty. Penalty.

SEC. 4. Whoever in the city shall resist any member of the police force in the discharge of his duty, or shall in any way interfere with, or hinder or prevent him from discharging his duty as such member, or shall offer or endeavor so to do, and whoever shall in any manner assist any person in custody of any member of the police force to escape or attempt to escape from such custody, or shall rescue or attempt to rescue any person so in custody, shall be fined not less than three dollars nor more than one hundred dollars. Resistance to. Penalty.

SEC. 5. It shall be the duty of all persons in the city, when called upon by any member of the police department, to promptly aid and assist him in the execution of his duties. Whoever shall neglect or refuse to give such aid and assistance, shall be fined not exceeding one hundred dollars; and if the person offending be a licensed hackman, cabman or drayman, or the driver of any licensed hackney coach, cab, omnibus, dray, wagon or other vehicle, the court or magistrate convicting shall be authorized to give judgment that the license for the said person or the driver of the vehicle be canceled and revoked. Citizens to aid. Penalty.

Personating.

SEC. 6. Any person who shall falsely represent any of the members of the police department of this city, or who shall, maliciously or with intent to deceive, use or imitate any of the signs, signals or devices adopted and used by the police department, or shall wear in public the uniform adopted as the police uniform, after having been removed or suspended, shall be subject to be fined not less than three dollars nor more than one hundred dollars, or be imprisoned for a term not exceeding three months, or both.

Penalty.

Hackmen, etc., to obey.

SEC. 7. Hackmen, cabmen, omnibus drivers, draymen, porters, runners and other persons, when at or about any railroad depot or station, or steamboat or canal-boat landing, or other public place in the city, shall obey the commands and directions of the police officer or officers who may be stationed or doing duty at or about such depots or stations, or landings, or other places, for the preservation of order and enforcing the ordinances. Whoever shall refuse to obey the commands and directions of a police officer as aforesaid, shall be subject to be fined not exceeding twenty dollars.

Penalty.

Mayor's police; appointment and duties.

SEC. 8. The mayor is hereby authorized and empowered to appoint not to exceed four men who are qualified by law to act as police officers, to be known as the mayor's police, whose duties shall be to look after and to prosecute any person or persons who shall vend or dispose of any article or thing of any kind whatsoever without first having obtained legal permission so to do, or who shall in any manner violate the ordinances of the said city of Chicago, and to discharge such other duties as the mayor may direct.

Tenure of office and compensation.

SEC. 9. The person or persons so appointed may be dismissed from said service by the mayor, at his discretion, and he or they shall receive the same compensation as is paid to the patrol police force, to be paid out of the contingent fund of said city.

Mayor to report, etc.

SEC. 10. It shall be the duty of the mayor to report the appointments made in accordance with the provisions of section eight, to the commissioners of the board of police, who shall legally empower the person or persons so appointed to discharge the duties of a police officer.

CHAPTER XXXIV.

PORTERS AND RUNNERS.

SECTION
1. License to porters and runners; bond; charge; expiration.
2. Employers may have license revoked and new one in lieu; no change or transfer to another house; employer liable, etc.
3. Not to act without license; badge; card.
4. Not to solicit travelers without license; proviso as to hackmen, etc.

SECTION
5. Not to act at depots, etc., except, etc.; proviso as to hackmen, etc.
6. Deceit, imposition, etc.
7. Fees.
8. Disturbance, profanity, etc.
9. Police may arrest; give directions; duty to obey.
10. Penalty for violations of this chapter.

SECTION 1. Any person of good moral character, on application to the mayor, in writing, shall be entitled to a license to act as "public porter and runner," upon his executing, for the use of the city of Chicago, a bond, with two or more good and sufficient sureties, to be approved by the mayor, in the penal sum of five hundred dollars, conditioned to observe and keep all ordinances on this subject, and upon the payment of the sum of twelve dollars per annum and no other fees: *Provided*, That all licenses issued or granted under this ordinance shall expire or be renewed on the first day of April in each and every year. License. Bond. Charge. Expire.

SEC. 2. The keeper or keepers of any hotel or public house, who shall have obtained a license for any porter or runner in his, her or their employ, may, at his, her or their option, have the same revoked, and be entitled to another for the remaining portion of the year for which such license shall originally have been granted, without additional charge or fee therefor: *Provided*, That no such license shall be changed or transferred to any other hotel or public house, without an order from the mayor or common council for that purpose first had and obtained; and each and every keeper or proprietor of any such hotel or public house shall be personally liable for each and every violation of this chapter, or any clause thereof, when committed by any porter or runner in his, her or their employ, or who shall be acting under the license granted to any such hotel or public house keeper or proprietor, or either of them, for the use of such hotel or public house. Revocation and substitution. Proviso as to transfer. Employer liable.

SEC. 3. No person shall act as public porter or runner, License.

either for himself or for any hotel or public house, or in any manner act in that capacity, or ask the patronage or custom of any traveler or other person for any public house, hotel, steamboat, canal-boat, propeller, railroad depot or station, transportation company, stage company, or line, canal or steamboat landing or dock, or other place of business, of the person or persons, company, line or corporation, by whom he shall be employed, unless he shall first obtain a license, or be furnished with one by the person or persons, company, line or corporation, for whom he is acting, according to the provisions hereof; nor unless he shall, when so acting as public porter or runner as aforesaid, wear conspicuously upon his breast a badge as follows, to wit: A brass plate, elliptical in form, with a catch or pin to attach the same to the front of the breast, upon which shall be painted or engraved in legible letters, of not less than three-eighths of an inch in length, the name of the public house, hotel railroad depot, or station, or line, boat or company, or other place for which the said porter or runner is acting, and also in legible letters, of not less than one-half of an inch in length, the word porter, or runner, as the wearer may be; and also in legible letters, not less than five-eighths of an inch in length, the number of the license of said porter or runner. The said plate shall not be less than three and one-half inches in length, nor less than two inches in width. And no person in said city shall in any manner act as runner for any public house, hotel, company, boarding house or person, unless such runner shall present to the person or persons solicited, a card plainly printed in a language understood by such person, containing the name of the person, company or place, and the business and location of the company, person or place for whom such runner may be acting, and if he be a runner for a boarding house, hotel or other place of entertainment, such card shall contain also the price of lodging, of board by the day, by the week, by the single meal, and the price of conveyance of persons and baggage to and from such boarding house, hotel or other place of entertainment, conspicuously printed on such card or bill.

Badge.

Card.

Soliciting without license.

SEC. 4. No person shall, at any railroad depot or station, steamboat, canal-boat, propeller, dock or landing, or other place in this city, ask or solicit any travelers, or other person or persons, to ride in or use any hackney coach, cab, omnibus or other vehicle, which runs for hire and for the conveyance of passengers, unless he or they shall have a license for that purpose first had and obtained: *Provided*, That nothing herein contained is intended to prevent the owner or licensed driver of any licensed hackney coach, cab or omnibus, from notifying any person that his hackney coach, cab or omnibus is licensed, and runs for hire for the conveyance of passengers. Proviso.

Runners, etc., at depots, etc.

SEC. 5. No person shall, as a runner or porter at any place on any railroad or railway grounds, or on any street adjacent thereto, ask, solicit or engage any person to repair to any tavern, hotel or public house in said city, or to any steamboat, railroad or other public conveyance, excepting such agents for other railroads, steamboats or other public conveyances as may be authorized thereto by the person having charge of the said passenger houses respectively, and persons so authorized shall, at all times when on duty, wear appropriate badges designating their employment: *Provided*, That the provisions of this section shall not apply to any licensed hackman asking or soliciting custom for his hack while wearing the badge specified in section five, of the chapter concerning Vehicles. Proviso.

Deceit, etc.

SEC. 6. No porter or runner shall at any time or place make use of any device, deceit, imposition or false representation, in relation to the charge of fare, character, custom or location of any public house or hotel, private house, street, place of business, locality or number, whatever in said city, or in relation to the time or place of the arrival or departure of any vessels, boat, stage, railroad car or train, or other conveyance, to any stranger, non-resident or citizen, or in any other manner use any deceit as to the arrival or departure of any stage, steamboat, railroad car or train, or other conveyance, or as to any locality, place, name or number, or be guilty of any misrepresentation or evil practice toward any emigrant or other person.

Fees.

SEC. 7. Public porters shall be entitled to charge, for each trunk or package which they may carry, twelve and a half cents for any distance not exceeding one-fourth of a mile, and twenty-five cents for any distance exceeding one-fourth of a mile; and no public porter shall demand or exact any greater sums than are herein permitted.

Profanity, etc.

SEC. 8. No porter or runner shall at any time or place, when engaged in his employment, make any unusual noise or disturbance, or make use of profane, obscene or boisterous language, or use any language or be guilty of any act calculated to disturb the public peace or the good order of the city, or harass, vex or disturb strangers or citizens.

Police may arrest.

SEC. 9. Any member of the police force shall have power to arrest and commit any porter or runner for examination, who shall be engaged in the commission of any act prohibited by this chapter. They shall also have power to give any directions which may be required for the preservation of the peace, or the convenience of the public at any railroad termination, steamboat or other public landings. And no person shall refuse to obey any such directions, or shall resist such officer in the discharge of any duty.

Penalty for violation.

SEC. 10. Any person who shall violate any section, or any clause or provision of any section of this chapter, or shall fail to perform any act or thing required hereby, shall, on conviction, be fined in a sum of money not less than five dollars nor more than one hundred dollars, and may be imprisoned in the bridewell for the space of ninety days at hard labor, or both, in the discretion of the court before whom such conviction shall be had; and if committed by any such licensed porter or runner herein provided for, his license may be revoked, in the discretion of the mayor.

CHAPTER XXXV.

POUNDS.

SECTION
1. Pounds to be constructed; appointment of keepers; if but one pound, provisions of this chapter to apply.
2. Cattle not to run in certain limits, nor horses nor swine in the city.
3. Penalty to owner for permitting animals to run at large.
4. Duty of keeper to impound; penalty for neglect.

SECTION
5. Power of citizens to impound; reward.
6. General duties of keeper; notice of sale, and sale.
7. Fees of keeper.
8. Application of proceeds of sales.
9. Redemption by owners of animals impounded.

SECTION
10. Person impounding or selling, not to be interested in purchase of animal sold; penalty.
11. Breaking pound, etc.; penalty.
12. Obstructing impounding; penalty.

SECTION
13. Keeper to report to comptroller; pay surplus proceeds of sales to treasurer; to keep record.
14. If proceeds deficient, suit for such deficiency.
15. Owner to have surplus proceeds, exceeding three dollars.

SECTION 1. The board of public works, when directed by the common council, shall construct in each of the divisions of the city, good and suitable pounds, to be placed under the care and direction of a pound keeper for each division, to be appointed in accordance with the provisions of section 16, of chapter 2, of the Revised Charter of 1863. Should but one pound for the whole city at any time be in use, then all the provisions of this chapter, as to pounds for, and animals at large in, each division, shall apply to such pound for, and animals at large in, the whole city. *Construction of.* *Appointment of keeper.* *If but one.*

SEC. 2. No cows, or cattle of any kind, shall be permitted to run at large within that part or portion of the city of Chicago bounded as follows: All that portion of the south division lying north of Thirty-first street, and east of Clark street, and all that portion of the south division lying north of Sixteenth street, and all that portion of the west division between Monroe street and Fulton street, and all that portion of the north division lying south of North avenue and east of Wells street, and all that portion of the north division lying south of Division street; nor shall any horse or swine be permitted to run at large within the corporate limits of the city of Chicago. *Cattle not to run in certain limits.* *Horses and swine.*

SEC. 3. Any owner or owners of any such animal or animals, who shall permit the same to run at large, contrary to the provisions of the last section, shall forfeit and pay a penalty of three dollars for each animal so permitted to run at large. *Penalty.*

SEC. 4. It shall be the duty of the pound keeper in each division, to take up and impound any such animal known to him to be running at large in his division, contrary to the provisions of section two; and for each refusal or neglect so to do, he shall forfeit and pay a penalty of ten dollars. *Duty of keeper to impound.*

SEC. 5. It shall be lawful for any person to take up any such animal running at large contrary to the provisions of section two, and take the same to the pound of that division *Power of others.*

of the city where such animal may be found. And for so doing he shall receive from the pound keeper, when collected, one-half of the penalty collected on account of such animal running at large.

Reward.

General duties of keepers.

SEC. 6. It shall be the duty of the pound keepers to receive into their pounds all animals brought there in pursuance of the provisions of the last section; to take proper care of, and provide proper sustenance for, all animals impounded; to deliver to the owners thereof all such animals as may be redeemed by such owners before sale thereof; and if such animals are not so redeemed within twenty-four hours after the same are impounded, then, forthwith (Sundays excepted), after the expiration of said twenty-four hours, to post three notices, one at the court-house, and the other two in two of the most public places in the division of the city where such animal or animals may be impounded, in substance as follows:

Notice.

POUND NOTICE.

Taken up and impounded in the Pound of the Division at (here insert location of the pound), on the day of , 18 , (here insert description of animal or animals,) which will, if not redeemed before sale, be sold at public auction to the highest bidder, for cash, at said Pound, at the hour of ten o'clock in the forenoon, on the day of , 18 .

———, *Pound Keeper.*

The day of sale fixed in such notice shall be the third day after the animal or animals therein mentioned were impounded, except when the same would fall upon a Sunday, Christmas, New Years, fourth of July, or election day, when it shall be the day after such holiday, or holidays, if two of them come together. And if said animal or animals are not redeemed, authority is hereby given to said pound keepers to sell the same in accordance with such notices.

Sale.

Fees.

SEC. 7. The pound keepers shall be entitled to the sum of fifty cents for their fees for each animal impounded, and fifty cents for providing sustenance for each animal impounded, for each day or part of day the same may be kept, and to all penalties received for all animals taken up and impounded, except so much as is paid to other persons under the provisions of section five, and to no other compensation.

Proceeds of sale.

SEC. 8. The proceeds of the sales of all animals sold

under the provisions of section six, shall be applied, first, to pay the pound keepers such sums as they may be entitled to receive for fees and sustenance, under the provisions of the last section; next, to the payment of the penalties incurred by the owner or owners of such animals; and any surplus of such proceeds shall be by the pound keepers accounted for as hereinafter provided.

SEC. 9. At any time before sale of such animal or animals, the owner or owners thereof may redeem the same by paying to the pound keepers such sums as they may be entitled to receive for fees and sustenance, under the provisions of section seven, and the penalties incurred under the provisions of section three. **Redemption.**

SEC. 10. No person shall purchase, or be interested, directly or indirectly, in the purchase of any animal taken up, impounded or sold by him under the provisions of this chapter, under a penalty of ten dollars for each animal, and, if a pound keeper, a forfeiture of his office. **Disability to purchase.** **Penalty.**

SEC. 11. If any person shall break open, or in any manner, directly or indirectly, aid or assist in, or counsel or advise, the breaking open of any city pound, such person or persons shall severally forfeit and pay the sum of twenty-five dollars. **Breaking pound.** **Penalty.**

SEC. 12. Any person who shall hinder, delay or obstruct any person or persons engaged in taking to any city pound any animal or animals liable to be impounded, shall forfeit and pay a fine of not less than five dollars and not more than fifty dollars, for each animal so being taken. **Obstructing.** **Penalty.**

SEC. 13. Each pound keeper shall render to the comptroller, at the end of each month, a full statement, on oath, of the animals by him received into his pound, of those redeemed by the owners, of those sold by him, and the amount of the sales thereof respectively, and of the moneys received by him as such pound keeper during such month; and at the same time he shall pay to the treasurer all surplus of proceeds of sales, as mentioned in section eight, and present to the comptroller, with the statement aforesaid, the treasurer's receipt therefor. He shall also keep a record in which he shall enter, from time to time as they occur, all the matters required to be shown by such statement, and **Keeper to report.** **Surplus proceeds.** **Record.**

upon which he shall take the receipts of the owners for the animals by them redeemed.

Deficiency of proceeds. SEC. 14. Whenever any animal shall be sold under the provisions of this chapter, and shall not bring enough to pay the fees, sustenance and penalty, the deficiency may be Suit. recovered by suit in the name of the city, prosecuted by the pound keeper, and when recovered, shall be disposed of as hereinbefore provided as to proceeds of sales.

Owner to have surplus proceeds. SEC. 15. When the surplus proceeds of the sale of any animal, as mentioned in section eight, shall have been paid to the treasurer and exceed three dollars, the owner of such animal, upon satisfactory evidence of his right thereto presented to the comptroller, may have a warrant on the treasurer for such excess.

CHAPTER XXXVI.

RAILROADS.

SECTION
1. Not to run at greater speed than six miles an hour in the city.
2. Not to stop on street-crossing longer than, etc.; proviso.
3. If crossing obstructed longer than, etc., how to proceed.
4. Light when running at night.
5. Obstructing streets by lumber, etc.; switch-house, etc.
6. Whistles not to be sounded in city.
7. Bell rung continually in city.
8. Sign-boards at entrance of city.

SECTION
9. Superintendents to furnish engineers and conductors with a copy of this chapter.
10. Cylinder cocks; steam escaping; proviso.
11. Flagmen; where to be stationed; duties.
12. Penalty for violations of foregoing provisions.
13. Empty cars on street-crossing; penalty.
14. Reward to informers.

Speed. SECTION 1. No locomotive engine, railroad passenger car or freight car shall be driven, propelled or run upon or along any railroad track within said city, at a greater speed than the rate of six miles per hour.

Stopping on crossing. SEC. 2. No railroad company, railroad engineer, train conductor, or other person, shall cause or allow any locomotive engine, car or cars, or train of cars, to stop in, or remain upon, any street and railroad crossing within said city, at which, by the provisions of this chapter, a flagman is ordered to be stationed and kept, for a longer period than five minutes at any one time, nor upon any other street and railroad crossing in said city for a longer period Proviso. than ten minutes: *Provided, however*, That in case a collision should take place at any or either of the crossings aforesaid, reasonable time shall be allowed to remove any obstruction that may be caused thereby.

SEC. 3. Should any street and railroad crossing in said city be and remain occupied and obstructed, in whole or in part, by any train of railroad cars for and during the period of five minutes, it shall be the duty of each and every railroad company upon whose line of road such obstruction may occur, their agents or employees, on or before the expiration of said five minutes, when from any cause the entire train cannot be propelled or removed to any one side of any street occupied and obstructed as aforesaid, to cause such cars as may be on or near said crossing to be uncoupled, and some one division of the train, as thus made, removed from off the aforesaid street and railroad crossing, in such manner as to leave said street entirely free and unobstructed, and said train, when again coupled, shall be removed forthwith from off any such crossing as aforesaid. **Crossing obstructed, how to proceed.**

SEC. 4. Every locomotive engine, railroad car or train of cars running in the night time on any railroad track in said city, shall have and keep, while so running, a brilliant and conspicuous light on the forward end of such locomotive engine, car or train of cars. **Light.**

SEC. 5. No company, corporation or person shall be allowed to deposit or place in the street, any lumber or other material, nor shall they load any car from the street with any material deposited there, nor erect or maintain any switch house, or other building, upon any street, highway, or alley within the city limits. **Obstructing streets.**

SEC. 6. No railroad company shall cause or allow the whistle of any locomotive engine to be sounded within the city, except necessary brake signals, and such as may be absolutely necessary to prevent injury to persons, and to property other than their own, and that in their possession as freight. **Whistle.**

SEC. 7. The bell of each locomotive engine shall be rung continually while running within said city. **Bell.**

SEC. 8. Each railroad company, running on any railroad within said city, shall erect at the entrance of such railroad **Sign-boards.**

within the city, a sign-board, having thereon the words, "*stop speed,*" "*ring the bell,*" legibly painted thereon, and keep the same so erected.

Copy of this chapter to engineers and conductors.

SEC. 9. Each superintendent of any railroad shall furnish each engineer and train conductor of any railroad running within the city, a certified or printed copy of this chapter, and shall moreover furnish to any officer of said city applying therefor, the name of any person in the employment of said railroad company who shall have been charged with having violated any of the provisions of this chapter.

Cylinder cocks.

SEC. 10. No railroad company shall cause or allow the cylinder cock or cocks, of any or either of their several locomotive engines, to be opened so as to permit steam to escape therefrom at any time while running upon or along any railroad track laid in any street, or when the engine is in immediate proximity to any street or railroad crossing in said city: *Provided, however*, That when such engine shall be standing at such point in said city, and for three revolutions of the driving wheel after being put in motion, the said cocks may be opened for the purpose of allowing condensed steam to escape.

Proviso.

Flagmen.

SEC. 11. All railroad companies whose track or tracks cross or intersect any of the streets in the city of Chicago east of the west line of Halsted street, approaching any bridge or bridges now erected or constructed, or which may hereafter be erected or constructed upon or across the Chicago river, or either of its branches, shall, when any such street or streets approaching any bridge or bridges, as aforesaid, are crossed or intersected by any such railroad track or tracks at any point within one mile from either end of any or either of said bridges, keep at such crossing a flagman, who shall at all times keep watch for the trains to prevent accidents, and also at all crossings of street or horse railways. In addition to keeping flagmen on bridge streets, and street railway crossings, all railroad companies whose track or tracks cross or intersect any of the following named streets at the points herein designated, to wit: On Harrison street, between Griswold and Sherman streets; on South Canal street, between Meagher and Sixteenth streets; on

Where to be stationed.

South Jefferson street, between Meagher and Sixteenth streets; on State street, near Sixteenth street; on South Clark street near Sixteenth street; on North Jefferson street, between Kinzie and Fulton streets; on the Archer road, at its intersection with Stewart avenue, and on South Clark street, at its intersection with Taylor street, and at all street crossings where they shall be required so to do by the mayor of said city, on the recommendation of the committee on railroads, shall station, keep, and maintain at all times, at their own expense, at each and every of said street and railroad crossings, a flagman, whose duty it shall be to signal persons traveling in the direction of any or either of the crossings aforesaid, and warn them of the approach of any locomotive engine, or other impending danger. **Duties.**

SEC. 12. Any railroad company or railroad corporation who shall, by themselves, their agents or employees, violate or fail to observe any of the foregoing provisions of this chapter, or any agent or employee of any railroad company or railroad corporation, or other person, who shall violate or fail to observe the same, shall, for each violation or failure to observe the same, be fined in a sum not less than twenty-five dollars nor exceeding one hundred dollars, to be recovered in any court of competent jurisdiction. **Penalty for violation.**

SEC. 13. Any railroad company or railroad corporation who shall, by themselves, their agents or employees, or any agent or employee of any railroad company or railroad corporation, who shall cause or allow any empty railroad car or cars to be detached from any locomotive engine and left to remain upon any street and railroad crossing within said city, east of the west line of Halsted street and north of the south line of Sixteenth street, for a longer period than five minutes, shall be fined in the sum of ten dollars for each and every consecutive five minutes after the lapse of the first five minutes any such empty railroad car or cars detached as aforesaid shall be so permitted to remain thereon. **Empty cars remaining on crossings.** **Penalty.**

SEC. 14. Any person or persons, excepting members of the police department, who shall make complaint to the police justices of this city or other proper authority, of the violation of any of the provisions of this chapter, by any **Reward to informers.**

railroad company or railroad corporation, whether committed by themselves, their agents or employees, and upon whose evidence a final verdict shall have been obtained in favor of said city, from any court of competent jurisdiction, before whom the case may be tried, shall be entitled to receive, in addition to the usual witness fees, one-half the fine imposed for each and every violation or failure to observe the same as aforesaid.

CHAPTER XXXVII.

SALE BY SAMPLE.

SECTION
1. License required.
2. License; expiration, and charge.

SECTION
3. Penalty for violating this chapter.

License required. SECTION 1. No person not being an actual and *bona fide* resident of the city of Chicago, having a regular place of business therein, and subject to pay a tax to the United States government as a wholesale or retail dealer in said city, shall sell by sample, without a license, or offer or contract by sample, to any person or persons within the limits of said city, any goods, wares or merchandise whatever, except agricultural products, provisions, and articles manufactured within the limits of the State of Illinois.

License. SEC. 2. The mayor of said city is hereby authorized to grant to any person a license under his hand, and attested by the clerk and the seal of said city, to sell by sample in said city, goods, wares and merchandise. Such licenses shall expire on the first day of July in each year; and any person receiving such license shall pay therefor the sum of one hundred dollars. (Expire. Charge.)

Penalty. SEC. 3. Any person who shall violate any of the provisions of this chapter, shall be fined for each violation thereof a sum not less than one hundred dollars and not more than five hundred dollars.

CHAPTER XXXVIII.

SCAVENGERS.

SECTION
1. Board of police to employ scavengers.
2. To give notice to have garbage, etc., ready for.
3. Penalty for neglect so to do.
4. Night scavengers defined; license required; bond; charge; expiration.
5. Regulations for night scavengers.

SECTION
6. Owners, etc., cleaning privies without scavenger, how and when permitted.
7. Fees of night scavenger; duty to complete work, etc.
8. Penalty for violation of this chapter.
9. Offensive privy; proceedings; penalty; expense.

SECTION 1. The board of police are hereby authorized to employ, from time to time, as many scavengers as they may deem necessary, upon such terms and with such appliances and conveyances as they may deem expedient, and to make, from time to time, such rules and regulations for the conduct of such scavengers as they may deem necessary. *Board of police to employ.*

SEC. 2. The board of police shall cause a printed notice to be left at each and every hotel, tavern, eating-house, and dwelling-house, in the city, stating that a scavenger will call for offal, garbage, swill (and, on improved streets, ashes,) at certain times mentioned in the notice, and requiring that such offal, garbage, swill, (and, on improved streets, ashes,) be ready in tight tubs, or other suitable vessels, for the scavenger when he calls for the same. A copy of the third section of this chapter shall be appended to such notice. *Notice to have garbage ready.*

SEC. 3. Any person who shall, after notice, neglect or refuse to have the offal, garbage, or swill, upon his or her premises, ready for the scavenger in the manner and at the time mentioned in said notice, shall pay a penalty of five dollars for each and every day such offal, garbage, or swill shall remain on such premises after the same has been called for by the scavenger. *Penalty for neglect.*

SEC. 4. Any person or company who shall engage in the business of removing the contents of privy vaults within the city for hire or profit, shall be deemed night scavengers within the meaning hereof. No person or company shall exercise the calling of night scavengers within the city, without first obtaining license in pursuance hereof. The mayor of said city is hereby authorized to license one or *Night scavengers defined.* *License required.*

Proviso. Bond. more night scavengers: *Provided*, The person applying therefor shall execute to the city of Chicago a bond, in the sum of five hundred dollars, with ample surety, to be approved by the mayor, conditioned, that such night scavengers shall well and truly keep and perform all and every of the provisions and restrictions of this chapter: *And Provided, further*, Such night scavenger shall pay, for the use of the city, the sum of seventeen dollars and no other fees. Such licenses shall each expire on the expiration of one year from the date thereof.

Charge.

Expire.

Regulations for night scavengers. SEC. 5. Such night scavengers, so licensed, shall each provide himself with a team and wagon, with a covered water-tight box, of the capacity of twenty-seven cubic feet, which said box, when filled, shall be deemed a load. Upon each side of said wagon-box shall be painted, in letters and figures, the name and the number of the license, and always upon the top of said box, when said wagon shall be in use, shall be kept, in a conspicuous position, a lighted lantern, with the number of the license aforesaid painted upon two of the glass sides thereof, in at least four-inch letters. It shall be the right and duty of such night scavengers, so licensed, (when requested by any owner, agent or occupant of any privy within the city,) to clean and remove the contents of the vaults thereof, and to deposit and bury the same, at least three feet below the surface of the earth, at such place or places as shall be designated by the written permit of the health officer of said city: *Provided*, No such privy vault shall be opened, nor the contents thereof disturbed or removed, between the hours of six o'clock A. M. and ten o'clock P. M. of any day, nor shall such contents be deposited or buried within the city, except upon the special permission of the board of police of said city, and in such manner and places as shall be by them directed: *And Provided, further*, That if any night scavenger shall not bury said contents as above provided, and cover the same so as to prevent any smell arising therefrom, his license shall immediately be forfeited and annulled.

Proviso.

Further proviso.

Owners, etc., cleaning privies. SEC. 6. Owners, occupants and agents of privy vaults within the city, desiring to clean and remove the contents thereof themselves, without the aid of night scavengers as aforesaid, shall not be allowed so to do except upon the written permission of the health officer of said city, and then only in such manner as he in said permit shall direct: *Provided*, Such health officer shall in no case permit any privy vault to be opened, or the contents removed, within the hours mentioned in the preceding section; nor shall he allow any deposit of such contents to be buried less than three feet deep, nor within the city, unless the board of police shall first by resolution authorize him so to do: *Provided*, No delay or refusal of such health officer to grant such permit, or of such board of police to pass such resolution, shall be an excuse or justification to any party for not cleaning any privy vault when directed so to do by the proper officers. **How and when.** **Proviso.** **Proviso.**

SEC. 7. Such night scavengers, so as aforesaid licensed, shall be allowed to charge and receive for each load so by them taken, removed and buried, a sum not exceeding five dollars: *Provided*, Such scavenger having undertaken such work shall speedily and without delay complete the same, in all cases leaving the privy in as good condition upon the vault as when undertaken by him. **Fees.** **Duty.**

SEC. 8. Any person without license as aforesaid, who shall engage in business as night scavenger, or who shall undertake to remove any contents of any privy vault within the city, without license or permit as aforesaid, shall, on conviction thereof, pay a fine of not less than ten dollars nor more than fifty dollars for each offense; and any night scavenger so as aforesaid licensed, or owner, agent or occupant so as aforesaid acting under permit as aforesaid, who shall violate any provision or section, or clause of any provision or section of this chapter, shall, on conviction thereof, pay a fine of not less than five dollars nor more than one hundred dollars, according to the nature of such violation, and shall, in the discretion of the health officer, forfeit his license. **Penalty for violation.**

SEC. 9. Whenever, in the opinion of the health officer, any privy vault shall be offensive and need cleaning, it shall be his duty to notify the owner, agent or occupant to cleanse the same within a period named in said notice; also, together with said notice, to serve a printed copy of this **Offensive privy.**

Proceedings. chapter. Unless the person so notified shall comply within the time mentioned, it shall be the duty of such officer to cause said vault to be cleaned by one or more of the night scavengers aforesaid; and such person so failing to comply Penalty. with said notice, shall, on conviction, be fined in a sum not less than twenty dollars nor more than one hundred dollars: Proviso. *Provided*, That nothing in this section contained shall discharge the owner, agent or occupant of the premises from any liability otherwise provided, to pay all the expenses of such cleaning. In case no owner or agent can be found in the city, such officer shall cause such offensive vault to be Expense. cleaned, and in either case the expenses shall be collected as in other cases of the removal or abatement of nuisances.

CHAPTER XXXIX.

SCHOOLS.

SECTION
1. Boundaries of school districts defined.
2. Terms of schools; proviso; how to be kept.
3. Board of education to control high school.
4. Free instruction in high school.
5. Qualifications for admission of pupils to high school.
6. Education in high school, of female teachers.

SECTION
7. Term of attendance for graduating.
8. Several donations and funds named, how to be used.
9. Interest thereof, regulations concerning.
10. School tax fund, when money to be paid out of.
11. Cleansing and other labor from bridewell, how to be paid for.

Districts. SECTION 1. The city of Chicago is hereby laid off and divided into school districts, as follows, to wit:

Dearborn School. That portion of the south division situated north of Jackson street.

Jones School. That portion of the south division situated between Jackson street on the north, and Peck court and Polk street on the south.

Scammon School. That portion of the west division commencing on Fulton street at the river, thence following Fulton street to Green, Green street to Adams, Adams street to the river, and bounded on the east by the river.

Kinzie School. That portion of the north division bounded on the west by the river, on the south by the river to Dearborn street, thence following Dearborn street to Ohio, Ohio street to Clark, Clark street to Huron, Huron street to

Wells, Wells street to Chicago avenue, and Chicago avenue to the river.

Franklin School. That portion of the north division bounded on the west by the river from Haines street to Chicago avenue, thence following Chicago avenue to Wells street, Wells street to Oak, Oak street to Clark, Clark street to Elm, Elm street to the lake, following the lake to Schiller street, Schiller street to Larrabee, Larrabee street to Division, Division street to Crosby, Crosby street to Haines, and Haines street to the river.

Washington School. That portion of the west division beginning on Fulton street at the river, thence following Fulton street to Ann, Ann street to Kinzie, Kinzie street to Noble, Noble street to Chicago avenue, Chicago avenue to Milwaukee avenue, Milwaukee avenue to Elston street, Elston street to the river, and the river to the place of beginning.

Moseley School. That portion of the south division situated between Eighteenth street and Thirty-first street, and east of Dyer avenue.

Brown School. That portion of the west division bounded on the west by the city limits from Taylor street to Kinzie street, thence following Kinzie street to Ann, Ann street to Fulton, Fulton street to May, May street to Randolph, Randolph street to Ann, Ann street to Madison, Madison street to Loomis, Loomis street to Taylor, and Taylor street to the city limits.

Foster School. That portion of the west division bounded on the east and south by the river, on the west by the city limits from the river to Taylor street, thence following Taylor street to Blue Island avenue, Blue Island avenue to Polk street, and Polk street to the river.

Ogden School. That portion of the north division bounded on the east by the lake, on the south by the river from the lake to Dearborn street, thence following Dearborn street to Ohio, Ohio street to Clark, Clark street to Huron, Huron street to Wells, Wells street to Oak, Oak street to Clark, Clark street to Elm, and Elm street to the lake.

Newberry School. That portion of the north and west divisions bounded on the east by the lake from Schiller street to the city limits, on the north by the city limits from the lake to Wheeling avenue, thence following Wheeling avenue to North avenue, North avenue to Elston street, Elston street to Hine street, Hine street to the river, the river to Haines street, Haines street to Crosby, Crosby street to Division, Division street to Larrabee, Larrabee street to Schiller, and Schiller street to the lake.

School No. 12. That portion of the west division bounded on the east by the river from Elston street to North avenue, thence following North avenue to the city limits, on the west by the city limits from North avenue to Kinzie street, thence following Kinzie street to Noble, Noble street to Chicago avenue, Chicago avenue to Milwaukee avenue, Milwaukee avenue to Elston street, and Elston street to the river.

Skinner School. That portion of the west division bounded on the east by the river from Polk street to Adams, thence following Adams street to Green, Green street to Fulton, Fulton street to May, May street to Randolph, Randolph street to Ann, Ann street to Madison, Madison street to Loomis, Loomis street to Taylor, Taylor street to Blue Island avenue, Blue Island avenue to Polk street, and Polk street to the river.

Haven School. All that portion of the south division situated between Peck court and Polk street on the north, and Eighteenth street on the south.

South Chicago School. All that portion of the south division lying south of Thirty-first street, and east of Dyer avenue.

Bridgeport School. Bounded on the north by the river from the city limits to Dyer avenue, thence following Dyer avenue south to the city limits, and on the south and west by the city limits.

Holstein School. All that portion of the west division lying north of North avenue, and west of Wheeling avenue.

Terms. SEC. 2. The terms of the district schools shall commence on the first Monday of September, the second day of January, and the Monday after the first Friday of May, and close on the twenty-fourth day of December, two weeks before the first Friday of May, and on the first Friday of

July: *Provided*, That when the second day of January occurs later than Wednesday, then the schools shall not commence till the following Monday, and when the fourth day of July occurs later than Wednesday, the schools shall close on the third day of July. The schools shall be continued five days in each week, at and during such hours, both forenoon and afternoon, as the board of education shall direct.

Proviso.

How kept.

SEC. 3. The board of education shall have the same control of the high school established for the improvement of the system of public schools now existing in this city, that it has of the other public schools; and it shall be the duty of the board to employ a principal and such other teachers as they may deem necessary and expedient, and prescribe rules for the discipline and instruction of the school, what studies shall be pursued, and what books and apparatus shall be used.

Board of education control high school.

SEC. 4. Free instruction shall be given to all pupils who may attend said high school, subject to the rules and regulations prescribed by the board of education.

Free instruction.

SEC. 5. Pupils shall not be admitted to the general department of said high school until they are thirteen years of age, nor to the normal department until sixteen years of age, and shall have sustained an examination upon those studies pursued in the district schools, to the approval of the superintendent of public schools and a committee to be appointed by the board of education.

Qualifications of pupils.

SEC. 6. There shall be a department in the high school expressly for the qualification of female teachers, which shall be styled the "normal department." Graduates of this department shall have preference, other things being equal, in the appointment of teachers for the district schools.

Education of teachers.

SEC. 7. The term of attendance upon the high school necessary for graduation shall be, in the normal department, two years; general and classical department, four years.

Term for graduating.

SEC. 8. The donation of one thousand dollars, and the bequest of ten thousand dollars, made by Flavel Moseley, accepted and denominated "The Moseley Public School Fund;" and the donation of one thousand dollars made by John H. Foster, accepted and denominated "The Foster

Donations.

Various funds named. Medal Fund;" and the donation of one thousand dollars made by William Jones, accepted and denominated "The Jones Fund for the benefit of the Jones School;" and the donation of one thousand dollars made by Walter L. Newberry, accepted and denominated "The Newberry Fund for the benefit of the Newberry School;" together with any donations that have been or may be made thereto, shall constitute a part of the school fund of the city, and shall be loaned upon the same terms and at the same rate of interest as other school funds are loaned: *Provided*, That a separate account shall be kept with said funds, and disbursed according to the provisions established by said donors respectively, under the direction of the board of education, upon whose order only the school agent shall be authorized to pay out said funds.

How used.

Proviso.

Interest, how used. SEC. 9. In case any part of the interest arising from the loan of said funds be unexpended at the close of any municipal year, the same may be added to the principal, or expended in the purchase of books for the libraries of the public schools, and philosophical and mathematical apparatus for the use of such schools, unless contrary to the provisions established by the donors, in the discretion of said board of education, and no other appropriation of said funds shall ever be made, except by order of the common council and board of education, and with the written consent of the donor or donors, or their legal representatives, which consent shall be placed upon file in the clerk's office.

School tax fund, money out of. SEC. 10. The comptroller shall pay no money out of the school tax fund, for improvements or repairs to any school premises, unless such improvements or repairs were previously ordered by him upon the certificate of the board of education, that such improvements or repairs were necessary; nor unless the board of education shall subsequently approve the bills. Nor shall he pay out of that fund any money for supplies of any kind, unless he shall have purchased them subsequent to a certificate of the board, that such supplies were necessary, nor unless the board shall approve of the bills after his purchase.

Labor from bridewell. SEC. 11. Such labor as may be required in cleansing school-houses, or for other purposes for the public schools, as can be supplied from the bridewell, shall be so supplied, and paid for out of the school tax fund, to the credit of the bridewell, at a reasonable price to be fixed by the mayor, or in default of his so doing, by the comptroller. Payment for.

CHAPTER XL.

SEAL.

SECTION 1. City seal established and described.

SECTION 1. The seal heretofore provided and used by and for the city of Chicago—(the impression on which is a representation of a shield, with a sheaf of wheat in the centre; a ship in full sail on the right; a sleeping infant on the top; an Indian with bow and arrow on the left; and with the motto, "*Urbs in Horto*," at the bottom of the shield; with the inscription, "*City of Chicago: Incorporated* 4*th March*, 1837," around the outer edge of said seal; which seal, represented as aforesaid, is hereunto annexed)—shall be, and is hereby established and declared to have been and now to be the seal of the city of Chicago. Description.

CHAPTER XLI.

SEWERS AND DRAINS.

SECTION
1. Notices of laying pipe, sewer or drain, or of same being exposed to injury; liability for damages.
2. Uncovering, etc., sewers, etc., without consent of board of public works; penalty.
3. Connecting, etc., with, without permit; penalty.
4. Laying, etc., not being licensed; penalty.

SECTION
5. Drains, etc., to conform to orders of board; penalty.
6. Depositing substances in sewers, etc.; penalty.
7. Board of public works, and agents, access to premises; penalty for refusing.
8. Injuring sewers, etc.; penalty.

Notice of laying pipe, sewer, or drain.

SECTION 1. The board of public works and the Chicago gas light and coke company, as to the south and north divisions of the city of Chicago, and the board of public works and the People's gas light and coke company, as to the west division of the city of Chicago, shall not lay down any pipes, sewer or drain in any of the streets, alleys, lanes or public ways of this city without giving to each other written notice of at least ten days, prior to the commencement of such work, of their intention to lay down such pipe, sewer or drain, together with either an accurate plan or clear description of the same; and it shall be the duty of the parties receiving such notice to acknowledge the same in writing forthwith. In case any damages or expense shall be caused in consequence of a default or neglect to give such notice, such damage or expense shall be paid by the party so in default. In all cases of repairs or alterations by either of the said parties, by which repairs or alterations any pipe, sewer or drain belonging to or under the charge or supervision of either of said parties, shall be uncovered, undermined, or in any way exposed to injury, the party making such repairs or alterations shall give immediate notice of the same to the party in charge of such pipe, sewer or drain, as may be affected thereby; and any party failing to give such notice, shall be liable for all injuries, damages and repairs resulting from such want of notice.

Damages.

Notice of pipe, sewer or drain being exposed.

Damages.

Uncovering sewers without consent.

SEC. 2. Any person who shall uncover, excavate under or around the brick or pipe sewers laid in this city, for any purpose whatever, without the written consent of said board, shall be subject to a fine of not less than ten dollars and not exceeding fifty dollars; the person or persons by whom the work is done, and their employers, shall be deemed guilty of a violation of this section. Penalty.

Connecting with sewers without permit.

SEC. 3. Any person who shall make any connection with or opening into the brick or pipe sewers laid in this city, without having first obtained a written permit in each case from the said board, shall be subject to a fine of not less than ten dollars and not exceeding fifty dollars, which fine shall be recoverable against the owner of the property in which such drain is made, or against the person or persons making the same or causing the same to be made, or their employers. Penalty.

Laying, etc., drains, etc., without license.

SEC. 4. Any person who shall lay, alter or disturb any part of a house drain or drains, catch-basin or strainer of said drain or drains, cess-pool or water closet, connected with any brick or pipe sewer belonging to said city, without being duly licensed to perform the same by said board, shall be subject to a fine of not less than ten dollars and not exceeding fifty dollars for each offense, which shall be recoverable against the person or persons performing the work, or their employers. Penalty.

Drains, etc., to conform to orders of board.

SEC. 5. It shall be the duty of any person or persons constructing or using any private drain, sewer, cess-pool, water closet pipe, or other pipe connecting with or emptying into any brick or pipe drain or sewer belonging to said city, to construct and use the same strictly in conformity with the orders and directions of the said board, which orders and directions shall be given in writing for such purpose; and any person who shall construct or use, or cause to be constructed or used, any such drain, sewer, cess-pool or water closet pipe in a different manner from that so ordered and directed by said board, or in violation of the orders of said board, shall be subject to a fine not exceeding fifty dollars, which shall be recoverable against the person or persons so constructing or using the said sewer, drain or pipe, or their employers, and the owner of the lot or lots, or premises, in which said work is constructed or used, shall be deemed and considered as authorizing such construction or use, and liable to such penalty. Penalty.

Obstructing.

SEC. 6. Any owner or occupant of premises who shall

deposit or cause to be deposited any substance, such as garbage, grease, rags, sand, earth, or such other substances as said board may find it necessary to exclude in any of said sewers, pipes, or house drains, gullies or catch-basins connected with said sewers, or allow any such substance to flow into the same, in such manner as to obstruct or tend to obstruct the same, shall be liable to a penalty of not less than five dollars and not exceeding fifty dollars for each offense, and shall be liable for all expenses incurred on account of removing said obstructions.

Penalty.

Board, etc., access to premises.

SEC. 7. The said board and their authorized agents shall have free and unobstructed access to any part of the premises where house drains, cess-pools, or water closets, connected with or draining into said sewers, are laid, for the purpose of examining the construction, condition and usage of the same, and making necessary alterations or repairs, at any time of the day between the hours of seven o'clock A. M. and six o'clock P. M.; and any owner, occupant or other person refusing to allow any officer or agent of said board access to any premises for such purposes, shall be liable to a fine of not less than five dollars nor exceeding fifty dollars.

Penalty.

Injuring sewers, etc.

SEC. 8. Any person who shall willfully or maliciously damage, injure or obstruct any sewer or house drain, cess-pool or water closet pipe, laid or constructed under the direction of the said board, shall be liable to a penalty of not less than ten dollars nor exceeding one hundred dollars, and to imprisonment not exceeding ninety days, and to pay all expenses incurred on account of repairs and damages arising from the same.

Penalty.

CHAPTER XLII.

SHOWS.

SECTION
1. License required; proviso.
2. How obtained.
3. What to contain; subject to all ordinances; good order to be kept.
4. Penalty for violating foregoing provisions.
5. Proviso against gaming, etc.; proceeding in case of breach; penalty for gaming, etc.
6. No concerts or exhibitions in, or through saloons or groceries; penalty.

SECTION 1. It shall not be lawful for any person or persons to own, conduct or manage, for gain, within the city, any theater, circus, caravan or other exhibition, show or amusement; or exhibit any natural or artificial curiosities, or panoramic or other show or device of any kind; or give any concert or musical entertainment, without a license: *Provided*, That, for musical parties or concerts, and exhibitions of paintings or statuary, given or made by citizens of this city, no license shall be required. **License required.** **Proviso.**

SEC. 2. Licenses shall be granted by the common council or by the mayor, as hereinafter provided, upon application therefor under the provisions hereof, for any of the purposes aforesaid, upon the payment into the treasury of such sum of money as the common council shall determine in each particular case: *Provided*, That if a meeting of the common council shall not intervene between the time of application for a license and the time of performance or exhibition, in that case the mayor is hereby authorized to determine the sum of money to be paid therefor; but not less than five dollars shall be fixed in any case, nor shall any license so granted continue in force beyond the next session of the common council. **How obtained.**

SEC. 3. All licenses issued under the provisions hereof shall specify the object and length of time for which the same shall have been respectively granted. The clerk shall register every license so issued, in the license register. Licenses granted under the provisions hereof, shall at all times be subject to the ordinances of the city existing when issued, or subsequently passed. It shall be the duty of the person licensed to keep good order about his place of exhibition or amusement, and for that purpose to keep at his own expense a sufficient police force. **Requisites of.** **Subject to ordinances.** **Good order.**

SEC. 4. If any person shall violate, or aid or assist in the violation of any of the foregoing provisions, or neglect or refuse to conform thereto, he shall be subject to a fine of not less than thirty dollars and not exceeding one hundred dollars, for every such violation; and to a revocation of his license, at the pleasure of the council. **Penalty for violation.**

SEC. 5. All licenses granted by the mayor or common council of the city of Chicago, for exhibitions, musical enter- **Proviso against gaming, etc.**

tainments, circuses, theatrical performances, panoramas, and all other shows and exhibitions where license is required, shall contain a proviso that no gaming, raffle, lottery or chance gift distribution of money or articles of value shall be connected therewith or allowed by the person obtaining said license, or in anywise permitted or held out as an inducement to visitors; and when any person or persons shall be charged by a credible person with having violated the provision of his or her license, as aforesaid, the mayor of the city is directed to give the parties accused reasonable notice thereof, and inquire into the truth of said charge; and if the accusation be sustained, he shall declare the license of said person or persons forfeited, and revoke the same. And any person or persons, whether licensed or unlicensed, getting up, carrying on, or permitting in any place occupied by them, any gambling, raffle, lottery or chance gift distribution, shall, on conviction, be fined not less than fifty dollars nor more than one hundred dollars.

Proceedings for breach.

Penalty for gaming, etc.

No concerts, etc., in or through saloon, etc.

SEC. 6. No person or persons shall be allowed to give concerts and exhibitions of any kind, in any licensed saloon or grocery, or in any place the entrance of which shall be through a saloon or grocery, within the city of Chicago, and any person or persons violating the provisions of this section, shall be fined in a sum not less than five dollars nor exceeding fifty dollars, and shall have his or her license revoked, in the discretion of the mayor.

Penalty.

CHAPTER XLIII.

SIDEWALKS.

SECTION

1. To be constructed to satisfaction of board of public works; width; curbing.
2. To be built according to grade; penalty.
3. Neglect to repair sidewalk or drain after notice; penalty.
4. Encroachments upon; penalty.
5. Posts upon; penalty; how to erect hitching posts.
6. How to erect awnings; penalty.
7. How may occupy with goods, etc.; not on Sunday; proviso; penalty.
8. Same; penalty; proviso; further proviso.
9. Auctions upon; penalty.
10. Fastening horses so as to obstruct; penalty.
11. Crossing with horses, etc.; penalty.
12. Obstructing cross-walks; penalty.
13. Cleaning snow and ice from; penalty.
14. Board of public works to remove obstructions, etc.; expenses; penalty for interference.
15. Curbing to be supported; raised to grade with street.

SECTION 1. All sidewalks which may be ordered by the common council, shall be constructed under the superintendence, and to the satisfaction, of the board of public works; and shall be of the width herein specified, unless a different width shall be specified in the order, to wit: On streets eighty feet and upwards in width, sixteen feet; on streets sixty-six feet, and under eighty feet in width, fourteen feet; on streets fifty feet, and under sixty-six feet in width, twelve feet; and on streets less than fifty feet in width, nine feet. When built of full width, a substantial curbing of stone or white oak plank, not less than three inches in thickness, well tied in, shall be laid on the outer edge of the sidewalk. How constructed. Width of curbing.

SEC. 2. The grade for sidewalks shall be given in the several divisions, by the board of public works, until a permanent grade shall be established by the common council. If any person shall build or assist in building any sidewalk, where no grade has been established, without first obtaining a grade therefor from the board of public works, or contrary to any grade which may be obtained from said board, or shall build or assist in building any sidewalk contrary to any grade which may be established by the common council, or contrary to any of the provisions of this chapter, he shall, in either case, be subject to a penalty of ten dollars for every offense, and to a like penalty for every day he shall fail to remove or reconstruct the same, after notice by the board of public works to move or re construct the same. Built according to grade. Penalty.

SEC. 3. Whenever the owner or occupant of real estate in said city shall be required and notified by the board of public works, pursuant to the provisions of section twenty-eight (28) of chapter seven (7) of the Revised Charter of 1863, to repair any sidewalk, or to repair or cleanse any private drain in front of, adjacent to, or upon any premises owned or occupied by him, it shall be the duty of such owner or occupant to cause the said improvement to be made in the manner and within the time prescribed by said board. If any such owner or occupant shall neglect or refuse to comply with any such requirement, he shall be Notice to repair. Penalty.

subject to a penalty of not less than one dollar nor more than ten dollars for each day's neglect.

Encroachments.

SEC. 4. No porch, gallery, stoop, steps, cellar door, stair railing or platform, erected or to be erected within the city, shall be allowed to extend into or upon any sidewalk, where the street is less than eighty feet in width, more than four feet, nor more than five feet where the street is eighty feet and upwards in width. No bow window or other window shall extend into any sidewalk more than fourteen inches, nor shall any cellar door rise or project above the surface of the sidewalk more than one inch at the outer side, nor more than three inches near the store or other building, nor shall the hinges thereof, or any other thing connected therewith, project or rise above the door; nor shall any staple, lock or other fastening be placed on the upper side thereof; under a penalty of five dollars for each offense, to every person violating any provision of this section, and a like penalty for every day such violation shall continue after the lapse of three days after notice from the board of public works to remove the same.

Penalty.

Posts.

SEC. 5. No sign or other post, except awning posts, as hereinafter provided, shall be erected or placed, or if heretofore erected or placed, shall be permitted to remain in or upon any sidewalk or street, or other public way, under a penalty of five dollars, and a like penalty for every day such post shall be allowed to remain after notice to the owner or occupant of the premises, from the board of public works, to remove the same. But nothing herein contained shall prevent the erection of one, and not to exceed two, posts in front of each building for the purpose of hitching horses. Every such post so erected shall, if of wood, be not less than four inches in diameter, and not to exceed four feet in height, and placed on a line within the outer edge or curb of the sidewalk.

Penalty.

How to erect hitching posts.

How to erect awnings.

SEC. 6. All awnings in such portions of the streets of the city of Chicago as are, or hereafter may be, lighted by public lamps, shall be covered with cloth, leather or other light and pliable substance, and securely attached to the building, and properly supported, without posts, by iron or other metallic fastenings and supports, and shall be elevated at least eight feet at the lowest part thereof, above the top of the sidewalk, and shall not project over the sidewalk to exceed three-fourths of the width thereof, so as to leave the sidewalk wholly unobstructed thereby; and no such awning shall be erected or repaired, either wholly or in part, of wood. All other awnings shall be elevated, in the lowest part thereof, at least eight feet above the top of the sidewalk, and may be supported by a rail placed on posts erected on the outer edge of the sidewalk. Any person who shall erect any awning contrary to the provisions hereof, or refuse or neglect forthwith to remove any awning or awning posts, heretofore or hereafter erected, contrary to the provisions hereof, shall be subject to a penalty of five dollars for every offense, and to a further penalty of five dollars for every day he shall fail to comply with a notice, after a lapse of three days from the service thereof, from the board of public works, to remove the same.

Penalty.

SEC. 7. No clothing, goods, merchandise, wares, signs, boxes, or other article or thing, shall be placed in front of any store, shop or other place in said city, on or above the sidewalk, or in or upon any alley, so as to occupy more than three feet next to the buildings or premises on such sidewalk or alley, or of the space above the sidewalk or alley, and such articles or things as may be placed on the sidewalk shall not be more than three feet high above the top of the sidewalk, and the articles or things that may be hung out or placed above the sidewalk shall be so placed or hung that the lowest part of such articles or things shall be at least seven feet and six inches above the top of the sidewalk, and shall not swing more than three feet from the building. No such article or thing shall be permitted to remain on any sidewalk or alley after ten o'clock at night, or on Sunday; nor shall any owner or occupant of any lot or premises lease the space aforesaid, or permit or allow the same to be used or occupied, except for his or their own business; nor shall said space be used for selling any article or thing whatever: *Provided*, That the occupants of buildings, on streets where the sidewalks are sixteen feet or more in width, be permitted to occupy five feet next the line of building, and on streets where the sidewalks are

How may be occupied with goods, etc.

Night and Sunday.

Proviso.

twelve feet and less than sixteen feet in width, such occupants be permitted to occupy four feet next the line of building, at all times, for the display or storage of goods, so placed as to be not more than five feet above the level of the sidewalk. Any person violating the provisions of this section shall suffer a penalty of five dollars for each offense, and a like penalty of five dollars for every forty-eight hours the same shall remain, after being requested to remove the same by any city officer.

Penalty.

Same. SEC. 8. No person or persons receiving or delivering goods, wares or merchandise, in said city, shall place or keep upon, or suffer to be placed or kept upon any sidewalk in said city, any goods, wares or merchandise which he or they may be receiving or delivering, without leaving a passage way clear upon such sidewalk where such goods may be, of six feet wide, for the use of foot passengers; and no person or persons receiving or delivering such goods shall suffer the same to be or remain on such sidewalk (subject, nevertheless, to the foregoing restrictions,) for a longer period than twenty-four hours; and any person or persons violating any of the provisions of this section, shall forfeit and pay to said city a sum of not less than three dollars nor more than ten dollars, and shall be subject to a like penalty for each hour the said goods, or any part thereof, shall remain as aforesaid, after notice to remove the same: *Provided*, That the board of public works is hereby authorized to grant permits to owners of manufacturing establishments, to occupy the outer edge of the sidewalk and space over the gutter fronting their premises, for the placing thereon such articles and things as may be necessary in their business: *Provided*, There shall always be a space of at least eight feet wide, left free and clear along the centre of such sidewalk, and that such permit shall terminate absolutely upon notice from the board of public works or common council.

Penalty.

Proviso.

Proviso.

Auctions upon. SEC. 9. Any person or persons, whether licensed as an auctioneer or not, who shall sell or attempt to sell, or shall cry for sale, at public auction in the city of Chicago, any goods, chattels or personal property whatever, to any person or persons, upon the sidewalks or streets within the said city, so as to collect a crowd of people upon the said sidewalks and streets, whereby the free passage thereof of any person or persons is prevented or hindered, shall be deemed guilty of a nuisance, and of obstructing the said sidewalks or streets, and shall be severally subject to a fine of ten dollars. Penalty.

SEC. 10. No person shall at any time fasten any horse or horses, in such a way that the horse, vehicle, reins or lines shall be an obstacle to the free use of the sidewalk, under a penalty of one dollar for each offense, and the person in whose possession or use such horse or horses shall then be, shall be deemed the offender, unless he can prove the contrary to the satisfaction of the magistrate before whom he shall be prosecuted. Fastening horses. Penalty.

SEC. 11. No person or persons shall push or draw back any horse, wagon, cart or other vehicle, over any sidewalk, or use, ride or drive any horse, wagon, sled or sleigh thereon, unless it be in crossing the same to go into a yard or lot, where no other suitable crossing or means of access is provided, under the penalty of not less than one dollar nor more than ten dollars for each offense. Crossing with horses, etc. Penalty.

SEC. 12. All cross-walks in the city shall be kept and reserved free from any sleighs, wagons, carts or carriages, and horses or other animals being placed or suffered to stand thereon, except so far as may be necessary in crossing the same; and the owner or driver of any sleigh, wagon, cart or other carriage, or horse or other animal, offending herein, shall forfeit and pay a penalty of three dollars. Obstructing crosswalks. Penalty.

SEC. 13. The occupant, or owner if there be no occupant, of each and every tenement, building or lot, in the city of Chicago, fronting upon any street the sidewalk of which shall be of plank, stone or brick, shall clear the sidewalk in front of such tenement, building or lot, of snow and ice, by nine o'clock in the forenoon of each day, and keep the same clear of such snow and ice, under a penalty of two dollars for a failure so to do, and the like penalty of two dollars for every twelve hours such sidewalk shall remain incumbered with snow or ice, after notice thereof to such occupant or owner from or by any officer of said city. Clearing from snow and ice. Penalty.

Board of public works to remove obstructions.

SEC. 14. The board of public works is authorized to cause any obstruction, encroachment, article or thing, which may be in violation of the provisions of this chapter, to be removed within a reasonable time after notice served upon the owner, agent or person in possession of the premises where such violation occurs, or in case the owner, agent or person in possession cannot be found, then by posting such notice upon the premises or sidewalk in front thereof, and the owner, agent or party causing such violation shall pay all expenses and costs of such removal, in addition to the penalties aforesaid. And any person who shall wrongfully interfere with such removal, shall suffer a penalty of not less than ten dollars nor more than one hundred dollars, and may be imprisoned in the bridewell not exceeding thirty days, in the discretion of the court or magistrate before whom such person may be convicted.

Expenses.

Penalty for interference.

Curbing to be supported.

SEC. 15. Where any streets are filled to the established grade, or filled to a grade requiring curbstone to be set on the line of sidewalk, it shall be the duty of the board of public works or person in charge of such filling, to deposit sufficient earth or other material on the sidewalk of such streets, to back up and permanently hold the curbstone; and they may use and obstruct the sidewalks to any extent necessary for that purpose. And where any street or portion of street shall be raised to the grade established by the common council, and curbed, or area walls constructed on the curb line of such street or portion of street, the report, order or resolution, directing such improvement, shall be deemed to embrace and include the raising of the sidewalk to such established grade, whether expressed in such report, order or resolution, or not.

Raising to grade.

CHAPTER XLIV.

SPIRITUOUS LIQUORS.

SECTION
1. License; bond and condition; charge; expiration.
2. Transfer; register; date; take effect only when issued or transferred.
SECTION
3. Revocation; posting; penalty for not posting license, or posting counterfeit.
4. Penalty for dealing without license; proviso as to druggists.

SECTION 1. The mayor is hereby authorized to grant license for the sale of spirituous, vinous and fermented liquors to any person who shall apply therefor to him in writing, upon such person executing to the city of Chicago a bond, with at least two sureties, to be approved by the mayor, in the penal sum of five hundred dollars, conditioned that the party so licensed shall faithfully observe and keep all ordinances heretofore passed or to be passed during the period of such license; and that he will not keep open his bar or place for the sale of such liquors, nor sell, give away or in any manner deal in, by himself, servant or any other person, any spirituous, vinous or mixed, fermented or intoxicating liquors upon Sunday; and that he will prohibit all gaming, with or without betting, by means of any cards, dominoes, dice or other articles of luck or chance; and paying for the use of the city fifty-two dollars, and no other fees. On compliance with these requirements, a license shall be issued to the applicant under the corporate seal, signed by the mayor and countersigned by the clerk, which shall authorize the person or persons therein named to sell, barter, give away and deliver wines and other liquors, whether vinous, ardent or fermented, in quantities less than one gallon, in the place designated in the application: *Provided*, All licenses issued in pursuance hereof shall expire on the first day of July in each year.

License. Bond. Condition of bond. Charge. Expire.

SEC. 2. No license shall be transferable without the permission of the mayor of said city. The clerk shall keep a license register, in which shall be entered the name of the person or persons licensed, the place of business, the date of the license, and the time the same will expire. The license shall be dated as of the day of application. No person shall be deemed to be duly licensed to whom a license has not been actually issued or transferred as aforesaid.

Transfer. Register.

SEC. 3. Any license so granted may be revoked upon written notice by the mayor, whenever it shall appear to his satisfaction that the party so licensed shall have violated any provision of any ordinance of the common council relating to spirituous liquors, or any condition of the bond aforesaid. Any and all persons licensed under this chapter

Revocation.

or any ordinance of the city for the sale of liquors, shall immediately cause to be and remain posted upon some conspicuous part of the room or bar kept or used for such purpose, his or their license. Any person so licensed, who shall not cause such license to be and remain posted as aforesaid, or who, not being so licensed, shall cause or permit any paper or document purporting to be a license, to be or remain posted as aforesaid, shall, on conviction, be fined in a sum not exceeding twenty dollars.

Posting.

Penalty.

Penalty for dealing without license.

SEC. 4. Any person who shall hereafter have or keep any tavern, grocery, ordinary, victualing or other house or place within the city, for the selling, giving away, or in any manner dealing in any vinous, spirituous, ardent, intoxicating or fermented liquors, in quantities less than one gallon; or who, by himself, his agent or servant, shall sell, give away or in any manner deal in any vinous, spirituous, ardent or fermented liquors, in less quantity than one gallon, without a license for that purpose in pursuance hereof, shall, upon conviction thereof, be subject to a fine of not less than ten dollars nor more than one hundred dollars: *Provided*, That druggists or persons whose chief business is to sell drugs and medicines, shall not be deemed to be within the provisions hereof in selling quantities less than as aforesaid, for purposes purely medicinal, mechanical or sacramental; and in all cases of conviction under this chapter, the court or magistrate shall have power, in its discretion, to sentence the offender to imprisonment in the bridewell or county jail for a period not exceeding two months, in addition to the penalty.

Proviso as to druggists.

CHAPTER XLV.

STREETS.

SECTION
1. Names and numbering.
2. Board of public works to assign numbers; maps and records; no number to be affixed without certificate from board.
3. Charge for certificate.
4. Size of, and place for, numbers.
5. Penalty for not numbering, under foregoing provisions.
6. Same.

SECTION
7. Incumbering, etc., streets, wharves, etc.; penalty.
8. Removal of obstructions; penalty and cost.
9. Thing removed may, unless reclaimed, be sold; disposition of proceeds.
10. Wagons, etc., without horses, etc., on streets; penalty; proviso.

SECTION
11. Removing building along street, etc., without permit; penalty.
12. Building remaining longer than permit; penalty.
13. Erecting building upon street, etc.; penalty.
14. Owner to remove building, etc., after notice; penalty.
15. Proceedings in case of neglect; expense; penalty for resisting.
16. Obstructions by teams, etc.; directions by officer; penalty for disobeying.

SECTION
17. Charge by board of public works for permits.
18. Street taken up, to be repaired, etc.; penalty.
19. Ashes, rubbish, etc., in streets; penalty.
20. Injuring pavement, etc., obstructing public work, etc.; penalty.
21. Fastening animals to, or injuring fences, trees, etc.; penalty.

SECTION 1. The several streets, avenues and places of the city of Chicago, shall hereafter be known and designated by the names applied thereto respectively on the map of the city of Chicago, published by Mr. J. Van Vechten in the year 1863, except as follows, to wit: The name of Josephine street is changed to Seeley street. And it is hereby made the duty of the owners or occupants of all buildings situated in the city of Chicago, to number them in the manner hereinafter provided.

Names.

Numbering.

SEC. 2. The board of public works shall assign a number to each lot or part of lot fronting on any street, avenue or public place of said city; said streets, avenues and public places being numbered progressively, and, where practicable, so that the odd number shall be on one side and the even number on the other side of each street, and so that there shall be a number for every twenty or twenty-five feet of land fronting on any street, or as near thereto as conveniently may be, and the record of such numbering in the books of said board shall be evidence of the respective numbers or designations aforesaid. Said board shall prepare the necessary maps and records of the numbers to be assigned to all lots situated in the city of Chicago, as above described, and no owner or other person shall affix a street number to a building in said city, without having first obtained from said board a certificate designating the number assigned to the lot on which such building is situated.

Board of public works to assign numbers.

Maps and records.

No number without certificate from board.

SEC. 3. The board of public works, to provide for the expenses of mapping the city and assigning the street numbers to the lots therein, are hereby authorized and directed to require payment for the certificates to be issued according to the foregoing section, at the rate of fifty cents for each number designated by said certificates.

Charge for certificate.

Size of, and place for, numbers.

SEC. 4. Each of the figures of every number shall be not less than three inches in length, being so marked as to be distinct and easily read. Said numbers shall be placed in a conspicuous place on the side of or above the front door of the buildings to which the same are attached.

Penalty for not numbering, under foregoing provisions.

SEC. 5. Any person being the owner or occupant of any building now erected in the city of Chicago, who, after being notified by the board of public works that the street numbers are on record at their office, shall for thirty days neglect or refuse to number any buildings owned or occupied by him, in conformity with the provisions of this chapter, or who shall number such building without having first obtained from the board of public works a certificate designating the proper number of such building, shall be subject to a penalty of five dollars, and a further penalty of five dollars for every thirty days thereafter that he shall neglect or refuse to number said building, or shall maintain thereon a number without having first obtained from said board said certificate, and a sufficient notice by said board to all owners or occupants that the street numbers are on record at their office, shall be an advertisement to such effect in the corporation newspaper, to be inserted for three days.

Same.

SEC. 6. Any owner or occupant of any building hereafter erected in the city of Chicago, who shall for thirty days after the same shall be erected, neglect or refuse to number said building according to the provisions of this chapter, or who shall number said building without having first obtained from said board a certificate designating the proper number, shall be subject to a penalty of five dollars, and a further penalty of five dollars for every thirty days thereafter that said building shall be without its number according to the provisions of this chapter, or shall have a number thereon without said certificate having first been obtained from said board.

Obstructing without permit.

SEC. 7. Any person who shall incumber or obstruct, or cause to be incumbered or obstructed, any street, alley, public landing, wharf or pier, or other public place in said city, by placing therein or thereon any building materials, or any article or thing whatsoever, without having first obtained written permission from the board of public works, shall be subject to a penalty of not less than five dollars nor more than fifty dollars for each offense, and a further penalty of ten dollars for each day or part of a day such incumbrance or obstruction shall continue. Penalty.

SEC. 8. The board of police, the mayor, any alderman, or any public officer, is hereby authorized to order any article or thing whatsoever which may incumber or obstruct any street, alley, public landing, wharf or pier within said city, to be removed; and if such article or thing shall not be removed within six hours after notice to the owner or person in charge thereof to remove the same, or if the owner cannot be readily found for the purpose of such notice, to cause the same to be removed to some suitable place, to be designated by the mayor or board of public works. And the owner of any article so removed shall forfeit a penalty of ten dollars, in addition to the cost of such removal. Removal of obstructions. Penalty and cost.

SEC. 9. Any article or thing which may be removed in accordance with the preceding section, shall be advertised ten days and sold by the board of public works, unless the same shall be sooner reclaimed, and the penalty and costs paid by the owners thereof. The proceeds of such sale shall be paid into the city treasury, and the balance if any, after deducting the penalty and costs, shall be paid to any person or persons furnishing satisfactory proof of ownership. Thing removed may be sold. Disposition of proceeds.

SEC. 10. No wagon, sleigh, sled, carriage, railway car, or vehicle of any kind or description, or any part of the samo, without horses or other beasts of burden, shall be permitted to remain or stand in any street or alley of this city for more than one hour, except for the purpose of being repaired, and then only in front of the premises of the person so repairing and within ten feet of the curbing, under a penalty of not less than one dollar nor more than twenty-five dollars; and any such wagon, sled, sleigh, car riage, railway car or vehicle, or any part of the same, may be removed by the board of public works, or any police officer, as provided in section eight, of this chapter: *Provided*, This section shall only apply to the district bounded on the south by Harrison street, west by Halsted Wagons, etc., on streets, etc. Penalty. Proviso.

street, and north by Chicago avenue—except so much thereof as prohibits railway cars from standing in the streets, which provision shall apply to the whole city.

Removing building in, without permit.

SEC. 11. If any person shall remove or cause to be removed, or aid and assist in removing, any building into, along or across any street, alley or public ground in the city, without first obtaining written permission from the board of public works, and conforming to such rules, regulations, requirements, restrictions and conditions as they may prescribe, he shall be subject to a penalty of twenty-five dollars, to be recovered from the owner of the building, or any person aiding or directing in its removal, and a like penalty for every twenty-four hours the same shall remain in or upon any street, alley or public ground; and the board of public works shall not have any anthority to allow a wood building to be moved into the present or future fire limits.

Penalty.

Building remaining on, longer than permit.

SEC. 12. The owner of any building, or the contractor for its removal, either or both, who shall suffer the same to be or remain in any of the streets or alleys, or upon any of the public grounds of the city, for any time longer than may be specified in the permission of the board of public works, shall forfeit a penalty of ten dollars, and a like penalty for every twenty-four hours the same shall be continued, and such building shall be deemed a nuisance, and be proceeded against as provided in section fifteen of this chapter.

Penalty.

Building upon.

SEC. 13. No person shall erect or place any building, in whole or in part, upon any street, alley, sidewalk or other public ground within this city, under a penalty of fifty dollars.

e nalty.

Owner to remove building, etc., after notice.

SEC. 14. The owner of any building, fence, porch, steps, gallery, or other obstruction, now standing, or which may hereafter be erected or placed upon any street, alley or sidewalk, or public ground within this city, or which may be left standing upon any new street that has been or may hereafter be opened, shall remove the same within such reasonable time, not exceeding thirty and not less than three days, as he shall be required so to do by a notice, signed by the mayor, secretary, or a member of the board of public works, under a penalty of not less than twenty-five dollars nor more than one hundred dollars, and a further penalty of one hundred dollars for every ten days the same shall so remain. Penalty.

SEC. 15. Whenever the owner of any building, fence, or other obstruction, upon any street, alley, sidewalk or public ground in this city shall refuse or neglect to remove the same after notice as prescribed in the preceding section, or if the owner cannot be readily found for the purpose of such notice, the same shall be deemed a nuisance, and it shall be lawful for either the mayor or the board of public works, and it is hereby made their duty, to cause the same to be removed or taken down, in their discretion, and the expense thereof shall be recoverable of the owner in an action of assumpsit; and every person who shall oppose or resist the execution of the orders of the mayor or the board of public works in the premises, shall forfeit a penalty of one hundred dollars. Proceedings in case of neglect. Expense. Penalty for resisting.

SEC. 16. Whenever, from any cause, any street or alley of the city shall be obstructed by a press of teams attached to vehicles loaded or otherwise, the mayor, any alderman, police officer, or commissioner of the board of public works, may give such directions in regard to the removal of such teams, vehicles, etc., as in the opinion of such officer may be required by the public convenience; and any person or persons refusing or neglecting to obey such directions shall forfeit and pay a sum of not less than five dollars nor exceeding twenty-five dollars, and may be arrested forthwith to answer for such refusal or neglect. Obstructions by teams, etc. Directions by officer. Penalty for disobeying.

SEC. 17. All permits which the board of public works is authorized by law to grant, shall be subject to such rules, requirements, regulations, conditions and restrictions, as said board, in its wisdom, may deem proper and just to impose, for the interests and protection of the city, and said board shall demand and receive, for the use of the city of Chicago, a reasonable compensation for the granting of such permits: *Provided*, That not less than one nor more than five dollars shall be chargeable in any one case. Charge for permits.

SEC. 18. When any part of any street, alley, sidewalk or other public place in the city of Chicago, shall be torn, Street taken up, to be repaired, etc.

dug or taken up for any purpose, the person, persons or corporation, so tearing, digging or taking up any earth, paving, planking, graveling or macadamizing, shall, immediately upon the completion of such purpose, and as fast as practicable during the accomplishment thereof, return the earth, ram and puddle the same as fast as returned, to a firm and solid bearing, and in a manner that will entirely prevent any settling of such earth, and shall also relay all paving, planking, graveling and macadamizing in a skillful and permanent manner, and in every case to the satisfaction of the board of public works, under a penalty, for any neglect or refusal so to do, of not less than twenty dollars nor more than one hundred dollars.

Penalty.

Rubbish, etc.

SEC. 19. No person shall place any straw, dirt, chips, shells, ashes, swill, or other rubbish, though not offensive to health, in any street or alley in the city of Chicago, (except that ashes may be placed in the middle of the carriage way of streets not improved, if leveled off so as not to obstruct the street,) under a penalty of five dollars for each offense, and a like penalty for every hour the same shall be suffered to remain after notice given by any officer or agent of the city to remove the same.

Penalty.

Injuring.

SEC. 20. No person shall injure or tear up any pavement, side or crosswalk, or any part thereof, dig any hole, ditch, or drain in, or dig or remove any sod, stone, earth, sand or gravel from any street, alley or public ground in the city of Chicago, without having first obtained, from the board of public works, written permission; or hinder or obstruct the making or repairing any public improvement or work ordered by the common council, or being done under lawful authority for the city of Chicago, under a penalty, for each offense, of not less than ten dollars nor more than one hundred dollars.

Obstructing public work.

Penalty.

Injuring fences, etc.

SEC. 21. No person shall fasten any animal to, or destroy or injure any fence, railing, ornamental or shade tree, or shrub, in or upon any public ground, street, alley or other public place in the city of Chicago, under a penalty of not less than five dollars nor more than one hundred dollars.

Penalty.

CHAPTER XLVI.

TREES.

SECTION
1. On sidewalk, where to be planted; penalty.
2. Injuring, etc.; penalty.

SECTION
3. Board of public works may transplant; proviso.
4. Obstructing lamps, to be trimmed, after notice; penalty.

SECTION 1. All shade and ornamental trees shall be planted on a line two feet inside of the outer line of the sidewalk as defined and established by the chapter relative to sidewalks. If any person shall plant any tree as aforesaid on any different line, he shall be subject to a penalty of five dollars. **Where planted.** **Penalty.**

SEC. 2. Any person who shall cut, break, or otherwise injure or destroy any shade or ornamental tree other than his own, upon any sidewalk, or elsewhere, shall be subject to a fine of not less than ten dollars nor exceeding fifty dollars, in every case. **Injuring.** **Penalty.**

SEC. 3. If any trees shall have been heretofore planted within or without the line established at the time the same were set out, or shall hereafter be planted in violation of this chapter, the board of public works shall have power, in their discretion, to cause the same to be taken up and properly set out: *Provided*, That in no case shall such discretion be exercised unless such tree shall form a material obstruction to the street or sidewalk; nor unless the season shall be favorable for transplanting the same. **Board of public works may transplant.** **Proviso.**

SEC. 4. If any trees shall be suffered by the owner or occupant of the premises to grow in such a manner as to obstruct the reflection of the public lamps, it shall be the duty of the board of public works to notify the owner or occupant of the premises forthwith to trim the same, in the manner to be specified in the notice. If any person shall refuse or neglect to comply with such notice, it shall be the duty of the said board to cause such trees to be trimmed; and the person so neglecting or refusing shall be subject to a penalty of one dollar for each tree he was so notified and refused or neglected to trim. **Obstructing lamps.** **Penalty.**

CHAPTER XLVII.

VEHICLES.

SECTION
1. License required; to whom issued; bond and condition; transfer; proviso.
2. Register; expiration.
3. Name and number painted on vehicle; to be erased at expiration of license.
4. Lamps on passenger vehicles; how painted.
5. Licensed drivers; regulations as to license; badges, what, and how worn.
6. Charges for licenses.
7. Charges for carrying passengers.
8. Drivers, etc., not to act as porters and runners, or solicit for other vehicles; racing; fast driving; keep to the right.

SECTION
9. Not to refuse or omit to carry passengers.
10. Charges for carrying goods; not to refuse, etc.; proviso.
11. Rates of fare to be posted in passenger vehicles.
12. Deceits, frauds, impositions, abuse, etc.
13. Decency and good order.
14. Police may arrest, etc.; give directions at depot, etc.; to be obeyed.
15. Stands for vehicles.
16. Order of taking places at stands.
17. Not to be more than ten feet from vehicle while awaiting at stand.
18. Disorderly conduct at depots.
19. Police to enforce last section.
20. Penalty for violating this chapter.

License required. SECTION 1. No person or persons shall hire out, keep or use for hire, or cause to be kept or used for hire, for the carrying or conveying of persons or any article or thing whatever within the city of Chicago, any hackney coach, cab, coach, omnibus, dray, cart, wagon, or other vehicle or vehicles, carriage or carriages, of any description or name whatever, without a license so to do. To whom. And the mayor is hereby authorized to license under his hand, attested by the clerk and the seal of the city, any person or persons, residents of said city, over the age of twenty-one years, and being the owner or owners of any or either of the said vehicles or carriages, to keep and use for hire and the conveyance of persons, or any article or thing as aforesaid, any or either of the said carriages or vehicles, upon his or their entering into bond, Bond and condition. with sufficient sureties to be approved by the mayor, in the penalty of three hundred dollars, conditioned for the payment of all penalties and damages which the said owner or owners, and the driver or drivers thereof, may incur or be liable to pay under any by-law or ordinance of the city of Chicago, now in force, or that shall hereafter be established. Transfer. All licenses granted under this section may be transferred by the mayor, in his discretion, attested by the clerk: Proviso. *Provided*, That the keeper or keepers of livery stables shall have the right to do the ordinary business of such stables without obtaining such license.

SEC. 2. It shall be the duty of the clerk to keep a register of the name of the person to whom each license is granted or transferred, the date when issued or transferred, the number of the license, and the description of the vehicle licensed. All licenses, unless revoked, shall continue in force until the first day of April after the date of the issuing thereof. Register. Expire.

SEC. 3. Every person so licensed, shall forthwith cause the name of the owner and the number of his license to be plainly painted in letters at least one and a half inches in size, in a conspicuous place on the outside of each side of such vehicle, and shall keep the same plain and distinct at all times, when used, during the continuance of such license; but upon the expiration of said license, (unless renewed,) such person shall immediately cause the said name and number to be erased from said vehicle, and shall not allow said vehicle to be used with said name or number thereon. Name and number painted on vehicle. Erased at expiration of license.

SEC. 4. Every hackney coach, cab, carriage, or vehicle, for the conveyance of passengers, except omnibuses running upon established lines, when driven or used, or waiting or standing for use, on any public street or place in the night time, shall have fixed upon some conspicuous part of each of the outsides thereof a lighted lamp, with plain glass fronts and sides, with the number of the license painted with black paint, on the sides and front of each of said lamps, in distinct and legible figures, at least one and a half inches in size, and so placed that said numbers and lamps may be distinctly seen from the inside and outside of such vehicle. All omnibuses running within the city, and required to be licensed, shall, when running in the night time, have fixed in some conspicuous place, in front thereof, so as to be distinctly seen from the inside and outside, a lighted lamp, with the number of license distinctly painted thereon in figures of one inch and a half in size. Lamps, and how painted.

SEC. 5. No person, except a licensed owner, shall hereafter drive any licensed hackney coach, cab, dray, cart or other vehicle, (except omnibuses on established lines,) for the conveyance of passengers or any article or thing whatever for hire or reward, without first obtaining a license, as Licensed drivers.

such driver, and no such driver shall drive any other carriage or vehicle than the one for which he shall be licensed; nor shall the owner or owners permit any person, except a licensed driver or owner, to drive any licensed carriage or vehicle owned or used by him or them; nor shall any such owner permit any licensed driver to drive any other carriage or vehicle than the one for which he shall be licensed. No more than one driver shall be licensed for each of said vehicles or carriages. Such drivers shall be licensed by the mayor and clerk, on request of the owner of any of the vehicles herein mentioned, and such licenses may be transferred on such request; and it shall be the duty of the clerk to keep a list of the drivers so licensed, and the number of the vehicle for which each driver shall be licensed, and of all transfers of such licenses. All such licenses shall expire on the first day of April after the date of the issuing thereof. All licenses granted under this chapter shall designate the coach, cab, omnibus, dray, wagon or vehicle, by their number or name, and the owner and owners, driver and drivers, shall be severally liable for each and every violation of this chapter, by such owner or owners, or their driver or drivers. And every person so licensed, (except drivers of omnibuses on established lines, running at regular hours, on regular routes, in cases where the name or names of the owner or owners of such line of omnibuses, together with the number of the vehicle, shall be legibly painted on the outside upon the door of such omnibus,) shall, while acting as driver of such vehicle, wear, conspicuously, a badge, consisting of a rectangular silver plate, or plated metal, one and three-fourths inches long and one and one-eighth inches wide, having the corners cut off; on said plate shall be engraved the word "hack," or other word designating his kind of vehicle, in letters not less than five-sixteenths of an inch long, and the number of the hack or other vehicle in figures not less than seven-sixteenths of an inch long; said letters and figures to be boldly cut in Roman characters and filled in with black; said badge shall be provided with a pin or other fastening, by which the same may be and shall be worn in a conspicuous place on the outside of the breast

Regulations as to license.

Badges, what, and how worn.

of the coat, so that it may not be hidden either by accident or design.

SEC. 6. All omnibuses and accommodation coaches, running in connection with hotels, shall be charged for license, each, the sum of ten dollars per annum. Charges for licenses.

All omnibuses and accommodation coaches, running upon established lines, and at stated periods, from place to place within the city, shall be charged for license, each, the sum of two dollars per annum.

All hackney coaches and carriages, drawn by two horses or other animals, and occupying any public stand, or that shall run for the conveyance of passengers, for hire or reward, within the city, shall be charged for license, each, the sum of twelve dollars per annum.

All cabs and other vehicles, drawn by one horse or other animal, and occupying any public stand, or that shall run for the conveyance of passengers, for hire or reward, within the city, shall be charged for license, each, the sum of five dollars per annum.

All baggage, express and furniture wagons and vehicles, drawn by two or more horses or other animals, shall be charged for license, each, the sum of ten dollars per annum.

All baggage, express and furniture wagons and vehicles, drawn by one horse or other animal, shall be charged for license, each, the sum of five dollars per annum.

All drays, carts, wagons, and other vehicles, running within said city, for hire or reward, and not otherwise expressly provided for, shall be charged for license, each, the sum of five dollars per annum.

All wagons and other vehicles, drawn by four or more horses or other animals, for the conveyance of any heavy article or thing for hire, from place to place in said city, shall be charged for license, each, the sum of ten dollars per annum: *Provided*, That nothing herein contained shall include omnibuses or baggage wagons running to and from hotels free of charge, and no fees shall be charged for any license issued under this section.

SEC. 7. The only prices to be charged, received or taken by the owner or owners or drivers of any hackney coach, carriage or other vehicle, except omnibuses, for the convey- Charges for carrying passengers.

ance of passengers for hire within said city, shall be as follows, to be regulated and estimated by the distance, on the most direct routes, namely:

For conveying a passenger not exceeding one mile, fifty cents.

For every additional passenger of the same family, or party, twenty-five cents.

For conveying a passenger any distance over a mile, and less than two miles, one dollar.

For each additional passenger of the same family or party, twenty-five cents.

For conveying a passenger any distance in said city exceeding two miles, one dollar and fifty cents.

For each additional passenger of the same family or party, when the distance is over two miles, fifty cents.

Children. For conveying children between five and fourteen years of age, half of the above prices may be charged for like distances; but for children under five years of age no charge shall be made: *Provided*, That the distance from any railroad depot, steamboat landing, or hotel, to any other railroad depot, steamboat landing or hotel, shall in all cases be estimated as not exceeding one mile.

By the day and hour. For the use by the day of any hackney coach, or other vehicle drawn by two horses or other animals, with one or more passengers, six dollars.

For the use of any such carriage or vehicle by the hour, with one or more passengers, with the privilege of going from place to place, and stopping as often as may be required, as follows:

For the first hour, one dollar and fifty cents.

For the second hour, seventy-five cents.

For each succeeding hour, fifty cents.

For the use of any cab or other vehicle drawn by one horse or other animal, by the hour, with the privilege of going from place to place, with one or more passengers, and stopping when required:

For the first hour, one dollar.

For the second hour, fifty cents.

For each succeeding hour, thirty cents.

For the use of any such carriage by the day, four dollars.

Every passenger shall be allowed to have conveyed upon such vehicle, without charge, his ordinary traveling baggage, not exceeding in any case one trunk and twenty-five pounds of other baggage. For every additional package, where the whole weight of baggage is over one hundred pounds, if conveyed to any place within the city limits, the owner or driver shall be permitted to charge fifteen cents. Baggage.

SEC. 8. No driver, agent, servant, owner or owners of any such hackney coach, cab, carriage or other vehicle herein referred to, shall act as public porter or runner without a license for that purpose, or solicit passengers, except for such vehicle as he may be licensed for; and no driver of any hackney coach, cab, omnibus, wagon, dray, car, carriage or other vehicle, shall engage in racing with another, or drive faster than a moderate trot, while passing in, along or through any of the public streets in the city; and all such vehicles shall keep to the right when in motion and passing along any of such public streets. Not to act as porters and runners. Racing. Keep to the right.

SEC. 9. No owner or driver of any hackney coach, cab, coach or other carriage or vehicle licensed as aforesaid, shall refuse to convey in said city any person with or without baggage as aforesaid, when applied to for that purpose; or, having undertaken to convey such person, shall omit or neglect so to do, or shall ask, take or extort from any person desiring to be, or having been, conveyed to any place in said city, as the price or rate of fare for such conveyance, any greater price or rate of fare than is herein established. Not to refuse or omit to carry passengers.

SEC. 10. Draymen, carters, expressmen, or wagoners, licensed as aforesaid, shall be entitled to receive and ask for the cartage of any articles, goods, wares and merchandise upon such cart, wagon or dray, when the distance shall not be greater than one mile, fifty cents, and for each additional mile or fractional part of a mile, twenty-five cents; and no person driving such licensed dray, cart or wagon, shall refuse to convey within said city the baggage, goods or merchandise of any person, when applied to for that purpose, or having undertaken to convey such baggage, goods or merchandise or other thing, shall omit or neglect to do so, or shall state to, ask, take or extort from any person desiring to have, or having had, conveyed to any place in said city Charges for carrying goods, etc. Not to refuse, etc.

such baggage, goods, merchandise or other thing, as the price or rate of fare for such conveyance, any greater price or rate of fare than that herein established: *Provided*, That this section shall not apply to teams with two or more horses or other animals used for conveying heavy articles.

Proviso.

Rates of fare to be posted in vehicle.

SEC. 11. Every driver and owner of a licensed hackney coach, cab or other vehicle for the conveyance of passengers, shall at all times keep fixed and posted, right side up, inside of the same, so as to be most conveniently seen and read, a card, to be furnished by the city at the expense of the owner, printed in plain, legible characters, containing the prices or rates of fare allowed by this chapter, and the name of the owner and driver of such vehicle, and the number of the license thereof.

Deceits, frauds, imposition, abuse, etc.

SEC. 12. No owner or driver of any licensed hackney coach, cab, coach or other carriage, vehicle, dray, cart or wagon, shall induce any person to employ him by either knowingly, wantonly or ignorantly misinforming or misleading such person as to the time or place of the arrival or departure of any railroad car, steamboat, canal-boat or other public conveyance whatever, or the location of any railroad depot, office, station or any railroad ticket office, or the location of any hotel, stage office, public place or private residence within said city, or shall induce any person to ride in or employ his vehicle, by falsely representing his vehicle to such person as running for or being in the employment of a public house, canal or steamboat line, railroad or stage company, with a view to exact, solicit or obtain fare, or anything of value from such person, or having so induced any person to ride in his vehicle, shall exact, solicit or take fare or anything of value from such person, for conveying him to such public house, canal or steamboat landing, railroad depot, ticket office, stage company office or other public place, or shall convey any passenger, with or without request, in such a vehicle, to any ticket office for the purpose of obtaining a ticket for any of the beforementioned conveyances, or for the purpose of inquiring as to the time of departure thereof, and thence to any of said public conveyances, or shall convey any person, without his request, to any place or house of ill-fame, or shall deceive any person in relation to any ticket, or shall sell or offer to sell any ticket or voucher for conveyance which is worthless, or shall make any false representation or statement in regard to any voucher or ticket for conveyance that may be shown to him, or shall not give his name and the number of his license on request of any person, or shall impose upon or deceive any person, in any manner or form, or shall charge any passenger a greater price than single fare or hire, or shall strike, threaten, insult or otherwise abuse or ill-treat any passenger under any pretense whatever. And no owner of any vehicle in this chapter specified shall aid or abet the driver thereof in any offense in this section specified, or shall know and conceal or connive at any such offense, or aid or assist him in escaping from punishment by preventing the appearance of witnesses, or by attempting so to do, or by any other mode whatever.

Decency and good order.

SEC. 13. No owner or driver of any hackney coach, cab, omnibus, coach, dray, cart, wagon or other carriage or vehicle, while waiting for employment at any stand, railroad depot or other public place in said city, shall unnecessarily snap or flourish his whip, or use indecent or profane language, or be guilty of boisterous or loud talking or any disorderly conduct, or vex or annoy travelers or citizens, or obstruct any sidewalk; and such owners and drivers are required to obey any and all regulations and rules adopted by any railroad company or other association or person, for the promotion of order at any public landing, railroad depot or other public place in said city, not inconsistent with the ordinances of the city and the police regulations thereof.

Police may arrest; give directions.

SEC. 14. Any police officer or member of the police department shall have power to arrest any person offending against any or either of the provisions of this chapter, or any person who refuses or neglects to desist from any such offense when commanded; and such officers or either of them shall have power to give any directions which they may deem necessary for the preservation of good order and the convenience of the public at any railroad depot, termination, public place, station or steamboat

Directions to be obeyed. landing within said city, and no owner or driver of any of the vehicles mentioned in this chapter shall refuse or neglect to obey such directions, or shall interfere with such officer as to such directions, or shall resist or interfere with any such officer in the discharge of his said duties.

Stands for vehicles. SEC. 15. No owner or driver of any licensed hackney coach, cab, coach or other carriage or vehicle for the conveyance of passengers, shall make any stand or stopping place for business with his vehicle in any street or other public place in the south division of said city north of the south line of Washington street, except in the places designated as follows, namely: The east side of La Salle street, between Randolph street and Washington street, the north side of Washington street between La Salle street and to within fifty feet of Clark street, except as hereinafter provided, and no owner or driver of any hackney coach, omnibus, cab, or other carriage for the conveyance of passengers, or of any wagon, dray, cart, or other carriage, for the conveyance of baggage, luggage or merchandise, shall make any stand or stopping place, with or without his vehicle, while waiting for employment, at any place on any railroad or railway grounds, or on any street adjacent to any railroad or railway depot, except in the place designated by the person having charge of such depot. Nor shall any such owner or driver make such stand or stopping place, either within or without the limits designated, within the distance of twenty feet of any street crossing; and in such other places and under such other regulations as may from time to time be established and designated by the common council: *Provided*, That hackney coaches may stand in front of any or either of the hotels, or other public buildings, in case the owners of such hackney coaches shall first obtain the written permission of the occupant or occupants of such hotel or building for that purpose, and the written permission of the mayor, and until such written permission shall be revoked by such occupant or the said mayor.

Order of taking places at stands. SEC. 16. All owners or drivers of hacks, hackney coaches, omnibuses, cabs, wagons, drays, carts or other carriages for the conveyance of passengers, baggage, luggage or merchandise, taking their stands, with their vehicles, at such places designated by the persons having charge of depots, as in the last section provided, shall have the right to stand at any vacant place, within the limits of the places designated, and no preference shall be shown between different vehicles of the same class, as to the choice of position within such limits; but different places may be designated for omnibuses, for other carriages for passengers, and for drays and baggage wagons, so as to keep each class of vehicles together.

SEC. 17. No person having in charge any hackney coach, cab, omnibus or other carriage for the conveyance of passengers, luggage or baggage, shall, while awaiting employment at any of the stands hereinbefore designated, be or remain more than ten feet from the vehicle which he has in charge, and no more than one driver will be allowed to any omnibus, hackney coach or other carriage intended for passengers.

Not to leave vehicle.

SEC. 18. No person shall, in or about any railroad passenger house in said city, make any loud noise or disturbance, or be guilty of any lewd or indecent conduct or behavior, to the annoyance or disturbance of citizens or travelers.

Disorderly conduct at depots.

SEC. 19. It shall be the duty of the depot and city police to see that the foregoing provisions are strictly observed, and in case of any violation thereof, forthwith to arrest the offender, and take him before a court having jurisdiction of the offense, to be dealt with according to law.

Police to enforce this chapter.

SEC. 20. Any person who shall violate any or either of the provisions of this chapter, or any section, clause or provision of any section of this chapter, or who shall neglect or fail to comply with any or either of the requirements thereof, shall on conviction, pay a fine of not less than five dollars nor more than one hundred dollars, and shall forfeit his license.

Penalty for violating.

CHAPTER XLVIII.

WATER WORKS.

SECTION
1. Fouling water near water works; penalty.
2. Public hydrants; opening, injuring, etc.; penalty.
3. Same; polluting or wasting water; penalty.
4. Firemen misusing wrenches; penalty.

SECTION
5. Rules and regulations for water takers.
6. Penalty for violating same.
7. Obstructing access to stop cocks; penalty.
8. Board of public works to attach meters to premises using large quantities of water; assessments to be proportioned to use.

Fouling water near. SECTION 1. No person or persons shall drive, lead or swim any horses, sheep, swine or other animals into or in the waters of lake Michigan within three blocks of the works on Chicago avenue, in said city, commonly called the "Water Works," nor shall any person or persons wash or clean any carriage or other vehicle whatever in the water of lake Michigan, within said limits, under a penalty of not less than two dollars nor more than twenty-five dollars for each and every offense. Penalty.

Public hydrants. SEC. 2. All the hydrants constructed, in the city of Chicago, for the purpose of extinguishing fires in said city, be and the same are hereby declared to be public hydrants, and no person or persons (other than the members of the fire department of said city, for the uses and purposes of said department, and those specially authorized by the board of public works,) shall open any of the said hydrants, or attempt to draw water from the same, or in any manner interfere with or injure any of said hydrants, under a penalty of not less than ten dollars nor exceeding fifty dollars for each and every offense. Opening, injuring, etc. Penalty.

Polluting or wasting water, etc. SEC. 3. Any person or persons who shall willfully or carelessly break or injure any of the public hydrants, or shall pollute, or unnecessarily waste the water at any such hydrants, shall, on conviction, be fined in a sum not less than ten dollars nor exceeding fifty dollars for each and every offense. Penalty.

Firemen. SEC. 4. Any member of the fire department who shall let out, or suffer or permit any person or persons to take, the wrenches furnished to the fire department of said city, to be used in cases of fire, or shall suffer or permit any of said wrenches furnished said department to be taken from the engine houses of said department, except as they accompany the engines on occasions of fire, or for other purposes connected with the fire department, shall forfeit and pay, on conviction, a sum not less than ten dollars nor exceeding fifty dollars for each and every offense.

Misuse of wrenches.

Penalty.

SEC. 5. The following rules and regulations for the government of water takers be and the same are hereby adopted and established, in the words and figures as the same are now established by the board of public works of the city of Chicago, as follows:

Rules and regulations for water takers.

The board of public works of the city of Chicago do establish the following rules and regulations for the government of water takers:

First. No occupant or owner of any building, in which the water is introduced, will be allowed to supply other persons or families. If found doing so, the supply will be stopped, and the amount of pay forfeited.

Second. Whenever two or more parties shall be supplied from one pipe connecting with the distribution main, the failure, on the part of any one of said parties to comply with the rules and regulations of this board, shall authorize the board to withhold a supply of water from such main, without any liability whatsoever, and all payments made shall be forfeited.

Third. No addition or alteration whatever, in or about any conduit, pipe or water-cock, shall be made or caused to be made by persons taking the water, without notice thereof being previously given to, and permission had, in writing, from the board.

Fourth. All persons taking the water shall keep their own service pipes, stop-cocks and apparatus in good repair, and protected from frost, at their own expense, and shall prevent all unnecessary waste of water; and it is expressly stipulated by the board that no claim shall be made against them or the city, by reason of the breaking of any service cock or service pipe.

Fifth. No hydrants will be permitted on the sidewalk or in the front area, neither will they be permitted to be kept running when not in actual use; taps at wash-basins, water-closets, baths and urinals must be kept closed in like manner.

Sixth. Applications for water must state, fully and truly, all purposes for which it is required; and when paying the semi-annual charges for it, parties must frankly and without concealment answer all questions put to them relating to its consumption. In case of fraudulent misrepresentation on the part of the applicant, or of uses of the water not embraced in the applicant's bill, or of willful or unreasonable waste of water, the board shall have the right to forfeit his payment, and the supply of water will be stopped, unless the party shall promptly pay such additional charge as the board may impose.

Seventh. The various officers employed by the board, and every person by them delegated for the purpose, must have free access, at proper hours of the day, to all parts of every building in which the water is delivered and consumed, to examine the pipes and fixtures, and to ascertain whether there is any unnecessary waste of water.

Eighth. Water rents must be paid semi-annually, in advance, on the first days of May and November, at the office of said board. If not paid at their office within thirty days thereafter, ten per cent. will be added for the expenses of collection. At the termination of thirty days, all rents or assessments remaining unpaid will be collected in the manner provided by law.

Ninth. For a violation of any of the preceding rules and regulations, this board reserves the right to stop the supply of water, without any further or preliminary notice; nor will it be restored, except upon payment of the expense of shutting it off and putting it on, and upon a satisfactory understanding with the party, that no future cause of complaint shall arise.

Penalty for violation.

SEC. 6. Any person who shall violate any or either of the "rules and regulations for the government of water takers," specified in section five hereof, shall, on conviction, in addition to the enforcement of the forfeitures, liabilities, stipulations and reservations therein contained, pay a fine of not less than three dollars nor more than twenty dollars.

SEC. 7. No person shall in any manner obstruct the

access to any stop-cocks connected with any water-pipe within any street, alley or common of said city, by means of any lumber, brick, building material or other article, thing or hindrance whatsoever, under a penalty of not less than five dollars nor more than fifty dollars.

Obstructing access to stop-cocks, etc.

Penalty.

SEC. 8. The board of public works shall attach meters at all hotels, manufacturing establishments using steam, bath houses, livery stables, and other premises using large quantities of water, to measure the quantities of water used at such premises, and the water rents and assessments at such premises shall be in proportion to the quantities used.

Water meters to be attached, where.

CHAPTER XLIX.

WEIGHTS AND MEASURES.

SECTION
1. Comptroller to procure standards.
2. Sealer to test weights, measures, etc.; persons refusing to exhibit, etc.; penalty.
3. Sealer to keep an office; person using incorrect weights, etc., after notice; penalty.
4. Fees and compensation of sealer.
5. Inspection charges not oftener than yearly, unless weights, etc., incorrect.

SECTION
6. Using unsealed weights, etc.; refusing to allow examination, etc.; alteration, etc.; penalties.
7. Sealer to keep a register, and report to council.
8. Peddlers, etc., to have weights, etc., sealed; penalty.
9. Frauds, etc.; penalty.

SECTION 1. The comptroller, at the expense of the city, shall procure correct and approved standards of weights and measures of the standard adopted by the State of Illinois, with their necessary subdivisions, together with the proper beams and scales, for the purpose of testing and proving the weights and measures of said standard used in the city.

Comptroller to procure standards.

SEC. 2. It shall be the duty of the sealer of weights and measures, at least once in every year, to examine and test the accuracy of all weights, measures, scales or other instruments or things used by any person for weighing or measuring any article for sale in said city of Chicago; and to stamp with a suitable seal all weights, measures and scales, so used, which he may find correct, and deliver to the owner thereof a certificate of their accuracy. Any person refusing to exhibit any weights, measures or scales, or instruments for weighing or measuring, to said sealer for the purpose of

Sealer to test weights, measures, etc.

Refusing to exhibit.

examination and inspection as aforesaid, or obstructing him in the performance of his duty, shall forfeit a penalty of not less than five dollars nor more than ten dollars for each offense.

Penalty.

Office.

SEC. 3. It shall be the duty of said sealer of weights and measures to establish and keep an office within the limits of the city of Chicago, and to designate, by card or otherwise, the time during which he may be found in such office. If upon examination he shall find any weights, measures, balances or scales of any kind untrue, he shall immediately notify the owner or owners thereof, and any person or persons who shall, after such notice, use such untrue weights, measures, balances or scales, before the same shall have been adjusted, corrected and sealed by the sealer, shall forfeit and pay to the city, for each offense, a sum not less than fifty dollars nor more than one hundred dollars, with costs of prosecution, for each and every day they are so used after such notification.

Using incorrect, after notice.

Penalty.

Fees.

SEC. 4. The sealer of weights and measures shall be allowed to demand and receive of the person for whom he shall perform services, the following fees and compensation:

For inspecting and sealing railroad or track scales of the capacity of twenty tons and upwards, each, five dollars.

For inspecting and sealing scales of from three to ten tons capacity, each, one dollar and fifty cents.

For inspecting and sealing hay and coal scales, each, one dollar.

For inspecting and sealing dormant scales, each, seventy-five cents.

For inspecting and sealing depot scales, each, one dollar.

For inspecting and sealing movable platform scales, each, fifty cents.

For inspecting and sealing beams weighing one thousand pounds and upwards, each, fifty cents.

For inspecting and sealing beams weighing less than one thousand pounds, each, twenty-five cents.

For inspecting and sealing hopper scales, each, one dollar.

For inspecting and sealing counter scales, each, twenty-five cents.

For inspecting and sealing any kind of scales other than above enumerated, each, twenty-five cents.

And with each scale sealed by him, he shall inspect and seal one set of weights, without any additional charge or compensation.

For inspecting and sealing any dry measure, each, five cents.

For inspecting liquid measures of a capacity of five gallons and upwards, each, ten cents.

For inspecting and sealing liquid measures of a capacity of not less than one gallon nor more than five gallons, each, seven cents.

For inspecting and sealing one-half gallon and one quart liquid measures, each, five cents.

For inspecting and sealing liquid measures of a less capacity than one quart, each, three cents.

For inspecting and sealing any board or cloth measure, each, five cents.

And in every case where he may, at the request of the owner, employ labor or material in making any scale, weight or measure, accurate, he shall be entitled to a just compensation therefor.

SEC. 5. It shall not be lawful for said sealer to make the aforesaid charges for inspecting and testing weights, measures and scales, as aforesaid, oftener than once in each year, unless the same shall be found not conformable to the standard of the State. **Inspecting annual, unless incorrect.**

SEC. 6. No person shall make use of any weight, scale, measure or other instrument for weighing or measuring any article for sale in the city, until the same has been duly examined and sealed by the sealer of weights and measures, under a penalty of not less than five dollars nor more than twenty-five dollars. All persons using weights, measures, scales or other instruments for measuring any article for sale in this city, which have been sealed, shall, upon application of the sealer of weights and measures, allow the same to be examined, tested and sealed, as herein provided, under a penalty of not less than five dollars, nor more than twenty-five dollars for failing so to do; and any person or persons altering any weights, measures or scales, causing the same **Using unsealed weights, etc.** **Penalty.** **Refusing to submit for examination, etc.** **Penalty.** **Alteration of, etc.**

Penalty. to weigh or measure incorrectly, unless to repair, shall, on conviction thereof, be fined in any sum not exceeding one hundred dollars.

Sealer to keep register and report. SEC. 7. It shall be the duty of the said sealer to make a regular register of all weights, measures, scale-beams, and steelyards, or other instruments inspected by him, in which he shall state the names of the owners of the same, and whether they are conformable to the standard of the State. And it shall also be his duty to report to the common council the names of all persons whose weights, measures, scale-beams or steelyards are incorrect, and to deliver a copy of his said register to the clerk.

Peddlers, etc., to have weights, etc., sealed. SEC. 8. All itinerant peddlers and hawkers using scales, balances, weights or measures, shall take the same to the office of the city sealer before using the same, and have the same sealed and adjusted annually; and any such person or persons failing to comply with the provisions of this section, shall each forfeit and pay to the said city a sum of not less than five dollars nor more than one hundred dollars, with costs of prosecution, for each and every day such person or persons shall use the same without having the same adjusted and sealed as hereinbefore provided. Penalty.

Frauds, etc. SEC. 9. Any person who shall sell, or offer for sale, any fruit, vegetables, berries or grains of any description, or any article of dry measurement, within the city of Chicago, in wine measures, or in any other than legal dry measures, which shall have been sealed by the city sealer, whether of pint, quart, or other contents, or who shall practice deceit or fraud in the sale of wood or coal, by selling for a cord of wood less than one hundred and twenty-eight cubic feet of wood, or for a ton of coal less than two thousand pounds of coal, shall be subject to a fine of not less than five dollars and not more than twenty-five dollars, for each offense. Penalty.

CHAPTER L.

WOOD.

SECTION
1. Appointment of inspector and assistants.
2. Duty to measure wood; fees; cord defined.
3. Boxes, racks or wagons, regulations concerning size, etc.; to be inspected by sealer.
4. Wood, how to be sold.

SECTION
5. Wood stands.
6. Inspector to measure, keep books, etc.
7. Badge when on duty; duty of owners, drivers, etc., of wood wagons.
8. Inspectors to be appointed policemen.
9. Penalty for violating this chapter.

SECTION 1. There shall be appointed by the common council by ballot, biennially, on the second Monday of May, or as soon thereafter as may be, one inspector of fire wood in said city, and such assistant inspectors as may be deemed by the common council necessary for the public interests. **Appointment of inspector.**

SEC. 2. It shall be the duty of such wood inspector and assistants to measure any and all loads or piles of wood in said city, on request of any person or persons, and to give a certificate to the person or persons making such request, stating the amount, the date of measuring, for whom measured, the kind and description thereof, for the following prices: For each wagon load, pile or parcel containing a cord or less, ten cents; for each pile or load containing more than one cord and not exceeding two cords, twenty cents; for each additional cord in the same load or pile, five cents. One hundred and twenty-eight cubic feet shall be deemed a cord of wood, and the length of wood shall be measured from point to butt, and not from point to point. **To measure wood.** **Fees.** **Cord defined.**

SEC. 3. Boxes for the sale or delivery of sawed and split wood shall contain one hundred and fifty cubic feet, measured on the inside, for one cord, and seventy-five and a half cubic feet, measured in like manner, for half a cord, and thirty-eight and one-quarter cubic feet for a quarter of a cord. If wood shall be sold or kept for sale in racks or wagons, or otherwise, and shall be piled lengthwise of the wagon or rack, there shall be only two lengths of the wood upon the wagon or in the rack, and such rack shall be four or eight feet long, and of a width and height sufficient to contain one-fourth, one-half or three-fourths of a **Boxes.** **Racks or wagons.** **Regulations concerning size, etc.**

cord, or one cord, measured in the inside of the rack. And if such wood shall be piled or placed crosswise of the wagon or rack, such wagon or rack may be either four, six, eight or ten feet in length, and shall have two stakes behind and two stakes before the place for piling the wood, firmly and permanently placed in the wagon or rack, and of such height as to contain one-fourth, one-half or three-fourths of a cord, or one cord or more in like proportions. And all such boxes, wagons or racks used for selling or exhibiting for sale, any wood in said city, shall be inspected, measured and numbered by the city sealer of weights and measures; and the owner or owners thereof shall, at all times, when such wagons or racks shall be in use, keep his or their name and number, and the quantity of wood such box, wagon or rack will contain, plainly and distinctly painted thereon in letters of at least one and a half inches in size. And all wagons, boxes, racks or vehicles, used at and about the wood yards of the city of Chicago, and all places for the measuring of wood in said city, for retail, shall be made, measured and marked in accordance with the provisions of this section. And the sealers of weights and measures shall, at least as often as once each month, and on the first of each month, furnish the city comptroller with a complete list of the boxes, vehicles and racks, and places so measured.

To be inspected by sealer, etc.

Sale of wood, how.

SEC. 4. No person in said city shall sell, exhibit for sale, or offer to sell, by the load, any fire wood in said city, except in accordance with the provisions of section three of this chapter, unless such wood shall have been previously measured by the said wood inspector, or one of his assistants.

Wood stands.

SEC. 5. The following are hereby designated places for wood stands in said city: In the centre of Market street, at least twenty feet from the sidewalks between Randolph and Madison streets. In the centre of Randolph street between Desplaines and Halsted streets, at least thirty feet from the sidewalks. In the centre of Michigan street, at least twenty feet from the sidewalk and market, between Clark and Wolcott streets. And no person shall be permitted to occupy any of such stands with a load of fire-wood, unless the vehicle, box, wagon or rack, shall be made, measured, marked and numbered, as required in section three of this chapter, or unless such load shall have been measured by one of the said wood inspectors.

Inspector to measure, keep books, etc.

SEC. 6. It shall be the duty of the wood inspector or one or more of his assistants, under his direction, at all reasonable times, to attend at each of the wood stands in said city, for the purpose of measuring wood. They shall be furnished with proper books, at the expense of the city, under the direction of the comptroller, in which shall be printed proper blank certificates and margins, and it shall be their duty to enter therein all necessary facts pertaining to their business, and such as shall be required, from time to time, by the said comptroller, and which books and entry shall, at all times, be subject to his inspection, and shall be delivered to him for safe keeping when required.

Badge.

SEC. 7. The wood inspector and assistants, while on duty, are required to wear an appropriate badge, marked "Wood Inspector;" and no person driving any wood wagon or vehicle occupying or standing about any wood stand or other place in said city, or upon or near any such load of wood, shall refuse to give his name and residence, or to answer any proper questions of such wood inspector or assistant, in regard to any load or loads of wood, or the owner or owners thereof; nor shall any driver or drivers, owner or owners of any wood wagons, boxes or vehicles, refuse to show any certificate of measurement of any such loads, wagons or vehicles, or show a different or fraudulent certificate thereof, to any officer of said city, or person requesting to purchase any load of wood, or commit any other fraudulent or deceitful practice whatever; and all persons selling wood in any other manner than as provided in section three of this chapter, shall deliver the certificate of measurement thereof to the purchaser.

Duty of owners, drivers, etc., of wood wagons.

Frauds.

Inspectors to be policemen.

SEC. 8. All such wood inspectors and assistants shall be appointed policemen of said city, and clothed with all the powers of policemen, while wearing their badges in the discharge of their duty as such wood inspectors and assistants; but shall not be entitled to pay as policemen, except by order or resolution of the common council.

SEC. 9. Any person who shall fail or neglect to comply

Penalty or violation. with any or either of the foregoing requirements of this chapter, or who shall violate any section, clause or provision of any of the preceding sections thereof, shall, on conviction, pay a fine of not less than three dollars nor more than one hundred dollars. And if such person shall be the owner or driver of any vehicle, licensed by the city, his license may be revoked, in the discretion of the mayor.

Passed October 23, 1865.

AMENDMENTS.

AN ORDINANCE to amend Chapter XXXV of "An Ordinance for revising and consolidating the General Ordinances of the City of Chicago."

SECTION
1. No person, other than police, to take up animals, unless he wears a badge.

SECTION
2. Pound master to furnish badges; penalty for wearing, unless furnished by him.
3. Ordinance to take effect, etc.

Persons, other than police, taking up animals, to wear badge. SECTION 1. *Be it ordained by the Common Council of the City of Chicago*, That chapter thirty-five (concerning pounds) of "An Ordinance for revising and consolidating the general ordinances of the city of Chicago," passed October 23rd, 1865, be, and the same is hereby so amended, that it shall not be lawful for any person, whether acting under the direction of the pound master or otherwise, except police patrolmen, to take up any animal running at large contrary to the provisions of section two of said chapter, unless he shall have in a conspicuous place upon the coat or outside garment, a metal badge, with the words "Assistant Pound Master" engraved thereon in letters not less than one-half inch in size.

Pound master to furnish badge. SEC. 2. It shall be the duty of the pound masters of the respective divisions of the city to procure such number of said badges as may be necessary, and furnish them to such persons of good character as they may deem proper, at the cost thereof, and any person who shall wear any such badge, unless furnished as aforesaid by the pound masters, Penalty for wearing, etc. shall be liable to a fine of not less than five dollars nor to exceed ten dollars.

SEC. 3. This ordinance shall take effect and be in force from and after its passage and due publication. Ordinance take effect.

Passed December 11, 1865.

AN ORDINANCE amending Chapter XLIII (Sidewalks) of the General Ordinances of the City of Chicago.

SECTION 1. Amending general ordinance as to notice to repair, etc., sidewalks and drains.

SECTION 1. *Be it ordained by the Common Council of the City of Chicago*, That Section 3, of Chapter XLIII, of the general ordinances of the city of Chicago, be amended by substituting for the words "to repair any sidewalk, or to repair or cleanse any private drain," in the fifth and sixth lines of said section, the words "to raise, lower, repair or relay any sidewalk, or to raise, lower, repair or cleanse any private drain." Notice to repair, etc.

Passed December 4, 1865.

SPECIAL LAWS AND ORDINANCES.

BONDS.

AN ORDINANCE providing for the indorsement of City Bonds.

SECTION
1. Bonds may be specially indorsed; affidavit of ownership.
2. Form of indorsement; fee.
3. Indorsement of coupons; fee.
4. Bonds held as school funds; form of indorsement; no fee.

Special indorsement. SECTION 1. *Be it ordained by the Mayor and Aldermen of the City of Chicago, in Common Council assembled,* That, by the indorsement of the comptroller upon any bonds of the city, payable to bearer, when presented for that purpose by the owner, such bond shall become payable only to the party named in such indorsement, his assignees or legal representatives, anything on the face of the bond to the contrary notwithstanding. Affidavit. The affidavit of the party presenting any such bond, or his authorized agent or attorney, that he is the owner thereof, shall be sufficient evidence to the comptroller of such ownership.

Form of indorsement. SEC. 2. The indorsement of the comptroller may be in the following form: "By virtue of the act of the General Assembly of Illinois, the ordinances of the city of Chicago, and the consent of (A. B.) the owner of this bond, this bond is made payable only to said (A. B.), his assignees or legal representatives, anything on the face thereof to the contrary notwithstanding. C. D., Comptroller." Fee. The cost of the requisite government stamp, and a fee of 50 cents for each indorsement, shall be paid, by the owner of the bond, into the city treasury.

Coupons. Fee. SEC. 3. Coupons may also be indorsed by the comptroller in a shorter form, and a fee of ten cents and the government stamp charged therefor.

School funds. SEC. 4. The bonds held as a part of the school funds may be indorsed as follows: "This bond is made payable by law only to the school agent of the city of Chicago, or his successors in office, anything on the face thereof to the contrary notwithstanding. C. D., Comptroller." No fee shall be charged for indorsing said last mentioned bonds or the coupons attached thereto. No fee.

Passed April 24, 1865.

"CHICAGO" GAS COMPANY.

AN ACT to incorporate the Chicago Gas Light and Coke Company.

SECTION
1. Incorporation; name; general powers.
2. To manufacture and sell gas, lay pipe in streets, etc., of Chicago; not to injure streets, etc., permanently; real estate not to exceed $50,000.

SECTION
3. Capital stock not to exceed $300,000; how subscribed and paid; by-laws; monopoly for ten years.

SECTION 1. *Be it enacted by the People of the State of Illinois, represented in the General Assembly,* That H. L. Stewart, W. S. Bennett, F. C. Sherman, P. L. Updike, P. Page, and their associates, be, and they are hereby created a body politic and corporate, with perpetual succession, by the name and style of the "Chicago Gas Light and Coke Company," and by that name they and their successors shall be capable in law of contracting and being contracted with, suing and being sued, defending and being defended, in all courts and places, and in all matters whatsoever, with full powers to acquire, hold, occupy and enjoy all such real and personal estate as may be necessary and proper for the construction, extension and usefulness of the works of said company, and for the management and good government of the same; and they may have a common seal, and the same may alter, break and renew at pleasure. Incorporation. Name. General powers.

SEC. 2. The corporation hereby created shall have full power and authority to manufacture and sell gas, to be made from any and all of the substances, or a combination thereof, from which inflammable gas is usually obtained, and to be used for the purpose of lighting the city of Chicago, or the streets thereof, and any buildings, manufactories, public places or houses therein contained, and erect all necessary works and apparatus, and to lay pipes for the purpose of Manufacture and sell gas. Lay pipe.

conducting the gas in any of the streets or avenues of said city: *Provided*, That no permanent injury or damage shall be done to any street, lane or highway in said city. The real estate which this corporation is entitled to hold, shall not exceed in value fifty thousand dollars.

Proviso.

Capital stock.

SEC. 3. The capital stock of said company shall not exceed three hundred thousand dollars, to be subscribed for and paid in such proportions as shall be prescribed by the by-laws and rules regulating the concerns of said company, as they shall think proper and necessary respecting the management and disposition of the stock, property and estate of said company, the duties of the officers, artificers and agents to be employed, the number and election of directors, and all such matters as appertain to the concerns of said company. Said company shall have the exclusive privilege of supplying the city of Chicago and its inhabitants with gas for the purpose of affording light, for ten years.

By-laws.

Monopoly for ten years.

Approved February 12, 1849.

AN ACT to amend an Act entitled "An Act to incorporate the Chicago Gas Light and Coke Company.

SECTION
1. Capital may be increased $1,000,000; may borrow money, issue bonds, and mortgage property; may purchase and hold all necessary real estate.

SECTION
2. Repealing conflicting parts of former act; this act in force from passage.

Capital increased.

SECTION 1. *Be it enacted by the People of the State of Illinois, represented in the General Assembly*, The Chicago Gas Light and Coke Company is hereby authorized to increase the capital stock of said company one million of dollars, at such times and in such manner as the board of directors shall from time to time direct. Said company is also authorized to borrow such an amount of money for the purpose of constructing, carrying on and completing its works, upon such terms as the board of directors shall judge best, and, for such purpose, may issue its bonds and mortgage its property; and all bonds heretofore issued for such purpose, and all mortgages executed to secure the same by the said company, are hereby legalized. Said company shall also have the right to purchase and hold such an

May borrow money, issue bonds, and mortgage.

Hold real estate.

amount in value and extent of real estate, in the city of Chicago, as may be necessary for its business, and to carry out the objects of its incorporation.

SEC. 2. So much of the act to which this is an amendment, as conflicts with this act, is hereby repealed. This act shall take effect from and after its passage. **Repealing.** **Act in force.**

Approved February 9, 1855.

"PEOPLE'S" GAS COMPANY.

AN ACT to incorporate the People's Gas Light and Coke Company.

SECTION
1. Incorporation; name; general powers.
2. Manufacture and sell gas; lay pipe in streets, without doing permanent injury; real estate not to exceed $100,000.
3. Capital stock not to exceed $500,000; by-laws.
4. Price of gas.

SECTION 1. *Be it enacted by the People of the State of Illinois, represented in the General Assembly,* That Matthew Laflin, L. C. Paine Freer, A. G. Throop, D. A. Gage, John S. Wallace, George W. Snow, H. B. Bay, and R. H. Foss, and their associates, be, and they are hereby created a body politic and corporate, with perpetual succession, by the name and style of "The People's Gas Light and Coke Company," and by that name they and their successors shall be capable in law of contracting and being contracted with, suing and being sued, defending and being defended, in all courts and places, and in all matters and places whatsoever, with full powers to acquire, hold, occupy and enjoy all such real and personal estate as may be necessary and proper for the construction, extension and usefulness of the works of said company, and for the management and good government of the same; and they may have a common seal, and the same may alter, break and renew at pleasure. **Incorporation.** **Name.** **General powers.**

SEC. 2. The corporation hereby created, shall have full power and authority forthwith, upon their due organization, under this act, to proceed to the erection of the necessary works for the manufacture of gas and coke within said city of Chicago, and on and after the 12th day of February, A. D. 1859, to manufacture and sell gas, to be made from **Manufacture and sell gas.**

any or all the substances, or a combination thereof, from which inflammable gas is usually obtained, and to be used for the purpose of lighting the city of Chicago, or the streets thereof, and any buildings, manufactories, public places, or houses therein contained, and to erect all necessary works and apparatus as aforesaid; and on and after the said 12th day of February, 1859, or sooner, by and with the consent of the Chicago Gas Light and Coke Company, to lay pipes for the purpose of conducting the gas in any of the streets or avenues of said city, with the consent of the city council: *Provided*, That no permanent injury or damage shall be done to any street, lane or highway in said city. The real estate which this corporation is entitled to hold, shall not exceed in value one hundred thousand dollars.

Lay pipe.

Capital stock.

SEC. 3. The capital stock of said company shall not exceed five hundred thousand dollars, to be subscribed for and paid in such proportions as shall be prescribed by the by-laws and rules for regulating the concerns of said company, as they shall think proper and necessary respecting the management and disposition of the stock, property and estate of said company, the duties of the officers and agents to be employed, the number and election of directors, and all such matters as appertain to the concerns of said company.

By-laws.

Price of gas.

SEC. 4. It is an express provision of the foregoing act of incorporation, that the said company shall furnish and supply to the city of Chicago, for all its public uses, at the election of the proper authorities of said city, a sufficient supply of gas, at a rate not exceeding two dollars per thousand feet; and the inhabitants of said city at a rate not exceeding two dollars and fifty cents per thousand feet.

Approved February 12, 1855.

AN ACT to amend an Act entitled "An Act to incorporate the People's Gas Light and Coke Company," approved February 12, 1855.

SECTION
1. Second section of former act amended, and powers enlarged.
2. Capital stock fixed at $500,000, and may be increased at pleasure; how divided, etc.

SECTION
3. Directors, election and powers; fourth section of former act repealed; price of gas.
4. Power to borrow money, etc.
5. This act public, and to take effect from passage.

SECTION 1. *Be it enacted by the People of the State of Illinois, represented in the General Assembly*, That the second section of said act be, and the same is, hereby so amended as to read as follows, viz.: The corporation hereby created shall have full power and authority forthwith to proceed to the erection and maintenance of the necessary works for the manufacture of gas and coke within said city of Chicago, and to manufacture, supply and sell gas, to be made from any and all substances, or a combination thereof, from which inflammable gas is usually obtained, and to be used for the purpose of lighting the city of Chicago, any streets, buildings, manufactories, public places or houses therein contained; and to erect and use all necessary works and apparatus for such purposes aforesaid, and, with the consent of the common council of said city, to lay down and use all necessary pipes for the conducting of gas, in and along any of the streets, alleys, avenues or public squares of said city: *Provided*, That no permanent injury or damage shall be done to any such street, alley, avenue or public square, by the laying down of any such pipes. **Second section of former act amended.**

SEC. 2. That section three of the said act be, and the same is hereby so amended as to read as follows, viz.: The capital stock of said company shall be five hundred thousand dollars, and may be increased from time to time, at the pleasure of said corporation; it may be divided into such shares, subscribed for, paid, and transferred, in such proportions and manner as shall be prescribed by the by-laws and regulations of said company. **Third section of former act amended.**

SEC. 3. All the corporate powers of said corporation shall be vested in, and exercised by, a board of directors, and such officers and agents as said board shall appoint. The board of directors shall consist of not less than three nor more than five stockholders, who shall be chosen by the stockholders at such time and in such manner as the said corporation shall, by its by-laws, prescribe, and shall hold their office until their successors are elected and qualified, and may fill any vacancies which may happen in the board of directors, by death, resignation or otherwise. **Directors.** They may adopt such by-laws, rules and regulations for the government of said corporation, and the management of its **By-laws.**

Fourth section of former act repealed. affairs and business, as they may think proper, not inconsistent with the laws of this State. And the fourth section of said act is hereby repealed; but ten years after the passage of this act, the common council of the city of Chicago Price of gas. may, by resolution or ordinance, regulate the prices charged by said company for gas, but said common council of the city of Chicago shall, in no case, be authorized to compel the said company to furnish gas at a less rate than three dollars per thousand feet.

Borrow money, etc. SEC. 4. The said company is hereby authorized to borrow money, and to mortgage or lease any of its property or franchises.

This act public and in force. SEC. 5. This act shall be deemed a public act, and noticed as such by all courts, without pleading, and take effect from and after its passage.

Approved February 7, 1865.

AN ORDINANCE concerning the People's Gas Light and Coke Company.

SECTION 1. Permission to lay pipe, etc., in streets, etc.; conditions; liability for damages; further conditions as to principal streets; proviso as to conflict with rights of the Chicago Gas Light and Coke Company.

Permission to lay pipe, etc. SECTION 1. *Be it ordained by the Common Council of the City of Chicago*, That permission and authority be, and the same are, hereby granted to the People's Gas Light and Coke Company, of the city of Chicago, and State of Illinois, to lay their gas mains, pipes, feeders, and service pipes, in any of the streets, alleys, avenues, highways, public parks or squares, throughout said city, subject at all times, however, to the resolutions and ordinances of the common Conditions. council of said city: *Provided*, That said company, when they shall open the ground to lay any pipe, or for any other purpose whatever, they shall restore the streets, pavements and sidewalks to a condition satisfactory to the city superintendent, with all convenient dispatch, and no more of any street or alley shall be opened or encumbered at any one time or in any one place, nor shall any street or alley be suffered to remain open or encumbered for a longer period than shall be strictly necessary to enable said company to proceed with their work; and said company shall be liable for all damages which may result from or by reason of opening or encumbering any street, alley or sidewalk in said city of Chicago: *And provided further*, That whenever said company shall desire to lay their pipes, or do other work in any of the principal streets of said city, before they commence doing so they shall consult the mayor or city superintendent of public works, and unless the mayor or superintendent consent to such work being done at the particular time, they shall not proceed with such work on any such principal street, without the express permission of the common council of said city of Chicago: *And provided further*, That nothing herein contained shall be construed to conflict with any rights or privileges heretofore given by the common council to the Chicago Gas Light and Coke Company, or in conflict with the provisions contained in the act of incorporation of the People's Gas Light and Coke Company, to first obtain the consent of the Chicago Gas Light and Coke Company, if pipes are laid previous to February 12th, A. D. 1859.

Liability for damages.

Further conditions as to principal streets.

Proviso.

Passed August 30, 1858.

HORSE RAILWAYS.

AN ACT to promote the construction of Horse Railways in the City of Chicago.

SECTION
1. The Chicago City Railway Company incorporated.
2. Authorized to construct, etc., railways on streets, etc., of south and west divisions of Chicago, upon certain terms specified.
3. Capital stock; amount and mode of issue and transfer.
4. Board of directors; election and term of office; by-laws, etc.
5. May extend railways through the county of Cook; power to take private property.

SECTION
6. May lay railway on highway in township, with assent, etc.; not to obstruct travel; other vehicles to give way.
7. Ordinances of city in favor of corporators confirmed.
8. Restrictions as to track on State street, and the use of steam power.
9. Two railways to be built within two years.
10. The North Chicago Railway Company incorporated, with same powers as to north division of Chicago.
11. This act public, and to take effect from passage.

SECTION 1. *Be it enacted by the People of the State of Illinois, represented in the General Assembly*, That Franklin Parmelee, Liberty Bigelow, Henry Fuller and David A. Gage, and their successors, be, and they are hereby created

The Chicago City Railway Company incorporated.

and constituted a body corporate and politic, by the name of "The Chicago City Railway Company," for the term of twenty-five years, with all the powers and authority incident to corporations, for the purposes hereinafter mentioned.

Name.

Power to construct.

SEC. 2. The said corporation is hereby authorized and empowered to construct, maintain and operate, a single or double track railway, with all necessary and convenient tracks for turn-outs, side tracks and appendages in the city of Chicago, and in, on, over and along such street or streets, highway or highways, bridge or bridges, river or rivers, within the present or future limits of the south or west divisions of the city of Chicago, as the common council of said city have authorized said corporators or any of them, or shall authorize said corporation so to do, in such manner and upon such terms and conditions, and with such rights and privileges as the said common council has, or may, by contract with said parties, or any or either of them, prescribe; but said corporation shall not be liable for the loss of any baggage carried on said railways, kept in and under the care of its owner, his servant or agent.

Terms and conditions.

Capital stock.

SEC. 3. The capital stock of said corporation shall be one hundred thousand dollars, and may be increased from time to time at the pleasure of said corporation. It shall be divided into shares of one hundred dollars each, and be issued and transferred in such manner and upon such conditions as the board of directors of said corporation may direct.

Directors.

SEC. 4. All the corporate powers of said corporation shall be vested in and exercised by a board of directors, and such officers and agents as said board shall appoint. The first board of directors shall consist of said Franklin Parmelee, Liberty Bigelow, Henry Fuller and David A. Gage, and thereafter of not less than three nor more than seven stockholders, who shall be chosen each and every year by the stockholders, at such time and in such manner as the said corporation shall by its laws prescribe. The said directors shall hold their offices until their successors are elected and qualified, and may fill any vacancies which may happen in the board of directors, by death, resignation or otherwise. They may also adopt such by-laws, rules and

By-laws, etc.

regulations, for the government of said corporation and the management of its affairs and business, as they may think proper, not inconsistent with the laws of this State.

Extend through county.

SEC. 5. The said corporation is hereby authorized to extend the said several railways herein authorized to be built, in the manner aforesaid, to any point or points within the county of Cook, in this State; and, to enable said corporation to construct any or all the railways herein authorized, or their appendages, the said corporation is hereby vested with power to take and apply private property for the purposes and in the manner prescribed by an act entitled "An Act to amend the law condemning right of way for purposes of internal improvement," approved June 22, 1852, and the several acts amendatory thereof, and may exercise all the powers conferred upon railroad corporations by the twenty-fifth and twenty-sixth sections of "An Act to provide for a general system of railroad incorporations," approved November 5, 1849, ascertaining and making recompense for all damages sustained agreeably to the provisions of the act herein before first mentioned.

May take private property.

May use highway.

SEC. 6. The said corporation is hereby authorized, with the assent of the supervisor of any township, to lay down and maintain its said railway or railways, in, upon, over and along any common highway in said township, but in such manner as not to obstruct the common travel of the public over the same. In all cases where vehicles shall meet the cars or carriages of said railways, either in the city or country, said vehicles shall give way to the cars or carriages on the railway.

Vehicles to give way.

Ordinances confirmed.

SEC. 7. All the rights and privileges granted, or intended so to be, to said Franklin Parmelee, Liberty Bigelow, Henry Fuller and their associates, in and by the ordinances of the common council, and the amendments thereto, are hereby, in all things, affirmed, and shall pass to and become vested in the corporation hereby created.

Restrictions on double tracks.

SEC. 8. Nothing herein contained shall authorize the construction of more than a single track, with the necessary turn-outs, which shall only be at street crossings, upon State street between Madison and Twelfth streets, except by the consent of the owners of two-thirds of the property, in lineal measurement, lying upon said State street between Madison and Twelfth streets aforesaid, nor shall anything herein contained be construed to authorize the company, hereby incorporated, to permit the cars of any other railroad company whatever, propelled by steam, to be run along or upon the railway of the company hereby incorporated.

Steam.

Two tracks to be built in two years.

SEC. 9. The said company hereby incorporated shall, within two years from the passage of this act, erect, maintain and operate two railways; one from Lake street to the southern boundary of the city, and one from the south branch of the Chicago river, on Madison street, to the western boundary of said city; and upon failure to do so, this act, and all the privileges and franchises hereby conferred, shall cease and determine.

The North Chicago Railway Company incorporated.

SEC. 10. All the grants, powers, privileges, immunities and franchises conferred upon, and all duties and obligations required of Franklin Parmelee, Liberty Bigelow, Henry Fuller and David A. Gage, by this act, for the south and west divisions of the city of Chicago and the county of Cook, are hereby conferred upon and required of William B. Ogden, John B. Turner, Charles V. Dyer, James H. Rees and Valentine C. Turner, by the name of "The North Chicago Railway Company," for the north division of said city and said county of Cook, as fully and effectually, to all intents and purposes, as if they had been, by a separate act, incorporated with all of said grants, powers, privileges, immunities and franchises conferred upon them, and all of said duties and obligations imposed upon them; and the said last named corporation may take, hold, mortgage and convey real estate.

Public act. Take effect.

SEC. 11. This act shall be deemed a public act, and noticed by all courts as such without pleading, and shall take effect from its passage.

Approved February 14, 1859.

AN ACT to authorize the extension of Horse Railways in the City of Chicago.

SECTION
1. The Chicago West Division Railway Company incorporated.
2. Powers and restrictions; proviso.
3. Board of directors; election and term of office; by-laws, etc.

SECTION
4. Special powers.
5. Penalty for obstructing railways.
6. Act public, and to take effect from passage.

SECTION 1. *Be it enacted by the People of the State of Illinois, represented in the General Assembly*, That Edward P. Ward, William K. McAllister, Samuel B. Walker, James L. Wilson, Charles B. Brown, Nathaniel P. Wilder, and their successors, be, and they are hereby created and constituted a body corporate and politic, by the name of "The Chicago West Division Railway Company," for the term of twenty-five years, with all the powers and authority pertaining to corporations for like purposes. **The Chicago West Division Railway Company incorporated.**

SEC. 2. The said corporation shall possess all the powers conferred by, and be subject to all the provisions contained in the second, third, fifth and sixth sections of an act entitled "An Act to promote the construction of horse railways in the city of Chicago," approved February 14th, 1859: *Provided*, That nothing herein contained shall be so construed as to in any manner invalidate or injuriously affect any of the rights of either of the corporations created by said act, or to authorize the corporation hereby created to construct or use any railway track in the north division of Chicago, except by the written consent of The North Chicago City Railway Company: *And further provided*, The consent of the owners of two-thirds of the property, by lineal measure, fronting upon the streets through which said railways shall pass, shall be obtained. **Powers and restrictions.** **Proviso.**

SEC. 3. All the corporate powers of said corporation shall be vested in and exercised by a board of directors, and such officers and agents as said board shall appoint. The first board of directors shall consist of said Charles B. Brown, James L. Wilson, William K. McAllister, Samuel B. Walker and Nathaniel P. Wilder, and thereafter of not less than three nor more than seven stockholders, who shall be chosen each and every year, by the stockholders, at such time and in such manner as the said corporation shall by its laws prescribe. The said directors shall hold their offices **Directors.**

until their successors are elected and qualified, and may fill any vacancies which may happen in the board of directors by death, resignation or otherwise. They may also adopt such by-laws, rules and regulations for the government of said corporation and the management of its affairs and business as they may think proper, not inconsistent with the laws of this State.

By-laws, etc.

Special powers.

SEC. 4. The corporation hereby created is authorized to purchase, hold and convey real or personal estate; to mortgage or lease its franchises and property; to acquire, unite and exercise any of the powers, franchises, privileges or immunities conferred upon The Chicago City Railway Company by the act aforesaid, or any ordinance of the common council of said city, upon such terms and conditions as may by contract between the said railway corporations be prescribed; and the consent of the board of directors of the said Chicago City Railway Company, manifested in writing, shall be a condition precedent to the corporation hereby created exercising the powers, or any of them, conferred upon it by the second section of the act aforesaid, as to any streets of said south and west divisions of Chicago, in which the said Chicago City Railway Company has acquired the right of laying down its track: *Provided*, That upon obtaining such contract or consent, as aforesaid, this corporation shall thereupon and thereby become entitled, as to the streets last above mentioned and no others, to use the same according to the provisions of said contract and the ordinances aforesaid, anything herein contained to the contrary notwithstanding.

Penalty for obstructing.

SEC. 5. If any person shall willfully and maliciously obstruct either of the corporations aforesaid, or that hereby created, in the use of any of their railway tracks, or the passing of the cars of either of said corporations thereon, such person, and all who shall be aiding or abetting, shall be punished by a fine not exceeding five hundred dollars, or may be imprisoned in a common jail for a period not exceeding three months.

Public act.

SEC. 6. This act shall be deemed a public act, and

noticed by all courts as such without pleading, and shall take effect from its passage. Take effect.

Approved February 21, 1861.

AN ACT to incorporate The Chicago and Evanston Railroad Company.

SECTION
1. The Chicago and Evanston Railroad Company incorporated.
2. General powers; restrictions as to laying tracks on certain streets.
3. Capital stock.

SECTION
4 Directors; election and term of office.
5. Proceedings to obtain right of way.
6. Act in force from passage, and for fifty years.

SECTION 1. *Be it enacted by the People of the State of Illinois, represented in the General Assembly,* That James G. Hamilton, George W. Thompson, Orrington Lunt, Hugh T. Dickey, Jabez K. Botsford, S. B. Chase, Henry Smith, Edwin Haskins, Thomas C. Hoag, Isaac N. Arnold, J. F. Willard and John Evans, and their associates, who may be such by becoming stockholders in this company, and their successors, be, and they are hereby created a body politic and corporate, by the name and style of "The Chicago and Evanston Railroad Company," with power to sue and be sued, plead and be impleaded, to adopt a common seal and alter it at pleasure; to adopt such by-laws, rules and regulations as they may deem expedient; and to have and exercise all other rights and powers necessary to carry out the intentions of this act. Incorporation. Name.

SEC. 2. They shall have power to locate, construct, maintain and operate, with horse or locomotive cars, from the city of Chicago to any point in the town of Evanston, a railroad, with a single or double track, turn-outs, sidings, depots and all other necessary appliances. They may contract with The North Chicago Horse Railroad Company, or any other company or party, to operate their road, or the road of such other party, either separately or jointly, as may be agreed upon. They may acquire, by donation, stock subscription or purchase, dispose of and convey, as they may deem expedient, real estate, not to exceed in value on hand at any one time the capital stock of the company; and, for the purpose of carrying out the intentions of this act, they shall have power to borrow money, not to exceed in amount the capital stock of the company, and to secure the General powers.

payment thereof by pledge or mortgage of any or all of its property, rights, credits and franchises. No authority is or shall be granted to said company, or to any other corporation or party, by the city of Chicago, to lay any railroad track in Wells, Dearborn, Wolcott, Cass, Rush, Pine, North or South Clark streets, or in Wabash or Michigan avenues, in the city of Chicago; but the laying of the same is hereby expressly prohibited.

Laying of track on certain streets prohibited.

Capital stock.

SEC. 3. The capital stock of the company shall be one hundred thousand dollars, which shall be divided into shares of one hundred dollars each. It may be increased by a two-thirds vote of all the stock of the company, at any regular meeting of the stockholders, to an amount not to exceed three hundred thousand dollars. Books may be opened for subscriptions to the stock of the company, as may be deemed expedient by the board of directors.

Directors.

SEC. 4. The affairs of the company shall be managed by a board of twelve directors, a majority of whom shall form a quorum. After the expiration of the term of the first board they shall be elected, annually, by the stockholders, as may be provided in the by-laws, and shall hold their office for one year, and until their successors are elected. The persons herein named as corporators shall be the first board of directors.

Right of way.

SEC. 5. In procuring the right of way for said railroad, they shall be entitled to such privileges and rights to cross or run along highways as may be granted by the commissioners of highways of the towns through which it may pass; and when, on account of non-residence, minority or other disability to sell, on the part of owners of property, or where parties refuse to grant their property, or fail to agree as to compensation for the right of way or depot grounds, said company may condemn and take the same, according to the provisions of "An Act to amend the law condemning the right of way for purposes of internal improvements," approved June 22, 1852.

Take effect.

SEC. 6. This act shall take effect and be in force from and after its passage, and continue for fifty years.

Approved February 16, 1861.

AN ACT concerning Horse Railways in the City of Chicago.

SECTION
1. Former acts extended.
2. Amendment of former act, enlarging the powers.
3. Ordinance of the city of Chicago, as to The Chicago and Evanston Railroad Company, confirmed.

SECTION
4. Power to hold real estate and manufacture materials.
5. This act public, and to take effect from passage.

Former acts extended.

SECTION 1. *Be it enacted by the People of the State of Illinois, represented in the General Assembly*, That the first section of an act of said General Assembly entitled "An Act to promote the construction of horse railways in the city of Chicago," approved February 14, 1859, and the first section of a certain other act of said General Assembly, entitled "An Act to authorize the extension of horse railways in the city of Chicago," approved February 21, 1861, be, and the same are hereby so amended as that all the words in said respective sections after the word "company" therein respectively, shall be and read as follows, viz.: For ninety-nine years, with all the powers and authority hereinafter expressed, or pertaining to corporations for the purposes hereafter mentioned.

General powers enlarged.

SEC. 2. That the second section of the act first above referred to by its title, and which section is included in and made a part of the act secondly above referred to by the title thereof, be, and the same is hereby, as to both of said acts, so amended as to read as follows, viz.: The said corporation is hereby authorized and empowered to construct, maintain and operate, a single or double track railway, with all necessary and convenient tracks for turn-outs, side tracks and appendages, in the city of Chicago, and in, on, over and along such street or streets, highway or highways, bridge or bridges, river or rivers, within the present or future limits of the south and west divisions of the city of Chicago, as the common council of said city have authorized said corporations, or any of them, or shall from time to time authorize said corporations, or either of them, so to do, in such manner, and upon such terms and conditions and with such rights and privileges, immunities and exemptions, as the said common council has, or may, by contract with said parties, or any or either of them, prescribe; and any and all acts or deeds of transfer of rights, privileges or franchises, between the corporations in said several acts named, or any two of them, and all contracts, stipulations, licenses and undertakings, made, entered into or given, and as made or amended by and between the said common council and any one or more of the said corporations, respecting the location, use or exclusion of railways in or upon the streets, or any of them, of said city, shall be deemed and held and continued in force during the life hereof, as valid and effectual, to all intents and purposes, as if made a part, and the same are hereby made a part of said several acts: *Provided*, That it shall be competent for the said common council, with the written consent or concurrence of the other party or parties, or their assigns, to any of said contracts, stipulations, licenses or undertakings, to amend, modify or annul the same. But said corporations shall not, or any or either of them, be liable for the loss of any property or thing carried on said railways, kept in and under the care of its owner, his servant or agent: *Provided*, That any contract hereafter made by the common council of the city of Chicago with either of the corporations referred to in this act, for a higher rate of fare than five cents, shall be subject to modification or repeal at any regular meeting of said common council, by a majority vote of all the aldermen elected, or by the General Assembly of the State of Illinois.

Ordinance confirmed.

SEC. 3. An ordinance of the common council of the city of Chicago, entitled "An Ordinance concerning the maintenance and operation of The Chicago and Evanston Railroad in the limits of the city of Chicago," as passed on the 17th day of August, A. D. 1864, is hereby confirmed, and shall be deemed and held to confer on The Chicago and Evanston Railroad Company, power and authority to construct and operate their road in the streets and over the bridge mentioned therein, until the same is altered, changed or amended by the common council, with the consent of said company. And such ordinance may, from time to time, be changed, altered or amended, and such other provisions be made as, to the common council, may seem proper, and be agreed to by said company. The prohibition as to the use of certain streets, in the second section of the charter of The Chicago and Evanston Railroad Company, is hereby re-enacted, and shall remain in force until altered, released or amended by the common council of the city of Chicago and said company.

SEC. 4. Each of said corporations shall be authorized to purchase, hold and convey real or personal estate, necessary for the use of such corporation, and to manufacture materials, machinery and rolling stock for the use of such corporation. Additional powers,

SEC. 5. This act shall be deemed a public act, and noticed by all courts as such, without pleading, and shall take effect from its passage. Act public. Take effect.

Passed by the Legislature over the veto of the Governor, February 6, 1865.

AN ORDINANCE to authorize the construction and operation of certain Horse Railways in the Streets of the City.

SECTION
1. Certain persons authorized to lay railway tracks in certain streets of the city of Chicago.
2. Steam power prohibited.
3. Use of railway limited.
4. Council may establish regulations.
5. Grading, paving, etc., of streets.
6. Kind of rail, and laying of track.
7. Rates of fare.

SECTION
8. When railways to be built.
9. Provisions as to incorporation.
10. Time during which right shall continue.
11. Purchase by city; terms of.
12. Saving of others' rights.
13. Assent of land owners required.
14. Agreement to be made.

SECTION 1. *Be it ordained by the Common Council of the City of Chicago*, That there is hereby granted to Roswell B. Mason, Charles B. Phillips, and such persons as may hereafter become associated with them, and to their executors, administrators or assigns, permission or authority and consent of the common council to lay a single or double track for a railway, with all necessary and convenient tracks for turn-outs, side tracks and switches, in any or all of the following streets in said city, to wit: Certain persons authorized to lay tracks in certain streets.

State street, in the south division, beginning at Randolph street and extending to the present and future southern city limits; thence east on Ridgely place to Cottage Grove avenue. Also, beginning in said State street at the intersection of Ringgold place; thence east upon Ringgold place to Cottage Grove avenue; thence on Cottage Grove avenue, southerly, to the present and future southern limits of the city. Also, beginning at State street at the intersection of South division.

Washington street; thence west on Washington street to Market street.

North division. Dearborn street, beginning at Kinzie street in the north division at the intersection of Dearborn street; thence north on Dearborn street to North street; thence west on North street to the Green Bay road; thence on the Green Bay road to the present and future north limits of the city.

Franklin street, beginning at Kinzie street in said north division at the intersection of Franklin street; thence north on Franklin street to Division street; thence west on Division street to Clybourne avenue; thence on Clybourne avenue to Racine street; thence on Racine street to the present and future north limits of the city. Also, beginning on Division street at the intersection of Sedgwick street; thence north on Sedgwick street to the Green Bay road.

Archer road. Archer street, or road, beginning at its intersection with State street; thence south-westerly on said Archer street, or road, to the present or future limits of the city.

And to operate railway cars and carriages thereon, in the manner, for the time, and upon the conditions hereinafter mentioned and prescribed.

Steam carriages prohibited. SEC. 2. No locomotive or engine propelled by steam shall ever be used upon any of said railways within the limits of the city; and the carriages used thereon shall be of the best style, with all the modern improvements, and shall be propelled by none other than animal power.

Use of railway limited. SEC. 3. The common council may at any time, or from time to time, limit the use of said railways, or any of them, or any part thereof, to the transportation of passengers and their ordinary baggage, and no cars of any railroad within the State shall ever be allowed to run upon any or either of the railways herein mentioned.

Council to establish speed, etc. SEC. 4. The common council may, from time to time, fix and establish the rate of speed of running carriages or cars upon said railways, or any of them, and the time or times of departure from the termini of such road or roads, of such carriages or cars; and when so fixed or established by the common council, the said parties shall conform to the same: *Provided*, That the common council shall not require said parties to run any carriage or car at any time when the ordinary demand for passage in the same would not be sufficient to remunerate said parties for running such carriage or car: *And provided further*, That the common council shall never restrict the said parties from running such number of carriages or cars as said parties may think proper.

Parties to grade streets.

SEC. 5. The streets whereon said railways are to be constructed and opened as aforesaid, shall be wholly graded at the expense and cost of the parties constructing said railways, upon such grade as the common council shall establish, which said grade shall not, during the continuance of said railways, be altered or changed at the cost or to the damage of said company; and the said streets may be, in the first instance, planked at least twenty-four feet wide in the centre, by and at the expense of said company: *Provided*, That the said company shall be required to pave, macadamize or otherwise improve the said twenty-four feet in each of said streets, or any portion thereof, whenever the common council shall direct the remaining portions, corresponding with and opposite, to be so paved, macadamized or otherwise improved. And all moneys expended by the city for the improvement, grading or planking of either of the said streets, of benefit or value to said parties, for the objects and purposes in this ordinance contained, between the time of the passage hereof and the completion of either or all of the railways aforesaid, shall be refunded to the city by said company: *Provided*, That if the said company shall occupy any street now planked, they shall be required either to pay for the plank now laid down, or to remove and relay the same upon the sides of said street, outside of the twenty-four feet to be occupied by said company.

Planking, etc., to be done.

Plank to be paid for.

Tracks, how laid.

SEC. 6. The track of said railways shall not be elevated above the surface of the street, shall be laid with the "O G" rail, (so called,) and shall be so laid that carriages and vehicles can easily and freely cross said track at any and all points thereof, with the least obstruction possible.

Rates of fare.

SEC. 7. The rates of fare for any distance less than one mile shall not exceed five cents, and for any distance more than a mile, and within the limits of the city, shall not exceed ten cents for each passenger.

Rights, when forfeited.

SEC. 8. The rights and privileges given to the said parties by virtue of this ordinance, shall be forfeited to the city, unless the construction of one or more of said railways shall be commenced before the first day of September, A. D. 1856, and so much of all the routes aforesaid as shall not be fully completed within four years from the passage hereof, shall be forfeited to the city, unless the time shall be extended by the common council; and in case any or either of said routes, or any part thereof, shall be abandoned by the parties aforesaid, all improvements, except the iron rails upon such track or route so abandoned, shall be forfeited to the city.

Should parties become incorporate.

SEC. 9. If the said parties shall hereafter become incorporated under an act of the legislature of the State of Illinois, the rights and privileges granted by virtue of this ordinance shall extend to such corporation for the time and upon the conditions herein prescribed, and when such act of incorporation shall have been obtained, such corporation shall have all the rights and privileges hereby granted, as the successor of said parties, without further action of the common council.

Rights to extend, how long.

SEC. 10. The right to operate said railways shall extend to the full expiration of twenty-five years from the passage hereof, and at the expiration of said time, the parties operating said railways shall be entitled to enjoy all of said privileges until the common council shall elect, by order for that purpose, to purchase said railways, depots, depot grounds, station grounds, station houses, carriages, cars, horses, animals, harnesses, equipage, furniture, and implements of every kind, name and description, used in the construction or operation of said railways, or any of the appurtenances in and about the same, and pay for the same in the manner hereinafter mentioned.

City may purchase, when.

Time of taking possession by city, how fixed.

SEC. 11. Such order shall fix the time when said common council will take such railways and other property before mentioned, which shall not be less than six months after the passage of said order; and at the time of taking said railways and other property above mentioned, the common council shall pay to the parties operating the same, a sum of money, to be ascertained by computing the interest at six per cent. for one year, on such amount to be paid, so that such interest will amount to a sum equal to the earnings of said railways for the year next preceding the time when the common council shall take and pay for the same, after deducting all expenses paid out for running the same during the said year. Payment by city.

SEC. 12. All rights heretofore vested in the water commissioners, sewerage commissioners, Chicago gas light and coke company, or other corporation, are not to be impaired or affected by this ordinance, but the rights and privileges hereby granted are subject thereto. Rights of other corporations.

SEC. 13. The said R. B. Mason and Charles B. Phillips, their associates, executors, administrators and assigns, shall not lay down said railway track in said streets, for the purposes mentioned in this ordinance, without the assent of the land owners fronting on such parts or portions of said streets as the said Roswell B. Mason and Charles B. Phillips and their associates may desire to use, until after an act of the legislature of the State of Illinois, authorizing such use, shall have been obtained. Assent of land owners, etc.

SEC. 14. The said R. B. Mason and Charles B. Phillips shall enter into an agreement, to be signed by them and the mayor, and countersigned by the clerk of the city, obliging the said R. B. Mason and C. B. Phillips, their associates and assigns, and said city, to abide by and perform the stipulations herein contained, which agreement, when so executed, shall be obligatory upon both parties, and until such agreement shall be so executed, this ordinance shall have no force or effect. Agreement with city.

Passed March 4, 1856.

AN ORDINANCE authorizing the construction and operation of certain Horse Railways in the Streets of the City of Chicago.

SECTION
1. Permission to persons named, to lay railway tracks on certain streets, and operate thereon, upon conditions; tracks not to be within twelve feet of sidewalk.
2. Streets named upon which tracks may be laid.

SECTION
3. Only animal power to be used; cars of other railroads not to be used.
4. Used only for passengers, etc.; cars to be best class; power of council to regulate speed and time of running.
5. Tracks, how to be laid.

SECTION
6. Fare not to exceed five cents, except, etc.
7. Liability to pave, repair, etc., streets; liability for damages; to pay for paving, etc., already done.
8. When railways to be built; forfeiture; proviso as to injunctions.
9. If said persons become incorporated, corporation to have same rights.

SECTION
10. Rights to continue twenty-five years; city may then purchase the property.
11. Terms and manner of purchase.
12. Rights of others not to be affected.
13. Said persons to give bond; terms thereof.
14. Repeal of former ordinances.

Permission to lay and operate railway, on streets.

SECTION 1. *Be it ordained by the Common Council of the City of Chicago*, That there is hereby granted to Henry Fuller, Franklin Parmelee and Liberty Bigelow, and such other persons as may hereafter become associated with them, and to their executors, administrators and assigns, permission or authority and consent of the common council, to lay a single or double track for a railway, with all necessary and convenient tracks for turn-outs, side tracks and switches, in and along the course of certain streets in the city of Chicago, hereinafter mentioned, and to operate railway cars and carriages thereon, in the manner, and for the time, and upon the conditions hereinafter prescribed: *Provided*, That said tracks shall not be laid within twelve feet of the sidewalks upon any of the streets.

Streets named.

SEC. 2. That said parties are hereby authorized to lay a single or double track, for a railway, in and along the course of the following streets in said city, and extending the same as follows: Commencing on State street, at the south side of Lake street; thence south to the present city limits. Also, commencing on State street, at the junction of Ringgold place; thence on Ringgold place to Cottage Grove avenue; thence on Cottage Grove avenue to the present limits of the city of Chicago. Also, commencing on State street, at the junction of the Archer road; thence along the said Archer road to the present limits of the city. Also, commencing on State street, at the intersection of Madison street, and extending west along said Madison street to the present city limits.

Power, and cars.

SEC. 3. The cars to be used upon said tracks shall be operated with animal power only; and said railways shall not connect with any other railroad on which other power is used, and no railway car or carriage, used upon any other railroad in this State, shall be used or passed upon said tracks.

SEC. 4. The said tracks and railways shall be used for no other purpose than to transport passengers and their ordinary baggage, and the cars or carriages used for that purpose shall be of the best style and class in use on such railways. The common council shall have power at all times to make such regulations, as to the rate of speed and time of running said cars or carriages, as the public safety and convenience may require. Passengers; cars; council may regulate.

SEC. 5. The tracks of said railways shall not be elevated above the surface of the street; shall be laid with modern improved rails, and shall be so laid that carriages and other vehicles can easily and freely cross said tracks, at any and all points, and in any and all directions, without obstruction. Tracks, how laid.

SEC. 6. The rate of fare for any distance shall not exceed five cents, except when cars or carriages shall be chartered for a specific purpose. Fare.

SEC. 7. The said parties, their associates and successors, shall pay one-third of the cost of grading, paving, macadamizing, filling or planking, on the streets or parts of streets on which they shall construct their said railways, and in the respects last mentioned shall keep such portion of the respective streets as shall be occupied by their said railways, or either of them, in good repair and condition during the whole time that the privileges hereby granted to said parties shall extend, in accordance with whatever orders may be passed, in that behalf, by the common council of the said city of Chicago; and said parties shall be liable for all legal or consequential damages which may be sustained by any person by reason of the carelessness, neglect or misconduct of any agent or servant of said parties, in the course of their employment in the construction or the use of the said tracks or railways, and said parties shall moreover pay to the property owners on any street so used by them, as aforesaid, for their said railways, which has, since the first day of January, A. D. 1858, been paved, macadamized or planked, and at any time between said date last mentioned, and the time of going into the occupation of either of said respective streets with the said railway by said parties, their associates or successors, may be Grading, paving, etc., of streets. Repairs. Damages. Pay for former paving.

paved, macadamized or planked, one-third of the reasonable cost and expense thereof so paid by said property owners respectively.

When railways to be built.

SEC. 8. The rights and privileges granted to said parties, by virtue of this ordinance, shall be forfeited to the city of Chicago, unless the construction of one of said railways shall be commenced on or before the first day of November, A. D. 1858; and unless the said railway commencing on the south side of Lake street and extending to Ringgold place, shall be fully completed and ready for use on or before the fifteenth day of October, A. D. 1859; and the Madison street railway, commencing at the intersection of State street, and running on said Madison street to the city limits, completed and ready for use on or before the fifteenth day of October, A. D. 1860; and said railway, from Ringgold place to Cottage Grove avenue, and along the same to the city limits, by the first day of January, A. D. 1861; and all the remaining railways herein before mentioned, on or before the first day of January, A. D. 1863, the said railways, together with all improvements made upon the same, shall be forfeited to said city of Chicago, unless the common council of said city shall grant to said parties a further extension of time: *Provided*, That if said parties are delayed by the order or injunction of any court, the time of such delay shall be excluded, and the same time, in addition to the periods above prescribed, shall be allowed for the completion of said railways, as that during which they may be so delayed.

Forfeiture.

Proviso as to injunctions.

Provision as to incorporation.

SEC. 9. If the said parties, their associates or successors, shall hereafter become incorporated, the rights and privileges granted to them, by virtue of this ordinance, shall extend to such corporation for the time and upon the conditions herein prescribed, and when such act of incorporation shall have been obtained, such corporation shall have all the rights and privileges hereby granted, as the successors of said parties, without further action of the common council.

Term of twenty-five years.

SEC. 10. The right to operate said railways shall extend to the full time of twenty-five years from the passage hereof, and at the expiration of said time, the parties operating said railways shall be entitled to enjoy all of said privileges until the common council shall elect, by order for that purpose, to purchase said tracks of said railways, cars, carriages, station houses, station grounds, depot grounds, furniture and implements of every kind and description, used in the construction or operation of said railways, or any of the appurtenances in and about the same, and pay for the same in the manner hereinafter mentioned. Purchase by city.

SEC. 11. Such order shall fix the time when said city of Chicago will take such railways, and other property before mentioned, which shall not be less than six months after the passage of said order, and at the time of taking said railways and other property, before mentioned, the city of Chicago shall pay to the parties operating the same, a sum of money to be ascertained by three commissioners, to be appointed for that purpose, as follows: One to be chosen from the disinterested freeholders of Cook county, by the said common council; one in like manner by the said parties, their associates or successors; and the two persons so chosen, to choose the third from said freeholders. Terms of purchase.

SEC. 12. All rights heretofore vested in the board of water commissioners and sewerage commissioners, or other corporations, are not to be impaired or affected by this ordinance, but the rights and privileges hereby granted are subject thereto. Rights of others.

SEC. 13. The said Henry Fuller, Franklin Parmelee and Liberty Bigelow, shall enter into a good and sufficient bond with the city of Chicago, in the penal sum of twenty-five thousand dollars, for the faithful performance of all the terms and conditions herein contained in this ordinance, and that said railways herein mentioned shall be completed at the times and manner herein stated, unless delayed by the order or injunction of some court having jurisdiction of such matters, from so completing the same, and until such bond shall be so executed by said parties, this ordinance shall have no force or effect whatever. Bond.

SEC. 14. All ordinances or parts of ordinances heretofore passed, respecting the subject-matter of this ordinance, (except that to which this is an amendment), or in conflict Repealing.

with this ordinance, or that to which the same is an amendment, is hereby repealed.

Passed August 16, 1858.

AN ORDINANCE to amend an Ordinance entitled "An Ordinance authorizing the construction and operation of certain Horse Railways in the Streets of the City of Chicago.

SECTION 1. Amending Section 7 of former ordinance as to paving, etc., of streets, and paying therefor, and amending Section 13 of former ordinance, as to bond.

SECTION 1. *Be it ordained by the Common Council of the City of Chicago*, That sections seven and thirteen of the above entitled ordinance be so amended as to read as follows, viz.:

Grading, paving, etc., of streets. That section seven be so amended as to read: The said parties and their associates shall, as respects the grading, paving, macadamizing, filling or planking of the streets, or parts of streets, upon which they shall construct their said railways, or any of them, keep so much of said respective streets as shall be occupied by the said railways, or either of them, in good repair and condition during all of the time to which the privileges hereby granted to said parties shall extend, in accordance with whatever orders or regulations respecting the ordinary repairs thereof, may be passed or adopted by the common council of said city; and the said parties shall be liable for all the legal consequential damages which may be sustained by any person, by reason of the carelessness or misconduct of any of the agents or servants of the said parties, in the course of their employment in the construction or use of the railways aforesaid, or either of them.

Damages.

Bond. And section thirteen be so amended as to read: The said Henry Fuller, Franklin Parmelee and Liberty Bigelow, shall enter into a penal bond, in the sum of twenty-five thousand dollars, with the said city of Chicago, conditioned for the faithful performance of all the terms and conditions in the said above entitled ordinance, as hereby amended, are contained and set forth; and that the railways aforesaid shall be completed at the time and in the manner in the aforesaid ordinance specified, unless delayed by the order or injunction of some court of competent jurisdiction, from so completing the same. And the giving of the bond above mentioned shall supercede the bond heretofore given by said parties under the original ordinance aforesaid, and the same shall be surrendered up and canceled.

Passed December 20, 1858.

AN ORDINANCE authorizing the extension and operation of certain Horse Railways in the Streets of the South and West Divisions of Chicago.

SECTION
1. Permission to The Chicago City Railway Company to lay and operate tracks on streets, upon conditions; tracks not to be within twelve feet of side walks, where, etc.
2. Streets named.
3. When railways to be completed.
4. Animal power only to be used; cars of other railroads not to be used.
5. Used only for passengers, etc.; cars to be best class; power of council to regulate speed and time of running.
6. Tracks, how to be laid.

SECTION
7. Fare not to exceed five cents, except, etc.
8. Grading, paving, etc., of streets; liability for damages.
9. Forfeiture for failure to complete railways according to third section; proviso as to injunctions.
10. Rights of others not to be affected.
11. Rights under former ordinances in favor of corporators, continued to corporation.
12. Corporators to give bond; terms thereof.

Permission to lay and operate railways on streets.

SECTION 1. *Be it ordained by the Common Council of the City of Chicago*, That under and by virtue of an act of the legislature of the State of Illinois, entitled "An Act to promote the construction of horse railways in the city of Chicago," approved the 14th day of February, A. D. 1859, constituting Franklin Parmelee, Liberty Bigelow, Henry Fuller, and David A. Gage, and their successors, a body corporate and politic, by the name of "The Chicago City Railway Company," and by virtue of the powers and authority in the said common council otherwise by law vested, consent, permission and authority are hereby unto the said "The Chicago City Railway Company" given, granted and duly vested, to lay a single or double track for a railway, with all necessary and convenient tracks for turn-outs, side tracks and switches, in and along the course of the streets and bridges of the south and west divisions of the city of Chicago hereinafter mentioned; and the same to keep, maintain and use, and to operate thereon railway cars and carriages, during all the term in the said act of the 14th February, A. D. 1859, specified and prescribed, in the manner and upon the conditions hereinafter prescribed: *Provided*, That said tracks shall not be laid within twelve feet of the sidewalk upon any of the streets hereinafter mentioned, in any case wherein it is practicable to be avoided.

Streets named.

SEC. 2. The said company is hereby, as above mentioned, authorized to lay a single or double track for such railways, in and along the course of the following streets of said south and west divisions of Chicago, and to extend the same as follows:

Commencing on Lake street, at the intersection of said Lake street with the east line of Market street, and thence west, with a single or double track, in and along the course of said Lake street, to Lake street bridge; thence westerly, with a single or double track, over said bridge, and in and along the course of said Lake street, to the present and future limits of the city.

Commencing on Randolph street, at the intersection with the State street railway, and thence west, with a single or double track, in and along the course of said Randolph street, to Union Park; thence in and along Park street to intersect with the said Lake street track.

Commencing on Desplaines street and intersecting with the said Lake street track, and thence northerly, with a single or double track, in and along the course of said Desplaines street, to Milwaukee avenue, and thence in and along the course of said Milwaukee avenue, to the present and future city limits.

Commencing on Canal street, at the point of intersection with said Lake street track, and thence southerly, with a single or double track, in and along the course of said Canal street, to intersect with the track to be upon Polk street, as hereinafter mentioned.

Commencing on Harrison street, at the intersection with Canal street aforesaid, thence westerly, with a single or double track, in and along said Harrison street to the southwestern plankroad.

Commencing on Market street, at the intersection with Lake street railway aforesaid, and thence southerly, with a single or double track, in and along the course of said Market street, to intersect with the Madison street railway.

Commencing on South Wells street, at the intersection with the said Randolph street track, and thence southerly, with a single or double track, in and along the course of said Wells street, to Polk street; thence westerly, with a like track, in and along the course of said Polk street, to Canal street, as aforesaid; and thence southerly, with a like track, in and along the course of said Canal street, to the Chicago, Burlington and Quincy Railroad.

Commencing on South Clark street, at a point intersecting said Randolph street track, and thence southerly, with a single or double track, in and along the course of said Clark street, to Polk street; and thence westerly, with a like track, in and along the course of said Polk street, to Wells street.

Commencing on State street, at the intersection of Van Buren street, thence westerly, on Van Buren street, and in and along said Van Buren street, to the southwestern plank-road.

Commencing on Harrison street, at its intersection with Canal street, and thence, with a like track, in and along said Harrison street, to Blue Island avenue; and thence, with a like track, in and along the course of said Blue Island avenue, to the Chicago, Burlington and Quincy Railroad.

Commencing on Twelfth street, at the intersection with State street railway, and thence easterly, with a single or double track, in and along the course of said Twelfth street, to Wabash avenue; thence south, with a like track, in and along said Wabash avenue, to Old street; thence, in and along said Old street, to Indiana avenue; thence, in and along Indiana avenue, to intersect with the Cottage Grove railway.

Also, commencing on Twelfth street, at the intersection of State street, thence westerly, in and along said Twelfth street, with a like track, to the intersection of Blue Island avenue.

SEC. 3. The said railway upon Randolph street, as aforesaid, is to be completed from said State street to Union Park, aforesaid, within three months, and from said Union Park to Robey street, within five months after the passage of

When to be completed.

this ordinance. The said railway upon Lake street, as aforesaid, to be completed, from said Market street to Union Park, as aforesaid; that upon South Wells street, as aforesaid, is to be completed from Randolph to Polk street, aforesaid; and that upon South Clark street, as aforesaid, is to be completed from said Randolph street to said Van Buren street, and in and along Van Buren street to the southwestern plankroad, severally, within eighteen months from the passage of this ordinance. And the said railway upon Canal street is to be extended and completed to the Chicago, Burlington and Quincy Railroad, and the said railways on Harrison street to Blue Island avenue, and on Blue Island avenue southerly to Twelfth street, are to be completed within one year from the passage of this ordinance. And the said railways upon Desplaines street and Milwaukee avenue are to be extended and completed to the city limits before the first day of the next session of the legislature of this State. The other of said railways included in the second section aforesaid, and not above in this section specified, shall be completed as soon after the passage hereof as may be practicable; but whenever the common council shall determine that the public interest requires any one of said railways last mentioned, to be constructed or extended, and shall by ordinance direct that such railway shall be constructed or extended, as the case may be, then said company shall be required to complete such construction or extension in sixty days after being notified of such ordinance: *Provided, however*, That such ordinance shall include but one street only; that then there shall be an interval of at least three months between such ordinances, and that the same shall not be made at an unseasonable time of year for doing such work.

Power, and cars.

SEC. 4. The cars to be used upon said tracks shall be operated with animal power only; and shall not connect with any other railroad on which other power is used, and no railway car or carriage used upon any other railroad in this State shall be used upon any of said tracks.

Passengers; cars; council may regulate.

SEC. 5. The said tracks and railways shall be used for no other purpose than to transport passengers and their ordinary baggage, and the cars and carriages for that purpose shall be of the best style and class in use on such railways. The common council shall have power at all times to make such regulations as to the rate of speed and time of running said cars or carriages as the public safety and convenience may require.

SEC. 6. The track of any such railways shall not be elevated above the surface of the street; shall be laid with modern improved rails, and shall be so laid that carriages and other vehicles can easily and freely cross said tracks, at any and all points, and in any and all directions, without obstruction: *Provided*, Whenever the said railway company construct two tracks on the same street, that the said tracks shall be constructed perfectly parallel, as far as practicable. **Tracks, how laid.**

SEC. 7. The rate of fare for any distance shall not exceed five cents, except when cars or carriages shall be chartered for special purposes. **Fare.**

SEC. 8. The said company shall, as respects the grading, paving, macadamizing, filling or planking of the streets or parts of streets upon which they shall construct their said railways, or any of them, keep eight feet in width along the line of said railway, on all streets whereon one track is constructed, and sixteen feet in width along the line of said railway, where two tracks are constructed, in good repair and condition during all the time to which the privileges hereby granted to said company shall extend, in accordance with whatever order or regulation respecting the ordinary repairs thereof, may be passed or adopted by the common council of said city. And the said company shall be liable for all legal consequential damages which may be sustained by any person by reason of the carelessness, negligence or misconduct of any of the agents or servants of the said company in the course of their employment in the construction or use of the railways aforesaid, or any or either of them. **Grading, paving, etc.** **Repairs.** **Damages.**

SEC. 9. If the said company shall fail to complete any of the aforesaid railways, in said second section mentioned, at the time mentioned and provided, and according to the conditions prescribed in the third section of this ordinance, then the rights and privileges granted by virtue hereof, respecting the said railways in the said second section mentioned, shall **Forfeiture for not completing.**

be forfeited, together with all or any improvements made upon any of the said railways, to the city of Chicago, unless the common council of said city shall grant to said company a further extension of time: *Provided*, That if said company is delayed by the order or injunction of any court, the time of such delay shall be excluded from the time above prescribed.

Rights of others.

SEC. 10. All rights heretofore vested in the board of water commissioners and sewerage commissioners, or other corporations, are not to be impaired or affected by anything herein contained, but the rights and privileges hereby granted are subject thereto.

Former rights continued.

SEC. 11. All the rights and privileges heretofore granted, or intended to be granted, to the said Franklin Parmelee, Liberty Bigelow and Henry Fuller, by an ordinance entitled "An Ordinance authorizing the construction and operation of certain horse railways in the streets of the city of Chicago," or any amendment thereto, are hereby granted and confirmed to the said "The Chicago City Railway Company," and its successors.

Bond.

SEC. 12. The said Franklin Parmelee, Liberty Bigelow, Henry Fuller and David A. Gage, shall enter into a bond with the city of Chicago in the penal sum of dollars, conditioned for the faithful performance by said company of all the terms and conditions of this ordinance, and that the railways aforesaid shall be completed at the time and in the manner in this ordinance specified, unless delayed by the order or injunction of some court of competent jurisdiction from so completing the same. And until such bond is made by the said parties, this ordinance is to have no force or effect whatever.

Passed May 23, 1859.

AN ORDINANCE amendatory of the Ordinance entitled "An Ordinance authorizing the extension and operation of certain Horse Railways in the Streets of the South and West Divisions of Chicago," passed May 23, 1859.

SECTION 1. Amending third section of last ordinance, by extending the time for constructing said railways.

SECTION 1. *Be it ordained by the Common Council of the City of Chicago*, That the third section of the ordinance entitled "An Ordinance authorizing the extension and operation of certain horse railways in the streets of the south and west divisions of Chicago," be, and the same is, hereby so amended that the time for the construction of the railway track on Clark street in said ordinance mentioned, be extended for the period of ten years, and that the time for the construction of the several railways, and each and every one thereof in said section mentioned or referred to, be extended for the period of five years beyond the time mentioned in said ordinance for the completion thereof: *Provided, however*, That the Blue Island avenue and the Milwaukee avenue lines shall severally be completed within the period of two years from the passage of this ordinance. **Extending time for construction**

Passed February 13, 1860.

AN ORDINANCE to accept a certain Resolution of the Chicago City Railway Company.

SECTION 1. Repealing ninth and twelfth sections of ordinance of May 23, 1859, by reference to a resolution of The Chicago City Railway Company, following this ordinance.

SECTION 1. *Be it ordained by the Common Council of the City of Chicago*, That the resolution of The Chicago City Railway Company, passed on the 18th day of February, 1860, tendered to this body, (to which reference is hereby made,) whereby the said company obligates itself to postpone the laying down of its track on South Clark street, for and during the period of ten years, be, and the same is, hereby in all things accepted, and said amendatory ordinance therein mentioned, affirmed. **Repealing by reference to resolution following this ordinance.**

Passed March 9, 1860.

Resolution referred to in foregoing Ordinance.

Resolved, That this company hereby accepts of the provisions of the ordinance of the common council of the city of Chicago, passed on the 13th day of February, 1860, amendatory of the 3rd section of an ordinance entitled "An ordinance authorizing the extension and operation of certain horse railways in the streets of the south and west divisions of Chicago," passed May 23, 1859. And in consideration thereof, and of the repealing by said council, (to be signified by acceptance hereof,) of the ninth and twelfth sections of the above entitled ordinance, this company, as to said South Clark street, will and hereby does agree to the postponement of laying down its track along said street, or any part thereof, for and during the time in said amendatory ordinance mentioned: *Provided*, That nothing herein contained shall prevent this company from using so much of said street as shall be necessary to make proper connections with the track of The North Chicago City Railway Company, in pursuance of any ordinance of the common council hereafter in that behalf to be passed.

CHICAGO CITY RAILWAY OFFICE, }
CITY OF CHICAGO. } ss. I, Geo. W. Fuller, Secretary of The Chicago City Railway Company, do hereby certify that the above is a true copy of a resolution passed by the board of directors of said company, at a meeting of said board, held on the 18th day of February, 1860.

Witness my hand and the corporate seal of said company, this 20th day of February, A. D. 1860.

GEO. W. FULLER,
[SEAL.] *Secretary Chicago City Railway Company.*

AN ORDINANCE exempting Canal Street and other Streets from Railway Uses, by substitution, and for other purposes.

SECTION
1. Change as to streets on which railways are to be constructed; certain streets to be kept free from railways.
2. Extension of time in which to construct railways upon certain streets; manner of construction and operation; time and rate of speed.
3. Forfeiture for failure to construct in time specified; proviso as to injunctions.

Change as to streets on which railways are to be constructed.

SECTION 1. *Be it ordained by the Common Council of the City of Chicago*, That in consideration of the extending by the Chicago City Railroad Company, of its railway upon West Lake street, from Robey street to the west limits of the city, within ninety days from the passage hereof, and the release and surrender by said company of any and all right to lay down a railway track along the course of either Canal street, Harrison street, or Lake street, from the east line of Market street to the same line of Desplaines street, and which said streets, so released, the said city is to preserve and keep at all times free from any such railway, authority and consent are hereby given and granted unto said company to lay down and use a single or double track for a railway, with all necessary and convenient tracks for turn-outs and switches in and upon Desplaines street, from Lake street, aforesaid, to Randolph street, and in, upon and along Halsted street, from said Lake street, southerly, to Blue Island avenue, and thence on Blue Island avenue to the city limits, but which last mentioned railway on said Halsted street and Blue Island avenue, said company shall not be required to construct at any time within three years from the passage hereof.

SEC. 2. That the ordinance entitled "An Ordinance authorizing the construction and operation of certain horse railways in the streets of the city of Chicago," passed August 16th, 1858, and also the ordinance entitled "An Ordinance authorizing the extension and operation of certain horse railways in the streets of the south and west divisions of Chicago," passed May 23rd, 1859, and all amendments thereof, be, and the same are, hereby so amended as that the time therein prescribed for the construction of the several railways therein mentioned, except said West Lake street, from Robey to the city limits, aforesaid, and also excepting the railway upon Desplaines street and Milwaukee avenue, north of Lake street, aforesaid, is extended for the period of five years. That both as to the construction and maintenance of each and every of the aforesaid railways, said company shall use suitable rails of not less than a five-inch flange, (except on Lake street west of Robey street,) for the purpose; shall avoid the unnecessary elevation of their tracks above the surface of the streets, and so lay, or where laid, so maintain the same as not necessarily to obstruct the passage of carriages or vehicles over them, or to impair the usefulness of the streets whereupon they are laid; shall run cars or carriages thereon of a suitable style and description, and at all such times and rate of speed as the public convenience and safety shall, to it, seem to require.

Extension of time in which to construct.

Manner of construction and operation.

SEC. 3. That if the said company shall fail to construct any portion of the railways aforesaid, within the time prescribed for doing the same, it shall thereupon forfeit all right to such portion; and if it fail to construct said railway on West Lake street, from Robey street to the city limits, within ninety days as aforesaid, it shall thereupon forfeit all and singular the rights, privileges, and extension of time by this ordinance granted, conferred, or intended, and all parts of the several ordinances aforesaid, inconsistent with any of the provisions of this ordinance, are hereby repealed: *Provided*, That if said company shall be delayed by the order or injunction of any court of competent jurisdiction from completing any of the railways aforesaid, the

Forfeiture for failure to construct in time specified.

Proviso as to injunction.

time of such delay shall be excluded from the period prescribed herein for completing the same.

Passed November 18, 1861.

Resolution and Release referred to in foregoing Ordinance.

Resolved, That upon the approval by the mayor of the city of Chicago, of an ordinance passed on the 18th day of November, 1861, by the common council of said city, entitled "An Ordinance exempting Canal street and other streets from railway uses, by substitution, and for other purposes," the president and secretary of this company are authorized to sign, seal and deliver to the said city of Chicago, on behalf of this company, a release in the following form, that is to say:

CHICAGO CITY RAILWAY OFFICE, }
CITY OF CHICAGO, } ss. I, Geo. W. Fuller, Secretary of The Chicago City Railway Company, do hereby certify that the above is a true copy of a resolution of record passed by the board of directors of said company, on the 19th day of November, A. D. 1861.

Witness my hand and the corporate seal of said company, this 19th day of November, A. D. 1861.

GEO. W. FULLER,
[SEAL.] *Secretary of the Chicago City R. W. Co.*

KNOW ALL MEN BY THESE PRESENTS, That The Chicago City Railway Company, for and in consideration of the passage by the common council, and the approval of the mayor of the city of Chicago, of a certain ordinance entitled "An Ordinance exempting Canal street and other streets from railway uses, by substitution, and for other purposes," have, and by these presents do hereby release and surrender unto the said city of Chicago, any and all right to lay down a railway track along the course of either Canal street, Harrison street or Lake street, from the east line of Market street to the same line of Desplaines street: *Provided, however*, That nothing herein contained shall be so construed as to affect the right of said railway company to cross said Canal street at the point of intersection therewith by any east and west street upon which said company has the right to a railway track, or to cross said Harrison street at the point of intersection therewith by Halsted street.

In Testimony Whereof, The said The Chicago City Railway Company has caused these presents to be signed by its president and secretary, and its corporate seal hereunto affixed, this 19th day of November, A. D. 1861.

W. H. WAITE, *Pres't.*
[SEAL.] GEO. W. FULLER, *Sec'y.*

AN ORDINANCE concerning the State Street Horse Railway.

SECTION
1. Permission to lay track for fair in 1862.

SECTION
2. Track to be taken up within twenty days after the fair.

Permission to lay track.

SECTION 1. *Be it ordained by the Common Council of the City of Chicago*, That the Chicago City Horse Railway Company be and is hereby permitted to build and lay down temporary tracks from Ringgold place to city limits on State street, and run cars thereon during the holding of the United States Horse Fair in September next.

Track to be taken up.

SEC. 2. That said company shall have the privilege and be compelled to take up said track within twenty days after the expiration of said fair, and leave said street in as good condition as it is at the present time.

Passed August 11, 1862.

AN ORDINANCE authorizing temporary Horse Railroad Tracks in the South Division.

SECTION
1. Permission to lay and operate track on certain streets during construction of sewer on other streets; removal; terms and conditions.

SECTION
2. Track to be under directions of board of public works.

SECTION 1. *Be it ordained by the Common Council of the City of Chicago*, That The Chicago City Railway Company is hereby authorized to lay a single or double track for a railway on State street, between Twenty-second and Twenty-third streets, and on Twenty-third street between State street and Cottage Grove avenue, and to operate the same in connection with the horse railroad of said company now on State street and Cottage Grove avenue: *Provided*, That said railway track shall be continued only during the construction of the main sewer now building on Twenty-second street between Cottage Grove avenue and State street, and that when said sewer is completed, the said track shall be removed by said company, and the said street be by them restored to as good condition as before being occupied by said track: *And provided further*, That said railway company, in the laying, maintaining and operating said temporary railway, shall be subject to all the general liabilities, regulations, restrictions and conditions concerning the same, and during its continuance in said streets as herein above provided, as by the laws of this State or the ordinances of the city of Chicago are imposed on said company concerning other railway tracks laid and operated by them in the south division of said city.

Permission to lay track.

Proviso for removal.

Terms and conditions.

SEC. 2. The said temporary railway track shall be laid by The Chicago City Railway Company, under the directions of the board of public works, subject, however, to any regulations as to the manner of laying the track required by any existing ordinances of the city.

Under direction of board of public works

Passed August 10, 1863.

AN ORDINANCE for the preservation of certain Streets of Chicago from Railway Uses.

SECTION
1. Certain streets named, to be kept from railway uses for twenty years.
2. Penalty for entering, etc., upon such streets to construct railway.
3. Saving of city from liability for damages.
4. Ordinance to take effect upon acceptance and execution of covenants by railway companies.

Certain streets named, to be kept from railway uses for twenty years.

SECTION 1. *Be it ordained by the Common Council of the City of Chicago*, That whereas, by an act of the general assembly of the State of Illinois, entitled "An Act to promote the construction of horse railways in the city of Chicago," approved February 14, 1859, and by an ordinance of the common council of said city entitled "An Ordinance authorizing the construction and operation of certain horse railways in the streets of the city of Chicago," passed August 16, 1858; and, also, by a certain other ordinance of said city, in pursuance of the act aforesaid, entitled "An Ordinance authorizing the extension and operation of certain horse railways in the streets of the south and west divisions of Chicago," passed May 23, 1859; and, also, by an ordinance of said city entitled "An Ordinance exempting Canal street and other streets from railway uses by substitution, and for other purposes," passed November 18, 1861, authority and consent were and are duly granted to, vested in and accepted by The Chicago City Railway Company and its assigns, to construct single or double track horse railways in, upon and along certain streets of said city, and to use the same for the period in said ordinances mentioned, among which said streets so mentioned are Wabash avenue and Lake street: and whereas, it is deemed and considered by the common council of said city that the permanent interest and welfare of said city demand the exclusion of all such railways from said Wabash avenue and from all of said Lake street east of the east line of Peck street, and from certain other streets hereinafter named, and that the same should be kept at all times free from such railways, and that no other railways than those above authorized should be permitted upon the streets in said ordinances mentioned, or those wherein they are now in use: whereas, also, The Chicago West Division Railway Company, in pursuance of an act of said general assembly, entitled "An Act to authorize the extension of horse railways in the city of Chicago," approved February 21, 1861, has acquired by contract with the said Chicago City Railway Company, all such right to use said streets as was and hereby is granted to said last named company as aforesaid, as to all the streets in said west division, and certain of the streets in the south division of Chicago, in said ordinances mentioned; and the said respective railway companies are now willing to give up and effectually to surrender to the city of Chicago any and all right to construct or use any railway along the course of any portion of said Wabash avenue, or of said Lake street east of the east line of Peck street, and also each of said corporations to enter into covenant, under their respective corporate seals, to and with the city of Chicago, to absolutely refrain, for all time hereafter, from constructing or using any railway along the course of either of said streets as last named, or of Michigan avenue, Third avenue, Washington street, Monroe street, Adams street or West Jackson street, (except necessary crossings of said streets), upon condition that the railways of all other persons or corporations shall likewise be excluded therefrom: now, therefore, in consideration of all and singular the premises, of said release and surrender as aforesaid, and of the making of the covenant by the said respective railway companies as aforesaid, the said common council do, by virtue and in pursuance of the said acts of the general assembly of the State of Illinois, and the powers therein otherwise vested by law, and for the promotion of the permanent interests of said city, ordain and declare that no railway track shall be constructed or used for or during the period of twenty years next hereafter, along the course of either Michigan avenue, Wabash avenue, Third avenue, Washington street, Lake street east of the east line of Peck street, Monroe street, Adams street or West Jackson street, or along any part or portion of the course thereof, nor shall the railway of any person or corporation, other than those above named and authorized as aforesaid, be constructed or used in, upon or along any of the several streets in said ordinances mentioned.

SEC. 2. That if any person or corporation shall enter

Penalty for entering, etc., upon such streets to construct railway.

upon either said Michigan avenue, Wabash avenue, Third avenue, Washington street, Lake street east of the east line of Peck street, Monroe street, Adams street or West Jackson street, or any portion of the same, (except at their crossings), or dig up any portion of said several streets, or bring upon any portion thereof any timber, ties, rails or other materials, with the intention of constructing any railway track along the course, in or upon either of said streets, said person or corporation, and all who shall be aiding or abetting, shall be subject to a fine of one hundred dollars for each and every offense.

Saving of city from liability.

SEC. 3. This ordinance shall not be construed to create any obligation, either express or implied, which shall in any event render the said city of Chicago liable to any action or claim for damages at the suit of either of the horse railway companies herein before mentioned, or their successors or assigns.

Ordinance to take effect, etc.

SEC. 4. This ordinance shall be in force and take effect as soon as the same shall have been duly accepted by the said Chicago City Railway Company and The Chicago West Division Railway Company, and the covenants herein before mentioned shall have been duly executed by said companies respectively.

Passed November 16, 1863.

Covenants referred to in foregoing Ordinance.

WHEREAS, At a regular meeting of the common council of the city of Chicago, held on the 16th day of November, A. D. 1863, an ordinance was passed, entitled "An Ordinance for the preservation of certain streets of Chicago from railway uses," to which reference is hereby made as a part hereof; and whereas, it is, amongst other things in substance recited in said ordinance, that The Chicago City Railway Company is willing to give up and effectually surrender to the city of Chicago any and all right to construct or use any railway along the course of any portion of Wabash avenue or of Lake street east of the east line of Peck street, in said city; and also to enter into covenant under its corporate seal, to and with the city of Chicago, to absolutely refrain for all time hereafter from constructing or using any railway along the course of either of said streets last named, or of Michigan avenue, Third avenue, Washington street, Monroe street, Adams street or West Jackson street, (except necessary crossings of said streets,) upon certain conditions in said ordinance mentioned. Now, therefore, to signify the acceptance of the said ordinance, by the said Chicago City Railway Company, and to cause the same to go into force and effect as therein provided, these articles of agreement, made and entered into this 21st day of November, A. D. 1863, between the said The Chicago City Railway Company, the party of the first, and the city of Chicago, party of the second part, witness, that the party of the first part, in consideration of the passage by the common council of the said ordinance as aforesaid, and the conditions and provisions therein contained, and in pursuance of a resolution of the board of directors of the said party of the first part, this day duly passed, has, and hereby does give up, effectually surrender and release to the said party of the second part, any and all right of the party of the first part to construct or use any railway along the course of any portion of Wabash avenue, or of Lake street east of the east line of Peck street, in said city, and does hereby covenant and agree to and with the said party of the second part, in pursuance of said ordinance, that it, the said party of the first part, will absolutely refrain, for all time hereafter, from constructing or using any railway along the course of either of said last named streets, or along the course of either Michigan avenue, Third avenue, Washington street, Monroe street, Adams street or West Jackson street, (except necessary crossings of said streets,) upon the conditions aforesaid: *Provided*, That nothing herein contained shall be so construed as to in any manner affect any of the rights of the said party of the first part to construct or use a railway upon any street of said city, not herein above specified.

Wherefore the said party of the first part has caused these presents to be signed by its president and secretary, and its corporate seal to be hereunto affixed, the day and year above written.

D. A. GAGE,
President Chicago City Railway Co.

[SEAL.] GEO. W. FULLER,
Secretary Chicago City Railway Company.

WHEREAS, At a regular meeting of the common council of the city of Chicago, held on the 16th day of November, A. D. 1863, an ordinance was passed, entitled "An Ordinance for the preservation of certain streets of Chicago from railway uses," to which ordinance reference is hereby made as a part hereof; and whereas, it is, amongst other things in substance recited in said ordinance, that The Chicago West Division Railway Company is willing to give up and effectually surrender to the city of Chicago any and all right to construct or use any railway along the course of any portion of Wabash avenue, or of Lake street east of the east line of Peck street in said city, and also to enter into covenant under its corporate seal to and with the city of Chicago, to absolutely refrain for all time hereafter, from constructing or using any railway along the course of either of said streets last named, or of Michigan avenue, Third avenue, Washington street, Monroe street, Adams street, or West Jackson street, (except necessary crossings of said streets,) upon certain conditions in said ordinance mentioned. Now, therefore, to signify the acceptance of the said ordinance by the said The Chicago West Division Railway Company, and to cause the same to go into force and effect as therein provided, these articles of agreement, made and entered into this twenty-first day of November, A. D. 1863, between the said The Chicago West Division Railway Company, the party of the first, and the city of Chicago, party of the second part, witness, that the party of the first part, in consideration of the passage by the common council of the said ordinance, as aforesaid, and the conditions and provisions therein contained, and in pursuance of a resolution of the board of directors of the said party of the first part, this day duly passed, has, and hereby does give up, effectually surrender and release to the said party of the second part, any and all right of the party of the first part to construct or use any railway along the course of any portion of Wabash avenue, or of Lake street east of the east line of Peck street, in said city, and does hereby covenant and agree to and with the said party of the second part, in pursuance of said ordinance, that it, the said party of the first part, will absolutely refrain, for all time hereafter, from constructing or using any railway along the course of either of said last named streets, or along the course of either Michigan avenue, Third avenue, Washington street, Monroe street, Adams street, or West Jackson street, (except necessary crossings of said streets,) upon the conditions aforesaid: *Provided*, that nothing herein contained shall be so construed as to in any manner affect any of the rights of the said party of the first part to construct or use a railway upon any street of said city not herein above specified.

Wherefore the said party of the first part has caused these presents to be signed by its president and secretary, and its corporate seal to be hereunto affixed, the day and year above written.

J. R. JONES,
President The Chicago West Division Railway Company.

[SEAL.] WM. H. OVINGTON,
Secretary The Chicago West Division Railway Company.

AN ORDINANCE for releasing of North Desplaines Street from Railway uses, and the substitution of North Halsted street.

SECTION
1. Track to be removed from Desplaines to North Halsted street; proviso against single track.
2. Grading, paving, repair, etc., of street, and condition of track.

SECTION
3. Time in which ordinance to be complied with; forfeiture for failure.
4. Ordinance to take effect on execution of release by railway company.

Track to be removed from Desplaines to North Halsted street.

SECTION 1. *Be it ordained by the Common Council of the City of Chicago*, That because of the numerous steam railway tracks now laid and in use on Kinzie street, whereby a horse railway upon said Desplaines street would be seriously obstructed in its connection with that upon Milwaukee avenue, and made both dangerous and inconvenient to the public, and in consideration of the release by The Chicago West Division Railway Company to the city of Chicago of any and all right to use said Desplaines street for railway purposes, authority and consent are hereby given and granted unto said railway company to remove its railway tracks from said Desplaines street, and to lay down and use a double track for a railway, with all necessary or convenient tracks for curves, turn-outs and switches, in and upon said North Halsted street, from the south line of West Lake street to the north line of Milwaukee avenue, subject to the conditions of the ordinances heretofore passed concerning said railway company or The Chicago City Railway Company, and all ordinances which may be hereafter passed concerning said West Division Railway Company: *Provided*, That no authority is hereby or shall be given to said company to construct or operate a single track on said North Halsted street.

Grading, paving, etc.

SEC. 2. The said Chicago West Division Railway Company, its successors or assigns, as respects grading, paving, macadamizing, filling or planking, shall, at their own expense, keep sixteen feet in width in repair on said North Halsted street, so far as the same is embraced in this ordinance, and keep their tracks in such condition that wagons, carriages and other vehicles can pass and repass at any and all points, and in any and all directions, and shall be subject to assessment for paving, repaving, planking, replanking, or any other kind of new improvement which may by ordinance be ordered at any time by the common council. Condition of track.

SEC. 3. The said railway company shall remove its track from said Desplaines street, and restore said street to its former state within thirty days from the time of the approval of this ordinance, and shall also within three months from said time construct a railway on said Halsted street, from the south line of said Lake street to said Milwaukee avenue, unless restrained by the order or injunction of some court of competent jurisdiction from so doing; and in case said company shall fail to remove said track from said Desplaines street, and construct a railway on Halsted street, according to the provisions of this ordinance, then the same shall forfeit all the rights and privileges by this ordinance granted or conferred. Time in which ordinance to be complied with. Forfeiture for failure.

SEC. 4. This ordinance shall be in force from the time of the execution of the said release by the said The Chicago West Division Railway Company, under the hands of its proper officers and corporate seal, and the delivery thereof to the clerk of the city of Chicago. Ordinance to take effect, etc.

Passed March 14, 1864.

AN ORDINANCE for the releasing of North Desplaines Street from Railway Uses, and the substitution of North Halsted Street.

SECTION
1. Track to be removed from Desplaines to North Halsted street; proviso against single track.
2. Grading, paving, repairing, etc., of street, and condition of track.

SECTION
3. Time in which ordinance to be complied with; forfeiture for failure
4. Ordinance to take effect on execution of release by railway company.

SECTION 1. *Be it ordained by the Common Council of the City of Chicago,* That because of the numerous steam railway tracks now laid and in use on Kinzie street, whereby Track to be removed from Desplaines to North Halsted street.

a horse railway upon said Desplaines street would be seriously obstructed in its connection with that upon Milwaukee avenue, and made both dangerous and inconvenient to the public, and in consideration of the release by The Chicago West Division Railway Company to the city of Chicago of any and all right to use said Desplaines street for railway purposes, authority and consent are hereby given and granted unto said railway company to remove its railway tracks from said Desplaines street, and to lay down and use a double track for a railway, with all necessary or convenient tracks for curves, turn-outs and switches, in and upon North Halsted street, from the south line of West Lake street to the north line of Milwaukee avenue, subject to the conditions of the ordinances heretofore passed concerning said railway company or The Chicago City Railway Company: *Provided*, That no authority is hereby or shall be given to said company to construct or operate a single track on said North Halsted street.

Grading, paving, etc.

SEC. 2. The Chicago West Division Railway Company, its successors or assigns, as respects grading, paving, macadamizing, filling or planking, shall, at their own expense, keep sixteen feet in width in repair on said North Halsted street, so far as the same is embraced in this ordinance, and keep their tracks in such condition that wagons, carriages and other vehicles can pass and repass at any and all points, and in any and all directions, and shall be subject to assessment for paving, repaving, planking, replanking, or any other kind of new improvement which may by ordinance be ordered at any time by the common council, on said Halsted street.

Condition of track.

Time in which ordinance to be complied with.

SEC. 3. The said railway company shall remove its track from said Desplaines street, and restore said street to its former state within thirty days from the time of the approval of this ordinance, and shall also, within three months from said time, construct a railway on said Halsted street, from the south line of said Lake street to said Milwaukee avenue, unless restrained by the order or injunction of some court of competent jurisdiction from so doing; and in case said company shall fail to remove said track from said Desplaines street and construct a railway on Halsted street,

Forfeiture for failure.

according to the provisions of this ordinance, then the same shall forfeit all the rights and privileges by this ordinance granted or conferred.

SEC. 4. This ordinance shall be in force from the time of the execution of the said release by the said The Chicago West Division Railway Company, under the hands of its proper officers and corporate seal, and the delivery thereof to the clerk of the city of Chicago. **Ordinance to take effect, etc.**

Passed March 28, 1864.

Release referred to in foregoing Ordinance.

KNOW ALL MEN BY THESE PRESENTS, That The Chicago West Division Railway Company, for and in consideration of the passage by the common council and the approval by the mayor of the city of Chicago, of a certain ordinance entitled "An Ordinance for the releasing of North Desplaines street from railway uses, and the substitution of North Halsted street," have, and, by these presents, do hereby release and surrender unto the said city of Chicago any and all right to lay down a railway track along the course of North Desplaines street, between Randolph street and Milwaukee avenue.

Witness the hands of the president and secretary of said company, and its corporate seal, this fourth day of April, A. D. 1864.

J. R. JONES, *President.*

[SEAL.] WM. H. OVINGTON, *Secretary.*

AN ORDINANCE authorizing temporary Horse Railway Tracks on Clinton Street, between Madison and Randolph Streets.

SECTION
1. Permission to lay track during building of Randolph street bridge; removal when bridge is completed; regulations, conditions, etc.
2. Track under direction of board of public works.
3. Penalty for not removing within twenty days after bridge is completed and in general use.
4. Ordinance to take effect, etc.

SECTION 1. *Be it ordained by the Common Council of the City of Chicago*, That The West Division Railway Company is hereby authorized to lay a single or double track for a railway on Clinton street, between Madison and Randolph streets, and to operate the same in connection with the horse railroads of said company, now on Randolph and Madison streets: *Provided*, That said railway track shall be continued only during the construction of the proposed new bridge across the Chicago river at Randolph street, and that when said bridge is completed, the said track shall be removed by said company, and the said street be by them restored to as good condition as before being occupied by said track: **Permission to lay track.** **Removal.**

27

Regulations, etc. *And provided further*, That the said railway company, in the laying, maintaining and operating said temporary railway, shall be subject to all the general liabilities, regulations and conditions concerning the same, during its continuance in said street, as herein above provided, as by the laws of the State and the ordinances of the city of Chicago are imposed on said company concerning other railway tracks operated by them in the city of Chicago.

Direction of board of public works. SEC. 2. The said temporary railway track shall be laid by the said West Division Railway Company, under the direction of the board of public works, subject, however, to any regulation, as to the manner of laying the track, required by any existing ordinance of this city.

Penalty for not removing. SEC. 3. Should the said company, its successors or assigns, fail or neglect to remove the said temporary railway track or tracks and superstructure from off said Clinton street, within the first twenty days next ensuing the day on which the proposed new bridge at Randolph street shall be completed and in general use, the said company, its successors or assigns, shall, for each and every day, after the lapse of said twenty days, that the said railway track or tracks and superstructure are allowed to be and remain upon said Clinton street, be fined in the sum of fifty dollars, to be collected as other fines.

Ordinance take effect. SEC. 4. This ordinance shall take effect and be in force from and after its passage and due publication.

Passed March 28, 1864.

AN ORDINANCE concerning Horse Railways on Clinton Street.

SECTION
1. Former ordinance amended so as to change temporary to permanent use of street for railway.

SECTION
2. Grading, paving, repair, etc., of street; condition of track.
3. Ordinance to take effect from its passage.

Former ordinance amended so as to change temporary to permanent use. SECTION 1. *Be it ordained by the Common Council of the City of Chicago*, That the ordinance entitled "An Ordinance authorizing temporary horse railway tracks on Clinton street, between Madison and Randolph streets," passed March 28th, 1864, be so amended as that the third section and the provisions of said ordinance for a temporary use only of said Clinton street, be, and the same are hereby repealed.

SEC. 2. That all the provisions and conditions contained in the second section of an ordinance entitled "An Ordinance for the releasing of North Desplaines street from railway uses, and the substitution of North Halsted street," passed March 28th, 1864, so far as the same applies to said Halsted street, be, and the same is hereby applied to said railway on Clinton street. **Grading, paving, etc.** **Condition of track.**

SEC. 3. This ordinance shall take effect from and after its passage. **Ordinance take effect.**

Passed July 11, 1864.

AN ORDINANCE creating new lines of Horse Railways, extending others, and regulating the use thereof.

SECTION
1. The Chicago West Division Railway Company authorized to construct and operate railways on certain streets named, with the consent of the owners of two-thirds of the property fronting on such streets.
2. Time in which such railways shall be constructed.
3. Grading, paving, repair, etc., of streets by the company; kind of rail, and general regulations.
4. Only animal power to be used; connection with, and use of track by other railway companies.
5. Facilities for funerals; fare, etc.
6. Ordinance in force from its passage.

SECTION 1. *Be it ordained by the Common Council of the City of Chicago,* That in consideration of the acceptance hereof, and the undertaking by The Chicago West Division Railway Company to comply with the provisions of this ordinance, authority and consent is hereby given and granted unto the said The Chicago West Division Railway Company, its successors and assigns, to construct, lay down, operate and maintain horse railways, with the necessary side tracks and switches, in the manner and upon and along the several streets hereinafter mentioned. Commencing on Clinton street, at its intersection with Madison street, and running south, with a single or double track, to Harrison street; thence south, with a single track only, to Twelfth street. Commencing on Meagher street, at its intersection with Canal street, and running west, with a single or double track, to Jefferson street; thence north, on Jefferson street, with a single or double track, to Twelfth street; thence north, with a single track only, to Harrison street; thence **The Chicago West Division Railway Company authorized to construct, etc., on certain streets named.**

north, with a single or double track, to Van Buren street. Commencing on Chicago avenue, at the river, so as to connect with the track of The North Chicago City Railway Company, and running west, with a single or double track, to the present or future city limits. Commencing on West Indiana street, at its intersection with Milwaukee avenue, and running west, with a single or double track, to the present or future city limits. Commencing on Catharine street, at its intersection with Blue Island avenue, and running west, with a single or double track, to Robey street. Commencing on Polk street, at the east line of Canal street, and running west, with a single or double track, to Jefferson street. Commencing on Desplaines street, at its intersection with Van Buren street, and running south, with a single or double track, to Sebor street; thence west, on Sebor street, to Halsted street. Commencing on Halsted street, at Harrison street, and running south, with a single or double track, to the south branch of the Chicago river. And commencing on Halsted street, at Milwaukee avenue, and running north, with a single or double track, to the centre of the north branch of the Chicago river: *Provided*, That the consent of the owners of two-thirds of the property, by lineal measure, fronting upon said streets, shall first be obtained.

Consent of owners of property.

Time of constructing.

SEC. 2. The said The Chicago West Division Railway Company, shall construct the railways aforesaid on Clinton street, Jefferson street and Meagher street, within ninety days from the passage of this ordinance, unless delayed by the order or injunction of some court of competent jurisdiction; and shall construct the railway on Chicago avenue, from Milwaukee avenue to Wood street, on West Indiana street, from Milwaukee avenue to Reuben street, and on Catharine street, from Blue Island avenue to Robey street, and on Halsted street, Desplaines street and Sebor street, within fifteen months from the passage of this ordinance.

Grading, paving, etc.

SEC. 3. The said The Chicago West Division Railway Company, its successors and assigns, shall, as respects the grading, paving, macadamizing, filling or planking of the streets or part of streets upon which they shall construct the said railways, or any of them, keep eight feet in width along the line of said railways, on all streets where one track is constructed, and sixteen feet in width along the line of said railways where two tracks are constructed, in good repair, so that wagons, carriages and other vehicles can pass and repass at any and all points, and in any and all directions; and when any new improvement, paving, repaving, planking or replanking, is ordered by the common council on any of said streets or parts of said streets, the said railway company shall, in the same manner and with like material as required of the owners of property as to other contiguous parts of the street, make such new improvements, on eight feet in width where a single track is used, or sixteen feet in width where a double track is used; and if the said company shall refuse or neglect to make such new improvement within a reasonable time, to be fixed by the ordinance, the work may be done by the city, and the cost thereof assessed by the board of public works on said company, and collected as other assessments, from any real or personal property of said company. But if the board of public works should deem it inexpedient that said new improvement should be so made by said company, then the same shall be done by the city as in other cases, and the costs thereof assessed upon and collected of said company in manner as aforesaid. And if the said company shall refuse or neglect to make any necessary repairs as aforesaid, or the repairs required by any ordinances heretofore passed, and now in force in respect to horse railway companies, after twenty days notice from the board of public works, the city may make the repairs and collect the cost thereof, by suit at law, in any court of competent jurisdiction. And said company shall construct all and singular its said respective railways of the kind of rail, and be subject to and governed by the ordinances in force respecting such railways in the south and west divisions of Chicago, except as herein otherwise provided.

Rail.

General regulations.

SEC. 4. The cars to be used on said several railways shall be operated by animal power only; and said railways shall not, or any of them, connect with any other railroad operated by other power; nor shall any other person or corporation operate or use any railway cars or carriages upon

Animal power.

Connection with other roads. or along any or either of said tracks or streets wherein such track is laid, without first having the consent, in writing, therefor of said railway company.

Facilities for funerals. SEC. 5. Said railroad company shall keep on hand a sufficient number of cars adapted to funeral purposes, in which shall be suitable compartments for carrying the corpse by itself; and, on application of any person, shall furnish not exceeding three cars, unless more shall be agreed upon, at some convenient point on the line of its said roads, so as not to hinder or delay other cars thereon, to convey the corpse and persons attending the funeral to any cemetery to which its lines or connections extend: *Provided*, That if its funeral cars shall all be engaged for funeral purposes before such application is made, the company shall not be bound to furnish the same until such prior engagement is fulfilled. And the said company shall make the best possible arrangement with the street railway companies whose lines do now or may hereafter extend to the cemeteries, to convey cars used for funeral purposes through to the cemeteries, so that the charge for conveying any corpse from points on said lines of railways through to the cemeteries, shall not exceed two dollars, and for each person attending such funeral not exceeding twenty-five cents for the round trip out and back. Fare.

Ordinance in force. SEC. 6. This ordinance shall be in full force and effect from and after its passage.

Passed August 17, 1864.

Stipulation in reference to foregoing Ordinance.

WHEREAS, The common council of the city of Chicago has passed an ordinance entitled "An Ordinance creating new lines of horse railways, extending others, and regulating the use thereof," on the 17th day of August, A. D. 1864; and whereas, the following provision occurs in the third section thereof, to wit: "And said company shall construct all and singular its said respective railways of the kind of rail, and be subject to and governed by the ordinances in force respecting such railways in the south and west divisions of Chicago, except as herein otherwise provided;" and whereas, some question has arisen as to whether the city of Chicago could, under said provision, regulate the kind of rail to be used by said company, now, for the purpose of removing all doubt on such question,

Resolved, by The Chicago West Division Railway Company, That said company admit, as a perpetual estoppel on it, its successors and assigns, that the said company are and shall be subject to the provisions of an ordinance passed by said common council on the 11th day of August, A. D. 1864, entitled "An Ordinance prescribing the gauge and rail to be used on horse railways in the city of Chicago," and any future ordinances hereafter passed by the common council on the kind of rail to be used in said city on horse railways. And the said ordinance first named is and shall be accepted by The Chicago West Division Railway Company, with the express understanding and condition that the construction herein set forth, shall be given to the clause quoted in the preamble hereof.

OFFICE OF THE CHICAGO WEST DIVISION RAILWAY COMPANY,
Chicago, August 25th, 1864.

I hereby certify, that the foregoing is a true copy of a preamble and resolution passed this 25th day of August, A. D. 1864, by the Board of Directors of The Chicago West Division Railway Company.

[SEAL.] WM. H. OVINGTON, *Secretary.*

AN ORDINANCE relating to Horse Railways in the South Division of Chicago.

SECTION
1. The Chicago City Railway Company authorized to construct and operate railways on certain streets named, with the consent of the owners of two-thirds of the property fronting on such streets.
2. Time in which such railways shall be constructed.
3. Kind of rail, and general regulations; grading, paving, repair, etc., of streets by the company.
4. Facilities for funerals; fare, etc.
5. Only animal power to be used; connection with, and use of track by other railway companies.
6. Ordinance in force from its passage.

SECTION 1. *Be it ordained by the Common Council of the City of Chicago,* That in consideration of the acceptance hereof, and the undertaking by The Chicago City Railway Company to comply with the provisions hereof, authority, permission and consent are hereby given, granted and duly vested in the said company, its successors and assigns, to construct, lay down, operate and maintain a single or double track railway, with all necessary turn-outs, side tracks and switches, in, upon and along Eighteenth street from State street railway to the east line of Wabash avenue; on State street from the south line of Lake street, northerly to the centre of Chicago river, and on Indiana avenue a single track, from Twenty-second street to the present or future city limits: *Provided,* That the consent of the owners of two-thirds of the property by lineal measure fronting upon said streets respectively, shall first be obtained.

The Chicago City Railway Company authorized to construct, etc., on certain streets named.

Consent of owners of property.

SEC. 2. The said railway on Eighteenth street and Indiana avenue shall be constructed within fifteen months after the passage of this ordinance, (unless restrained by a court of competent jurisdiction,) and the residue thereof as soon after the passage hereof as may be practicable; but whenever the common council shall duly determine that the

Time of constructing.

public interest requires any of said lines to be constructed, then said company may be required, by ordinance of said city, to construct the same within ninety days after the passage and actual notice of such ordinance.

Rail.

SEC. 3. Said company shall construct said several railways of the kind of rail prescribed by the ordinance passed August 11th, 1864, entitled "An Ordinance prescribing the gauge and rail to be used on horse railways in the city of Chicago," and all others hereafter passed on the subject of the kind of rails to be used by horse railways, and shall be subject to and governed by the ordinances of the common council of said city respecting horse railways in the south and west divisions, in force, except as herein otherwise provided. The said railway company, its successors or assigns, as respects grading, paving, macadamizing, filling or planking, shall, at their own expense, keep eight feet in width where a single track is used, and sixteen feet in width where a double track is used, of said streets, or parts thereof, so occupied, in good repair, so that wagons, carriages and other vehicles can pass and repass at any and all points, and in any and all directions, and when any new improvement, paving, repaving, planking or replanking, is ordered by the common council in any of said streets or parts of streets, the said railway company shall, in the same manner and with like material as required of the owners of property as to other contiguous parts of the street, make such new improvements, on eight feet in width where a single track is used, or sixteen feet in width where a double track is used; and if the said company shall refuse or neglect to make such new improvement within a reasonable time, to be fixed by the ordinance, the work may be done by the city, and the costs thereof assessed by the board of public works on said company, and collected as other assessments from any real or personal property of said company. But if the board of public works should deem it inexpedient that said new improvements on said streets should be made by said company, then the same shall be done by the city, as in other cases, and the cost thereof assessed upon and collected of said company in manner as aforesaid. And if the said company shall refuse or neglect to make any necessary

General regulations.

Grading, paving, etc.

repairs as aforesaid, or the repairs required by any ordinance heretofore passed and now in force in reference to the said railway company, after twenty days notice from the board of public works, the city may make the repairs and collect the cost thereof by suit at law in any court of competent jurisdiction.

SEC. 4. Said railroad company shall keep on hand a sufficient number of cars adapted to funeral purposes, in which shall be suitable compartments for carrying the corpse by itself; and, on the application of any person, shall furnish not exceeding three cars, unless more shall be agreed upon, at some convenient point on the line of said roads, so it will not hinder or delay other cars thereon, to convey the corpse, and persons attending the funeral, to any cemetery to which its lines or connections extend: *Provided*, That if its funeral cars shall be all engaged for funeral purposes before such application is made, the company shall not be bound to furnish the same until such prior engagement is fulfilled. And the said company shall make the best possible arrangement with the street railway companies whose lines do now or may hereafter extend to the cemeteries, to convey cars used for funeral purposes through to the cemeteries, so that the charge of conveying any corpse from points on said lines of railways through to the cemeteries, shall not exceed two dollars, and for each person attending such funeral not exceeding twenty-five cents for the round trip out and back. **Facilities for funerals.** **Fare.**

SEC. 5. The cars to be used on said several railways shall be operated by animal power only. Said railways shall not, or any of them, except as herein otherwise provided, connect with any other railroad operated by other power; nor shall the railway cars or carriages of any other person or corporation be used or operated upon or along any of the said railways, or any or either of the above mentioned streets, except with the consent of the said company. The said company is hereby permitted to operate or use upon or along any of said railways the cars or vehicles of any other railway company, person or corporation, for funeral processions. **Animal power.** **Connection with other roads.**

Ordinance in force.

SEC. 6. This ordinance shall be in full force from and after its passage.

Passed August 22, 1864.

AN ORDINANCE to promote the construction of Horse Railways to the Public Fairs.

SECTION
1. Kind of rail on Indiana avenue and State street.

SECTION
2. Fare to fair grounds; time during which this ordinance shall remain in force.

Kind of rail on Indiana avenue and State street.

SECTION 1. *Be it ordained by the Common Council of the City of Chicago*, That in order to afford increased and competent facilities for going to and from the public fair grounds in the southern suburbs of said city, The Chicago City Railway Company is hereby authorized to use, in extending its railways on Indiana avenue and State street, in said city, the pattern of rail therefor known as the Cleveland city pattern, all which rails to be so used on said streets to have a tram of not less than three inches in width, and to be laid within three months from the passage hereof.

Fare to fair grounds.

SEC. 2. That the said Chicago City Railway Company shall be authorized to collect and receive as fare for each passenger conveyed by it for any such fair, the sum of ten cents. The cars actually used for the purpose aforesaid, and those only, shall be properly designated, but shall not be so appropriated as to interfere with the ordinary street travel, and the carriage thereof. Nor shall anything herein contained be deemed in any manner to authorize said company to charge a sum exceeding five cents as to any other passengers than those carried for said fairs: *Provided*, That this ordinance shall cease to be of any force and effect from and after the 15th day of September A. D. 1865: *And provided further*, That if said State fair shall be postponed, that this ordinance shall remain in force for and until three days after the close of said fair in the year A. D. 1865.

Time during which this ordinance shall remain in force.

Passed June 12, 1865.

AN ORDINANCE authorizing the construction and operation of Horse Railways in the North Division of the City of Chicago.

SECTION
1. Permission to The North Chicago City Railway Company to lay and operate tracks on streets, upon conditions: tracks not to be within twelve feet of sidewalks when, etc.
2. Streets named.
3. Animal power only to be used; used only for passengers, etc.; cars to be best class.
4. Power of council to regulate speed and time of running.
5. Tracks, how to be laid.
6. Fare not to exceed five cents, except, etc.

SECTION
7. Grading, paving, etc., of streets; liability for damages.
8. Forfeiture for failure to complete railways within times specified; proviso as to injunctions.
9. Rights of others not to be affected.
10. Rights, etc., under this ordinance to continue twenty-five years, and no longer.
11. Company to give bond; terms thereof; ordinance not to take effect until bond is given.

SECTION 1. *Be it ordained by the Common Council of the City of Chicago*, That there is hereby granted to The North Chicago City Railway Company the consent, authority and permission of the common council to lay a single track for a railway, with all necessary and convenient tracks for turn-outs, side tracks and switches, in and along the course of certain streets in the city of Chicago, hereinafter mentioned, and to operate railway cars and carriages thereon, in the manner and for the time and upon the conditions hereinafter prescribed: *Provided, however*, That, except in turning street corners, said tracks shall not be laid within twelve feet of the sidewalk upon any of the streets. **Permission to lay and operate railways on streets.**

SEC. 2. The said company is hereby authorized to lay a single or double track for a railway in and along the course of any or all the following streets in said city, to wit: **Streets named.**

Commencing on Clark street, in the north division of said city, at its intersection with North Water, and extending thence north on Clark street to Green Bay road; thence on Green Bay road to the present or future northern city limits.

Also, beginning on said Clark street at the intersection of Division street, thence west upon Division street to Clybourn avenue; thence on Clybourn avenue to Racine road; thence in the same direct line to the northern city limits, whenever a street shall be opened on said line to said city limits.

Also, beginning on said Clark street at its intersection with Michigan street, and extending thence east on Michigan street to Rush street; thence north on Rush street to Chicago avenue; thence on Green Bay road to Wolcott street; thence north on Wolcott street to Elm street; thence west on Elm street to Clark street.

Also, commencing on Wells street at its intersection with North Water, and running thence north to Division street; thence west on Division street to Sedgwick street; thence north on Sedgwick street to its intersection with Green Bay road.

Also, commencing on Chicago avenue at its intersection with Rush street, and running thence west on Chicago avenue to the north branch of the Chicago river.

Power, and cars.

SEC. 3. The cars to be used upon said tracks shall (within the limits of the city) be propelled by animal power only, and the said tracks and railways shall be used for no other purpose than to transport passengers and their ordinary baggage, and the cars or carriages used for that purpose shall be of the best style and class in use on such railways.

Council may regulate.

SEC. 4. The common council shall have power at all times to make such regulations as to the rate of speed and time or times of running said cars or carriages as the public safety and convenience may require: *Provided*, That the common council shall not require said company to run any carriage or car earlier than five o'clock in the morning, nor later than eleven o'clock in the night.

Tracks, how laid.

SEC. 5. The tracks of said railways shall not be elevated above the surface of the streets, shall be laid with modern improved rails, and shall be so laid that carriages and other vehicles can easily and freely cross said tracks at any and all points, and in any and all directions, with the least obstruction possible.

Fare.

SEC. 6. The rates of fare for any distance within the city limits shall not exceed five cents for each passenger, except when cars and carriages shall be chartered for a specific purpose.

Grading, paving, etc.

SEC. 7. The said company shall, as respects the grading, macadamizing, paving, filling or planking of the streets or parts of streets upon which they shall construct their said railways or any of them, keep eight feet in width along the line of said railway, on all streets whereon one track is constructed, and sixteen feet in width along the line of said railway where two tracks are constructed, in good repair and condition during all the time to which the privileges hereby granted to said company shall extend, in accordance with whatever order or regulation respecting the ordinary repairs thereof may be passed or adopted by the common council of said city, and the said company shall be liable for all the legal consequential damages which may be sustained by any person, by reason of the carelessness, negligence or misconduct of any of the agents or servants of said company in the course of their employment in the construction or use of said railways or either of them. **Repairs.** **Damages.**

SEC. 8. Unless the said railway, commencing on said Clark street at its intersection with North Water street, and extending north to Green Bay road, and thence on Green Bay road to the present or future northern city limits, shall be completed and ready for use on or before the first day of January, A. D. 1860; and unless the said railway, commencing on Clark street at its intersection with Division street, and extending thence west on Division street to Clybourn avenue, thence on Clybourn avenue to Racine road, thence on the same direct line to the northern limits of the city, shall be completed on or before the first day of July, A. D. 1862, or within six months after a street shall have been opened from the intersection of Clybourn avenue and Racine road, on the same direct line with said Clybourn avenue, to the northern city limits; and unless the said railway, beginning on said Clark street at its intersection with Michigan street, and running thence east on Michigan street to Rush street, thence north on Rush street to Chicago avenue, thence on Green Bay road to Wolcott street, thence north on Wolcott street to Elm street, thence west on Elm street to Clark street, shall be completed on or before the first day of January, A. D. 1861; and unless all the remaining railways herein mentioned shall be completed on or before the first day of January, A. D. 1862, then the rights and privileges granted to said company by virtue of this ordinance shall be forfeited to said city of Chicago, unless the common council thereof shall grant to said company a further extension of time to construct the same: *Provided, however*, That nothing in this ordinance shall be so construed as to **Forfeiture for not completing.**

cause a forfeiture of any of said lines which shall be completed previous to the time herein specified for their respective completion: *And provided further*, That if said company shall be delayed by order or injunction of any court having competent jurisdiction, the time of such delay shall be excluded, and the same time in addition to the periods above prescribed shall be allowed for the completion of said railways as that during which they may be so delayed.

Rights of others. SEC. 9. All rights heretofore vested in the boards of water commissioners and sewerage commissioners or other corporations, are not to be affected by this ordinance, but the rights and privileges hereby granted are subject thereto.

This ordinance to continue twenty-five years. SEC. 10. The rights and privileges granted to the said company by this ordinance, or intended so to be, shall continue and be in force for the benefit of said company for the full term of twenty-five years from the passage of this ordinance, and no longer.

Bond to be given. SEC. 11. The North Chicago City Railway Company shall enter into a bond with the city of Chicago in the penal sum of twenty-five thousand dollars, conditioned for the faithful performance by said company of all the terms and conditions of this ordinance; and that the railways aforesaid shall be completed at the times and in the manner specified in this ordinance, unless delayed by the order or injunction of some court of competent jurisdiction from so completing the same; and until such bond is made by said parties, this ordinance is to have no force or effect whatever.

Passed May 23, 1859.

AN ORDINANCE supplementary to and explanatory of an Ordinance entitled "An Ordinance authorizing the construction and operation of Horse Railways in the North Division of the City of Chicago."

SECTION 1. Amending the foregoing ordinance as to grading, paving, repair, etc., of streets by the company; liability of company for damages.

Amending. SECTION 1. *Be it ordained by the Common Council of the City of Chicago*, That section 8 [7] of the ordinance entitled "An Ordinance authorizing the construction and operation of horse railways in the north division of the city of Chicago," passed May 23, 1859, be, and the same is hereby declared to read as follows: The said company shall, as respects the grading, paving, macadamizing, filling or planking of streets or parts of streets upon which they shall construct their said railways, or any of them, keep eight feet in width along the line of said railway on all streets where one track is constructed, and sixteen feet in width along the line of said railway on all streets where two tracks are constructed, in good repair and condition during all the time to which the privileges hereby granted to said company shall extend, in accordance with whatever order or regulation, respecting the ordinary repairs thereof, may be passed or adopted by the common council of said city. And the said company shall be liable for all legal consequential damages which may be sustained by any person by reason of the carelessness, negligence or misconduct of any of the agents or servants of the said company, in the course of their employment in the construction or use of the railways aforesaid, or any or either of them. Grading, paving, etc. Liability for damages.

Passed June 20, 1859.

AN ORDINANCE amendatory of an Ordinance authorizing the construction and operation of Horse Railways in the North Division of the City of Chicago.

SECTION 1. Tracks permitted to remain ten years.

SECTION 1. *Be it ordained by the Common Council of the City of Chicago*, That the tracks of The North Chicago City Railway Company, as now laid, be permitted to so remain for the period of ten years from and after this date. Tracks to remain ten years.

Passed March 9, 1860.

AN ORDINANCE extending the time for the construction of certain Horse Railways therein mentioned, and compelling The North Chicago City Railway Company to abandon their right to run upon and construct a Railway in North Wells Street.

SECTION 1. Time to construct certain railways by The North Chicago City Railway Company extended ten years, on condition that they release Wells street, and the right to use Franklin street, granted.

SECTION 1. *Be it ordained by the Common Council of the City of Chicago*, That The North Chicago City Railway Company shall have ten years in addition to the time fixed by the ordinance entitled "An Ordinance authorizing the construc- Extending time to construct, etc.

tion and operation of horse railways in the north division of the city of Chicago," for the construction of the several railways, or any parts thereof, named therein, as follows: On Michigan street to Rush street; thence north, on Rush street, to Chicago avenue; thence, on Green Bay road, to Wolcott street; thence north, on Wolcott street, to Elm street; thence west, on Elm street, to Clark street; from Division street to Sedgwick street; thence, on Sedgwick street, to Green Bay road; also, from Rush street, on Chicago avenue, to Clark street: *Provided, however*, and this extension is upon this express condition, That the said North Chicago City Railway Company shall release all the right they now have, or may hereafter acquire, to construct and run a railway on North Wells street in said city, and the right is hereby granted to said company to construct and operate a horse railway, in accordance with the ordinance hereby extended, on Franklin street, from its intersection with Chicago avenue, north to its intersection with Division street.

Substitution of Franklin for Wells.

Passed December 17, 1860.

AN ORDINANCE authorizing the connection of the Tracks of the Horse Railways of The North Chicago City Railway and The Chicago City Railway Companies.

SECTION
1. The North Chicago City Railway Company and The Chicago City Railway Company, authorized to connect their tracks, across the river at Wolcott and State streets.
2. Construction and operation subject to ordinance of May 23, 1859, in favor of first named company.
3. Companies to pave, etc.; rail; forfeiture for non-compliance.

Connection between north and south railways over State street bridge authorized.

SECTION 1. *Be it ordained by the Common Council of the City of Chicago*, That The North Chicago City Railway Company is hereby authorized to lay a single or double track, with the necessary curves and appendages, in and along Wolcott street, in the city of Chicago, from its intersection with Michigan street, to the centre of the Chicago river, at such points and in such way as that they may make connections with the tracks of The Chicago City Railway Company (by arrangement with said company) at such centre of the river, thereby making continuous lines of horse railway between the different divisions of the city;

and for this purpose the last named company is authorized to lay a single or double track, with the necessary curves and appendages, from the present point of intersection of the tracks of said last named company on State street, with Lake street, in said city of Chicago, in and along said State street to the centre of the Chicago river.

SEC. 2. The construction and operation of any road or roads that may be built under this ordinance, shall be subject to all the rules and limitations and restrictions that are prescribed in the ordinance heretofore passed by the common council, entitled "An Ordinance authorizing the construction and operation of horse railways in the north division of the city of Chicago," approved May 23, 1859. **Subject to provisions of former ordinance.**

SEC. 3. That the said companies shall, if a single track be laid, pave, macadamize, gravel or otherwise improve, in accordance with such ordinances as may be passed by the common council, eight feet in width, on the street occupied by said track; and if a double track be laid, they shall pave, macadamize, gravel or otherwise improve, in accordance with such ordinances as may be passed by the common council, sixteen feet in width, on the street occupied by said track: *Provided*, The form of rail to be used on said railroads, shall be the best and most modern improved tram rail: *And provided further*, In case any or either of said railroad companies should fail to comply with the provisions of this ordinance, or any previous ordinance granting railroad privileges to said companies, that the privileges hereby granted shall cease and become forfeited. **Paving, etc.** **Rail.** **Forfeiture.**

Passed January 18, 1864.

AN ORDINANCE authorizing The North Chicago City Railway Company to extend their Tracks on certain Streets.

SECTION
1. The North Chicago City Railway Company authorized to construct, etc., railways on certain streets named.
2. Time when such railways are to be completed.

SECTION
3. Subject to ordinance of May 23, 1859, in favor of said company, except as otherwise herein provided; right to regulate laying of track, and kind of rail, reserved.
4. Facilities for funerals; fare.
5. Grading, paving, repairs, etc.

SECTION 1. *Be it ordained by the Common Council of the City of Chicago*, That permission and authority be and is **Permission to construct, etc., on certain streets.**

hereby granted to The North Chicago City Railway Company to construct, maintain and operate a single or double track railway, with the necessary curves and side tracks, as an extension of the lines of railway now operated by said company, on the following streets, to wit: commencing at Chicago avenue and running on Larrabee street to Little Fort road, and thence on Little Fort road to the present or future city limits; and commencing at Larrabee street and running east on Linden street and Eugenie street to Wells street, and thence across Wells street, and on any street that may hereafter be laid out, to Green Bayr oad; except that on Larrabee street, from Chicago avenue to the north side of Hawthorne avenue, only a single track shall be laid.

Time for completion. SEC. 2. The line on Larrabee street, between Clybourn avenue and Centre street, shall be completed within sixty days after the passage of this ordinance, unless restrained by a court of competent jurisdiction, and the other lines of railways herein before mentioned shall be completed as soon as practicable after the passage of this ordinance; but whenever the common council shall determine that the public interest requires any of said lines to be constructed, and pass an ordinance that any of said lines shall be constructed in a period of time not less than ninety days after the passage of said ordinance, and actual notice thereof to said company, it shall be the duty of said company to comply with said ordinance: *Provided*, The work shall not be required to be done between the first day of November and the first day of May.

Subject to former ordinance. SEC. 3. The permission and authority hereby granted are made subject to all the restrictions and conditions, the rights and privileges mentioned in the ordinance passed by the common council on the 23rd day of May, 1859, entitled "An Ordinance authorizing the construction and operation of horse railways in the north division of the city of Chicago," except as otherwise herein provided, reserving to the common council the right to regulate the laying down of tracks, and the kind of rail to be used. **Power to regulate, etc**

Funeral facilities. SEC. 4. The said railway company shall keep on hand a sufficient number of cars adapted to funeral purposes, in which shall be suitable compartments for the carrying of the corpse by itself; and on the application of any person, shall furnish not exceeding three cars, unless more shall be agreed upon, at any designated point on the lines of any of its roads, to convey the corpse and persons attending the funeral to any cemetery to which their lines or connections extend: *Provided*, That, if their funeral cars are all engaged for funeral purposes before any such application is made, the company shall not be bound to furnish the same until such prior engagement is fulfilled. Said company shall be entitled to charge not exceeding two dollars for each corpse, and not exceeding twenty cents for the round trip for each person conveyed on such funeral occasion.

Fare.

The said company shall, on its part, make an arrangement with The Chicago City Railway Company, and The Chicago West Division Railway Company, as soon as the bridge is built across Chicago river at State street, to convey the cars of either of said companies, used for funeral purposes, over the tracks of said North Chicago City Railroad Company, to any cemetery to which its lines extend, so that the charge for conveying any corpse from any part of the city on any of the lines of said companies, shall not exceed three dollars, and for each person attending said funeral, shall not exceed twenty-five cents for the round trip to and from any such cemetery, which shall be in full for all the charges to all of said companies.

Arrangements with other railway companies.

Fare.

SEC. 5. The said railway company, its successors or assigns, as respects grading, paving, macadamizing, filling or planking, shall, at their own expense, keep eight feet where a single track is used, and sixteen feet where a double track is used, of said streets, or parts thereof, so occupied, in good repair, so that wagons, carriages and other vehicles can pass and repass at any and all points, and in any and all directions, and when any new improvement, paving, repaving, planking or replanking, is ordered by the common council in any of said streets or parts of streets, the said railway company shall, in the same manner and with like material as required of the owners of property as to other parts of the street, make such new improvements, on eight feet where a single track is used, or sixteen feet where a double track is used; and if the said company shall refuse

Grading, paving, repairs, etc.

or neglect to make such new improvement within a reasonable time to be fixed by the ordinance, the work may be done by the city, and the cost thereof assessed by the board of public works on said company, and collected as other assessments, from any real or personal property of said company. But if the board of public works should deem it inexpedient that said new improvement should be so made by said company, then the same shall be done by the city as in other cases, and the cost thereof assessed upon and collected of said company in manner as aforesaid. And if the said company shall refuse or neglect to make any necessary repairs as aforesaid, or the repairs required by any ordinances heretofore passed, after twenty days notice from the board of public works, the city may make the repairs and collect the cost thereof, by suit at law in any court of competent jurisdiction.

Passed August 11, 1864.

Stipulation in reference to foregoing Ordinance.

AUGUST 18, 1864.

At a meeting of the directors of The North Chicago City Railway Company, held at the office of said company this eighteenth day of August, A. D. 1864, the following resolutions were adopted:

"*Resolved*, That The North Chicago City Railway Company will and do hereby accept an ordinance passed by the common council of the city of Chicago on the 11th day of August, A. D. 1864, entitled 'An Ordinance authorizing The North Chicago City Railway Company to extend their tracks on certain streets,' and in so accepting the said ordinance, the said railway company declare that wherever the words 'eight feet' and 'sixteen feet' occur in the fifth section thereof, they mean, and shall be held to mean, 'eight feet in width,' and 'sixteen feet in width.'

"*Resolved*, That a certified copy of these resolutions be delivered to the city of Chicago."

JOHN J. GRAHAM,
Sec'y pro tem.

[SEAL.]

AN ORDINANCE concerning the maintenance and operation of the Chicago and Evanston Railroad in the limits of the City of Chicago.

PREAMBLE. Recital of incorporation, and location of line; first section of road designated; desirable to secure facility of access to the cemeteries.

SECTION
1. Permission to lay and operate railways on certain streets named, subject to certain ordinances, etc.
2. Grading, paving, repairs, etc.; cars; fare; funeral facilities and fare.
3. To keep an office, where and how, where application may be made for funeral facilities, and how to furnish.
4. Bridge at La Salle street; provisions concerning.
5. Time for completion; forfeiture for failure.
6. Ordinance in force from its passage.

WHEREAS, Under and by virtue of an act of the general assembly of the State of Illinois, entitled "An Act to incorporate The Chicago and Evanston Railroad Company," approved February 16, 1861, certain persons therein named, their associates and successors, are created a body politic and corporate by the name and style of "The Chicago and Evanston Railroad Company," and are authorized to locate, construct, maintain and operate with horse power or locomotive cars from the city of Chicago (excepting certain streets in said city) to Evanston; and whereas, as the said railroad company have, in pursuance of said act, commenced the location of their line of railroad, and desire to locate as follows: Commencing at the intersection of Madison street and La Salle street, and running thence north on La Salle street to Erie street; thence west on Erie street to Roberts street; thence with a single track, until the street shall be widened to the usual width, on Roberts street (or that street now opened and used by the public as Roberts street) to Larrabee street; thence north on Larrabee street with a single track to Hawthorne street; thence northwesterly on Hawthorne street to Halsted street; thence north on Halsted street to the northern limits of the city of Chicago; also, on Halsted street from the centre of the north branch of the Chicago river north to Hawthorne street: that portion of said road lying between Madison street and the northern limits of the city of Chicago being designated as the first section of said road. And whereas, among other advantages to be derived from the operation of said railroad, it is desirable to secure to the people of the city of Chicago facilities and convenience for transportation, and at reasonable rates, to and from the several cemeteries or burial grounds lying north of the city; therefore, Preamble.

SECTION 1. *Be it ordained by the Common Council of the City of Chicago*, That permission is given to said Chicago and Evanston Railroad Company to lay a single or double track railway, except on Larrabee street from Chicago avenue to Hawthorne street, and on Roberts street until widened as hereinafter mentioned, where there is to be a Permission to lay tracks on certain streets named.

single track only, with all the necessary and convenient switches, side tracks and turn-outs, in and along the course of the following streets in the city of Chicago, to wit:

Commencing at the intersection of Madison street and La Salle street, and running thence north on La Salle street to Erie street; thence west on Erie street to Roberts street; thence north on Roberts street (or that street now opened and used by the public as Roberts street) to Larrabee street, with a single track until said Roberts street is widened to the width of Larrabee street; thence north on Larrabee street with a single track to Hawthorne street; thence north-westerly on Hawthorne street to Halsted street; thence north on Halsted street to the northern limits of the city of Chicago; also, on Halsted street from the centre of the north branch of Chicago river north to Hawthorne street, and to keep and maintain, use and operate therein railway cars and carriages, in the manner and upon the conditions set forth and required by the various ordinances passed and now in force in relation to The Chicago City Railway Company and The Chicago West Division Railway Company, except as the same are herein modified.

Subject to certain ordinances.

Grading, paving, repairs, etc.

SEC. 2. The said railway company, its successors or assigns, as respects grading, paving, macadamizing, filling or planking, shall, at their own expense, keep eight feet in width where a single track is used, and sixteen feet in width where a double track is used, of said streets, or parts thereof, so occupied, in good repair, so that wagons, carriages and other vehicles can pass and repass at any and all points and in any and all directions; and when any new improvement, paving, repaving, planking or replanking, is ordered by the common council in any of said streets or parts of streets, the said railway company shall, in the same manner and with like material as required of the owners of property as to other parts of the street, make such new improvements on eight feet in width where a single track is used, or sixteen feet in width where a double track is used; and if the said company shall refuse or neglect to make such new improvement within a reasonable time, to be fixed by the ordinance, the work may be done by the city, and the costs thereof assessed by the board of public works on said company, and collected as other assessments from any real or personal property of said company. But if the board of public works should deem it inexpedient that said new improvement should be so made by said company, then the same shall be done by the city as in other cases, and the cost thereof assessed upon and collected of said company in manner as aforesaid. And if the said company shall refuse or neglect to make any necessary repairs as aforesaid, or the repairs required by any ordinances heretofore passed, after twenty days notice from the board of public works, the city may make the repairs, and collect the cost thereof by suit at law in any court of competent jurisdiction. The cars and carriages used on this road shall not be inferior to the best street railway cars or carriages now in ordinary use in said city; the rate of fare for any distance over said road within the city limits shall not exceed five cents, and the fare shall not exceed twenty-five cents for a round trip to each person attending funerals at Calvary, Graceland, Rose Hill or other cemeteries on the route, and shall not exceed forty cents for each adult person and twenty cents for each child under fifteen years of age for a round trip to and from either of said cemeteries on any and all other occasions, except when cars or carriages are chartered for a specific purpose for a number of persons less than a car load. And the said company, its successors or assigns, shall at all times keep on hand ready for use a sufficient number of cars expressly adapted, by compartments or otherwise, to the conveying or removal of the remains of deceased persons separate and apart from ordinary passengers or persons attending funerals, and shall not charge over the sum of two dollars for any one deceased person so carried from any point on the line of said railway in the city of Chicago to Graceland, Rosehill, Calvary or either of the cemeteries, on its route to Evanston; and whenever said company, its successors or assigns, shall be called upon and required to furnish cars for funeral purposes, such funeral train or car shall have priority over all other business on said railway.

Cars. Fare. Funeral facilities. Fare.

SEC. 3. Said company shall have an office in or near the business centre of the city, which shall be kept open every day from 7 o'clock A. M. to 7 o'clock P. M., where

Office where application may be made for

funeral facilities; and how to furnish.

application can be made for the use of cars for funeral purposes; and shall, when such application shall have been made, furnish at the nearest convenient point on the line of said railway, to any house or other place in this city where the corpse of any person or persons may be awaiting burial, as many cars for such purpose as the party making such application may desire, but shall not be bound thereby to furnish more than three cars, unless a larger number shall be agreed upon with such party, and shall proceed thence from said point to such cemetery on the line of said railway, as the relatives or friends of such deceased person or persons may direct; and when application as aforesaid shall be made at any time during the forenoon of any day, cars shall be furnished as early as three o'clock and thirty minutes in the afternoon of the same day, and when application shall be made in the afternoon of any day, cars shall be furnished as aforesaid in the forenoon of the following day.

Bridge at La Salle street; provisions concerning.

SEC. 4. That said company is hereby authorized to construct a bridge to cross the Chicago river at La Salle street, on the same general plan as the bridges at Clark and Wells streets, but the particular plans and specifications shall be furnished by the board of public works, and said bridge shall be constructed in accordance therewith, and under the direction of said board. Said bridge, when constructed, shall be subject at all times to the city regulations and management for the benefit of the public, the city to pay one-half the cost of said bridge: *Provided*, The whole cost of constructing said bridge and approaches does not exceed twenty-two thousand dollars: *And provided further*, That, if it shall be ordered by the common council that said bridge shall be constructed as that proposed for the bridge at State street, then, and in that event, the city shall pay the same as it pays for State street bridge.

Time for completion.

SEC. 5. The first section of said road shall be completed within fifteen months from the passage of this ordinance, and the balance of the track, from the south terminus of said road to Calvary Cemetery and Evanston, shall be completed within two years from the passage of this ordinance. If this company, its successors or assigns, shall fail to have its road constructed and in operation between Madison street, in the city of Chicago, and the village of Evanston, within two years from and after the passage of this ordinance, the common council of this city shall have the right to annul and declare void this ordinance, and order the superstructure and rails of said company, its successors or assigns, which may have been laid within the city limits, taken up and removed from the streets of the city; and if at any time, or for any cause, the rights, privileges or easements of said company, its successors or assigns, shall become forfeited, and the common council order their superstructure and rails removed from the street, they shall, without delay, and at their own cost and expense, remove the same, and put each and every street or part of street on which their railway track or tracks may have been laid at any time, in as good repair as the same was immediately preceding the time when said tracks were first laid: *Provided*, That if said company is delayed by order or injunction of any court, the time equal to such delay shall be added to the time specified above, and the forfeiture for not laying down track between the points above specified shall not be made until the company shall have had two full years to build its road, exclusive of the time it may be detained by order or injunction of any court: *And provided further*, That if the common council shall deem that there is any unreasonable delay on the part of said company in raising such injunction, they may direct the city attorney to take the management of such suit or suits, so far as to bring the same to a speedy decision. **Forfeiture for failure.**

SEC. 6. This ordinance shall take effect and be in force from and after its passage. **Ordinance in force.**

Passed August 17, 1864.

Stipulation in reference to foregoing Ordinance.

WHEREAS, The common council of the city of Chicago did, on the 17th day of August, A. D. 1864, pass an ordinance entitled "An Ordinance concerning the maintenance and operation of The Chicago and Evanston Railroad, in the limits of the city of Chicago; and whereas, the mayor of said city has not yet approved the said ordinance, and hesitates and refuses to approve the same on account of certain doubts which the said mayor has in relation to the proper construction of the said ordinance, and on account of certain objections thereto; now, for the purpose of removing the said doubts and objections, and in consideration of the approval by the mayor of the said ordinance, it is hereby

Resolved, That it was the intention, and is the proper construction of said ordinance, that "The Chicago and Evanston Railroad Company" should operate the cars and carriages used upon their railway tracks within the limits of said city of Chicago, with animal power only, and that the said railway should not connect with any other railroad on which any other power is used; and that as to the gauge and kind of rail to be used on the tracks of the said company, they are to be governed in all respects by an ordinance entitled "An Ordinance prescribing the gauge and rail to be used on horse railways in the city of Chicago," passed by the common council of said city, August 11th, 1864.

Resolved, That it was not the intention, and is not the proper construction of section four of said ordinance, that the said company should have the power to contract for the bridge therein mentioned, but the intention and proper construction of said section is, that the work upon the said bridge, and the building of the same, should be let, by contract, by the board of public works of said city as provided in and by the charter of said city; and it is further expressly agreed, that when the said company are desirous of having the said bridge constructed, they shall, as a condition precedent to the undertaking of the said work by the said city, or the letting of the contract for the same, deposit with the board of public works of said city a sum of money equal to half the estimated cost and expense of said work, or shall secure the payment of the said money by security satisfactory to the city comptroller and board of public works of said city.

Resolved, That the said ordinance, subject to the aforesaid construction of the same, and the aforesaid agreement as to the said bridge, is hereby accepted, and that a properly certified copy of these resolutions be delivered to the city of Chicago.

OFFICE OF THE CHICAGO AND EVANSTON RAILROAD COMPANY,
Chicago, Ill.

I do hereby certify, that the above and foregoing is a true copy of original preamble and resolutions, this day passed and adopted by the Board of Directors of The Chicago and Evanston Railroad Company, and duly entered upon the records of said corporation.

In witness whereof, I have hereunto set my hand and affixed the seal of said company, this 25th day of August, A. D. 1864.

[SEAL.] J. F. WILLARD, *Secretary.*

ICE.

AN ORDINANCE concerning the cutting of Ice in the Basin between Michigan Avenue and the Tracks of the Illinois Central Railroad.

SECTION
1. Comptroller to let the privilege of cutting ice.
2. To advertise for proposals.
3. Terms of contract to be made.
4. Bond for performance.
5. Other persons than contractor prohibited from cutting, etc.; penalty.
6. Furnishing ice from basin for domestic use; penalty.
7. This ordinance in force.

Comptroller let, etc.

SECTION 1. *Be it ordained by the Common Council of the City of Chicago,* That the comptroller of said city be, and he is hereby authorized and required to let the privilege of cutting and using the ice formed in the basin between Michigan avenue and the tracks of the Illinois Central Railroad, to the highest bidder or bidders, and on the terms as to payment as he shall deem best for the interests of said city.

SEC. 2. That annually before letting said privilege, said comptroller shall advertise in the corporation newspaper for bids or proposals, stating the time and place of receiving and opening the same, for at least ten days before said time. Advertising.

SEC. 3. On making the award, said comptroller shall require the party or parties to whom such award shall be made, to enter into a written contract to save and keep the city harmless from any and all damages that may in any way result from cutting or taking out said ice, and that the travel on Michigan avenue shall not in any wise be interfered with, and that said ice shall not be retailed, sold or supplied to any person or family for domestic uses or purposes. Terms of contract.

SEC. 4. Said comptroller shall also require the party or parties entering into said contracts, to execute and deliver to the said city good and sufficient bond or bonds for the faithful performance of such contracts. Bond.

SEC. 5. That all other persons be, and they are hereby prohibited from cutting or using the ice found in said basin, under the penalty of not less than five dollars nor more than one hundred dollars for each and every offense. Penalty for cutting, etc.

SEC. 6. That any person or persons, whether a contractor or otherwise, who shall sell, retail or furnish any ice from said basin for family or domestic uses or purposes, shall be liable to a fine of not less than five dollars nor more than one hundred dollars for each and every offense. Penalty for selling, etc.

SEC. 7. This ordinance shall be in force from and after its passage and due publication. Ordinance in force.

Passed November 27, 1865.

LAKE VIEW AVENUE.

CERTIFICATE OF INCORPORATION.

Object of corporation; directors and other officers; capital stock; name.

The undersigned, in pursuance of the provisions of an act of the general assembly of the State of Illinois, entitled

"An Act to provide for constructing, maintaining and keeping in repair, plank, gravel or macadamized roads or pikes, by a general law," approved February 21, 1859, hereby certify and declare their intention to construct, maintain and keep in repair a gravel or macadamized road, commencing at some convenient point on the shore of lake Michigan, within the limits of the north division of the city of Chicago, county of Cook, and State of Illinois, and running along the said shore, as near to the water as practicable and convenient, to the north line of the township of Lake View in said county of Cook; and we hereby further certify and declare, that for this purpose we have elected Uranus H. Crosby, William C. Goudy, Timothy S. Fitch, and Samuel H. Kerfoot, as directors in the corporation hereby created, to hold their office for the term of one year, or until such time as may hereafter be determined, according to the rules and by-laws of the said corporation, and until their successors are elected and enter upon their duties, and that we have elected the said Crosby to be the president of said corporation, and William B. Howard as secretary of the same.

We do further certify and declare, that the capital stock of said corporation shall be one hundred and fifty thousand dollars until increased under the provisions of said act, or otherwise, which shall be divided into shares of one hundred dollars each; and we do assume and certify the corporate name of ourselves and associates who may hereafter become holders of the capital stock aforesaid, to be "The Lake View Avenue Company."

In testimony whereof, we have hereunto subscribed our names this 30th day of December, A. D. 1864.

U. H. CROSBY.
W. C. GOUDY.
T. S. FITCH.
WM. B. HOWARD.
SAM'L H. KERFOOT.

I hereby certify the foregoing to be a correct copy of a certificate of organization filed in my office the 16th day of January, A. D. 1865.

Witness my hand and official seal this 17th day of January, A. D. 1865.

[SEAL.] LAURIN P. HILLIARD,
Clerk of Cook County Court, Illinois.

AN ACT to amend the charter of "The Lake View Avenue Company."

PREAMBLE. Reciting organization.
SECTION
1. Power to hold and sell real estate; make by-laws; invest funds.
SECTION
2. Common council may fix tolls, etc.; restrain by penalties.
3. Act public, and in force from its passage.

WHEREAS, "The Lake View Avenue Company" has been organized under and according to the provisions of an act entitled "An Act to provide for constructing, maintaining and keeping in repair, plank, gravel or macadamized roads or pikes, by a general law," approved February 21st, 1859, for the purpose of constructing, maintaining and keeping in repair a gravel or macadamized road in the county of Cook; therefore, Organization.

SECTION 1. *Be it enacted by the People of the State of Illinois, represented in the General Assembly,* That said corporation, in addition to its powers under said general law, be and is hereby authorized to take and hold by purchase, gift, grant or devise, real estate, not exceeding at any one time in value the sum of one hundred and fifty thousand dollars ($150,000), and to sell and convey the same, and to make and establish such by-laws and regulations in regard to the duties of its officers and agents, the use of its road and property, and the investments of its profits and funds, as are not inconsistent with the constitution of the State of Illinois or of the United States. Powers as to real estate, by-laws and investments

SEC. 2. The common council of the city of Chicago may fix and determine by contract with said company the rates of toll to be received by said corporation within the limits of said city, but the rates either within or without the said limits shall not exceed the following, to wit: For each horse, one cent and a half per mile; for each vehicle drawn by one horse, the same rate; and for each vehicle drawn by two or more horses, two and a half cents per mile. And the common council of said city may pro- Council may fix tolls, etc.

Restrain by penalties. vide by ordinance against the charge and receipt of greater rates within said city, and enforce the same by adequate penalties against said corporation, its officers or agents.

Act public and in force. SEC. 3. This act shall be deemed a public act, and shall take effect and be in force from and after its passage.

Approved February 16, 1865.

AN ORDINANCE concerning the right of way of The Lake View Avenue Company.

PREAMBLE. Reciting incorporation, etc.
SECTION
1. Right of way over property of city granted.
2. Conditions; to complete road and improve ground; how and when.
3. Where toll-gates may be erected.
4. Improvements to be approved, etc.
5. Not to obstruct passage on cross streets.
SECTION
6. To keep in repair; forfeiture for failure.
7. So much of road as may be within the city to become public at end of thirty years.
8. Tolls to be charged according to charter.
9. When ordinance in force.

Preamble. WHEREAS, The Lake View Avenue Company, by virtue of a general act of the legislature, approved February 21, 1859, and also of a special act, approved February 16, 1865, have acquired a right to condemn for roadway purposes, for a period of thirty years, commencing Dec. 30, 1864, a strip of land one hundred feet in width, along the shore of lake Michigan, in the north division of the city of Chicago, and the town of Lake View; and, whereas, it is considered necessary, in order to make such roadway available, that said roadway should be increased fifty feet in width; and, whereas, said roadway, as now located, passes over lands owned by the city of Chicago; therefore,

Right of way granted. SECTION 1. *Be it ordained by the Common Council of the City of Chicago*, That the right of way be and is hereby granted to the Lake View Avenue Company over the property of the city of Chicago, one hundred and fifty feet wide, next and adjacent to the present high water mark of lake Michigan, commencing at the south line of the grounds now used as the Chicago City Cemetery, North avenue, and running thence along the shore of lake Michigan to Asylum place, and commencing again at Fullerton avenue, and running thence along said shore to the north line of the southeast quarter of section twenty-eight (28), in township forty

(40) north, of range fourteen (14) east of the third principal meridian.

SEC. 2. The foregoing grant is made upon the express conditions named in this and the following sections. That the said Lake View Avenue Company shall, on or before the first day of August, A. D. 1866, make and complete in good order a road across said property at least fifty feet wide, and shall finish and improve the ground for the full width hereby granted, within one year thereafter. Conditions. Complete road. Improve ground.

SEC. 3. Said Lake View Avenue Company shall not erect any toll-gate south of Schiller street, or the street now known and designated by that name, nor shall said company erect or maintain more than one toll-gate within the corporate limits of the city of Chicago. Toll gates.

SEC. 4. That all improvements of said roadway or avenue, which are made on grounds not actually used as a road bed or passage way for carriages, etc., which are made between North avenue and Asylum place, shall be first approved by the board of public works, or such board or person or persons as shall, by virtue of any law or ordinance now or hereafter in force, have charge of the Chicago City Cemetery and Lincoln Park. Improvements to be approved.

SEC. 5. Said road shall be so constructed as not to interfere with the passage on, to or across such road or avenue from any street or streets which now are or may hereafter be laid out and opened to the water line of said lake Michigan, or the line of said avenue. Not to obstruct cross streets

SEC. 6. That said company shall keep said road or avenue in good repair and condition at their own expense, and if at any time said road or avenue shall be abandoned by said company, or suffered to become so out of repair as not to be safe for the passage of teams or carriages over and upon it, the said city shall have the right to enter upon said road, or so much thereof as may be in the city of Chicago, and declare the same a public highway, the same as other streets and avenues in said city. Repair. Forfeiture.

SEC. 7. That at the end of thirty years from the thirtieth (30th) day of December, A. D. 1864, so much of said road or avenue as shall then be in the corporate limits Term of the city of Chicago shall become a public street or avenue, and all toll gates shall be removed therefrom.

Tolls.

SEC. 8. Said company shall have the right to charge tolls at the rate named in their amended charter, approved February 16, 1865, and no more.

Ordinance in force.

SEC. 9. This ordinance shall be in force from and after its passage and due publication.

Passed October 5, 1865.

NEWSBOYS.

This Ordinance was passed after page 370, where it properly belongs, was in print.

AN ORDINANCE amendatory of Chapter XXVI of an Ordinance for revising and consolidating the General Ordinances of the City of Chicago.

SECTION
1. Newsboys' badge changed.

SECTION
2. This ordinance to take effect January 1, 1866.

Badge changed.

SECTION 1. *Be it ordained by the Common Council of the City of Chicago*, That Section 3, of Chapter XXVI, of "An Ordinance for revising and consolidating the general ordinances of the city of Chicago," passed October 23rd, 1865, be, and the same is hereby so amended that the words "shall wear a black leather badge upon his hat or cap, with the word 'licensed' and the number of his license painted thereon with white letters and figures at least one-half inch in size," be stricken out, and the following words inserted instead thereof: "Shall wear a white metal badge upon his hat, cap, coat or outside garment, with the words 'Newsboy, No. —,' engraved thereon in letters and figures not less than one-eighth of an inch in size."

Take effect.

SEC. 2. This amendment shall be in force and take effect from and after January 1st, 1866.

Passed December 18, 1865.

RAILROADS.

AN ORDINANCE concerning the Galena and Chicago Union Railroad.

SECTION
1. The Galena and Chicago Union Railroad Company to enter the city on Kinzie street, to the north branch of Chicago river; construction of road; reservation of right to regulate, etc.

SECTION
2. Temporary tracks on other streets; room and crossings for carriages; removal of such tracks.
3. Tracks eastwardly to the limits of the city, where and how; location as council may direct.
4. Drawbridge over north branch of Chicago river.

SECTION 1. *Be it ordained by the Common Council of the City of Chicago*, That permission be, and is hereby granted to the Galena and Chicago Union Railroad Company to introduce their road into the city on the line of Kinzie street, commencing at the west bounds of the city and extending to the north branch of the Chicago river, and to occupy so much of said street as may be necessary for the purpose of constructing, maintaining, using and occupying a single or double railroad track through said street, with such turn-outs, turn-tables and branches extending to adjoining lands as may be deemed necessary to the successful use and occupation of said road: *Provided*, The space occupied by said road, except when turn-outs, turn-tables and branches occur, does not exceed twenty-two feet in width of the centre of said street: *And provided*, Said work be so constructed that carriages may pass along either side of said road, and may conveniently cross the same: *And provided, also*, The common council reserve to itself the right to regulate running of locomotives on said road within the limits of the city.

Permission to enter city on Kinzie street.

Road, how constructed.

SEC. 2. Said company may also construct and use a temporary track or branch from Kinzie street to Fulton street, and occupy such portion of Fulton street and the streets between Kinzie and Fulton streets as may be necessary for that purpose, and terminate the same at or near the junction of Fulton street with the north branch of the Chicago river: *Provided*, That sufficient room be left for the free passage of carriages along said streets, and convenient crossings be made where the said track crosses the line of streets: *And provided, also*, That said company bind

Other streets may be occupied by temporary track.

Carriage-way.

itself to remove said temporary track when the common council shall so direct.

Road may be constructed eastwardly from north branch.

SEC. 3. Said company may lay down, maintain, use and occupy a single or double railroad track, with suitable turnouts and turn-tables, on the most suitable route from Kinzie street, at or near the north branch of the Chicago river to the proposed new street, or proposed new location of North Water street, proposed to be established about where the alley between Kinzie and North Water streets now is, and may extend the same along said proposed new street, when laid out, to Wolcott street; or if said new street shall be extended through block two, in Kinzie's addition, to North Water street, may extend said single or double track, if they shall elect to do so, on said new street when extended to North Water street, and thence along North Water street part of the way or all of the way to the east limits of the city; or said company may occupy the alley through block two, in Kinzie's addition, from Wolcott to Kinzie street, with their railroad track as aforesaid, and extend it thence along Kinzie street to North Water street, and thence across or along said North Water street all of the way or part of the way to the east limits of the city as aforesaid: *Provided, however*, That the said railroad track or tracks shall be located in said streets in such manner as the common council may hereafter direct.

Draw-bridge.

SEC. 4. Said company may construct a railroad draw-bridge over the north branch of the Chicago river, on or near the line of Kinzie street, or the street about to be laid out between Kinzie and North Water streets.

Passed July 17, 1848.

AN ORDINANCE in relation to the Chicago and Rock Island Railroad.

SECTION
1. The Chicago and Rock Island Railroad Company to lay track in certain streets, from the south line of the city to Van Buren street.
2. Tracks on their own land; depots; subject to laws and ordinances that may be passed.
3. Drawbridge over south branch of Chicago river, where and how.
4. Locomotives may run at speed not exceeding five miles per hour, subject to ordinances regulating.
5. Tracks to be laid so as to interfere as little as possible with travel; space to be left.

Authority to lay track in streets, and limits.

SECTION 1. *Be it ordained by the Common Council of the City of Chicago*, That the Rock Island and Chicago Railroad Company may lay down in any one of the streets of said city, between the west line of State street and the west line of Halsted street, from the south line of said city as far north as the north line of Polk street, a single railroad track, with the necessary turn-outs and turning tables. Said company may extend said track northwardly as far as the south line of Van Buren street, upon any street between the west line of Clark street and the west line of said Halsted street, and build all necessary turn-outs and turning tables.

SEC. 2. Said company may also construct in said city one or more railroad tracks within the boundaries aforesaid, upon any land they may procure by purchase or otherwise, and may also construct and use all depots which may be necessary to accommodate the business of said company. Said company to be subject to all laws and ordinances that may hereafter be passed to regulate railroads within the city. May lay track on their own land.

SEC. 3. Said company may construct and maintain a railroad draw-bridge across the south branch of the Chicago river, at any point south of the south line of Van Buren street, provided said bridge shall be so constructed as not to interrupt or impede the navigation of said south branch. Draw-bridge.

SEC. 4. Said company may run their trains by locomotives, within the limits before described herein, at a speed not exceeding five miles per hour, subject to such ordinances as may, from time to time, be passed by the common council of said city, regulating speed and motive power within said city. Speed of locomotives.

SEC. 5. In laying down said tracks, turn-outs and turning tables in said streets, they shall be so laid down as to interfere with the ordinary travel and use of said streets as little as possible, and a sufficient space for the passage of teams shall always be left on either side of said streets. Not to interfere with travel.

Passed May 26, 1851.

AN ORDINANCE in relation to the Chicago and Rock Island Railroad. (Supplemental.)

SECTION
1. The Chicago and Rock Island Railroad Company to extend track, etc., to and through Market to South Water street; proviso as to use of South Water and River streets.
2. Track on the west side of the south branch of the Chicago river to Kinzie street; when to be laid.
3. Tracks, grade, speed, motive power, etc., subject to control of council; use of tracks, etc., by other roads.
4. Use by company of tracks laid by any other company.
5. Company to indemnify city for damage and expense, etc.

Authority to extend track, and limits.

SECTION 1. *Be it ordained by the Common Council of the City of Chicago*, That permission and authority is hereby given to the Chicago and Rock Island Railroad Company to extend, construct and maintain their track, with necessary switches, turn-tables and side tracks, from the depot ground belonging to said company on the south branch of the Chicago river, northward through such streets as the city may hereafter designate, or through such lands as the company may procure for that purpose, to the southern terminus of Market street; thence through Market street to South Water street: *Provided*, That if hereafter permission shall be given to any railroad company to construct a track through South Water street and River street, the same privilege to lay down a track, or use the track of such company as shall lay down a track from Market street to the west line of Wabash avenue, shall be granted to the said Chicago and Rock Island Railroad Company, upon such terms as shall be safe, just and equitable, to be prescribed by the common council.

Track on west side of river.

SEC. 2. Permission and authority is hereby given to said railroad company to extend their track, and to construct, maintain and use the same, with all necessary switches, turn-tables and side tracks, from the bridge across the south branch of the Chicago river, heretofore by ordinance authorized to be constructed by said company; thence northerly on the west side of said south branch, through such streets as the city may hereafter designate, to Kinzie street: *Provided*, That if the city shall designate the streets, or furnish the right of way for the track provided for in this section, so as to allow the track to be built within the time hereinafter mentioned, in such case said company shall, within eighteen months after the completion of the track

When to finish track.

on the east side, lay down and finish the track in this section provided.

SEC. 3. The tracks, side tracks and switches authorized by the foregoing section, shall be laid on such side or part of the street that may be used for the same, as the common council may prescribe; and the grade of the tracks, side tracks and switches herein authorized, and the manner of laying down the same, shall be subject to the direction and supervision of such committee of the common council as may be appointed by the common council for that purpose; and the speed and the motive power to be used on said tracks, and the tracks, side tracks and switches and turn-tables built in connection with said tracks and along the same, shall be subject to such general regulations as the common council may prescribe for railroads within the city. Said tracks, side tracks, switches and turn-tables, so far as the same are laid in any street, shall be open to the use of other railroad companies and railroad corporations whose cars come into the city, with all proper, necessary and suitable connections for such companies as may desire to use said tracks, upon just, safe and equitable terms, to be agreed upon by the parties interested, and, in case of disagreement, by arbitration.

Track, etc., to be laid as council may prescribe.

Use of tracks, etc., by other roads.

SEC. 4. If any other railroad company shall desire to lay down tracks in any of the streets herein authorized to be used, and, having obtained permission, shall proceed to lay down tracks before said Chicago and Rock Island Railroad Company shall have done so, said Chicago and Rock Island Railroad Company may use and occupy the same jointly with such company, upon just and equitable terms, and so as to accommodate both companies so far as practicable; said terms to be agreed upon by the parties interested, and, in case of disagreement, by arbitration.

Use by company of tracks of other roads.

SEC. 5. The permission and authority hereby granted is upon the express condition, that the railroad company shall indemnify the city for any damage and expense to which it may be legally subjected by reason of the occupying of any of the streets, alleys or grounds of the city, with its track or other fixtures.

To indemnify city against damage.

Passed April 2, 1852.

AN ORDINANCE to aid the Illinois Central Railroad Company to obtain an Amendment to their Charter.

SECTION
1. Mayor instructed to unite with the Illinois Central Railroad Company in an application for an amendment of their charter.

SECTION
2. Members of the legislature from Cook county requested to aid in same.

Mayor to unite with company to procure amendment to charter.

SECTION 1. *Be it ordained by the Common Council of the City of Chicago,* That the mayor be instructed to unite with the Illinois Central Railroad Company in an application to the legislature of the State of Illinois, for such amendment or addition to the act incorporating said company as will confer upon it power to construct and operate such branch as may be stipulated for between the common council of the city of Chicago and the said company.

Members of legislature, request to.

SEC. 2. That the senators and representatives of the county of Cook, in the legislature, be respectfully requested to aid in carrying out the object of the foregoing section.

Passed June 7, 1852.

AN ORDINANCE concerning the Illinois Central Railroad.

SECTION
1. The Illinois Central Railroad Company to lay and operate railroad within the city, where and how; no undertaking or liability on the part of the city.
2. May use a width of 300 feet, to be not less than 400 feet east of west line of Michigan avenue.
3. May fill into the lake at the south pier; limitation of grant by the city; company responsible for damage to the harbor.
4. Tracks from main track to various points mentioned; crossing river with bridges, etc.
5. Construction, etc., of tracks; subject to regulations of council; use of tracks by other roads.
6. Protection of track against animals; manner thereof; gates; provision in case of outside harbor; regulation of speed by council.
7. Company to erect and maintain a protection for city front against the action of the lake, when and how.

SECTION
8. Company not to intrude on Lake Park, except by consent of council, while constructing or repairing, etc.
9. No buildings or obstructions to the view of the lake, between north line of Randolph street and south line of Lake Park, to be erected or placed; how works between those points to be used; cars, etc., not to remain.
10. Culverts for the flow of water through the works in front of Lake Park.
11. Track to connect with the tracks of the Chicago and Rock Island Railroad Company, when and how to be laid; city to furnish right of way.
12. Within ninety days company to execute an agreement with the city to comply with this ordinance.

Permission to lay and operate railroad, etc.

SECTION 1. *Be it ordained by the Common Council of the City of Chicago,* That permission is hereby granted to the Illinois Central Railroad Company to lay down, construct, and maintain, within the limits of the city of Chicago and along the margin of the lake within and adjacent to the same, a railroad with one or more tracks, and to operate the same with locomotive engines and cars, under such rules and regulations with reference to speed of trains, the receipt, safe keeping and delivery of freight, and arrangements for the accommodation and conveyance of passengers, not inconsistent with the public safety, as said company may from time to time establish, and to have the right of way and all powers incident to and necessary therefor, in the manner and upon the terms and conditions following, to wit:

The said road shall enter said city at or near the intersection of its south boundary with lake Michigan, and following the shore on or near the margin of said lake northerly to the southern bounds of the open space known as Lake Park, in front of canal section fifteen, and continue northerly across the open space in front of said section fifteen to such grounds as the said company may acquire between the north line of Randolph street and the Chicago river, in the Fort Dearborn addition to said city, upon which said grounds shall be located the depot of said railroad within the city, and such other buildings, slips or apparatus, as may be necessary and convenient for the business of said company. **Where located.**

But it is expressly understood, that the city of Chicago does not undertake to obtain for said company any right of way, or other right, privilege or easement, not now in the power of said city to grant or confer, or to assume any liability or responsibility for the acts of said company.

SEC. 2. The said company may enter upon and use in perpetuity for its said line of road, and other works necessary to protect the same from the lake, a width of three hundred feet from the southern boundary of said public ground, near Twelfth street, to the northern line of Randolph street; the inner or west line of the ground to be used by said company to be not less than four hundred feet east from the west line of Michigan avenue, and parallel thereto. **Width to be occupied.**

SEC. 3. The said company may extend their works and fill out into the lake to a point in the southern pier not less than four hundred feet west from the present east end of the same, thence parallel with Michigan avenue to the north **May fill out into lake.**

line of Randolph street extended, but it is expressly understood that the common council does not grant any right or privilege beyond the limits above specified, nor beyond the line that may be actually occupied by the works of said company.

Company liable for damage.

It is further expressly understood that, should any damage or obstruction occur to the harbor of Chicago, clearly traceable to the construction of said works contemplated by sections two and three hereof, then the said company shall be held responsible for the same.

Side track, where located.

SEC. 4. Permission and right of way are hereby given to the said company to construct and maintain a side track from its main track, beginning at or south of Twelfth street, proceeding through said street, or such line as may be prescribed by the common council, westerly to the south branch of the Chicago river; thence crossing the said south branch by a bridge, or other mode to be approved by the common council, which shall not obstruct navigation; thence proceeding northerly to Kinzie street, following as far as practicable the streets nearest to said branch, on such sides of the centre of streets as the common council may prescribe; said track not to be laid west of the west line of Canal street; and also a track leading from the last mentioned track, at or near its intersection with the eastern line of the said south branch of the Chicago river, along the line of said south branch, into Market street, following as far as possible the streets nearest the river, and on such sides of such streets as the common council may direct; thence along the west line of Market street northerly to Lake street. And they may also extend the track of said road from their track or grounds south of the south pier, across the Chicago river to North Water street, by means of a draw-bridge or other mode, which shall not obstruct navigation, and which may be approved by the common council.

May extend track.

Tracks to accommodate business.

SEC. 5. And the said tracks shall be so constructed, furnished and operated as to meet the demands of business upon the streets and lines through and along which they shall run. The said side tracks, the stations, depots, turnouts, switches, turn-tables, buildings and bridges along said lines, as well as the motive power to be used and the rate of speed thereon, to be subject to such regulations as the common council may from time to time prescribe for the government of side tracks of railroads within the inhabited portions of the city. Said side tracks shall be open to the use of other railroad companies, and railroads connecting therewith, upon just and equitable terms, to be agreed upon by the parties interested, and, in case of disagreement, by arbitration. **Powers of council.**

SEC. 6. The said company shall erect and maintain, on the western or inner line of the ground pointed out for its main track on the lake shore, as the same is herein before defined, such suitable walls, fences or other sufficient works, as will prevent animals from straying upon or obstructing its tracks, and secure persons and property from danger. **Fences, etc.**

Said structure to be of suitable materials and sightly appearance, and of such height, as the common council may direct, and no change therein shall be made except by mutual consent: *Provided, however*, That the company shall construct such suitable gates at proper places at the ends of the streets, which are now or may hereafter be laid out, as may be required by the common council, to afford safe access to the lake: *And provided, also*, That in case of the construction of an outside harbor, streets may be laid out to approach the same, in manner provided by law, in which case the common council may regulate the speed of locomotives and trains across them. **Fences, etc., how made.** **Gates.** **Harbor and streets.**

SEC. 7. The said company shall erect and complete within three years after they shall have accepted this ordinance, and shall forever thereafter maintain, a continuous wall or structure of stone masonry, pier-work or other sufficient material, of regular and sightly appearance, and not to exceed in height the general level of Michigan avenue opposite thereto, from the north side of Randolph street to the southern bound of Lake Park before mentioned, at a distance of not more than three hundred feet east from and parallel with the western or inner line pointed out for said company, as specified in section two hereof, and shall continue said works to the southern boundary of the city, at such distance outside of the track of said road **Protection against lake.**

as may be expedient, which structure and works shall be of sufficient strength and magnitude to protect the entire front of said city between the north line of Randolph street and its southern boundary from further damage or injury from the action of the waters of lake Michigan, and that part of the structure south of Lake Park shall be commenced and prosecuted with all reasonable dispatch after the acceptance of this ordinance.

Not to intrude upon Lake Park. SEC. 8. The said company shall not in any manner, nor for any purpose whatever, occupy, use or intrude upon the open ground known as Lake Park, belonging to the city of Chicago, lying between Michigan avenue and the western or inner line before mentioned, except as far as the common council may consent, for the convenience of said company, while constructing or repairing their works in front of said ground.

Nor obstruct view. SEC. 9. The said company shall erect no buildings between the north line of Randolph street and the south line of the said Lake Park, nor occupy nor use the works proposed to be constructed between these points, except for the passage of, or for making up or distributing their trains; nor place upon any part of their works between said points any obstruction to the view of the lake from the shore, nor suffer their locomotives, cars or other articles to remain upon their tracks, but only erect such works as are proper for the construction of their necessary tracks and the protection of the same.

Culverts through protection. SEC. 10. The said company, in constructing the said line of works in front of Lake Park and the public grounds, shall make and keep open through the same such culverts or ways as the common council shall prescribe, from the open lake to the space inside of the western line before mentioned, as will afford room for the uninterrupted flow of the water through the same.

Shall lay track to connect with Rock Island railroad. SEC. 11. The said company shall lay down, construct, operate and maintain a track, with suitable turn-outs, switches and turn-tables, through Twelfth street, or through such other street north of North street as the common council may designate, from their main track on the lake shore, to connect with the said tracks to be constructed by the Chicago and Rock Island Railroad Company, or procure the same to be done, as provided by an ordinance of the city of Chicago, passed April 2, 1852, so soon as the said track on the east side of the south branch of the river shall be completed: *Provided*, That the city of Chicago shall furnish the right of way to the said company, free of cost, before requiring said track to be constructed.

SEC. 12. Upon the acceptance of this ordinance by the said company, (which shall be within ninety days of the passing of the same), a contract or agreement embodying the provisions herein contained, and stipulating that the permission, rights and privileges hereby conferred upon said company shall depend upon the performance on their part of the requirements made upon them by this ordinance, shall be executed, sealed and delivered on the part of the city of Chicago by the mayor thereof, and on the part of the Illinois Central Railroad Company by the president thereof, both in usual legal form. **Agreement to be made with city.**

Passed June 14, 1852.

AN ORDINANCE concerning the Illinois and Wisconsin Railroad Track.

SECTION 1. The Illinois and Wisconsin Railroad Company to lay track, etc., on their own land, and cross streets in certain limits of the west division; reservation to the city, of power to control construction, motive power and speed.

SECTION 1. *Be it ordained by the Common Council of the City of Chicago*, That the Illinois and Wisconsin Railroad Company are hereby authorized to lay down through their own land, or such land as they may acquire by purchase or otherwise, the track, switches, turn-tables and turn-outs, as said company may deem proper, within the following described limits of the west division of the city of Chicago: **Authority to lay track.**

All of Waubansia addition west to the centre of Jefferson street, and that part of Russell, Mather & Roberts' addition lying north of Owen street, and those parts of sections four, five and eight, lying between Milwaukee avenue and the north branch of the Chicago river, and for the purposes of such track, to intersect and cross any street or streets said company may deem proper; the city hereby reserving to itself the power to control the manner of con- **Limits.**

structing said track, and the motive power to be used, and the speed of the same.

Passed October 4, 1852.

AN ORDINANCE in relation to the Chicago, St. Charles and Mississippi Air-line Railroad.

SECTION
1. The Chicago, St. Charles and Mississippi Air-Line Railroad Company to construct railroad in certain limits in west division of the city on their own land; crossings and warning tables; subject to laws and ordinances.

SECTION
2. May construct track in street in certain other limits in west division, and use for three years; contract to vacate; not to occupy more than ten feet in width; construct so that carriages may pass.
3. Speed not to exceed five miles per hour, subject to ordinances.
4. Ordinance not to take effect until company execute bond to pay all damages.

Permission to lay track, and limits. SECTION 1. *Be it ordained by the Common Council of the City of Chicago*, That permission be and is hereby granted to the Chicago, St. Charles and Mississippi Air-line Railroad Company to construct in the west division of said city, one or more railroad tracks upon any land south of Madison street or north of Lake street, which they may procure by purchase or otherwise, and to lay down said track or tracks across any street within the boundaries aforesaid, wherever any such street crosses their intended line of railroad, and also to construct and use all depots necessary to accommodate the business of said company: *Provided*, That convenient crossings be made by said company where the said track crosses the line of streets, and sufficient warning tables be erected in some conspicuous place at or near said crossings; said company to be subject to all laws and ordinances that are now in force or may hereafter be passed to regulate railroads within this city.

Crossings, etc.

Road, where constructed. SEC. 2. Said company may also introduce their road into said city on any street or streets in the west division of the said city, south of Polk street, and extend the same to the south branch of the Chicago river, or on any street or streets north of Fourth street (north of Kinzie street), and extend the same to the north branch of the Chicago river; and may occupy so much of said street or streets as may be necessary for the purpose of constructing, maintaining, using and occupying a single railroad track, with the necessary switches, turn-tables and turn-outs, for the period of three years: *Provided*, That said company will enter into a contract with the city of Chicago to vacate said streets of their railroad track or tracks at the expiration of that time, and place the street so vacated in good order for ordinary travel, subject to the approval of the street commissioner and aldermen of the west division: *Provided*, The space occupied by said road, except when turn-outs, turn-tables or switches occur, does not exceed ten feet in width of the centre of said street or streets: *And provided*, Said work be so constructed that carriages may pass along either side of said road, and may conveniently cross the same. **Contract with city.**

SEC. 3. Said company may run their trains by locomotives within the limits before described herein, at a speed not exceeding five miles per hour, subject to such ordinances as may from time to time be passed by the common council of said city, establishing and regulating speed and motive power within said city. **Speed of locomotives**

SEC. 4. This ordinance shall not take effect until said company shall have entered into a bond with the city of Chicago, conditioned for the payment of all damages for which the said city may become liable to any person or persons by reason of the said road entering said city, or by reason of said company constructing, laying down, using or occupying said railroad track or tracks within said city, and conditioned also for the payment of all damages which may arise to the said city of Chicago and to any person or persons whomsoever, by reason of said company constructing, laying down, maintaining, using and occupying said railroad track or tracks within the said city of Chicago. **Bond.**

Passed April 11, 1853.

AN ORDINANCE to amend an Ordinance in relation to the Chicago, St. Charles and Mississippi Air-line Railroad.

SECTION
1. Limits in which railroad may be constructed changed; crossings and warning tables; subject to laws and ordinances.
2. Speed not to exceed five miles per hour, subject to ordinances.

SECTION
3. May construct draw-bridge across south branch of Chicago river, south of Twelfth street; not to impede navigation; join and connect with other companies.

Permission to construct track, and limits.

SECTION 1. *Be it ordained by the Common Council of the City of Chicago*, That permission be, and is hereby granted to the Chicago, St. Charles and Mississippi Air-line Railroad Company to construct, maintain and operate in the west division of said city one or more railroad tracks upon any land south of Madison street or north of Lake street, and also any other railroad track within said city, west of the west line of sections twenty (20), seventeen (17), and eight (8), which said company may procure by purchase or otherwise; and to lay down said track or tracks across any street within the boundaries above described, wherever any such street crosses their intended line of railroad; and also to construct and use all depots which may be necessary to accommodate the business of said company: *Provided*, That convenient crossings be made by said company where the said track or tracks cross the line of streets, and sufficient warning tables be erected in some conspicuous place at or near said crossings; said company to be subject to all laws and ordinances that are now in force or may hereafter be passed to regulate railroads within said city.

Crossings.

Speed of locomotives

SEC. 2. Said company may run their trains by locomotives within the limits herein described, at a speed not exceeding five miles per hour, subject to such ordinances as may, from time to time, be passed by the common council of said city establishing and regulating speed and motive power within said city.

Draw-bridge, where and how constructed.

SEC. 3. Said company may construct, maintain and use a railroad draw-bridge across the south branch of the Chicago river, at any point south of Twelfth street in said city, for the purpose of connecting their track with the track of any other railroad company, which may be approved by the common council: *Provided*, Said bridge shall be so constructed as not materially to interrupt or impede the navigation of said south branch. And the said company may join any other railroad company in the erection and use of any railroad bridge heretofore authorized or which may hereafter be authorized to be constructed across said south branch, and the said company and any other railroad company may jointly use each other's track or tracks and bridge, and form material connection within

May join other company.

said city, upon such terms as may be agreed upon by the parties interested.

Passed August 8, 1853.

AN ORDINANCE in relation to the Fort Wayne and Chicago Railroad Company.

SECTION
1. The Fort Wayne and Chicago Railroad Company to lay, etc., track in certain limits, in street.
2. Same, on their own land, in same and additional limits; crossings and warning tables; subject to laws and ordinances.
3. May use locomotive engines, under rules and regulations of council.
4. Draw-bridge or tunnel, across or under south branch of Chicago river; not to impede navigation; may join therein with other company.
5. May construct and operate with horse power on street or their own ground in additional limits; planking carriage-way; consent of property holders.
6. Ordinance not to take effect until company give bond to the city, conditioned for payment of damages.

SECTION 1. *Be it ordained by the Common Council of the City of Chicago*, That permission and authority be, and is hereby given to the Fort Wayne and Chicago Railroad Company to lay down, maintain and operate a single railroad track in any one street in the city of Chicago west of the west line of Clark street, from the southern boundary of said city as far north as the south line of North street, and all such turn-outs, switches and turn-tables as shall be deemed necessary. **Permission granted to lay track.** **Limits.**

SEC. 2. Said company may and shall have the power to lay down, maintain and operate one or more railroad tracks, with such turn-outs and switches as they shall deem necessary, on any ground which they may acquire by purchase, donation or otherwise, within the district and boundaries aforesaid, and also from the north line of the district and boundary aforesaid as far north as the south line of Van Buren street, and west of the west line of Clark street, and to lay down, and maintain and operate any such track or tracks, and turn-outs, across any street or streets, or alleys, within the districts aforesaid, and also to acquire, as aforesaid, and use all depot grounds, and to erect all depot buildings necessary to accommodate the business of said company: *Provided*, That convenient crossings shall be made and maintained by said company where such track or tracks cross any such street or alleys, and **Additional limits.** **Crossings, etc., to be constructed.**

Warning tables. Company subject to ordinances of city. proper warning tables shall be erected in conspicuous places at or near such crossings. Said company shall be subject to all laws and ordinances that are now in force or may hereafter be passed to regulate railroads within said city.

Locomotive power. SEC. 3. Said company may use and operate said railroad tracks, within the districts aforesaid, with locomotive engines and cars, under such rules and regulations with reference to the speed, motive power and manner of running the same as the common council of said city may, from time to time, impose and make.

May erect bridge or tunnel in south branch. SEC. 4. Said company may construct, maintain and use a railroad draw-bridge across the south branch of the Chicago river, or a tunnel under the same, at any point south of the south line of Twelfth street in said city: *Provided*, Said bridge or tunnel shall be so constructed as not materially to interrupt or impede the navigation of the south branch of the Chicago river; and the said company may join any other railroad company in the erection and use of said bridge or tunnel, heretofore authorized or which may be hereafter authorized to construct a bridge across the said south branch, and said companies thus uniting may jointly use each other's track or tracks, bridge and depots, and form mutual connection within said city upon such terms as may be agreed upon by the parties interested.

Not to obstruct navigation. May unite with other railroad.

May operate horse power tracks. SEC. 5. And said company shall have the power to construct and maintain a single railroad track, and operate the same with horse power only, in any one street of said city, or may lay down and use one or more tracks on grounds which may be acquired by said company by purchase, donation or otherwise, within the following limits, viz.: west of the east line of Canal street, and between the south line of Harrison street and the north line of Kinzie street, and to cross any and all intervening streets and alleys in the track and course thereof: *Provided*, Said company shall plank the carriage-way of the street so occupied, in and on each side of said track, so as to render the same convenient for the passage of teams and travel: *And provided, also*, That said railroad company shall get the consent of a majority in interest of the property holders on said street so occu-

Limits. To plank streets. To obtain consent of property owners.

pied, before they proceed to lay down and operate said horse tracks.

SEC. 6. This ordinance shall not take effect until the said company shall have entered into a bond with the city of Chicago, conditioned for the payment of all damages for which the said city may become liable to any person or persons by reason of the said road entering said city, or by reason of said company constructing, laying down, using or occupying said railroad track or tracks within said city; and conditioned also for the payment of all damages which may arise to the said city of Chicago, and to any person or persons whomsoever, by reason of said company constructing, laying down, maintaining, using and occupying said railroad track or tracks within said city of Chicago.

Bond to be given city.

Conditions of bond.

Passed February 13, 1854.

AN ORDINANCE concerning the Chicago and Mississippi Railroad Company.

SECTION
1. The Chicago and Mississippi Railroad Company to lay side tracks from the track of the Chicago and Rock Island Railroad Company; depots, etc., on its own grounds.

SECTION
2. Tracks, where to be laid; crossings subject to ordinances; street not to be obstructed; right of council to rescind reserved; company liable for damages.

SECTION 1. *Be it ordained by the Common Council of the City of Chicago*, That permission and authority is hereby granted to the Chicago and Mississippi Railroad Company to lay down and use two such side tracks as its business may require, from the track of the Chicago and Rock Island Railroad, as the same is located on block one hundred and nine (109) in the school section addition, south across Taylor street, and on block one hundred and eight (108.) And said company, on its own grounds procured for that purpose, may erect such depots, stations, buildings and shops as it thinks proper.

Permission to lay tracks granted.

Location of tracks.

SEC. 2. The side tracks herein authorized shall be laid down east of Griswold street and west of Clark street, and the crossing at Taylor street shall be completed and finished under the direction of the committee on streets and alleys of the south division of the city; such tracks at the crossings of Taylor street shall be subject to all the ordinances

To be laid between Griswold and Clark streets.

Crossing at Taylor street.

that now are or hereafter may be made by the city to regulate the crossing of railroads across the streets of the city: *Provided*, That said street shall not at any time be obstructed by the stoppage of cars therein, nor shall the said street be obstructed longer than three minutes at any one time by the crossing of trains under way: *And provided*, The city council reserve the right to rescind at any time the rights hereby granted: *Provided*, *also*, The said company shall be liable for all damages that may accrue by reason of the crossing, occupying or using said tracks.

Street not to be obstructed.

Right to rescind this grant.

Company liable for all damages.

Passed September 11, 1854.

AN ORDINANCE authorizing the use of Clark Street, (by Railroads,) upon making the Improvements specified herein.

SECTION
1. The Chicago and Rock Island Railroad Company, and the Michigan Southern and Northern Indiana Railroad Company, to lay additional track in Clark street on conditions; where laid; planking and sewers; materials and grade; paving.

SECTION
2. Supervision of the city superintendent.
3. Companies to indemnify city against damages.

Certain companies authorized to lay track, etc.

SECTION 1. *Be it ordained by the Common Council of the City of Chicago*, That the Chicago and Rock Island Railroad Company, and the Michigan Southern and Northern Indiana Railroad Company, be and are hereby authorized to lay down an additional track in Clark street from its southern terminus to where their present track diverges from said street, and to maintain and use the same on the following terms and conditions:

Conditions.

Tracks to be laid, where.

First. That the east rail of the east track shall be placed in the centre of the street, and the additional track hereby authorized be placed west, and as near the east track as practicable.

Planking and sewers.

Second. That such companies shall plank the whole surface of each street, including sidewalks, between the points first above indicated, and put in good, complete and proper sewers on both sides, and forever maintain such planking and sewers in good order and condition, and cross sewers, if necessary.

Materials.

Third. That the planks shall be of oak, not less than three (3) inches, and laid upon oak stringers with proper bearings, and upon the grade fixed by the city; and whenever the city shall pave the balance of South Clark street, then such companies shall pave the portion used by them in the same manner, free of expense to the city. Construction, etc.

SEC. 2. The work provided in this ordinance is to be done under the supervision of the city superintendent. Superintendent to oversee work.

SEC. 3. The powers herein granted are upon the conditions that such companies shall fully indemnify the city against all damages to which the city may be subjected by property holders on said street, in consequence of the powers herein granted. Companies responsible for damages.

Passed January 7, 1856.

AN ORDINANCE concerning the Illinois Central Railroad.

PREAMBLE. Reciting former grant to the Illinois Central Railroad Company, of right to use ground, and that the ground granted is too narrow.

SECTION

1. Bounds of ground granted enlarged, upon condition to be subject to conditions of former ordinance.

WHEREAS, The common council of this city, by an ordinance of the 14th day of June, 1852, granted to the Illinois Central Railroad Company, the right to enter and use in perpetuity for its line of railroad and other works necessary to protect the same from the lake, a width of three hundred feet from the southern boundary of the public ground on Twelfth street to the northern line of Randolph street, the inner or the west line of which ground so to be used by the company, to be not less than four hundred feet east from the west line of Michigan avenue and parallel thereto; and whereas, the ground granted is shown to be too narrow to afford to said company a convenient means of approaching and using a part of their station grounds between Randolph street and Chicago river; therefore, Preamble.

SECTION 1. *Be it ordained by the Common Council of the City of Chicago,* That permission is hereby granted to the said Illinois Central Railroad Company to enter upon and use in perpetuity, for its line of railroad, and other works necessary to protect the same from the lake, the space between its present breakwater, and a line drawn from a point on Permission to use certain land.

said breakwater, seven hundred feet south of the north line of Randolph street extended, and running thence on a straight line to the south-east corner of its present breakwater, and thence to the river: *Provided, however,* and this permission is only given upon the express condition, That the portion of said line which lies south of the north line of Randolph street extended, shall be kept subject to all the conditions and restrictions, as to the use of the same, as are imposed upon that part of said line by the said ordinance of June 14, 1852.

Subject to conditions of former ordinance.

Passed September 15, 1856.

AN ORDINANCE amendatory of an Ordinance passed February 13th, 1854, concerning the Fort Wayne and Chicago Railroad Company, now the Pittsburgh, Fort Wayne and Chicago Railroad Company.

SECTION 1. Company to lay tracks, etc.; to execute bond to the city, conditioned, etc.; right of council to authorize slips reserved; privileges granted, subject to general ordinances; tracks, how laid; grading, etc., of streets; compliance with former ordinance.

Company to lay tracks, etc.

SECTION 1. *Be it ordained by the Common Council of the City of Chicago,* That permission and authority be and is hereby given the Pittsburgh, Fort Wayne and Chicago Railroad Company to lay down, maintain and operate a railroad track or tracks, with necessary switches, turn-outs and side tracks in the street in the city of Chicago, running north and south on the centre line of section twenty-one, in township thirty-nine north, of range fourteen east of third principal meridian, from the south line of North street to the north line of Twelfth street, and thence in Beach street to Harrison street.

Bond and condition.

Provided, Said railroad company shall enter into bonds with the city of Chicago, to be filed in the clerk's office of said city, conditioned that said railroad company will afford facilities to the owners of property on said streets running north and south, for doing business on said railroad, by putting in side tracks necessary for that purpose, and operate the said track so as to carry the cars of said railroad company, and of all other connecting railroads, on fair and reasonable terms, to and from said property, and also to hold and save harmless the said city of Chicago from all damages in consequence of this act: *And provided, also,* That nothing herein granted shall prevent the common council of the city of Chicago authorizing the construction of a slip or slips across said streets. Slips.

And provided further, That the privileges hereby granted, shall be enjoyed subject to all general ordinances that now are or hereafter may be in force concerning railroads in said city. Subject to general ordinances.

Provided, The tracks of said road shall be so laid as to interfere as little as possible with the usefulness of said streets, as road or carriage-ways, by grading, filling, and planking or macadamizing them in such way as to allow free passage for carriages across and alongside its tracks, and in such manner as the common council shall direct, and also by changing the grade of said streets at any time it may be ordered by the common council, and that they will comply with all the restrictions imposed by the ordinance to which this is an amendment. Tracks, how laid. Grading, etc. Comply with former ordinance.

Passed November 17, 1856.

AN ORDINANCE in relation to the Joliet and Chicago Railroad Company.

SECTION
1. May lay tracks in certain streets on conditions, as to paving, etc., of streets; width occupied, and manner of construction.
2. Contract between the city and the company to be made.

SECTION
3. Supervision of officers of city.
4. To save city harmless from damages.
5. Subject to general ordinances.
6. Side tracks for convenience of adjoining property.
7. Maintain bridges.

SECTION 1. *Be it ordained by the Common Council of the City of Chicago,* That permission be, and the same is hereby given and granted to the Joliet and Chicago Railroad Company to introduce said railroad into the city on the street known as the Archer road, from a point commencing on the section line between sections twenty-eight and twenty-nine, to Grove street, and from thence through Grove street to the north line of North street; and to use and occupy so much of said streets as may be necessary for the purpose of constructing, maintaining and using and occupying a single or double railroad track through said streets, with such turn-outs and branches, ex- Permission to lay track.

tending to adjoining lands, as may be deemed necessary for the successful use and occupation of said road, upon the following conditions:

Conditions.

Paving, etc. *First.* That said company shall plank, pave or macadamize the whole surface of said streets between the points indicated above, and forever maintain such planking, paving or macadamizing in good order and condition.

Width occupied. *Second.* That the space occupied by said railroad shall not exceed fifteen feet in width on the Archer road, and shall not exceed twenty-four feet in width on Grove street, and shall be taken from the north-west side of Archer road.

Carriages. *Third.* That said company shall so construct said work that carriages may pass along said streets, and may also conveniently cross said road.

Contract between city and company. SEC. 2. Upon the acceptance of this ordinance by the said company (which shall be within ninety days from the passage hereof,) a contract embracing the provisions herein contained shall be executed, sealed and delivered, on the part of the city of Chicago, by the mayor thereof, and on the part of the Joliet and Chicago Railroad Company, by the president thereof, both in the usual legal form.

Supervision of city officers. SEC. 3. The work provided in this ordinance shall be done under the supervision of the city superintendent, or such other officer or agent as the common council may direct.

Damages. SEC. 4. Said railroad company shall save the city harmless from all costs, damages and suits arising from the occupation of said streets, by said company, from any and all persons whomsoever.

Subject to general ordinances. SEC. 5. This permission is granted subject to all general railroad ordinances of the city of Chicago now in force, or that may hereafter be passed, in relation to crossing streets, rates of speed, and other matters of public convenience and necessity.

Side tracks. SEC. 6. Said railroad company shall afford all necessary facilities to the owners of property on said streets for doing business on said road, by putting in side tracks necessary for such purpose, and to operate said tracks so as to carry the cars of said road, and all other railroads connecting, or desirous of making connections with said road, on fair and reasonable terms to and from said property.

SEC. 7. Said company shall make, maintain, and keep in good repair, all road and slip bridges between the said points. Bridges.

Passed January 5, 1857.

AN ORDINANCE allowing the South Branch Canal Company to lay down Railroad Track in Streets in the West Division.

SECTION
1. May lay tracks, etc., in certain limits of west division, on their own land.
2. May cross streets; construct depots; to make convenient crossings.
3. May lay tracks on their own lands, and occupy certain streets in Green's south branch addition to Chicago.

SECTION
4. May join any railroad company in construction of bridge across south branch of Chicago river, and in use of tracks.
5. May run trains by locomotives, at a speed not exceeding six miles per hour, subject to laws and ordinances.

SECTION 1. *Be it ordained by the Common Council of the City of Chicago*, That permission be and is hereby granted to the Chicago South Branch Canal Company to construct, maintain and operate, in the west division of said city, one or more railroad tracks, with all necessary switches, turn-outs, turn-tables, in, upon or through any and all lands owned or controlled by said company, between the air-line railroad track and South street. May lay tracks, etc.

SEC. 2. Said company may lay down said track or tracks across any street within the boundaries aforesaid, wherever any such street crosses their intended line of railroad; also the right to construct and use all depots necessary to accommodate the business of said company: *Provided*, That convenient crossings be made by said company, where the said tracks cross the line of streets. Crossing streets. Depots.

SEC. 3. Said company may construct, maintain and operate one or more railroad tracks through or upon any lands they own or control, in Green's south branch addition to Chicago; and, also, occupy such portion of the streets in said addition, for railroad purposes, as were provided for by reservation in the record of the plat of said addition. May lay tracks, etc.

SEC. 4. Said company may join any railroad company, in the erection and use of any railroad bridge heretofore authorized, or which may hereafter be authorized, to be May join other company as to bridge and use of tracks constructed across the south branch of the Chicago river, and the said South Branch Canal Company, and any railroad company, may jointly use each other's track or tracks, and bridge or bridges, within the city, and form material connections, upon such terms as may be agreed upon by the parties interested.

Locomotives. Speed. Subject to ordinances. SEC. 5. Said company may run their trains, by locomotives, within the limits herein described, at a speed not exceeding six miles per hour, subject to such laws and ordinances as are now in force, or that may, from time to time, be passed by the common council of said city, establishing and regulating speed and motive power within said city.

Passed January 5, 1857.

AN ORDINANCE concerning the Chicago and Milwaukee Railroad Company.

SECTION 1. May lay track in streets to connect with the Galena and Chicago Union Railroad Company.

Permission to lay track. SECTION 1. *Be it ordained by the Common Council of the City of Chicago*, That the Chicago and Milwaukee Railroad Company be and the same is hereby authorized to lay down and maintain the track for its railroad, with all necessary side tracks and switches through and along so much of Jefferson street and West Kinzie street as shall be necessary to connect the track of said railroad with the track of the Galena and Chicago Union Railroad on Kinzie street.

Passed February 2, 1857.

AN ORDINANCE to authorize the Chicago and Milwaukee Railroad Company to lay down a Track for its Railroad in Jefferson and West Kinzie streets.

SECTION
1. May lay track in streets to connect with the Galena and Chicago Union Railroad Company; how laid, location, repair and grade.

SECTION
2. Filling, paving, etc., of street.

Permission to lay track. SECTION 1. *Be it ordained by the Common Council of the City of Chicago*, That the Chicago and Milwaukee Railroad Company is hereby authorized and empowered to lay down, use and maintain the track of its railroad through so much of Jefferson street and West Kinzie street as shall be necessary to connect the track of the railroad of said company with the track of the Galena and Chicago Union Railroad Company on West Kinzie street; said track to be laid down and used by said company and its agents as not unnecessarily to interfere with the public use of said streets, and the location of said track to be fixed by the agents of said company, under the direction of the city superintendent, and said road to be kept in repair, at the expense of said company, and the grades to be altered when directed by the common council or city superintendent. **How laid.** **Location.** **Repair and grade.**

SEC. 2. In consideration of the right granted to it by the foregoing section, said company shall fill said street up to grade with gravel, or other suitable material, and shall, also, plank or pave said street, when required so to do by order of the common council. **Filling, paving, etc., of street.**

Passed April 20, 1857.

AN ORDINANCE to allow a connection between the Pittsburgh, Fort Wayne and Chicago, and the Chicago, St. Paul and Fond du Lac Railroad Companies, and such other Railroad Companies as may unite with them.

SECTION
1. May lay tracks, etc., in certain limits, upon their own grounds.
2. May use for same purpose certain streets and alleys, if they improve the same as may be ordered by council.
3. May cross streets and alleys; shall go under streets on which may be bridges; how to be done; pay all damages; not to obstruct travel.
4. Terms and manner of associating other companies in the powers and privileges conferred hereby.
5. Depots, freight houses, etc.
6. Rules and regulations by council as to speed, motive power and manner of running; if steam locomotives used, coke or coal to be used for fuel, and speed not to exceed five miles per hour.
7. To indemnify city against damages.
8. Subject to general ordinance.
9. Companies accepting this ordinance to execute contract and bond to the city.

SECTION 1. *Be it ordained by the Common Council of the City of Chicago*, That permission is hereby granted to the Pittsburgh, Fort Wayne and Chicago, and the Chicago, St. Paul and Fond du Lac Railroad Companies, and all other railroad companies that may unite with them, to lay down, construct, maintain and operate a single or double railroad track, with all the necessary switches, side tracks, turn-outs and turn-tables, across and upon any grounds that they may acquire or obtain the use of, between Van Buren and Kin- **May lay tracks, etc., on their own grounds.**

zie streets, and the south and north branches of the Chicago river and Canal street.

May use streets if they improve them, etc.

SEC. 2. Like permission and authority are hereby granted to said companies, or either of them, to use for the purposes and in the manner mentioned in the foregoing section, West Water street, in the city of Chicago, and that portion of Canal street which is between the south line of Fulton and the north line of Kinzie streets, and also use for such purposes the alleys through blocks number twenty-two (22), twenty-nine (29), and forty-four (44), of the original town of Chicago: *Provided*, Said companies shall improve and maintain the public highways so used by them, as may, from time to time, be ordered by the common council.

May cross streets and alleys.

SEC. 3. The said companies shall have full power and authority to cross all streets and alleys that may intersect the route of the tracks granted by the preceding section. The tracks of said roads, at their intersection with all streets that are now or hereafter may be bridged to cross either branch of the river, shall be carried under the streets in tunnels, so constructed as to protect the public from accidents or injuries. And if, for these purposes, it is necessary to raise the grade of such streets, or of the approaches to the bridges, the same shall be done by and at the expense of said railroad companies, and under the direction and to the satisfaction of the city superintendent of public works, or such other person or committee as the common council may direct or appoint to superintend such work, and said companies shall pay and shall hold the city harmless from all damages arising from such raising of grades and filling and tunneling of approaches; and at the intersections of said track with the unbridged streets, where no tunnels are required, the said railroad companies shall construct and maintain such crossings as to obstruct the ordinary travel as little as possible.

Tunnels under bridge streets.

Pay all damages.

Not obstruct travel.

Terms and manner of associating other companies.

SEC. 4. Said companies may associate with themselves in the construction and use of such tracks, any and all railroad corporations, and any corporations so associated shall possess all the powers herein granted to the said Pittsburgh, Fort Wayne and Chicago, and the Chicago, St.

Paul and Fond du Lac Railroad Companies, and said latter companies shall allow and permit the use of the tracks constructed under this ordinance by any other railroad corporations upon such terms and conditions as shall be fair and equitable, to be determined, in case of disagreement between the companies, by two disinterested and competent civil engineers, one to be selected by each party, and in case of their disagreement, a third shall be appointed by the judge of the Cook county court of common pleas; and the award and decision of said referees shall be final, conclusive and binding upon the parties.

SEC. 5. Said companies may establish, construct, maintain and use at any place or places between Lake and Van Buren streets, all such depots, freight houses and station buildings as the business of said companies, or of any and all companies that may use said tracks may require. And in case the depot shall be of such length, and so located as to extend over and require the use of grounds upon two adjoining lots or blocks, said companies may use the street between said lots or blocks for that purpose: *Provided*, Such street is not used as a public thoroughfare for crossing the river, and is legally vacated for the purpose. **Depots, etc.**

SEC. 6. Said companies may use and operate said railroad tracks, within the district aforesaid, under such rules and regulations with reference to speed, motive power, and manner of running the same, as the common council may from time to time impose and make; and if steam power locomotives be used, said companies shall use only coke or coal for fuel for the same, and the speed shall not exceed five miles per hour. **General regulations.**

SEC. 7. The permission and authority hereby granted to said railroad companies are upon the express condition that they shall each and all of them indemnify the city for any and all damage and expense to which it may be subjected by reason of the using and occupying of any of the streets and alleys and grounds, in the district aforesaid, by said companies, or either of them. **Damages.**

SEC. 8. All powers and privileges herein granted are subject to the ordinance entitled "An Ordinance supplemental to all ordinances concerning railroads," as the same **Subject to general ordinance.**

is found incorporated in the "Municipal Laws," chap. 49, pp. 363, 364 and 365.*

Contracts and bonds to fulfill this ordinance.

SEC. 9. This ordinance shall not take effect or be in force unless the said Pittsburgh, Fort Wayne and Chicago, and the Chicago, St. Paul and Fond du Lac Railroad Companies, shall, within ninety days of the passage hereof, file, with the comptroller, contracts in legal form, binding their respective companies to fulfill the same so far as any of its provisions apply to them, and also shall file as above the bonds of their respective companies, satisfactory in form and amount to the mayor and comptroller, to secure the fulfillment of said contract; nor shall any other railroad companies be entitled to participate in the rights and privileges herein granted, or any of them, until they respectively shall execute and file contracts and bonds in accordance with this section.

Passed August 16, 1858.

AN ORDINANCE in relation to the Chicago, St. Paul and Fond du Lac Railroad Company.

SECTION 1. Time for said company to file contract and bond, under preceding ordinance, extended thirty days.

Time to file contract and bond extended.

SECTION 1. *Be it ordained by the Common Council of the City of Chicago,* That section nine of an ordinance passed August 16th, 1858, entitled "An Ordinance to allow a connection between the Pittsburgh, Fort Wayne and Chicago, and the Chicago, St. Paul and Fond du Lac Railroad Companies, and such other railroad companies as may unite with them," be so far amended as to grant to said Chicago, St. Paul and Fond du Lac Railroad Company, thirty days additional to the ninety days therein specified, in which to file the "contract" and the "bond" of said company as required by said section number nine.

Passed November 8, 1858.

---

* Chapter 36, page 316, of this edition.

AN ORDINANCE permitting the laying down of a temporary Railroad Track in a portion of Canal Street.

SECTION
1. Permission to lay temporary track in Canal street from Van Buren to Randolph street; restrictions on use; not to remain, etc.

SECTION
2. Repair of Canal street; removal of track.
3. Provisions of former ordinance applied.

SECTION 1. *Be it ordained by the Common Council of the City of Chicago*, That permission is hereby granted to the Pittsburgh, Fort Wayne and Chicago Railroad Company, and such other railroad companies as may unite with them, to lay down and to use one railway track from the south line of Van Buren street northwesterly across said street; thence along the west side of Canal street to the south line of Madison street; thence northeasterly across Madison street; thence along the east side of Canal street to the south line of Randolph street. Said track to be used only in the conveyance of passengers and their ordinary baggage, and not for freighting purposes. Also to be used only until said company can perfect a right of way and construct their track on the locality now selected and recorded for their permanent track, and not in any event to be used or to remain in said streets for a term longer than one year from the passage hereof, unless two-thirds in frontage feet of property owners owning lots abutting said section of Canal street, shall consent in writing to a longer continuance of said track in said street.

Permission to lay temporary track

Restrictions on use.

SEC. 2. The permission and authority herein granted, are upon the express condition that said railroad company shall, at their own expense, during their occupancy of a portion of the same hereunder, put and maintain Canal street, from the south line of Van Buren street to the south line of Randolph street, in such condition and repair as the common council and the city superintendent of public works, or either of them, shall require, and within ten days after the expiration of said time, shall remove said track from said streets, and leave said streets in condition satisfactory to the city superintendent of public works.

Repair of Canal street.

Removal of track.

SEC. 3. Sections four (4), six (6), seven (7), eight (8), and nine (9), of the ordinance passed August sixteenth, eighteen hundred and fifty-eight, entitled "An ordinance to

Former ordinance applied.

allow a connection between the Pittsburgh, Fort Wayne and Chicago, and the Chicago, St. Paul and Fond du Lac Railroad Companies, and such other railroad companies as may unite with them," so far as the same are applicable, shall apply to, qualify and control the privileges and authority herein granted, and the action of all officers and parties hereunder.

Passed November 22, 1858.

AN ORDINANCE permitting the laying down of a temporary Railroad Track in a portion of Canal Street.

SECTION
1. Permission to lay temporary track in Canal street, from Van Buren to Randolph street; restrictions on use.
2. Repair and condition of Canal street.
3. Provisions of former ordinance applied.

SECTION
4. Companies to give bond, for benefit of property owners, conditioned to remove the track, etc.
5. When track to be laid.
6. Last preceding ordinance repealed.

Permission to lay temporary track

SECTION 1. *Be it ordained by the Common Council of the City of Chicago*, That permission is hereby granted, on the conditions herein expressed, to the Pittsburgh, Fort Wayne and Chicago Railroad Company, and such other railroad companies as may unite with them, to lay down and to use for two years from May 1st, 1859, one railroad track along the east side of Canal street, from the south line of Van Buren street to the south line of Randolph street, said track to be used only in the conveyance of passengers and their ordinary baggage, and not for freighting purposes, except that, on an average, one freight train per day from north to south, and the same from south to north, may pass over the said track, the same to move not less than two nor more than five miles per hour, and not to stop at any point on the way.

Restrictions on use.

Repair, etc., of street.

SEC. 2. In consideration of the privileges herein granted, and as an express condition ot the right to use and enjoy them, the said railroad companies shall, at any time when so ordered by the common council, or by any person or persons acting under their authority, supply gravel filling one foot deep the whole width of the roadway of Canal street from Van Buren street to Randolph street, and also shall, during the full time of their using the privileges herein granted, keep in repair, to the satisfaction of the council or any person or persons acting under their authority, the portion of Canal street so to be filled by them, and the said companies shall lay down and maintain said track and approaches at its sides in such way that it may be conveniently crossed at all points.

SEC. 3. Sections four (4), six (6), seven (7), eight (8), and nine (9), of the ordinance passed August sixteenth, eighteen hundred and fifty-eight, entitled "An Ordinance to allow a connection between the Pittsburgh, Fort Wayne and Chicago, and the Chicago, St. Paul and Fond du Lac Railroad Companies, and such other railroad companies as may unite with them," so far as the same are applicable, shall apply to, qualify and control the privileges and authority herein granted, and the action of all officers and parties hereunder. **Former ordinance applied.**

SEC. 4. In addition to the contracts and bonds required under section nine (9) of said ordinance of August sixteenth, eighteen hundred and fifty-eight, the Pittsburgh, Fort Wayne and Chicago Railroad Company, or any other railroad company taking action hereunder, which shall lay down the said temporary railroad track in a portion of Canal street as herein provided, shall, within sixty days of the passage hereof, and before proceeding so to lay down said track, file with Robert H. Foss, Joshua L. Marsh and Eber J. Chapin, of Chicago, as trustees for the persons owning lots or lands fronting on the portion of Canal street between Van Buren street and Randolph street, the bonds of said railroad company in the penal sum of five hundred thousand dollars, conditioned that said railroad tracks shall be taken up, and said roadway restored to good passable condition, on or before the first day of May, eighteen hundred and sixty-one, and that in case said railroad tracks be not so taken up from said portion of Canal street, and the street so restored to good passable condition at or before the time specified, to wit, on the first day of May, eighteen hundred and sixty-one, then in that case said bonds shall become due and payable in their full amount to said trustees as aforesaid, as liquidated damages for the indemnification of said owners of lots proportionate to the frontage feet of property be- **Bond, and condition thereof.**

longing to them respectively on the part of Canal street so to be occupied.

When track to be laid. SEC. 5. The privileges herein granted are on the express condition that said temporary railroad track in Canal street, from Van Buren street to Randolph street, shall be laid down on or before the fifteenth day of May next.

Last preceding ordinance repealed. SEC. 6. The ordinance passed November twenty-second, eighteen hundred and fifty-eight, entitled "An Ordinance permitting the laying down of a temporary railroad track in a portion of Canal street," is hereby repealed.

Passed February 28, 1859.

AN ORDINANCE granting permission to lay a Railroad Track through School Blocks 87 and 88.

SECTION 1. Permission to lay track and connect with railroads named, subject to removal by council.

May lay track, etc. SECTION 1. *Be it ordained by the Mayor and Aldermen of the City of Chicago, in Common Council assembled,* That permission is hereby given to lay so much of railroad track upon blocks 87 and 88, school section addition to Chicago, as may be necessary for business purposes upon said blocks, and that the same be connected with the Southern Michigan and Northern Indiana and Rock Island Railroads, at such points as the committee on schools of the common council may deem proper and necessary: *Provided,* That said track may be removed at the option of the common council.

Passed August 13, 1860.

AN ORDINANCE to vacate parts of First and Second Streets, and an Alley intersecting said Streets.

SECTION
1. Certain parts of certain streets vacated for railroad purposes.
2. Certain parts of an alley vacated for railroad purposes.
3. Mayor and comptroller to release to the Chicago and Northwestern Railway Company, and to the Chicago and Milwaukee Railroad Company, respectively, the interest of the city in different portions of the streets and alley vacated.

SECTION
4. Interest to revert to the city when use for railroad purposes shall cease; proviso, that no vacation except where railroad companies own on both sides.

SECTION 1. *Be it ordained by the Common Council of the City of Chicago,* That so much of First street as extends eastwardly from Halsted street to Union street, and between blocks seventy-eight (78) and seventy-nine (79), in Russell, Mather and Roberts' addition to the city of Chicago, and also so much of Second street as extends eastwardly from Halsted to Union street, and between blocks seventy-seven (77) and seventy-eight (78), in Russell, Mather and Roberts' addition to the city of Chicago, be and the same are hereby vacated and discontinued so long as they may be used for railroad purposes, and no longer. **Parts of streets vacated.**

SEC. 2. That so much of the alley as extends south from Chicago avenue to Third street, and intersecting blocks seventy-nine (79), seventy-eight (78), and seventy-seven (77), in Russell, Mather and Roberts' addition to the city of Chicago, be and the same hereby is declared vacated and discontinued, so long as it may be used for railroad purposes, and no longer. **Part of alley vacated.**

SEC. 3. The mayor and comptroller shall execute and deliver, on behalf of the city, such proper release or releases, conveyance or conveyances, as may be necessary, of the city's right, title and interest in said vacated and discontinued streets and alleys, to the Chicago and Northwestern Railway Company, and to the Chicago and Milwaukee Railroad Company, and each of said companies, as follows: To the Chicago and Northwestern Railway Company all that part of said First street which lies west of the east line of the alley through said blocks seventy-nine and seventy-eight, and the south half of that part of First street which lies between the west line of Union street and the east line of said alley, through said blocks seventy-eight and seventy-nine; also as much of Second street as lies between the west line of Union street and a line drawn from a point on the north line of lot one (1), in block seventy-seven (77), one hundred and eight (108) feet west of the north-east corner of said block seventy-seven (77), to a point on the south line of lot eight (8), in block seventy-eight (78), one hundred and seventy feet west of the south-east corner of said lot eight (8); also all of the alley through said block seventy-eight (78), except that part which **Release of interest of city to railroad companies.**

lies between the north line of Second street and a line drawn from a point on the east line of lot fifteen (15), in said block seventy-eight (78), sixty (60) feet north from the south-east corner of lot sixteen (16), in said block, measured on the west line of said alley, to a point on the west line of lot eight (8), in said block seventy-eight (78), thirty-one and a half feet north of the south-west corner of said lot eight (8). And to the Chicago and Milwaukee Railroad Company, the north half of said First street, between the west line of Union street and the east line of the alley through said blocks seventy-eight (78) and seventy-nine (79); the whole of the alley through said block seventy-nine (79); the whole of said alley through block seventy-seven (77); so much of the alley through block seventy-eight (78), as lies south of a line drawn from a point on the east line of lot fifteen (15), in block seventy-eight (78), sixty feet north of the south-east corner of lot sixteen (16), in said block seventy-eight (78), to a point on the west line of lot eight (8), in said block seventy-eight (78), thirty-one and a half (31½) feet north of the south-west corner of said lot eight (8), in said block seventy-eight (78); also, so much of Second street as lies between Halsted street and a line drawn from a point on the north line of lot one (1), in block seventy-seven (77), one hundred and eight (108) feet west of the north-east corner of said block seventy-seven (77), to a point on the south line of lot eight, in block seventy-eight (78), one hundred and seventy feet west of the south-east corner of said lot eight. And in each of which deeds, releases, conveyances, or other instruments, this ordinance shall be fully recited.

Interest to revert when railroad use ceases.

SEC. 4. The said First street, the said Second street, and the said alley, or so much of the same as is herein vacated and released to the before named railroad companies, shall immediately revert to the city of Chicago when the said railroad companies shall cease to use the streets and alleys vacated and released herein for railroad purposes, and all right and title thereunto shall again become vested in the city of Chicago, as before the passage of this ordinance: *Provided*, That no streets or alleys shall be vacated

No vacation except rail-

except where the railroad companies own upon both sides thereof. roads own both sides.

Passed August 13, 1860.

AN ORDINANCE to amend an Ordinance passed August 16, 1858, entitled "An Ordinance to allow a connection between the Pittsburgh, Fort Wayne and Chicago, and the Chicago, St. Paul and Fond du Lac Railroad Companies, and such other Railroad Companies as may unite with them."

SECTION
1. Permission to lay temporary tracks across Lake, Randolph and Madison streets, while permanent tracks and tunnels are constructing; time during which they may be used.
2. Flagmen at crossings.
3. Diligence required in locating depot grounds, constructing permanent tracks and tunnels; injunctions.
4. Provisions to secure discontinuance of use, and removal, of temporary tracks.
5. Mode of using temporary tracks regulated.
6. Ordinance not to take effect until railroad companies execute contract to perform it.
7. Grade of streets over tunnels fixed at twenty-two feet.

Permission to lay temporary track while permanent track and tunnels are constructing.

SECTION 1. *Be it ordained by the Common Council of the City of Chicago*, That the ordinance passed August 16, 1858, entitled "An Ordinance to allow a connection between the Pittsburgh, Fort Wayne and Chicago, and the Chicago, St. Paul and Fond du Lac Railroad Companies, and such other railroad companies as may unite with them," be and the same is hereby so modified as to permit a temporary track to be laid and used over Lake, Randolph and Madison streets, for the period of one year from the time when they shall first use said temporary track, or any part thereof, for the transportation of freight and passengers over either Lake, Randolph or Madison streets; said track to be laid in the alley in crossing blocks twenty-two, twenty-nine and forty-four, old town of Chicago. Whenever the permanent track and tunnels shall have been made, the right to use the said temporary track shall cease, although the twelve months shall not have expired: *Provided*, That if the said companies, or either of them, shall be enjoined by the order or injunction of any court of competent jurisdiction from proceeding with the making of any or either of said last mentioned tunnels, or the laying of said temporary track, the time during which they are so enjoined shall be added to the time above limited for continuing the use of said temporary track and completing said tunnels; but in no

Injunction.

event shall said railroad companies, or either of them, be permitted to have or use said temporary track over either Madison, Lake or Randolph streets for a longer period than three years from the passage of this ordinance, except as provided for in the fourth section hereof.

Flagmen.

SEC. 2. The said companies shall station and keep a flagman upon every street crossed by the track aforesaid, and at the junction of Canal and West Water streets, whenever a train or locomotive shall be crossing any of said several streets on said track.

Depot grounds.

SEC. 3. The said Pittsburgh, Fort Wayne and Chicago Railroad Company shall commence and complete the location of its depot grounds, between Madison and Adams streets in the west division, as soon after the passage of this ordinance as it legally can, and at all events within six months after the passage of this ordinance. And the aforesaid railroad companies shall, immediately upon the passage hereof, begin and persistently follow the making of the permanent connection in and by said original ordinance contemplated, and the making and finishing of the several tunnels under Lake, Randolph and Madison streets, in the manner in said ordinance specified; of which said tunnels, they shall finish that under Madison street in four months, under Lake street in eight months, and under Randolph street in ten months from the passage hereof. In the event of an injunction being obtained against proceeding with the permanent track or the tunnels, or either of them, the said railroad companies shall press for a hearing and dissolution as soon as possible, and the citizens of the west division may employ counsel to aid the counsel of said railroad companies in the same, and said railroad companies shall comply with all lawful orders of the court in the premises, and fairly and fully insist upon their right to make such track and tunnels.

Permanent track and tunnels.

Injunction.

Removal of temporary tracks.

SEC. 4. At the expiration of the time as in the first section of this ordinance provided, all right to have, continue or use the said temporary track by any or either of the railroad companies above mentioned or referred to, shall utterly cease and determine; and the said railroad companies, and each and every one of them, shall, and by the acceptance of this ordinance and in consideration of the privileges hereby granted, expressly will and do jointly and severally covenant and agree to and with S. S. Hayes, David J. Lake, John C. Haines, C. N. Holden and William W. Farwell, and the survivors of them, severally and not jointly, as trustees of the rights and interests of the present owners, their grantees or assigns, of property situate in the west division of Chicago, without the power in said trustees of releasing or acquitting the said railroad companies or either of them therefrom, that the said temporary track or appurtenances shall not be continued beyond the period aforesaid, nor shall said railroad companies, or any of them, or any one for them, apply to the common council to extend the said term of such continuance thereof, or accept, or in any manner receive any extension or renewal of the said term, except upon the petition hereinafter mentioned; and any act, attempt, or authority from any source whatever, except as hereinafter provided, purporting to authorize the continuance of the said track across the said streets above mentioned, or either of them, beyond the said period, shall be absolutely null and void as to the said trustees and each of the property owners and inhabitants of said west division; and the said trustees, their agents or servants, or any inhabitant of said west division, may, if said track be continued across either of said streets beyond the period aforesaid, enter upon, tear up and remove the portion of said track crossing said street or streets as aforesaid, and be forever discharged and acquitted from any action by or liability to said railroad companies, or their assigns, or any or either of them, for so doing: *Provided, however*, That upon the presentation of the petition in writing of the owners of two-thirds, in lineal measurement, of the property fronting either of said streets crossed by such temporary track, counting from the river or the branch thereof which said street crosses west to the city limits, at least one month prior to the expiration of said year, the common council may, in its discretion, extend the use of said temporary track on such street for a longer period: *Provided, also*, That such petition shall designate the length of time for which such extension of use is sought to be granted.

Mode of using temporary tracks.

SEC. 5. The said temporary track is to be used by the said railroad companies, as aforesaid, with the utmost care and caution, and every locomotive in coming in from the north shall come to a full stop near to and before crossing Kinzie street, and in coming in from the south in like manner, before crossing Van Buren street. The rate of speed on such temporary track shall be subject to the control and regulation of the common council, and shall in no place thereon exceed the rate of five miles per hour; trains shall not be made up on said temporary track, and all locomotives used thereon shall use coke or coal for fuel, and a clear violation of any of the provisions of this ordinance by any of the railroad companies aforesaid, shall render the same absolutely null and void, and all the rights herein and hereby granted shall thereupon cease and determine: *Provided*, There shall be no switch or switches located at the crossing of any street or alley.

Contracts to be executed before ordinance takes effect.

SEC. 6. This ordinance shall not take effect, nor shall either of the railroad companies aforesaid commence the construction or use of said temporary track or any part thereof, until the Pittsburgh, Fort Wayne and Chicago, and the Chicago and Northwestern Railway Companies, shall have first respectively, in writing under seal and in due form, bound themselves to the acceptance and performance of this ordinance, and filed such written acceptance with the comptroller of the city of Chicago, and made and delivered a duplicate of the same personally to either William W. Farwell or David J. Lake aforesaid, for the said trustees above mentioned. Nor shall this ordinance take effect as to any other railroad company proposing to construct or use such track, until such company shall have first filed and served the obligation in this section required.

Grades.

SEC. 7. The grade of said streets at the several points at which the tunnels shall be located, are hereby fixed at twenty-two feet above low water mark in the Chicago river.

Passed August 18, 1860.

AN ORDINANCE to amend an Ordinance, passed August 16, 1858, entitled "An Ordinance to allow a connection between the Pittsburgh, Fort Wayne and Chicago, and the Chicago, St. Paul and Fond du Lac Railroad Companies, and such other Railroad Companies as may unite with them."

SECTION 1. Permission to cross Van Buren street at present grade, subject to future orders of council; ordinance to be void unless passenger depot located, etc.

SECTION 1. *Be it ordained by the Common Council of the City of Chicago,* That the ordinance passed August 16, 1858, entitled "An Ordinance to allow a connection between the Pittsburgh, Fort Wayne and Chicago, and the Chicago, St. Paul and Fond du Lac Railroad Companies, and such other railroad companies as may unite with them," be so modified as to permit the Pittsburgh, Fort Wayne and Chicago Railroad Company, and such other railroad companies as may unite with them, to cross Van Buren street at its present grade until the common council shall order otherwise, for the purpose of making said railroad companies comply with any grade it may hereafter establish, either by running over or under said street: *Provided,* That the common council shall give six months notice of said change. But this ordinance shall be void, and all the rights, privileges and immunities under it, unless the Pittsburgh, Fort Wayne and Chicago Railroad Company shall locate their passenger depot on the west side of the river, between Madison and Adams streets, within six months after the passage of this ordinance, and the marshal shall at once proceed to take up the track.

May cross Van Buren street on present grade, subject to future orders, etc.

Location of passenger depot.

Passed August 18, 1860.

AN ORDINANCE in relation to connecting School Blocks 87 and 88, School Section, by rail, with the Michigan Southern and Rock Island Railroads.

SECTION 1. Ordinance of August 18, 1860, repealed.

SECTION 1. *Be it ordained by the Common Council of the City of Chicago,* That all ordinances or parts of ordinances heretofore passed, relative to laying a railroad track connecting school blocks 87 and 88, school section, with the

Permission to lay track epealed.

Michigan Southern and Rock Island Railroad, be and the same are hereby repealed.

Passed July 15, 1861.

AN ORDINANCE to vacate Monroe Street, between Canal Street and the South Branch of the Chicago river, in accordance with the provisions of an Ordinance passed August 16th, 1858, entitled "An Ordinance to allow a connection between the Pittsburgh, Fort Wayne and Chicago, and the Chicago, St. Paul and Fond du Lac Railroad Companies, and such other Railroad Companies as may unite with them."

PREAMBLE. Reciting reasons for vacating part of Monroe street.
SECTION
1. Vacating part of Monroe street for railroad passenger depot purposes.
2. Mayor and comptroller to convey the interest of the city in such part of the street to the company.
SECTION
3. If the company cease to use such part for a passenger depot, or neglect to pay certain damages, such part of the street to immediately revert to the city.

Reasons for vacating.

WHEREAS, The said Pittsburgh, Fort Wayne and Chicago Railroad Company have purchased and are the owners in fee of blocks 71 and 72, in school section addition to Chicago, and have permanently located thereon a union depot for the accommodation of said company, the Chicago and Northwestern Railroad Company, and such other railroad companies as may unite with them, and for the purpose of constructing upon said blocks such buildings and improvements as may be required for the business of said companies, it is desirable that Monroe street, lying between said blocks, should be vacated, in accordance with the provisions of said ordinance of August 16th, A. D. 1858; therefore,

Vacation of part of Monroe street.

SECTION 1. *Be it ordained by the Common Council of the City of Chicago*, That so much of West Monroe street as extends from the east line of Canal street to the dock line which may at any time hereafter be established by the authorities of the city of Chicago on the west bank of the south branch of the Chicago river, and lying between blocks 71 and 72, in school section addition to Chicago, be and the same is hereby vacated and discontinued, so long as it may be used for railroad passenger depot purposes, and no longer.

Conveyance of interest of city.

SEC. 2. The mayor and comptroller shall execute and deliver, on behalf of the city, such proper deed or conveyance as may be necessary to convey all the right, title and interest of the city in said vacated and discontinued street to the Pittsburgh, Fort Wayne and Chicago Railroad Company, and in such deed or conveyance, or other instrument, this ordinance shall be fully recited.

SEC. 3. If the said Pittsburgh, Fort Wayne and Chicago Railroad Company shall at any time cease to use for railroad passenger depot purposes that portion of Monroe street which is hereby vacated, or if said railroad company shall at any time hereafter refuse or neglect to reimburse said city of Chicago for any amount of money it may be compelled by legal process to pay any person or persons, as damages caused by reason of the vacation and discontinuance of said portion of Monroe street, the same shall immediately revert to the city of Chicago, and any deed or conveyance given by the city of Chicago by virtue hereof shall be void, and all right and title thereunto shall again become vested in the city of Chicago as before the passage of this ordinance. When to revert to the city.

Passed August 12, 1861.

AN ORDINANCE to vacate certain Streets and Alleys in the West Division.

SECTION
1. Parts of certain streets and alleys vacated for purpose of a depot for the Chicago and Northwestern Railroad Company, only so long as they may be so used, and city to have the right to enter as to water pipes and sewers.
2. Mayor and comptroller to convey the interest of the city in such streets, etc., to the company.
3. If the company cease to use such streets, etc., for depot, or neglect to pay certain damages, such streets, etc., to immediately revert to the city.
4. The city may take any part of said streets, etc., vacated, if necessary in establishing dock lines, without making compensation; forfeiture for neglect of company to comply with this section.

SECTION 1. *Be it ordained by the Common Council of the City of Chicago,* That so much of Fourth street as lies between the east line of Desplaines street and the west line of Jefferson street; also so much of Jefferson street as lies between the north line of West Indiana street and the north line of Fourth street; also so much of Water street as lies between the south line of Indiana street and the north line of Cook street, and from the north line of Indiana street to Jefferson street; also the alley running north from Indiana Parts of certain streets and alleys vacated for depot purposes.

street to the north branch of the Chicago river, between Desplaines street and Jefferson street; also the alley between lots seventeen (17) and eighteen (18), and lots seven (7) and eight (8), in Waubansia addition; also the alley running east and west, north and adjoining lot eleven (11), in block sixty-one (61), in Russell, Mather and Robert's addition to Chicago, be and the same are hereby vacated and discontinued: *Provided, however,* That such vacation and discontinuance shall continue only so long as they may be used for railroad depot purposes and no longer: *Provided further,* That the city authorities shall have the right to enter upon any or such portions of said streets and alleys as they shall deem necessary for the purpose of laying down or repairing water pipes or sewers or either.

City may enter, etc.

Conveyance of interest of city.

SEC. 2. That the mayor and comptroller shall execute and deliver in behalf of the city such proper conveyance as may be necessary to convey to the Chicago and Northwestern Railroad Company so much of the right and title of said city to said streets and alleys hereby vacated, as is contemplated by the provisions of this ordinance, and subject to all the conditions in this ordinance prescribed.

When to revert to the city.

SEC. 3. That if the said Chicago and Northwestern Railroad Company shall at any time cease to use for railroad depot purposes the streets and alleys that are hereby vacated, or if said railroad company shall at any time hereafter refuse or neglect to immediately pay over to said city of Chicago any and all amount of moneys it may be judicially determined that said city should pay as damages or costs, by reason of the property of any person or persons being damaged by reason of the vacation and discontinuance of such streets and alleys, then such streets and alleys shall immediately revert to the said city of Chicago as before the passage of this ordinance, and any deed or conveyance given by virtue hereof shall in such event become immediately null and void.

Dock lines.

SEC. 4. If the authorities of the said city of Chicago shall at any time hereafter establish a dock line on the west bank of the north branch of the Chicago river, which shall necessitate the taking or cutting away of any portion of the streets and alleys hereby vacated, said railroad company shall thereupon cease to use, and shall surrender to said city such portion or portions of such streets and alleys without charge or cost to said city, and said railroad company shall not be entitled to receive damages for the portion of streets or alleys so taken or cut away. Any neglect on the part of said railroad company to comply with the provisions of this section, shall forfeit all right of said company to occupy or longer use the streets and alleys herein vacated. Forfeiture.

Passed October 21, 1861.

AN ORDINANCE to allow a connection between the Galena and Chicago Union Railroad Track, and the Warehouse of L. Newberry & Co.

SECTION 1. Permission to connect railroad with elevator; bond to save city harmless; subject to ordinances and to repeal.

SECTION 1. *Be it ordained by the Common Council of the City of Chicago*, That permission and authority are hereby given to L. Newberry & Co., to lay down, maintain and operate a railroad track in, upon and along North Market street, from the track of the Galena and Chicago Union Railroad to Carroll street; thence, on Carroll street, to connect with the elevator of L. Newberry & Co., in block 14, original town of Chicago: *Provided*, Said Newberry & Co. shall enter into bonds with said city, to be approved by the mayor, to hold and save the city harmless from all damages in consequence of this act: *And provided*, The privilege hereby granted shall be enjoyed subject to all ordinances now in force concerning railroads, or which may be hereafter passed regulating or in any way concerning the track laid in conformity with this ordinance: *Provided*, That this ordinance shall at all times be subject to repeal by the common council, and if so repealed, all the privileges hereby granted shall cease and determine. Permission to lay track on giving bond. Subject to ordinances and repeal.

Passed February 10, 1862.

AN ORDINANCE to vacate DePuyster Street.

SECTION
1. Part of street vacated for railroad purposes; right of city to enter as to sewers and water pipes.

SECTION
2. Unless used for railroad purposes, and other conditions performed, to revert immediately to the city.

Part of street vacated for railroad purposes.

SECTION 1. *Be it ordained by the Common Council of the City of Chicago,* That the street running east and west through block sixty-seven (67), school section addition to Chicago, known as DePuyster street, (except a strip of the same, through the centre thereof, twenty (20) feet in width, running from Canal street east a distance of one hundred and twenty (120) feet,) be and the same is hereby vacated and discontinued: *Provided, however,* That such vacation and discontinuance shall continue so long, and so long only, as the same may be used for railroad purposes; and it is further provided, that the authorities of said city shall at all times have and possess, without charge or hindrance, the right to enter upon that portion of said street hereby vacated, or any part thereof, for the purpose of laying down or repairing either sewerage or water pipes.

Right of city to enter.

To revert to the city unless certain conditions complied with.

SEC. 2. That if the Pittsburgh, Fort Wayne and Chicago Railway Company, and the Joliet and Chicago Railroad Company, shall at any time cease to use for railroad purposes the portion of the street hereby vacated and discontinued, or if said companies, or either of them, shall at any time refuse or neglect to fully indemnify the said city of Chicago against, and save it harmless from all judgments or decrees, with the costs and expenses of the same, which may be recovered or obtained against said city, in any judicial proceeding which may ensue from or in consequence of the vacation and discontinuance of said street, or if said companies shall not, immediately after the passage of this ordinance, widen and dedicate to public use (without charge or cost to said city), the alley in the rear of lots sixteen (16) to twenty-six (26) inclusive, in said block, to the width of twenty (20) feet, and extend the same through a portion of said vacated street, so as to intersect with that portion of said street herein before reserved or excepted, then this ordinance shall immediately become null and void, and said street shall thereupon revert to and become vested in the said city of Chicago, as before the passage of this ordinance.

Passed July 28, 1862.

AN ORDINANCE approving the plans for a Bridge, to be erected by the Illinois Central Railroad Company across the Chicago River.

PREAMBLE. Reciting former ordinance.
SECTION
1. Plans of bridge approved, subject to conditions.
2. Construction and management of bridge; company to pay all damages.

WHEREAS, The common council, by ordinance passed June 14, 1852, (see Section 4, page 350, of Municipal Laws,)* did authorize the Illinois Central Railroad Company to extend the track of said road from their track or grounds south of the south pier, across the Chicago river to North Water street, by means of a bridge, the plans of which were to be approved by the common council; therefore, Former ordinance recited.

SECTION 1. *Be it ordained by the Common Council of the City of Chicago*, That the plans for a pivot bridge presented by the Illinois Central Railroad Company, to cross the Chicago river at a point designated in the foregoing preamble, be and the same is hereby approved; subject, however, to this express condition, that the breaking of ground for the erection of said bridge, or the taking of any measures by the said company or its agents towards the building of the same, shall be taken and construed as an acceptance of, and agreement on the part of said company to all the conditions, provisions, restrictions and requirements of this ordinance, and the same shall be binding upon said company. Plans of bridge approved, subject to conditions.

SEC. 2. Said railroad company shall construct said bridge under the charge and superintendence of the board of public works; and said company shall be liable for and chargeable with all damages that may accrue and become payable to the owners or occupants of any real estate, or to the owners or charter party of any vessel, float or water craft, by reason of the construction, operation or improper care and management of said bridge; and said company shall, at its own cost, tend said bridge, and shall so operate Construction and management of bridge; liability for damages.

* Page 456 of this edition.

and manage the same as to cause the least possible obstruction to navigation; and said railroad company shall indemnify and save the city of Chicago harmless from any and all costs, damages, charges and expenses whatsoever, that may in any manner arise by reason of the erection or use of a bridge at that point.

Passed December 1, 1862.

AN ORDINANCE relative to the use of a part of Lumber Street by the Pittsburgh, Fort Wayne and Chicago Railroad Company.

SECTION
1. Permission to lay tracks; construction, repair, etc., of streets; use of tracks.

SECTION
2. Forfeiture for neglect to comply with orders or ordinances.
3. Ordinance not to take effect until bond to pay all damages is given by the company.

Permission to lay tracks SECTION 1. *Be it ordained by the Common Council of the City of Chicago*, That permission and authority be and is hereby given to the Pittsburgh, Fort Wayne and Chicago Railroad Company, to lay down, maintain and operate a single railroad track on the east side of Lumber street, from the intersection of said railroad with Lumber street to South street, together with all such turn-outs and side tracks leading into the property adjoining such said part of Lumber street as may be desired by the owners or occupants of such adjoining property: **Construction.** *Provided, however*, That said single track be laid immediately over the ditch on the east side of said Lumber street, and it and all side tracks and turn-outs shall be laid in conformity with the directions of the board of public works of said city of Chicago, and in such a manner as to interfere as little as possible with Lumber street for the ordinary purposes and uses as a highway: *And provided further*, **Repair, etc., of streets.** That said railroad company shall at all times keep that portion of Lumber street which lies between the points above mentioned in good repair, and shall repair, grade, plank or pave all that portion of said Lumber street as the said board of public works or said common council shall order or direct, and shall, **Use of tracks.** in the use of said track or tracks, be subject to all rules and regulations relative to motive power, speed, and manner of running thereon, that the said common council have or hereafter may, either by general or special ordinance, make or impose.

Forfeiture for neglect. SEC. 2. If at any time the said railroad company shall refuse or neglect to comply with any order of said board of public works, or with any order or ordinance of said common council relative to the repairing, grading, planking or paving of said part of Lumber street, or relative to the laying of said track or tracks, or using the same, then all rights herein or hereby granted, or intended to be granted, shall cease and determine, and the said city of Chicago, its officers, agents, servants or workmen, shall have the right at once to take up and remove any or all of said tracks laid in said Lumber street.

Bond to be given. SEC. 3. This ordinance shall not take effect until the said railroad company shall have entered into a bond with the city of Chicago, to be filed with and approved by the city comptroller of said city, and conditioned for the payment of any and all costs, expenses, fees, charges and damages for which the said city of Chicago may become or be held liable to any person or persons by reason of any act of said railroad company, in laying down said track or tracks in said Lumber street, or using or operating on the same, or by reason of said railroad company's neglect or refusal to keep said Lumber street, between the points above mentioned, in good repair, or to keep that portion of said Lumber street repaired, graded, planked or paved, as directed by said common council or said board of public works.

Passed December 1, 1862.

AN ORDINANCE concerning the Chicago, Burlington and Quincy Railroad Company.

SECTION
1. Permission to lay tracks on alley and lands of company, and to cross streets within limits named.
2. Permission to lay tracks on their own lands, within other limits, and to cross streets; make connections with other roads; depots and buildings; crossings and warning tables; subject to laws and ordinances.

SECTION
3. Track in North street in west division.
4. Operate engines and cars under regulations of council.
5. To keep that portion of North street in which track is laid in repair, and pay all damages which city may sustain.

Permission to lay tracks, etc., on alley and lands of company, and cross streets, within certain limits.

SECTION 1. *Be it ordained by the Common Council of the City of Chicago*, That permission and authority be and is hereby given to the Chicago, Burlington and Quincy Railroad Company to lay down, maintain and operate one or more railroad tracks, together with all such turn-outs, switches and turn-tables as may be deemed necessary, on the alley next north of North street in said city, and on such lands as said company may acquire next south of and adjoining said alley, and in continuation of the same, from the south branch of the Chicago river to and across May street, and from May street, on such lands as it may acquire, to or near the point on the western limits of the city at which Evans street crosses said limits, with the right to cross all intervening streets.

Permission to lay tracks on their own lands in other limits.

SEC. 2. Said company is also hereby authorized to lay down, maintain and operate one or more railroad tracks, with such turn-outs and switches as they shall deem necessary, on any ground which they now own or may hereafter acquire by purchase, donation, condemnation or otherwise, from its depot grounds on North street to South street, east of the east line of Stewart avenue, to Lumber street, and east of the east line of Lumber street, from its intersection with Stewart avenue to South street, and west of the south branch of the Chicago river, and from the south branch of the Chicago river to Stinson street, on any lands it may acquire within one block on either side of South street, and from South street to the St. Charles and Mississippi Air-line Railroad, on any lands it may acquire between Stinson street and Lisle or Reuben street, and to lay down, maintain and operate any such track or tracks and turn-outs across any street or streets and alleys within the district aforesaid, and also all such as may be necessary to the convenient use of any depot grounds the said company may now own or hereafter acquire in the vicinity of or adjoining said line of road, and the grounds of the Union track road as now laid between the said south branch of the Chicago river and the Illinois Central Railroad, and to form connections with it and other roads, and also to acquire and use all such depot grounds, and to erect thereon such buildings as said company may deem necessary for the convenient

To cross streets.

Connections with other roads and depots.

transaction of its business: *Provided*, That convenient crossings shall be made and maintained by said company, where such track or tracks cross any such street or alley, and proper warning tables shall be erected in conspicuous places at or near such crossings; said company shall be subject to all laws and ordinances that are now in force, or may hereafter be passed, to regulate railroads within the said city. **Crossings and warning tables.**

SEC. 3. Said company is hereby authorized to lay down, maintain and operate a single railroad track in North street, and fifteen feet south of the north line thereof, from a point two hundred feet west of the west end of the freight depot of said company, on block forty-eight (48), in Canal Trustees' subdivision of the north-west quarter of section twenty-one (21), in township thirty-nine (39) north, of range fourteen (14) east to the slip constructed in North street, at its intersection with the south branch of the Chicago river. **Track in North street**

SEC. 4. Said company may use and operate said railroad tracks with locomotive engines and cars, under the regulations and rules with reference to speed, motive power and manner of running the same as the common council of said city may from time to time impose and make. **Engines and cars.**

SEC. 5. Said company shall be required to keep that portion of North street, in which said track shall be laid, in good repair, and pay all damages said city may sustain by reason of suits or otherwise on account of the laying down and using said track, on said part of North street, as provided for by section three of this ordinance. **Repair of street. Damages.**

Passed December 15, 1862.

AN ORDINANCE granting permission to George Steele and Isaac Taylor to lay down and operate a Railroad Track.

SECTION
1. Permission to connect elevator by railroad track with railroads named, for removing grain only; limit on liability of the city.

SECTION
2. To plank and repair streets; build and repair culverts; give bond to pay damages.
3. Subject to all laws and ordinances.
4. Ordinance to take effect from its passage.

SECTION 1. *Be it ordained by the Common Council of the City of Chicago*, That permission is hereby granted to **Permission to connect** elevator with railroads. George Steele and Isaac Taylor to lay down and operate a railroad track across all intervening streets from their elevator, situated on lots 8, 9 and 10, in block 4 of the Canal addition to Chicago, to the track or tracks of the Chicago, Alton and St. Louis, and the Fort Wayne and Chicago railroads, on the most direct practicable route, for the purpose of removing grain to and from said elevator, and none other. But it is expressly understood that the city of Chicago does not undertake to obtain for said Steele and Taylor any right of way, or other right, privilege or easement not now in the power of said city to grant or confer, or to assume any liability or responsibility for the acts of the said George Steele and Isaac Taylor or their successors.

City not liable.

SEC. 2. The permission hereby granted is with the following express conditions, to wit:

Plank and repair streets.

First. That the said Steele and Taylor, or their successors, shall, at their own expense, plank the carriage-way of all streets across which their track or tracks when so laid shall pass, to the width of twenty-four feet, on a line of all such streets, and extending from a point not less than twenty feet from the outside rail on the one side of said track or tracks, to a point not less than twenty feet from the outside rail on the other or opposite side of said track or tracks, and said rails and planking shall be so laid that teams, carriages, and all other vehicles can easily and freely cross said track or tracks with the least obstruction possible, and shall at all times keep said planking and street and railroad crossings in good order and repair.

Build and repair culverts.

Second. That the said Steele and Taylor and their successors shall, at their own expense, and subject to the direction of the board of public works, build good and substantial culverts, and keep the same in good order and repair, on all streets where their track or tracks pass over or intersect any street or alley.

Bond to pay damages.

Third. That the said Steele and Taylor, for themselves and their successors, shall enter into a good and sufficient bond with the city of Chicago, conditioned that they will indemnify the city for any damage and expense to which it may be legally subjected by reason of the occupying of any of the streets or alleys of the city with their tracks or other fixtures.

SEC. 3. The said George Steele and Isaac Taylor and their successors, shall be subject to all laws and ordinances that are now in force or may hereafter be passed, to regulate railroads within this city. **Subject to laws and ordinances.**

SEC. 4. This ordinance shall take effect and be in force from and after its passage. **Ordinance in force.**

Passed September 7, 1863.

A CONTRACT

Between the Galena and Chicago Union Railroad Company and the city, ratified by an Ordinance at the end thereof, in relation to State Street Bridge, etc.

This Indenture, made this thirtieth day of May, A. D. 1864, by and between the Galena and Chicago Union Railroad Company, party of the first part, and the city of Chicago, party of the second part, witnesseth:

That whereas, the said city of Chicago proposes to erect and maintain a pivot or draw-bridge across the Chicago river, on or near the line of State street, in the south division, and Wolcott street in the north division of said city, the approach to which proposed bridge from the north will cross water lots one (1), two (2), and three (3), in Kinzie's addition to the city of Chicago, or parts of them, which water lots are owned by the said party of the first part;

And whereas, by virtue of a certain ordinance of the city of Chicago, passed July 17th, 1848, the said party of the first part has heretofore laid and constructed, and has been and is now using and operating railroad tracks, in connection with its railroad, upon and across Wolcott street, between Kinzie street and the Chicago river;

And whereas, it is believed that the public interests and convenience, as well as those of the Galena and Chicago Union Railroad Company, would be promoted by carrying the approach-way of the proposed bridge on the north side, over the railroad tracks of said company, in the form of a viaduct, instead of raising and filling Wolcott street from Kinzie street to the river up to the necessary grade;

And whereas, the said party of the first part is willing to grant, convey and confirm unto the said party of the second part so much and such portions of the said water lots one (1), two (2), and three (3), in Kinzie's addition to Chicago, as is required for the extension of Wolcott street, through, sixty-six feet in width, to the Chicago river, in return for and in consideration of the rights, privileges and benefits hereinafter secured by the said party of the second part to the said party of the first part:

Now, therefore, the said party of the first part, in consideration of the construction and maintenance of said bridge and viaduct, and of other valuable considerations in this agreement hereinafter contained, to be kept and performed by said party of the second part, and upon the conditions hereinafter specified, does hereby grant, convey and confirm unto the said party of the second part, all that portion of water lots one (1), two (2), and three (3), in Kinzie's addition to Chicago, in the county of Cook and State of Illinois, which is embraced or included within the east and west lines of Wolcott street, in said city of Chicago, produced and extended southerly to the main Chicago river; the said party of the second part and its successors forever, to thereafter have and hold the same, for the purposes of a public street, but subject to the stipulations and conditions hereinafter mentioned.

And in consideration of the above agreement to grant and convey as aforesaid, the said party of the second part hereby stipulates and agrees to and with the said party of the first part, that whenever the proposed bridge shall be erected across the Chicago river at the point above indicated, it shall be constructed in accordance with the plan and profile prepared for that purpose by the board of public works of the city of Chicago, and appended hereto, and when displaced by accident, or because worn out and requiring to be repaired or built anew, it shall be renewed or reconstructed without unnecessary delay, in accordance with the same plan and profile, unless the parties hereto mutually agree otherwise, a general description of which plan and profile is as follows:

The said bridge shall be one hundred and eighty-four (184) feet long, revolving on a pivot at the centre, having two openings for vessels, each seventy-four (74) feet wide in the clear. The said central pivot shall be fixed at a point in the river about one hundred and twenty-one (121) feet from that point in the northerly line of the river, which is intersected by the centre line of said bridge. The top of the floor of said bridge shall be twenty-one feet and three inches above the base line of the city level heretofore established. The northerly approach-way to said bridge shall be carried over the tracks of said railroad company on Wolcott street, in the form of a viaduct, on such a grade line, that the under side of the three-inch oak plank floor of the said viaduct shall be twenty-one feet above the base line of the said city level, to the end that the roadway over the bridge and the viaduct shall be level, and that the locomotives and cars of the said railroad company may always have free and uninterrupted passage to and fro along the said tracks beneath said viaduct; and to establish this definitely, it is hereby expressly agreed that the grade of Wolcott street, under the proposed viaduct, for the entire distance occupied by the tracks of said company, and of North Water street, at its intersection with Wolcott street, shall be and is hereby established at seven feet above the base line of said city level, and the grade of North Water street, east and west of Wolcott street, shall ascend from Wolcott street at the rate of one (1) foot rise to one hundred (100) feet horizontal distance, until such inclined grade shall intersect and connect with the established grade of said North Water street; and the grade of Wolcott street, where occupied by the tracks of said company as above, and of North Water street within the limits above specified, shall never be changed or modified, except by the mutual consent of both parties to this indenture.

The said viaduct is to be sustained at proper intervals by piers constructed of stone, or a double row of piles, well capped and cased in with two-inch oak plank, and is to extend from the north end of said bridge to a point ten (10) feet north of the centre line of the track entering the east door of the more northerly brick freight house of said railroad company, near the corner of Wolcott street and (new) North Water street, where it is to rest on an abutment pier, to be constructed of stone, or a double row of piles extending across the said viaduct thirty-eight (38) feet wide; from thence the approach-way will descend at the same width by such a grade as may be proper, to Kinzie street. From the said abutment to the south line of Kinzie street the approach-way is to be constructed, for the present, of piles and timber, with a roadway twenty-three feet and four inches wide, to be covered with three-inch oak plank, and with a sidewalk on each side of the roadway, and raised eight inches above it, seven feet and four inches wide, to be covered with two-inch oak plank. But nothing herein contained shall be so construed as to prevent the widening of this approach-way to the said viaduct, and the widening of said viaduct to the extent of the entire width of Wolcott street, or to prevent the raising and filling of Wolcott street, from the northerly abutment of said viaduct to Kinzie street, to such grade as will furnish to the public easy and convenient access to said viaduct and bridge.

It is further mutually agreed, that the said Galena and Chicago Union Railroad Company shall have the right to construct and maintain, at its own expense, and for its own accommodation and convenience, a passage-way for teams and foot passengers from the said viaduct, and connecting therewith on the westerly side thereof, to such point south of the south warehouse of said company as may be agreeable to said company, and in case the alley now used by said company, running along the northerly side of its north warehouse, across lots five (5), six (6), seven (7) and eight (8), in block one (1), in the original town of Chicago, should be hereafter extended easterly to Wolcott street, through lot or block one (1) in Kinzie's addition to Chicago, the said company shall also have the right to construct and maintain at its own expense another passage-way for teams and foot passengers from the approach-way to the said viaduct, and connecting therewith to the said alley: *Provided*, That these passage-ways and the use of the same, shall at no time be permitted to cause any obstruction or delay to the public travel across the said bridge and viaduct or the approach thereto.

And the said party of the second part further agrees to take immediate steps to vacate a portion of the alley running through block two (2) in Kinzie's addition to Chicago, the portion to be vacated being described as follows:

Beginning at its intersection with Wolcott street and running thence northeasterly to the south-west corner of lot one (1) in said block two (2); and, in consideration thereof, the said party of the first part hereby covenants and agrees, to and with the said party of the second part, that immediately after the vacating of the above described portion of the aforesaid alley, it will cause to be laid out, opened and dedicated to the public use, without expense or cost to the city of Chicago, a free passage-way from the remaining part of said alley into North Water street, along the easterly side of lot eleven (11) in block two (2) aforesaid, said passage-way to be eighteen feet wide.

The said party of the second part further agrees to take immediate steps to vacate all that portion of (old) North Water street situated in Kinzie's addition to Chicago, and lying west of the west line of Wolcott street produced to the Chicago river.

It is further mutually covenanted and agreed, that the said party of the second part shall never grant to any other party the right to use or occupy any portion of the premises herein before conveyed by said party of the first part to said party of the second part for the extension of Wolcott street to the river, without the consent of the said party of the first part, nor shall the said party of the first part be hereafter excluded from such restricted use of the said granted premises as may be compatible with the full exercise and enjoyment by the said city of Chicago and the public at large of all the paramount rights, privileges and facilities which are by the foregoing terms of this instrument vested in or secured to the said party of the second part, or intended so to be.

And the said party of the second part further stipulates and agrees, that the said railroad company shall at all times hereafter have the right uninterruptedly, to stand, move, or propel its locomotives and cars along North Water street and across Wolcott street, beneath the said proposed viaduct, any past, present or future ordinance of the city to the contrary notwithstanding; provided, however, that no locomotive when in active service, shall stop or stand directly under the said viaduct, and further, that so much of (new) North Water street at this point shall be left open and unobstructed as to allow always a free passage for teams through and along the same.

And the said party of the first part, in consideration of the foregoing stipulations and agreements to be observed and performed by said party of the second part, further covenants and agrees, to and with the said party of the second part, that it, the said party of the first part, will contribute and pay to the said party of the second part, the sum of fifteen hundred dollars towards the construction of the said bridge and viaduct; such payment to be made whenever demanded by said party of the second part, after the final execution and ratification of this contract, and at any time after commencing to build said bridge. And further, that the said party of the first part shall and will, annually hereafter, as long as said bridge, viaduct and approach-way are maintained, on the first day of April in each and every year, contribute and pay to the said city of Chicago, the sum of four hundred dollars towards maintaining the said viaduct, and renewing and keeping the same in repair—said annual payments to commence on the first day of April next succeeding the opening of the bridge and viaduct to public use; and the first payment to be computed for such fractional part of the year as may intervene between such opening and such first day of April, at said rate of four hundred dollars per annum.

It is further mutually agreed by the parties hereto, that this contract shall take effect and become binding and obligatory upon both parties, as soon as the same shall be duly ratified and confirmed by the common council of the city of Chicago; such ratification and confirmation to be evidenced by the passage of an ordinance prepared by the board of public works, and hereby declared to be a part of this agreement, and providing as follows, to wit:

AN ORDINANCE approving a certain Contract with the Galena and Chicago Union Railroad Company.

SECTION
1. Preceding contract ratified and confirmed.
2. Grades of parts of Wolcott and North Water streets fixed; not to be changed without consent of company.
3. Part of an alley and part of North Water street vacated on condition that company open new alley.
4. Ordinance in force from its passage.

Contract ratified and confirmed.

SECTION 1. *Be it ordained by the Common Council of the City of Chicago*, That the contract made and executed by and between the Galena and Chicago Union Railroad Company, party of the first part, and the city of Chicago, through the board of public works, party of the second part, bearing date the thirtieth day of May, A. D. 1864, in relation to the construction of a bridge across the Chicago river on the line of State street in the south division, and Wolcott street in the north division, a copy of which is hereto appended, be and the same hereby is in all respects approved, ratified and confirmed.

Grades of Wolcott and North Water streets.

SEC. 2. That pursuant to the terms of said contract, the grade of Wolcott street, between the Chicago river and a point ten feet north of the centre line of the track of the Galena and Chicago Union Railroad Company, entering the east door of the more northerly brick freight house of said company, near the corner of Wolcott and (new) North Water streets, be and the same is hereby permanently established at seven feet above the base line of the city level heretofore established; and that the grade of (new) North Water street, at its intersection with Wolcott street, be and the same is hereby permanently established at seven feet above the base line of the city level, and the grade of said (new) North Water street shall ascend east and west from Wolcott street at the rate of one foot rise to one hundred feet in horizontal distance, until such inclined grade shall intersect and connect with the general grade of said (new) North Water street, as now or as it may be hereafter established. The grades hereby established shall never be changed without the consent of the said Galena and Chicago Union Railroad Company. **Not to be changed.**

SEC. 3. That a portion of the alley running through block two (2) in Kinzie's addition to Chicago, beginning at its intersection with Wolcott street, and running thence northeasterly to the south-west corner of lot one (1) in said block two (2), and all that portion of (old) North Water street, situated in Kinzie's addition to Chicago, lying west of the west line of Wolcott street produced to the Chicago river, be and the same are discontinued and vacated: *Provided*, That a new alley shall be laid out and opened by the Galena and Chicago Union Railroad Company, from the remaining portion of the alley above referred to, into North Water street along the easterly side of lot eleven (11) in block two (2) of Kinzie's addition to Chicago, without charge or expense to said city, said alley to be eighteen feet wide. **Portion of alley and (old) North Water street vacated, if new alley opened by the company**

SEC. 4. This ordinance shall take effect from and after its passage. **Ordinance in force.**

In testimony whereof, The party of the first part have caused this contract to be signed by its President and Secretary, and affixed the seal of the said company, and the said party of the second part, through the board of public works, have also executed the same and caused to be affixed hereto the signatures of the commissioners of said board.

W. H. BROWN, *President.*

Attest:

[SEAL.] W. M. LARRABEE, *Secretary.*

J. G. GINDELE,
FRED LETZ,
O. J. ROSE,
Board of Public Works.

Ordinance passed July 11, 1864.

AN ORDINANCE amending an Ordinance entitled "An Ordinance amending an Ordinance passed February 13th, 1854, concerning the Fort Wayne and Chicago Railroad Company, now the Pittsburgh, Fort Wayne and Chicago Railroad Company," passed November 17th, 1856.

PREAMBLE. Reciting extension of city limits and former rights of company.
SECTION
1. Permission to lay tracks in Stewart avenue.
SECTION
2. Limiting construction of last section.
3. Subject to all general ordinances.
4. Repair of street; condition of tracks and kind of rail.

Extension of city limits.

WHEREAS, Since the passage of the ordinance to which the following is an amendment, the legislature of the State of Illinois has, by the passage of the act approved February 13th, 1863, entitled "An Act to reduce the charter of the city of Chicago, and the several acts amendatory thereof, into one act, and to revise the same," extended the limits of said city upon the south by including in the city section No. thirty-three (33) in township thirty-nine (39) north, range fourteen (14) east of third principal meridian; and whereas, before the passage of said act, the Pittsburgh, Fort Wayne and Chicago Railway Company had acquired from the commissioners of highways of the town of South Chicago, and from the various property owners along the street or highway known as Stewart avenue, as the same was laid out and dedicated, through the centre of section thirty-three (33), the right of way for their track or tracks in said street or highway running through said section; and whereas, by the several ordinances to which this is an amendment, said railroad company were authorized and empowered to use said street as the same is located through the centres of sections No. twenty-one (21) and twenty-eight (28), in the manner therein specified, from the south line of North (now Sixteenth) street to the city limits; now, therefore,

Former rights of company.

Permission to lay tracks

SECTION 1. *Be it ordained by the Common Council of the City of Chicago*, That permission and authority is hereby given to the Pittsburgh, Fort Wayne and Chicago Railroad Company to lay down, maintain and operate a railroad track or tracks — not exceeding two in number — with the necessary switches, turn-outs and side tracks, in the street known and designated as Stewart avenue, in the city of

Chicago, as the same is laid out and dedicated, running north and south on the centre lines of sections twenty-one (21), twenty-eight (28), and thirty-three (33), in township thirty-nine (39) north, range fourteen (14) east of the third principal meridian, from the south line of Sixteenth (formerly North) street to the southern boundary of said city.

SEC. 2. Nothing in the foregoing section shall be construed as conferring upon said railway company the right to use any other street than the one therein named, nor as extending the right to use Stewart avenue between said points to any greater extent than is provided by the ordinance passed November 17th, 1856, granting to said company permission to use said street north of the south line of North (now Sixteenth) street, to which this is an amendment. Last section limited.

SEC. 3. That the privileges hereby granted shall be enjoyed subject to all general ordinances that now are or hereafter may be in force concerning railroads in said city. Subject to ordinances.

SEC. 4. The privileges granted by this ordinance are upon this express condition: That said railway company, its successors and assigns, shall, as respects grading, paving, macadamizing, filling, or planking, at its own expense, keep eighteen feet in width in repair on said Stewart avenue, so far as the same is embraced in this ordinance, and keep its tracks in such condition that wagons and other vehicles can pass and repass at any and all points and in any and all directions, and shall be subject to assessment for paving, repaving, planking, replanking, or any other kind of improvement, of eighteen feet in width of said avenue, whenever the common council shall by ordinance order said improvement to be made in said Stewart avenue, and shall then use the kind of rail and lay it in said avenue in the manner directed by the board of public works. Repair of street. Condition of tracks. Rail.

Passed August 22, 1864.

AN ORDINANCE concerning the Chicago, Burlington and Quincy Railroad Company.

SECTION
1. Permission to lay track on streets named, in certain limits, on condition of dedicating land to open a street named.

SECTION
2. May operate with steam, etc.; subject to general ordinances.
3. Repair of streets; condition of track.
4. Ordinance in force from its passage.

Permission to lay track in streets named.

SECTION 1. *Be it ordained by the Common Council of the City of Chicago*, That permission and authority is hereby given to the Chicago, Burlington and Quincy Railroad Company and its successors, to put down, construct and maintain a railroad with a single track, and with the necessary switches and turn-outs in that part of Brown street in said city which extends from Sixteenth to Twenty-second street, with the right to cross said last mentioned streets at the intersection of Brown street with the same, or at such other points near such intersections as may be necessary to connect said railroad with said company's main line near Sixteenth street, and with a railroad track to be built by said company on the fifty feet south of and adjoining the south line of Twenty-second street, and extending from the east to the west line of Green's south branch addition to Chicago: *Provided, however*, and this permission and authority is given upon the express condition, That said company shall procure and dedicate to said city so much land as shall be necessary to open Brown street northward from its present terminus to Sixteenth street; and in case the same or any part thereof is opened by or under the authority of said city, said company shall pay to the said city the costs and expenses of procuring land and opening the same, and shall indemnify and secure said city from any costs or expenses on account of the procuring of land for the opening of said part of said street.

On condition to open street.

Operate with steam, subject to ordinances.

SEC. 2. Said company and its successors are hereby authorized to operate said railroad track with steam or such other motive power as it shall deem best; the privileges hereby granted, however, shall be enjoyed subject to all general ordinances that now are and hereafter may be in force concerning railroads in said city.

epair of streets.

SEC. 3. The privileges granted by this ordinance are upon this express condition: That said railway company, its successors and assigns, shall, as respects grading, paving, macadamizing, filling or planking, at its own expense, keep ten feet in width, exclusive of and on one side of its track, in repair on said Brown street, so far as the same is embraced in this ordinance, and keep its tracks in such condition that wagons and other vehicles can pass and repass at any and all points and in any and all directions, and shall be subject to assessment for paving, repaving, planking, replanking, or any other kind of improvements, of ten feet in width of said street, exclusive of and on one side of its track, whenever the common council shall by ordinance order said improvement to be made. **Condition of tracks.**

SEC. 4. That this ordinance be in force from and after its passage. **Ordinance in force.**

Passed November 2, 1864.

AN ORDINANCE concerning the Chicago, Burlington and Quincy Railroad Company.

SECTION
1. Permission to lay track on streets named, in certain limits, on condition of dedicating land to open a street named.
2. May operate with steam; subject to general ordinances.
3. Repair of streets; condition of track.
4. No preferences to be shown between lumber yards as to facilities for transportation.
5. Ordinance in force from its passage.

SECTION 1. *Be it ordained by the Common Council of the City of Chicago*, That permission and authority is hereby given to the Chicago, Burlington and Quincy Railroad Company and its successors, to put down, construct and maintain a railroad with a single track, and with the necessary switches and turn-outs, in that part of Brown street in said city which extends from Sixteenth to Twenty-second street, with the right to cross said last mentioned street at the intersection of Brown street with the same, or at such other points near such intersections as may be necessary to connect said railroad with said company's main line near Sixteenth street, and with a railroad track to be built by said company on the fifty feet south of and adjoining the south line of Twenty-second street, and extending from the east to the west line of Green's south branch addition to Chicago: *Provided, however*, and this permission and authority is given upon the express condition, That said company **Permission to lay track in streets named.** **On condition to open street.**

shall procure and dedicate to said city so much land as shall be necessary to open Brown street northward from its present terminus to Sixteenth street; and in case the same or any part thereof is opened by or under the authority of said city, said company shall pay to the said city the costs and expenses of procuring land and opening the same, and shall indemnify and secure said city from any costs or expenses on account of the procuring of land for the opening of said part of said street.

Operate with steam, subject to ordinances.

SEC. 2. Said company and its successors are hereby authorized to operate said railroad track with steam or such other motive power as it shall deem best; the privileges hereby granted, however, shall be enjoyed subject to all general ordinances that now are and hereafter may be in force concerning railroads in said city.

Repair of streets.

SEC. 3. The privileges granted by this ordinance are upon this express condition: That said railway company, its successors and assigns, shall, as respects grading, paving, macadamizing, filling or planking, at its own expense, keep ten feet in width, exclusive of and on one side of its track, in repair, on said Brown street, so far as the same is embraced in this ordinance, and keep its tracks in such condition that wagons and other vehicles can pass and repass at any and all points and in any and all directions, and shall be subject to assessment for paving, repaving, planking, replanking, or any other kind of improvements, of ten feet in width of said street, exclusive of and on one side of its track, whenever the common council shall by ordinance order said improvement to be made.

Condition of tracks.

No preferences to be shown between lumber yards as to facilities far transportation.

SEC. 4. The right hereby granted shall not be used for the purpose of building up a lumber business in one locality in said city and destroying it in another; and it is hereby expressly provided, and the authority hereby conferred is granted, upon the distinct understanding, that said Chicago, Burlington and Quincy Railroad Company shall receive all lumber delivered at its depot, in said city, for transportation over its road, and transport the same in the order of its delivery, so far as practicable, and if it shall take or send its cars off its own tracks, and to or into the lumber yards of any one locality in said city to be loaded, it shall, in like manner, take or send its cars to and into the lumber yards of every other locality in said city, which is reached by railroad, and over which railroad the said company shall have the right or privilege to run its engine and cars, and said cars, when sent, shall be taken or sent to the respective lumber yards in said city in the order in which application shall be made for the same, so far as may be practicable: *Provided, however*, That said company shall have the right to refuse cars to such persons or parties as shall, by their own fault or neglect, detain cars delivered at their yards to be loaded, over twenty-four hours at any one time.

SEC. 5. That this ordinance be in force from and after its passage. **Ordinance in force.**

Passed November 28, 1864.

AN ORDINANCE for the vacation of that portion of Adams Street lying between Canal Street and the South Branch of the Chicago River, and for the construction of a Tunnel at Washington Street.

SECTION
1. Portion of Adams street vacated upon conditions named in following sections.
2. Pittsburgh, Fort Wayne and Chicago Railroad Company to pay $20,000, and $80,000 to be raised by subscription, in aid of tunnel at Washington street.
3. Proceeds of one hundred bonds of the city, of $1,000 each, appropriated for same purpose.

SECTION
4. When appropriation to take effect.
5. On compliance with second section, the interest of the city in portion of street vacated to be conveyed to company; reservation of right to the city to construct a tunnel or bridge at Adams street, upon certain terms.

SECTION 1. *Be it ordained by the Common Council of the City of Chicago*, That all that portion of Adams street which lies between Canal street and the south branch of the Chicago river, be and the same is hereby vacated and discontinued upon the conditions hereinafter contained. **Portion of Adams street vacated on conditions.**

SEC. 2. That the vacation herein before provided for shall take effect when and so soon as the Pittsburgh, Fort Wayne and Chicago Railway Company shall have paid the comptroller of the city the sum of twenty thousand dollars, for the purpose of aiding in the construction of a tunnel under and across the Chicago river at Washington street, and an additional sum shall have been raised by subscription sufficient to make in all the sum of one hun- **Railroad company and subscription to pay $100,000 to aid in building tunnel.**

dred thousand dollars for building said tunnel, besides the proceeds of the bonds hereinafter provided for.

$100,000 appropriated by city for same purpose.

SEC. 3. That the proceeds of one hundred bonds of the city of Chicago, of one thousand dollars each, bearing seven per cent. interest, payable half-yearly on the first days of July and January in each year, and the principal payable twenty-five years after their date, in the city of New York, to be issued by the mayor and comptroller, for the payment of which the faith of the city is hereby pledged, be and the same are hereby appropriated for the construction of said tunnel at Washington street by the city of Chicago, under the supervision of the board of public works, in accordance with the provisions of the city charter, which tunnel shall be forever free for the passage of teams and persons.

Appropriation, when to take effect.

SEC. 4. That the appropriation aforesaid shall not take effect until proper authority shall be obtained from the legislature of the State of Illinois for the issuing of the said bonds, nor until the further sum, as provided in section two, shall be raised by subscription among the citizens and property holders, to construct said tunnel in accordance with a plan to be adopted by the board of public works.

Conveyance of interest of city.

SEC. 5. That after the payment of said sum of twenty thousand dollars, as provided in section two, by the said Pittsburgh, Fort Wayne and Chicago Railway Company to the comptroller, and the subscription and payment of said additional subscription of $80,000, a proper conveyance shall be executed by said city, conveying by quit-claim all of its right, title and interest in that portion of said street so vacated to said company: *Provided, however*, That the right and privilege shall be and is hereby reserved to said city to construct a tunnel under the Chicago river at said Adams street at any time hereafter, and to use so much of the street hereby vacated as may be necessary for that purpose: *And provided further*, That the right and privilege of constructing a bridge across the river at said Adams street, at any time within ten years from the completion of the tunnel first above provided for, shall be and is hereby also reserved to said city, upon refunding to said railroad company the aforesaid sum of twenty thousand dollars, and

Proviso for future use by city for tunnel or bridge.

said city shall have the right to use so much of the street hereby vacated as may be necessary or convenient for that purpose; and all buildings or erections that may be placed on said premises by said railroad company, its successors or assigns, which shall interfere in any way with the full exercise or enjoyment of the rights hereby reserved to said city, shall be removed by said railroad company, its successors or assigns, at its or their own cost, and without expense to said city.

Passed January 9, 1865.

AN ORDINANCE for the appropriation of the proceeds of one hundred Bonds for construction of a Tunnel at Washington Street, in accordance with the provisions of an Ordinance passed by the Common Council, on the 9th day of January, A. D. 1865.

SECTION
1. Making absolute the appropriation contained in former ordinance.

SECTION
2. Former ordinance ratified and confirmed.

SECTION 1. *Be it ordained by the Common Council of the City of Chicago*, That in accordance with the terms and provisions of the ordinance mentioned and referred to in the foregoing title, and in order to carry out the objects and purposes thereof, the proceeds of one hundred bonds of the city of Chicago, of one thousand dollars each, bearing seven per cent. interest, payable half-yearly, on the first days of July and January in each year, and the principal payable twenty-five years after their date, in the city of New York, to be issued by the mayor and comptroller, for the payment of which the faith of the city is hereby pledged, be and the same is hereby appropriated for the construction of said tunnel at Washington street by the city of Chicago, under the supervision of the board of public works, in accordance with the provisions of the city charter, which tunnel shall be forever free for the passage of teams and persons. **Appropriation made absolute.**

SEC. 2. Nothing in the foregoing section contained shall be deemed, taken or construed to invalidate any of the provisions, terms or conditions of the ordinance therein referred **Former ordinance ratified.**

to, but the same, and every part and portion thereof, are hereby ratified and confirmed.

Passed March 25, 1865.

RECORDER'S COURT.

AN ACT to establish the Recorder's Court of the City of Chicago.

SECTION
1. Recorder's court of the city of Chicago established; jurisdiction; duties and election of judge and clerk.
2. Judge to be called "the recorder of the city of Chicago;" his salary and fees.
3. Seal of, and place of holding said court.
4. Process tested in name of clerk.
5. Recognizances, except in treason and murder, taken in the city, returnable to said court; fines, etc., to be paid into city treasury.
6. Appeals from justices of the peace in the city to be taken to said court, except, etc.

SECTION
7. State's attorney to be prosecuting attorney of said court; his salary and fees, and how paid.
8. Sheriff of Cook county, his duties; fees of sheriff and clerk.
9. Provisions concerning grand and petit jurors in said court.
10. Changes of venue from said court.
11. Appeals from said court to circuit court of Cook county.
12. Terms of said court, when to be held.
13. Vacancies in the office of judge or clerk, how filled.
14. State's attorney *pro tem.* in case of absence of the State's attorney, and his compensation.
15. Act in force from March 1, 1853.

Title and jurisdiction of recorder's court.

SECTION 1. *Be it enacted by the People of the State of Illinois, represented in the General Assembly*, That there shall be established in the city of Chicago an inferior court of civil and criminal jurisdiction, which shall be a court of record, by the name of the "Recorder's Court of the City of Chicago," and shall have concurrent jurisdiction within said city with the circuit court in all criminal cases, except treason and murder, and of civil cases where the amount in controversy shall not exceed one hundred dollars. Said court, and the judge and clerk thereof, shall respectively have the like power, authority and jurisdiction, and perform the like duties as the circuit court, and the judge and clerk thereof, in relation to all matters, suits, prosecutions and proceedings within the city of Chicago, so far as the same are not otherwise limited by this act. Said judge and clerk shall be elected by the qualified voters of said city, and shall respectively hold their offices for five years, and until their successors shall be elected and qualified. The first election thereof shall be held at the next annual election for mayor of said city, to be held on the first Tuesday of March, 1853; and like elections shall be held every five

Judge and clerk to be elected.

years thereafter. The person having the highest number of votes for said offices respectively shall be declared elected thereto, and shall be commissioned by the governor.

SEC. 2. The said judge shall be called "the recorder of the city of Chicago," and shall receive an annual salary of one thousand dollars, to be paid quarterly from the State treasury, and shall receive the like fees, in addition thereto, as is received by the judge of the Cook county court of common pleas, to be paid and collected in the same manner as the fees of said judge last named are paid and collected; and the provisions of the statute in relation to the said Cook county court of common pleas, in relation to the duties, compensation and liabilities of the clerk of said Cook county court of common pleas, so far as the same can be made applicable and are not inconsistent with the provisions of this act, shall apply to and govern the clerk of said recorder's court, and be in force in relation to him and his duties and powers: *Provided*, That in case the compensation and emoluments of said judge shall exceed the sum of fifteen hundred dollars per annum, then the excess shall be paid into the State treasury.

Name and salary of judge.

Compensation.

SEC. 3. Said recorder's court shall have a seal, to be provided by the city of Chicago; and said court shall be held in such place as shall be provided by said city, and the expenses thereof, except as herein otherwise provided for, shall be paid by said city.

Seal, etc.

SEC. 4. The process of said court shall be tested in the name of the clerk thereof.

Process, how tested.

SEC. 5. All recognizances, except in cases of treason and murder, taken before any judge, justice or magistrate in said city, in criminal cases, shall be made returnable to said recorder's court; and it shall be the duty of the officer taking the same to return all the papers in said criminal cases to the said court; and all fines, penalties and forfeitures had or taken in any such criminal proceeding, shall enure to the benefit of said city, and shall, when collected, be paid into said city treasury.

Recognizances.

SEC. 6. All appeals from decisions of justices of the peace within said city shall be taken to said recorder's court: *Provided*, That when a term of the circuit court or Cook

Appeals from justices.

county court of common pleas shall intervene between the taking of any such appeals and the next term of the recorder's court, it shall be optional with the appellant to take his appeal to any one of said courts.

State's attorney to be prosecuting attorney; his compensation.

SEC. 7. The State's attorney of the judicial circuit in which said city is situated shall be the prosecuting attorney of said court, and for his services therein shall receive an additional compensation of five hundred dollars per annum, to be paid out of the same fund in the same manner as his salary as State's attorney for said circuit is paid; and the board of supervisors of said county may allow and pay said State's attorney his fees in all cases of conviction in any court in said county.

Duties of sheriff.

SEC. 8. The sheriff of the county of Cook shall perform the same duties, and have the same powers, and be liable to the same penalties in the said court as in the circuit court; and said sheriff and the clerk of the said recorder's court shall respectively be entitled to the like fees in all civil and criminal cases as are now allowed by law for similar services in criminal cases, to be collected out of defendants, if convicted: *Provided*, That if said defendant has no property on which to levy, the said fees shall be paid out of the city treasury.

Grand and petit jury, how drawn.

SEC. 9. The grand and petit jurors of said court shall be selected from the voters of said city who have paid a city tax for the preceding year, in the following manner: Said council shall annually select five hundred names, who are qualified to act as jurors, and who are not exempt from such service, from the list of such voters, and transmit the same to the clerk of said court, who shall keep a record thereof in a book to be provided for that purpose, and deposit such names upon separate pieces of paper in a jury box, from which he shall draw the names of the grand and petit jurors, in the presence of the recorder of said court, the sheriff or his deputy, and such persons as may see fit to attend, at least ten days before the first day of each term of said court, notices of the time and place of such drawing having been given by said clerk, by posting the same upon the door of his office for five days immediately preceding such drawing: *Provided*, That the name of no person shall be put into said box who has been drawn as a juror therefrom for the preceding year, nor shall the names drawn therefrom in any year be replaced in said box during said year, but the names in said box shall be annually renewed: *Provided*, That if for any cause said grand and petit jurors shall not be selected and drawn in the manner aforesaid, or in cases of vacancies in the panel thereof, or of the exhaustion of the same, said court may direct the same to be summoned by the sheriff, as now provided by law. All venires for jurors in said court shall be issued by the clerk of said court and executed by said sheriff as in other cases; and all laws in relation to jurors, their compensation, duties, powers, authority and proceedings, as far as not inconsistent with the provisions of this act, shall be applied to said court.

Venires, how issued.

SEC. 10. Changes of venue in all cases, civil or criminal, may be taken from said court to either the circuit court or the Cook county court of common pleas of said county, in all cases, when the party praying for such change of venue, or his attorney, shall make affidavit that in his or her belief justice and a fair and impartial trial requires such change of venue, stating in such affidavit the particular facts and circumstances upon which such belief is founded, and the judge of said court being satisfied of the truth of such affidavit; and no other or further change of venue shall be allowed.

Change of venue, how obtained.

SEC. 11. Appeals may be taken from said court to the circuit court of Cook county in all cases, in the same manner that appeals may be taken to the supreme court; and upon such appeals errors may be assigned and the like proceedings had as upon assignments of error in the supreme court.

Appeals, where and how taken.

SEC. 12. The regular terms of said court shall be held on the first Monday of each month: *Provided*, That the common council of said city may diminish the number of terms or abolish any term or terms that they may deem unnecessary, not exceeding six in any one year.

Terms of court.

SEC. 13. Any vacancies in the office of judge or clerk of said recorder's court may be filled by election at such time as may be appointed by the common council of said

Vacancies, how filled.

city; and the person elected to fill such vacancy shall hold his office until the next regular election for such office, as provided in this act: *Provided*, That a clerk *pro tem.* may be appointed by the judge thereof, when necessary.

Attorney *pro tem.*

SEC. 14. In case the State's attorney should fail to attend upon said court at any term thereof, his place shall be supplied by a State's attorney *pro tem.*, who shall be appointed by the judge, and who shall, in the meantime, receive for his services such compensation as is allowed to the State's attorney under the provisions of this act.

When act to take effect.

SEC. 15. This act shall take effect and be in force from and after the first day of March next.

Approved February 12, 1853.

AN ACT to amend the Act entitled "An Act to establish the Recorder's Court of the City of Chicago."

SECTION
1. City of Chicago to pay fees, expenses, etc., of prisoners.

SECTION
2. Act in force from its passage.

City of Chicago to pay expenses, etc.

SECTION 1. *Be it enacted by the People of the State of Illinois, represented in the General Assembly*, That the city of Chicago shall pay all fees, expenses and charges for dieting, committing, discharging and retaining in custody, any and all persons committed or convicted of any offense within the limits of the city of Chicago, and over which said court may have jurisdiction.

When act to be in force.

SEC. 2. This act shall be in force and take effect from and after its passage.

Approved February 28, 1854.

(See Sec. 10, Ch. 17, of Charter.)

AN ACT concerning Inferior Courts in the Cities.

SECTION
1. Inferior courts in cities to have jurisdiction concurrent with circuit courts, except in cases of murder and treason, and rules of practice to conform, etc.; this act not to interfere with police magistrates' courts.

SECTION
2. If amount in controversy in any case in the recorder's court exceeds one hundred dollars, defendant may have cause transferred to the circuit court of Cook county, or Cook county court of common pleas.

SECTION
3. Ten days notice of issuing writs of *ne exeat*, injunction, etc., from the recorder's court.

SECTION
4. Party against whom writ of *ne exeat*, injunction, etc., is applied for, may have application transferred to other courts named.
5. Act in force from its passage.

SECTION 1. *Be it enacted by the People of the State of Illinois, represented in the General Assembly*, That the inferior courts, now or which may be hereafter established, in the cities in this State, shall have concurrent jurisdiction with the circuit courts in all civil and criminal cases, except in cases of murder and treason, any law now in force to the contrary notwithstanding; and the rules of practice in such inferior courts shall conform as near as may be to the rules of practice in the circuit court of the county in which the particular inferior court may be established: *Provided*, That this act shall not be held in any way to interfere with the act approved February 27, 1854, providing for police magistrates' courts.

Inferior courts to have concurrent jurisdiction with circuit courts.

SEC. 2. That in all cases where any suit, either at law or in chancery, shall be commenced in the recorder's court of the city of Chicago, and the amount in controversy shall exceed one hundred dollars, and the defendant or defendants, or either of them, or his, her or their attorney, shall at any time before final trial therein, file in said court a written request to have such suit transferred to either the circuit court of Cook county, or to the Cook county court of common pleas, all further proceedings in said recorder's court shall thereupon cease; and said suit shall be transferred agreeable to said request, and in the manner now required by law in cases of change of venue.

When causes to be transferred.

SEC. 3. That neither the said recorder's court, nor the judge thereof, shall grant any writ of *ne exeat*, injunction, or other writ or process which said court or judge shall have power to issuc in civil cases, excepting original writs of summons, capias and attachment, and attachments in cases of contempt, unless the person against whom such writ is granted shall have had ten days notice in writing, of the time and place of making application for such writ.

Writs of *ne exeat* and injunctions.

SEC. 4. That in all cases when any application shall be made to said recorder's court of the city of Chicago, or to the judge thereof, for any writ of *ne exeat*, injunction or

Causes transferred upon application.

other writ or process, except as excepted in the third section of this act, and the person or persons or either of them against whom such application shall be made, or his, her or their attorney, shall, in writing, filed with said recorder's court or judge, request a transfer of such application to the circuit court of Cook county, or to the Cook county court of common pleas, all further proceedings upon such application before said recorder's court, or the judge thereof, shall be thereupon suspended; and the said application, and all papers connected therewith, shall be transmitted to said circuit court of Cook county, or to the Cook county court of common pleas, as the person making said request shall desire; and if neither of said courts shall be in session, then to either judge of said courts, as the party making such request shall desire.

When act in force. SEC. 4. This act shall be in force from and after its passage.

Approved February 15, 1855.

RIVER AND CANAL.

AN ORDINANCE to provide for cleansing the Chicago River, and appropriating the proceeds of two hundred and fifty Bonds therefor.

SECTION
1. Plan of the board of public works for cutting down the canal approved, and work authorized.
2. Board authorized to make necessary contract with trustees of canal.

SECTION
3. Contract for temporary pumping from river into canal authorized.
4. Appropriation for foregoing purposes of proceeds of two hundred and fifty bonds, of one thousand dollars each.

Plan of cutting down canal approved. SECTION 1. *Be it ordained by the Common Council of the City of Chicago*, That the plan of the board of public works for cleansing the Chicago river and its branches, by cutting down the summit of the Illinois and Michigan canal to below the level of lake Michigan, so as to draw from it at a low stage of water in the lake not less than twenty-four thousand (24,000) cubic feet of water per minute, is hereby approved, and said board are hereby authorized to execute said work.

SEC. 2. That the board of public works are hereby

authorized and empowered, for the purpose of prosecuting the work described in the previous section, to make any contract necessary to carry into effect such purpose, with the trustees of the Illinois and Michigan canal, in conformity with and subject to the general provisions of the city charter. **Contract and work authorized.**

SEC. 3. That, as a temporary expedient for cleansing the south branch of the Chicago river, the said board are hereby authorized and empowered to contract with the said trustees for the pumping from the river into the canal, by the hydraulic works at Bridgeport, and discharging through the canal, of such amount of water as shall be found necessary and practicable for such purpose. **Temporary pumping.**

SEC. 4. That, for the purpose of carrying out the improvement specified in the foregoing sections, the board of public works be, and they are hereby authorized to issue two hundred and fifty bonds, of the denomination of one thousand dollars each, to be dated July 1st, 1865, and payable in New York twenty-five years after the date thereof, with coupons for interest at the rate of seven per centum per annum, payable semi-annually in New York; the said bonds to be issued in conformity with the provisions of an act of the general assembly of the State of Illinois, approved February 15th, 1865, and entitled "An Act to amend an act entitled 'An Act to reduce the charter of the city of Chicago, and the several acts amendatory thereof, into one act and to revise the same,' approved February 13th, 1863." **Bonds, proceeds of, appropriated.**

Passed June 5, 1865.

SLAUGHTERING.

AN ORDINANCE concerning Slaughtering within the limits of the City of Chicago.

SECTION
1. Monopoly to John Reid & Co., on conditions, for ten years, to have all slaughtering done on their premises.
2. To erect buildings, etc., with all necessary conveniences, etc.; butchers to slaughter there; conditions.
3. Condition of premises; disposition of garbage, etc.
4. Penalty for slaughtering elsewhere; proviso for establishing other slaughter-houses.

SECTION
5. Entitled to offal as compensation for use of buildings, etc.; parties slaughtering to pay United States tax.
6. To employ special policemen; inspection by health officer.
7. Limit of liability of the city.
8. Bond, security and condition.
9. Ordinance may be repealed, and rights annulled, if premises become a nuisance.

Monopoly for ten years.

SECTION 1. *Be it ordained by the Common Council of the City of Chicago*, That in consideration of the acceptance by John Reid & Co., of said city, and their guaranty (provided by bond as hereinafter mentioned within ten days from the date of the passage of this ordinance,) that they will faithfully comply with the provisions of this ordinance, and all existing laws and ordinances, and all laws and ordinances that may hereafter be enacted or passed relating to nuisances, authority and consent is hereby given and granted to said John Reid & Co., their heirs and assignees, for a period of ten years from the first day of April, A. D. 1866, to have the exclusive right to have all the slaughtering (except that done at the regular packing houses for packing purposes,) carried on and done on their premises, described as follows, to wit: The south half of block ten (10), in the South Branch addition to the city of Chicago, in Cook county, in the State of Illinois.

Buildings, etc.

SEC. 2. The said John Reid & Co. shall, before the 1st day of April, A. D. 1866, erect good, ample and complete buildings and yards, with all the necessary conveniences, fixtures and arrangements, including hot and cold water, and gas or other lights, for the slaughtering and taking care of all animals that may be brought to said place by the butchers and dealers in meat in said city; and all such butchers and dealers in meat shall, at any and all times during the continuance in force of this ordinance, have the right and privilege of slaughtering therein, on the conditions hereinafter set forth; and any butcher who kills as many as four cattle per day, shall have a bed allotted to him, and shall not, without his consent, be changed from such bed to any other, but shall have the privilege of its use at any time he shall demand it.

Butchers to slaughter.

Good condition, garbage, etc.

SEC. 3. The said John Reid & Co. shall keep said buildings and yards and premises in good condition, and daily take and dispose of all the filth, manure and garbage, as is now or may hereafter be required by the ordinances or laws now in force, or that may hereafter be enacted or passed concerning nuisances.

Penalty for slaughtering elsewhere.

SEC. 4. After the first day of April, A. D. 1866, no other slaughtering establishment or establishments shall be suffered or permitted within the limits of the city of Chicago, nor shall any slaughtering by butchers or others be suffered or permitted, except as provided in section one of this ordinance, under a penalty of not less than twenty-five dollars nor exceeding one hundred dollars for each and every offense: *Provided*, That the city shall have the right to establish at any time hereafter, two additional slaughter-houses, one to be located in the west division, and one in the north division. **Other slaughter-houses.**

SEC. 5. The said John Reid & Co. are hereby authorized to charge for the use of their buildings, yards, water, gas or other lights, and all the arrangements, machinery and appointments of said slaughter-house, for each head of cattle, hogs, calves and sheep, the usual offal, and no other pay or compensation, and the parties slaughtering therein shall pay the United States revenue tax chargeable upon such slaughtering. **Compensation.**

SEC. 6. The said John Reid & Co. shall at all times keep and employ at their own expense at said slaughtering establishment, one or more special policemen; and said slaughtering establishment, and every department thereof, shall at all times be open to the inspection of the city health officer or any of his deputies. **Policemen.** **Health officer.**

SEC. 7. The city of Chicago shall only be answerable to said John Reid & Co. to the extent of the exercise of reasonable diligence in enforcing that portion of sections one and four of this ordinance, which gives and grants unto said John Reid & Co. the exclusive right to have all slaughtering within the limits of the city of Chicago done at the said slaughtering-house of said John Reid & Co., subject to the conditions and exceptions expressed in said sections one and four of this ordinance. And in case this ordinance or any part thereof shall be declared inoperative or void by the supreme court of the State of Illinois, then and in that event the city of Chicago shall not in any case be held answerable to said John Reid & Co. for any damages they may sustain by the failure or neglect of the city of Chicago to enforce this ordinance or such parts as may be declared inoperative or void by said supreme court. **Liability of city.**

SEC. 8. That said John Reid & Co. shall, within ten **Bond.**

days after the passage of this ordinance, execute to the city of Chicago a bond, with two or more securities, to be approved by the mayor, in the penal sum of ten thousand dollars, conditioned that they will well and truly perform and abide by all the provisions of this ordinance and by the provisions of any other ordinances or laws that hereafter may be passed or enacted concerning nuisances.

Nuisance. SEC. 9. If at any time during the continuance in force of this ordinance, said John Reid & Co. shall suffer or permit the slaughter-house hereby authorized to be established, to become a nuisance, and it shall be so adjudged by any Forfeiture. court of record, or declared by the common council, then, and in that event, the common council shall have the right to repeal this ordinance, and annul the rights and privileges hereby granted.

Passed December 18, 1865.

STATE'S ATTORNEY.

AN ORDINANCE fixing the Conviction Fees of the State's Attorney.

SECTION 1. Fees of State's attorney for convictions in the recorder's court to be paid out of city treasury; certificates of clerk; receipts by the attorney.

Fees to be paid by city. SECTION 1. *Be it ordained by the Common Council of the City of Chicago*, That all conviction fees legally accruing to the State's attorney of this judicial circuit for prosecutions in the recorder's court, from and after July 1st, 1857, where said attorney cannot collect the same from the defendants in the respective cases, shall hereafter be paid to said attorney by the city comptroller, out of any money in Certificate of clerk. the city treasury not otherwise appropriated: *Provided*, No money shall be paid as aforesaid except upon the certificate or certificates of the clerk of said court, at the conclusion of the terms thereof, setting forth in detail the names of the convicted parties, the crimes of which they are severally convicted, the sentences passed upon them, and the fee Receipt. legally due the prosecutor therefor: *And provided, also,*

Said attorney shall, in each case of receiving money hereunder, receipt for the same, as being in full of all demands, both in law and equity, against the city.

Passed November 9, 1857.

TELEGRAPHS.

AN ORDINANCE concerning the United States Telegraph Company.

SECTION 1. United States Telegraph Company authorized to construct lines in the city, subject to future ordinances.

SECTION 1. *Be it ordained by the Common Council of the City of Chicago,* That the United States Telegraph Company is hereby authorized to construct and maintain a line or lines of telegraph through the streets, and under the bed of Chicago river and its branches, so as in nowise to interfere now or hereafter with the navigation of said river and its branches; the line or lines to be constructed along such streets, and across the river or branches at such points, and in such manner, as to the kind and position of the telegraph poles, the height of the wires above the streets, and in all other particulars, as the board of public works may direct: *Provided, however,* That all the doings of said telegraph company under this ordinance shall be subject to any ordinance which may hereafter be passed by the council concerning the same. **Telegraph lines authorized.**

Passed September 21, 1863.

AN ORDINANCE to provide for the construction of a Fire-Alarm, Police and Water Telegraph in and for the City of Chicago.

SECTION
1. Board of public works authorized to contract for construction of telegraph.
2. Letting of contract; how work done, and payment therefor.
3. Appropriation for paying for telegraph.
4. Location of boxes.
5. Ordinance to take effect from its passage.

SECTION 1. *Be it ordained by the Common Council of the City of Chicago,* That the board of public works be and **Telegraph authorized.**

they are hereby authorized and empowered to contract, in the name and in behalf of the city of Chicago, for the immediate construction of a fire-alarm, police, and water telegraph, in and for said city; said telegraph to be constructed in accordance with the general plan herewith submitted for that purpose by John F. Kennard & Co., or that of any other responsible company or party, but subject to such modification of the details thereof as to the said board of public works shall seem expedient.

Contract.

SEC. 2. Said contract shall be let to some skillful and responsible party or parties, at such price, not exceeding seventy thousand dollars, as may be agreed upon. The work shall be done under the superintendence and subject to the approval of the board of public works, and the payments therefor shall be made as follows: On the satisfactory completion of the whole work, and the presentation to the city comptroller of a certificate of the completion and acceptance thereof, signed by the board of public works, the said contractor shall be entitled to receive a sum equal to the entire amount that shall then have accumulated in the city treasury to the credit of the special fund provided by section 8, chapter 12, of the revised charter, for a fire-alarm telegraph; and the balance of the contract price shall be payable in successive annual installments, at the expiration of each and every year ensuing the date of the aforesaid certificate, of ten thousand dollars each (provided so much shall remain due,) until the whole amount shall have been fully paid; the said deferred payments to bear interest at the rate of six per cent. per annum from the date of said certificate, payable semi-annually. But the right shall be reserved to the city, in and by said contract, to make such additional payments on the first day of January and July of each or any year, as it may be prepared and choose to make.

Work and compensation.

Appropriation for paying for telegraph.

SEC. 3. The whole amount now in the treasury of said city standing to the credit of the fire-alarm telegraph fund aforesaid, together with seven-eighths of the entire proceeds of all fire insurance rates that shall be hereafter paid into the city treasury, agreeably to the provisions of the revised charter, are hereby appropriated to provide for the cost and expense of the work hereby authorized, and to meet the payments for the same in the manner and at the times contemplated and provided for in the foregoing section. In case the said fund should be insufficient or unavailable to meet any one or more of said deferred payments, or the interest accruing thereon, when the same shall have matured, such deficiency shall be supplied from the general fund of said city; but the said general fund shall be reimbursed for all such advances from the proceeds of said insurance rates as soon as a sufficient amount shall have accumulated for that purpose.

SEC. 4. That a committee of three, composed of one from each division, to be appointed by the president, together with the chief engineer of the fire department, shall together meet with the board of public works, and locate the boxes mentioned in the proposed plan of a fire-alarm telegraph. **Boxes, how located.**

SEC. 5. This ordinance shall take effect from its passage. **Ordinance in force.**

Passed April 25, 1864.

AN ORDINANCE to provide for the care and management of the Police and Fire Telegraph.

SECTION
1. Penalty for causing false alarms of fire by telegraph.
2. Penalty for making or using keys, etc., without authority.
3. Cutting or removing telegraph wires; penalty.
4. When ordinance to take effect.

SECTION 1. *Be it ordained by the Common Council of the City of Chicago*, That should any person or persons knowingly give, or cause to be given, any false alarm of fire by means of the telegraph boxes connected with the police and fire-alarm telegraph, such person or persons shall be subject to a fine of not less than fifty dollars nor more than one hundred dollars, to be recovered as other fines are recoverable. **Penalty for giving false alarm.**

SEC. 2. And be it ordained: That should any person or persons make, or cause to be made, any key or keys of any fire engine, hose, truck house, or fire-alarm telegraph box, or use, or cause to be used, the same, except the mayor, **Penalty for making false keys.**

board of police, board of public works and chief fire marshal, without the consent of the proper authority, such person or persons shall be subject to a fine of not more than one hundred dollars, to be recovered as other fines are recoverable.

Cutting, etc. wires.

SEC. 3. That all persons whatsoever, except the duly authorized agents or officers of the board of police, are hereby forbidden to cut or remove, or in any way alter or interfere with any fire-alarm, police, water or other telegraph wire belonging to the city of Chicago; and any person violating this section shall be subject to a penalty of fifty dollars, to be recovered as other fines for the violation of city ordinances are recoverable.

Penalty.

Ordinance in force.

SEC. 4. This ordinance shall be in force and take effect from and after its passage and due publication.

Passed May 29, 1865.

TUNNEL, LAKE.

This ordinance was passed without a title.

SECTION
1. Tunnel under lake Michigan two miles, authorized.
2. Issue of one hundred and fifty bonds, of one thousand dollars each, authorized.

SECTION
3. Further issue of two hundred and twenty-five bonds, of one thousand dollars each, authorized.

Tunnel authorized.

SECTION 1. *Be it ordained by the Common Council of the City of Chicago*, That the board of public works are hereby authorized to extend the inlet pipe of the water works, two miles out into lake Michigan, by the construction of a brick tunnel under the bed of the lake, according to the specifications prepared by the board of public works for the same, entitled "specifications for lake tunnel," and appended herewith, and to contract for the doing of the work.

Bonds appropriated.

SEC. 2. The board of public works are hereby authorized to issue one hundred and fifty (150) water loan bonds, of the denomination of one thousand dollars each, to be dated July 1st, 1863, and payable in New York July 1st, 1888, with coupons attached for interest, at the rate of seven per cent. per annum, payable semi-annually in New York, the said bonds to be issued in conformity with the provisions of an act of the general assembly of the State of Illinois, entitled "An Act in amendment of, and supplemental to, an act, entitled 'An Act to incorporate the Chicago City Hydraulic Company,'" approved February 16th, 1857; and also of an act of the general assembly of the State of Illinois, entitled "An Act to reduce the charter of the city of Chicago, and the several acts amendatory thereof, into one act, and to revise the same," approved February 13th, 1863.

SEC. 3. The board of public works are hereby authorized to issue, in addition to the bonds above named, two hundred and twenty-five (225) water loan bonds, of the denomination of one thousand dollars each, to be dated July 1st, 1864, and payable in New York twenty-five years after the date thereof, with coupons for interest, at the rate of seven per cent. per annum, payable semi-annually in New York, the said bonds to be issued in conformity with the provisions of an act of the general assembly of the State of Illinois, entitled "An Act to reduce the charter of the city of Chicago, and the several acts amendatory thereof, into one act, and to revise the same," approved February 13th, 1863. Additional bonds appropriated.

Passed October 5, 1863.

TUNNEL, RIVER.

AN ORDINANCE authorizing the construction of a Tunnel under the South Branch of the Chicago River at Washington Street, and the issue and sale of Bonds of the City of Chicago, to aid in defraying the expense thereof.

SECTION
1. Tunnel under river at Washington street, authorized.
2. Issue of one hundred bonds, of one thousand dollars each, authorized.

SECTION
3. Proceeds of bonds appropriated for cost of tunnel.
4. Comptroller authorized to receive subscriptions in aid of construction of tunnel.

SECTION 1. *Be it ordained by the Common Council of the City of Chicago,* That the board of public works be and they are hereby authorized and empowered to construct a tunnel under the south branch of the Chicago river, at Tunnel authorized.

Washington street, according to the plans and specifications heretofore, or that may be hereafter, adopted by the board of public works of said city.

Bonds to be issued. SEC. 2. That the mayor and comptroller of said city of Chicago be and they are hereby authorized to issue and negotiate, on behalf of said city of Chicago, one hundred bonds, of one thousand dollars each, bearing seven per cent. interest, said interest to be payable semi-annually on the first days of January and July in each year, in the city of New York, and said bonds to be due and payable in thirty years from date: *Provided*, The sum of one hundred thousand dollars be first contributed by other parties.

Proceeds appropriated. SEC. 3. That the proceeds of the sale of said bonds be and the same are hereby appropriated toward the payment of the cost and construction of said tunnel.

Subscriptions in aid. SEC. 4. That the comptroller of said city of Chicago be and he is hereby authorized and required to receive, by subscription or otherwise, any sum or sums of money that may be offered to aid in the construction of said tunnel.

Passed July 27, 1865.

WHARFING PRIVILEGES.

AN ORDINANCE to abate and remove Obstructions and Encroachments upon those portions of the City of Chicago called Wharfing Privileges.

SECTION
1. Parts of streets called wharfing privileges, or adjoining river, not to be occupied or obstructed without authority of council; penalty.

SECTION
2. Authority to be in writing.

Streets adjoining river not to be obstructed. SECTION 1. *Be it ordained by the Common Council of the City of Chicago*, That no person shall occupy, encumber or obstruct any portion of those parts of the streets of the city of Chicago called wharfing privileges, or any portion of a street adjoining the Chicago river or either of its branches, with a wharf, building, lumber, stone, or any other substance or material, without special authority and permission from the common council; and every occupier of any building or wharf, or owner of any building or wharf, lumber, stone, or other substance or material, which is now placed or remaining upon any portion of any such parts of said streets as are sometimes called wharfing privileges, or any portion of a street adjoining the Chicago river, or either of its branches, without the permission or authority of said council, shall remove the same from said portions of said streets, within ten days from the passage of this ordinance. And any person who shall be guilty of a breach of any provision of this ordinance, or shall place any building, wharf, lumber, stone, or other substance or material, without special authority and permission from the common council, upon any of such portions of said streets, and every occupier of any such building or wharf, or owner of any such building, wharf, lumber, stone, or other material, who shall suffer the same to remain on any of such portions of said streets, contrary to the provisions of this ordinance, shall forfeit and pay to said city a penalty of twenty dollars for each day or part of day such building, wharf, lumber, stone or other substance or material shall remain or continue upon any of such portions of said streets. **Penalty.**

SEC. 2. The permission or authority required in the first section of this ordinance shall be in writing, and no other shall be valid. **Permission to be in writing.**

Passed March 19, 1852.

APPENDIX

AN ACT to change the Corporate Powers of the Town of Chicago.

SECTION 1. *Be it enacted by the People of the State of Illinois, represented in the General Assembly*, That John H. Kinzie, Gurdon S. Hubbard, Ebenezer Goodrich, John K. Boyer, and John S. C. Hogan, be and they are hereby constituted a body politic and corporate, to be known by the name of the "Trustees of the Town of Chicago," and by that name they and their successors shall be known in law, have perpetual succession, sue and be sued, implead and be impleaded, defend and be defended, in courts of law and equity, and in all actions and matters whatsoever ; may grant, purchase and receive and hold property, real and personal, within the said town, and no other (burial grounds excepted), and may lease, sell and dispose of the same for the benefit of the town, and shall have power to lease any of the reserved lands which have been or may hereafter be appropriated to the use of said town, and may do all other acts as natural persons ; may have a common seal, and break and alter the same at pleasure.

SEC. 2. That all that district of country contained in sections nine and sixteen, north and south fractional section ten, and fractional section fifteen, in township thirty-nine north, of range fourteen east of the third principal meridian, is hereby declared to be within the boundaries of the town of Chicago : *Provided*, That the authority of the board of trustees of the said town of Chicago shall not extend over the south fractional section ten, until the same shall cease to be occupied by the United States.

SEC. 3. That the corporate powers and duties of said town shall be vested in nine trustees, (after the term of the present incumbents shall have expired, to wit, on the first Monday of June next, and to be chosen and appointed as hereinafter directed,) who shall form a board for the transaction of business.

SEC. 4. The members composing the board of trustees shall be elected annually, on the first Monday in June, by the persons residing within said town (qualified to vote for representative to the legislature), to serve for one year ; they shall be at least twenty-one years of age, citizens of the United States, and inhabitants of said town, and shall possess a freehold estate within the limits thereof.

SEC. 5. That the board of trustees shall appoint their president from their own body ; shall appoint all other officers of their board, and shall be the judges of the qualifications, elections and returns of their own members ; a majority shall constitute a board to do business, but a smaller number may adjourn from day to day ; may compel the attendance of absent members, in such manner and under such penalties as the board may provide ; they may determine the rule of proceeding, and make such other rules and regulations for their own government as to them may seem proper and expedient.

SEC. 6. That the board of trustees shall have power to levy and collect taxes upon all real estate within the town, not exceeding the one-half of one per centum upon the assessed value thereof, except as hereinafter excepted ; to make regulations to secure the general health of the inhabitants ; to prevent and remove nuisances; to establish night watches ; erect lamps in the streets, and lighting the same; to regulate and license ferries within the corporation ; to lease the wharfing privilege of said town, giving to the owner or owners, occupant or occupants of the lots fronting the river, the preference of such privilege ; to erect and keep in repair bridges ; to provide for licensing, taxing and regulating theatrical and other shows, billiard tables and other amusements; to restrain and prohibit gaming houses, bawdy houses, and other disorderly houses; to build market-houses; establish and regulate markets; to open and keep in repair streets, avenues, lanes, alleys, drains and sewers; to keep the same clean and free from incumbrances; to establish and regulate a fire department, and to provide for the prevention and extinguishment of fires; to regulate the storage of gunpowder and other combustible materials; to erect pumps and wells in the streets for the convenience of the inhabitants; to regulate the police of the town; to regulate the election of the town officers; to fix their compensation; to establish and enforce quarantine laws; and, from time to time, to pass such ordinances to carry into effect the ordinances of this act, and the powers hereby granted, as the good of the inhabitants may require, and to impose and appropriate fines and forfeitures for the breach of any ordinance, and to provide for the collection thereof: *Provided*, That said trustees shall, in no case, levy a tax upon lots owned by the State.

SEC. 7. That upon the application of the owners of two-thirds of real estate on any street or parts of a street, it shall be lawful for the board of trustees to levy and collect a special tax on the owners of the lots on the said street or parts of a street, according to their respective fronts, for the purpose of grading and paving the sidewalks on said street.

SEC. 8. That the board of trustees shall have power to regulate, grade, pave and improve the streets, avenues, lanes and alleys within the limits of said town, and to extend, open and widen the same, making the person or persons injured thereby adequate compensation; to ascertain which, the board shall cause to be summoned twelve good and lawful men, freeholders and inhabitants of said town, not directly interested, who (being first duly sworn for that purpose,) shall inquire into, and take into consideration, as well the benefits as the injury, which may accrue, and estimate and assess the damages which would be sustained by reason of the opening, extension, widening of any street, avenue, lane or alley; and shall, moreover, estimate the amount which other persons will be benefited thereby, and shall contribute towards compensating the persons injured; all of which shall be returned to the board of trustees, under their hands and seals; and the person or persons who shall be benefited and so assessed, shall pay the same in such manner as shall be provided, and the residue, if any, shall be paid out of the town treasury.

SEC. 9. All ordinances shall, within ten days after they are passed, be published in a newspaper printed in said town, and posted in three of the most public places thereof.

SEC. 10. That when any real estate in said town shall have been sold by the authority of the corporation thereof, for the non-payment of any tax that may have been levied upon the same, the same shall be subject to redemption by the owner or owners thereof, his, her or their agent or agents, within one year after the same shall have been sold, on paying to the treasurer of the board of trustees of said town, double the amount of the taxes for which the same was sold, together with costs for the selling of the same. But should the said lots or parts of lots so sold for the non-payment of the taxes aforesaid, not be redeemed within the time specified, then, in that event, it shall be the duty of the president of the board of trustees of the said town to execute a deed, with a special warranty, signed by the president of said board, and countersigned by the clerk thereof.

SEC. 11. It shall be the duty of the board of trustees to cause to be paid to the purchasers of lots, all moneys which may have been paid to the treasurer, over the costs for selling the same.

SEC. 12. The officers of said town (in addition to the trustees,) shall consist of one clerk, one street commissioner, one treasurer, one assessor and collector of taxes, one town surveyor, two measurers of wood and coal, two measurers of lumber, two measurers and weighers of grain, and such other officers as the trustees of said town may deem necessary for the good of said town.

SEC. 13. That the president and trustees of said town shall, whenever they may deem necessary, order the formation of fire engine companies, and fire hook-and-ladder companies. The fire engine companies each to contain from twenty-five to forty able-bodied men, of between the ages of eighteen and fifty years, and no more. Which companies shall be officered and governed by their own by-laws; shall be formed only by voluntary enlistment. Every member of each company shall be exempted from jury and military duty; and whenever a member of such company shall have served twelve years, he shall receive a discharge from the incorporation, signed by the president, and shall forever thereafter be exempted from further jury duty, and from further military duty, except in case of invasion.

SEC. 14. That the members of the board of trustees, and every officer of said corporation, shall, before entering on the duties of his office, take an oath or affirmation, before some judge or justice of the peace, to support the constitution of the United States and of this State, and faithfully to demean themselves in said office.

SEC. 15. That this incorporation shall be divided into three districts, to wit: All that part which lies south of the Chicago river, and east of the south branch of said river, shall be included in the first district; all that part which lies west of the north and south branches of said river, shall be included in the second district; and all that part which lies north of the Chicago river, and east of the north branch of said river, shall be included in the third district; and the taxes collected within the said respective districts shall be expended, under the direction of the board of trustees, for improvements within their respective districts; but all elections for trustees in said town shall be by general ticket.

Approved February 11, 1835.

AN ACT to amend an Act entitled "An Act to change the Corporate Powers of the Town of Chicago."

SECTION 1. *Be it enacted by the People of the State of Illinois, represented in the General Assembly*, That so much of the sixth section of the act to which this is an amendment, relating to the power of the trustees of said town to lease the wharfing privileges, shall not be so construed as to empower said trustees to create or make any lease of said privileges for any one term longer than five years, nor shall any lease as aforesaid be so construed as to give any lessee power to erect any building, storehouse or other building than a wharf, for loading or unloading goods, wares, merchandise or other articles, on said wharfing privileges; and all houses, buildings, stores and outhouses hereafter erected upon any ground or land situate, lying and being between the south line of South Water street and the north line of North Water street, in said town, as laid out by the commissioners of the Illinois and Michigan canal, shall be deemed nuisances, and may and shall be abated: *Provided*, In no case shall said trustees have, use or exercise the right of leasing or disposing of any wharfing privilege which may be in front of any lot or lots owned by any individual or individuals, or in front of any lot or lots belonging to the State or to the canal.

SEC. 2. That so much of the sixth section of the act to which this is an amendment, as empowers the trustees to levy and collect taxes upon all real estate within the town, not exceeding the one-half of one per centum upon the assessed value thereof, be and the same hereby is repealed; and the said trustees shall have power to levy and collect taxes upon all real estate within the town, not exceeding the one-fourth of one per centum upon the assessed value thereof.

Approved January 15, 1836.

AN ACT to incorporate the Chicago Hydraulic Company.

WHEREAS, The health and convenience of the inhabitants of the town of Chicago, in the county of Cook, as well as the security of property against the ravages of fire, would be greatly promoted by the introduction of a plentiful supply of pure and wholesome water in said town; therefore,

SECTION 1. *Be it enacted by the People of the State of Illinois, represented in the General Assembly*, That James B. Campbell, Gholson Kercheval, Robert A. Kinzie, Richard J. Hamilton, Henry G. Hubbard, David Hunter, Peter Cohen, Ed. W. Casey, Gurdon S. Hubbard, G. W. Dole, John H. Kinzie, William Forsythe, and Solomon Wills, and their heirs and assigns, be and they hereby are constituted a body politic and corporate, under the style and title of the "Chicago Hydraulic Company," with the sole power to them and their successors, by their corporate name, to sue and be sued, plead and be impleaded, answer and be answered, defend and be defended, in all courts of law and equity in this State; and to make, have and use a common seal, and the same break, alter or renew at their pleasure; and to take and hold such property, real, personal or mixed, as may be necessary to carry into effect the object of said company or incorporation; and the same to sell, exchange or otherwise dispose of; and also to ordain, establish and put in execution such by-laws, ordinances and regulations as may be necessary, proper or convenient for the government of said incorporation, not contrary to law or the constitution.

SEC. 2. The capital stock of said company shall not exceed two hundred thousand dollars.

SEC. 3. The charter of incorporation shall be and continue in force for and during the term of seventy years, from and after the passage of this act: *Provided*, That the said company shall, within four years from this date, commence the construction of the necessary works for the introduction into said town of the water of lake Michigan.

SEC. 4. The said company, for the more effectually completing the object of said corporation, shall have power and authority to build and construct fountains, reservoirs and other necessary works; to make and lay conduits, pipes or tunnels, for the conveyance of said water, under and along the public highways, streets, lanes, alleys and sidewalks, or any of them, in said town of Chicago; to put up fire-plugs or hydrants, at such places as they may deem convenient for public use, and the same from time to time to renew and repair, leaving at all times, during the progress of said work, one-half of said streets or alleys unobstructed; and immediately after the laying of said pipes or conduits, restore the street or alley through which the same may pass, or which has been dug up or opened, to its former condition. And further, said company shall have the sole privilege to grant to all persons whomsoever, to all bodies corporate and politic, the privilege of using said water, so introduced, as aforesaid, in such manner and upon such terms and conditions, and in such quantities respectively, as they shall think fit.

SEC. 5. If any person or persons shall willfully pollute said water, by throwing or depositing in any pipe, tunnel, hydrant, reservoir or fountain conducting or containing the same, any impure, unwholesome or offensive substance; or by bathing or washing clothes in said reservoir; or shall injure any of the works or machinery used in raising, containing, forcing or conducting said water, the person or persons so offending, shall be liable to a fine of not exceeding one hundred dollars, to the use of said company, for each and every offense, recoverable before any court of competent jurisdiction; and shall also be compelled to remove all nuisances by him or them created as aforesaid, forthwith, under the penalty of ten dollars for every twenty-four hours said nuisances shall continue, to the use of said company aforesaid: *Provided*, That said fines and penalties shall not prevent said company from recovering damages in a civil suit, for any injury done to said works.

SEC. 6. The officers of said company shall consist of a president and four directors, who shall be annually chosen from among the members of the company, at the time such election may be held, and in such manner as they ordain and direct. The first election therefor shall take place at such time as the members, or a majority of them, may deem expedient, each member at said first election having one vote; and in case of the death or resignation of the president, or either of one or more of the directors, then the vacancy shall be filled by the board.

SEC. 7. The directors, or a majority of them, shall have full power to appoint and employ, and, in their discretion, to remove or dismiss a secretary, treasurer and all such other officers, clerks, agents, mechanics, laborers and servants, as they shall deem necessary, from time to time, to attend to and transact or execute all the affairs and business of the company, and fix their compensation; to contract, agree for and purchase, rent or hire, all such lands, chattels, materials, rights, privileges and effects whatever, and to sell or otherwise dispose of the same, in their discretion; to divide the capital stock into shares among the members of said company, and to call for such installments on each share as the board of directors may deem necessary for the interests of the company; and in case of a failure on the part of any of the members of said company, or their assignee or assignees, to pay said installments when required, or within thirty days thereafter, all the interest they may have or possess in said company shall be forfeited to the members thereof: *Provided*, That six weeks notice, either in writing, of such call, shall be given, or in some one of the newspapers printed in Chicago.

Approved January 18, 1836.

AN ACT to incorporate the City of Chicago.

SECTION 1. *Be it enacted by the People of the State of Illinois, represented in the General Assembly*, That the district of country in the county of Cook, in the State aforesaid, known as the east half of the south-east quarter of section thirty-three, in township forty, and fractional section thirty-four in the same township, the east fourth part of sections six, seven, eighteen and nineteen, in the same township, also fractional section three, section four, section five, section eight, section nine, and fractional section ten, excepting the south-west fractional quarter of section ten, occupied as a military post, until the same shall become private property, fractional section fifteen, section sixteen, section seventeen, section twenty, section twenty-one, and fractional section twenty-two, in township thirty-nine north, range number fourteen east of the third principal meridian, in the State aforesaid, shall hereafter be known by the name of the City of Chicago.

SEC. 2. The inhabitants of said city shall be a corporation, by the name of the City of Chicago, and may sue and be sued, complain and defend in any court, make and use a common seal, and alter it at pleasure, and take, hold, purchase and convey such real and personal estate as the purposes of the corporation may require.

SEC. 3. The said city shall be divided into six wards, as follows: All that part of the city which lies south of Chicago river and east of the centre of Clark street following the centre of Clark street to the south line of section sixteen, thence following the said south line of section sixteen, to the centre of State street, and a line parallel with the centre of said street, to the southern boundary of said city, shall be denominated the first ward of said city; all that part of said city which lies south of said Chicago river, west of the first ward, and east of the south branch of said Chicago river, shall be denominated the second ward of said city: all that part of the said city, lying west of the aforesaid south branch of the Chicago river, and south of the centre of Randolph street, and by a line parallel with the centre of said Randolph street to the western boundary of said city, shall be denominated the third ward; all that part of said city which lies north of the said third ward, and west of the said Chicago river, and the north and south branches thereof, shall be denominated the fourth ward of said city; all that part of said city which lies north of the Chicago river, and east of the north branch thereof, and west of the centre of Clark street, to the centre of Chicago avenue, and lying south of the centre of Chicago avenue, to the centre of Franklin street, and lying west of Franklin street, and a line parallel with the centre thereof, to the northern boundary of said city, shall be denominated the fifth ward; and all that part of said city lying north of the Chicago river, and east of the said fifth ward, shall be denominated the sixth ward of said city.

SEC. 4. There shall be in and for said city, except as herein afterwards provided, one mayor, twelve aldermen, one clerk, one treasurer, six assessors, one or more collectors, and such other officers as are hereinafter authorized to be appointed, which said mayor, aldermen and assessors shall be freeholders in the said city.

SEC. 5. An election shall be held in each of the wards of said city, on the first Tuesday in March in each year, after the year eighteen hundred and thirty-seven, at such place as the common council of said city may appoint, and of which six days previous public notice shall be given in writing, in three public places in each ward, by the inspectors thereof.

SEC. 6. At the first election under this act, and at each annual election thereafter, there shall be elected two aldermen and one assessor from each ward, each of whom shall be an actual resident of the ward in which he was elected: *Provided, however*, That the aforesaid wards, denominated the third and fifth wards, shall be entitled to elect but one alderman from each ward, until the annual election for the year A. D. 1839.

SEC. 7. The common council shall appoint three inspectors of election for each ward, who shall be inspectors of elections after the first. Such inspectors shall have the same power and authority as the inspectors of a general State election.

SEC. 8. The manner of conducting and voting at the elections to be held under this act, and the keeping of the poll lists thereof, shall be the same, as nearly as may be, as is provided by law, at the general State election: *Provided*, That the common council may hereafter, if expedient, change the mode of election to that by ballot, and prescribe the manner of conducting the same.

SEC. 9. Every person voting at such election, shall be an actual resident of the ward in which he is to vote, shall be a householder within the city, or shall have paid a city tax of not less than three dollars, within twelve months next preceding such election, and shall have resided in said city at least six months next preceding such election, and shall, moreover, if required by any person qualified to vote thereat, before he is permitted to vote, take the following oath: "You swear (*or* affirm) that you are of the age of twenty-one years, that you have been a resident of this city for six months immediately preceding this election, that you are a householder therein, or that you have paid a city tax of not less than three dollars within twelve months next preceding this election, and that you are now a resident of this ward, and have not voted at this election."

SEC. 10. The persons entitled to vote at any election held under this act, shall not be arrested on civil process within said city on the day on which said election is held.

SEC. 11. The trustees of the town of Chicago, for the time being, shall appoint the inspectors of the first election to be held under this act. Such election shall be held and conducted, and the votes thereat canvassed by said inspectors, and the result determined in the manner herein before provided; the said trustees shall also appoint the time and place of holding such first election, which time shall be some day after the passage of this act, and on or before the first day of June next.

SEC. 12. Vacancies in the offices of mayor and aldermen occurring in any manner, may be filled at a special election called and appointed by the common council, and conducted in the same manner as an annual election; vacancies in all other offices shall be filled by appointment by the common council. All appointments to fill a vacancy in an elective office under this act, and all appointments of clerk, treasurer, attorney for the city, police constables, collectors, street commissioners and city surveyors, shall be by warrant under the corporate seal, signed by the mayor as presiding officer of the common council, and clerk. In case of a failure to elect aldermen at an annual election, or if from any cause there shall be no aldermen, the clerk shall appoint the time and places for holding a special election, and appoint inspectors; all officers appointed or elected annually, and except to fill a vacancy, shall hold their respective offices for one year, and until others are chosen and have taken the oath of office.

SEC. 13. The common council shall appoint as many police constables as they shall think proper, not exceeding one in each ward, who shall not have power to serve any civil process out of the limits of said city, except in cases of persons fleeing from said city, and to commit on execution where the defendant shall have been arrested in the said city.

SEC. 14. The mayor for the said city shall be chosen by the qualified electors of the said city, at the same time and in the same manner as is prescribed for the choosing of aldermen, whose term of service shall be for one year, until his successor shall be chosen and qualified. At the time of voting for aldermen, the electors of said city shall also vote in their respective wards, for some qualified person as mayor of said city, which votes shall be canvassed and certified at the same time and in the same manner as those given for aldermen, and the person having the highest number of votes given in the several wards at such election, shall be mayor.

SEC. 15. The mayor and aldermen of the said city shall constitute the common council of said city. The common council shall meet at such times and places as they shall by resolution direct, or as the mayor, or in his absence any two of the aldermen, shall appoint. The mayor when present, shall preside at all meetings of the common council, and shall have only a casting vote; in his absence, any one of the aldermen may be appointed to preside. A majority of the persons elected as aldermen, shall constitute a quorum. No member of a common council shall, during the period for which he was elected, be appointed to, or be competent to hold any office of which the emoluments are paid from the city treasury, or paid by fees directed to be paid by any act or ordinance of the common council, or be directly or indirectly interested in any contract, the expenses or consideration whereof are to be paid under any ordinance of the common council. But this section shall not be construed to prevent the mayor from receiving his salary or any other fees permitted by this act.

SEC. 16. The common council shall meet annually, after the year 1837, on the second Tuesday in March, and in 1837, on the day following the election, and, by ballot, appoint a clerk, treasurer, city attorney, street commissioner, police constables, clerk of the market, one or more collectors, one or more city surveyors, one or more pound masters, porters, carriers, cartmen, packers, beadles, bellmen, sextons, common criers, scavengers, measurers, surveyors, weighers, sealer of weights and measures, and gaugers. If for any cause the officers above named are not appointed on the second Tuesday of March, on the day after the election, in the year eighteen hundred and thirty-seven, the common council may adjourn from time to time until such appointments are made.

SEC. 17. If any inhabitant of said city, elected or appointed to any office in pursuance of this act, shall refuse or neglect to accept such office, and take and subscribe the oath of office prescribed by the constitution of this State, for five days after personal notice in writing, from the clerk, of his election, he shall forfeit the sum of ten dollars.

SEC. 18. Every person chosen or appointed to an executive, judicial or administrative office, under this act, shall, before he enters on the duties of his office, take and subscribe, before some justice of the peace, the oath of office prescribed in the constitution of this State, and file the same, duly certified by the officer before whom it was taken, with the clerk of the city.

SEC. 19. The treasurer, street commissioner, and collector or collectors of said city, shall, severally, before they enter on the duties of their respective offices, execute a bond to the city of Chicago, in such sum and with such sureties as the common council shall approve, conditioned that they shall faithfully execute the duties of their offices, and account for and pay over all moneys received by them respectively; which bonds, with the approval of the common council certified thereon by the clerk, shall be filed with the clerk of the city.

SEC. 20. Every person appointed to the office of constable, in said city, shall, before he enters upon the duties of his office, with two or more sureties, to be approved by the common council, execute in presence of the clerk of the city, an instrument in writing, by which such constables and sureties shall jointly and severally agree to pay to each and every person who may be entitled thereto, all such sums of money as the said constable may become liable to pay, by reason or on account of any summons, execution, distress warrant or other process which shall be delivered to him for collection. The clerk of the city shall certify the approval of the common council on such instrument, and file the same; and a copy of such instrument, certified by the clerk under the corporate seal, shall be presumptive evidence in all courts, of the execution thereof by such constable and his sureties; and all actions on any such instrument shall be prosecuted within two years after the expiration of the year for which the constable named therein shall have been elected or appointed, and may be brought in the name of the person or persons entitled to the money collected by virtue of such instruments.

SEC. 21. The treasurer shall receive all moneys belonging to the city, and keep an accurate account of all receipts and expenditures, in such manner as the common council shall direct; all moneys shall be drawn from the treasury in pursuance of an order from the common council, by warrant signed by the mayor or presiding officer of the common council, and countersigned by the clerk; such warrant shall specify for what purpose the amount specified therein is to be paid; and the clerk shall keep an accurate account of all orders drawn on the treasury, in a book to be provided for that purpose. The treasurer shall exhibit to the common council, at least fifteen days before the annual election in each year, a full and detailed account of all receipts and expenditures, after the date of the last annual report, and also of the state of the treasury, which account shall be filed in the office of the clerk.

SEC. 22. It shall be the duty of the common council, at least ten days before the annual election held under this act in each year, to cause to be published in two or more of the public newspapers in said city, a full and correct statement of the receipts and expenditures by the said common council, for the contingent expenses of the said city from the date of the last annual report published in pursuance of this section to the date of said reports, and also a distinct statement of the whole amount of money assessed, received and expended in the respective wards for making and repairing roads, highways and bridges, in said city for the same period, together with such other information in their power to furnish, as may be necessary to a full understanding of the financial concerns of the said city.

SEC. 23. The clerk shall keep the corporate seal, and all the papers belonging to said city, and make a record of the proceedings of the common council, at whose meetings it shall be his duty to attend; and copies of all papers duly filed in his office, and transcripts from the records of the proceedings of the common council, certified by him under the corporate seal, shall be evidence in all courts in like manner as if the original were produced.

SEC. 24. It shall be the duty of the street commissioner to superintend the making of all public improvements ordered by the common council, and to make contracts for the work and materials which may be necessary for the same, and shall be the executive officer to carry into effect the ordinances of the common council relative thereto, and shall keep accurate accounts of all moneys expended by him in performance of any work, together with the cause of such expenditures, and to render such account to the common council monthly.

SEC. 25. That the city surveyor or surveyors, appointed by the said common council, shall have the sole power, under the direction and control of the said common council, to survey within the limits of said city; and he and they shall be governed by such rules and ordinances as the said common council shall direct, and receive such fees and emoluments for his or their services as the common council shall appoint.

SEC. 26. The mayor of said city, for the time being, shall be allowed an annual salary of five hundred dollars, payable out of the treasury, and the other officers of said corporation shall be paid out of the treasury such compensation for their services, when the same are not herein provided for, as the said common council may deem adequate and reasonable.

SEC. 27. If any person, having been an officer in said city, shall not, within ten days after notification and request, deliver to his successor in office all the property, papers and effects of every description, in his possession belonging to said city, or appertaining to the office he held, he shall forfeit and pay, for the use of the city, one hundred dollars, besides all damages caused by his neglect or refusal so to deliver.

SEC. 28. The common council shall hold stated meetings, and the mayor or any two aldermen may call special meetings, by notice to each of the members of said council, served personally, or left at their usual place of abode. Petitions and remonstrances may be presented to the common council. The common council shall have the management and control of the finances, and all the property, real and personal, belonging to the corporation, and shall have power, within said city, to make and establish, publish, alter, modify, amend and repeal ordinances, regulations, rules and by-laws, for the following purposes:

First. To prevent all obstructions in the waters which are public highways in said city.

Second. To prevent and punish forestalling and regrating, and to prevent and restrain every kind of fraudulent device and practice.

Third. To restrain and prohibit all descriptions of gaming and fraudulent devices in said city, and all playing of dice, cards and other games of chance, with or without betting, in any grocery, shop or store.

Fourth. To regulate the selling or giving away of any ardent spirits, by any storekeeper, trader or grocer, to be drank in any shop, store or grocery, outhouse, yard, garden or other place within the city, except by innkeepers, duly licensed.

Fifth. To forbid the selling or giving away of ardent spirits or other intoxicating liquors, to any child, apprentice or servant, without the consent of his or her parent, guardian, master or mistress, or to any Indian.

Sixth. To regulate, license or prohibit the exhibition of common showmen, and of shows of every kind, or the exhibition of any natural or artificial curiosities, caravans, circusses or theatrical performances.

Seventh. To prevent any riot or noise, disturbance, or disorderly assemblage.

Eighth. To suppress and restrain disorderly houses and groceries, houses of ill-fame, billiard tables, nine or ten pin alleys or tables, and ball alleys, and to authorize the destruction and demolition of all instruments and devices used for the purpose of gaming.

Ninth. To compel the owner or occupant of any grocery, cellar, tallow-chandler's shop, soap factory, tannery, stable, barn, privy, sewer, or other unwholesome, nauseous house or place, to cleanse, remove or abate the same, from time to time, as often as may be necessary for the health, comfort and convenience of the inhabitants of said city.

Tenth. To direct the location and management of all slaughter-houses, markets, and houses for storing powder.

Eleventh. To regulate the keeping and conveying of gunpowder, and other combustibles and dangerous materials, and the use of candles and lights in barns and stables.

Twelfth. To prevent horse-racing, immoderate riding or driving in the streets, and to authorize persons immoderately riding or driving as aforesaid, to be stopped by any person.

Thirteenth. To prevent the incumbering of the streets, sidewalks, lanes, alleys, public wharves and docks, with carriages, carts, sleighs, sleds, wheel-barrows, boxes, lumber, timbers, firewood, or any other substance or material whatsoever.

Fourteenth. To regulate and determine the times and places of bathing and swimming in the canals, rivers, harbors, and other waters in and adjoining said city.

Fifteenth. To restrain and punish vagrants, mendicants, street beggars and common prostitutes.

Sixteenth. To restrain and regulate the running at large of cattle, horses, swine, sheep, goats and geese, and to authorize the distraining, impounding, and sale of the same, for the penalty incurred and the costs of proceeding.

Seventeenth. To prevent the running at large of dogs, and to authorize the destruction of the same when at large, contrary to the ordinance.

Eighteenth. To prevent any person from bringing, depositing or having within the limits of said city, any dead carcass or any other unwholesome substance, and to require the removal or destruction by any person who shall have upon or near his premises any such substance, or any putrid or unsound beef, pork or fish, hides or skins of any kind, and on his default, to authorize the removal or destruction thereof by some officer of said city.

Nineteenth. To prevent the rolling of hoops, playing at ball, or flying of kites, or any other amusement or practice having a tendency to annoy persons passing in the streets or on the sidewalks of said city, or to frighten teams and horses within the same.

Twentieth. To compel all persons to keep the snow and ice and dirt from the sidewalks in front of the premises owned or occupied by them.

Twenty-first. To prevent the ringing of bells, blowing of horns and bugles, crying of goods and other things within the limits of said city.

Twenty-second. To abate and remove nuisances.

Twenty-third. To regulate and restrain runners for boats and stages.

Twenty-fourth. To survey the boundaries of said city.

Twenty-fifth. To regulate the burial of the dead.

Twenty-sixth. To direct the returning and keeping of bills of mortality, and to impose penalties on physicians, sextons and others, for any default in the premises.

Twenty-seventh. To regulate gauging, the place and manner of selling and weighing hay, of selling pickled and other fish, and of selling and measuring of wood, lime and coal, and to appoint suitable persons to superintend and conduct the same.

Twenty-eighth. To appoint watchmen, and prescribe their duties and powers.

Twenty-ninth. To regulate cartmen and cartage.

Thirtieth. To regulate the police of said city.

Thirty-first. To establish, make and regulate public pumps, wells, cisterns and reservoirs, and to prevent the unnecessary waste of water.

Thirty-second. To establish and regulate public pounds.

Thirty-third. To erect lamps, and regulate the lighting thereof.

Thirty-fourth. To regulate and license ferries. The said common council shall have the power to prohibit the use of locomotive engines on any railroad within the inhabited parts of said city, and may require the cars to be used thereon, within the inhabited portions thereof, to be drawn or propelled by other power than that of steam. The common council may erect and establish a bridewell or house of correction, in said city, and may pass all necessary ordinances for the regulation thereof; may appoint a keeper and as many assistants as may be necessary, and shall prescribe their duties and compensation, and the securities to be given by them. In the said bridewell, or house of correction, shall be confined all rogues, vagabonds, stragglers, idle or disorderly persons who may be committed thereto by the mayor or any alderman in said city; and all persons sentenced by any criminal court, in and for said city, for any assault and battery, petit larceny, or other misdemeanor punishable by imprisonment in any county jail, shall be kept therein in the same manner as prisoners of that description are required to be kept in the county jails. The common council may, by ordinances, require every merchant, retailer, trader and dealer in merchandise or property of any description which is sold by measure or weight, to cause their weights and measures to be sealed by the city sealer, and to be subject to his inspection, and may impose penalties for any violation of any such ordinances; the standard of which weights and measures shall be agreeable to those now established by law.

SEC. 29. The common council shall have power, from time to time, to prescribe the duties of all officers and persons appointed by them to any office or place whatsoever, subject to the provisions of this act, and may remove all such persons or officers at pleasure.

SEC. 30. The common council may make, publish, ordain, amend and repeal all such ordinances, by-laws and police regulations, not contrary to the laws of this State, for the good government and order of said city, and the trade and commerce thereof, as may be necessary to carry into effect the powers given to said council by this act, and enforce observance of all rules, ordinances, by-laws and police regulations made in pursuance of this act, by imposing penalties upon any person violating the same, not exceeding one hundred dollars for any offense, to be recovered with costs, in an action of debt, before the mayor or any justice of the peace of the said city. Every such ordinance or by-law, imposing any penalty or forfeiture for a violation of its provisions, shall, after the passage thereof, be published for three weeks successively, in the corporation newspaper printed and published in said city; and proof of such publication by the affidavit of the printer or publisher of said newspaper, taken before any officer authorized to administer oaths, and filed with the clerk of the city, or any other competent proof of such publication, shall be conclusive evidence of the legal publication and promulgation of such ordinance or by-law in all courts and places.

SEC. 31. The common council, at their annual meeting on the second Tuesday in March, in each year, after eighteen hundred and thirty-seven, and at their first meeting in that year, or within ten days thereafter, shall designate one public newspaper printed in said city, in which shall be published all ordinances and other proceedings and matters required in any case by this act, or the by-laws and ordinances of the common council, to be published in a public newspaper.

SEC. 32. All actions brought to recover any penalty or forfeiture incurred under this act, or the ordinances, by-laws or police regulations made in pursuance of it, shall be brought in the corporate name; and in any such action it shall be lawful to declare generally in debt for such penalty or forfeiture, stating the section of this act, or the by-laws or ordinances under which the penalty is claimed, and to give the special matter in evidence under it. The first process in any such action shall be by warrant, and execution may be issued thereon immediately on the rendition of judgment. If the defendant in any such action have no goods or chattels, lands or tenements, whereof the judgment can be collected, the execution shall require the defendant to be imprisoned in close custody in the jail of Cook county, for a term not exceeding thirty days. All expenses incurred in prosecuting for the recovery of any penalty or forfeiture, when collected, shall be paid to the treasurer for the use of the city.

SEC. 33. No person shall be an incompetent judge, justice, witness or juror by reason of his being an inhabitant or freeholder in the city of Chicago, in any action or proceeding in which the said city is a party in interest.

SEC. 34. The common council of said city shall have power to revise, alter and correct the several assessment rolls of the different assessors of said city, and to prescribe the rate of assessment, the form of the assessment roll, and to make such rules in relation thereto as they may deem expedient and proper.

SEC. 35. The common council shall have power in each year to raise a sufficient sum by tax upon real or personal estate in said city, not exceeding the one-half of one per centum upon the assessed value thereof, to defray the expenses of lighting the streets, supporting a night watch, and making and repairing streets, roads, highways and bridges in the said city, and to defray the contingent and other expenses of said city: *Provided*, That the said common council shall in no case levy a tax upon lots or land owned by the State, nor any tax for making and repairing streets, roads and highways contrary to the subsequent provisions of this act.

SEC. 36. The said common council are hereby authorized to require every male resident of the city over the age of twenty-one years, to labor at least three days in each and every year upon the streets and alleys of said city, at such time and in such manner as the street commissioner shall direct; but any person may, at his option, pay at the rate of one dollar for every day he shall be so bound to labor, and such labor or payment shall be in lieu of all labor required to be performed upon any roads, streets or alleys, by any law of this State; and in default of the payment of such money, or the performance of such labor, the said common council may sue for and collect such money before the mayor or any justice of the peace.

SEC. 37. The said common council shall have the exclusive power to regulate repair, amend and clear the streets and alleys of said city, bridges, side and crosswalks, and of opening said streets, and putting drains and sewers therein, and to prevent the incumbering of the same in any manner, and to protect the same from encroachments and injury; they shall also have power to direct and regulate the planting and preserving of ornamental trees in the streets of said city.

SEC. 38. The common council shall have power to lay out, make and assess streets, alleys, lanes and highways in said city, and make wharves and slips at the end of streets, on property belonging to said city, and to alter, widen, contract, straighten and discontinue the same; but no building exceeding the value of one thousand five hundred dollars shall be removed, in whole or in part, without the consent of the owner. They shall cause all streets, alleys, lanes or highways laid out by them to be surveyed, described and recorded in a book to be kept by the clerk, and the same, when opened and made, shall be public highways. Whenever any street, alley, lane, highway, wharf or slip is laid out, altered, widened or straightened, by virtue of this section, the common council shall give notice of their intention to appropriate and take the land necessary for the same, to the owner or owners thereof, by publishing said notice for fourteen days in the corporation newspaper printed in said city; and after the expiration of the said fourteen days, the common council shall give notice to the said owner or owners, by publishing the same for thirty days in the corporation newspaper, that such owner or owners may file a notice with the clerk of the city, of a claim for damages on account of appropriating the land of such owner or owners for the uses specified in this section; and if such owner or owners shall, within said thirty days, file, or cause to be filed, such notice of a claim for damages as aforesaid, with the clerk of the city, the common council shall choose by ballot five discreet and disinterested freeholders, residing in said city, as commissioners to ascertain and assess the damages and recompense due the owner or owners of such land, and at the same time to determine what persons will be benefited by such improvement, and to assess the damages and expense thereof, on the real estate of persons benefited, in proportion, as nearly as may be, to the benefits resulting to each. A majority of all the aldermen authorized by law to be elected, shall be necessary to constitute a choice of such commissioners. The commissioners shall be sworn by the mayor or any justice of the peace in said city, faithfully and impartially to execute their duty in making such assessment, according to the best of their ability. The commissioners shall view the premises, and, in their discretion, receive any legal evidence, and may, if necessary, adjourn from day to day. The commissioners shall, before entering upon the duties assigned them by this section, give notice to the persons interested of the time and place of the meeting of the said commissioners for the purpose of viewing the premises and making such assessment, at least five days before the time of such meeting, by publishing said notice in the corporation newspaper printed in said city. The said commissioners shall determine and award to the owner or owners of said land, such damages as they shall judge such owner or owners to sustain in consequence of such street, lane, alley, highway, wharf or slip having been laid out, altered, widened or straightened, after taking into consideration and making due allowance for any benefit which said owner or owners may derive from such improvement. The said commissioners shall, at the same time, assess and apportion the said damages and expenses of said improvement on the real estate benefited thereby, as nearly as may be, in proportion to the benefit resulting therefrom, and shall describe the real estate upon which any such assessment is made. If there be any building on any land taken for such improvement, the owner thereof shall have ten days, or such time as the common council may allow after the final assessment of the commissioners is returned to and confirmed by the common council, to remove the same, and in case said owner removes such building, the value thereof to the owner to remove, shall be deducted from the amount of damages awarded to the owner thereof, and such value shall be, at the time of the assessment, determined by the commissioners. The determination and assessment of the commissioners shall be returned in writing, signed by all the commissioners, to the common council, within thirty days after their appointment by the common council as aforesaid; the common council may, if sufficient objections are made to the appointment of any of said commissioners, or if any such commissioners shall be unable to serve, by sickness or other cause, appoint other commissioners to serve in their places, in the manner as herein provided. And the said common council, after the determination and assessment of the commissioners as aforesaid is returned to them, shall give two weeks notice, in the corporation newspaper, printed in said city, that such determination and assessment of the commissioners will, on a day to be specified in said notice, be confirmed by the common council, unless objections to such determination and assessment aforesaid are made by some person interested; all objections to such determination and assessment as aforesaid, shall be briefly stated in writing and filed with the clerk; if no objections are made as aforesaid, the said determination and assessment shall be confirmed by the common council. If the objections are made as aforesaid, any person interested may be heard before the common council, touching the said determination and assessment of the commissioners, on the day specified in the aforesaid notice, or on such other day or days as the common council shall for that purpose appoint; and the said common council, in consideration of the objections made, shall have power, in their discretion, to confirm such determination and assessment of the commissioners, or to annul the same, and refer the same subject-matter back to the same commissioners, or appoint five other commissioners for the purpose and in the manner herein provided; and the said commissioners shall make the second determination and assessment, and return the same to the common council in like manner, and give like notices, as they are herein required in relation to the first determination and assessment and returns thereof, and the parties in interest shall have the like notices and rights, and the common council shall perform like duties, and have like powers in relation to the second determination and assessment of said commissioners, as are herein given and required in relation to the first determination and assessment of said commissioners; and in case the common council shall confirm the second determination and assessment, the same shall be final and conclusive to all persons interested. But in case the common council shall annul the same, then all the proceedings in relation to laying out, altering, widening or straightening such street, alley, lane, highway, wharf or slip, shall be null and void. But nothing herein contained shall authorize the said common council to discontinue or contract any street or highway, or any part thereof, except for the purpose of widening and improving the rivers and making basins and slips within said city, without the consent, in writing, of all persons owning land adjoining such street or highway. That in all cases where the whole of any lot or parcel of land or other premises under lease or other contract shall be taken for any of the purposes aforesaid by virtue of this act, all the covenants, contracts and engagements between landlord and tenant, or any other contracting parties, touching the same or any part thereof, shall, upon confirmation of such report in the premises as shall be confirmed by the common council aforesaid, respectively cease and determine and be absolutely discharged; and in all cases where part only of any lot or parcel of land or other premises so under lease or other contract, shall be so taken for any of the purposes aforesaid, all contracts and engagements respecting the same, upon the confirmation of such report in the premises as shall be confirmed as aforesaid, shall cease, determine and be absolutely discharged, as to the part thereof so taken, but shall remain valid and obligatory as to the residue thereof, and the rents, considerations and payments, reserved, payable and to be paid for or in respect to the same, shall be so apportioned as that the part thereof justly and equitably payable, or that ought to be paid for such residue thereof, and no more, shall be demanded or paid or recoverable for in any respect of the same. No power is given by virtue of this act to alter, change, lay out in lots, or lease, that part of the city of Chicago originally laid out by the commissioners of the Illinois and Michigan canal on section nine, in township thirty-seven north, range fourteen east of the third principal meridian, which lies between the river and North and South Water streets, or is comprised within said streets.

SEC. 39. All taxes and assessments imposed, voted and assessed by the said common council, shall be collected by the collector of said city, in the same manner and with the same power and authority as taxes in and for any county of the State are collected, by virtue of a warrant or warrants under the corporate seal, signed by the mayor or presiding officer, or by suit in the corporate name, with interest and costs, and the assessment roll of the said common council shall in all cases be evidence on the part of the corporation. And taxes or assessments imposed or assessed on or in respect of any real estate, within the said city, shall be a lien, on filing the roll with the clerk of the city, on such real estate, and in case such taxes or assessments are not paid, the common council may cause such real estate to be sold for the payment and collection of such taxes and assessments as aforesaid, together with the expenses of the sale, in the manner and with the effect and subject to the provisions specified in the forty-first section of the act relative to the sale of real estate, for the non-payment of assessments or taxes. All taxes and sums of money raised and collected by virtue of this section, shall be paid to the treasurer of the city. In all cases where there is no agreement to the contrary, the owner or landlord, and not the occupant or tenant, shall be deemed the person who ought to bear and pay every assessment made for the expenses of any public improvement in said city. Where any such assessment shall be made upon or paid by any person, when by agreement or by law, the same ought to be borne or paid by any other person, it shall be lawful for one so paying, to sue for and recover of the person bound to pay the same, the amount so paid, with interest, in action for the money so paid, laid out and expended for the benefit of such defendant. Nothing herein contained shall impair, or in any way affect any agreement between any landlord or tenant, or other persons, respecting the payment of such assessments.

SEC. 40. The common council shall have power to cause any street, alley, lane or highway in said city. to be graded, leveled, paved, repaired, macadamized or graveled; to cause cross and sidewalks, drains, sewers and aqueducts to be constructed and made in the said city; and to cause any sidewalks or drains, sewers and aqueducts to be relaid, amended and repaired; and to cause the expenses of all improvements (except sidewalks) made and directed under this section, to be assessed upon the real estate in any ward in said city, deemed benefited by such improvements, in proportion to the benefits resulting thereto, as nearly as may be. which assessment shall not exceed two per centum per annum on the property assessed. The common council shall determine the amount to be assessed for all improvements to be made or directed under this section, except sidewalks, and shall appoint, by a majority of all the aldermen authorized by law to be elected, five reputable freeholders of said city, by ballot, to make such assessment. The assessors shall be sworn before the mayor or any justice of the peace in said city, faithfully and impartially to execute their duty as such assessors according to the best of their ability; and before entering upon the duties assigned them by this section, the assessors shall give notice to all persons interested, of the time and place of meeting of said assessors, at least four days before the time of such meeting, by publishing such notice in the corporation newspaper printed in said city, and they may, if necessary, adjourn from day to day. The said assessors shall assess the amount directed by the common council to be assessed for any such improvement, on the real estate deemed by them to be benefited thereby, in proportion to the benefit resulting thereto as nearly as may be, and the said assessors shall briefly describe in the assessment roll to be made by them, the real estate on or in respect to which any assessment is made under this section. When the assessment is completed, they shall give like notice, and also publish the same in the corporation newspaper, and have the same power to make corrections as in case of the assessment of taxes. They shall deliver a corrected copy of the assessment roll, signed by all the assessors, to the clerk of the city, within sixty days after their appointment as aforesaid. and any person interested may appeal to the common council for the correction of the assessment; such appeal shall be in writing, and shall be delivered to the clerk or presiding officer of the common council, within ten days after the corrected copy of the assessment roll is filed with the clerk. In case of appeal, the common council shall appoint a time within ten days thereafter, for the hearing of those who are interested, and shall cause a notice to be published in the corporation newspaper, designating the time and place and object of hearing, and they may adjourn said hearing from time to time, as may be necessary, and the common council shall, in case of appeal as aforesaid, have power in their discretion, to confirm their assessment, or to annul the same, and direct a new assessment to be made in the manner herein before directed, by the same assessors, or by five other assessors, to be appointed as aforesaid, by the common council, and sworn as aforesaid. which shall be final and conclusive on all parties interested, in case the common council shall confirm the same. But in case the common council shall set aside the last aforesaid assessment, all the proceedings in relation to the grading. leveling, paving, repairing, macadamizing or graveling such street, alley, lane or highway in said city, shall be null and void. If the first assessment to be made and confirmed under this or the preceding sections proves insufficient, the common council may cause another to be made in the same manner, or if too large an amount shall at any time be raised, the excess shall be refunded ratably to those by whom it was paid. The said assessors may, if in their opinion any owner or owners of land situated on such street. alley, lane or highway, as shall be graveled or leveled, will sustain damages over and above the benefit which may accrue to the owner or owners of such land by such improvement, assess such an amount as they may deem a reasonable recompense to such owner or owners thereof, upon the real estate in said city, deemed by them to be benefited by such improvement, in proportion to the benefit resulting thereto, as nearly as may be, and the said assessors shall add such amount to the assessment roll which they are herein required to make, and certify the said amount to the common council, at the time of filing said roll with the clerk as aforesaid. If any vacancy shall happen in the office of assessor for any of the causes mentioned in the thirty-eighth section of this act, the same shall be filled by the common council in the manner therein provided.

SEC. 41. All assessments for improvements authorized by this act, shall be made upon the real estate, and be paid to or collected by the collector, except as herein otherwise directed. A corrected copy of the assessment roll shall in all cases be filed in the office of the clerk of the city, and the assessment shall be a lien upon the premises assessed, for one year only after the final corrected copy of the assessment roll shall have been filed as aforesaid. In case of non-payment, the premises may be sold at any time within the year from the time of the filing of the said assessment roll. Before any such sale, an order shall be made by the common council, which shall be entered at large in the records of the city kept by the clerk, directing the attorney of the city to sell, and particularly describing the premises to be sold and the assessment for which the sale is to be made, a copy of which order shall be delivered to the said attorney. The said attorney shall then advertise the premises to be sold in the manner and for the time required in the case of sales of real estate for taxes, and the sale shall be conducted in the same manner. The proceedings may be stopped at any time before the sale, by any person paying to said attorney the amount of the assessment, interest, and the expenses of advertising. All sales in such cases shall be made for the smallest portion of ground for which any person will pay the assessment, interest and expenses of advertising; certicates of the sale shall be made and subscribed by the said attorney, one of which shall be filed by him within ten days after the day of sale, in the office of the clerk of the city, and one in the office of the recorder of Cook county, and shall contain a description of the property and the price for which it was sold, and state the amount of the assessment, interest and expenses for which the sale was made, and the time at which the right to redeem will expire. If the proceedings are stopped before a sale is made, the attorney may include one dollar and no more in the expenses, for his fees. If the premises are sold, the attorney may include two dollars in the amount of expenses, for his fees, and no more. The right of redemption in all cases of such sales in the same manner and to the same extent, shall exist to the owner and his creditors as is allowed by law in the cases of sales of real estate for taxes. The money in case of redemption may be paid to the purchaser or for him to the clerk of the city. In case of no redemption, or of redemption by the creditor or creditors, the common council shall make to the purchaser or his legal representatives, or the person entitled thereto, a deed with a special warranty, signed by the mayor of said city, and countersigned by the clerk of said city, containing a description of the said premises sold for taxes or assessments as aforesaid.

SEC. 42. Any person interested may appeal from any order of the common council for laying out, opening, making, altering or widening any street, alley, lane, highway, to the circuit court of the county of Cook, or to the municipal court of said city, by notice in writing, delivered to the mayor or clerk of the city, at any time before the expiration of twenty days after the passage of the ordinance therefrom by the common council. The only ground of appeal shall be the want of conformity in the proceedings to this act. The propriety or utility of the streets, alleys, lanes, highways, or other improvements, or the correctness of the assessments of damage, if made in conformity to this act, shall not constitute a ground of appeal. In case of appeal, the common council shall make a return within twenty days after notice thereof; and the said circuit or municipal court shall, at the next term after the return, which shall be filed in the office of the clerk of said court, proceed to hear and determine the appeal, and shall confirm or annul the proceedings of the common council.

SEC. 43. The land required to be taken for the making, opening or widening of any street, alley, lane or highway in said city, shall not be so taken and appropriated by the common council, until the damages assessed and awarded therefor to any owner thereof, under this act, shall be paid or tendered to such owner, or his agent or legal representative, or, in case the said owner or his agent or legal representative cannot be found in said city, shall be deposited, to his or their credit, or for his or their use, in some safe place of deposit, other than the hands of the treasurer of said city; and then and in such cases, and not before, such lands may be taken and appropriated by the common council, for the purposes required in making such improvements, and such streets, alleys, lanes, highways, wharves or slips, may be made and opened.

SEC. 44. Where any known owner residing in said city or elsewhere shall be an infant, and proceeding shall be had under sections thirty-eight and forty of this act, the circuit court of the county of Cook, the judge thereof, the municipal court of said city, or any such judge of the supreme court or judge of probate for said county, may, upon the application of the common council or such infant, or his next friend, appoint a guardian for such infant, taking security from such guardian for the faithful execution of such trust, and all notices and summons required by either of said sections shall be served on such guardian.

SEC. 45. All owners or occupants, in front of whose premises the common council shall direct sidewalks to be constructed or repaired, shall make or repair such sidewalks at their own cost and charges, but if not done in the manner and of the materials and within the time prescribed by the common council, the said council may cause them to be constructed, and assess the expenses thereof upon such lots respectively, and collect the same in the manner directed by the thirty-eighth and fortieth and forty-first sections of this act, and such assessments shall be a lien upon such lot in like manner as assessments under the said thirty-eighth. fortieth and forty-first sections.

SEC. 46. The common council shall have power to order the grading, paving, graveling, raising, closing, fencing, amending, cleansing and protecting any public square or area, now or hereafter laid out in said city, and to improve the same by the construction of walks, and the rearing and protecting of ornamental trees therein, and to cause such part of the expenses thereof as they shall deem just, to be assessed and collected in the manner prescribed in the thirty-eighth, fortieth and forty-first sections of this act, for assessing and collecting the expenses of improvements mentioned in those sections, and to cause the sale of any real estate, on which such expenses are assessed, to be sold as provided in said thirty-eighth, fortieth and forty-first sections. But nothing herein shall empower the common council to divest or obstruct the interest of any individual in or to any such square or area.

SEC. 47. The common council shall have power to establish and regulate a market or markets in said city, and to restrain and regulate the sale of fresh meats and vegetables in said city, to restrain and punish the forestalling of poultry, fruits and eggs, and to license, under the hand and seal of the mayor, annually, such and so many butchers as they shall deem necessary and proper, and to revoke such license for any infraction of the by-laws and ordinances of the common council or other malconduct of such butchers in the course of their trade.

SEC. 48. The common council, for the purpose of guarding against the calamities of fire, shall have power to prescribe the limits in said city, within which wooden buildings shall not be erected or placed without the permission of the said common council, and to direct that all or any buildings within the limits prescribed shall be made or constructed of stone or brick, with partition walls, fire-proof roofs, and brick or stone cornices and eave-troughs, under such penalties as may be prescribed by the common council, not exceeding one hundred dollars for any one offense, and the further sum of twenty-five dollars for each and every week any building so prohibited shall be continued.

SEC. 49. The common council shall have power to regulate the construction of chimneys so as to admit chimney sweeps, and to compel the sweeping and cleaning of chimneys, and to prevent chimney sweeps from sweeping, unless licensed as they shall direct; to prevent the dangerous construction and condition of chimneys, fire-places, hearths, stoves, stove-pipes, ovens, boilers and apparatus used in any building or manufactory, and to cause the same to be removed or placed in a safe and secure condition, when considered dangerous; to prevent the deposit of ashes in unsafe places, and to appoint one or more officers to enter into all buildings and inclosures, to discover whether the same are in a dangerous state, and to cause such as may be dangerous to be put in safe condition; to require the inhabitants of said city to provide so many fire buckets, and in such manner and time as they shall prescribe, and to regulate the use of them in times of fire, and to regulate and prevent the carrying on of manufactories dangerous in causing or promoting fire, and to prevent the use of fire-works and fire-arms in said city, or any part thereof; to compel the owners and occupants of houses and other buildings, to have scuttles in the roofs, and stairs and ladders leading to the same; to authorize the mayor, aldermen, fire-wardens or other officers of said city, to keep away from the vicinity of any fire, all idle and suspicious persons, and to compel all officers of said city and other persons, to aid in the extinguishment of fires, and in the preservation of property exposed to danger thereat; and generally to establish such regulations for the prevention and extinguishment of fires, as the common council may deem expedient.

SEC. 50. The common council shall procure fire engines and other apparatus used for the extinguishment of fires, and have the charge and control of the same, and provide fit and secure engine-houses and other places for keeping and preserving the same, and shall have power to organize fire, hook, hose, bag, ladder and ax companies; to appoint during their pleasure a competent number of able and reputable inhabitants of said city firemen, to take the care and management of the engines and other apparatus and implements used and provided for the extinguishment of fires; to prescribe the duties of firemen, and to make rules and regulations for their government, and to impose such reasonable fines and forfeitures upon such firemen for a violation of the same, as the council may deem proper, and for incapacity, neglect of duty or misconduct, to remove them and appoint others in their places. And the qualified electors of said city may, at the annual election to be held for said city, choose a chief engineer and two assistant engineers of the fire department, whose term of office shall be for one year, who, with the other firemen, shall take the care and management of the engines and other apparatus and implements used and provided for the extinguishment of fires, and whose duties and powers shall be defined by the common council: *Provided, however*, That if the said qualified electors shall for any reason fail to elect a chief engineer and two assistant engineers, or either of them, as aforesaid, or if any of the offices shall become vacant in any way, then such vacancy may be filled by the common council in the same manner as other officers are appointed by them.

SEC. 51. The members of the common council shall be fire-wardens, and shall have power to appoint such other fire-wardens as they may deem necessary.

SEC. 52. The members of the common council, hook-and-ladder men, ax-men and firemen appointed by virtue of this act, shall, during their term of service as such, be exempt from serving on juries in all courts, and in the militia except in case of war, insurrection or invasion. The name of each person appointed fireman, hook-and-ladder man or ax-man, shall be registered with the clerk of the city, and the evidence to entitle him to the exemption as provided in this section, shall be the certificate of the clerk, made within the year in which the exemption is claimed.

SEC. 53. The present firemen of the town of Chicago shall be firemen of the city of Chicago, subject to be removed by the common council in like manner as other firemen of said city.

SEC. 54. Every fireman, hook-and-ladder man or ax-man who shall have faithfully served as such in said city or town of Chicago, or both, for the term of ten years, shall be thereafter exempt from serving on juries in all courts, or in the militia except in case of war, invasion or insurrection; and the evidence to entitle such person to the exemption as provided in this section, shall be a certificate under the corporate seal, signed by the mayor and clerk.

SEC. 55. The common council may authorize the mayor, or any other proper officer of the corporation, to grant license to tavern keepers, grocers, and keepers of ordinaries or victualing houses, to sell wines and other liquors, whether ardent, vinous or fermented, in the manner prescribed by the laws of this State; and also to license billiard tables, hackmen, draymen, carters, porters, omnibus drivers and auctioneers, and to adopt rules and regulations for their government, and to impose duties upon the sale of goods at auction; and may moreover direct the manner of issuing, countersigning and registering of such licenses, and may determine upon the fees to be paid for such licenses, not less than five nor more than fifty dollars, to be paid to the city treasurer; and the sum to be paid to the mayor or other officer for granting such license shall not exceed one dollar. Bond shall be taken on the granting of such license, for the due observance of the regulations of the common council in respect thereto. They shall be filed and may be prosecuted, and the money collected shall be applied in such manner as the common council shall direct.

SEC. 56. The common council shall have power to pass such ordinances as they shall deem proper for regulating or restraining tavern keepers, grocers, keepers of ordinaries or victualing houses, hackmen, draymen, carters, porters, omnibus drivers and auctioneers.

SEC. 57. The said common council shall be and are hereby authorized to appoint annually, three commissioners as a board of health for said city, and the mayor of said city or presiding officer of the common council shall be president of said board; and the clerk of said city shall be clerk of said board, and shall keep minutes of the proceedings thereof. The said common council shall, at their pleasure, appoint a health officer annually, and as often as the office may become vacant, and may remove him at pleasure, whose duty it shall be to visit every sick person who may be reported to the board of health as hereinafter provided, and to report with all convenient speed his opinion of the sickness of such person to the clerk of the said board of health; and it shall be the duty of the said officer to visit and inspect, at the request of the president of said board, all boats and vessels running to or being at the wharves, landing places or shores in said city, which are suspected of having on board any pestilential or infectious disease, and all stores or buildings which are suspected to contain unsound provisions or damaged hides or other articles, and to make report of the state of the same with all convenient speed to the clerk of the board of health.

SEC. 58. In case any boat or vessel shall be at [or] near any of the wharves, shores or landing places in said city, and the said board of health shall believe that such boat or vessel is dangerous to the inhabitants of said city in consequence of its bringing and spreading any pestilential or infectious disease among said inhabitants, or have just cause to suspect or believe that if said boat or vessel is suffered to remain at or near the said wharves, shores or landing places, it will be the cause of spreading among the said inhabitants any pestilential or infectious disease, that it shall and may be lawful for the said board, by an order in writing signed by the president for the time being, to order such boat or vessel to any distance from said wharves, shores or landing places, not exceeding three miles beyond the bounds of said city, within six hours after the delivery of such order to the owner or consignee of said boat or vessel; and if the master, owner or consignee to whom such order shall be delivered, shall neglect or refuse to comply therewith, the said president may enforce such removal, and such master, owner or consignee shall be considered guilty of a misdemeanor, and on conviction shall be fined a sum not exceeding two hundred and fifty dollars, and imprisoned not exceeding three months, in the jail of the county of Cook, by any court having cognizance thereof; the said fine, when paid, to be applied by the said board to the support of the treasury of the city of Chicago.

SEC. 59. Every person practicing physic in the said city who shall have a patient laboring under any malignant or yellow fever or other infectious or pestilential disease, shall forthwith make report thereof in writing to the clerk of said board of health; and for neglecting so to do shall be considered guilty of a misdemeanor, and liable to a fine of fifty dollars, to be sued for and recovered in any action of debt in any court having cognizance thereof, with cost, for the use of the treasury of said city.

SEC. 60. All persons in said city not being residents thereof, who shall be infected with any infectious or pestilential disease, and all things within said city which in the opinion of said board shall be infected by or tainted with pestilential matter, and ought to be removed so as not to endanger the health of the city, shall, by order of the said board of health, be removed to some proper place not exceeding three miles beyond the bounds of said city, to be provided by the said board at the expense of the said city, and the said board may order any furniture or wearing apparel to be destroyed whenever they may judge it to be necessary for the health of the city; and the said common council shall have power to erect one or more hospitals within the said city, and to control and regulate the same.

SEC. 61. All the estate, real and personal, vested in, or belonging to, or held in trust by the trustees of the town of Chicago, at the time this act shall take effect as a law, shall be and is hereby declared to be vested in the city of Chicago, and the said common council shall be bound and holden in the same manner, to all persons whomsoever, for all causes whatsoever, as the trustees of the town of Chicago were bound and holden under and by virtue of any law of this State.

SEC. 62. The said common council are hereby authorized and empowered to borrow, upon the faith and pledge of the city of Chicago, such necessary sum or sums of money, for any term of time, and at such rate of interest and payable at such place as they may deem expedient, not exceeding one hundred thousand dollars for any one year, and to issue bonds or scrip therefor under the seal of the said corporation, signed by the mayor and countersigned by the clerk, such sum or sums so borrowed, to be expended and applied in the liquidation of the debts of the said city of Chicago, and in the permanent and useful improvements of the said city, and to pledge the revenues accruing to the said city for the re-payment of the said sum or sums so borrowed, with the interest upon the same.

SEC. 63. The said common council shall, in all improvements strictly local in their character, such as improving streets, making drains and sewers, expend annually in each ward such proportion of the public moneys, as shall correspond with the amount of the assessed value of the property in each ward, as exhibited in the last assessment roll.

SEC. 64. The mayor of the said city for the time being shall have power to administer any oath required to be taken by any person under this act.

SEC. 65. Any person who shall hereafter be elected to the office of mayor or alderman of said city, may tender his resignation of such office to the common council of said city.

SEC. 66. The common council of the said city shall determine the rules of its own proceedings, and be the judge of the elections and qualifications of its own members, and have power to compel the attendance of absent members.

SEC. 67. The said common council are hereby authorized to levy an annual tax upon the owner of every dog kept or owned in said city by such person, not exceeding five dollars for every dog so owned or kept by such person.

SEC. 68. That the mayor of the said city of Chicago shall have the same jurisdiction within the limits of the said city, and shall be entitled to the same fees and emoluments which are given by the laws of this State to the justices of the peace, upon his conforming to the requirements, restrictions and directions of the laws of this State regulating the office of justice of the peace.

SEC. 69. That there shall be established in said city of Chicago, a municipal court, which shall have jurisdiction concurrent with the circuit courts of this State in all matters, civil or criminal, arising within the limits of said city, and in all cases where either plaintiff or defendant or defendants shall reside, at the time of commencing suit, within said city, which court shall be held within the limits of said city in a building provided by the corporation.

SEC. 70. Said court shall be held by one judge, who shall be appointed by joint ballot of both branches of the general assembly and commissioned by the governor, and shall hold his office during good behavior, and shall, during his continuance in office, reside within the limits of said city, and shall receive a salary of one thousand dollars annually, payable quarter-yearly by the common council of said city, which salary shall not be diminished but may be increased by said common council: *Provided, always*, That the said judge may and shall be removed from office for the same causes and in the same manner that the constitution of this State provides for the removal of other judges.

SEC. 71. That the docket fees now authorized and required by law to be paid to the clerk of the circuit court, shall be paid in all suits arising in said municipal court to the clerk thereof, and shall by him be paid to the city treasurer, out of which fees, together with the other revenues of said city, the salary of the judge and the other expenses of said court shall be paid.

SEC. 72. That the grand and petit jurors of said municipal court, shall be selected from the qualified inhabitants of said city by the common council thereof, in the same manner as other jurors are selected by the county commissioners' courts of this State, which jurors shall possess the same qualifications, and shall be liable to the same punishments and penalties, and have the benefits of the same excuses and exemptions as are imposed upon and allowed by the laws of this State to other jurors, and they shall take the same oaths, possess the same powers and be governed in all their proceedings as is prescribed in the case of other jurors by the laws of this State.

SEC. 73. That the said jurors shall be summoned by the high constable of said town, in the same manner as other jurors are summoned by the sheriffs of this State, and the said jurors shall be impanneled by the officers of the said municipal court, in the same manner as jurors of circuit courts; and the judge of said municipal court shall have all the powers concerning jurors that are given by the laws of this State to judges of the circuit courts.

SEC. 74. The jurors of said municipal court shall receive, out of the city treasury, the same compensation for their services as is allowed to jurors of the circuit courts, to be paid upon the certificate of the clerk of said municipal court, which certificate said treasurer shall file as his voucher.

SEC. 75. The judge of said municipal court shall hold six terms of said court in each year, for the transaction of civil and criminal business, and shall continue each term until the business before it shall be disposed of. The said terms shall respectively commence on the first Monday of January, March, May, July, September, and

November: *Provided, always,* That the common council of said city shall have power to increase the number of the terms of said court or to alter the same, by giving four weeks notice thereof in the corporation newspaper.

SEC. 76. The clerk of said court shall be appointed by the judge thereof, and shall be qualified and shall enter into bonds as clerks of the circuit courts are now required to do, and shall receive the same emoluments as are allowed to the clerks of the circuit courts for similar services, which fees shall be collected in the same manner.

SEC. 77. There shall be chosen by the qualified electors of said city, at the same time and in the same manner as is provided in this act, for the election of mayor, one high constable, whose term of service shall be for one year, and until his successor shall be chosen and qualified, who shall have and exercise all the powers and functions as an officer of said municipal court within the limits of said city, as sheriffs are allowed to exercise within the limits of their respective counties, and shall be entitled to the same fees for his services.

SEC. 78. Said municipal court shall be a court of record, and have a seal, to be furnished by the common council; the process of said court shall be tested by the judge, and issued in the same manner as in the circuit courts, and shall be directed to the high constable of said city, to be executed within the limits of the same, but where the defendant or defendants, or either of them, may reside without the limits of said city, and in Cook county, the process shall be directed to the sheriff of said county, who shall execute the same and make return thereof to the clerk of said court.

SEC. 79. The said high constable shall, before he enters upon the duties of his office, execute a bond with sufficient sureties payable to the city of Chicago, to be approved by the common council, in the penal sum of ten thousand dollars, conditioned as the sheriffs' bonds in this State are required by law to be conditioned, and may be prosecuted in the same manner in behalf of any person aggrieved, and the said high constable shall be required to take the same oath as the sheriffs of this State are required to take, as far as is consistent with the provisions of this act, before he enters upon the duties of his office, and the said high constable shall have power to appoint from among the city constables, one or more deputies, who shall be qualified in the same manner, shall have the same powers under the said high constable, so far as is consistent with the provisions of this act, as deputy sheriffs have under the high sheriffs.

SEC. 80. All judgments rendered in said municipal court shall have the same lien on real and personal estate, and shall be enforced and collected in the same manner as judgments rendered in the circuit courts of this State, and all appeals from any judgment rendered by the mayor of said city, or any justice of the peace within the limits of said city, shall be taken to the next circuit or municipal court whose term shall first happen.

SEC. 81. The said common council shall have power, from time to time, to establish, alter and regulate a tariff of fees to be allowed to the party or parties prosecuting or defending any suit or action in the said municipal court, to be taxed against the party failing in said suit, and to be recovered and collected in the same manner as fees are recovered and collected in the circuit courts of this State.

SEC. 82. All rules and proceedings of the said municipal court, not herein otherwise provided for, shall conform as near as may be to the rules and proceedings of the circuit courts of this State, and appeals from the municipal court to the supreme court, shall be taken and conducted in the same manner as is provided by the laws of this State for the taking of appeals or writs of error from the circuit court.

OF COMMON AND OTHER SCHOOLS.

SEC. 1. [83.] That the common council of the city of Chicago shall, by virtue of their offices, be commissioners of common schools in and for the said city, and shall have and possess all the rights, powers and authority necessary for the proper management of said schools.

SEC. 2. [84.] The said common council shall have power to lay off and divide the said city into school districts, and from time to time alter the same and create new ones, as circumstances may require.

SEC. 3. [85.] The common council shall annually appoint a number of inspectors of common schools in said city, not exceeding twelve, and not less than five; and in case of a vacancy in the office, the common council shall, from time to time, appoint others; which inspectors, or some of them, shall visit all the public schools in said city at least once a month, inquire into the progress of the scholars, and the government of the schools, examine all persons offering themselves as candidates for teachers, and when found well qualified, give them certificates thereof gratuitously, and remove them for any good cause; and it shall be the duty of the said inspectors to report to the common council, from time to time, any suggestions and improvements that they may deem necessary or proper for the prosperity of said schools.

SEC. 4. [86.] That the legal voters in each school district shall annually elect three persons to be trustees of common schools therein, whose duty it shall be to employ qualified and suitable teachers, to pay the wages of such teachers, when qualified, out of the money which shall come into their hands from the commissioner of school lands, so far as such money shall be sufficient for that purpose, and to collect the residue of such wages from all persons liable therefor. They shall call special meetings of the inhabitants of the district liable to pay taxes whenever they shall deem it necessary and proper, shall give notice of the time and place for special district meetings at least five days before said meeting shall be held, by leaving a written or printed notice thereof, at the place of abode of each of said inhabitants, make out a tax list of every district tax which the inhabitants of said district may, by a vote of a majority present, direct at any meeting called as aforesaid for that purpose, which list shall contain the names of all the taxable inhabitants residing in the district at the time of making out the list, and the amount of tax payable by each inhabitant, set opposite to his name, which tax may be levied upon the real or personal estate of said inhabitants; they shall annex to such tax list a warrant directed to one of the city constables residing in the ward in which said district may be, for the collection of the sums in said list mentioned, and said constable shall receive five cents on each dollar thereof, for his fees. The said trustees shall have power to purchase or lease a site for the district school-house, as designated by a meeting of the district, and to build, hire or purchase, keep in repair and furnish said school-house with necessary fuel and appendages, out of the funds collected and paid to them for such purposes.

SEC. 5. [87.] The trustees of each district shall, at the end of every quarter, make a report to the school inspectors in writing, setting forth the number of schools within the district, the time that each has been taught during the previous quarter, and by whom, the number of scholars at each school, and the time of their attendance during the quarter, to be ascertained from an exact list or roll of the scholars' names to be kept by the teacher for that purpose, which list shall be sworn to or affirmed by said teacher.

SEC. 6. [88.] That it shall be the duty of the commissioner of school lands in Cook county to make, semi-annually, to the common council of said city, a full and correct report, in such manner as they shall direct, of the state of the school fund arising from the sale or lease of school lands in township thirty-nine north, range fourteen east, in Cook county, with the interest accruing thereon.

SEC. 7. [89.] The school inspectors shall quarterly apportion said school money among the several districts in said city according to the number of scholars in each school therein between the ages of five and twenty-one, and also according to the time that each scholar has actually attended such school during the previous quarter, to be ascertained by the reports of said trustees and teachers.

SEC. 8. [90.] Whenever the said apportionment shall have been made, the school inspectors shall make out a schedule thereof, setting forth the amount due to each district, the person or persons entitled to receive the same, and shall deliver the said schedule, together with the report of the trustees and the lists or rolls of the teachers, to the common council, and thereupon the said common council shall issue a warrant directed to the commissioner of school lands, to pay over such part of the interest of the school moneys of said township as shall be therein expressed: *Provided*, That nothing herein contained shall authorize the expenditure of the principal of any part of the said school fund.

SEC. 9. [91.] The freeholders and inhabitants of any school district in the said city, by a vote of two-thirds of the persons present and entitled to vote, at a meeting of such district, convened after notice of the object of such meeting shall have been published for one week in the corporation newspaper of the said city, and after said notice shall have been served on every such freeholder or inhabitant, by reading the same to him, or, in case of his absence, by leaving the same at his place of residence at least five days previous to such meeting, determine, either separately or in conjunction with any other school district or districts in the said city, to have a high school created for such district or districts as shall so agree to unite for that purpose, and may vote a sum not exceeding five thousand dollars, to be raised for erecting a building for such high school. And on evidence of such vote, and of such notice having been published and served as above provided, being presented to the common council, they may, in their discretion, authorize the erecting of a high school in such district, or may authorize the several districts so agreeing, to be erected into one district, which shall thereafter form one school district, and all the property, right and interest of the several districts so united, shall belong to and be vested in the trustees of said united districts, and the trustees thereof shall have all the powers of trustees of school districts, shall be elected in the same manner, and shall be subject to all the duties and obligations of trustees of common school districts.

SEC. 10. [92.] The common council shall annually publish, on the second Tuesday of February, in the corporation newspaper of the city, the number of pupils instructed there in the year preceding, the several branches of education pursued by them, and the receipts and expenditures of each school, specifying the sources of such receipts, and the object of such expenditures. That the act entitled "An Act to incorporate the inhabitants of such towns as may wish to become incorporated," approved on the 12th day of February, 1831; and so much of an act entitled "An Act for the incorporation of fire companies," approved the 12th day of February, 1835; and so much of an act entitled "An Act to change the corporate powers of the town of Chicago;" and so much of an act entitled "An Act to amend an act entitled 'An Act to change the corporate powers of the town of Chicago,'" approved January 15, 1836, and all other acts and parts of acts, as are inconsistent with and repugnant to the provisions of this act, in so far as relates to the said city of Chicago, be and the same are hereby repealed.

Approved March 4, 1837.

AN ACT supplemental to an Act to incorporate the City of Chicago.

SECTION 1. *Be it enacted by the People of the State of Illinois, represented in the General Assembly*, That so much of the said act as permits the licensing of billiard tables in the said city be repealed; that all persons residing in the said county of Cook may, at their option, have recourse to the municipal court of said city, and the said municipal court shall have concurrent jurisdiction with the circuit court in all matters arising within said county; that only so much of an act entitled "An Act to incorporate the inhabitants of such towns as may wish to be incorporated," approved on the 12th day of February, 1831, shall be repealed as is inconsistent with the provisions of the act incorporating the said city of Chicago, and only in so far as the same relates to the said city of Chicago.

Approved March 4, 1837.

AN ACT to repeal part of "An Act to incorporate the City of Chicago."

SECTION 1. *Be it enacted by the People of the State of Illinois, represented in the General Assembly*, That so much of an act entitled "An Act to incorporate the city of Chicago," approved March 4th, in the year of our Lord one thousand eight hundred and thirty-seven, as establishes a municipal court in the said city of Chicago, and all matters connected therewith, be and the same is hereby repealed.

SEC. 2. That all suits or matters, both at law and in equity, now pending and undetermined, in the said municipal court, shall be heard, tried and prosecuted to final judgment and execution, in the circuit court of the county of Cook, in the same manner as they would be if the said suits or matters had been originally made returnable, or had in the circuit court for the said county of Cook; and all records, dockets and papers, belonging to, arising from or connected with the said municipal court shall, by the clerk of the said municipal court, be transferred and delivered over to the clerk of the circuit court for the said county of Cook: *Provided*, That this section shall not be construed as a release of errors that might have been taken advantage of in said municipal court: *Provided further*, That it shall be no ground of error in or to any judgment heretofore rendered in the said municipal court, that it does not appear by the record or proceedings that the defendant resided in the said county of Cook.

SEC. 3. It is hereby made the duty of the high constable, elected under the provisions of the said act entitled "An Act to incorporate the city of Chicago," hereby in part repealed, to make returns of all process of summons, executions, or of whatever nature, to the said circuit court of the county of Cook; which said circuit court is hereby invested with the same powers to enforce a compliance with the law in this behalf, that it would have had if the process had been originally issued from the said circuit court; and all executions hereafter to be issued upon any judgment rendered in the said municipal court, shall be directed to the sheriff of Cook county.

SEC. 4. That the transcript of any record of the said municipal court, of any judgment rendered therein, may and shall be furnished by the clerk of the circuit court of the said county of Cook; and any such transcript shall have the same force and effect, to all intents and purposes, that the same would have had if the suit, process or proceeding, whether in law or equity, had been originally commenced or instituted in the said circuit court.

SEC. 5. That the clerk of the said municipal court shall deliver over the records, dockets and papers, as provided in the second section of this act, within six weeks after the passage hereof: *Provided*, That nothing in this act contained shall be so construed as to prevent the clerk of the said municipal court from collecting his fees in the manner now provided by law; and the clerk of the said municipal court shall, for that purpose, have free access to the said records, dockets and papers, and copies thereof, without cost or charge.

SEC. 6. That the sheriff of Cook county is hereby authorized to give deeds of conveyance for any real estate which may have been sold by the high constable of the city of Chicago, as fully and effectually as he might or could do if the said real estate had been sold by the sheriff of said county.

SEC. 7. That nothing in this act contained shall be construed to prevent the high constable of said city of Chicago from proceeding to collect executions which have been levied.

Approved February 15, 1839.

AN ACT relating to Common Schools in the City of Chicago, and for other purposes.

SECTION 1. *Be it enacted by the People of the State of Illinois, represented in the General Assembly*, That the school lands and school funds of township thirty-nine north, range fourteen east of the third principal meridian, be and the same are hereby vested in the city of Chicago; and the common council of said city shall at all times have power to do all acts and things in relation to said school lands and school funds which they may think proper to their safe preservation and efficient management, and to sell or lease said lands on such terms and at such times as the said common council shall deem most advantageous, and, on such sale or sales, leasing or leasings, to make, execute and deliver all proper conveyances therefor; which said conveyances shall be signed by the mayor of said city, and countersigned by the clerk thereof, and sealed with the corporate seal of said city: *Provided*, That the proceeds arising from such sales shall be added to, and constitute a part of, the school fund of said township: *And provided*, That nothing shall be done to impair the principal of said fund, or to appropriate the interest accruing from the same to any other purpose than the support of public schools in said township: *And provided further*, That any schools established in said township, and without the limits of said city, shall be entitled to the same benefits and advantages from said fund as they would be without the passage of this act.

SEC. 2. It shall be the duty of the commissioners of school lands for Cook county to deliver to such person or persons as the common council of the city of Chicago shall direct, all the books, papers, notes, mortgages or other evidences of debt belonging to said school fund of said township thirty-nine, and all moneys belonging to the same, taking the receipt of such person or persons therefor; which said receipt shall be a full indemnity to him for so doing.

SEC. 3. The common council of Chicago shall have power to raise all sufficient sum or sums of money, by taxing the real and personal estate in said city, for the following purposes, to wit: To build school-houses; to establish, support and maintain common and public schools, and to supply the inadequacy of the school fund for the payment of teachers; to purchase or lease a site or sites for school-houses; to erect, hire or purchase buildings suitable for said school-houses; to keep in repair and furnish the same with necessary fixtures and furniture, whenever they may deem it expedient; and the taxes for that purpose shall be assessed and collected in the same manner that other city taxes are or may be. The said common council shall also have power to fix the amount of the compensation to be allowed to teachers in the different schools, to prescribe the school books to be used, and the studies to be taught in the different schools, and to pass all such ordinances and by-laws as they may from time to time deem necessary in relation to said schools, and the government and management of the same, and of the school lands and funds belonging to the said township.

SEC. 4. The said common council shall annually appoint seven persons for inspectors of common schools, and three persons in each district to be trustees of common schools in and for said district, whose powers and duties shall be prescribed by the said common council.

SEC. 5. Sections eighty-five, eighty-six, eighty-seven, eighty-eight, eighty-nine, ninety and ninety-one, of the act entitled "An Act to incorporate the city of Chicago," passed 4th March, 1837, and all other acts and parts of acts coming within the purview of this act, be and the same are hereby repealed so far as they relate to the said township thirty-nine, or the city of Chicago.

Approved March 1, 1839.

AN ACT to amend "An Act to incorporate the City of Chicago," approved the fourth day of March, one thousand eight hundred and thirty-seven, and for other purposes.

SECTION 1. *Be it enacted by the People of the State of Illinois, represented in the General Assembly,* That so much of the fourth section of the act to which this is an amendment, as provides that the mayor, aldermen and assessors of the city of Chicago, shall be freeholders in the said city; and section nine of said act, and so much of section twenty-six of said act as allows an annual salary of five hundred dollars to the mayor of said city; and section fifty-two of said act, be and the same are hereby repealed.

SEC. 2. Every person voting at the election for mayor, aldermen, assessors and other officers of said city, shall be an actual resident of the ward in which he so votes, and shall have resided in said city at least six months next preceding such election, and shall moreover, if required by any person qualified to vote thereat, before he is permitted to vote, take the following oath: "I swear (*or* affirm) that I am of the age of twenty-one years, that I have been a resident of this city for six months immediately preceding this election, that I am now a resident of this ward, and have not voted at this election."

SEC. 3. That so much of the forty-first section of said act, as provides that all sales of real estate for taxes and assessments within said city of Chicago, shall be made by the city attorney; and so much of said section as provides that the said city attorney shall receive one dollar, if proceedings in the sale of lots be stopped before the sale is made, and two dollars if the premises are sold, as his fees, be and the same is hereby repealed; and that hereafter all sales of real estate in the said city, for any tax or assessment, shall be made by the city collector, in the manner and at the time prescribed by the said act, and shall receive therefor the same fees and compensation as are allowed county clerks for similar services.

SEC. 4. The qualified electors of the said city shall elect annually, at the election for mayor and aldermen, a city marshal, whose duties shall be prescribed, and whose salary shall be fixed by the common council of said city, and that the seventy-seventh section of said act to incorporate the said city of Chicago, be repealed.

SEC. 5. That so much of the fourth and sixth sections of said act as provides for the election of one assessor from each ward of said city, be repealed; and the common council, at their first meeting annually after the charter election in said city, or as soon thereafter as may be, shall appoint one assessor, with the privilege at any time of increasing the number to three, whose duties shall be the same in all respects as are prescribed in the act to which this is an amendment.

SEC. 6. All deeds made to purchasers of lots sold for taxes by order of the council, as is provided in the act to which this is an amendment, shall be *prima facie* evidence in all controversies and suits in relation to the right of the purchaser, his or her heirs or assigns, to the premises thereby conveyed, of the following facts: *First,* That the land or lot conveyed was subject to taxation at the time the same was advertised for sale, and had been listed and assessed in the time and manner required by law; *Second,* That the taxes were not paid at any time before the sale; *Third,* That the lands conveyed had not been redeemed from the sale at the date of the deed; and shall be conclusive evidence of the following facts:

First. That the land or lot was advertised for sale in the manner and for the length of time required by law.

Second. That the land was sold for taxes, as stated in the deed.

Third. That the grantee in the deed was the purchaser.

Fourth. That the sale was conducted in the manner required by law. And in all controversies and suits involving the title to land claimed and held under and by virtue of a deed executed by the mayor and clerk, as provided in the act to which this is an amendment, the person or persons claiming title adverse to the title conveyed by such deed, shall be required to prove, in order to defeat the said title, either that the land was not subject to taxation at the date of the sale; that the taxes had been paid; that the land had never been listed and assessed for taxation; or that the same had been redeemed according to the provisions of this act, and that such redemption was had or made for the use and benefit of the persons having the right of redemption under the laws of this State; but no person shall be permitted to question the title acquired by the said deed, without first showing that he, she or they, or the person under whom he, she or they claims title, had title to the land at the time of the sale, or that the title was obtained from the United States, or this State, after the sale, and that all taxes due upon the lands have been paid by such person or the person under whom he claims title as aforesaid.

SEC. 7. That the common council of the city of Chicago have power and authority to inflict such penalties, not inconsistent with the constitution and laws of this State, as they may deem necessary and expedient, for a non-compliance with such ordinances as they may pass in relation to the regulating, restraining or licensing the sale of vinous, spirituous or fermented liquors within the city aforesaid; and also, that the said council have full and ample power over the streets and alleys, and public buildings of said city, (except such as belong to the county of Cook,) and to authorize, if they may deem it necessary, the location of any market or market buildings, in any of the streets or alleys of said city, with power to establish and regulate the markets so located by such ordinance or ordinances, for the restraining or licensing of the sale of meats and vegetables therein, as they may deem expedient, with such penalties as they may see proper to affix thereto for a violation thereof, not inconsistent with the laws and constitution of this State.

SEC. 8. That the said common council shall have power to assess and levy a tax upon all improvements on canal lots, or forfeited canal lots, as other lots are taxed in said city, so as to make the said improvements or the rents thereof liable therefor, and that the personal property of the person or persons in said city owning said improvements or renting or leasing the ground of said lots, shall be liable therefor, and upon a failure or refusal to pay said taxes, it shall be the duty of the collector of said city to obtain from the common council of said city a warrant in the nature of an execution against all such delinquents, authorizing him to levy upon and sell their goods and chattels, as in case of an execution from a justice of the peace, for the payment of said taxes and costs, and in case the said persons so owning the said improvements or renting the ground aforesaid, shall have no personal estate upon which to levy for the payment of the said taxes and costs, then and in that case the tenant or tenants, after notice given, shall be liable for the said taxes and costs to the extent of the rents in their hands unpaid, if sufficient to pay said taxes and costs; and upon refusal to pay the same, may be proceeded against in the same manner as the persons owning said improvements or leasing said lots.

SEC. 9. That the thirty-fifth section of the act to which this is an amendment, be so amended, that whenever the word "or" occurs in said section, it shall be taken and construed to mean "and," and in all respects shall have the same meaning and signification as the word "and."

SEC. 10. That the forty-first section of the said act, to which this is an amendment, or so much thereof as provides that the right of redemption shall in all cases of sale of real estate for taxes, exist to the same extent to the owner and his creditors, as is allowed by law in cases of sale of real estate for taxes, be so amended as to make the late revenue law, approved February twenty-six, one thousand eight hundred and thirty-nine, the law to which reference shall be expressly had in all cases.

This act to take effect from and after the first day of March next.

Approved February 27, 1841.

AN ACT to legalize the recorded Plat of School Section Addition to Chicago, and for other purposes.

SECTION 1. *Be it enacted by the People of the State of Illinois, represented in the General Assembly,* That the recorder of the county of Cook is hereby authorized to certify upon the maps or plat of the school section, recorded in his office, in book "A," page three hundred and fifteen, that the same is the plat of the school section addition, an addition to the town of Chicago, and to make such other certificates upon said maps as the common council of Chicago shall direct, to remedy any omission or defect in the same; and the said plat or map, when so certified, is hereby declared and made good, valid and legal, for all purposes whatever, any omission or defect in the same to the contrary notwithstanding; and the same shall hereafter be deemed good, valid and legal, and all omissions and defects in the same cured by this law, and the common council of said city are hereby authorized to cause said school section to be resurveyed, and the same run out so as to correspond with said plat.

SEC. 2. The said common council shall have power to enforce all such rules, ordinances and public regulations made in pursuance of the powers heretofore granted to said city, by imposing penalties of fine and imprisonment, either or both, in the discretion of the magistrate or magistrates before whom conviction shall be had: *Provided,* Such fine shall not exceed one hundred dollars, and the imprisonment sixty days.

SEC. 3. The cemetery lots which have or may be hereafter laid out and sold by said city for private places of burial, shall, with the appurtenances, forever be exempt from execution and attachment.

SEC. 4. The assignee of any tax certificate, of any lot sold for taxes under the authority of said city, shall be entitled to receive the deed of such lot in his own name, with the same effect as though he had been the original purchaser.

SEC. 5. The south-east and north-east quarters of the south-west quarter, south-west and north-west quarters of the south-east quarter of section number five, township thirty-nine, range fourteen east, and the west half of the north-east quarter of section number eight, in township thirty-nine, range fourteen east of the third principal meridian, are hereby stricken out of the corporate limits of the said city of Chicago.

SEC. 6. This act to take effect from its passage.

Approved March 3, 1843.

AN ACT supplementary to an Act to incorporate the City of Chicago, approved March 4, 1837.

SECTION 1. *Be it enacted by the People of the State of Illinois, represented in the General Assembly,* That the district of country, in the county of Cook and State of Illinois, known and described as follows, to wit: All that part of township thirty-nine (39) north, range fourteen (14) east of the third principal meridian, which lies north of the north line of sections twenty-seven (27), twenty-eight (28), twenty-nine (29), and thirty (30), of said township, and the east half of section thirty-three (33), in township forty (40) north, of range fourteen (14), and fractional section thirty-four (34), in said township forty (40), shall hereafter be included in, constitute and be known by the name of the City of Chicago.

SEC. 2. The city of Chicago shall be divided into nine wards, as follows: All that part of the city which lies south of the centre of Chicago river, and east of the centre of State street and a line running due south from the centre of the last named street, shall be denominated the first ward of said city.

All that part of said city which lies south of the centre of said Chicago river, west of the first ward, and east of the centre of Clark street and a line running due south from the centre of the last named street, shall be denominated the second ward of said city.

All that part of said city which lies south of the centre of the said Chicago river, west of the second ward, and east of the centre of Wells street and a line running due south from the centre of the last named street, shall be denominated the third ward of said city.

All that part of said city which lies south of the centre of the said Chicago river, west of the third ward, and east of the centre of the south branch of the Chicago river, shall be denominated the fourth ward of said city.

All that part of said city which lies west of the centre of the south branch of the Chicago river, and south of the centre of Randolph street and a line running due west from the centre of the last named street, shall be denominated the fifth ward of said city.

All that part of said city lying west of the centre of Chicago river and north and south branches thereof, and north of the centre of Randolph street and a line running due west from the centre of the last named street, shall be denominated the sixth ward of said city.

All that part of said city which lies east of the centre of the north branch of the Chicago river, and north of the centre of the Chicago river, and west of the centre of La Salle street and a line running due north from the centre of the last named street, shall be denominated the seventh ward of said city.

All that part of said city which lies north of the centre of Chicago river, and east of the seventh ward, and west of the centre of Wolcott street and a line running due north from the centre of the last named street, shall be denominated the eighth ward of said city.

All that part of said city which lies north of the centre of Chicago river, east of Wolcott street and a line running due north from the centre of the last named street, shall be denominated the ninth ward of said city.

SEC. 3. Two aldermen shall be elected in each of said wards, in the manner provided in the act to which this is supplementary, for the election of aldermen, who shall perform the same duties and possess like powers as are performed by the present aldermen of said city, except as hereinafter provided.

After the next election of aldermen, the common council of said city, who shall be chosen at said election, shall divide said aldermen from each ward into two classes, by lot; the first class shall respectively hold their offices for one year, and until their successors are elected and qualified; and the second class shall hold their offices respectively for two years, and until their successors are elected and qualified; and thereafter one alderman shall annually be elected in each ward, who shall hold his office for the term of two years, and until his successor shall be elected and qualified: *Provided*, That any person who may be elected to fill a vacancy, shall hold his office only for the term of time that shall be unexpired between the date of his election and qualification and the next regular election of alderman in his place as is hereinbefore provided; and the aldermen shall be conservators of the peace in their respective wards.

SEC. 4. It shall be the duty of the mayor of said city to give bond and be qualified as a justice of the peace of Cook county; and upon his filing such bond, and qualifying, as aforesaid, he shall possess the like power and jurisdiction as any other justice of the peace, and shall be entitled to the like fees and emoluments.

SEC. 5. In case of a vacancy in the office of mayor, or of his being unable to perform the duties of his office by reason of temporary or continued absence or sickness, the common council shall appoint, by ballot, one of their number as acting mayor, whose official designation shall be such, to preside at their meetings. And the alderman so appointed shall be vested with all the powers and perform all the duties of mayor, except in regard to qualifying as justice of the peace, until the mayor shall resume his office, or the vacancy be filled by a new election.

SEC. 6. There shall be elected at each annual election in said city, one city attorney, one city treasurer, one city collector and one city surveyor, by the legal voters thereof.

Second. There shall also be elected at such election, one street commissioner and one assessor, by the legal voters of the first, second, third and fourth wards, and one street commissioner and one assessor by the legal voters of the fifth and sixth wards, and one street commissioner and one assessor by the legal voters of the seventh, eighth and ninth wards of said city.

Third. The said assessors shall meet together and revise and correct their assessment rolls, before the same shall be returned to the council as required by law.

Fourth. There shall also be elected at each annual election, one police constable in each ward of said city, by the legal voters thereof: *Provided*, That nothing in this clause shall be so construed as to take away from the common council the power to appoint any additional number when an emergency or the public interest may require it.

Fifth. The city marshal shall possess all the powers and authority of a constable in common law, and under the statutes of this State, and shall receive the same fees and emoluments. He shall also enter into bond for the performance of his duties as constable, to be approved by the common council as in other cases.

SEC. 7. Every person appointed to any office by the common council, or elected to any office in said city, may be removed from such office by a vote of two-thirds of the aldermen of said city authorized by law to be elected. But no officer shall be removed except for cause, nor unless the accused shall be first furnished with the charges against him, that he may be heard in his defense.

Second. Whenever any vacancy shall happen by the death, removal or resignation of any officer of the city, elected by the people, such vacancy shall be filled by a new election by the people, and the common council shall order such new election, within ten days after the happening of such vacancy; and in the meantime the council may fill such vacancy by an appointment *pro tem.*, to expire upon the election and qualification of the officer elected to fill such vacancy.

Third. Any vacancy occurring by the death, removal or resignation of any officer authorized to be appointed by the common council, may be filled by appointment of the council.

SEC. 8. The common council shall have power to define the powers and duties of all officers elected by the people, or appointed to office by the common council, and to fix the compensation of such officers.

SEC. 9. Every male resident of the city over the age of twenty-one years, and under the age of sixty years, shall hereafter labor three days in each and every year upon the streets and alleys of said city, at such time and in such manner as the street commissioner shall direct; but any person may, at his option, pay at the rate of fifty cents for every day he shall be so bound to labor: *Provided,* The same shall be paid on or before the first day of the three days upon which he is notified to labor by the street commissioner; and such labor or payment shall be in lieu of all labor required to be performed upon any roads, streets or alleys, by any law of this State; and in default of the payment of such money as aforesaid, or the performance of such labor, the common council may sue for and collect the sum of three dollars of every person so in default, before any justice of the peace, and no set-off shall be allowed the defendant in any such case: *Provided,* This section shall not take effect until after the first day of March, A. D. 1847.

Second. The street taxes shall be expended in the several wards where the persons paying the same may reside respectively. Section sixty-three of the act to which this is supplementary is hereby repealed.

SEC. 10. The common council of said city shall have no power to remit any fine imposed upon any person for the violation of the laws or ordinances of said city, unless two-thirds of all the aldermen authorized to be elected shall vote for such remission; nor shall anything in this act contained, or that to which it is supplementary, or in any act relating to said city, be so construed as to oust any court of jurisdiction to abate and remove nuisances in the streets or any other parts of said city, by indictment or otherwise.

Second. No vote of the common council shall be reconsidered or rescinded at a special meeting of said council, unless, at such special meeting, there be present as large a number of aldermen as were present when such vote was taken.

SEC. 11. The common council shall have power to lay out, make and assess streets, alleys, lanes and highways in said city, and make wharves and slips at the end of streets, and to alter, widen, contract, straighten and discontinue the same. They shall cause all streets, alleys, lanes or highways, laid out by them, to be surveyed, described and recorded in a book to be kept by the clerk; and the same, when opened, shall be public highways.

Second. Whenever the common council shall desire to take or appropriate any land or town lot, or any part thereof, not the property of the city, for any of the purposes aforesaid, they shall cause an application to be made in writing to some court of record in the county of Cook, or judge thereof in vacation, for the condemnation of such land or town lot, or part thereof, for such purposes, and shall give notice of such application by publishing a notice thereof for thirty days in the corporation newspaper. And upon such application and proof of such notice being filed in the office of the clerk of said court, the said court or judge shall appoint three commissioners to examine and report upon the necessity of such appropriation, and the value of such land, town lot or part thereof, and the injury to the owner or owners thereof, respectively, in consequence of such appropriation, and at the same time to assess and apportion the said damages and expenses of said improvement on real estate deemed by them benefited thereby, as nearly as may be in proportion to the benefit resulting therefrom, after taking into consideration and making due allowance for any benefit which said owner or owners may derive from such improvement, and shall describe the real estate upon which such assessment is made. If there be any building on any land taken for such improvement, the owner thereof shall have ten days, or such time as the common council may allow after the final assessment of the commissioners and the proceedings of the court are confirmed by the common council, to remove the same, and in case such owner remove such building, the value thereof to the owner to remove shall be deducted from the amount of damages to be awarded to the owner thereof, and such value shall be, at the time of the assessment, determined by the commissioners, and in case of removal deducted *pro rata* from the assessments upon the real estate deemed benefited by such improvements.

Third. The said commissioners shall be sworn faithfully and impartially to execute their duty in making such assessment, according to the best of their ability. They shall appoint time or times, and place or places, for the purpose of viewing the premises and making their assessment, and give notice thereof by publication for the space of ten days in the corporation newspaper, and personal notice shall be given to all persons interested, where the same are known, or left at their last usual place of abode. When any person known to be an owner or interested in any such land, town lot or part thereof, shall be an infant, a guardian shall be appointed for such infant by such judge in court, in the manner pointed out in the forty-fourth section of the act to which this is supplementary.

Fourth. The commissioners shall view the premises, and in their discretion receive any legal evidence, and may, if necessary, adjourn from day to day.

Fifth. The said commissioners shall make their determination and assessment in the manner aforesaid, and the determination and assessment of said commissioners shall be reduced to writing and signed by all of said commissioners, and reported and returned to said court, as soon after such hearing as may be; and upon filing such report in the office of the clerk of said court, the said clerk shall publish a notice of such fact in the corporation newspaper for the space of ten days; and any person interested may appear and file their objections to the confirmation of such report at any time within fifteen days from the first publication of such notice last aforesaid. At the next term of the court, or in vacation, if ten days notice aforesaid shall have been published of the time and place of hearing, and said fifteen days shall have expired, the judge of the court in which such proceedings shall be had, shall examine said report and hear all persons interested therein; and if the proceedings of said commissioners shall be found fair and regular, said report shall be confirmed, and said land, lot or part thereof be condemned by said judge for such purpose or purposes. And thereupon the said court, or judge in vacation, shall cause the proceedings to be certified to the common council, and if the same shall be confirmed by the council, an order shall be entered at large upon the records of the common council, confirming the same and directing a warrant to be issued to the collector for the collection of said assessment as in other cases, and the same proceedings shall be had in all respects for the collection of the same, as for the collection of other taxes or assessments. All orders and judgments required to be entered by the court in the progress of the proceedings under this section, may be entered by the judge thereof in vacation; and the said judge shall have power to refer the assessment back to the commissioners for correction and revisal, upon such principles as he may consider equitable and just, and appoint other commissioners in the place of such as may be unable or refuse to serve. And if in his opinion such improvement is not required by the public interests, he shall have the power of setting the proceedings aside.

Sixth. But in case such council shall refuse to confirm the same, then all the proceedings in relation to the laying out, altering, widening or straightening such street, alley, lane, highway, wharf or slip, shall be null and void. But if the order of said court shall not be confirmed, the common council shall reimburse the parties, defendants, interested in the said proceedings, all reasonable costs and charges, including counsel fees.

Seventh. The commissioners of assessment appointed under this act, or the act to which this is supplementary, shall be allowed two dollars per day each for every day's actual services, and it shall be the duty of the city attorney to prepare all such papers and make all such examinations as they may request.

Eighth. *Provided,* That no portion of the thirty-eighth section of the act to which this is supplementary shall be deemed to be repealed by this section, except so far as the same provides for the making, opening and assessing alleys, streets, highways, wharves and slips; and for all other purposes the said section shall be continued in force.

SEC. 12. The common council of the city of Chicago may lay, make, maintain and repair all main drains or common sewers in the city of Chicago, and all the main drains or common sewers which have heretofore been, or which may hereafter be constructed by said common council, shall be taken and deemed to be the property of said city.

Second. Every person who may hereafter enter his particular or private drain into any main drain or common sewer so constructed as aforesaid, for the draining of his cellar or land, or in obedience to the ordinance of said city, or who, by any more remote means, shall receive any benefit thereof for draining his cellar or land, shall pay to the city a proportional part of the charge of making and repairing such main drain or common sewer, to be ascertained and determined by a committee of the common council, and by them certified to the council, and approved by the latter, and notice thereof given to the party to be charged therewith, or his tenant or lessee, who shall have the right to appeal therefrom as in other cases.

Third. All assessments so made shall constitute a lien on the real estate assessed for one year after they are levied, and may, together with all incidental costs and expenses, be levied by sale thereof, if the assessment be not paid within thirty days after a written demand of payment made either upon the person assessed, or upon any person occupying the estate; such sales to be conducted in like manner as sales for the non-payment of taxes.

SEC. 13. The common council of the city of Chicago shall have exclusive power to erect and construct, or to permit or cause or procure to be erected and constructed, float or draw-bridges over the navigable waters within the corporation limits of said city, said bridges to have draws of suitable width, so as not to prevent or interrupt the free navigation of said waters. And any person or persons who shall injure or destroy any bridge, the construction of which may have been heretofore or may be hereafter authorized or permitted by the common council, or shall cause or procure the same to be injured or destroyed, shall be subject to a penalty of one hundred dollars for each offense, to be recovered by the city in an action of debt, and may be imprisoned for a term not exceeding three months, in the discretion of the magistrate before whom such conviction may be had, and such person or persons shall also be liable in a civil action at the suit of the city for the damages occasioned by such injury or destruction.

SEC. 14. The common council shall have power to cause any streets or highways in the city to be planked, and also to build and construct a breakwater or barrier, along the shore of lake Michigan, for the protection of the said city against the encroachments of the water, and also to construct, or authorize to be constructed, a tunnel or tunnels under the Chicago river or either of its branches, at the crossing of any street, and to cause the expenses of either of the said improvements to be assessed and collected in the manner prescribed in the thirty-eighth, thirty-ninth, fortieth and forty-first sections of the act to which this is supplementary: *Provided*, That nothing contained in this section shall authorize the common council to assess or collect any expenses incurred in the construction of a breakwater, or on account of any public grounds, (excepting streets and alleys,) upon any particular portion or part of said city, but all such expenses hereafter incurred shall be paid by assessing the same on the city at large, in the same manner as general taxes are now assessed and collected.

SEC. 15. The common council shall have power to pass all such ordinances as they may think proper and necessary to preserve the harbor; to prevent and punish the casting or depositing therein any earth, ashes, or other substances, filth, logs, or floating matter; to prevent and remove all obstructions therein, and to punish the authors thereof; to regulate and prescribe the mode and speed of entering and leaving the harbor, and of coming to and departing from the wharves and streets of the city by steamboats, canal boats, and other craft and vessels, and the disposition of the sails, yards, anchors and appurtenances thereof, while entering, leaving or abiding in the harbor; and to regulate and prescribe, by such ordinances or through their harbor master, such a location of every canal boat, steamboat, or other craft or vessel, or float, and such changes of station in and use of the harbor as may be proper in order to promote order therein, and the safety and equal convenience, as near as may be, of all such boats, vessels, craft and floats. The common council may annually appoint one or more harbor masters, whose especial duty it shall be to enforce all such ordinances; and may impose penalties and fines not exceeding one hundred dollars for any offense against any such ordinance; and may by such ordinance charge any such penalty upon the steamboat, canal boat, or other vessel, craft, or boat, the captain, master, owner, consignee or person in charge of which, is thereby liable therefor. The word "*harbor*," as used in this section, shall be taken and deemed to include so much of lake Michigan as lies within the distance of one mile from the shore thereof into the lake, and the Chicago river and its branches, including the piers.

SEC. 16. The common council shall have power to lease for any term of years not exceeding ten years in any term, lot number five (5), in block number four (4), lot number nine (9), in block number fifty (50), and lot six (6), in block fifty-five (55), all in the original town of Chicago, heretofore donated to the city of Chicago, for the use of schools, under "An Act to provide for the dedication of lots in towns situate on canal lands to public purposes," passed 1839; or exchange the same or any part thereof; and for this purpose to execute a deed or deeds to the purchaser, for the lots or parts of lots in the city, which may be more eligible for the purposes of the original donation. The common council shall also have power to sell and dispose of the whole or any part of lot number five (5), in block number four (4), in the original town above described, and execute to the purchaser a good and sufficient deed, so as to vest in him the legal title to the same: *Provided*, That in case the common council shall lease all or either of said lots, or sell or dispose of said lot number five (5), in block number four (4), of the original town, or any part thereof, the rents, issues and proceeds of such leases or sale shall not be appropriated at any time hereafter to any other purpose than the support of common schools in the city, or the purchase of suitable sites for school-houses, as contemplated in the original donation of the same.

SEC. 17. Every assessment or tax levied or assessed by the common council, the collection of which shall be delayed by injunction or other judicial proceedings, shall be a lien upon the premises assessed for the period of one year after the final disposition of the injunction or other judicial proceedings, unless said injunction shall be sustained. The collector of the city may seize personal goods and chattels, for the satisfaction of any taxes or assesments levied or assessed by the common council, in virtue of any of its corporate powers, in the manner prescribed by the revenue laws of the State.

Second. If at any sale of real or personal estate for taxes or assessments levied or assessed by the common council, no bid shall be made for any parcel of land, or any goods or chattels, the same shall be struck off to the city; and thereupon the city shall receive in the corporate name a certificate of the sale thereof, and shall be vested with the same rights as other purchasers at such sales.

SEC. 18. The common council shall have power to pass ordinances to regulate, restrain or prohibit the keeping of any billiard table or tables, or any ball alley within said city, under penalties not exceeding one hundred dollars for each and every violation thereof. And also to restrain and prohibit the running at large [of] any horses or hogs within the city, and for this purpose shall have power to impose a penalty upon the owner or owners of said horses or hogs, not exceeding ten dollars, for the violation of any ordinance concerning horses or hogs, or both, which the common council may enact and ordain.

SEC. 19. In all prosecutions for any violation of any ordinance of said city, the first process shall be a summons, unless oath or affirmation be made by some officer of said city or other person for a warrant, as in other cases before justices of the peace.

Second. In all suits for the violation of ordinances the writ shall specify the particular clause or offense of the ordinances violated.

Third. It shall be lawful for the Cook county court and the circuit court of Cook county, respectively, in passing sentence upon any person hereafter found guilty by the verdict of a jury, or upon confession of any offense, for which the punishment is fine and imprisonment in the county jail, or either, to make an order that during the term of imprisonment such person shall be required to labor upon the streets of the city of Chicago. And that unless such fine and costs shall be paid upon demand, or property sufficient to satisfy the same be turned out, to be taken in execution, such prisoner shall also be required to labor upon the streets of the city at the rate of fifty cents per day, under the direction of the street commissioners of the city, until the whole fine and costs shall be fully paid.

Fourth. Every person who may be hereafter committed upon any execution issued by any court of record or justice of the peace of Cook county, upon a judgment recovered by the city for penalty, fine for a breach of any provision of this act or the act incorporating the said city, or any act amendatory thereof, or for a violation of any by-law or ordinance of said city, shall be required to labor on the streets of the city at the rate aforesaid, until the whole of such judgment and costs shall be fully paid; and the jailer of Cook county is hereby authorized to deliver any prisoner sentenced or committed in execution as aforesaid, to any street commissioner of said city under an order of the mayor or acting mayor of the city, for the purpose of laboring on the streets as aforesaid; and the city shall pay to the jailer the sum of thirty-seven and a half cents per day for board for each day such prisoner shall actually labor, and not otherwise: *Provided*, That such prisoner may be excused from labor by a vote of two-thirds of the common council.

Fifth. The officers of said city who may be authorized to receive such prisoner, may secure him in such manner as may be necessary to compel him to labor on the streets, and shall return such prisoner to the custody of the jailer before sunset of each day.

SEC. 20. All ordinances hereafter passed by the common council imposing penalties shall take full force and effect in one week after their publication.

Approved February 16, 1847.

AN ACT in relation to that part of Township 39 north, of Range 14 east of the Third Principal Meridian, in relation to Schools.

SECTION 1. *Be it enacted by the People of the State of Illinois, represented in the General Assembly*, That all that part of township thirty-nine north, of range fourteen east of the third principal meridian, in Cook county, which lies south of the corporate limits of the city of Chicago, shall constitute a school district, by the name of "South Chicago School District," and the legal voters of said district shall have authority to levy and collect a school tax, annually, upon all the estate, both real and personal, in said district, for school purposes, not exceeding one-quarter of one per centum upon the assessed value thereof, as the same shall be valued by the assessor of Cook county.

SEC. 2. The inhabitants of said district shall meet together at such time and place as shall be appointed by the clerk of the county commissioners' court of Cook county, in each year, and appoint three inspectors of elections, who shall be qualified in the same manner as judges of precinct elections, and shall be governed, as nearly as may be, by the laws relating to judges of precinct elections, and make returns of the election to the clerk of said court. At such elections, there shall be elected, by ballot, three directors of said district, who shall be freeholders therein at the time of their election, and who shall have the same power, and perform the like duties, within their district, that are possessed and performed by the trustees and inspectors of common schools in the city of Chicago. The said directors shall hold their offices for one year, and until their successors are elected and qualified. At such election the inhabitants of said district shall determine, by vote, what tax, not exceeding the said one-fourth of one per centum, shall be levied upon the real and personal estate within said district. The inspectors of said election shall make return of said election, and the votes taken thereat, to said clerk, within ten days after such election. Said returns shall be opened by said clerk in the presence of two justices of the peace, and he shall grant a certificate of election to the three persons who shall appear, by said returns, to have received the greatest number of votes thereat. In case of contested elections, the contest shall be determined in the manner provided by law for contesting the election of justices of the peace.

SEC. 3. Upon said return being made and filed in the office of said clerk, he shall add to the tax list levied by the county commissioners' court upon the estate in said district, in a separate column, the tax voted by said district, and the same shall be collected by the sheriff or county collector, as other taxes, in money, and paid unto the agent of the school fund appointed by the common council of the city of Chicago, who shall keep a separate account of the same, and disburse it only upon the written order of said directors.

SEC. 4. If any such director or directors shall draw an order upon said agent for any part of said money thus collected as a district tax, except so much thereof as shall be allowed by them to said clerk for his services in the premises, or shall appropriate the same to any purpose other than the building of a school-house or school-houses in said district, or the support of schools therein, he or they shall forfeit and pay to any person who may sue for the same, three times the amount of such order or appropriation, to be recovered by action of debt before any justice of the peace or court, and besides, shall be liable to indictment and punishment by fine, not exceeding five hundred dollars, and imprisonment in the county jail not exceeding six months, at the discretion of the court.

SEC. 5. The said directors shall be authorized to draw from the agent of the school fund of the city of Chicago, monthly, such an amount as said district shall be entitled to, in proportion to its number of inhabitants, between the ages of five and twenty-one years, as compared with the whole number of such inhabitants in said city, out of the interest of the school fund in said township: *Provided*, That a common school be established and maintained in said district, and said money be drawn and appropriated solely for the payment of teachers' wages.

Approved February 23, 1847.

AN ACT to exempt the Members of the Fire Department in the City of Chicago from paying a Street or Road Tax.

SECTION 1. *Be it enacted by the People of the State of Illinois, represented in the General Assembly*, That the several persons in the city of Chicago, who are members of the fire department of said city, shall be and they are hereby exempted from working out any road or street tax within said city, or from paying any money in lieu thereof.

Approved February 10, 1849.

AN ACT to reduce the Law incorporating the City of Chicago, and the several Acts amendatory thereof, into one Act, and to amend the same.

CHAPTER I. CITY AND WARD BOUNDARIES.
" II. OFFICERS: THEIR ELECTION AND APPOINTMENT.
" III. POWERS AND DUTIES OF OFFICERS.
" IV. OF THE COMMON COUNCIL, ITS GENERAL POWERS AND DUTIES.
" V. OF TAXATION.
" VI. ASSESSMENTS FOR OPENING STREETS AND ALLEYS.
" VII. ASSESSMENTS FOR PUBLIC IMPROVEMENTS.
" VIII. COLLECTION OF TAXES AND ASSESSMENTS.
" IX. FIRE DEPARTMENT.
" X. BOARD OF HEALTH.
" XI. SCHOOLS AND SCHOOL FUND.
" XII. MISCELLANEOUS PROVISIONS.

CHAPTER I.

CITY AND WARD BOUNDARIES.

SECTION 1. *Be it enacted by the People of the State of Illinois, represented in the General Assembly*, That the district of country in the county of Cook and State of Illinois, known and described as follows, to wit: All that part of township thirty-nine north, range fourteen east of the third principal meridian, which lies north of the north line of sections twenty-seven, twenty-eight, twenty-nine and thirty, of said township, and the east half of section thirty-three and fractional section thirty-four in township forty north, range fourteen east, is hereby erected into a city, by the name of the "City of Chicago."

SEC. 2. The inhabitants of said city shall be a corporation by the name of the "City of Chicago;" and by that name sue and be sued, complain and defend in any court; make and use a common seal, and alter it at pleasure; and take, hold and purchase, lease and convey, such real and personal or mixed estate as the purposes of the corporation may require, within or without the limits aforesaid.

SEC. 3. The city of Chicago shall be divided into nine wards, as follows:

First Ward. All that part of the city which lies south of the centre of Chicago river, and east of the centre of State street and a line running due south from the centre of the last named street, shall be denominated the first ward.

Second Ward. All that part of said city which lies south of the centre of said Chicago river, west of the first ward, and east of the centre of Clark street and a line running due south from the centre of the last named street, shall be denominated the second ward.

Third Ward. All that part of said city which lies south of the centre of the said Chicago river, west of the second ward, and east of the centre of Wells street and a line running due south from the centre of the last named street, shall be denominated the third ward.

Fourth Ward. All that part of said city which lies south of the centre of the said Chicago river, west of the third ward, and east of the centre of the south branch of the Chicago river, shall be denominated the fourth ward.

Fifth Ward. All that part of said city which lies west of the centre of the south branch of Chicago river, and south of the centre of Randolph street and a line running due west from the centre of the last named street, shall be denominated the fifth ward.

Sixth Ward. All that part of said city lying west of the centre of Chicago river and north and south branches thereof, and north of the centre of Randolph street and a line running due west from the centre of the last named street, shall be denominated the sixth ward.

Seventh Ward. All that part of said city which lies east of the centre of the north branch of the Chicago river, and north of the centre of the Chicago river, and west of the centre of La Salle street and a line running due north from the centre of the last named street, shall be denominated the seventh ward.

Eighth Ward. All that part of said city which lies north of the centre of the Chicago river, and east of the seventh ward, and west of the centre of Wolcott street and a line running due north from the centre of the last named street, shall be denominated the eighth ward.

Ninth Ward. All that part of said city which lies north of the centre of the Chicago river, east of Wolcott street and a line running due north from the centre of the last named street, shall be denominated the ninth ward.

CHAPTER II.

OFFICERS: THEIR ELECTION AND APPOINTMENT.

SECTION 1. The municipal government of the city shall consist of a common council, composed of the mayor, and two aldermen from each ward. The other officers of the corporation shall be as follows:

A clerk; an attorney; a treasurer; a school agent; a marshal; a board of school inspectors; a board of health; one chief, and a first and second assistant engineers of the fire department; one or more collectors; one or more surveyors; one street commissioner and one assessor for each natural division of the city; one or more harbor masters; three trustees of schools for each school district; one or more health officers; one or more market clerks; three inspectors of elections for each ward; and as many firemen, fire-wardens, constables, policemen, watchmen, sealers of weights and measures, inspectors, measurers, weighers, gaugers, sextons or keepers of burial grounds; keepers and assistants of almshouses, workhouses, public buildings, hospitals and bridewell or house of correction; bellmen, common criers, scavengers; and such other officers and agents as the common council may, from time to time, direct and appoint.

SEC. 2. An election shall be held in each of the wards of said city on the first Tuesday of March in each year, at such place as the common council may appoint, and of which six days previous public notice shall be given in written or printed notices, in three public places in each ward, by the city clerk.

SEC. 3. At the annual election there shall be elected by the qualified voters of said city, a mayor, marshal, treasurer, collector, surveyor, attorney, and chief and assistant engineers; and the person having the highest number of votes in the whole city for either of such offices, shall be declared elected. At the same time the electors in their respective wards shall vote for one alderman and one police constable, and the persons receiving the highest number of votes cast in the ward for such offices respectively, shall be declared elected.

SEC. 4. There shall also be elected at such election, one street commissioner by the legal voters of the south division, being the first, second, third and fourth wards; one street commissioner by the legal voters of the west division, being the fifth and sixth wards; and one street commissioner by the legal voters of the north division, being the seventh, eighth and ninth wards of said city; and the person having the highest number of votes in each division respectively, shall be declared elected.

SEC. 5. The officers elected by the people under this act, (except aldermen), shall respectively hold their offices for one year, and until the election and qualification of their successors respectively. All other officers mentioned in this act, (except aldermen and firemen), and not otherwise specially provided for, shall be appointed by the common council by ballot, on the second Tuesday of March in each year, or as soon thereafter as may be, and respectively continue in office one year, and until the appointment and qualification of their successors. But the council may specially authorize the appointment of watchmen by the mayor or marshal, to continue in office during the pleasure of the council: *Provided*, The mayor or marshal may be authorized by the council to remove them for good cause. Officers elected or appointed to fill vacancies, shall respectively hold for the unexpired term only, and until the election or appointment and qualification of their successors.

SEC. 6. The several wards of the city shall be respectively represented in the common council by two aldermen, who shall be residents thereof, and hold their offices respectively for two years from and after their election, and until the election and qualification of their successors. They shall be divided into two classes, consisting of one alderman from each ward, so that one from each ward may be annually elected. The first class shall be elected at the annual election in March next, and be successors to the members of the present common council whose offices expire at that time. The second class shall be elected one year thereafter, and succeed those members who are entitled to hold over one year after the next election. The members of each class, hereafter elected, shall respectively continue in office two years. If from any cause there shall not be a quorum of aldermen, the clerk shall appoint the time and places for holding a special election, and appoint inspectors thereof, if necessary. If any alderman remove from the ward represented by him, his office shall thereby become vacant.

SEC. 7. If, for any cause, the officers herein named shall not be appointed on the second Tuesday in March, the common council may adjourn from time to time, until such appointments are made. If there should be a failure by the people to elect any officers herein required to be elected, the common council may forthwith order a new election.

SEC. 8. Every person appointed to any office by the common council, or elected to any office by the people, may be removed from such office by a vote of two-thirds of all the aldermen authorized by law to be elected. But no officer shall be removed except for cause, nor unless first furnished with the charges and heard in his defense, and the common council shall have power to compel the attendance of witnesses and the production of papers, when necessary for the purposes of such trial, and shall proceed within ten days to hear and determine upon the merits of the case, and if such officer shall neglect to appear and answer to such charges, then the common council may declare the office vacant: *Provided*, This section shall not be deemed to apply to any officer appointed by the common council; such officer may be removed at any time by a vote of two-thirds as aforesaid, in the discretion of the council. But any officer may be suspended until the disposition of charges, when preferred.

SEC. 9. Whenever any vacancy shall happen by the death, removal, resignation or otherwise, of any officer elected by the people, such vacancy shall be filled by a new election, and the common council shall order such new election within ten days after the happening of such vacancy. Any vacancy occurring by the death, removal or resignation of any officer authorized to be appointed by the common council, may be filled by appointment of the council; but no special election shall be held to fill vacancies (except of mayor and aldermen,) if more than six months of the term have expired.

SEC. 10. All citizens of the United States, qualified to vote at any election held under this act, shall be qualified to hold any office created by this act, but no person shall be eligible to any office or place under this or any other act in relation to said city, who is now, or hereafter may be, a defaulter to said city, or to the State of Illinois, or any county thereof, and any person shall be considered a defaulter who has refused or neglected, or may hereafter refuse or neglect, for thirty days after demand made, to account for and pay over to the party authorized to receive the same, any public money which may have come into his possession. And if any person holding any such office or place shall become a defaulter whilst in office, the office or place shall thereupon become vacant.

SEC. 11. When two or more candidates for an elective office shall have an equal number of votes for the same office, the election shall be determined by the casting of lots in the presence of the common council.

SEC. 12. The manner of conducting and voting at elections to be held under this act, and contesting the same, the keeping of the poll lists, canvassing of the votes and certifying the returns, shall be the same, as nearly as may be, as is now or may hereafter be provided by law at general State elections: *Provided*, The council shall have power to regulate elections. The voting shall be by ballot, and the inspectors of elections shall take the same oath, and shall have the same power and authority as inspectors of general elections. After the closing of the polls, the ballots shall be counted in the manner required by law, and the returns shall be returned sealed to the city clerk within three days after the election, and thereupon the common council shall meet and canvass the same, and declare the result of the election. It shall be the duty of the clerk to notify all persons elected or appointed to office of their election or appointment, and unless such persons shall respectively qualify within ten days thereafter, the offices shall become vacant.

SEC. 13. No person shall be entitled to vote at any election under this act, who is not entitled to vote at State elections, and has not been a resident of said city at least six months next preceding the election; he shall moreover have been an actual resident of the ward in which he votes for ten days previous to the election, and if required by any person qualified to vote thereat, shall take the following oath before he is permitted to vote: *Provided*, That the voter shall be deemed a resident of the ward in which he is accustomed to lodge:

"I swear (*or* 'affirm') that I am of the age of twenty-one years, that I am a citizen of the United States, (*or* 'was a resident of this State at the time of the adoption of the constitution,') and have been a resident of this State one year, and a resident of this city six months immediately preceding this election, and am now, and have been for ten days last past, a resident of this ward, and have not voted at this election."

SEC. 14. The persons entitled to vote at any election held under this act, shall not be arrested on civil process within said city upon the day in which said election is held, and all persons illegally voting at any election under this act, shall be punishable according to the laws of this State.

CHAPTER III.

POWERS AND DUTIES OF OFFICERS.

SECTION 1. Every person chosen or appointed to an executive, judicial or administrative office under this act, shall, before he enters on the duties of his office, take and subscribe the oath of office prescribed in the constitution of this State, and file the same, duly certified by the officer before whom it was taken, with the clerk of the city.

SEC. 2. The mayor shall, before he enters upon the duties of his office, in addition to the usual oath, swear or affirm that he will devote so much of his time to the duties of his office as an efficient and faithful discharge thereof may require. He shall preside over the meetings of the common council, and take care that the laws of the State and ordinances of the city are duly enforced, respected and observed, and that all other executive officers of the city discharge their respective duties. He shall, from time to time, give the common council such information, and recommend such measures as he may deem advantageous to the city. He shall have a salary of twelve hundred dollars per annum; and he may give bond and qualify as a justice of the peace, and when qualified shall possess the same powers and jurisdiction as are herein vested in such justices of the peace as may be designated by the common council under this act, and be entitled to like fees. But he shall account for and pay over to the city treasurer, when required, all fines, fees, or other moneys received by him in his judicial capacity, and keep a docket subject at all times to the inspection of the common council. All ordinances and resolutions shall, before they take effect, be placed in the office of the city clerk, and if the mayor approve thereof, he shall sign the same; and such as he shall not sign, he shall return to the council with his objections thereto. Upon the return of any ordinance or resolution, by the mayor, the vote by which the same was passed shall be reconsidered; and if, after such reconsideration, a majority of all the members elected to the council shall agree, by ayes and noes, which shall be entered of record, to pass the same, it shall go into effect. And if the mayor shall neglect to approve or object to any such proceedings for a longer period than three days after the same shall be placed in the clerk's office, as aforesaid, the same shall go into effect. The mayor shall likewise have the power, *ex officio*, to administer any oath required to be taken by this act.

SEC. 3. In case of a vacancy in the office of mayor, or of his being unable to perform the duties of his office, by reason of temporary or continued absence or sickness, the common council shall appoint by ballot one of their number to preside over their meetings, whose official designation shall be, acting mayor. And the alderman so appointed shall be vested with all the powers, and perform all the duties of mayor, except in regard to qualifying as justice of the peace, until the mayor shall resume his office, or the vacancy be filled by a new election.

SEC. 4. The members of the common council shall be fire wardens and conservators of the peace, and shall be exempted from jury duty, and the payment of street taxes, during their term of office.

SEC. 5. The clerk shall keep the corporate seal and all papers belonging to said city, and make a record of the proceedings of the common council, at whose meetings it shall be his duty to attend; and copies of all papers duly filed in his office, and transcripts from the records of the proceedings of the common council, certified by him under the corporate seal, shall be evidence in all courts, in like manner as if the originals were produced. He shall likewise draw all warrants on the treasury and countersign the same, and keep an accurate account thereof in a book to be provided for that purpose; he shall also have power to administer any oath required to be taken by this act.

SEC. 6. It shall be the duty of the city attorney to perform all professional services incident to the office, and, when required, furnish written opinions upon subjects submitted to him by the mayor or the common council, or its committees.

SEC. 7. The treasurer shall receive all moneys belonging to the city, and keep an accurate account of all receipts and expenditures in such manner as the common council shall direct. All moneys shall be drawn from the treasury in pursuance of an order from the common council, by warrant signed by the mayor or presiding officer of the common council, and countersigned by the clerk; such warrant shall specify for what purpose the amount specified therein is to be paid. The treasurer shall exhibit to the common council, at least fifteen days before the annual election of each year, and oftener, if required, a full and detailed account of all receipts and expenditures after the date of the last annual report, and also of the state of the treasury; which account shall be filed in the office of the clerk.

SEC. 8. The marshal shall perform such duties as shall be prescribed by the common council, for the preservation of the public peace, the collection of license money and fines, or otherwise. He shall possess the power and authority of a constable at common law and under the statutes of this State, and receive like fees, but shall not serve civil process without first entering into bonds as such constable, to be approved by the common council as in other cases.

SEC. 9. The city surveyor or surveyors, shall have the sole power, under the direction or control of the common council, to survey within the city limits, and he and they shall be governed by such rules and ordinances, and receive such fees and emoluments, for his or their services, as the common council shall appoint and direct. He shall possess the same powers in making surveys and plats, within the city, as is given by law to county surveyors, and the like effect and validity shall be given to his acts, and to all plats and surveys heretofore or hereafter made by any such surveyor, as are or may be given by law to the acts, plats and surveys of county surveyors.

SEC. 10. It shall be the duty of the collector or collectors to collect all taxes and assessments which may be levied by said city, and perform such other duties as may be herein prescribed or ordained by the common council.

SEC. 11. Assessors shall perform all the duties in relation to the assessing of property, for the purpose of levying the taxes imposed by the common council. In the performance of their duties, they shall have the same powers as are or may be given by law to county or town assessors, and be subject to the same liabilities. On completing their assessment rolls, they shall meet together and revise and correct the same, and having completed the revision, they shall sign the several rolls and return the same to the common council.

SEC. 12. It shall be the duty of the harbor master to enforce all ordinances, and provisions of this act, in relation to the harbor.

SEC. 13. It shall be the duty of the street commissioners to superintend all local improvements in their respective divisions, and carry into effect all orders of the common council in relation thereto. They shall keep accurate account of all expenditures made by them, and render monthly accounts thereof to the common council.

SEC. 14. Every person appointed or elected to the office of constable, shall, before he enters upon the duties of his office, with two or more sureties, to be approved by the common council, execute, in presence of the clerk of the city, an instrument in writing by which such constable and securities shall jointly and severally agree to pay to each and every person who may be entitled thereto, all such sums of money as the said constable may be liable to pay by reason or on account of any summons, execution, distress warrant or other process which shall be delivered to him for collection. The clerk shall certify the approval of the common council on such instrument, and file the same; and a copy certified by the clerk, under the corporate seal, shall be presumptive evidence, in all courts, of the execution thereof by such constable and his sureties; and all actions thereon shall be prosecuted within two years after the expiration of the year for which the constable named therein shall have been appointed or elected, and may be brought in the name of the person or persons entitled to the money collected by virtue of such instruments. No constable appointed or elected, under this act, shall have power to serve any civil process out of the city limits, except in cases of persons fleeing therefrom, and to commit on execution, where the defendant shall have been arrested within the city.

SEC. 15. The common council shall have power, from time to time, to require further and other duties of all officers whose duties are herein prescribed, and prescribe the powers and duties of all officers appointed or elected to any office under this act, whose duties are not herein specifically mentioned, and fix their compensation. They may also require bonds to be given to the city of Chicago by all officers, for the faithful performance of their duties.

SEC. 16. The treasurer, collectors, marshal, street commissioners and school agent shall, severally, before they enter on the duties of their respective offices, execute a bond to the city of Chicago, in such sum and with such sureties as the common council shall approve, conditioned that they shall faithfully execute the duties of their offices, and account for and pay over all moneys and other property received by them; which bonds, with the approval of the common council certified thereon by the clerk, shall be filed with the clerk.

SEC. 17. The common council, at their annual meeting on the second Tuesday in March, in each year, or within not to exceed thirty days thereafter, shall designate one public newspaper printed in said city, in which shall be published all ordinances and other proceedings and matters required in any case by this act, or by the by-laws and ordinances of the common council, to be published in a public newspaper.

SEC. 18. If any person, having been an officer in said city, shall not, within ten days after notification and request, deliver to his successor in office all the property, papers and effects of every description in his possession belonging to said city, or appertaining to the office he held, he shall forfeit and pay, for the use of the city, one hundred dollars, besides all damages caused by his neglect or refusal so to deliver. And such successor shall and may recover possession of the books, etc., appertaining to his office, in the manner prescribed by the laws of this State.

SEC. 19. All persons elected or appointed, under this act, to the office of clerk, marshal, attorney, treasurer, collector, assessor, surveyor, street commissioner or constable, shall be commissioned by warrant under the corporate seal, signed by the mayor or presiding officer of the common council, and clerk.

CHAPTER IV.

OF THE COMMON COUNCIL: ITS GENERAL POWERS AND DUTIES.

SECTION 1. The mayor and aldermen shall constitute the common council of said city. The common council shall meet at such times and places as they shall by resolution direct. The mayor, when present, shall preside at all meetings of the common council, and shall have only a casting vote. In his absence, any one of the aldermen may be appointed to preside. A majority of the persons elected as aldermen shall constitute a quorum.

SEC. 2. No member of the common council shall, during the period for which he was elected, receive any compensation for his services, or be appointed to, or be competent to hold, any office of which the emoluments are paid from the city treasury, or paid by fees directed to be paid by any act or ordinance of the common council, or be directly or indirectly interested in any contract, the expenses or consideration whereof are to be paid under any ordinance of the common council.

SEC. 3. The common council shall hold stated meetings, and the mayor or any two aldermen may call special meetings by notice to each of the members of said council, served personally, or left at their usual place of abode. Petitions and remonstrances may be presented to the common council, and the council shall determine the rules of its own proceedings, and be the judge of the election and qualifications of its own members, and have power to compel the attendance of absent members.

SEC. 4. The common council shall have the management and control of the finances, and all the property, real, personal and mixed, belonging to the corporation; and shall likewise have power within the jurisdiction of the city, by ordinance—

First. To lease the wharfing privileges of the river, at the ends of streets, upon such terms and conditions as may be usual in the leasing of other real estate, reserving such rents as may be agreed upon, and employing such remedies in case of non-performance of any covenants in such lease, as are given by law in other cases. But no buildings shall be erected thereon: *Provided*, No lease for a longer period than three years shall at any time be executed, and the owner or owners of the adjoining lot or lots shall, in all cases, have the preference in leasing such property; but a free passage over the same for all persons, with their baggage, shall be reserved in such lease: *Provided, further*, Nothing in this section shall be so construed as to impair or prejudice any rights which any person may have acquired by the acceptance of any proposition heretofore made by said city respecting the wharfing privileges.

Second. To remove and prevent all obstructions in the waters which are public highways in said city, and to widen, straighten and deepen the same.

Third. To prevent and punish forestalling and regrating, and to prevent and restrain every kind of fraudulent device and practice.

Fourth. To restrain and prohibit all descriptions of gaming and fraudulent devices, and all playing of dice, cards and other games of chance, with or without betting.

Fifth. To regulate the selling or giving away of any ardent spirits by any shop-keeper, trader or grocer, to be drunk in any shop, store or grocery, out-house, yard, garden or other place within the city, except by inn-keepers duly licensed.

Sixth. To forbid the selling or giving away of ardent spirits or other intoxicating liquors, to any child, apprentice or servant, without the consent of his or her parent, guardian, master or mistress, or to any Indian.

Seventh. To license, regulate and restrain tavern-keepers, grocers, and keepers of ordinaries or victualing or other houses or places, for the selling or giving away wines and other liquors, whether ardent, vinous or fermented.

Eighth. To license, tax, regulate, suppress and prohibit billiard tables, pin alleys, nine or ten pin alleys, and ball alleys.

Ninth. To license, regulate and suppress hackmen, draymen, carters, porters, omnibus drivers, cabmen, packers, carmen, and all others who may pursue like occupations with or without vehicles, and prescribe their compensation.

Tenth. To tax, license and regulate auctioneers, distillers, brewers and pawnbrokers, and to impose duties upon the sale of goods at auction.

Eleventh. To license, tax, regulate and suppress hawkers and pedlars.

Twelfth. To regulate, license, suppress and prohibit all exhibitions of common showmen, shows of every kind, concerts or other musical entertainments, by itinerant persons or companies, exhibitions of natural or artificial curiosities, caravans, circusses, theatrical performances, and all other exhibitions and amusements.

Thirteenth. To authorize the mayor, or other proper officer of the city, to grant and issue licenses, and direct the manner of issuing and registering thereof, and the fees to be paid therefor. No license shall be granted for more than one year: *Provided*, Not less than five nor more than five hundred dollars shall be required to be paid for any license under this act, and the fee for issuing the same shall not exceed one dollar; but no license for the sale of wines or other liquors, ardent, vinous or fermented, at wholesale or retail, or by inn-keepers or others, as aforesaid, shall be less than fifty dollars. Bond shall be taken on the granting of license, for the due observance of the ordinances or regulations of the common council.

Fourteenth. To prevent any riot or noise, disturbance or disorderly assemblage.

Fifteenth. To suppress and restrain disorderly houses and groceries, houses of ill-fame, billiard tables, nine or ten pin alleys or tables, and ball alleys, and to authorize the destruction and demolition of all instruments and devices used for the purpose of gaming.

Sixteenth. To compel the owner or occupant of any grocery, cellar, tallow chandler shop, soap factory, tannery, stable, barn, privy, sewer, or other unwholesome, nauseous house or place, to cleanse, remove or abate the same, from time to time, as often as may be necessary for the health, comfort and convenience of the inhabitants of said city.

Seventeenth. To direct the location and management of, and regulate breweries, tanneries and packing-houses, and to direct the location, management and construction of, and regulate, restrain, abate and prohibit, within the city, and the distance of four miles therefrom, distilleries, slaughtering establishments, establishments for steaming or rendering lard, tallow, offal, and such other substances as can or may be rendered; and all establishments or places where any nauseous, offensive or unwholesome business may be carried on: *Provided*, That for the purposes of this section, the Chicago river and its branches to their respective sources, and the land adjacent thereto, or within one hundred rods thereof, shall be deemed to be within the jurisdiction of the city.

Eighteenth. To establish and regulate markets and other public buildings, and provide for their erection, determine their location, and authorize their erection in the streets or avenues of the city.

Nineteenth. To regulate, and license or prohibit butchers, and to revoke their licenses for malconduct in the course of trade, and to regulate, license and restrain the sale of fresh meats and vegetables in the city, and restrain and punish the forestalling of poultry, fruit and eggs.

Twentieth. To direct and prohibit the location and management of houses for the storing of gunpowder or other combustible and dangerous materials within the city.

Twenty-first. To regulate the keeping and conveying of gunpowder and other combustible and dangerous materials, and the use of candles and lights in barns, stables and out-houses.

Twenty-second. To prevent horse-racing, immoderate riding or driving in the streets, and to authorize persons immoderately riding, or driving, as aforesaid, to be stopped by any person; and punish or prohibit the abuse of animals; to compel persons to fasten their horses, oxen or other animals attached to vehicles or otherwise, while standing or remaining in the street.

Twenty-third. To prevent the encumbering of the streets, sidewalks, lanes, alleys, public grounds, wharves and docks, with carriages, carts, sleighs, sleds, wheelbarrows, boxes, lumber, timber, fire-wood, posts, awnings, signs, or any substance or material whatever.

Twenty-fourth. To regulate and determine the times and places of bathing and swimming in the canals, rivers, harbors or other waters, in and adjoining said city, and to prevent any obscene or indecent exhibition, exposure or conduct.

Twenty-fifth. To restrain and punish vagrants, mendicants, street-beggars and prostitutes.

Twenty-sixth. To restrain and regulate, or prohibit the running at large of cattle, horses, swine, sheep, goats and geese; and to authorize the distraining, impounding and sale of the same for the penalty incurred, and the cost of the proceedings; and also to impose penalties on the owners of any such animals for a violation of any ordinances in relation thereto.

Twenty-seventh. To prevent and regulate the running at large of dogs, and to authorize the destruction of the same, when at large contrary to the ordinance.

Twenty-eighth. To prevent and regulate the rolling of hoops, playing of ball, flying of kites, or any other amusement or practice having a tendency to annoy persons passing in the streets or on the sidewalks, or to frighten teams and horses.

Twenty-ninth. To make regulations to prevent the introduction of contagious diseases into the city; to make quarantine laws, and enforce the same within the city, and not to exceed fifteen miles beyond the city bounds.

Thirtieth. To have exclusive power over the streets and alleys, and to remove and abate any obstructions and encroachments therein.

Thirty-first. To compel all persons to keep the snow, ice and dirt from the sidewalk, in front of the premises owned or occupied by them.

Thirty-second. To prevent the ringing of bells, blowing of horns and bugles, crying of goods, and all other noises, performances and devices tending to the collection of persons on the streets or sidewalks, by auctioneers or others, for the purposes of business, amusement or otherwise.

Thirty-third. To abate and remove nuisances, and punish the authors thereof, by penalties, fine and imprisonment, and to define and declare what shall be deemed nuisances, and authorize and direct the summary abatement thereof.

Thirty-fourth. To license, regulate and restrain runners for boats and stages, cars and public houses.

Thirty-fifth. To regulate the burial of the dead, and registration of births and deaths; to direct the returning and keeping of bills of mortality, and to impose penalties on physicians, sextons and others for any default in the premises.

Thirty-sixth. To appoint watchmen and policemen, and prescribe their duties and powers.

Thirty-seventh. To regulate the measuring and inspecting of lumber, shingles, timber, posts, staves and heading, and all building materials, and appoint one or more inspectors.

Thirty-eighth. To regulate the place and manner of selling pickled and other fish, and inspecting the same.

Thirty-ninth. To regulate the weighing, and place and manner of selling hay.

Fortieth. To regulate the measuring of wood and the weighing and selling of coal, and the place and manner of selling the same.

Forty-first. To regulate the inspection of flour, meal, pork, beef and other provisions, and salt to be sold in barrels, hogsheads and other packages.

Forty-second. To regulate the inspection of whisky and other liquors, to be sold in barrels, hogsheads and other vessels.

Forty-third. To appoint inspectors, weighers, gaugers, and regulate their duties and prescribe their fees.

Forty-fourth. To create and regulate the police of said city.

Forty-fifth. To establish, make and regulate public pumps, wells and cisterns, hydrants and reservoirs, and to prevent the unnecessary waste of water.

Forty-sixth. To establish and regulate public pounds.

Forty-seventh. To erect lamps, and regulate the lighting thereof, and from time to time to create, alter and extĕnd lamp districts.

Forty-eighth. To regulate and license ferries.

Forty-ninth. To regulate and prohibit the use of locomotive engines within the city, and may require the cars to be used thereon, within the inhabited portions thereof, to be drawn or propelled by other power than that of steam; to direct and control the location of railroad tracks and depot grounds, and prohibit railroad companies from doing storage and warehouse business, or collecting pay for storage.

Fiftieth. To erect and establish a bridewell or house of correction, pass all necessary ordinances for the regulation thereof, and appoint a keeper and as many assistants as may be necessary. In the said, bridewell or house of correction, shall be confined all vagrants, stragglers, idle or disorderly persons who may be committed thereto by the mayor, any alderman or other conservator of the peace; and all persons sentenced by any criminal court, or magistrate, in and for the city, for any assault and battery, petit larceny or other misdemeanor punishable by imprisonment in any county jail, shall be kept therein, subject to labor or solitary confinment.

Fifty-first. To require every merchant, retailer, trader and dealer in merchandise or property of any description, which is sold by measure or weight, to cause their weights and measures to be sealed by the city sealer, and to be subject to his inspection; the standard of which weights and measures shall be conformable to those now established by law.

Fifty-second. Exclusively to erect and construct, or to permit, or cause or procure to be erected and constructed, float or draw bridges over the navigable waters within the jurisdiction of said city, and keep the same in repair; said bridges to have draws of suitable width.

Fifty-third. To preserve the harbor; to prevent any use of the same, or any act in relation thereto, inconsistent with, or detrimental to, the public health, or calculated to render the waters of the same, or any part thereof, impure or offensive, or tending in any degree to fill up or obstruct the same; to prevent and punish the casting or depositing therein any earth, ashes, or other substance, filth, logs or floating matter; to prevent and remove all obstructions therein, and to punish the authors thereof; to regulate and prescribe the mode and speed of entering and leaving the harbor, and of coming to and departing from the wharves and streets of the city, by steamboats, canal boats, and other crafts and vessels, and the disposition of the sails, yards, anchors and appurtenances thereof, while entering, leaving, or abiding in the harbor; and to regulate and prescribe by such ordinances, or through their harbor master or other authorized officer, such a location of every canal boat, steamboat, or other craft or vessel, or float, and such changes of station in, and use of, the harbor, as may be necessary to promote order therein, and the safety and equal convenience, as near as may be, of all such boats, vessels, crafts and floats; and may impose penalties not exceeding one hundred dollars, for any offense against any such ordinance; and by such ordinance charge such penalties, together with such expenses as may be incurred by the city in enforcing this section, upon the steamboat, canal boat or other vessel, craft or float. The harbor of the city shall include the piers and so much of lake Michigan as lies within the distance of one mile into the lake, and the Chicago river and its branches to their respective sources.

Fifty-fourth. To exclusively control, regulate, repair, amend and clear the streets and alleys, bridges, side and cross walks, and open, widen, straighten and vacate streets and alleys, and put drains and sewers therein, and prevent the encumbering of the streets in any manner, and protect the same from any encroachments and injury.

Fifty-fifth. To direct and regulate the planting and preserving ornamental trees in the streets and public grounds.

Fifty-sixth. To borrow money, not exceeding one hundred thousand dollars in any one year, and pledge the revenue of the city for its payment, and issue bonds therefor.

Fifty-seventh. To fill up, drain, cleanse, alter, relay, repair and regulate any grounds, yards, basins, slips, cellars, private drains, sinks and privies, direct and regulate their construction, and cause the expenses to be assessed and collected in the same manner as sidewalk assessments.

Fifty-eighth. To erect and establish one or more hospitals or dispensaries, and control and regulate the same.

Fifty-ninth. To abate all nuisances which are or may be injurious to the public health, in any manner they may deem expedient.

Sixtieth. To do all acts and make all regulations which may be necessary or expedient for the preservation of health and the suppression of disease.

Sixty-first. To prevent any person from bringing, depositing or having within the limits of said city, any dead carcass, or any other unwholesome substance, and to require the removal or destruction by any person who shall have, place or cause to be placed upon or near his premises, any such substance, or any putrid or unsound beef, pork or fish, hides or skins of any kind, and, on his default, to authorize the removal or destruction thereof by some officer of said city.

Sixty-second. To authorize the taking up, and provide for the safe-keeping and education, for such periods of time as may be deemed expedient, of all children who are destitute of proper parental care, wandering about the streets, committing mischief, and growing up in mendicancy, ignorance, idleness and vice.

Sixty-third. The common council shall have power to make, publish, ordain, amend and repeal all such ordinances, by-laws and police regulations, not contrary to the constitution of this State, for the good government and order of the city and the trade and commerce thereof, as may be necessary or expedient to carry into effect the powers vested in the common council, or any officer of said city, by this act; and enforce observance of all rules, ordinances, by-laws, and police and other regulations, made in pursuance of this act, by penalties not exceeding one hundred dollars for any offense against the same. The common council may also enforce such rules, ordinances, by-laws, and police and other regulations, as aforesaid, by punishment of fine or imprisonment, or both, in the county jail, bridewell or house of correction, in the discretion of the magistrate or court before which conviction may be had: *Provided*, Such fine shall not exceed five hundred dollars, nor the imprisonment six months.

CHAPTER V.

OF TAXATION.

SECTION 1. The common council shall have power, within the city, by ordinance—

First. To annually levy and collect taxes, not exceeding three and one-half mills on the dollar, on the assessed value of all real and personal estate in the city, made taxable by the laws of this State, to defray the contingent and other expenses of the city, not herein otherwise especially provided for; which taxes shall constitute the general fund.

Second. To annually levy and collect a school tax, not exceeding two mills on the dollar, on all real and personal estate, to meet the expenses of purchasing grounds for school-houses, and building and repairing school-houses, and supporting and maintaining schools.

Third. To levy and collect a tax, not exceeding one-half mill on the dollar per annum, on real and personal estate, to meet the interest accruing on the bonded debt of the city.

SEC. 2. To levy and collect taxes on real and personal estate, when required—

First. For the erection of a barrier to protect the city from the lake.

Second. For the erection of a city hall, markets, hospital, bridewell or workhouse, the purchase of market grounds, public squares or parks, or any other permanent improvements: *Provided*, The estimated cost of a city hall or bridewell may be apportioned by the common council, and collected by a series of annual assessments: *Provided further*, That the cost of market grounds, markets, public squares or parks, and the lake barrier, or any other improvement, shall be levied upon all the property in the natural division of the city in which such markets, squares or barrier may be located, except such part of the cost as the common council may cause to be specially assessed upon real estate in such division immediately benefited by such improvements, in the manner herein prescribed for the assessment of like improvements in chapter seven: *Provided*, That no tax or taxes shall be levied in any one year, under this section, which shall exceed two per cent. upon the value of the property assessed, for either or all of the purposes herein specified: *Provided further*, That no local improvement under this section shall be ordered in any division, unless a majority of the aldermen thereof shall vote in favor of the same. *Provided further*, The common council may negotiate a loan for the purpose of building a market house in any division, and apply the revenues therefrom towards paying the interest on such loan, and liquidating the principal. But should the net revenues from such market be insufficient to pay such interest and principal, when they shall respectively become due, the common council shall levy and collect a tax upon the real and personal property in the division in which such market may be located, to make up the deficiency of such interest or principal, or both.

SEC. 3. To levy and collect, on the real and personal estate in such districts as they shall from time to time create, a sufficient tax to defray three-fourths of the expense of erecting lamps, and lighting the streets in such district or districts respectively: *Provided*, The money thus raised shall be exclusively expended for such purposes in the district paying the same.

SEC. 4. To require (and it is hereby made the duty of) every male resident of the city, over the age of twenty-one years, and under the age of sixty years, to labor three days in each year upon the streets and alleys; but every person may, at his option, pay at the rate of fifty cents for every day he shall be so bound to labor: *Provided*, The same shall be paid on or before the first of the three days upon which he may be notified to labor by the street commissioner. In default of payment, as aforesaid, the sum of three dollars may be collected, and no off-set shall be allowed in any suit brought to recover the same. Street taxes shall be expended in the several wards where the persons paying the same may respectively reside.

SEC. 5. The common council shall, hereafter, in all expenditures for purposes strictly local, expend annually in the several natural divisions of the city, such proportion of the whole expenditures for like purposes, during the same period, as will correspond to the several sums contributed respectively by each division to the general fund.

SEC. 6. If it shall appear, at the close of any municipal year, that a greater sum has been expended, for purposes strictly local, in any division or divisions, than its or their relative proportion, it shall be the duty of the common council, the ensuing year, to increase the general tax in such division or divisions respectively, by the amount of such excess, in such proportions thereof as each may be justly chargeable therewith. They shall, at the same time, abate such excess from the assessment in the other division or divisions respectively, in like proportions. For the purposes of this section, it may be lawful for the common council to levy a tax in any division, for general purposes, not exceeding four-tenths of one per cent. per annum.

SEC. 7. All improvements on any school or canal lands or lots, and all improvements on the wharfing privileges in said city, together with the interest of the lessees or occupants in the premises, whether by lease, covenant or deed, shall be subject to taxation, as real estate. And the personal property of the owner of such improvements, shall be liable for such taxes, and upon a failure to pay the same, the collector may levy upon and sell the goods and chattels of such occupant, or lessee, for the payment thereof and costs. And in case such lessee or occupant shall have no personal estate, or neglect to pay the taxes, the interest of such lessee or occupant in such premises, together with the improvements, may be sold as real estate: *Provided*, The purchaser shall acquire no greater rights in the land than the tenant or occupant thereof had, but shall take the same, subject to all the covenants and agreements in relation thereto.

CHAPTER VI.

ASSESSMENTS FOR OPENING STREETS AND ALLEYS.

SECTION 1. The common council shall have power to lay out public squares or grounds, streets, alleys, lanes and highways, and to make wharves and slips at the ends of streets, and alter, widen, contract, straighten and discontinue the same. They shall cause all streets, alleys, lanes, highways, wharves, slips, or public squares or grounds, laid out by them, to be surveyed, described and recorded in a book to be kept by the clerk, showing particularly the proposed improvements, and the real estate required to be taken; and the same, when opened and made, shall be public highways.

SEC. 2. Whenever any street, alley, lane, highway, wharf, slip, or public square or ground, is laid out, altered, widened or straightened, by virtue hereof, the common council shall give notice of their intention to appropriate and take the land necessary for the same, to the owner or owners thereof, by publishing said notice for ten days in the corporation newspaper; at the expiration of which time, they shall choose, by ballot, three disinterested freeholders, residing in said city, as commissioners to ascertain and assess the damages and recompense due the owners of such lands, respectively, and at the same time to determine what persons will be benefited by such improvement, and assess the damages and expenses thereof, on the real estate of persons benefited, in proportion, as nearly as may be, to the benefits resulting to each. A majority of all the aldermen authorized by law to be elected, shall be necessary to the choice of such commissioners.

SEC. 3. The commissioners shall be sworn, faithfully to execute their duties according to the best of their ability. Before entering on their duties, they shall give notice to the persons interested, of the time and place of their meeting, for the purpose of viewing the premises and making their assessment, at least ten days before the time of such meeting, by publishing the same in the corporation newspaper. They shall view the premises, and, in their discretion, receive any legal evidence, and may, if necessary, adjourn from day to day.

SEC. 4. If there should be any building standing, in whole or in part, upon the land to be taken, the commissioners, before proceeding to make their assessment, shall first estimate and determine the whole value of such building to the owner, aside from the value of the land, and the injury to him in having such building taken from him, and secondly, the value of such building to him to remove.

SEC. 5. At least five days personal notice shall be given to the owner, of such determination, when known, and a resident of the city, or left at his usual place of abode. If not known, or a non-resident, notice to all persons interested shall be given, by publication for ten days in the corporation newspaper; such notice shall be signed by the commissioners, and specify the building and the award of the commissioners. It shall also require parties interested to appear, by a day to be named therein, or give notice of their election, to the common council, either to accept the award of the commissioners, and allow such building to be taken, with the land condemned or appropriated, or of their intention to remove such building, at the value set thereon by the commissioners to remove. If the owner shall agree to remove the building, he shall have such time for this purpose as the common council may allow.

SEC. 6. If the owner refuse to take the building at the value to remove, or fail to give notice of his election, as aforesaid, within the time prescribed, the common council shall have power to direct the sale of such building, at public auction, for cash, giving five days public notice of the sale. The proceeds of the sale shall be paid to the owner, or deposited to his use.

SEC. 7. The commissioners shall thereupon proceed to make their assessment, and determine and appraise, to the owner or owners, the value of the real estate appropriated for the improvement, and the injury arising to them, respectively, from the condemnation thereof, which shall be awarded to such owners respectively, as damages, after making due allowance therefrom for any benefit which such owners may respectively derive from such improvement. In the estimate of damage to the land, the commissioners shall include the value of the building, (if the property of the owner of such land,) as estimated by them, as aforesaid, less the proceeds of the sale thereof; or if taken by the owner at the value to remove, in that case they shall only include the difference between such value and the whole estimated value of such building.

SEC. 8. If the damage to any person be greater than the benefit received, or if the benefit be greater than the damage, in either case the commissioners shall strike a balance, and carry the difference forward to another column, so that the assessment may show what amount is to be received or paid by such owners, respectively, and the difference only shall in any case be collectable of them, or paid to them.

SEC. 9. If the lands and buildings belong to different persons, or if the land be subject to lease or mortgage, the injury done to such persons, respectively, may be awarded to them, by the commissioners, less the benefits resulting to them, respectively, from the improvement.

SEC. 10. Having ascertained the damages and expenses of such improvement, as aforesaid, the commissioners shall thereupon apportion and assess the same, together with costs of the proceedings, upon the real estate by them deemed benefited, in proportion to the benefits resulting thereto from the improvements, as nearly as may be, and shall describe the real estate upon which their assessments may be made. When completed, the commissioners shall sign and return the same to the common council, within forty days of their appointment.

SEC. 11. The clerk shall give ten days notice, in the corporation paper, that such assessment has been returned, and, on a day to be specified therein, will be confirmed by the common council, unless objections to the same are made by some person interested. Objections may be heard before the common council, and the hearing may be adjourned from day to day. The council shall have power, in their discretion, to confirm or annul the assessment, or refer the same back to the commissioners. If annulled, all the proceedings shall be void. If confirmed, an order of confirmation shall be entered, directing a warrant to issue for the collection thereof. If referred back to the same or other commissioners, they shall proceed to make their assessments and return the same, in like manner, and give like notices, as herein required, in relation to the first; and all parties in interest shall have the like notices and rights, and the common council shall perform like duties and have like powers in relation to any subsequent determination, as are herein given in relation to the first.

SEC. 12. The common council shall have power to remove commissioners, and, from time to time, appoint others in the place of such as may be removed, refuse, neglect, or be unable, from any cause, to serve.

SEC. 13. Nothing herein contained shall authorize the common council to discontinue or contract any street or highway, or any part thereof, except for the purpose of widening and improving the river, and making basins and slips, without the consent, in writing, of all persons owning land adjoining said street or highway.

SEC. 14. The land required to be taken for the making, opening or widening any street, alley, lane or other highway, shall not be appropriated until the damages awarded therefor, to any owner thereof, under this act, shall be paid or tendered to such owner or his agent, or, in case the said owner or his agent cannot be found in said city, deposited to his or their credit in some safe place of deposit other than the hands of the treasurer, and then, not before, such lands may be taken and appropriated for the purpose required in making such improvements, and such streets, alleys, lanes, highways, wharves and slips, may be made and opened.

SEC. 15. Where the whole of any lot or parcel of land or other premises under lease or other contract, shall be taken for any of the purposes aforesaid by virtue of this act, all the covenants, contracts and engagements between landlords and tenants, or any other contracting parties, touching, the same or any part thereof, shall, upon confirmation of such report, respectively cease and be absolutely discharged.

SEC. 16. Where part only of any lot or parcel of land or other premises so under lease or other contract, shall be taken for any of the purposes aforesaid, by virtue of this act, all the covenants, contracts, agreements and engagements respecting the same, upon the confirmation of such report, shall be absolutely discharged, as to the part thereof so taken, but shall remain valid as to the residue thereof, and the rents, considerations and payments reserved, payable and to be paid for or in respect to the same, shall be so proportioned as that the part thereof justly and equitably payable, for such residue thereof, and no more, shall be paid or recoverable for, in any respect, of the same.

SEC. 17. Any person interested may appeal from any final order of the common council, for opening or widening any street, alley, public ground or highway, to any court of record in Cook county, by notice in writing to the mayor or clerk, at any time before the expiration of thirty days after the passage of such final order. In case of appeal, the common council shall make a return within thirty days after notice thereof, and the court shall, at the next term after return filed in the office of the clerk thereof, hear and determine such appeal, and confirm or annul the proceedings; from which judgment, no appeal or writ of error shall lie. Upon the trial of the appeal, all questions involved in said proceedings, including the amount of damages, shall be open to investigation by affidavit or oral testimony, addressed to the court, and the burden of proof shall, in all cases, be upon the city, to show that the proceedings are in conformity with this act.

SEC. 18. The common council may, by ordinance, make any changes they may deem advisable, in the proceedings herein prescribed for ascertaining the damages and injury occasioned to any person or real estate by reason of the condemnation of any real estate upon which any buildings may be situate, in whole or in part, and the assessment of such damage and injury upon persons or real estate benefited by the improvement; and in such other respects as experience may suggest.

SEC. 19. In all cases where there is no agreement to the contrary, the owner or landlord, and not the occupant or tenant, shall be deemed the person who ought to bear and pay every assessment made for the expense of any public improvement. Where any such assessment shall be made upon or paid by any person, when by agreement or by law the same ought to be borne or paid by any other person, it shall be lawful for one so paying, to sue for and recover of the person bound to pay the same, the amount so paid, with interest. Nothing herein contained shall impair, or in any way affect, any agreement between any landlord and tenant, or other persons, respecting the payment of such assessments.

CHAPTER VII.

ASSESSMENTS FOR PUBLIC IMPROVEMENTS.

SECTION 1. The common council shall have power, from time to time—

First. To cause any street, alley or highway to be graded, leveled, paved, macadamized or planked, and keep the same in repair.

Second. To cause cross and sidewalks, main drains and sewers, private drains, and aqueducts, to be constructed and laid, relaid, cleansed and repaired, and regulate the same.

Third. To cause or authorize a tunnel, or tunnels, to be constructed under the Chicago river and its branches, at the intersection of any street.

Fourth. To grade, improve, protect and ornament any public square, now or hereafter laid out.

SEC. 2. The expenses of any improvement mentioned in the foregoing section, (except sidewalks and private drains,) shall be assessed upon the real estate in any natural division benefited thereby, with the costs of the proceedings therein, in proportion, as nearly as may be, to the benefits resulting thereto: *Provided*, Such assessment shall not exceed three per cent. per annum on the property assessed.

SEC. 3. The amount to be assessed for any such improvement, (except sidewalks and private drains,) shall be determined by the common council; and they shall, by ballot, appoint, by a majority of all the aldermen authorized by law to be elected, three reputable freeholders of the city to make such assessment. The commissioners shall be sworn, faithfully and impartially to execute their duty to the best of their ability.

SEC. 4. Before entering on their duties, the commissioners shall give six days notice in the corporation newspaper, of the time and place of meeting, to all persons interested, and they may, if necessary, adjourn from day to day. The commissioners shall assess the amount directed by the common council to be assessed, on the real estate by them deemed benefited by any such improvement, in proportion to the benefit resulting thereto, as nearly as may be, and briefly describe in the assessment roll to be made by them, the real estate in respect to which any assessment is made, and the value thereof.

SEC. 5. If the commissioners shall be of opinion that any owner of land situate upon any street, alley or other highway, graded or leveled under this section, will sustain damages over and above the benefits which may accrue to the owner of such land, by the improvement, they may assess such an amount as they may deem a reasonable recompense to such owner, upon the real estate benefited in the manner aforesaid; and such sum shall be added to their assessment roll, and the amount certified to the council, at the time of filing the roll.

SEC. 6. When the commissioners shall have completed their assessment, and made a corrected copy thereof, they shall deliver the same to the city clerk, within forty days after their appointment, signed by all the commissioners. The clerk shall thereupon cause a notice to be published in the corporation newspaper for six days, to all persons interested, of the completion of the assessment, and the filing of the roll. Time and place shall be designated therein for hearing objections.

SEC. 7. Any person interested may appeal to the common council for the correction of the assessment. Appeals shall be in writing, and filed in the clerk's office, within ten days after the first publication of said notice. The council may adjourn such hearing, from day to day, and shall have power, in case of appeal or otherwise, in their discretion, to revise and correct the assessment, and confirm or annul the same, and direct a new assessment to be made, in the manner herein before directed, by the same commissioners, or by three others, which shall be final and conclusive on all parties interested, if confirmed When confirmed, the assessment shall be collected as in other cases, and no appeal or writ of error shall lie in any case from such order and determination. If any assessment be set aside by order of any court, the common council may cause a new one to be made in like manner, for the same purpose, for the collection of the amount so assessed.

SEC. 8. If any vacancy happen in the office of commissioners, at any time, by reason of removal, failure or refusal, or inability, from sickness or other cause, to serve, the common council may fill such vacancy.

SEC. 9. If the first assessment prove insufficient, another may be made in the same manner; or, if too large a sum shall at any time be raised, the excess shall be refunded, rateably, to those by whom it was paid.

SEC. 10. All owners or occupants, in front of or upon whose premises the common council shall order and direct sidewalks, or private drains, communicating with any main drain, to be constructed, repaired, relaid or cleansed, shall make, repair, relay or clease such sidewalks or private drains at their own cost and charges, in the manner and within the timo prescribed by ordinance or otherwise, and if not done in the manner and within the time prescribed, the council may cause the same to be constructed, repaired, relaid or cleansed, and assess the expenses thereof, by an order to be entered in their proceedings, upon such lots, respectively, and collect the same, by warrant and sale of the premises, as in other cases. A suit may also be maintained against the owner or occupant of such premises, for recovery of such expenses, as for money paid and laid out to his use at his request.

SEC. 11. In all cases where expenses may be incurred in the removal of any nuisance, the common council may cause the same to be assessed against the real estate chargeable therewith, in the manner prescribed in the foregoing section. Such expenses shall be likewise collectable of the owner or occupant of such premises, in a suit for money expended to his or their use. In case the same should not be chargeable to any real estate, suit may, in like manner, be brought for such expenses, against the author of such nuisance, when known, or any person whose duty it may be to remove or abate the same.

SEC. 12. Commissioners appointed under this act may be sworn into office by the city clerk. They shall be allowed two dollars per day, each, for actual services, which, together with all other expenses in relation to any assessment made in pursuance of this act, shall be deemed part of the expenses of the improvement, and included therein. The city attorney shall prepare such papers and make such examinations as they may request.

SEC. 13. When any known owner residing in said city, or elsewhere, shall be an infant, and any proceedings shall be had under this act, the circuit court of the county of Cook, the judge thereof, the municipal court of said city, or any judge of the supreme court, or judge of probate of said county, may, upon the application of the common council, or such infant, or his next friend, appoint a guardian for such infant, taking security from such guardian for the faithful execution of such trust, and all notices and summons, required by this act, shall be served on such guardian.

CHAPTER VIII.

COLLECTION OF TAXES AND ASSESSMENTS.

SECTION 1. The common council shall have power, by ordinance, to prescribe the form of assessment rolls, and prescribe the duties and define the powers of assessors. They may also make such rules and give such directions in relation to revising, altering or adding to the rolls, as they may deem proper and expedient.

SEC. 2. The annual assessment rolls shall be returned by the assessors on or before the first Monday of August, in each year; but the time may be extended by order of the common council. On the return thereof, the common council shall fix a day for hearing objections thereto, and the clerk shall give notice of the time and place of such hearing; and any person feeling aggrieved by the assessment of his property, may appear at the time specified, and make his objections. The common council shall have power to supply omissions in said assessment roll, and for the purpose of equalizing the same, to alter, add to, take from, and otherwise correct and revise the same, or to refer the same back to the assessors, with instructions to revise and correct the same: *Provided*, The common council shall not have power to increase the aggregate amount of said roll, except by the value of such property, real or personal, as may have been omitted by the assessors.

SEC. 3. When the assessment rolls shall have been corrected and revised, the same shall be filed, and an order confirming the same, and directing the warrant to be issued for the collection thereof, shall be entered by the clerk. The common council shall thereupon, by an ordinance or resolution, levy such sum or sums of money, as may be sufficient for the several purposes for which taxes are herein authorized to be levied, (not exceeding the authorized per centage), particularly specifying the purpose for which the same are levied, and if not for general purposes, the division of the city upon which the same are laid.

SEC. 4. All taxes and assessments, general or special, levied or assessed by the common council under this act, shall be a lien upon the real estate upon which the same may be imposed, voted or assessed, for two years from and after the corrected assessment roll shall have been confirmed, and on personal estate from and after the delivery of the warrant for the collection thereof, until paid, and no sale or transfer shall affect the lien. Any personal property belonging to the debtor, may be taken and sold for the payment of taxes on real or personal estate: *Provided*, That in case the collection of any assessment shall be delayed by injunction or other judicial proceedings, the same shall continue a lien (unless set aside) upon such real estate, for the period of two years from and after the final disposition of such injunction or other judicial proceedings.

SEC. 5. The clerk shall issue a warrant or warrants for the taxes, and rule therein separate columns, in which the taxes levied shall be respectively set down opposite the name of the person or real estate subject thereto; each column shall be headed with the name of the tax therein set down.

SEC. 6. All warrants issued for the collection of general or special taxes and assessments, shall be signed by the mayor and clerk, with the corporate seal thereto attached, and shall contain true and perfect copies of the corrected assessment rolls upon which the same may be respectively issued. They shall be delivered to the collector or collectors of the city for collection within six weeks after the filing of the corrected rolls, unless further time shall be given for this purpose by the common council. If not otherwise paid, the collector shall have power to collect said taxes, with interest and cost, by suit in the corporate name, or by distress and sale of personal property, as aforesaid, after a demand and refusal to pay the same. The assessor's roll shall in all cases be evidence on the part of the corporation: *Provided*, A notice published by the collector for ten days in the corporation paper, shall be deemed a demand, and a neglect to pay taxes for twenty days thereafter, shall be deemed a refusal.

SEC. 7. All taxes and assessments, general or special, shall be collected by the collector or collectors, in the same manner and with the same power and authority as are given by law to collectors of county and State taxes. He shall pay the same, as fast as collected, into the city treasury; and his duty in regard to returning warrants, and settling with the city, and his liabilities in case of default or misconduct, shall be the same as prescribed by law: *Provided*, The common council shall have power to prescribe the powers, duties and liabilities of collectors, by ordinance.

SEC. 8. In case of the non-payment of any taxes or assessments levied or assessed under this act, the premises may be sold for the payment thereof, at any time within two years after the confirmation of the assessment by the common council. Before any such sale, an order shall be made by the common council, which shall be entered at large in the records kept by the clerk, directing the collector to sell, particularly describing the delinquent premises to be sold, and the assessment for which the sale shall be made; a certified copy of which order, under the corporate seal, signed by the mayor or presiding officer, and clerk, shall be delivered to the collector, which, together with the warrant, shall constitute the process upon which such sale may be made.

SEC. 9. The collector shall then advertise such premises in the corporation paper, for sale, for the period of thirty days from and after the first publication of such notice, describing the same by figures or otherwise, with the name of the owner when known, and the several amounts of the taxes or assessments thereon, and costs. Said notice shall also contain the time and place of sale, and shall be published at least four times. The proceedings may be stopped at any time on the payment of the taxes or assessments and interest, with expense of advertising.

SEC. 10. All sales shall be conducted in the manner required by law, but the common council shall have power to prescribe the manner of conducting the same. The sale shall be made for the smallest portion of ground (to be taken from the east side of the premises) for which any person will take the same and pay the taxes or assessments thereon, with interest and costs of sale. Duplicate certificates of sale shall be made and subscribed by the collector, one of which shall be delivered to the purchaser, and the other filed in the office of the clerk; which certificate shall contain the name of the purchaser, a description of the premises sold, the amount of tax or assessment, with the interest and expenses for which the same was sold, and the time when the right to redeem will expire. The collector shall be entitled to the same fees for selling as are allowed by law for similar services. The clerk shall keep a record of such sales, which shall be open to public inspection at all reasonable times.

SEC. 11. The right of redemption in all cases of sales for taxes or assessments, shall exist to the owner, his heirs, creditors or assigns, to the same extent as is allowed by law in the case of sales of real estate for taxes, on the payment, in specie, of double the amount for which the same was sold, and all taxes accruing subsequent to the sale, with interest. If the real estate of any infant, *feme covert*, or lunatic, be sold under this act, the same may be redeemed at any time within one year after such disability be removed. In case of redemption, the money may be paid to the purchaser, or for him to the city clerk, who shall make a special deposit thereof with the treasurer, taking his receipt therefor. If not redeemed according to law, the common council shall, upon the return of the certificate, or proof of its loss, direct a deed to be executed to the purchaser, under the corporate seal, signed by the mayor or presiding officer of the council, and countersigned by the clerk, conveying to such purchaser the premises so sold and unredeemed as aforesaid. An abstract of all deeds so made and delivered shall be entered by the clerk in the book where tax sales are recorded. A fee of one dollar may be charged by the clerk for every deed so issued.

SEC. 12. The assignee of any tax certificate, of any premises sold for taxes or assessments under authority of said city, shall be entitled to receive a deed of such premises, in his own name, and with the same effect as though he had been the original purchaser.

SEC. 13. If, at any sale of real or personal estate for taxes or assessments, no bid shall be made for any parcel of land, or any goods and chattels, the same shall be struck off to the city; and thereupon the city shall receive, in the corporate name, a certificate of the sale thereof, and shall be vested with the same rights as other purchasers at such sales.

SEC. 14. All deeds made to purchasers, of lots sold for taxes or assessments, by order of the council, shall be *prima facie* evidence, in all controversies and suits, in relation to the right of the purchaser, his or her heirs or assigns, to the premises thereby conveyed, of the following facts:

First. That the land or lot conveyed was subject to taxation or assessment at the time the same was advertised for sale, and had been listed or assessed in the time and manner required by law.

Second. That the taxes or assessments were not paid at any time before the sale.

Third. That the land conveyed had not been redeemed from the sale at the date of the deed. And shall be conclusive evidence of the following facts:

First. That the land or lot was advertised for sale in the manner and for the length of time required by law.

Second. That the land was sold for taxes or assessments as stated in the deed.

Third. That the grantee in the deed was the purchaser.

Fourth. That the sale was conducted in the manner required by law. And in all controversies and suits involving the title to land claimed and held under and by virtue of such deed, the person or persons claiming title adverse to the title conveyed by such deed, shall be required to prove, in order to defeat the said title, either that the land was not subject to taxation at the date of the sale; that the taxes or assessments had been paid; that the land had never been listed and assessed for taxation or assessment, or that the same had been redeemed according to the provisions of this act; and that such redemption was made for the use and benefit of the persons having the right of redemption under the laws of this State; but no person shall be permitted to question the title acquired by the said deed, without first showing that he, she or they, or the person under whom he, she or they claim title, had title to the land at the time of the sale, or that the title was obtained from the United States, or this State, after the sale, and that all taxes due upon the lands have been paid by such persons, or the person under whom he claims title as aforesaid.

CHAPTER IX.

FIRE DEPARTMENT.

SECTION 1. The common council, for the purpose of guarding against the calamities of fire, shall have power to prescribe the limits within which wooden buildings shall not be erected, or placed, or repaired, without the permission of the common council, and to direct that all and any buildings, within the limits prescribed, shall be made or constructed of fire-proof materials, and to prohibit the repairing or rebuilding of wooden buildings within the fire limits, when the same shall have been damaged to the extent of fifty per cent. of the value thereof, and to prescribe the manner of ascertaining such damage.

SEC. 2. The common council shall also have power—

First. To regulate the construction of chimneys so as to admit chimney sweeps, and to compel the sweeping and cleaning of chimneys.

Second. To prevent the dangerous construction and condition of chimneys, fire-places, hearths, stoves, stove pipes, ovens, boilers and apparatus used in and about any building or manufactory, and to cause the same to be removed, or placed in a safe or secure condition, when considered dangerous.

Third. To prevent the deposit of ashes in unsafe places, and to appoint one or more officers to enter into all buildings and inclosures, to discover whether the same are in a dangerous state, and to cause such as may be dangerous to be put in safe condition.

Fourth. To require the inhabitants to provide as many fire buckets, and in such manner and time as they shall prescribe, and to regulate the use of them in times of fire.

Fifth. To regulate and prevent the carrying on of manufactories dangerous in causing or promoting fire.

Sixth. To regulate and prevent the use of fire-works and fire-arms.

Seventh. To compel the owners or occupants of houses or other buildings, to have scuttles in the roofs, and stairs or ladders leading to the same.

Eighth. To authorize the mayor, aldermen, fire-wardens, or other officers of said city, to keep away from the vicinity of any fire, all idle and suspicious persons, and to compel all officers of said city, and other persons, to aid in the extinguishment of fires, and in the preservation of property exposed to danger thereat.

Ninth. And generally, to establish such regulations for the prevention and extinguishment of fires as the common council may deem expedient.

SEC. 3. The common council shall procure fire engines and other apparatus used for the extinguishment of fires, and have the charge and control of the same, and provide fit and secure engine houses and other places for keeping and preserving the same; and shall have power—

First. To organize fire, hook, hose, bag, ladder and ax companies.

Second. To appoint, during their pleasure, a competent number of able and reputable inhabitants of said city, firemen, to take the care and management of the engines, and other apparatus and implements used and provided for the extinguishment of fires.

Third. To prescribe the duties of firemen, and to make rules and regulations for their government, and to impose reasonable fines and forfeitures upon them for a violation of the same; and, for incapacity, neglect of duty or misconduct, to remove them.

SEC. 4. The chief and assistant engineers of the fire department, with the other firemen, shall take the care and management of the engines, and other apparatus and implements used and provided for the extinguishment of fires, and their duties and powers shall be defined by the common council.

SEC. 5. The members of the common council and firemen shall, during their term of service as such, be exempt from serving on juries in all courts of this State, and in the militia, and shall likewise be exempt from working out any road or street tax. The name of each fireman shall be registered with the clerk of the city, and the evidence to entitle him to the exemption provided in this section, shall be the certificate of the clerk, made within the year in which the exemption is claimed.

SEC. 6. Every fireman, who shall have faithfully served as such, in said city, for the term of ten years, shall be thereafter exempt from serving on juries in all courts in this State, or in the militia, except in case of war, invasion or insurrection; and the evidence to entitle such person to such exemption, shall be a diploma under the corporate seal, signed by the mayor and clerk.

CHAPTER X.

BOARD OF HEALTH.

SECTION 1. The board of health shall consist of three or more commissioners, to be appointed annually by the common council; and the mayor or presiding officer of the common council shall be president of said board, and the city clerk shall be clerk thereof, and keep minutes of its proceedings.

SEC. 2. It shall be the duty of health officers to visit every sick person who may be reported to the board of health, as hereinfter provided, and to report with all convenient speed, their opinion of the sickness of such person, to the clerk of the said board of health; and to visit and inspect, at the request of the president of said board, all boats or vessels coming or lying and being within the harbor of the city, which are suspected of having on board any pestilential or infectious disease, and all stores and buildings which are suspected to contain unsound provisions or damaged hides, or other articles, and to make report of the state of the same with all convenient speed to the clerk of the board of health.

SEC. 3. All persons in said city, not resident thereof, who shall be infected with any pestilential or infectious disease, and all things which in the opinion of said board shall be infected by or tainted with pestilential matter, and ought to be removed so as not to endanger the health of the city, shall, by order of said board, be removed to some proper place, not exceeding fifteen miles beyond the city bounds, to be provided by the board, at the expense of the person who may be removed, if able; and the board may order any furniture or wearing apparel to be destroyed, whenever they may judge it necessary for the health of the city, by making just compensation.

SEC. 4. In case any boat or vessel shall come or be within the harbor or jurisdiction of the city, and the said board of health shall believe that such boat or vessel is dangerous to the inhabitants of said city, in consequence of her bringing and spreading any pestilential or infectious disease among said inhabitants, or have just cause to suspect or believe that if said boat or vessel is suffered to remain within the harbor or jurisdiction aforesaid, it will be the cause of spreading among the said inhabitants any pestilential or infectious disease, it shall and may be lawful for the said board, by an order in writing, signed by the president for the time being, to order such boat or vessel to be forthwith removed to any distance, not exceeding fifteen miles beyoud the bounds of said city, after the delivery of such order to the owner or consignee of said boat or vessel, to quarantine, under such regulations and for such time as the council or the board of health may prescribe; and if the master, owner or consignee to whom such order shall be delivered, shall neglect or refuse to comply therewith, or if, after such removal, such master, owner or consignee shall neglect or refuse to obey the regulations which may be prescribed, the said president may enforce such removal or other regulations in such manner as the council may by ordinance direct; and such master, owner or consignee shall be considered guilty of a misdemeanor, and on conviction, shall be fined a sum not exceeding two hundred and fifty dollars, and imprisoned not exceeding six months in the jail of Cook county, or in the city bridewell or house of correction, by any court having cognizance thereof. The said fine shall be paid into the treasury.

SEC. 5. The health officers may be authorized by the common council, when the public interests require, to exercise, for the time being, such of the powers and perform such of the duties of marshal, street commissioner and constable, as the common council may, in their discretion, direct, and shall be authorized to enter all houses and other places, private or public, and boats or other vessels, at all times, in the discharge of any duty under this act.

SEC. 6. The common council shall have power to prescribe the powers and duties of the board of health, and to punish by fine or imprisonment, or both, any refusal or neglect to observe the orders and regulations of the board.

SEC. 7. Every person practicing physic in the city who shall have a patient laboring under any malignant or yellow fever, or other infectious or pestilential disease, shall forthwith make report thereof in writing to the clerk of said board; and for neglecting so to do, shall be considered guilty of a misdemeanor, and be liable to a fine of fifty dollars, to be sued for and recovered in any action of debt, in any court having cognizance thereof, with costs, for the use of said city.

CHAPTER XI.

SCHOOLS AND SCHOOL FUND.

SECTION 1. The school lands and school fund of township thirty-nine north, range fourteen east of the third principal meridian, shall be and the same are hereby vested in the city of Chicago. The common council shall at all times have power to do all acts and things in relation to said school lands and school fund, which they may think proper to their safe preservation and efficient management; and sell or lease said lands, and all canal or other lots or lands, or other property, which may have been or may hereafter be donated to the school fund, on such terms and at such times as the common council shall deem most advantageous; and, on such sale or sales, lease or leasings, to make, execute and deliver all proper conveyances, which said conveyances shall be signed by the mayor and countersigned by the clerk, and sealed with the corporate seal: *Provided*, That the proceeds arising from such sales shall be added to and constitute a part of the school fund.

SEC. 2. Nothing shall be done to impair the principal of said fund, or to appropriate the interest accruing from the same to any other purpose than the payment of teachers in the public schools in said township; and any school established in said township, without the limits of said city, shall be entitled to the same benefits and advantages from said fund, as it would be without the passage of this act, except as to donations which may have been or may hereafter be made to the same.

SEC. 3. The common council shall have power—

First. To erect, hire or purchase buildings suitable for school-houses, and keep the same in repair.

Second. To buy or lease sites for school-houses, with the necessary grounds.

Third. To furnish schools with necessary fixtures, furniture and apparatus.

Fourth. To establish, support and maintain schools, and supply the inadequacy of the school fund for the payment of city teachers, from school taxes.

Fifth. To fix the amount of compensation to be allowed to teachers.

Sixth. To prescribe the school books to be used, and the studies to be taught, in the different schools.

Seventh. To lay off and divide the city into school districts, and, from time to time, alter the same, or create new ones, as circumstances may require.

Eighth. To appoint seven inspectors, to be denominated "Board of School Inspectors;" also, three trustees of schools in each district.

Ninth. To establish and prescribe the powers and duties of the board of school inspectors and school trustees.

Tenth. And generally have and possess all the rights, powers and authority necessary for the proper management of schools, and the school lands and funds belonging to the township, with power to enact such ordinances as may be necessary to carry their powers and duties into effect.

SEC. 4. The school agent shall have the custody and management of the money, securities and property belonging to the school fund, subject to the direction of the common council.

SEC. 5. The school agent, before entering upon his duties, shall give bond in such amount and with such conditions and sureties as the common council may require. His compensation shall be paid out of the school fund; and he shall be subject, for misconduct in office, to the same penalties and imprisonment as school commissioners are or may be subject to by law.

SEC. 6. The school fund shall be kept loaned at interest at the rate of twelve per cent. per annum, payable semi-annually in advance. No loan shall be made hereafter for a longer period than ten years, and all loans, exceeding one hundred dollars, shall be secured by unincumbered real estate of double the value of the sum loaned, exclusive of the value of perishable improvements thereon. For sums of one hundred dollars and less, two good sureties, besides the principal, shall be required: *Provided*, The common council shall have power to reduce the rate of interest by a vote of two-thirds of all the aldermen elected.

SEC. 7. All notes and securities shall be taken, to the city of Chicago, for the use of the inhabitants of said township for school purposes, and in that name all suits, actions and every description of legal proceedings may be had.

SEC. 8. All expenses of preparing or recording securities shall be paid exclusively by the borrower.

SEC. 9. In the payment of debts of deceased persons, those due the school fund shall be paid in preference to all others, except expenses attending the last illness and funeral of the deceased, not including the physician's bill.

SEC. 10. If default be made in the payment of interest, or of the principal, when due, interest at the rate of fifteen per cent. upon the same, shall be charged from the default, and may be recovered by suit or otherwise. Suits may be brought for the recovery of interest only, when the principal is not due.

SEC. 11. All judgments recovered for interest or principal, or both, shall respectively bear interest at twelve per cent. per annum, from the rendition of judgment until paid; and in case of the sale of real estate thereon, the city of Chicago may become the purchaser thereof for the use of the school fund, and shall be entitled to the same rights given by law to other purchasers. On redemption, twelve per cent. interest shall be paid from the time of sale.

SEC. 12. No costs made in the course of any judicial proceedings, in which the city of Chicago, for the use of the school fund, may be a party, shall be chargeable to the school fund.

SEC. 13. If the security on any loan should, at any time before the same is due, become, in the united judgment of the school agent and common council, insecure, the agent shall notify the person indebted thereof; and unless further satisfactory security shall be forthwith given by the debtor, judgment may be recovered thereon as in other cases, although no condition to that effect be inserted in the note or other security.

SEC. 14. The common council shall annually publish, on the second Tuesday in February, in the corporation newspaper of the city, the number of pupils instructed in the year preceding, the several branches of education pursued by them, and the receipts and expenditures of each school, specifying the sources of such receipts, and the objects of such expenditures.

SEC. 15. The school tax shall be paid into the city treasury, and be kept a separate fund for the building of school-houses, and keeping the same in repair, and supporting and maintaining schools.

CHAPTER XII.

MISCELLANEOUS PROVISIONS.

SECTION 1. The common council shall, at least ten days before the annual election, in each year, cause to be published in two newspapers in said city, a full and correct statement of the receipts and expenditures from the date of the last annual report, together with the sources from whence the former are derived, and their mode of disbursement; and also a distinct statement of the whole amount assessed, received and expended in the respective wards and divisions for making and repairing roads, highways and bridges, for the same period, together with such other information as may be necessary to a full understanding of the financial concerns of the city.

SEC. 2. Neither the mayor or common council shall remit any fine or penalty imposed upon any person for the violation of the laws or ordinances of said city, or release from imprisonment, unless two-thirds of all the aldermen authorized to be elected, shall vote for such release or remission; nor shall anything in this act be so construed as to oust any court of jurisdiction to abate and remove nuisances, in the streets, or any other parts of said city, or within its jurisdiction, by indictment or otherwise.

SEC. 3. No vote of the common council shall be reconsidered or rescinded at a special meeting, unless at such special meeting there be present as large a number of aldermen as were present when such vote was taken.

SEC. 4. The cemetery lots which have or may hereafter be laid out and sold by said city for private places of burial, shall, with the appurtenances, forever be exempt from execution and attachment.

SEC. 5. Every ordinance, regulation or by-law, imposing any penalty, fine, imprisonment or forfeiture for a violation of its provisions, shall, after the passage thereof, be published one week in the corporation newspaper; and proof of such publication by the affidavit of the printer or publisher of said newspaper, taken before any officer authorized to administer oaths, and filed with the city clerk, or any other competent proof of such publication, shall be conclusive evidence of the legal publication and promulgation of such ordinance or by-law in all courts and places.

SEC. 6. All actions brought to recover any penalty or forfeiture incurred under this act, or the ordinances, by-laws or police regulations made in pursuance of it, shall be brought in the corporate name. It shall be lawful to declare, generally, in debt for such penalty or forfeiture, stating the clause of this act or the by-laws or ordinances under which the penalty or forfeiture is claimed, and to give the special matter in evidence under it.

SEC. 7. In all prosecutions for any violation of any ordinance, by-law, police or other regulation, the first process shall be a summons, unless oath or affirmation be made for a warrant, as in other cases.

SEC. 8. The common council shall have power to designate two or more justices of the peace in said city, who shall have jurisdiction in any actions for the recovery of any fine or penalty, under this act, or any ordinance, by-law or police regulation of the city council, anything in the laws of this State to the contrary notwithstanding; such justices shall have power to fine or imprison, or both, in their discretion, where discretion may be vested in them by the ordinance or regulation, or by this act. The mayor may hold a police court.

SEC. 9. Execution may be issued immediately on the rendition of judgment. If the defendant, in any such action, have no goods or chattels, lands or tenements, whereof the judgment can be collected, the execution shall require the defendant to be imprisoned in close custody in the jail of Cook county, or bridewell, or house of correction, for a term not exceeding six months, in the discretion of the magistrate or court rendering judgment; and all persons who may be committed under this section, shall be confined one day for each fifty cents of such judgment and costs. All expenses incurred in prosecuting for the recovery of any penalty or forfeiture, when collected, shall be paid to the treasurer for the use of the city.

SEC. 10. And any person or persons who shall injure or destroy any bridge, the construction of which may have been heretofore or may be hereafter authorized or permitted to be built by the common council, or any other public buildings or property belonging to said city, or shall cause or procure the same to be injured or destroyed, shall be subject to a penalty not exceeding five hundred dollars for each offense, to be recovered by the city in an action of debt, and may be imprisoned for a term not exceeding six months in the discretion of the magistrate before whom such conviction may be had, and such person or persons shall also be liable in a civil action at the suit of the city, for the damages occasioned by such injury or destruction.

SEC. 11. No person shall be an incompetent judge, justice, witness or juror, by reason of his being an inhabitant or freeholder in the city of Chicago, in any action or proceeding in which the said city shall be a party in interest.

SEC. 12. All ordinances, regulations and resolutions now in force in the city of Chicago, and not inconsistent with this act, shall remain in force. under this act, until altered, modified or repealed by the common council, after this act shall take effect.

SEC. 13. All actions, rights, fines, penalties and forfeitures, in suit or otherwise, which have accrued under the several acts consolidated herein, shall be vested in, and prosecuted by, the corporation hereby created.

SEC. 14. All property, real, personal or mixed, belonging to the city of Chicago, is hereby vested in the corporation created by this act; and the officers of said corporation, now in office, shall respectively continue in the same until superseded in conformity to the provisions hereof; but shall be governed by this act, which shall take effect from and after its passage.

SEC. 15. All ordinances of the city, when printed and published by authority of the common council, shall be received in all courts and places without further proof.

SEC. 16. This act shall be deemed a public act, and may be read in evidence without proof; and judicial notice shall be taken thereof in all courts and places.

SEC. 17. This act shall not invalidate any legal act done by the common council of the city of Chicago, or by its officers; nor divest their successors under this act, of any rights of property or otherwise, or liability which may have accrued to, or been created by, said corporation prior to the passage of this act.

SEC. 18. All officers of the city, created conservators of the peace by this act, shall have power to arrest, or cause to be arrested, with or without process, all persons who shall break or threaten to break the peace, commit for examination, and, if necessary, detain such persons in custody over night in the watch-house, or other safe place, and shall have and exercise such other powers as conservators of the peace, as the common council may prescribe.

SEC. 19. The city of Chicago shall not be liable in any case for the board or jail fees of any person who may be committed by any officer of the city, or by any magistrate, to the jail of Cook county, for any offense punishable under the laws of this State.

SEC. 20. Nothing in this act contained shall be so construed as to deprive the common council of said city of any power or authority conferred upon the same by the act incorporating said city, and the various acts amendatory thereto. But the common council shall possess and enjoy all the powers and authority heretofore conferred upon the same, except so far as such powers and authority have been expressly modified or repealed by this act, or the acts heretofore mentioned.

This act shall be deemed a public act, and take effect from and after its passage.

Approved February 14, 1851.

AN ACT to incorporate the Chicago City Hydraulic Company.

SECTION 1. *Be it enacted by the People of the State of Illinois, represented in the General Assembly*, That John B. Turner, Horatio G. Loomis, and Alson S. Sherman, be, and they are hereby named and constituted as a board of water commissioners for the city of Chicago; who, and their successors in office, shall be a body politic and corporate, by the name and style of the "Board of Water Commissioners of the City of Chicago," and by that name shall have perpetual succession, with power to contract, sue and be sued, to purchase, hold and convey personal and real estate, to have a common seal, to alter and break the same at pleasure, to make by-laws, and do all legal acts which may be necessary and proper to carry out the effect, intent and object of this act.

SEC. 2. The said commissioners shall hold their offices respectively for the term of three, four and five years; said commissioners shall, within sixty days after the passage of this act, decide by lot their respective terms, which decision shall be notified by a written statement to the common council of said city, which shall be entered of record on the books of said common council; and on the first Tuesday of April, in the year of our Lord one thousand eight hundred and fifty-four, and annually thereafter, there shall be an election held by the qualified voters of said city, in the same manner that elections are held for the election of mayor, for the election of one or more commissioners to fill all vacancies occasioned by the termination, in any manner, of the term of any commissioner under this act. All commissioners elected subsequent to the first election aforesaid, shall hold their office for the term of three years. And in case of the death or resignation of any of said commissioners, the remaining commissioners shall nominate some citizen of said city, being a qualified voter, to fill such vacancy, and shall present said citizen to the common council of said city for confirmation, who, if confirmed by said common council, shall have full power to act as such commissioner; but if the said common council shall refuse to confirm such nomination, said commissioners shall nominate another, and so on, until such confirmation shall be made; such person, when so confirmed, shall fill such vacancy until the next regular election of a commissioner, to be held after such confirmation.

SEC. 3. The said commissioners shall have power to loan, from time to time, for such time as they shall deem expedient, a sum of money not exceeding two hundred and fifty thousand dollars, upon the credit of said city of Chicago, and shall have authority to issue bonds pledging the faith and credit of said city for the payment of the principal and interest of said bonds; which bonds shall issue under the seal of said board of commissioners, and shall be signed by them, or a majority of them, and bear interest not exceeding ten per centum per annum. And it shall be the duty of said commissioners to keep an accurate register of all bonds issued by them, showing the number, date and amount of each bond, and to whom the same was issued; and it shall also be their duty to furnish to the clerk of said city a copy of such register, as soon as the same is made, which shall be preserved by said clerk, and copied into the records of said city.

SEC. 4. It shall be the duty of said commissioners to examine and consider all matters relative to supplying the city of Chicago with a sufficient quantity of pure and wholesome water, to be taken from lake Michigan, for the use of its inhabitants.

SEC. 5. The said commissioners shall have power, and it is made their duty, to employ engineers, surveyors, and such other persons as, in their opinion, may be necessary to enable them to perform their duties under this act.

SEC. 6. Said commissioners shall have the power, and it is hereby made their duty, as soon as may be after the necessary funds shall have been procured, as herein provided, to purchase such lot or lots of land, and to construct such buildings, machinery and fixtures, as shall be deemed necessary or desirable to furnish a full supply of water for public and private use in said city.

SEC. 7. Said commissioners shall have power to construct reservoirs, jets, and public and private hydrants, and to lay pipes in and through all the alleys and streets of said city; and also across all rivers and streams, not interfering with the navigation of the same; and with the consent of the common council of said city, to construct fountains in the public squares, or such other public grounds of said city as they shall deem expedient.

SEC. 8. The said commissioners shall, from time to time, assess the water rents to be paid for water used at each house or other building, against the occupant or occupants, owner or owners of such house or other building, upon such basis as they shall deem equitable; and such water rents shall become a continuing lien upon such house or other building, for the accommodation of which water shall have been introduced, and upon the land, or lot and house or other building, on which such house or other building stands, when said lot or land and building are owned by the same person or persons, from the time the water shall have been introduced as aforesaid.

SEC. 9. It shall be the duty of said commissioners to collect the rents so assessed; and in case any person or persons, so assessed, shall neglect to pay any such assessment for ten days after the time fixed for the payment thereof, of which notice shall be given in some newspaper published in said city, such notice to be at least ten days before the time fixed for the payment of such rents, said commissioners shall issue their warrants, under the seal of said corporation, directed to the marshal or any constable of said city, commanding him to make the amount specified in such warrant, being the amount due for water rent as aforesaid, together with the costs of advertising the same, and such fees as constables are entitled to by the laws of this State, in the levy and sale of personal property upon execution, out of goods and chattels of the person or persons so assessed as aforesaid; and the marshal or constable in such case may levy, under said warrant, upon any personal property of the person or persons against whom the same is issued, and sell the same at public auction, after giving ten days notice of the time and place of sale in some newspaper published in said city; and such warrants shall authorize the sale of any house or building on which any lien shall have attached as aforesaid, subject only to such *bona fide* incumbrances as shall have existed prior to the time of the introduction of such water as aforesaid.

SEC. 10. And when any such warrants shall be returned by said officer unsatisfied, the said commissioners shall proceed to sell said lands and lots, and building or buildings, when owned by the same person or persons as aforesaid, in the same manner and after having given the like notice as is required by the laws of this State for the sale of lands for taxes; and the certificate of sale in such cases, signed by either of said commissioners, shall have the same force and effect as the certificate required by law on the sale of lands for taxes as aforesaid. In case the said real estate shall be sold as aforesaid, and the person or persons owning the same shall neglect to redeem the same in manner provided by the laws of this State for the redemption of real estate on sale for taxes, the said commissioners may give a deed, under the seal of said corporation, of the said real estate so sold as aforesaid, to the purchaser or purchasers thereof, which deed shall be, as near as may be, the same, and shall have the like force and effect, as deeds given upon the sale of lands for taxes as provided by the laws of this State.

SEC. 11. The said commissioners shall also, from time to time, assess upon the person or persons occupying or owning any house or other building situated in the vicinity of any public hydrant, when said house or other building is not supplied by a private hydrant, such amount as, in their judgment, the occupant of such house or other building might be benefited by the use of such public hydrant; and such assessment, when so made, shall be a lien upon such house or other building, and upon the lot upon which the same may stand, when said house or other building and lot are owned by the same individual, in the same manner as herein before provided in case of private hydrants, and such assessments may be collected in the manner, in all respects, as herein before provided.

SEC. 12. It shall be the duty of said commissioners to construct hydrants of sufficient size and capacity, and in such localities as they shall deem desirable for the purpose of extinguishing fires; and they shall assess the houses and other buildings in the vicinity of the said hydrants, in the proportion in which they shall deem the same respectively benefited; and the said assessment shall be collected in the same manner as herein provided for the collection of the water rent assessed by said corporation.

SEC. 13. The said commissioners shall keep an accurate record of all proceedings, together with a list of all assessments for water rents, which shall be subject to inspection at all times; and may elect one of their own number to act as secretary of said board, or employ some other competent person for the purpose, as they may deem desirable.

SEC. 14. It shall be the duty of said commissioners to make report to the common council of said city, semi-annually, which report shall embrace a statement of the funds and securities of said corporation, and all debts due and owing to and from said corporation, together with an accurate account of their expenditures; which statement shall be certified by said commissioners, under oath, and shall be entered of record by the clerk of said city, and published in some newspaper in said city of Chicago.

SEC. 15. Whenever the receipts of said corporation, from water rents or other sources, shall accumulate so that there shall be a surplus, amounting to a sum of not less than five hundred dollars, not needed for the payment of the current expenses of said corporation, it shall be the duty of the commissioners to invest the same in some safe stocks, or upon other real or personal securities, under the direction and approval of the judge of the circuit court of Cook county, or some other judge in said county having chancery jurisdiction; such approval to be signified in writing under the hand of such judge. Such investment shall be made in the name of said corporation, and in such manner as to make the same available for the payment of the interest and principal of the bonds issued as aforesaid, as soon as may be. It shall be the duty of said commissioners to pay the interest on such bonds as fast as such surplus fund will permit, and also the principal as the bonds become due, as funds for such purpose shall, from time to time, accumulate. The said commissioners may, when they have funds for that purpose, purchase the bonds so issued as aforesaid, whether the same become due or not; and in case the said commissioners shall at any time not have funds on hand sufficient to meet any of the said bonds, at the time when they shall become due, they shall have the right to issue new bonds, for such amount, and on such time as they shall deem expedient, in the place of bonds so becoming due as aforesaid; the said old bonds to be canceled in the registry thereof, and the said new bonds to be recorded in the manner herein before provided.

SEC. 16. It shall be the duty of said commissioners, at least thirty days before the time fixed by the ordinance of said city for assessing city taxes, to make a special report to the common council of said city, what, if any, sum will be needed by said commissioners over and above the revenue of said corporation, to meet the payment of interest or principal of the bonds issued as aforesaid; and it shall be the duty of the common council to raise said amount by a special tax, in the same manner as general taxes, to be designated as water tax; and the said amount shall be paid over to the said corporation by the collector of said city.

SEC. 17. The salary of said commissioners, and also of the secretary of said board, shall be fixed by the common council of said city, from time to time, as soon as may be after the passage of this act, and after each election as herein provided, and the amount of such salary shall not be reduced during the term for which said commissioners shall be elected.

SEC. 18. Each commissioner, before entering upon the duties of his office, shall give bond to said city in such sum and with surety to the satisfaction of the common council of said city, conditioned for the faithful performance of his duties as such commissioner, and that he will faithfully disburse and account for all moneys coming under his control as such commissioner, the amount of which bond may be increased at any time, as the said common council may deem expedient.

SEC. 19. Said commissioners may purchase the corporate rights, and real and personal property, fixtures and stock of every name and description, of the Chicago hydraulic company, on such terms as may be agreed upon between said commissioners and said company; and when such purchase shall be made, the said commissioners shall succeed to and become invested with all the powers, rights, privileges and immunities exercised and enjoyed by the Chicago hydraulic company, under their charter, and shall continue to supply water to the citizens of Chicago, under the same, and collect the money and rents therefor, in all respects as fully and effectually as the Chicago hydraulic company can or may do, until the said commissioners, acting under the provisions of this act, shall have completed their arrangements, machinery, engines, pipes, buildings, and other things provided for in this act, for the purpose of supplying the said city with pure and wholesome water; after which time the said Chicago hydraulic company, and their said charter, shall become extinct and null: *Provided, always*, That if the said commissioners cannot agree with the said Chicago hydraulic company as to what sum shall be paid the said Chicago hydraulic company for their property, rights and privileges, then the said company shall have the right to establish, by satisfactory proof, the actual cost of their said property, before the judge of the circuit court of Cook county, upon petition to him in term time or vacation; and no greater sum shall be paid for the same than the said judge shall decide the actual cost to have been.

SEC. 20. This act may at any time be altered, repealed or amended.

SEC. 21. All materials procured, or partially procured, under a contract with the commissioners, shall be exempt from execution, but it shall be the duty of the commissioners to pay the money due for such materials to the judgment creditor of the contractor under whose execution such materials might otherwise have been sold, upon his producing to them due proof that his execution would have so attached, and such payment shall be held a valid payment on the contract.

SEC. 22. No one or more of the said commissioners shall be interested, either directly or indirectly, in any contract entered into by them with any other person; nor shall they be interested, directly or indirectly, in the purchase of any material to be used or applied in and about the uses and purposes contemplated by this act.

SEC. 23. The said commissioners, or either of them, may be removed from office by the judge of the circuit court of Cook county, upon petition presented to him in term time or in vacation, by the common council of the city of Chicago, or if it shall appear, after hearing and proof before said judge, that the said commissioners, or either of them, have been guilty of misfeasance or malfeasance in office, or any breach of duty, either of commission or omission, under this act; and if the said judge shall remove any two or more of said commissioners from office for any cause before the expiration of the term of their office, he is hereby authorized and empowered to appoint others in their stead, who shall fill such offices for and during the unexpired term of such commissioners so removed.

SEC 24. The said commissioners shall adopt such plan as in their opinion shall be most advantageous for procuring such supply of water, and shall ascertain, as near as may be, what amount of money will be necessary to carry the same into effect. The said commissioners shall make a report of their proceedings, containing a full statement and description of the plans adopted by them, an estimate of the expense thereof, together with an estimate of the probable amount of revenue to accrue to the city, upon the completion of the work, with the reason and calculations upon which their opinions may be formed, and all such other information connected with the object of their appointment as they may deem important.

SEC. 25. Such report shall be made and presented to the common council by the said commissioners, together with all such conditional contracts as may have been made by them by virtue of this act, on or before the first day of January, which will be in the year of our Lord one thousand eight hundred and fifty-two.

SEC. 26. The said commissioners are hereby authorized to enter upon any land or water, for the purpose of making surveys, and to agree with the owner of any property which may be required for the purposes of this act, as to the amount of compensation to be paid to such owner.

SEC. 27. In case of a disagreement between the commissioners and the owners of any property which may be required for the said purposes, or affected by any operation connected therewith, as to the amount of compensation to be paid to such owner, or in case any such owner shall be an infant, a married woman, or insane, or absent from the State, the judge of the circuit court of Cook county may, upon the application of either party, nominate and appoint three different persons to examine such property, and to estimate the value thereof, or damage sustained thereby, and to report thereon to the said court without delay.

SEC. 28. Whenever such report shall have been confirmed by the said circuit judge of Cook county, the said commissioners shall, within two months thereafter, pay to the said owner, or to such person or persons as the court may direct, the sum mentioned in said report, in full compensation for the property required, or for the damage sustained, as the case may be, and thereupon the said commissioners shall become seized in fee of such property so required, and shall be discharged from all claim by reason of any such damage.

SEC. 29. If any person shall willfully do, or cause to be done, any act whereby any work, materials or property whatever, enacted or used within the city of Chicago or elsewhere, by the said commissioners, or by any person acting under their authority, for the purpose of securing or keeping a supply of water, shall in any manner be injured, or shall willfully pollute the water, shall be guilty of a misdemeanor, and, upon conviction, shall be punished therefor as other misdemeanors are punished.

SEC. 30. All contracts for materials, or for the construction of the work, shall be in writing, and of each contract two copies shall be taken, which shall be numbered, and indorsed with the date of the contract and with the name of the contractors, and a summary of the work to be done or materials to be furnished; one copy of which shall be retained by the said commissioners, and the other copy of which shall be filed with, and kept and preserved by, the clerk of the common council among the files of said office.

SEC. 31. Public notice shall be given of the time and place at which sealed proposals will be received for entering into contracts. All sealed proposals for contracts shall be for a sum certain as to the price to be paid or received, and no proposition which is not thus definite and certain, or which contains any alternative condition or limitation as to price, shall be received or acted upon.

SEC. 32. No more than one proposition shall be received from any one person for the same contract, and all the propositions of the person offering more than one shall be rejected.

SEC. 33. Every person who shall enter into any contract for the supply of materials or the performance of labor, shall give satisfactory security to the commissioners for the faithful performance of his contract according to his terms.

Approved February 15, 1851.

AN ACT concerning Fines and Forfeitures within the Limits of the Cities of Belleville and Chicago.

SECTION 1. *Be it enacted by the People of the State of Illinois, represented in the General Assembly*, That hereafter all fines and forfeitures collected for penalties incurred within the incorporated limits of the city of Belleville, in St. Clair county, shall be paid into the treasury of said city by the officers collecting the same.

SEC. 2. The provisions of the preceding section shall apply to and be in force in the city of Chicago.

SEC. 3. This act shall be in force from and after its passage.

Approved February 17, 1851.

AN ACT to provide for Township Organization.

ARTICLE TWENTY-FIFTH—SEC. 3.

The several wards in the city of Chicago shall be entitled to elect one supervisor in each ward, in addition to the township supervisors, and the several supervisors so elected shall be members of the board of supervisors of Cook county, and shall have, possess and enjoy, all the rights, powers and privileges that are now, or hereafter shall be possessed and enjoyed by the several township supervisors when voting as a county court. The election for such supervisors to be held at the same time and in the same manner as the election for township supervisors.

* * * * * * * * * *

Approved February 17, 1851.

AN ACT to amend an Act entitled "An Act to incorporate the Chicago City Hydraulic Company."

SECTION 1. *Be it enacted by the People of the State of Illinois, represented in the General Assembly*, That the commissioners named in "An Act to incorporate the Chicago city hydraulic company," approved February 15, 1851, and their successors in office, be and they are hereby authorized and empowered to loan, from time to time, as they shall deem expedient, in addition to the sum named in the said act, the sum of one hundred and fifty thousand dollars, in the same manner and upon the same terms, conditions, guarantees and securities named in the same act; and this act to be an amendment to and form a part of the said act to incorporate the Chicago hydraulic company herein mentioned: *Provided*, That no higher rate of interest than seven per centum per annum shall be paid for any such loan made by authority of this act.

Approved June 15, 1852.

AN ACT to amend an Act entitled "An Act to reduce the Law incorporating the City of Chicago, and the several Acts amendatory thereof, into one Act, and to amend the same," and to amend an Act to charter the City of Peru.

SECTION 1. *Be it enacted by the People of the State of Illinois, represented in the General Assembly*, That so much of the thirteenth division of the fourth section of the fourth chapter of the act entitled "An Act to amend an act to reduce the law incorporating the city of Chicago, and the several acts amendatory thereof, into one act, and to amend the same," approved February fourteenth, eighteen hundred and fifty-one, as authorizes the issuing or granting of licenses for the sale of wines or other liquors, ardent, vinous or fermented, at retail, and all and every other section or part of said herein named and recited act as authorizes the issuing or granting of licenses for the sale of wines or other liquors, ardent, vinous or fermented, at retail, in less quantities than one quart, be and the same is and are hereby repealed.

SEC. 2. That so much of section one, article fifth, of an act entitled "An Act to charter the city of Peru," approved February thirteenth, eighteen hundred and fifty-one, as authorizes the city council to license, tax and regulate groceries, taverns, tippling houses and dram shops, and all and every other section or part of section of said act as authorizes the issuing or granting licenses for the sale of spirituous liquors, be and the same are hereby repealed.

Approved June 23, 1852.

AN ACT to prohibit the Sale of Intoxicating Drinks.

SECTION 1. *Be it enacted by the People of the State of Illinois, represented in the General Assembly*, That all laws or parts of laws which were in force in relation to the granting of license to persons for the purpose of retailing spirituous, vinous or mixed liquors, at the time of the passage of an act entitled "An Act to prohibit the retailing of intoxicating drinks," approved February first, eighteen hundred and fifty-one, be and are hereby re-enacted and in full force and effect, as if never repealed: *Provided*, That no license shall be granted to any person for a less sum than fifty dollars, nor more than three hundred dollars per annum. This act shall take effect from and after its passage. *And provided further*, That a grocery shall be deemed to include all houses and places where spirituous or vinous liquors are retailed by less quantity than one gallon. The act entitled "An Act to amend 'An Act to reduce the law incorporating the city of Chicago, and the several acts amendatory thereof, into one act, and to amend the same,' and to amend an act to charter the city of Peru," be and the same hereby is repealed, and the provisions therein repealed are hereby revived and re-enacted.

Approved February 12, 1853.

AN ACT amendatory of an Act entitled "An Act to reduce the Law incorporating the City of Chicago, and the several Acts amendatory thereof, into one Act, and to amend the same," approved February 14, 1851.

SECTION 1. *Be it enacted by the People of the State of Illinois, represented in the General Assembly*, That the corporate limits and jurisdiction of the city of Chicago, shall be and the same are hereby so extended as to embrace and include within the same, the several tracts of land hereinafter described, which shall be deemed parts of the divisions of the said city named in connection therewith, as follows:

North Division. All those parts of sections thirty-one and thirty-two, in township forty north, range fourteen east, lying east of the centre of the north branch of the Chicago [river,] and the west half of section thirty-three in the same township and range.

South Division. All of fractional section twenty-seven, in township thirty-nine north, range fourteen east, and so much of the shore and bed of the lake as lie within one mile east of the said section, and all of that part of section twenty-eight in the same township and range, lying south and east of the south branch of the Chicago river.

West Division. And all those parts of sections twenty-eight, twenty-nine and thirty, in township thirty-nine north, range fourteen east, lying north of the south branch of the Chicago river, and the branch thereof running west through said section thirty.

SEC. 2. The land above described as constituting a part of the north division of said city, shall form a part of the seventh ward; the land above described as constituting a part of the west division, shall form a part of the fifth ward; and the boundary lines of the first, second, third and fourth wards of said city, shall be respectively extended south over the lands above described as constituting a part of the south division.

SEC. 3. Hereafter it shall be lawful for the city clerk to compute together as one tax, any two or more of the taxes levied by the common council, which may be general to the whole city or to any division thereof, and include the total amount of the taxes so computed together as one tax, in all warrants, orders of sale, or other proceedings in relation to the collection of taxes under the act to which this is amendatory: *Provided*, That in all cases where taxes may be so computed together, the clerk shall designate at the head of the proper column, the names and rates of the several taxes which may be included together.

SEC. 4. This act shall be deemed a public act, and shall take effect from and after its passage. So much of the act approved February 23, 1847, creating South Chicago school district, as includes the lands herein described within said district, is hereby repealed. And no tax shall hereafter be levied upon the same by virtue of said act.

Approved February 12, 1853.

AN ACT to remedy a Defect in the Laws in relation to Elections in the Towns of North Chicago, South Chicago and West Chicago.

SECTION 1. *Be it enacted by the People of the State of Illinois, represented in the General Assembly*, That each and every ward of the city of Chicago shall constitute an election precinct, and the judges of election, and the place of holding elections therein, for State and county officers, shall be appointed by the common council of said city, in the same manner that inspectors and judges of city elections are appointed; and so much and such parts of the respective towns of North Chicago, West Chicago and South Chicago, as are not included in any ward of said city, if any, shall respectively constitute election precincts, to be styled, respectively, North Chicago precinct,

South Chicago precinct, and West Chicago precinct, and the judges of elections, and respective places of holding elections therein, shall be appointed by the board of supervisors of Cook county: *Provided*, That there shall be but one place of holding elections in each of said precincts. All elections for State and county officers in said wards and precincts shall be conducted, and returns thereof made to the county clerk, as provided by the law regulating State and county elections.

This act shall take effect and be in force from and after its passage.

Approved February 12, 1853.

AN ACT amendatory of an Act entitled "An Act to reduce the Law incorporating the City of Chicago, and the several Acts amendatory thereof, into one Act, and to amend the same, approved February 14, 1851.

SECTION 1. *Be it enacted by the People of the State of Illinois, represented in the General Assembly*, That the corporate limits and jurisdiction of the city of Chicago shall be and the same are hereby extended to lake Michigan, and shall include so much of the waters and bed of said lake as lie within one mile of the shore thereof, and east of the present boundaries of the city.

SEC. 2. That whenever, at any general or special election, there shall be more than one vacancy in the office of alderman, to be filled at each election in any ward, the candidate having the highest number of votes for such office shall be declared elected for the longest term, and the candidate having the next highest number for the shortest; and in case any two or more candidates shall have an equal number of votes for such office, the election, as also the terms of service to which the successful candidates shall be respectively entitled, shall be determined by the casting of lots in the presence of the council: *Provided*, The common council may, in its discretion, direct the clerk, in its presence, to cast lots for the purposes aforesaid; as also, in any case where two or more candidates for any other elective office shall have an equal number of votes for the same office.

SEC. 3. That the vacancy occurring by operation of law in the board of water commissioners on the first Tuesday of April next, shall be filled by a qualified voter of the west division; the vacancy in like manner occurring therein in April, 1855, shall be filled by a qualified voter of the north division, and the vacancy in like manner occurring therein in April, 1856, shall be filled by a qualified voter of the south division. The said commissioners shall be elected by the general vote of the city, and the respective successors of the persons so elected shall thenceforth be elected or appointed from the divisions respectively represented by them: *Provided*, No person shall be eligible to such office who has not been a resident of the division in which such vacancy shall occur, for at least one year prior to the election or appointment; and a removal from the division by any member of said board for which he was elected, shall be deemed a resignation of his office.

SEC. 4. Every fireman who shall have faithfully served as such in the said city for the term of seven years, shall be entitled to the exemptions of the act to which this is amendatory.

SEC. 5. That the city marshal shall be elected at the next election for the term of two years, and biennially thereafter, and shall be ineligible to the same office for the term next succeeding the term for which he was elected.

SEC. 6. That the common council shall have power to borrow, upon the faith of the city, one hundred thousand dollars for the use of the water works, if the council shall hereafter deem such loan advisable: *Provided*, Two-thirds of all the aldermen elected shall concur therein.

SEC. 7. That it shall be lawful for the recorder's court to sentence criminals convicted of offenses committed in the city of Chicago, punishable by imprisonment in the county jail, to imprisonment in the city bridewell, to be there kept at labor.

SEC. 8. The common council may, whenever it shall deem it expedient so to do, elect a superintendent of special assessments, whose duty it shall be, when required, to act as one of the commissioners of special assessments, in any case where commissioners of special assessments are required to be selected or chosen by the council, and in no such case shall it be necessary to choose more than two other commissioners of special assessments; and the council may, in their discretion, appoint the said superintendent to act alone in making such assessments, in which case he shall be governed by the law in making such assessments, so far as the same may be applicable.

SEC. 9. Such superintendent shall have the general management of all special assessments and enforcement thereof, subject to the control of the council; and shall, when appointed, hold his office until the council shall elect another person in his place, or declare the office vacant.

SEC. 10. That the city council shall have power to purchase and improve suitable grounds for a house of refuge and correction, to erect buildings thereon, and adopt such rules and regulations for the government and the punishment of juvenile offenders therein, as they may from time to time deem expedient and just.

SEC. 11. That the common council shall have power to authorize the building of a tunnel or tunnels under the Chicago river and branches, and allow toll to be charged on the same, and to fix the rate thereof.

SEC. 12. That the common council shall have power to pay to the recorder of the city of Chicago, such compensation from time to time as said council may deem proper, in addition to the salary now prescribed by law.

SEC. 13. Any person owning or interested as proprietor in any real estate in said city, whose interests or property shall be injuriously affected by any encroachment upon, or occupying, or use of the public grounds, waters, streets, alleys or other public property of said city, or situate therein for private use or for the use of any corporation, or individual or individuals, without authority of law, shall have the right to apply to the courts by petition, for the protection of his or her rights, and upon such application, or the hearing of such petition, the court shall grant him or her such relief, by injunction or otherwise, as may be necessary to protect him or her from such injury: *Provided*, That nothing herein contained shall affect or apply to the settlement or adjustment, or acts authorized under the following acts, to wit: "An act to adjust and settle the title to the wharfing privileges in Chicago, and for other purposes," approved February 27, 1847, and "An Act to amend an act entitled 'An Act to adjust and settle the title to the wharfing privileges in Chicago, and for other purposes,' approved February 27, 1847, and 'in relation to wharves and docks in said city,'" approved February 11, 1853, but all such acts are hereby ratified and confirmed.

SEC. 14. The city shall cause a map or maps of the wharfing lots in the original town of Chicago to be made and certified by the city surveyor, and acknowledged by the mayor, and recorded in the recorder's office of Cook county. And the premises contained therein may be hereafter known and described in all conveyances or other papers, by the number of the wharfing lots as laid down on such map or maps. The map of the wharfing lots on the south side of Chicago river, heretofore caused to be recorded by the mayor in the recorder's office of Cook county, shall be taken to be made and recorded in conformity with this section, and shall have the same effect as if made and recorded subsequently to the passage of this act.

SEC. 15. To regulate and prohibit the keeping of any lumber yard, and the placing, piling or selling lumber, timber, wood or other combustible material within the fire limits of said city.

SEC. 16. That hereafter the said city of Chicago may annually levy and collect a tax, not exceeding one mill on the dollar per annum, on the real and personal estate, to meet the interest accruing on the bonded debt of the city, and that section two, of article one, chapter five, of the act to which this is amendatory, be and the same is hereby repealed.

SEC. 17. Whenever the expenditures in any division of the city shall have exceeded the amount to which it is entitled, in proportion to the annual revenue for general purposes derived from each division, the common council shall have power to collect such excess of expenditures by special *pro rata* assessment on the division, based upon the valuation of real and personal estate as contained in the last annual assessment roll, and may immediately issue a warrant for the same, and enforce the collection thereof in the manner heretofore prescribed for the collection of the annual revenue.

SEC. 18. This act shall take effect from and after its passage.

Approved February 28, 1854.

AN ACT to incorporate a Board of Sewerage Commissioners for the City of Chicago.

SECTION 1. *Be it enacted by the People of the State of Illinois, represented in the General Assembly*, That as soon as practicable after the next regular election for city officers in the city of Chicago, and within thirty days thereafter, there shall be elected by the common council of said city, three persons to serve as sewerage commissioners, one for the south, north and west divisions of said city respectively, who shall each be residents and freeholders of the respective districts for which they are elected: *Provided*, That no election shall be gone into by the said common council, of the said sewerage commissioners, until such election shall have been duly ordered at a previous meeting of said council; and such persons shall be named and constituted as a board of sewerage commissioners for the said city of Chicago, who, and their successors in office, shall be a body politic and corporate, by the name and style of the "Board of Sewerage Commissioners," and by that name shall have perpetual succession, with power to contract, sue and be sued, to purchase, hold and convey personal and real estate, to have a common seal, to alter and break the same at pleasure, and to make by-laws, and to do all legal acts which may be necessary and proper to carry out the effect, intention and object of this act: *Provided*, That if from any cause an election shall fail to be made within said thirty days, the same may be made at any time thereafter: *And provided further*, That no person shall be considered elected to said office unless he shall receive a majority of the votes of all the aldermen by law authorized to be elected: *Provided*, That no real estate shall be purchased without the approval of the council first had to each purchase, and that the title to all real estate purchased shall be taken in the name of the city of Chicago for the use of said commissioners.

SEC. 2. The said commissioners first elected shall hold their offices for the term of two, three and four years; the common council shall, forthwith after the election of said commissioners, decide by lot their respective terms, which decision shall be notified to the said commissioners by a written statement, signed by the clerk of said city, which shall also be entered of record on the books of the said common council, and at the same time provided by law for the election of water commissioners for said city; or in case no such election shall be had, then, on the first Tuesday in May, 1857, and annually thereafter, there shall be elected, by the qualified voters in said city, in the same manner that elections are made of mayor, one commissioner, to fill the vacancy occasioned by the termination of the term of one of the said commissioners under this act. All commissioners elected subsequent to said first election shall hold their office for the term of three years, and in case of the death, resignation or removal of any one of said commissioners, the vacancy shall be filled by the election, by the common council, of some citizen of said city, duly qualified and resident as aforesaid, who shall have power to act as such commissioner until the expiration of the term of the said commissioner in whose place he is appointed.

SEC. 3. The said commissioners shall have power to borrow, from time to time, as they shall deem expedient, a sum not exceeding five hundred thousand dollars, upon the credit of the said city of Chicago, and shall have authority to issue bonds pledging the faith and credit of said city for the payment of the principal and interest of said bonds, which shall be signed by them, and may be payable at such place and in such currency as they shall deem expedient, and bear interest not exceeding seven per cent. per annum. And it shall be the duty of said commissioners to keep an accurate register of all bonds and all interest coupons issued by them, showing the number, date and amount of each bond and coupon, to whom payable, and on account of which sewerage district the same was issued, and to whom the same was issued; and it shall also be their duty to furnish to the clerk of the said city, a copy of such register as soon as the same is made, which shall be preserved by said clerk, and copied into the records of said city, which said list shall particularly specify the bonds and coupons issued for each respective sewerage district: *Provided*, That the said commissioners shall not sell the said bonds, whatever rate of interest the same may bear, at a rate which will yield over seven per cent. per annum: *Provided further*, That no bonds shall be issued until the common council shall have approved of such issue, by a vote of a majority of all the aldermen by law authorized to be elected: *And provided*, That all bonds issued, before they shall be binding upon said city, shall be marked approved by the mayor and clerk of said city, under the seal of said city, and that such signature and seal shall be conclusive evidence to the holders of said bonds of the fact of such approval.

SEC. 4. It shall be the duty of the said commissioners to examine and consider all matters relative to the thorough, systematic and effectual drainage of the city of Chicago, not only of surface water and filth, but also of the soil on which said city is situated, to a sufficient depth to secure dryness in cellars and entire freedom from stagnant water, and in such manner as best to promote the healthfulness of said city.

SEC. 5. The said commissioners shall have power to offer rewards for the best system of drainage for said city, to call the attention of scientific men to the subject by advertisement of such rewards in the papers of other cities of the United States, and in foreign papers. and generally to do whatever in their judgment shall be found necessary or desirable to obtain the benefit of all the information and experience on said subject which is to be had.

SEC. 6. The said commissioners shall have power to employ engineers, surveyors, and such other persons as, in their opinion, may be necessary to enable them to perform their duties under this act; also to purchase such books, charts and other works as may be found necessary or useful, and to cause such surveys to be made of said city as may be required.

SEC. 7. There shall be three sewerage districts in said city, corresponding to the three divisions of the city, which districts shall be known and designated as south sewerage district, north sewerage district, and west sewerage district; and the entire amount of tax raised in each of said districts, as hereinafter provided, shall be expended in such district, and the accounts of the receipts and expenditures for each district shall always be kept separate and distinct from the other districts.

SEC. 8. It shall be the duty of the said commissioners, before entering upon the construction of any sewer in either of said districts, to fix upon a plan or system of sewerage for said entire district, of such a nature that all the subsequent sewerage of said district may be executed upon said plan: *Provided, also*, That the respective sewers which are constructed under this act, shall be constructed in such manner that every sewer, so far as built, shall be capable of beneficial use, independent of the further extension of such sewer or of the construction of any other sewer or sewers.

SEC. 9. After the said commissioners shall have fixed upon a plan for the sewerage of either of the said districts, they shall publish the same in full, with the estimates of the cost thereof, and with such drainage plans, maps and explanations as shall enable the public to fully understand the same, and shall cause copies of the same to be circulated in the said city.

SEC. 10. The commissioners shall cause to be printed with said plan, and also in the corporation newspaper of said city, a notice to the effect that the said board had fixed upon the said plan of sewerage specified in said printed publication for the said district, and would receive written objections to the same at any time within thirty days after the date of said notice.

SEC. 11. Any person, whether a citizen of said city or not, shall have the right of filing with the said commissioners, written objections to the said plan, stating therein the nature and reasons of their said objections, and may also suggest improvements to said plan.

SEC. 12. It shall be the duty of the said board to report officially to the common council the adoption of said plan, and to send a copy of the same to them immediately upon the publication thereof; and the common council shall thereupon take the same into consideration, and subject the same to the examination of one or more engineers or mechanics, if they shall deem expedient, and shall return to the said board as soon as practicable and within the said thirty days from their receiving a copy of said plan, a statement in writing, properly attested, of their objections to the said plan, if any, or of any alterations and improvements thereof which they may deem desirable: *Provided*, That an extension of the time for making such objections to a period not exceeding sixty days shall be allowed by said board, if so requested at a regular meeting of the council, by a vote of two-thirds of the members present at such meeting.

SEC. 13. After tho expiration of the time limited for making objections to the said plan, the said board shall revise and reconsider the same with all the objections, if any, which may have been made to the same, and shall thereupon proceed to adopt, or reject, or modify the same, as they shall find necessary or advisable.

SEC. 14. If the said board shall, upon such reconsideration, find it necessary or expedient to reject the said plan so published as aforesaid, they shall forthwith prepare another plan, which shall be published and subjected to the same course of objection and revision as herein provided for the first plan, and so on until some plan so published shall be substantially adopted by them: *Provided, however*, That the said board shall be at liberty, after receiving said objections to said published plan, to modify and change said plan in such a way as to obviate any of the difficulties suggested, without causing the said amended or altered plan to be submitted to the public for further objections.

SEC. 15. In case the said board shall, after receiving the said objections, make any material alteration in said plan, but not of such a character as to amount to an entirely new plan, they shall forthwith report the said plan, so altered and amended, to the common council, who shall, within ten days, report in writing to the said board their objections, if any, to said amended plan, and the said board shall thereupon reconsider said amended plan and said objections, and may adopt or reject the same, or make further changes therein, and such course shall be pursued until the said board shall adopt, without material alteration, the plan as by them last submitted to said common council. It being the intention hereof that every essentially new plan proposed shall be submitted to the examination and objections of the citizens of said city and of the common council for thirty days, and that every material change or improvement of such plan, not amounting to an entire change of plan, shall be submitted to the examination and objections of the common council for ten days, and so on until the said board shall, after such revision and objection, have adopted the plan as proposed or amended, without further material alteration; but the final responsibility of adopting a plan shall in all cases rest upon said board, and it shall have the right to adopt any plan which it shall decide upon, notwithstanding the objections made thereto, if, after giving the said objections such consideration as said board shall deem requisite, the said board shall deem said plan the most expedient.

SEC. 16. After said commissioners shall have adopted a plan of sewerage for any sewerage district, they may, in their discretion, advertise for proposals to let out the work on contracts, or may cause the same to be done under their own immediate direction: *Provided, however*, That in all cases the work shall always be subject to the superintendence and direction of the engineer of the said board, and no contractor shall be entitled to demand compensation for any work executed by him, or to recover for the same in any form of action, unless such work shall have been approved by the chief engineer of said board, or by some person by him or by said board of commissioners substituted for said purpose: *Provided further*, That the first construction of the main sewers shall in all cases be offered at public letting.

SEC. 17. The said board shall, after the adoption of a plan of sewerage for any district, have power to issue, in manner herein before provided, the whole amount of bonds which shall be required to defray the cost of the execution of the said plan, or such parts thereof as they shall deem expedient; such bonds shall not run for more than twenty-five years.

SEC. 18. It shall be the duty of the board to report to the common council, twenty days prior to the time fixed by the ordinance of said city for the assessment of city taxes, the amount which will be required to be raised in each sewerage district for the municipal year next ensuing, to meet the payment of interest to accrue, due during said year on all the bonds theretofore issued, or which are during said year to be issued, for the sewerage of the said district.

SEC. 19. It shall be the duty of the said board further to report to the common council at the time named in said last section, such amount as they shall, upon calculation, find necessary, in order to provide a sinking fund for the liquidation of the bonds so issued as aforesaid at the maturity thereof: *Provided*, That the amount to be raised for such sinking fund shall not exceed two per cent. of the amount of bonds theretofore issued, and which are during said year to be issued, for the sewerage of such district.

SEC. 20. The said commissioners shall also report to the said common council the sum which will be by them required to pay salaries and incidental expenses, for the payment of which the said commissioners shall not deem it expedient to issue bonds, and which amount shall be apportioned by them equally between the said districts.

SEC. 21. The amount which shall be so reported to the common council, as required for each sewerage district, as provided in said last three sections, shall be raised by the said common council by a special tax on the property of the respective sewerage districts, for which the sum is required, to be designated sewerage tax, which shall be collected in like manner with the other taxes of said city, and the said amount shall be paid over by the collector of said city to the said board of commissioners.

SEC. 22. It shall be the duty of the said commissioners to pay the interest on such bonds as the same becomes due, and also the principal as the said bonds become due.

SEC. 23. It shall be the duty of the said commissioners to invest the amount raised to provide a sinking fund for the liquidation of said bonds, which amount shall be first invested in the purchase of said bonds if they can be purchased at or below par, if not, then in United States or State government stocks, or upon bond and mortgage upon unincumbered real estate in the county of Cook, of at least double the value of the amount loaned, under the direction and approval of the mayor and the committee on finance of the common council, or a majority of them, such approval to be signified in writing, under the hand of such mayor or finance committee, or a majority of them, and also to invest the interest received upon such loans in like manner, and to invest and re-invest the same and the interest thereof in such manner as to create and constitute the same a sinking fund, and to make the same available for the liquidation of the said bonds. At the time of the maturity thereof, such investments shall be made in the name of the said corporation, and shall be designated as the sewerage sinking fund, and shall in no case be used or appropriated for any other purpose whatsoever than the liquidation of the said bonds. The semi-annual report of said board shall specify in full the nature and amount of the respective securities in which the said sinking fund is invested.

SEC. 24. If from any cause the said commissioners shall not have the amount necessary to pay the said bonds when due, they shall have the right to issue new bonds, in manner herein before provided, for such amount and at such time as they shall deem expedient, in the place of the old bonds so becoming due as aforesaid; the old bonds to be canceled on the registry thereof, and the said new bonds to be recorded as herein before provided.

SEC. 25. Each commissioner, before entering upon the duties of his office, shall give bond to said city in such sum and with surety to the satisfaction of the common council of said city, conditional for the faithful performance of his duties as such commissioner, the amount of which bond may be increased at any time, as the common council may deem expedient.

SEC. 26. Said commissioners shall have the power to purchase such lot or lots, in the manner herein before provided, and to construct such buildings, machinery and fixtures as shall be deemed necessary to effect the objects for which the said board is constituted.

SEC. 27. Said commissioners shall have power to construct reservoirs and to lay sewers or drains in and through all the alleys and streets of the said city, and also across all rivers and streams, not interfering with the navigation of the same, and through any or all breakwaters into lake Michigan, and also in any highways in said county of Cook, whether within the limits of said city or not: *Provided*, That it shall be their duty to repair the streets and alleys upon the completion of such drains or sewers, and to arrange the said drains and sewers with respect to the water and gas pipes in such manner as the council shall by ordinance direct.

SEC. 28. The cost of the private drains and sewers connecting the respective lots in said city with the public sewers, shall not be included in the estimate of the cost of the general plan of sewerage, but the same shall be a special charge upon the lot or lots for whose benefit such private drain or sewer shall be constructed.

SEC. 29. It shall be the duty of the said board to prescribe the location, arrangement, form, material and construction of every private drain or sewer emptying into the said public drains or sewers, and to determine the manner and plan of such connection; and the work of constructing the same shall be in all cases subject to the superintendence and control of the said board, and shall be executed strictly in compliance with their orders.

SEC. 30. It shall be the duty of the said board to see that proper drains or sewers are constructed from every lot in the said city which, in their judgment, requires it, and that such private drains or sewers are made to communicate with the public drains or sewers in a proper manner, and they shall [have] power to require such number of drains or sewers to be thus constructed as they shall deem expedient.

SEC. 31. The said board shall give notice in writing to the owners of the respective lots, in or for the benefit of which they deem it expedient to have private drains or sewers constructed, if such owners are known and reside in said city, and if not, by a printed notice, published for thirty days in the corporation newspaper, specifying the description of the lot or lots in which, or for the benefit of which, such drains are to be built, and notifying the respective parties in interest (naming them when their names are known, and if unknown, designating them as the unknown owners of said lot,) who desire to construct said drains for themselves, to appear at the office of the board of commissioners and receive the necessary instructions and specifications for the execution of said work: *Provided*, That during the said thirty days it shall be the duty of said board to have at their office, ready for examination of the parties in interest, the specification of the work referred to in said notice.

SEC. 32. In case the party in interest shall fail to go on with the execution of the said work forthwith after the expiration of the said thirty days notice, or prosecute the same in a manner satisfactory to said board, it shall be lawful for the said board, or their agents, to enter upon any of said lot or lots, and to construct thereon such drain or sewer, and for that purpose to have free ingress and egress upon said lot or lots, with men and teams, and to deposit all the necessary building materials, and generally to do and perform all things necessary to a complete execution of the work.

SEC. 33. After the completion of such private sever or drain, the said commissioners shall make out a report to the common council, specifying the amount expended by them in the construction of any private drain or sewer, and the description of the lot or lots to which the said cost and expense are chargeable, which report shall have the like effect as is given by the ordinance of said city to the report of the street commissioner, of the expense incurred by him in the construction of sidewalks; and the common council shall, upon the receipt of such report, take the same proceedings for the collection of the amounts due for such drains or sewers, as, or may hereafter be provided by the ordinance of said city for the collection of the amount due for sidewalk assessments, when reported as aforesaid, and the amount, when collected, shall be paid over to the said board.

SEC. 34. The said board shall appoint some other person to act as secretary, and shall also appoint one of their own number to act as treasurer of said board.

SEC. 35. It shall be the duty of the board to make report in writing to the common council of said city, semi-annually, which report shall embrace a detailed statement of the progress and condition of the work entrusted to them, as well as a statement of the funds and securities of said corporation, and all debts owing to and from said corporation, together with an accurate account of their expenditures, which statement shall be verified by said commissioners under oath, and shall be entered of record by the clerk of said city, and published in the corporation newspaper of said city.

SEC. 36. The salaries of said commissioners, and also of the secretary and chief engineer of said board, shall be fixed by the common council of said city as soon as may be after the passage of this act, and annually thereafter, and the amount of salary of either one of said commissioners shall not be changed during the year for which the same was fixed as aforesaid.

SEC. 37. All materials procured, or, partly procured, under a contract with the commissioners, shall be exempt from attachment or execution, but the commissioners may be served as garnishees and proceeded against as in other cases of attachment, and shall in such case retain the amount due to the contractor against whom said attachment or execution issued, and dispose of the same as adjudged by law, and such payment shall apply as a payment on such contract.

SEC. 38. No one or more of said commissioners or any of the officers of said board, nor any member of the common council, during the term for which they were elected, shall be interested, either directly or indirectly, in any contract entered into by said board with any other person, nor in the purchase of any material to be used or applied in or about the uses and purposes contemplated by said act.

SEC. 39. The said commissioners, or either of them, may be removed from office by the judge of the circuit court or judge of the court of common pleas of Cook county, upon petition addressed to either of said judges at any time by the common council of said city. The said petition shall be voted by a majority of all the members of said council, and when presented to such judge shall be accompanied by specifications of the charges made against said commissioners; no technical form shall be required for the said statement of said charges, so that the same are stated in such form as to be specific and intelligible. The judge to whom said petition is addressed, upon presentation of said petition, shall order a copy thereof to be filed in the court of which he is judge, and notice of the filing thereof to be issued forthwith by the clerk of said court to said commissioners, and that the same would be taken up in twenty days after the service of such notice upon said commissioners. The said judge shall sit as a special commissioner to try said charges, and the course of proceedings in such trial shall be governed by the general rules of procedure in the trial of misdemeanors in the courts of this State, excepting that no jury shall be allowed. Evidence shall be given orally or by deposition as in civil cases, and the said commissioners may be interrogated upon oath, touching the matters contained in said charges, and if it shall appear to the satisfaction of the said judge that the said commissioner or commissioners, charged as aforesaid, have been guilty of malfeasance in office or of any breach of duty, either of commission or omission under this act, which shall have been charged as aforesaid, the said judge shall order the removal of such commissioner or commissioners, and if the said judge shall for any cause remove any one or more of said commissioners from office before the expiration of their term of office, the common council shall thereupon appoint a commissioner or commissioners in the stead of those so removed, who shall fill such office for and during the unexpired term of such commissioner or commissioners so removed: *Provided further*, That the common council shall have the right to remove the said commissioners, or either of them, or the chief engineer of said board, by a vote of two-thirds of all the aldermen authorized by law to be elected, and in case of such removal, the said common council may elect one or more commissioners to fill the unexpired term of the commissioner or commissioners so removed.

SEC. 40. The said commissioners are hereby authorized to enter upon any land or water for the purpose of making surveys or constructing any of the work authorized by this act, and to agree with the owners of any property which may be required for the purpose of this act as to the amount of compensation to be paid to such owner for the property so taken, or the amount of damages to be paid to such owner or owners by reason of the construction of any of the work hereby authorized.

SEC. 41. The said commissioners are authorized to construct such canals, ditches, sewers, embankments, reservoirs, or other works, as they may find necessary or useful for the carrying out of the purposes of this act, whether the same are to be made within or without the limits of said city.

SEC. 42. In case of disagreement between the commissioners and the owners of property, which may, in the judgment of said commissioners, be required for any of the purposes specified in this act, as to the amount of compensation to be paid to such owners, or in case any such owner shall be an infant, a married woman, or insane, or absent from this State, or in case of disagreement between the said board and any owner or owners of property touching the amount of damages arising from the construction of any part of the work hereby authorized, the said board shall have the right to condemn said property, or to have the amount of such damages as ascertained, or both, and the proceedings for the condemnation of such property, or the ascertainment of such damages, or both, shall conform, as nearly as may be, to those specified and provided in the act entitled "An Act to amend the law condemning right of way for purposes of internal improvement," approved June 22, 1852, and the act or acts of which the same is in amendment.

SEC. 43. No person shall willfully or maliciously obstruct, damage or injure any public or private sewer or drain in said city, or willfully injure any of the materials employed and used in said city for the purposes specified in this act.

SEC. 44. All contracts for materials, or for construction of the work, shall be made in writing, and of each contract two copies shall be taken, which shall be numbered and indorsed with the date of the contract and with the names of the contractors, and a summary of the work to be done or materials to be furnished, one copy of which shall be retained by the said commissioners on file in their office, and the other copy of which shall be recorded in a well-bound book, to be by them safely kept in their office for that purpose.

SEC. 45. Public notice shall be given of the time and place at which sealed proposals will be received for entering into contracts, and all sealed proposals for contracts shall be for a sum certain as to the price to be paid or received, and no proposition which is not thus definite and certain, or which contains any alternative, condition, or limitation as to price, shall be received or acted upon.

SEC. 46. No more than one proposition shall be received from any one person for the same contract, and all the propositions of the person offering more than one shall be rejected.

SEC. 47. Every person who shall enter into any contract for the supply of materials, or the performance of labor, shall give satisfactory security to the commissioners for the faithful performance of his contract according to its terms.

SEC. 48. The said commissioners shall have power to regulate the construction of privies, and the manner of cleaning the same, and to construct and regulate the construction of cess-pools, and provide for the proper draining of privies and cess-pools at the cost of the proprietors, the mode of collecting such cost to be the same, substantially, as is provided in section thirty-three hereof.

SEC. 49. The said commissioners shall have the right, and it shall always be their duty, when directed by the common council as hereinafter provided, to employ in each sewerage district, such a number of scavengers and scavengers' carts as may be necessary to remove all filth from the streets and alleys of said city, and from the premises and inclosures of the citizens, and for that purpose may enter upon any yard, lot or other inclosure, and remove any filth, garbage or noxious matter therefrom: *Provided*, That the said work shall be done by said commissioners under the direction of the common council of said city, and in conformity with ordinances to be by the said common council passed, respecting the same, and shall be paid for out of the same fund as the said work is now paid for, according to the charter and ordinances of said city: *Provided*, That no power shall be exercised by said board under this section until an ordinance conferring such power, and specifying the mode of its exercise, shall have been passed by the common council, if said common council shall deem it necessary so to do.

SEC. 50. No account or claim against the said board shall be allowed except by a vote of a majority of the said board.

SEC. 51. No member or officer of said board, and no member of the common council, shall, either directly or indirectly, receive any interest or profit whatsoever on account of the deposit of any of the funds belonging to the said board, nor shall any member or officer of the said board, or any member of the common council, either directly or indirectly, make use of or borrow any of the funds of said board, or of the said sinking fund, for his own private benefit or advantage. The funds of said board remaining on hand, shall at all times, until disposed of, be kept deposited in such place or places of deposit, as shall, by an order of said board, be directed, which order shall be entered upon the records of said board: *Provided, however*, That such place or places of deposit shall first be approved by the common council: *And provided further*, That whenever the said common council shall pass a resolution disapproving of such place or places of deposit, it shall be the duty of said board forthwith to select other place or places of deposit for said funds, such as shall be approved by the said common council. And if either of the commissioners, or any of the officers of said board, shall, directly or indirectly, receive or appropriate for his own use or benefit, any of the funds, money or property of the said board, or of the said sinking fund, or any of the interest thereon, or shall take, pledge or borrow any of the said funds or property of the said board, or of the said sinking fund, for his own use or benefit, such commissioner or such officer of said board shall be deemed guilty of embezzlement, and shall be liable to indictment, and on conviction thereof, shall be fined not exceeding one thousand dollars, or imprisoned not exceeding one year in the county jail.

SEC. 52. The said commissioners shall have the power, and it shall be their duty, to make such changes in the grade of streets and alleys, and in the construction and arrangements of the gutters along the same, as shall serve effectually to carry out the purposes of this act, and to cause a rapid and effectual removal of the surface water from the same; and to this end may enter upon, use and obstruct the said street for such time as may be necessary to effect the said object: *Provided*, That no such change of grade in any street or alley shall be made until the common council have first approved of such change.

SEC. 53. The said board, while constructing the said drains or sewers as herein provided, may construct such additions to the same as they shall deem expedient to furnish the proper plans of connection with the private drains or sewers to be thereafter constructed, and the cost of such additions may be charged and assessed as a part of the expense of said private drains or sewers connecting therewith, when such private drains or sewers shall be constructed, and shall be chargeable to the lot or lots for the benefit of which the same are constructed, and collected in the same manner as herein before provided for the collection of the cost of such private drains or sewers.

SEC. 54. It shall be the duty of the common council to fix by ordinance the penalty to attach for the violation of any of the provisions of this act not herein specified, which penalty may be enforced in any court having jurisdiction of offenses against any of the ordinances of said city.

SEC. 55. The said board shall have the power to raise, by loan, upon the credit of said city of Chicago, with the approval of the common council, such sum or sums as they may from time to time require, prior to the receipts of the first money derived from the sale of bonds as herein provided, for preliminary expenses incurred by them prior to the commencement of the sewerage hereby authorized, or the city council may appropriate to the use of said board such sum as they shall require as aforesaid and in case the same shall be appropriated by the city council, the amount so appropriated shall be refunded to the city treasury out of the amount received from the first sale of bonds or of the first sewerage tax next thereafter collected.

SEC. 56. The board shall further report to the common council, in addition to the amounts provided in sections eighteen, nineteen and twenty, what, if any, sum is required during said year from each sewerage district, to meet the payment of any of the principal of the said bonds falling due in said year and not otherwise provided for, and it shall be the duty of the common council to make provision for the payment of the same, by taxation or by loan, or by the issue of the bonds of said city, and to that end they may issue such amount of the bonds of said city as shall be requisite for such purposes.

SEC. 57. The funds of the said board shall be drawn out upon checks or drafts, regularly numbered, and payable to the order of the respective person or persons for whose benefit the same are intended, and briefly specifying for what purpose or account the same are drawn; a careful register of said checks or drafts shall be kept in the office of said board, and the original checks or drafts when returned to said board shall be carefully filed and preserved among the vouchers of the said board, and the said register and the said returned checks or drafts shall always be subject to the examination of the finance or any other committee of the said common council; and it shall be the duty of said finance committee, or of some other committee appointed by the common council, to examine the said register and the cash account and checks and drafts of the said board at least once in three months, and oftener if the common council shall deem expedient.

SEC. 58. The chief engineer in the employ of the said board shall reside in the city of Chicago, and shall give his entire time and services to the duties of his said office, and said engineer shall employ no assistant who shall not have first been approved by a vote of said board, and the said engineer or any of his assistants, may at any time be discharged by a vote of the said board.

SEC. 59. It shall be the duty of the said commissioners to keep books of account showing with entire accuracy the amount of the receipts and expenditures of each sewerage district in such manner as to enable the same to be readily understood and investigated, and also to carefully preserve on file in their office, vouchers for all their expenditures, which books and vouchers shall at all times be open to the examination of the finance committee of the common council, or any other committee appointed by the common council for such purpose, and it shall be the duty of the said finance committee, or any special committee appointed for such purpose, at the time of the presentation of the semi-annual report of the said board to the council, as herein provided, to make a thorough examination of the books, accounts and vouchers of the said corporation, and to report in writing to the common council the results of said investigation.

SEC. 60. The provisions herein before contained, for the establishment of a sinking fund, shall be deemed and taken as a part of the contract with the parties purchasing said bonds, and shall not be repealed or modified so as in any manner to impair the security thereby afforded to the said bond holders.

SEC. 61. The said board may make such provisions and arrangement for securing the payment of interest on the amount realized from the said bonds, and not required by them for immediate use, as shall be consistent with the entire security of the fund and its availability, for use, when required: *Provided*, That such arrangement shall first be approved by the common council of the said city.

SEC. 62. This act may be at any time altered, repealed or amended, and shall take effect from and after its passage.

Approved February 14, 1855.

AN ACT in amendment of and supplemental to an Act entitled "An Act to incorporate the Chicago City Hydraulic Company."

SECTION 1. *Be it enacted by the People of the State of Illinois, represented in the General Assembly*, That the persons hereafter to be elected water commissioners of said city shall be taken successively from the south, north and west divisions of said city, in the following order: The first election after the passage hereof, shall be of a commissioner from the south division, the next from the north division, and the next from the west division, and so on in the same order, so that one commissioner shall be elected for one of said divisions each year, and shall hold his office for three years from the time of his election No person shall be elected from any division unless he shall, at the time of his election, be a freeholder, and have been a resident of said city for at least three years, and of said division for at least six months next preceding such election. In case of any vacancy in office of any one or more of said commissioners, the vacancy shall be filled by the election, by the common council, of some citizen of said city duly qualified and resident as aforesaid, who shall have power to act as such commissioner until the expiration of the full term for which the commissioner was elected in whose place he is appointed: *Provided*, That no person shall be considered elected by said common council unless he shall receive a majority of the votes of all the aldermen by law authorized to be elected. The first election under this act shall be for a commissioner from the south division, and shall be held on the first Tuesday in May, A. D. 1855, and the succeeding elections shall be annually thereafter.

SEC. 2. If any commissioner shall, during his term of office, remove his place of residence from the division from which he was elected, such removal shall vacate the office of such commissioner, and the common council shall forthwith declare said office vacant, and proceed to elect some person duly qualified and resident as aforesaid, who shall act as commissioner during the unexpired term of the commissioner whose office is thus vacated.

SEC. 3. The said board shall have the power and it shall be their duty to assess as water rents such amounts as they shall deem equitable upon the owner or owners, occupant or occupants of any building or buildings which shall be situated on lots adjoining any street, avenue or alley in said city, through which the distributing water pipes are or may hereafter be laid, from which such building or buildings can be conveniently supplied with water, whether the said owner or owners shall make use of such water or not; and said water rates shall be and become a continuing lien or charge upon all such buildings, and the lot or lots upon which such buildings are situated, if owned by the same person or persons as such building or buildings, and shall be collected in like manner with other water rates of said city, as provided by the act of which this is an amendment.

SEC. 4. The said commissioners may make such division of duties among themselves for each year of their term as they shall deem expedient, and shall report in writing to the common council the nature and extent of the duties assigned to each commissioner, which report shall be made on the third Monday of May, or as soon thereafter as may be, in each year; and the council shall thereupon fix the salary to be paid to each of said commissioners during the year next succeeding, for the performance of the duties so specially assigned to him, and such salary shall attach to the performance of the said respective duties, and shall not be changed during the year for which it was fixed.

SEC. 5. The said commissioners shall have power to borrow, from time to time, as they and the common council shall deem expedient, a sum not exceeding three hundred thousand dollars, upon the credit of said city of Chicago, and shall have power, by and with the approval of the common council of said city, to issue bonds pledging the faith and credit of the said city for the payment of the principal and interest of said bonds, which bonds shall be issued under the seal of said board, and shall be signed by them, and may be made payable at such place and in such currency as they shall deem expedient, and bear interest not exceeding seven per centum per annum: *Provided*, That the said commissioners shall not sell the said bonds, whatever rate of interest the same may bear, at a rate which will net to the said board less than par value for seven per cent. bonds: *Provided further*, That no bonds shall be issued until the common council shall have approved of such issue by a vote of a majority of all the aldermen by law authorized to be elected, and provided that all bonds issued by the said board, before they shall be binding upon said city, shall be marked approved by the mayor and clerk of said city, under the seal of said city, and that such signature and seal shall be conclusive evidence to the holder of said bonds of the fact of such approval. It shall be the duty of the said commissioners to keep an accurate register of all bonds and all interest coupons issued by them, showing the number, date and amount of each bond and coupon, and to whom issued and where payable; and it shall be the duty of the city clerk to register the said bonds when approved as aforesaid, in the same manner as the other indebtedness of said city is registered: *Provided further*, That all funds derived from the sale of the bonds of the said board, or from water rents or otherwise, shall be exclusively used for and appropriated by said board to the objects and purposes specified in said act, of which this is an amendment, nor shall the same or any part thereof be loaned to or used by the said city of Chicago.

SEC. 6. It shall be the duty of the said board, at any time when they shall desire to make an issue of bonds for any of the purposes specified in the said act, to which this is an amendment, to make a report to the common council, setting forth in detail the nature and amount of the work proposed to be executed, and the amount which will be required by them for any of the purposes for which said board was constituted, within a period not exceeding six months from the date of said report; which report shall specify in detail the amount and nature of the work, and of the different kinds of work proposed to be executed in said time, and the estimated cost of said work, and of each kind of work, and the amount of materials required to be purchased, and the estimated cost of the same; and the common council may thereupon approve the issue of the whole amount of bonds called for by such report, or such part thereof as the said common council may deem expedient.

SEC. 7. The said board shall cause to be printed on each water permit issued to any party using the water, a copy of all rules and restrictions regulating the use of the water, which shall be adopted by them, and they shall further report a copy thereof to the common council, who shall thereupon pass an ordinance establishing such rules and regulations, and providing penalties for their violation, which penalties may be enforced in any court having jurisdiction of any offenses against any of the ordinances of said city. In all cases where said rules are not complied with, the said board shall have the right to stop or cut off the supply of water from any person or persons refusing or neglecting such compliances.

SEC. 8. It shall be the duty of the said board to return to the common council, as often as said board shall deem necessary, the warrants for the collection of water rents issued by them, as provided in the ninth section of the act of which this is an amendment, which have been returned to said board unsatisfied, and shall report to the common council, at the same time, the building or buildings, lot or lots, to which the amounts specified in such warrants are respectively chargeable; and the common council shall, thereupon, take the same proceedings for the collection of such amounts as are or may hereafter be provided by the charter and ordinances of said city, for the collection of the amount due in any warrant for the collection of sidewalk assessments, after such warrant has been returned unsatisfied; and the amount, when so collected, to be paid to the said board.

SEC. 9. Whenever the receipts of the said corporation, from water rents or other sources, shall accumulate so that there shall be a surplus amounting to a sum not less than five hundred dollars, not needed for the current expenses of the said corporation, it shall be the duty of the commissioners to invest the same, first in the payment of the interest on said bonds as it becomes due, or in the purchase of the outstanding bonds of said company, if they can be purchased at or below par; if not, then in the purchase of United States or State government stock, or upon unencumbered real estate in the county of Cook, of at least double the value of the amount loaned, with the approval of the mayor and committee of finance of the common council, or a majority of them; such approval to be signified in writing, under the hand of the said mayor and committee on finance, or a majority of them. Such investment shall be made in the name of said corporation, and in such manner as to make the same available for the payment of the interest and principal of the bonds issued by them. The semi-annual report of the said board shall specify. in full, the nature and amount of the respective securities in which the said surplus fund is invested.

SEC. 10. No one or more of said commissioners, nor any of the officers of said board, nor any member of the common council, during the term for which they were elected, shall be interested, directly or indirectly, in any contract entered into by said board, with any other person, nor in the purchase of any other materials to be used or applied in or about the uses and purposes contemplated in this act.

SEC. 11. The said commissioners, or either of them, may be removed from office by the judge of the circuit court, or the judge of the court of common pleas of Cook county, upon petition addressed to either of said judges, at any time, by the common council of said city. The said petition shall be voted by a majority of all the members of said council, and when presented to such judge, shall be accompanied by specifications of the charges made against said commissioner or commissioners. No technical form shall be required for the statement of said charges, so that the same are stated in such form as to be specific and intelligible. The judge to whom such petition is addressed, upon presentation of said petition, shall order a copy thereof to be filed in said court of which he is judge, and notice of the filing thereof to be issued forthwith by the clerk of said court to said commissioner, and that the same would be taken up in twenty days after the service of such notice upon said commissioner. The said judge shall sit as a special commissioner to try said charges, and the course of proceedings in said trial shall be governed by the general rules of procedure in the trial of misdemeanors in the courts of this State, excepting that no jury shall be allowed. Evidence may be given either orally or by deposition, as in civil cases, and the said commissioners may each be interrogated upon oath, touching the matter contained in said charges; and if it shall appear to the satisfaction of such judges, that the said commissioner or commissioners charged as aforesaid, have been guilty of malfeasance in office, or of any breach of duty, either of commission or omission, under this act, which shall have been charged as aforesaid, the said judge shall order the removal of any one or more of said commissioners; and if the said judge shall, for any cause, remove any one or more of said commissioners from office before the expiration of the term of office, the common council shall, thereupon, appoint a commissioner or commissioners in the stead of those so removed, who shall fill such office for and during the unexpired term of the commissioner or commissioners so removed.

SEC. 13. In case of disagreement between the commissioners and owners of property which may, in the judgment of the commissioners, be required for any of the purposes specified in this act, as to the amount of compensation to be paid such owners, or in case any such owner shall be an infant, a married woman or insane, or absent from this State, or in case of disagreement between the said commissioners and any owner or owners of property, touching the amount of damages arising from the construction of any part of the work authorized by this act, or the act of which this is an amendment, the said commissioners shall have the right to condemn said property, or to have the amount of such damages ascertained, or both, and the proceedings of the condemnation of such property, on the ascertainment of such damages, or both, shall conform, as nearly as may be, to those specified and provided in the act entitled "An Act to amend the law condemning right of way for purposes of internal improvements," approved June 22, 1852, and the act or acts of which the same is an amendment.

SEC. 14. It shall be the duty of said board of water commissioners to cause such connections to be made between the water pipes and the sewers or drains of said city, as they shall be requested to make by the board of sewerage commissioners, and to furnish such amount of water for the purpose of clearing out such drains or sewers as the said board of water commissioners shall deem requisite, and the said board of water commissioners can conveniently supply: *Provided*, That such connections shall be made under the superintendence of the board of water commissioners, and that said board shall regulate the times, and manner, and amount of such supply of water. In case of disagreement between the two boards in respect to the matters herein before provided, the common council shall have the right to regulate the manner in which such connections shall be made, and water supplied, for the purposes herein mentioned.

SEC. 15. No account or claim against the said board shall be allowed, except by the vote of a majority of the said board.

SEC. 16. No member, or other officer of said board, and no member of the common council, shall, either directly or indirectly, receive any interest or profit whatsoever, on account of the deposit of any of the funds belonging to the said commissioners, nor shall any member or other officer of the said board, or any member of the common council, either directly or indirectly, make use of or borrow any of the funds of the said commissioners for his own private benefit or advantage. The funds of the said commissioners remaining on hand, shall, at all times, until disposed of, be kept deposited in such place or places of deposit as shall, by an order of said board, be directed, which order shall be entered upon the records of the said board; and if either of said commissioners, or any of the officers of the said board, shall, either directly or indirectly, receive or appropriate for his own use or benefit, any of the funds, money or property of the said board, or shall, directly or indirectly, take, pledge or borrow any of the said funds or property for his own use or benefit, such commissioner or such officer of said board, shall be deemed guilty of embezzlement, and shall be liable to indictment, and on conviction thereof, shall be fined not exceeding one thousand dollars, or imprisoned not exceeding one year in the county jail. The said commissioners shall be liable, upon their bond, for the loss of any or all money coming into their possession or control, as such commissioners.

SEC. 17. The funds of the said board shall be drawn out upon checks or drafts, regularly numbered, and payable to the order of the respective person or persons for whose benefit the same are intended, and briefly specifying for what purpose or account the same are drawn. A careful register of the checks or drafts shall be kept in the office of said board, and the original checks or drafts, when returned to said board, shall be carefully filed and preserved among the vouchers of the said board; and the said register, and the said returned checks or drafts, shall always be subject to the examination of the finance or any other committee appointed by the common council for such purpose; and it shall be the duty of the said finance committee, or some other committee, or of such other person or persons as may be appointed by the common council for such purpose, to examine the said register and the cash accounts, and the checks and drafts of the said board, at least once in three months, and oftener, if the common council shall deem it expedient.

SEC. 18. The chief engineer and superintendent in the employ of the said board shall reside in the city of Chicago; and said engineer shall employ no assistant who shall not have first been approved by a vote of the said board; and the said engineer, superintendent, or any of his assistants, may at any time be discharged by a vote of the said board.

SEC. 19. It shall be the duty of the said commissioners to keep books of account, showing, with entire accuracy, the amount of the receipts and expenditures of such board, in such manner as to enable the same to be readily understood and investigated, and also to carefully preserve, on file in their office, vouchers for all their expenditures, which books and vouchers shall at all times be open to the examination of the finance committee of the common council, or any other committee, person or persons appointed by the common council for such purpose; and it shall be the duty of the said finance committee, or any special committee appointed for such purpose, at the time of the presentation of the semi-annual reports of the said board to the council, as herein provided, to make a thorough examination of the books, accounts and vouchers of the said corporation, and to report in writing to the common council the results of said investigations.

SEC. 20. The present commissioners shall hold their offices, unless removed for cause, in manner herein before provided to fill their respective places.

SEC. 21. Sections ten, twenty-seven and twenty-eight of the act of which this is an amendment, and all laws or parts of laws, or parts of said acts, which may be in conflict with the provisions of this act, are hereby repealed.

SEC. 22. This act shall take effect from and after its passage.

Approved February 15, 1855.

AN ACT to amend the Act entitled "An Act to reduce the law incorporating the City of Chicago, and the several acts amendatory thereof, into one Act, and to amend the same," approved February 14, 1851.

SECTION 1. *Be it enacted by the People of the State of Illinois, represented in the General Assembly,* In order to carry out fully the object and intent of the sixty-second section of the fourth chapter of the act to which this is an amendment, the common council of the city of Chicago is hereby authorized and empowered to establish and maintain at its option, either within or without the corporate limits of said city, a reform school, and to assess a tax upon the real estate in said city, year by year, for the support of the same, not exceeding, however, two mills, and to be levied and collected in the same manner and at the same time that the general taxes of the city are now; but no such tax shall be levied or collected in any year when there shall remain, from the taxes assessed for such purpose for any previous year or years, and collected and paid into the treasury and unexpended for the purposes of such school, a sum of money that, in the estimation of the board of guardians of such school, shall be deemed sufficient for the support of the reform school for such year.

SEC. 2. The reform school now established by the ordinance of the common council of the city of Chicago, is hereby declared to have been and to be established in conformity with the provisions of the said sixty-second section mentioned in the foregoing section, and the said ordinance and the amendments thereto are hereby continued in force and effect until altered, changed or amended by said common council, and the said common council is hereby authorized to alter, change, amend or repeal, in its option, the said ordinance, at any and all times when it shall deem proper; but not so as to contravene any provisions contained herein, or any laws of the State now or hereafter existing.

SEC. 3. Each and all courts having criminal jurisdiction in the county of Cook, and each and all police magistrates in the city of Chicago, shall sentence to the said reform school, every male under the age of seventeen years and over the age of six years, who shall be convicted before such court or magistrate, of vagrancy, or of any offense punishable by law by fine or imprisonment, and who the said courts or police magistrates shall be of opinion would be a fit and proper subject for commitment to said reform school, and an order to such effect shall be entered of record in the proceedings of said court or magistrate; and thereupon it shall be the duty of said court or magistrate, by warrant in due form of law, to commit such boy to said reform school, and all warrants of commitments of such boys, shall express the crime or complaint for which such commitment is made, and the age of the boy, but no such warrant of commitment shall be considered bad for want of form or technicality, and the same may be directed to the sheriff or any constable of Cook county or of the city of Chicago, who shall execute the same and deliver the boy or boys named in such warrant to the superintendent of the reform school, with the warrant, and for such services shall be paid the same fees and in the same manner as are now provided in case of the commitment of a criminal to the Cook county jail, for a misdemeanor or offense punishable by imprisonment in the county jail.

SEC. 4. Each and every boy above the age of six years and under the age of seventeen years, who shall be legally committed to said school as provided in the foregoing section, shall be kept, disciplined, instructed, employed and governed under the direction of the board of guardians of said school, until he be either reformed and discharged, or be bound out by said guardians, or until he shall have arrived at the age of twenty-one years; and all commitments to said reform school shall be to such effect, and need not express the time for which such boy shall be committed, and the said board of guardians are hereby clothed with the sole power to discharge any boy or boys from said reform school, who have been or may hereafter be legally committed to such reform school, and such power of discharge shall rest solely with said board of guardians, and with no other person or body politic or corporate, but it shall be the duty of the said board of guardians, and they shall have power to return any boy to the authorities of the county or city from which any such boy may be or shall have been received, whom the said guardians may deem to be an improper subject for their care and management, or who shall be found to be incorrigible, or whose continuance in the school they may deem prejudicial to the management and discipline thereof, or who in their judgment ought for any cause to be removed from said school, and in every such case it shall be the duty of said guardians to transmit to the court or magistrate by whom the said boy was committed to said school, a statement of the reasons for said discharge, and it shall be the duty of the authorities of the city or county, to whom such boy shall be returned, to produce such boy before the court or magistrate by whom such boy was committed, as soon as the same can reasonably be done, and such court or magistrate shall have power thereupon to make such order and have such proceedings as would have been legal in the first instance, and as would have been made or had in case said boy had not been sent to said reform school.

SEC. 5. Said guardians shall have power to bind out all boys committed to their charge for any term of time until they shall have arrived at the age of twenty-one years, as apprentices or servants to any inhabitant of this State, and the said guardians and master or mistress, apprentice or servant, shall respectively have all the rights and privileges and be subject to all the duties set forth in chapter sixth of the Revised Statutes, entitled "Apprentices," in the same manner as if said binding or apprenticing were made by any two overseers of the poor, or by the mayor or any two aldermen of any city; and the same clauses and provisions required to be inserted in the indentures of apprentices in such cases, shall be inserted in all indentures that may be executed by the said guardians. No person receiving an apprentice under the provisions of this act, shall be at liberty to assign or transfer the indenture of apprenticeship without the consent in writing of said guardians, and in case the master or mistress of such apprentice shall be dissatisfied with his behavior, or for any other cause may desire to be relieved from said contract, upon application, said guardians may in their discretion cancel the said indenture and resume the charge and management of such boy, and shall have the same power and authority in regard to him as before such indenture was made; and if any master or mistress shall be guilty of any cruelty, misusage, refusal or neglect to furnish necessary provisions, clothing, or any other violation of the terms of the indenture toward any boy so bound to service, such boy may make complaint to the board of guardians of said school, or to any court or magistrate having power to commit boys to said school, who shall thereupon summon the parties before said court or magistrate and examine into, hear and determine said complaint, and if upon examination such complaint shall appear to be well founded, such court or magistrate shall, by certificate under seal, discharge such boy from all obligations of future service, and restore him to said school, to be managed and taken care of in like manner and with the same powers as before such indenture, and a right of action shall immediately accrue against such master or mistress as for a violation of the covenants of such indenture. Upon the death or removal from the State of Illinois, of any master or mistress to whom any boy may be bound as aforesaid, the executor or administrators of such master or mistress that may have so deceased, or said master or mistress in person who are about to remove, with the consent of the boy so bound to service, signified in a writing acknowledged and approved by the said guardians, may assign the indenture or contract of services to some other person, which assignment shall transfer and vest in such assignee all the rights of the original master or mistress, and also make the assignee subject to all the obligations of such original master or mistress; and it shall be the duty of every person to whom any boy is so apprenticed as aforesaid, to report to said guardians as often as once in each year, and at all other times when required of by said guardians, the conduct, behavior, the condition and health of such apprentice, and whether such apprentice is still living with him or them, and if not, where such apprentice may be, and such other facts with regard to such apprentice as may be important for said guardians to know.

SEC. 6. In case a reform school, or schools, or other institution of a like character, and for a like purpose, should at any time be established by the State as a State institution, the common council of the city of Chicago are hereby authorized and empowered to remove and transfer to such State institution, as soon as the same shall be in operation, or at any time thereafter, all the boys that may at such time be in the Chicago reform school, and thereafter all such boys so removed, and all other boys that may at any time thereafter be sent to the Chicago reform school, or that the board of guardians of said Chicago reform school would otherwise be authorized to take and receive into the Chicago reform school, shall be sent to and received and taken by such State reform school, and shall be under the control, guardianship and custody of the board of guardians or other governing board of such State reform school or institution, in the same way and manner, and to the same extent in all respects, as if such boy and boys had been sent or sentenced to any such State reform school or institution in the first instance, and agreeably to the law or laws that may be or have been for such case made and provided; such removal and removals of such boys from said Chicago reform school to such State reform school, or other similar institution, shall be made under the direction of the mayor and common council of the city of Chicago, and any police officer or constable, one or more, of said city of Chicago, that may be directed by said mayor and common council to make such removal, are hereby clothed with the same power to take such boys through any county in the State and deliver such boys to such State reform school or other institution established for similar purposes, as a sheriff now has by law to remove a convict from the county where convicted to the State penitentiary.

SEC. 7. By permission of the common council of the city of Chicago, male juvenile delinquents, between the ages of six years and seventeen years, that may be proper subjects for said reform school, may in like manner as herein before provided for, in the case of male juvenile delinquents in said city of Chicago, be sentenced by any court of criminal jurisdiction, or police magistrate, or police justice, in any county or city of this State, to said Chicago reform school, subject, however, to such rules and regulations as the said common council may establish; and the expense at said school of such boys so committed, shall be respectively borne and paid by the counties or cities where such boys may be respectively convicted

SEC. 8. This act shall take effect and be in force from and after its passage.

Approved February 14, 1857.

AN ACT to amend the Act entitled "An Act to reduce the Law incorporating the City of Chicago, and the several Acts amendatory thereof, into one Act, and to amend the same," approved February 14, 1851.

SECTION 1. *Be it enacted by the People of the State of Illinois, represented in the General Assembly*, The common council shall, before the next annual election, divide the wards of said city into so many and such convenient election districts, as to the said common council shall seem proper, and to appoint places for holding elections therein, and appoint the board of inspectors therefor as now provided by the law; and for this purpose they are hereby authorized to appoint three additional inspectors of election for each election district so created, whose qualifications and duties shall be as now prescribed by the city charter.

SEC. 2. All ordinances, petitions and communications to the common council shall, unless by unanimous consent, be referred to appropriate committees, and only acted on by the council at a subsequent meeting, on the report of the committee having the same in charge; and any report of a committee of the council shall be deferred to the next regular meeting of the same, and the publication of the said report in the corporation paper may be required, by the request of any two aldermen present.

SEC. 3. Every act, ordinance or resolution, passed by the common council, before it shall take effect, shall be presented, duly certified by the city clerk, to the mayor for his approbation. If he approve, he shall sign it; if not, he shall return it with his objections in writing to said common council, who shall enter said objections upon their record and proceed to reconsider it; and if, after such reconsideration, two-thirds of all the members elected shall agree to pass the same, it shall take effect as an act or law of the corporation.

SEC. 4. If the mayor shall not return any act, ordinance or resolution so presented to him, within five days, it shall take effect in the same manner as if he had signed it.

SEC. 5. No contracts shall be hereafter made by the common council or any committee or member thereof, and no expense shall be incurred by any of the officers or departments of said city government, whether the object of expenditure shall have been ordered by the common council or not, unless an appropriation shall have been previously made concerning such expense. The making of contracts and superintendence of all public works undertaken at the expense of said city, shall be committed by law or ordinance of the corporation to some proper officer or department, under proper rules and regulations preventive of fraud or collusion therein. And no member of the common council, head of a department, clerk, city officers, assistant or employee in any department of said city, shall be directly or indirectly interested in any contract, work or business, or the sale of any article, the expense, price or consideration of which is paid from the city treasury, under the penalty of his immediate removal from office.

SEC. 6. All officers of the city whose election by the people is not provided for in this act, or the act to which this is an amendment, shall, after the next annual election, be appointed by the mayor of said city, by and with the advice and consent of the common council; any provision of law in relation to the appointment or election of such officers, now in force, providing for such appointment or election in any other manner, being hereby expressly repealed.

TREASURY DEPARTMENT.

SEC. 7. There shall be after the next annual election, and there is hereby established in the city of Chicago, an executive department of the municipal government of said city, to be known and styled the "Treasury Department," which shall embrace a city comptroller, the city treasurer, and the city collector or collectors, and all or any receivers of the city revenues which are now or may be appointed by law, and all such clerks and assistants, including an auditor, as the common council may, by ordinance, see fit to prescribe and establish.

SEC. 8. The said treasury department shall have control of all the fiscal concerns of the said corporation, and shall prescribe the forms of keeping and rendering all city accounts whatever, and all accounts rendered to or kept in the several departments of the city government, shall be subject to the revision and inspection of the officers of this department. It shall settle and adjust all claims whatever for the corporation or against them, and all accounts whatsoever in which the corporation is concerned either as debtor or creditor.

SEC. 9. There shall, after the next annual election in said city, be appointed by the mayor, with the advice and consent of the common council, some discreet and able accountant, to be styled the "City Comptroller," who shall be chief of said treasury department, and hold his office until removed or a successor be appointed, who shall receive such compensation for his services as may be established by law, and who shall be removable at all times at the pleasure of the mayor, with the concurrence of the common council, and he shall give bonds with securities to the amount of not less than ten thousand dollars, and the amount of his bond may be increased to such sum as may be fixed by the common council; said bond to be approved by the mayor and common council, and filed in the city clerk's office, and entered on record. He shall also be sworn, the same as other officers, to the faithful discharge of the duties of his office.

SEC. 10. The comptroller shall, immediately after his appointment, open and keep in a neat, methodical manner, a complete set of books, under the direction of the mayor and finance committee, wherein shall be stated, among other things, the appropriations of the year for each distinct object and branch of expenditure, and also the receipts from each and every source of revenue so far as he can ascertain the same. Said books and all papers, vouchers, contracts, bonds, receipts and other things kept in said office, shall be subject to the examination of the mayor, the members of the common council, or any committee or committees thereof.

SEC. 11. The comptroller shall be charged with, and shall exercise a general supervision over, all the officers of the city charged in any manner with the receipt, collection or disbursement of the city revenues, and the collection and return of such revenues into the city treasury. He shall be the fiscal agent of said city, and as such shall have charge of all deeds, mortgages, contracts, judgments, notes, bonds, debts, choses in action, belonging to said city, and shall possess and carefully preserve all assessment and tax warrants, and the returns thereof made by any collector or receiver of taxes and assessments, and all leases of markets, wharfing privileges and other public property of said city. He shall also have supervision over the city debts, contracts, bonds, obligations, loans and liabilities of the city, the payment of interest, and over all the property of the city and the sale or the disposition thereof; over all legal or other proceedings in which the interests of the city are involved, and with the approval of the mayor to institute or discontinue such proceedings, and to employ additional counsel, where he thinks the city interests require it, and generally, in subordination to the mayor and common council, to exercise such supervision over all interests of said city, as in any manner may concern or relate to the city finances, revenues and property.

SEC. 12. It shall be the comptroller's duty to examine, adjust and audit all accounts, claims and demands for or against the city; and no money shall, after his appointment as aforesaid, be drawn from the treasury, or paid by the city to any person or persons, unless the balance due or payable be first settled and adjusted by the said comptroller; and for the purpose of ascertaining the true state of any balance or balances so due, he shall have and he is hereby clothed with full power and authority to administer an oath or oaths to the claimant or claimants, or any other person or persons whom he may think proper to examine as to any fact, matter or thing concerning the correctness of any account, claim or demand presented, and the person so sworn shall, if he swear falsely, be deemed guilty of willful and corrupt perjury, and be subject to punishment accordingly, the same as in all other cases.

SEC. 13. All money found to be due and payable by the comptroller to any person or persons, shall be drawn for by said comptroller by warrant on the treasurer, which shall be countersigned by the mayor, stating therein the particular fund or appropriation to which the same is chargeable and the person to whom payable; but if said comptroller should, upon any examination of any account as aforesaid, still doubt as to its correctness, he shall submit the same to the mayor and finance committee for their decision thereon, which decision shall be binding upon the city and filed among his other vouchers in the comptroller's office; and after the appointment of said comptroller, no money shall be drawn from the treasury, except on the warrant of the comptroller drawn as aforesaid.

SEC. 14. It shall be the duty of said comptroller, as nearly as may be, to charge all officers in the receipt of revenues or moneys of the city, with the whole amount, from time to time, of such receipts; and in regard to all tax and assessment warrants for the collection of revenue, and all licenses or permits whatever, issued or granted under any ordinance or law of the city, by virtue of which money is receivable or to be received or paid into the city treasury, from or by any person or persons, he shall countersign the same, charging the proper officer the amount collectable thereon; and no tax or assessment warrant, license or other permit issued or granted, under which the collection of any money for said city may be authorized, shall be of any validity or force whatever, unless countersigned by said comptroller. He shall also require of all officers in receipt of city moneys, that they shall submit reports thereof, with vouchers and receipts of payment therefor into the city treasury, weekly or monthly, or as often as he shall see fit to require the same by any regulation which he may adopt; and if any such officer shall neglect to make an adjustment of his accounts when so required as aforesaid, and to pay over such moneys so received, it shall then be the duty of the said comptroller to issue a notice in writing, directed to such officer and his securities, requiring him or them within ten days to make settlement of his said accounts with the comptroller, and to pay over the balance of moneys found to be due and in his hands belonging to said city, according to the books of said comptroller; and in case of the refusal or neglect of such officer to adjust his said accounts, or pay over said balance to the treasury as required, it shall then be the duty of the said comptroller to make report of the delinquency of such officer to the mayor, who shall at once suspend him from office; and the mayor of said city is hereby authorized, upon the happening of such event, to declare said office vacant, with the concurrence of the common council, and to nominate a successor, in case of removal, who shall be appointed, by and with the advice and consent of the common council, to fill said office for the unexpired term of the officer so dismissed as aforesaid.

SEC. 15. The comptroller shall make out an annual statement for publication, in the month of February in each year, two weeks at least before the annual election, giving a full and detailed statement of all the receipts and expenditures of money during the year ending on the first day of said month. The said statement shall also detail the liabilities and resources of said city, the condition of all unexpended appropriations and contracts unfulfilled, and the balances of money then remaining in the treasury, with all sums due and outstanding; the names of all persons who may have become defaulters of the city, and the amount in their hands unaccounted for, and all other things necessary to exhibit the true financial condition of the city; which statement, when examined and approved by the finance committee, shall be published by him in the corporation newspaper at least one week before the annual election.

SEC. 16. The said comptroller shall, also, in the month of April in each year, before the annual appropriations are made by the common council, submit to the same a report of the estimates necessary, as nearly as may be, to defray the expenses of the city government during the ensuing fiscal year, commencing on the first day of the said month of April; he shall, in said report, class the different objects and branches of said city expenditure, giving, as nearly as may be, the amount required for each; and for this purpose he is authorized to require of all city officers and heads of departments, their statements of the condition and expense of their respective departments and offices, with any proposed improvement and the probable expense thereof, of contracts already made and unfinished, and the amount of any unexpended appropriations of the preceding year. He shall also, in such report, show the aggregate income of the preceding fiscal year from all sources; the amount of liabilities outstanding upon which interest is to be paid, and of bonds and city debts payable during the year, when due, and where payable, so that the common council may fully understand the money exigencies and demands of the city for the ensuing year; but in no event shall the common council make the current appropriations of any year exceed in amount the income of the city during the preceding year as ascertained by the comptroller in his said statement, unless in the payment of interest on the public debts of the city they shall provide according to law by taxation or otherwise, some additional fund out of which such excess of appropriations may be made to meet such indebtedness.

SEC. 17. The comptroller shall also keep in his office a correct list of all local and public improvements ordered by the common council and under contract by the city, copies of which shall be furnished him by the city clerk, and all contracts and estimates made by the common council or any officer of said city in relation to such improvements, for any work contracted or undertaken, done or finished, shall be filed in said comptroller's office; and no contract made, shall be of any validity, unless countersigned by said comptroller.

DUTIES OF THE TREASURER.

SEC. 18. The city treasurer shall, hereafter, keep his office in some place to be designated by the common council, appropriated to the keeping of such office, in the treasury department. He shall keep his books and accounts in such manner as the city comptroller or common council may prescribe, and such books and accounts shall be always subject to the inspection of said comptroller and the finance committee.

SEC. 19. All warrants drawn upon the treasurer must be signed by the comptroller and countersigned by the mayor, stating therein the particular fund or appropriation to which the same is chargeable, and the person to whom payable, and no money shall be otherwise paid than upon such warrants so drawn.

SEC. 20. He shall keep a separate account of each fund or appropriation, and the debts and credits belonging thereto.

SEC. 21. He shall give every person paying money into the city treasury a duplicate receipt therefor, specifying the date of payment and upon what account paid; and he shall also file copies of such receipts with the city comptroller at the date of his monthly reports, as herein provided.

SEC. 22. The treasurer shall, at the end of each and every month, and oftener if required, render an account to the comptroller, showing the state of the treasury at the date of such account, and the balance of moneys in the treasury. He shall also accompany such account with the duplicate of all receipts issued by him for moneys received into the treasury, together with all warrants redeemed and paid by him, which said receipts and warrants, with any and all other vouchers held by him, shall be delivered over to the comptroller, and filed with his said account in the comptroller's office upon every day of such settlement.

SEC. 23. The treasurer shall keep all moneys in his hands belonging to the city, in such place or places of deposit as the common council may hereafter by ordinance provide, order, establish or direct; and such moneys shall be kept distinct and separate from his own moneys; and he is hereby expressly prohibited from using, either directly or indirectly, the corporation money or warrants in his custody and keeping for his own use and benefit, or that of any other person or persons whomsoever; and any violation of this provision shall subject him to immediate removal from office by the mayor, with the concurrence of the common council, who are hereby authorized to declare said office vacant; and the mayor, in case of said removal, shall nominate a successor, who shall be appointed to said office upon the confirmation of the said common council, and hold his office for the remainder of the unexpired term of such officer so removed.

SEC. 24. The treasurer shall also report to the common council annually, in the month of February, at least two weeks before the election, and oftener if required, a full and detailed account of all receipts and expenditures, and the state of the treasury. He shall also keep a register of all warrants redeemed and paid into the treasury during the year, describing such warrant, its date, amount, number, the fund from which payable, and persons to whom paid, specifying also the time of receipt thereof, and all such warrants shall be examined at the time of the making such annual report to the common council by the finance committee, who shall examine and compare the same with the books of the comptroller, and report discrepancies, if any, to the common council.

CITY COLLECTORS.

SEC. 25. The city collector hereafter to be elected by the people, shall keep his office in such place or places as may be designated and provided by the common council, appropriated to the keeping of such office in the treasury department, and shall keep in said office, besides his collection and revenue warrants, such other books, vouchers, records and accounts, as the comptroller may, by regulation of the department, direct and prescribe, which books and records, with all other papers, shall remain in and pertain to said office, and be handed over to the successor or successors of said officer.

SEC. 26. All the city collector's papers, books, warrants and vouchers, shall be examined by, and the same are hereby placed under the supervision of the treasurer and comptroller, together with the finance committee; and the said collector and his assistants shall, on receipt of the same, pay over all moneys collected by him of any person or persons to the city treasurer, taking his receipt therefor, which said collector or assistant shall immediately file in the comptroller's office.

SEC. 27. From and after the passage of this act, there shall be no special collectors of the city revenue or assessments appointed by the common council, other than as assistants to the said city collector, who shall be, in all cases, principal in the collector's bureau of the treasury department.

SEC. 28. The city collector shall make report, in writing, to the comptroller weekly, or oftener, if required, of the amount of all moneys collected by him, and the account upon which collected; and shall file with him the vouchers or receipts of the treasurer for the amount so collected.

SEC. 29. The city collector is hereby expressly prohibited from keeping the moneys of the city in his hands, or that of any person or corporation to his use, beyond the time prescribed for the payment of the same to the city treasurer; and any violation of this provision shall subject him to removal from office, in the manner now provided by law; and it is hereby declared to be the duty of the mayor, upon such removal being made, to nominate and appoint a successor, with the advice and consent of the common council. Each assistant collector shall be subject to removal at the pleasure of the finance committee, whenever they may deem the public interest to require it, and their places be filled as provided by law.

SEC. 30. The city collector shall, on the first day of February of each year, submit to the common council and finance committee, a statement of all the moneys by him collected during the year, and the particular warrant, assessment or account upon which collected, and the balance of moneys uncollected on the warrants in his hands or returned to the comptroller, and a copy of such statement shall also be filed with the comptroller.

SEC. 31. The finance committee and the comptroller shall annually meet in the month of February, and compare all such reports and statements as are made by the comptroller, treasurer and collector, and report thereon to the common council.

SEC. 32. In the adjustments of the accounts of the treasurer and collector with the comptroller, there shall be an appeal to the finance committee, whose decision in all matters of controversy arising between said officers in the treasury department shall be binding, unless the common council shall otherwise direct and provide.

SEC. 33. The comptroller, city treasurer and city collector, shall nominate and, by and with the advice and consent of the common council, appoint such various assistant collectors, clerks and subordinates, in their respective offices, as the common council may authorize. Said subordinates shall in all cases be sworn to the faithful discharge of their duties, as other officers.

SEC. 34. The said comptroller, collector and treasurer, shall perform such other duties, and be subject to such other rules and regulations, as the common council may from time to time by ordinance provide and establish.

SEC. 35. The treasurer and city collector, and collectors and all receivers of city moneys, are hereby required to keep safely, without loaning or using, all the city or public moneys collected by them, or otherwise at any time placed in their custody or disposal, till the same is paid over, or directed by the proper officer, warrant, law, or order of the corporation, to be transferred or paid out, and to make all payments and transfers promptly when thereto required by any law or order of said corporation, or under any regulation of the comptroller. And if any one of said officers, or of those connected with them, in the collection, safe keeping or disbursing of said city revenues, shall convert to his or their own use, in any way whatever, or shall use by way of investment in any kind of property or merchandise, or shall loan, with or without interest, any portion of said city moneys entrusted to him or them for safe keeping, disbursement, payment, transfer, or for any other purpose, every such act shall be deemed and adjudged to be an embezzlement of so much of the said moneys as shall be thus taken, converted, invested, used or loaned, which is hereby declared a felony; and any officer or agent of said city, and all persons advising or participating in such act, or being a party thereto, shall, upon conviction before any court of competent jurisdiction in this State, be sentenced to imprisonment for a term of not less than six months nor more than ten years, in the penitentiary of this State, and also be fined in a sum equal to the amount of the money embezzled.

SEC. 36. All returns and accounts made or required to be rendered under this act, by any of the officers in said treasury department, shall be verified by the oath of the person rendering it; in which said oath it shall be declared that said statement, so far as he knows or has reason to believe, is a fair, accurate and full statement of all the moneys in his hands, or which he or any one for him has received since his last official account was rendered; and that he has not, directly or indirectly, used, loaned, invested or converted to his own use, or suffered any one to use, loan, invest or convert to their or his use, any of the moneys receivable or received by him, but that he has acted diligently and without any collusion or fraud in the collection of the public moneys of said city, and that he hath rendered a true and full account thereof in his said statement; which oath shall be attached to and filed with said accounts in the proper office of the comptroller or city clerk, as the case may be; and in case the said statement, or any of them, shall be false, the said person so making such statement shall be deemed guilty of willful and corrupt perjury, and shall be punished accordingly.

COLLECTION OF TAXES AND ASSESSMENTS.

SEC. 37. The annual assessment rolls shall hereafter be returned to the common council, who shall proceed in the manner now prescribed by law to revise and correct the same; and when revised, corrected and confirmed by them, the common council shall then proceed by ordinance, passed as in other cases, to levy the annual taxes authorized by law.

SEC. 38. All orders issued for the collection of the annual taxes, and all special warrants issued for the collection of any special assessments or tax authorized by law, shall be made out in the manner now required by the city charter, be countersigned by the comptroller, and delivered to the city collector on or before the 2nd Tuesday of October, in every year after the passage of this act.

SEC. 39. The collector shall forthwith publish a notice in the corporation newspaper, that such warrants are in his hands for collection, briefly describing the nature of each, and requesting all persons forthwith to make payment thereof at his office, or that the same will be collected at the cost and expense of the persons liable to the payment of such taxes and assessments; said notice to be published for thirty days.

SEC. 40. If, from any cause, the taxes and assessments charged in said collection warrants are not collected or paid on the lands or lots described in such warrants, on or before the first Tuesday in January, ensuing the date of said warrants, it shall be the duty of the collector to prepare and make report thereof to some court of general jurisdiction to be held in Chicago, at any vacation, special or general term thereof, for judgment against the lands, lots and parcels of land, for the amount of taxes, assessments, interest and costs respectively due thereon; and he shall give ten days notice of his intended application before the first day of the said term of the said court, briefly specifying the nature of the respective warrants upon which such application is to be made, and requesting all persons interested therein to attend at such term; and the advertisement so published shall be deemed and taken to be sufficient and legal notice, both of the aforesaid intended application by the collector to said court for judgment, and a refusal and a demand to pay the said taxes and assessments.

SEC. 41. The collector shall obtain a copy of the said advertisement or advertisements, together with a certificate of the due publication thereof, from the printer or publisher of the newspaper in which the same was published, and shall file the same with the clerk of said court at the said term, together with a copy of said report.

SEC. 42. The clerk of said court, upon the filing of such report or reports, and certificate of publication, by the collector, in each case, shall receive and record the same in a book kept for that purpose, in which shall be entered all judgments, orders and other proceedings of said court in relation thereto, and the same shall be preserved as other records of his office; and the said clerk shall place the said report or reports and the certificate attached to each, at the head of the common law docket for said term, in the following form as nearly as may be, to wit:

CITY OF CHICAGO *vs.* JOHN DOE AND OTHERS—Suit for Taxes.

Or, if it be an assessment for some specified improvement, shall also enter said report or reports returned by said collector, in similar forms as nearly as may be, or as follows:

CITY OF CHICAGO *vs.* JOHN DOE AND OTHERS—Suit for assessment on warrants for paving —— street, ——, or the opening of —— street, ——.

Or such other title as will sufficiently indicate the nature of the improvement for which the charge or assessment is due; entering a separate suit upon each of said warrants upon which such reports are made.

SEC. 43. It shall be the duty of the court upon calling the docket of said term, if any defense be offered by any of the owners of said property, or any person having a claim or interest therein, to hear and determine the same in a summary way, without pleadings; and if no defense be made, the said court shall pronounce judgment against the said several lots, lands, pieces or parcels of land, as described in said collector's reports; and shall thereupon direct said clerk to make out and issue an order for the sale of the same, which said order shall be in form as nearly as may be of that prescribed in the twenty-ninth section of an act entitled "An Act concerning the public revenue," approved February 26th, 1839, by the general assembly of this State: *Provided*, That in all such cases, where a defense is interposed, the trial of any issue or issues therein shall have priority over all other cases in said court, and shall be disposed of with as little delay as possible consistently with the demands of public justice at said term. But should justice require that, for any cause, the suit as to one or more owners should be delayed for more than twenty days, judgment shall then be rendered as to the other owners and lands, and process shall issue for the sale thereof the same as in all other cases.

SEC. 44. It shall be the duty of the clerk of such court, within twenty days after such order is granted as aforesaid, to make out under the seal of said court a copy of said collector's report in such case, together with the order of the court thereon, which shall constitute the process on which all lands, lots, sub-lots, pieces and parcels of land shall be sold for the amount of any taxes, assessments, interest and costs so levied, assessed or charged upon them, as provided in this act, or the act to which this is an amendment, or under any section or provision hereof, and the said city collector is hereby expressly authorized and empowered in like manner, as sheriffs may do, acting under process of *fi. fa.* under the laws of the State, to make sale of such lands, lots, pieces or parcels of land, upon twenty days notice, which, instead of posting, he shall publish in some newspaper printed in said city.

SEC. 45. The said notice, so to be published in each case of a judgment upon any special or general collection warrants, and reports as aforesaid, shall contain a list of the delinquent lands and town lots to be sold; the names of the owners, if known; the amount of taxes, interests and costs, or the amount of the assessments, interests and costs, as the case may be, due respectively thereon, and the account upon which the same is due; the court which pronounced the judgment; and that the same will be exposed to public sale at a time and place to be named in said advertisement by said collector. The proceedings may be stopped at any time upon payment of said taxes or assessments, interests and costs, to said collector.

SEC. 46. In all proceedings and advertisements for the collection of such taxes and assessments and the sale of lands therefor, figures may be used to denote lots, sub-lots, lands and blocks, sections, ranges and parts thereof, the year and the amounts, as now provided by law in like places.

SEC. 47. The sale shall be conducted in the manner provided by law in like cases, and shall be of the smallest portion of ground (to be taken from the east side of the premises) for which any person may take the same and pay the amount of assessments or taxes thereon, with interest and costs.

SEC. 48. In all other respects the same proceedings shall be had as to issuing certificates of sale, the making of deeds, and the redemption in cases of sale, as are now provided in the act to which this is an amendment, except that all duplicate certificates of the sale of any premises made by such collector, shall be hereafter filed by the comptroller, and redemption shall be made by the payment of the amount of redemption money to the treasurer, and taking his voucher therefor, and filing the same in the office of said comptroller, who shall thereupon cancel and annul said certificate and sale upon his records.

SEC. 49. The deeds made to purchasers shall be *prima facie* and conclusive evidence to the same extent as to facts, and have the same conclusive force and effect as to the rights of purchasers at such sales, as is now provided by law in the act to which this is an amendment.

SEC. 50. Any change made in the incumbent of the office of the city collector during the pendency of any such proceedings, shall not operate to affect or delay the same, but the successor or successors in office of such collector shall be authorized to do all acts necessary to complete such proceedings the same as if his predecessor had continued in office. In case of a vacancy occurring in any such office, the proceedings shall be prosecuted by the city comptroller until such vacancy is filled by election or otherwise.

SEC. 51. After the next annual election, all sales of property for the non-payment of taxes and assessments, for any improvement of what kind soever, shall be held at the same time with the general sale of property for non-payment of city taxes in each year, unless in particular cases said sale is stayed by examination or process of law, the intent hereof being that there shall be but one general collection by sale of all taxes and assessments whatsoever in each and every year, which sale shall take place in the manner herein before provided and at the same time in each year.

SEC. 52. The common council may direct all special warrants for the collection of any special assessments levied on any property for any improvement, to issue and be delivered to the city collector forthwith, who shall notify by advertisement all persons interested to pay the same immediately; but in all cases where said assessments are not paid on or before the day of the filing of the collector's report for judgment in any court of general jurisdiction, ten per cent. shall be collected as additional costs, and be added to and collected with the other assessments and expenses authorized to be collected on the property assessed; and for this purpose the collector shall add to his said report, on a separate column, the amount of such additional cost: *Provided*, That from and after the expiration of thirty days notice, to be published in the corporation newspaper by the city collector, that he has received such special warrant for collection, he shall be authorized and he is hereby required to demand and collect, for the use of said city, at the rate of ten per cent. per annum on the amount of every assessment made upon any real estate within said city, computed from the day of the date of said warrant to the day of the payment thereof.

POLICE COURT.

SEC. 53. That after the next municipal election, the common council of said city shall designate the two or more justices of the peace, now provided for under the act to which this is an amendment, and who are to have jurisdiction in all actions for the recovery of any fine and penalty under the laws, ordinances and police regulations of said city.

SEC. 54. The said justices of the peace so designated shall hereafter constitute and be styled the police court of said city, and said justices shall continue under such designation to take jurisdiction as justices of the peace for one year, or until their successors be appointed, in all actions for the recovery of any fine or penalty under the laws of said city, and all ordinances, by-laws or police regulations thereof; that while so employed under such designation, as such justice, one of them shall hold a session of said police court daily (Sundays excepted), at the city hall, in such place as the said common council may provide and appoint, until the business before them or him is disposed of.

SEC. 55. The said justice may be compensated by a salary, to be fixed by the common council, to do the business of said police court, in lieu of all other compensation or fees whatever, accruing from the business to be disposed of; and the said justices so designated shall not enter upon their duties nor be appointed to hold such court as justices of the peace aforesaid, unless they first sign and execute an express relinquishment in writing in favor of the city, of all other fees, emoluments, or compensation whatever, than what may be provided by a salary to be fixed as aforesaid by the common council under this act, and such express relinquishment shall be filed in the comptroller's office, and thereafter all justices' fees and costs collected in all actions brought for said city, under the city charter, shall be paid into the city treasury as other revenue of the city.

SEC. 56. There shall be elected by the people at the next municipal election, and biennially thereafter, one "police court clerk," who shall hold his office for two years, and until his successor is elected and qualified. He shall take an oath, the same as other officers elected under this act and the act to which this is amendatory, and shall execute a bond, with sufficient security to the city to be approved by the comptroller and mayor, in such sum as shall be fixed by the common council. He shall receive a fixed salary for his services, the amount thereof to be determined by the common council under this act. He shall have power to administer oaths and appoint deputies when in the opinion of the common council it may be necessary; in which case said deputies shall be nominated by said clerk and approved by the common council, and the common council may prescribe the duties and fix the compensation of such deputies.

SEC. 57. In case of the temporary inability or absence, or in case of a vacancy of the clerk, and there is no deputy, the police court may appoint some competent person to discharge the duties of the office until the vacancy is filled or ceases.

SEC. 58. The duties of the police clerk shall be to keep a full, detailed and complete account on his docket of all cases and persons arrested and brought before the police court, or any of them; how tried and disposed of; the number of cases disposed of; the cases in which moneys have been collected; and the cases in which money is to be collected; the amount of all forfeitures, penalties, and fines assessed, or the punishment fixed in each case, with the fees and costs accrued and accruing thereon, and to collect, prosecute and receive payment of all such fees, fines, penalties and forfeitures, and all judgments and executions, and all moneys whatever accruing or to be paid in for the use of said city from the enforcement of any of the laws thereof, and forthwith to pay over the same to the treasurer of said city, except the constables' and witness' fees, which shall be paid to the respective parties entitled thereto.

SEC. 59. It shall be his duty to see that all cases are properly prosecuted before said police court in the absence of the city attorney. He shall take care that said fines, penalties, forfeitures, fees, judgments and executions, are collected in all cases as speedily as may be, and the police justices shall, so far as is possible, aid said clerk in the collection thereof.

SEC. 60. The said police clerk shall, at the end of every week, make a report to the comptroller of the amount of such fines, fees, penalties and forfeitures, as he may have collected, and pay over the same to the city treasurer, and file his receipt therefor with the said comptroller. He shall also specify in his said reports the number of cases pending; the number of cases in which any fine, forfeiture or penalty has been inflicted, and the amount thereof, and also the amount of moneys outstanding to be collected in such cases; and the state of each case respectively; and upon making each and every such statement, he shall verify the same by oath taken before some competent officer, that such statement is a full, fair and complete statement of the moneys received and collected by him.

SEC. 61. In case of the failure of such clerk to make such report, and pay over said moneys weekly, as herein required, a notice shall be served upon him by the comptroller, that, within ten days, he is required to make such returns, and pay over all moneys received, and, in case of the failure of said clerk to pay over said moneys, and make such report to the satisfaction of said comptroller, he shall be suspended and removed from office, and thereupon the mayor, by and with the advice and consent of the common council, shall appoint his successor to fill the vacancy during the unexpired term.

SEC. 62. It shall be the duty of the clerk of said police court to receive and safely keep in his possession, in such place as may be provided by the common council therefor, all articles of stolen property, of every description, found upon or taken from the possession of any person or persons arrested for, or charged with, crime within said city, by any police officer, constable, or conservator of the peace therein, or any sheriff or officer of the county of Cook.

SEC. 63. Upon the finding of any articles of property stolen, or taken from any person or persons charged with crime, it shall be the duty of all officers finding the same, or arresting such persons, to lodge the said property in possession of said police clerk, and take his receipt therefor.

SEC. 64. The said police court clerk shall keep a record of all such articles, and number the same, stating the description of the article or articles, from whom taken, by what officer or person deposited, where found, and the person losing the same (if known); and it shall be his duty to deliver said articles over to such person or persons as may be entitled thereto, under the order of the court in which the person upon whose possession the property is found, or from whom it is taken, is tried, discharged or convicted.

SEC. 65. In all cases where such person or persons are discharged upon arrest, and there is no legal claimant appearing to replevy or try the right of property, as against such persons arrested, it shall be the duty of the court to order the restitution of the property in all cases.

SEC. 66. In case of the neglect or refusal of any officer or conservator of the peace, to so deposit the property taken or found upon the possession of any person or persons arrested, he shall be subject to indictment, and be fined in a sum not exceeding three thousand dollars, and in no case less than the value of the property, and be imprisoned in the county jail not to exceed one year, and the sentence of the court, in such cases, *ipso facto*, shall vacate the office of the person so convicted.

SEC. 67. The common council, if it think proper, may, by ordinance, provide for the appointment of a prosecuting attorney for said police court, to manage all city cases before it, and, in such case, may provide for his compensation by a salary.

SEC. 68. In case of the appointment of such prosecuting attorney of the police court, he shall prosecute all cases before it, and also superintend the collection of fees, fines, forfeitures, judgments and executions, and keep a docket thereof, and file a monthly report of the number of all cases commenced, and all cases disposed of, with the names of the parties sued, and the amount of fines, fees and forfeitures collected; with the number of cases where moneys are uncollected, and the amount thereof; and file such reports in the city comptroller's office.

SEC. 69. The clerk of the police court and police prosecuting attorney (if any), shall perform such other duties as may be prescribed by ordinance of the common council from time to time.

SEC. 70. Appeals and change of venue may be taken from the police justices, in all cases, the same as before other justices of the peace; but all such appeals shall hereafter be taken to the recorder's court of the city of Chicago.

FEES AND SALARIES.

SEC. 71. From and after the first Tuesday of March next, all fees, perquisites and emoluments of office whatever, by way of compensation for the performance of any official duty or duties, are hereby expressly prohibited to be retained by any officer whose compensaton is provided to be paid by salary, to be fixed by the common council under this act; and all fees, perquisites and emoluments whatever, received or paid, or payable, to any officer, justice of the peace, mayor, clerk, attorney, collector, treasurer, commissioner of public works, comptroller, or other person, whose compensation is to be so paid by a fixed salary, shall belong to and be paid, by such person or persons, into the city treasury of said city, the same as all other revenues belonging thereto; and any violation of this provision shall subject the offender to removal from his office, and the amount received by him shall be recoverable by action of debt or assumpsit, in favor of such city.

SEC. 72. The mayor of said city shall, after the next annual election, receive an annual salary of thirty-five hundred dollars, in lieu of all other compensation whatever.

SEC. 73. The said salaries shall be payable monthly or quarterly out of the appropriate fund, voted by the common council to pay the same, upon the warrant of the comptroller, as in other cases.

SEC. 74. The common council may, by ordinance, establish salaries, as a fixed compensation for such other officers of said city as are not named herein, in their discretion, and may provide for their removal from office, in case they receive or retain other or greater fees than so paid or fixed by the corporation for their services.

SCHOOLS AND SCHOOL FUND.

SEC. 75. The said common council shall have power to annually levy and collect a school tax, not exceeding two mills on the dollar, on all real and personal estate within said city, to meet the expenses of purchasing grounds for school-houses, and building and repairing school-houses, and supporting and maintaining schools.

SEC. 76. It is also hereby enacted that the school tax levied on said real and personal estate, for the year A. D. eighteen hundred and fifty-six, by the common council of said city, be and the same is hereby expressly legalized; and the collector of said city is hereby directed and authorized to collect the same, as in all other cases, the same as if such levy had been authorized by law, all other provisions of any law or enactment, now in force, in conflict with the exercise of the power hereby conferred being hereby expressly repealed.

SEC. 77. The common council of said city shall, before the first Tuesday of May after the passage of this act, appoint fifteen school inspectors, who shall be denominated and styled the board of education of said city. The said board shall be divided into three classes, of five members each; those of the first class shall vacate their seats at the expiration of the first year; those of the second class at the expiration of the second, and those of the third class at the expiration of the third year; so that five new members shall be appointed in every year to succeed those whose terms of office will expire. The board of aldermen, in electing the first board, shall designate the class or term of office to which each inspector is to belong; and the members of said board so elected shall enter upon the discharge of their duties on the said first Tuesday of May, and shall hold their offices for one, two and three years, according to their respective class, as designated by the said board of aldermen when they are so elected, and the same shall be entered upon the journal of proceedings of said board.

SEC. 78. After the first annual election of said board of inspectors, the board of aldermen shall annually thereafter, on or before the first Tuesday of May in every year, appoint five inspectors of said board of education, who shall hold their offices for three years and until their successors are elected and qualified, and shall enter upon the discharge of their duties on the said first Tuesday of May in each year.

SEC. 79. The duties of said board of education shall be the same as now are or may be hereafter prescribed by the laws or ordinances of said city.

SEC. 80. All provisions of law providing for the appointment or election of school trustees in said city, after the first Tuesday in March next, are hereby expressly repealed.

CITY CEMETERIES.

SEC. 81. The city of Chicago is hereby authorized to purchase, hold, take and convey, such tracts of land without the city limits, for the purpose of establishing such cemeteries for the interment of the dead therein, as they may think necessary, which shall be exempt from taxation under any law of this State.

SEC. 82. The common council of said city is hereby authorized and empowered to pass such ordinances, rules and regulations, with regard to the improvement, preservation, laying out, ornamenting, and the sale of burial places or lots in such cemeteries as they may think necessary for the interment of the dead therein, which ground or grounds so laid out shall be placed under the superintendence of the board of public works of said city.

SEC. 83. As soon as said grounds are regulated and laid out, a map or plat thereof shall be made out by the city mayor, and a copy thereof filed in the comptroller's office, who shall have charge of the sale and disposition of all lots therein, under the ordinances and regulations of the common council. The proceeds of such sales shall be paid into the city treasury, and be credited and charged on the books of the treasury department to a "cemetery fund," to be kept distinct from all other funds of said city.

SEC. 84. The said common council is also fully empowered and authorized to provide for the punishment, by ordinance, of all persons who shall, without said city limits, be guilty of any violation of the regulations, rules and ordinances, established by said city in relation to such cemeteries; and such violations may be punished by fine and imprisonment, as in other cases, by any court of competent jurisdiction within said city, and all process issued for the arrest of any person or persons guilty of such violation, may be executed without said city limits, by any officer or constable thereof, the same as if such offense had been committed within the boundaries of the corporation.

MISCELLANEOUS PROVISIONS.

SEC. 85. All ordinances, regulations and resolutions, now in force in the city of Chicago, and not inconsistent with this act, shall remain in force under this act, until altered, modified or repealed by the common council, after this act shall take effect.

SEC. 86. All actions, rights, fines, penalties and forfeitures, in suit or otherwise, which have accrued under any act to which this act is an amendment, or under any ordinance of said city now in force, shall be vested in and be prosecuted by the corporation, and all proceedings now or hereafter commenced for the opening of any street or streets in said city, and the assessment of real estate for any such improvement, is hereby expressly legalized and affirmed, and the common council is hereby expressly authorized to continue such proceedings, and open said street or streets; any defect, decree or order of any court to the contrary notwithstanding.

SEC. 87. All such parts of the act to which this is an amendment, and the several acts amending or in any manner affecting the same, or as are inconsistent with this act, are hereby repealed; but so much and such parts thereof as are not inconsistent with the provisions of this law, shall not be construed as repealed, altered or modified, or in any form affected thereby, but shall continue and remain in full force and virtue.

SEC. 88. All that part of the city which lies west of the south branch of the Chicago river, and south of a line running east and west along the centre of Randolph street, and north of the centre of Harrison street, shall be denominated the fifth ward; and all that part of said city which lies west of the south branch of the Chicago river, and south of a line in the centre of Harrison street, shall be denominated the tenth ward.

SEC. 89. All aldermen and officers now elected or appointed in and for the said fifth ward of said city, shall continue in their respective offices to the end of their respective terms for which they were elected or appointed, any provision of law now in force to the contrary notwithstanding.

SEC. 90. An election shall be held in and for the said tenth ward at the next annual election, for two aldermen to represent such ward in the common council, as also a police constable for said ward; and all provisions of law relating to the several wards of said city shall, so far as they may be applicable, apply to said tenth ward; and in all such elections the qualifications and duties of aldermen shall be the same as required by law in other cases.

PUBLIC PARKS.

SECTION 1. The judge of the Cook county court of common pleas shall, within six months after the passage of this act, or so soon after the annual election as may be, appoint three discreet and disinterested freeholders of said city, as commissioners of estimate and assessment, to lay out a public park in the south division of said city.

SEC. 2. Upon the appointment of said commissioners, they shall severally take an oath before some authorized person, that they will proceed faithfully and impartially to discharge the duties required of them under this act. In case of the death, resignation, disqualification or refusal of either of, or any of said commissioners to act, the said judge of said court shall appoint some disinterested and discreet freeholder of said city to act in the place or stead of the commissioner so dying, resigning, or refusing to act.

SEC. 3. Upon the qualification of said commissioners, they shall proceed to have surveyed, laid out and appropriated, a public park in said south division of Chicago, which shall embrace an area of not less than one hundred acres of land, nor more than three hundred acres, which shall forever remain open and dedicated to the free use and exercise of all citizens of said city, subject to the regulation of the common council thereof.

SEC. 4. The said land so to be taken shall be laid out and appropriated as aforesaid, south of Twelfth street, west of Michigan avenue and east of Stewart avenue, and as nearly central as may be between lake Michigan and the south branch of the Chicago river; and from such blocks, pieces and parcels of land within said territory as may lie contiguous to each other, extending southwardly to the southern limits of said city, and widening the area southward of such park, in such places and in such proportion as the commissioners may think will combine taste and utility with cheapness of price in the land to be taken.

SEC. 5. The said commissioners may require the assistance of the city surveyor and engineer, in making all necessary surveys, plats and profiles of said public grounds; and as soon as said commissioners shall determine upon the grounds to be appropriated and taken, they shall file a plat thereof in the city clerk's office, and shall submit one other copy with a report signed by said commissioners to the court of common pleas, in vacation or term time, which shall be spread upon the records of said court; and thereupon the said lands, lots and pieces and parcels of land designated on such plat, shall be and they are hereby declared to be a public park and common, in said city; said reports shall be filed within three months from the appointment of said commissioners.

SEC. 6. After the filing of said report, it shall be the duty of said commissioners, as soon as conveniently may be, to make just and true estimates of the loss and damage to the respective owners, lessees, parties and persons respectively entitled unto or interested in the lands designated in their said report and included within the boundaries of said public park or common, together with the tenements, hereditaments and premises and their appurtenances, and each and every part and parcel thereof, as far as can be ascertained by them; and shall state in their report, in general terms, the respective sums to be allowed and paid to the owner or owners and proprietors generally of such lands, tenements, hereditaments and premises, or the appurtenances and privileges to the same belonging or appertaining, and the loss and damages to the owners thereof (if known, and if unknown, shall so state in said report,) in respect to the whole estate and interest of whomsoever may be entitled unto or interested in said lands, by and in consequence of relinquishing the same to the city of Chicago for said public park.

SEC. 7. It shall not be necessary to specify the name of the estates of the different owners, proprietors or parties interested, or of any or either of them, but generally to put down the damage to the property taken or described in such report.

SEC. 8. Upon the coming in of such report, signed by said commissioners or any two of them, the said court shall, by rule or order, after hearing any matter or thing which shall be alleged against the same, either confirm the said report, or refer the same back to the said commissioners for revisal and correction, or to new commissioners to be appointed by said court, to reconsider the subject-matter thereof, and the same being returned by such new commissioners, the court shall proceed in like manner as before provided, as right and justice may require, until a report shall be made or returned in the premises, which the said court shall confirm, and such report when so confirmed, shall be final and conclusive, as well upon said city as upon all owners or others interested in the lands so appropriated and designated as aforesaid, and from thenceforth the said city shall be seized of all said premises to the use of a public park for the people of Chicago forever.

SEC. 9. The said commissioners shall also in their said proceedings, assess the said damages and costs, or so much thereof as is just and equitable, upon all property benefited, in proportion, as nearly as may be, to the benefit resulting thereto from such improvement to the owners of all such property benefited; and shall in like manner include the same in their said report, with the description of all the said property benefited, and the names of the owners where known, and where unknown shall so state in their said report, and upon the confirmation of said report, the said court shall enter an order against said lands assessed for the amount of such assessment, including all costs and expenses of said proceedings; under which order the collector of said city shall be designated to collect the same of the respective owners, and in case of default, to sell such lands and all interest therein at public sale, upon twenty days notice, in the same manner that other sales are authorized to be made for the non-payment of taxes and assessments of said city.

SEC. 10. For the payment of so much of the damages awarded by the commissioners of estimate and assessment, and the expenses, disbursements and charges in the premises, as shall exceed the amount or sums that may be assessed by said commissioners upon the parties and persons, lands and tenements deemed by them benefited by the laying out of such public park, it shall be lawful for the mayor and common council to raise such excess by loan, by the creation of a public fund or stock to be called the "Chicago Park Stock," which shall bear an interest not exceeding ten per centum per annum, and shall be redeemed within a period of time not exceeding fifty years after the passage of this act, and for the payment of which, the piece of land so taken, as aforesaid, shall be irrevocably pledged.

SEC. 11. The mayor and common council shall determine what shall be the nominal amount or value of each share of stock, and of what number of shares the same shall consist, and the mayor of said city is hereby authorized to sell and dispose of such shares on such terms as the common council may prescribe.

SEC. 12. In order to pay the interest on said stock hereby authorized, the common council of said city shall, and they are hereby authorized and empowered to order, and cause to be raised annually by tax on the property, real and personal, subject to taxation within the south division of said city, a sum of money sufficient to pay the interest annually accruing on said stock, which amount shall be levied and collected in addition to the ordinary taxes yearly and every year, for the payment of such interest.

SEC. 13. After the report and order of confirmation is entered by the court as herein provided, the city shall make provision for the payment of all damages within six months from the confirmation thereof, and in case the same is not paid to the persons entitled thereto, or deposited to their use with the clerk of the said court of common pleas, an action may be maintained by any person or persons entitled thereto against the corporation for the amount of his share of said damages.

SEC. 14. In case at any time that all the aldermen of the west or north divisions of said city, shall agree in presenting a petition to the said Cook county court of common pleas, for the laying out a park in their respective divisions, the court shall proceed to appoint commissioners, and all the provisions of this act shall in like manner apply to the respective divisions, where the laying out such park is desired, in the manner aforesaid, the same as if said divisions were respectively named herein.

This act to take effect and be in force from and after its passage.

Approved February 16, 1857.

AN ACT to define, confirm and legalize the Acts of a Fish Inspector of the City of Chicago.

SECTION 1. *Be it enacted by the People of the State of Illinois, represented in the General Assembly,* That from and after the passage of this law, no fresh water fish shall be sold, or received for sale, or on consignment, in or at the city of Chicago, without being first duly inspected by the legal inspector of and for the city of Chicago, appointed by virtue of this act, as hereinafter mentioned.

SEC. 2. It shall be the duty of every person or persons bringing or causing to be brought to the city of Chicago, for the purpose of sale, any fresh water fish, to have the same duly inspected by the legal inspector of the city of Chicago, before such fish shall be sold or in any way disposed of; and it shall be the duty of every person or persons receiving such fish, by consignment, for and on account of any other party, to have such fish duly inspected by the fish inspector of the city of Chicago, before delivering them to the owner or his agent or other person; and such consignee shall pay the fees of inspection, and shall have a lien upon such fish in his possession for the fees so advanced by him; and it shall be the duty of every person having such fish in his possession, for the purpose of selling or of dealing in the same, and of every consignee having fish on consignment, before the said fish shall be sold or in anywise disposed of, to give notice to the inspector, and have such fish duly inspected and branded; and for this purpose, such person shall arrange the packages in a convenient manner, and have them in some suitable place.

SEC. 3. It shall be the duty of the fish inspector, on due application of any person or persons having such fish in possession, to repair to the place of deposit of such fish, if the same shall be within the city limits of the city of Chicago, and shall inspect the same with as little delay as possible.

SEC. 4. It is hereby made the duty of the fish inspector to procure sealed weights, and carefully weigh all fish offered for inspection; and to entitle said inspector to grant a certificate of due inspection, or to brand the packages as duly inspected, he shall first find that the contents and weights of the several packages are as follows, viz.: Each barrel shall contain two hundred pounds; each half barrel shall contain one hundred pounds; each quarter barrel shall contain fifty pounds; and each eighth barrel shall contain twenty-five pounds. Such inspector shall, also, on branding any package of fish as inspected, plainly and distinctly mark on the head of each package, in some indelible manner, the kind, quantity and quality of fish contained in each package respectively, together with his name and the year and month in which the same shall have been inspected.

SEC. 5. The inspector shall be liable, by suit, in any court having jurisdiction of the cause, for all damages that may accrue to any person or persons, or company, by reason of misfeasance or malfeasance in the inspection of any package of fish.

SEC. 6. The inspector shall be entitled to the following fees for the performance of his duties, viz.: For unheading, heading, weighing, repacking, brining, and inspecting and branding each barrel, twenty-five cents; each half barrel, fifteen cents; each quarter barrel, ten cents; each extra hoop, five cents; each extra head, twenty-five cents.

SEC. 7. The inspector shall not put his brand upon any package of fish, as duly inspected, unless the same be well hooped and headed, and in all respects sufficient to retain brine, and also be in good shipping condition.

SEC. 8. No person holding the office of fish inspector for said city of Chicago, nor shall his employees or assistants, or either of them, buy or sell, or deal in, or in anywise be interested, in any fish to be sold or consigned to the city of Chicago.

SEC. 9. Every fish inspector, appointed by virtue hereof, shall keep a record of the number of packages and sizes, and of the kinds and qualities of fish, and for whom inspected by him, each year; and shall make a report of the same to the common council, on the first day of January in each year.

SEC. 10. It shall be the duty of the fish inspector to keep an office at a convenient place, on or near the Chicago river, which shall be kept open during business hours, and in which the inspector shall at all times have some person, during his absence, to receive orders.

SEC. 11. It shall be the duty of the inspector of fish to see to the enforcement of this law, and that all violations of the same are prosecuted.

SEC. 12. Any fish inspector violating, refusing or failing to comply with any of the provisions of this law, so far as they are made incumbent upon him, shall, for every offense, be liable to a fine of not less than five dollars nor more than one hundred dollars; which said fine may be collected in the same way as is provided by the Revised Statutes for the collection of fines in cases of misdemeanors.

SEC. 13. Every inspector of fish, who shall be appointed in pursuance hereof, shall, before entering upon the discharge of the duties of his said office, give bond, with two good and sufficient sureties, in the penal sum of five thousand dollars, and running to the people of the State of Illinois, and conditioned that he will well and faithfully perform the duties of said office, and satisfy all damages that may legally be demanded of him by virtue of the provisions hereof.

SEC. 14. The inspector appointed by virtue hereof shall have the right to appoint, and the same to remove at pleasure, one or more assistants, who shall have the same right to brand all packages inspected by either of them in the name of the said inspector; but each assistant shall have some distinctive mark, with which he shall designate each package inspected by himself, so as to indicate by whom the inspection was actually made; and the said inspector shall have the right to take bond, with sufficient penalty and security, running to himself, from each of the assistants appointed by himself, and to the same tenor, as the bond herein required to be executed by said inspector; and the said inspector shall be liable for the acts of his said assistants, and may sue on the bonds of any of them, to recover any damages that he may have suffered by reason of their misfeasance or malfeasance.

SEC. 15. The said inspector shall have the right to sue, in any court having jurisdiction of the action, for his fees for services performed, either by himself or his assistants, by virtue hereof.

SEC. 16. The inspector, to be appointed as herein provided, shall be appointed by the common council of the city of Chicago as soon as convenient after the annual election of said body; and he shall hold his office for the term of two years and until his successor be legally qualified.

SEC. 17. The present inspector of fish, heretofore appointed by the common council of the city of Chicago, and now in office, shall be and continue such inspector until his successor shall be appointed and qualified, at the time herein mentioned.

SEC. 18. This act shall become a law immediately on its passage.

Approved February 18, 1857.

AN ACT in addition to an Act entitled "An Act to incorporate a Board of Sewerage Commissioners for the City of Chicago," approved February 14th, 1855.

SECTION 1. *Be it enacted by the People of the State of Illinois, represented in the General Assembly,* That the board of sewerage commissioners for the city of Chicago, shall have power to borrow (in addition to the sum heretofore authorized) a further sum, not exceeding five hundred thousand dollars, upon the credit of the city of Chicago, and shall have authority to issue bonds pledging the faith and credit of said city for the payment of the principal and interest of said bonds.

SEC. 2. The said bonds shall, in all respects, be issued and registered and the principal and interest provided for and paid in the same manner and subject to the same regulations as provided in the original act to which this is an addition, and all the provisions of the said original act establishing a sinking fund, or securing in any manner the payment of the principal and interest of the bonds authorized to be issued by the said act to which this is an addition, shall apply to the bonds authorized to be issued by this act, in the same manner and to the same extent, to all intents and purposes, as if the said bonds hereby authorized had been issued under and by authority of the said original act.

SEC. 3. The said board of sewerage commissioners shall hold, retain, apply and appropriate the said bonds and the proceeds thereof for the same objects and purposes, and subject in all respects to the same terms, conditions, restrictions, penalties and liabilities as are contained in the act to which this is an addition; and the said act shall apply in the like manner, to all intents and purposes, to the said bonds hereby authorized to be issued, and the proceeds thereof, and to the rights, duties and liabilities of said sewerage commissioners, respecting the same, as if the said bonds hereby authorized to be issued had been issued under and by virtue of the act to which this is an addition.

SEC. 4. The said bonds shall not be sold at a rate less than that which is provided by the said act to which this is an amendment, unless the common council of said city shall, by a vote of a majority of all the aldermen elected, authorize the said board of sewerage commissioners to sell the same at a lower rate, and then only at such a rate as shall be fixed by said city council: *Provided, however*, That reasonable commissions to brokers or agents employed in procuring the sale or negotiation of said bonds may be paid by said board.

Approved February 14, 1859.

AN ACT to amend an Act approved February 16, 1857, which was entitled "An Act to amend the Act entitled 'An Act to reduce the Law incorporating the City of Chicago, and the several Acts amendatory thereof, into one Act, and to amend the same,'" approved February 14, 1851.

WHEREAS, on the 16th day of February, 1857, the general assembly of the State of Illinois passed "An Act to amend the act entitled 'An Act to reduce the law incorporating the city of Chicago, and the several acts amendatory thereof, into one act, and to amend the same,'" approved February 14th, 1851; and whereas, in said act, under the head of "Public Parks," the judge of the Cook county court of common pleas was directed and requested to appoint three discreet and disinterested freeholders of said city, as commissioners of estimate and assessment, to lay out a public park in the south division of said city; and whereas, the authority to lay out a public park was immature, and not demanded by the interests of the people in the south division of said city; now therefore,

Be it enacted by the People of the State of Illinois, represented in the General Assembly, That all that portion of said act, aforesaid, which concerns public parks, and which authorizes the appointment of commissioners and the laying out a public park in the south division of the city of Chicago, be and the same is hereby repealed.

This act to take effect and be in force from and after its passage.

Approved February 19, 1859.

AN ACT to amend an Act to amend the Act entitled "An Act to reduce the Law incorporating the City of Chicago, and the several Acts amendatory thereof, into one Act, and to amend the same," approved February 14, 1851, and to reduce the several Acts amendatory of said Act into one Act, and to amend the Act entitled "An Act to incorporate the Chicago City Hydraulic Company," approved February 15, 1851, and to reduce the several Acts amendatory of said last mentioned Acts into one Act, and to amend the Act entitled "An Act to incorporate a Board of Sewerage Commissioners for the City of Chicago," approved February 14, 1855.

SECTION 1. *Be it enacted by the People of the State of Illinois, represented in the General Assembly*, That the municipal elections in said city shall be held on the third Tuesday in April, at which time there shall be elected by the qualified voters of said city, all officers to be elected at the general municipal election. The first election shall be held on the third Tuesday in April, 1861, and no special election shall be hereafter held in said city, for the election of city officers, except as in this act provided.

SEC. 2. The term of office of the mayor, aldermen, water commssioners, sewerage commissioners, and of all officers now elected or appointed in and for said city, except as is in this act specially provided, is hereby extended, and shall continue until the first Monday in May, 1861, and until their successors are elected and qualified. The present city marshal shall continue in office until the expiration of the term for which he was elected, when the office of city marshal shall expire, and there shall be no "city marshal" in said city after the fourth day of March, 1862. The term of office of all water commissioners and of all sewerage commissioners in said city shall expire on the first day of May, A. D. 1861, any provision of law now in force to the contrary notwithstanding.

BOARD OF PUBLIC WORKS.

SEC. 3. That so much of the act to which this is an amendment as provides for the election of a street commissioner in the north, south and west divisions of said city, at the annual election, and for the appointment of a city superintendent by the common council of said city, is hereby repealed. All provisions in relation to the duties of said officers, mentioned in this section, shall continue in force to the first Monday in May next, at which time the same shall cease to have any force or effect whatosever: *Provided*, That the city shall have the right to enforce the performance of all contracts heretofore entered into, and the rights and liabilities accrued or to accrue, under any provisions of law now in force, and to continue and complete all proceedings commenced under any law or ordinance of said city, and to assess the costs and expenses of any improvement or work heretofore ordered, and the assessment for the same, the same as if said provisions of law remained in full force and effect; and the commissioners of the board of public works hereby created, shall carry out such contracts and complete all such improvements or works heretofore commenced.

SEC. 4. After the first Monday in May, 1861, there shall be organized in said city, an executive department of the municipal government, to be known as the "Board of Public Works."

SEC. 5. The said board of public works shall consist of three commissioners, to be chosen, one from the north, one from the south, and one from the west division of said city, who shall constitute said board. At the next city election to be holden in said city on the third Tuesday in April, 1861, there shall be elected by the qualified voters of said city, three commissioners of said board, from the said divisions, who when elected shall be the first commissioners of said board of public works, and who shall respectively hold their offices for two, four and six years, and until their successors are duly elected and qualified.

SEC. 6. The said commissioners herein named, shall, within ten days after the first Monday in May, A. D. 1861, proceed to organize said board, and decide by lot their respective terms of office, which decision shall be filed and deposited in the office of the city clerk.

SEC. 7. On the third Tuesday of April, A. D. 1863, and biennially thereafter, there shall be elected at the general city election, held in said city, one commissioner of said board of public works, to succeed the member thereof whose term of office expires; which commissioner shall be elected from the division of said city represented by the commissioner whose term of office expires; and said commissioner, when elected, shall hold his office for the term of six years, and until his successor in office is duly elected and qualified; should a vacancy occur, it shall be filled by appointment by the mayor, with the advice and consent of the common council of said city, until the next regular city election, when the qualified voters of said city may, as in other cases, fill such vacancy by an election of a successor, who shall hold his office for the unexpired term; said commissioners shall be elected in the same manner as is now provided by law for the election of general city officers, by general ticket, by the qualified voters of the whole city; and no person shall be elected a commissioner of said board of public works, unless he has been a resident of said city for at least three years, and a resident in the division of said city for which he is elected, at least one year immediately preceding his election.

SEC. 8. Before entering on the discharge of his duties, each of said commissioners shall give bond to said city in the sum of one hundred thousand dollars, with sureties to the satisfaction of the acting judge of the circuit court for Cook county, which bond shall be conditioned for the faithful discharge and performance of his duties as such commissioner; and that he will well and truly pay over any and all moneys, and surrender any and all property, books and papers which may come into his hand as such commissioner, on the expiration of his term of office, or when required so to do by the common council.

SEC. 9. Said board of public works shall have the charge and superintendence of all streets, alleys, lanes or highways in said city, and of all walks and cross-walks in the same, and of all bridges, docks, wharves, public places, public landings, public grounds and parks in said city, and of all markets, market places and market houses, engine houses, hospitals, armories and all other public buildings in said city, belonging to the city, except school-houses, and of the location and erection of all public buildings, of all lamps and lights for the lighting of the streets, alleys, lanes, highways, bridges, parks, public places and public buildings of the city, and of the erection and repair of such lamps and lights, and the creation of new lamp districts; of all works for the widening, deepening or dredging of the Chicago river, or either of its branches; of all sewers and the works pertaining thereto; of the water works of said city; of all public improvements hereafter to be commenced by said city; and they shall perform all the duties by this act prescribed, and such other duties as the common council may prescribe by ordinance.

SEC. 10. Said board is authorized to employ, from time to time, such superintendent or superintendents, engineers, surveyors, clerks, assistants and workmen, in the discharge of their duties, as they may deem necessary, and shall pay their employees such salaries or wages as they shall deem proper.

SEC. 11. Two of said commissioners shall constitute a quorum to do business; they shall keep a record of all their acts and doings, and adopt rules for their government and the government of their employees; and they shall keep and preserve copies of all contracts, estimates, receipts, plans, profiles, and the papers of the board; and shall report their acts and doings in detail to the common council, on or before the first Monday in January and July in each year, and oftener when required so to do by the common council.

SEC. 12. All applications for a change of grade, the erection of bridges, the creation of lamp districts, the lighting of streets and public places, the grading, regrading, paving, repaving, graveling and regraveling, macadamizing, planking, replanking of streets, alleys, highways or lanes, and the cleaning thereof, the construction and repairs of sidewalks, the improvements of public grounds or buildings belonging to the city, the widening, deepening or dredging of the Chicago river, or either of its branches, the opening, straightening, widening or closing of any street, alley, lane or highway, or for any other improvement, the doing of which is now placed by law under the care and within the control of the municipal government of said city, shall hereafter be first made to the said board of public works. Upon receiving any such application, the said board shall proceed to investigate the same; and if they shall determine that such improvement is necessary and proper before recommending the same to the common council, they shall cause an estimate of the expense and cost of the making of such improvement, or doing such work, to be made; which estimate, together with a plan or profile of the work to be done, or improvement to be made, shall accompany such recommendation of said board to the common council; and if they do not approve of such application, they shall report such application, with the reason for their disapproval; and the common council may then order the doing of such work, or the making of such improvement, having first ordered an estimate of the expense thereof.

SEC. 13. The said board shall have the exclusive privilege to grant permits, according to the ordinances of the city, for the moving of houses through the streets of the city; and shall regulate the building or placing of vaults under the sidewalks, and all open spaces for the basement stories; and the use of the public streets in any legal and proper manner, except for railroad tracks; and no building material or obstruction of any kind shall be placed in the public streets, alleys, or on the public grounds, without the written permit of said board. Said board shall have full power to regulate and control the manner of using the streets, alleys, highways and public places of the city, for the laying down of gas or water pipes and sewers, and to cause the prompt repair of the streets, alleys, highways and public places, whenever the same may be taken up or altered; and they are hereby authorized and empowered to charge and collect by suit or otherwise, in the name of the city of Chicago, the expense of such repairs to and from the person or persons by whom such street, alley, highway or public ground may have been taken up or altered.

SEC. 14. The said board shall have the exclusive privilege of granting permits for the erection of wooden buildings within the fire limits of said city, and to regulate and superintend the erection of the same.

SEC. 15. The said board shall hereafter superintend and direct the labor required to be performed, by law, by male residents over twenty-one years of age, upon the streets and alleys of said city, and to give the notices now required to be given by the street commissioners in said city; and they shall report to the city comptroller the number of persons so liable to labor upon said streets and alleys, when notified, and the number and names of the persons in default and refusing to work, so that the comptroller may take such measures to collect the street tax due from such persons, in lieu of said labor, and properly charge the same in like manner as other revenues of said city; and said board of public works are hereby vested, for the purposes of this section, with all powers now conferred by law on the street commissioners in said city.

SIDEWALKS.

SEC. 16. Said board shall, when they may deem it proper and necessary to repair or construct any sidewalk, direct the occupant or owner, where he may be known, of any lot, sub-lot, piece or parcel of ground fronting the same, upon any street, alley, lane or highway, to repair or construct such sidewalk at his own proper cost and charge, under the superintendence of said board, in such manner and of such material as they may prescribe, and within such reasonable time as they shall direct, and if the same is not so completed within such time, the board shall cause an estimate of the expense of repairing or constructing such sidewalk to be made, and shall report the same to the common council, together with recommendation that the proper ordinance be passed for the doing of such work; on the passage of such ordinance the board of public works shall proceed to make an assessment of the cost, damages and expenses for the making of such improvement, or for the doing of such work, the members of the said board being hereby appointed special commissioners to make such assessment. The damages, costs and expenses of making such contemplated improvement shall be assessed on the lot, sub-lot, piece or parcel of land, fronting, bounding or abutting thereon, and shall be in proportion to the number of front feet of the said lot, sub-lot, piece or parcel of land so bounding, abutting or fronting on such improvement.

GRADING, CURBING, PAVING, PLANKING AND REPAIRING OF STREETS.

SEC. 17. Whenever the board of public works may consider it necessary that any street, alley, lane or highway should be graded, curbed, paved, with wood, stone or other material, or repaved, or planked, replanked, macadamized or repaired, graveled, regraveled, they shall report the same to the common council of said city, accompanied with a plan or profile of the work to be done, an estimate of the expense for the doing of the same, accompanied with a proper ordinance for the ordering of such work to be done; and if the common council shall order such work to be done, or such public improvement to be made, the said board of public works shall proceed to make an assessment of the benefits and the damages, costs and expenses of the doing of such work, and the making of such contemplated improvement, the said board of public works being hereby appointed commissioners to make such assessments. The damages, costs and expenses of making such improvements shall be assessed on the lot, sub-lot, piece or parcel of land fronting, bounding or abutting thereon, and shall be in proportion to the number of front feet of the said lot, sub-lot, piece or parcel of land so bounding, abutting or fronting on such improvement.

OPENING OF STREETS AND PUBLIC GROUNDS.

SEC. 18. Whenever said board of public works shall deem it for the interest of said city to open, widen, lay out, extend, alter, narrow, straighten or close any public street, alley, lane, highway, park or public ground of said city, or to improve any park or public ground, they shall report the same to the common council, accompanied with a plan or profile of the contemplated work or improvement, and an estimate of the expense of the same, and they shall also specially report what damages it will be necessary to assess, and whether, in their opinion, lands, tenements and hereditaments, with any or all interests to be benefited or assessed can be found benefited to the extent of the damages, costs and expenses necessary to be incurred in the making of such contemplated improvement; and if the common council shall order such public improvement to be made, the said commissioners of said board of public works shall proceed to make an assessment of the benefits and damages, cost and expenses of the doing of such work, and the making of such contemplated improvement, the said board of public works being hereby appointed commissioners to make such assessment in accordance with the extent of the benefits accruing, and of the reports theretofore made by said board, and the damages, costs and expenses of making such improvement shall be assessed by the commissioners on the real estate deemed benefited by such improvement in proportion to the benefits resulting therefrom as nearly as may be.

WIDENING, DEEPENING AND DREDGING OF THE CHICAGO RIVER AND ITS BRANCHES.

SEC. 19. Whenever said board of public works shall deem it for the interest of said city to widen, deepen or dredge out the Chicago river or either of its branches, or any part or parts of the same, it shall report such fact to the common council of said city, together with an estimate of the cost and expense of the making of such improvement, accompanied with a plan or profile of the contemplated improvement, with an ordinance ordering the doing of such work, and the making of such improvement, and if the common council shall order such work to be done, the commissioners of said board of public works shall proceed to make an assessment of the benefits and damages, costs and expenses of the doing of such work, or the making of such improvement, said board of public works being hereby appointed commissioners to make such assessments. The damages, costs and expenses of making such improvement shall be assessed on the property, by the commissioners, deemed benefited by the making of such improvement.

SURVEYING AND CLEANING STREETS, AND REPAIRING PUBLIC BUILDINGS.

SEC. 20. The cost and expense of surveying streets, alleys, lanes and highways, and the cleaning thereof, and the cleansing of public places, markets and gutters, all improvement at the intersection of streets or alleys, or of streets and alleys, and the repair of public buildings within said city, and the construction of cross-walks, shall be chargeable upon and paid out of the general fund of said city: *Provided*, The common council of said city shall have the same power, as is now provided by law, to punish all violations of any ordinance or regulation in relation to the public health of the city.

BUILDING BRIDGES.

SEC. 21. When the board shall deem it for the interest of said city that any bridge should be hereafter constructed over the Chicago river, or either of its branches, they shall estimate the whole expense thereof, and submit such estimate, with a proper plan, to the common council, who may then direct the construction thereof, under the superintendence of said board: *Provided*, Whenever a suitable number of persons shall agree to secure to the board of public works the full expense of constructing any bridge, the common council may, in their discretion, authorize the persons agreeing to bear the expense thereof, to contract for the building of such bridge. In such case, however, the board of public works shall have the entire charge and superintendence of such work, and the plans for the same shall be subject to their approval.

SEC. 22. All public improvements, not herein specified to be paid for by special assessment, shall be paid for out of the general fund of said city, or in such manner as the common council of said city shall direct.

SEC. 23. Whenever said board of public works shall recommend to the common council the passage of an ordinance directing the doing of any work, or the making of any public improvement, to be paid for by a special assessment, they shall with such recommendation certify to said common council whether the doing of such work, or the making of such public improvement, is asked for by the petition of the owners of three-fourths of the property so to be assessed for the doing of such work, or the making of such public improvement, and if the owners of three-fourths of the property so to be assessed shall fail to petition for the making of such public improvement, or the doing of such work, the same shall only be ordered by the votes of three-fourths of all the aldermen elected, such vote to be entered by ayes and noes on the record of the common council. The certificate of said board of public works shall be *prima facie* as to the number of said petitioners, and of the interest of those asking for the doing of such work, or the making of such public improvement.

SEC. 24. So much of the act to which this is an amendment as provides for the appointment by the common council of said city, of commissioners to make special assessments, is hereby repealed, and said commissioners of said board of public works shall in all cases act as commissioners to make special assessments whenever the same may be ordered, for the making of which assessments they shall receive no fees.

SEC. 25. The said commissioners of said board of public works shall, before proceeding to make any assessment, give six days notice, by publication in the corporation newspaper, of the time and place, when and where they will proceed to make such assessment, in which notice they shall specify what such assessment is to be for, the amount of such assessment, and the premises to be assessed, as near as may be done by general description. The meeting of said commissioners, when engaged in making an assessment, shall be held in a public place in said city, to be specified in said notice, and all persons interested in any such assessment shall have the right to be present and be heard, either in person or by counsel, at the making of such assessment, and to introduce witnesses at such hearing, for the purpose of proving the true value of the premises assessed, or of the damages sustained by the reason of the making of such improvement; and the said commissioners, for this purpose, are hereby authorized to administer oaths to all witnesses produced before them, and they may require the city attorney to appear before them at such hearing, to represent the interests of the city, and said commissioners, when engaged in making an assessment, may adjourn from time to time, until such assessment is completed.

SEC. 26. When any assessment shall have been completed by the board of public works, and the assessment roll shall have been made up, a copy of the same shall be filed in the office of said board, and a duplicate thereof shall be filed in the office of the city clerk, signed by the acting president of said board of public works, and six days notice shall be given by said commissioners, by publication in the corporation newspaper, of the filing of such copy of such assessment roll in the office of the city clerk, and that at the next regular meeting of the common council after the expiration of such publication, the said commissioners will apply to the common council for a confirmation of such assessment. All parties interested in said assessment shall have the right to be heard at such meeting of the common council, both for and against such assessment. All parties objecting to such assessment shall file their objections to the same in writing, in the office of the city clerk, at least two days prior to such meeting of the common council, and the council shall have power to adjourn such hearing from time to time, and shall have the power in their discretion to revise and correct the assessment, and confirm or annul the same, and direct a new assessment to be made. Said assessments, when confirmed by the common council, shall be final and conclusive to all parties interested therein, except as is hereinafter provided; and when said assessment is confirmed by the common council, and no appeal is taken, as herein provided, a warrant shall issue for the collection of the same, signed by the mayor and city clerk. If any assessment shall be set aside, the board of public works shall proceed to make a new assessment, in like manner, for the same purpose, for the collection of the amount so assessed. Any person interested in any special assessment made by the board of public works, at any time within ten days after the confirmation of such assessment by the common council, and not after that time, having first given notice of his, her or their intention so to do, to the city attorney, by leaving a written notice at his usual place of business with some white person over the age of ten years, of such intention, specifying in such notice the court to which the appeal is to be taken, shall have the right to pray an appeal to any court of record for Cook county, from the order of the common council confirming such assessment, first giving bond to said city, approved by the judge or judges of the court to which such appeal is taken, conditioned to save the city harmless from all damages caused by the taking of such appeal; and which bond, together with the objection to such assessment roll, specifying with such objection the land for which such objection is made, having been filed in the office of the clerk of the court to which such appeal shall be taken, shall be by such clerk docketed in the name of the person taking such appeal against the city of Chicago, "appeal from assessment," and on the filing of a copy of the assessment roll, as confirmed by the common council, the same shall be at issue, and shall have the preference in order of trial over all civil causes pending in said court. Such appeal shall be tried before the judge and jury, and on such trial the only question to be passed on by the jury shall be, whether the valuation of the property specified in such objections, is the true value of the property, and whether such assessment is a fair and impartial assessment.

SEC. 27. If the first assessment prove insufficient, the board of public works shall make a second in the same manner, and so on, until sufficient moneys shall have been realized to pay for such public improvement. If too large a sum shall at any time be raised, the excess shall be refunded rateably to those by whom it was paid.

SEC. 28. If the damage to any person by reason of any public improvement be greater than the benefit received, or if the benefit be greater than the damage, in either case the commissioners shall strike a balance and carry the difference forward to another column, so that the assessment roll may show what amount is to be received or paid by such owners respectively, and the difference only in any case shall be collectable of them or paid to them.

SEC. 29. If the lands and buildings which may be in any case taken, either in whole or in part, in the making of any public improvement, belong to different persons, or if the land be subject to lease or mortgage, the injury done to such persons respectively may be awarded to them by the commissioners, less the benefits resulting to them respectively from the improvements.

SEC. 30. Whenever in the making of any public improvement which the common council is authorized to order or make, either in pursuance of the powers conferred by this act, or by the act to which this is an amendment, it shall be necessary to appropriate any land, the assessment by the board of public works, of benefits and damages, costs and expenses for the making of such improvement, when confirmed by the common council as is herein provided for the confirmation of assessments, and no appeal having been taken therefrom, shall be a sufficient condemnation of such land, so appropriated. On confirmation of said assessment, said board of public works shall pay or tender to the owner of such land, or to his agent, the amount of damages, over and above all benefits, which may have been awarded therefor; and in case the owner or agent of such land cannot be found in said city, the amount of such damage, over and above all benefits, for the making of such public improvement, shall be deposited to the credit of such owner by said board of public works, in some safe place of deposit in said city, other than the hands of the city treasurer, or any officer of said city; for the safety of which the city shall be responsible; and ten days notice shall be given of the making of such deposit by publication in the corporation newspaper; and then, and not before, shall the board of public works enter upon, take possession of, and appropriate such land. In case the damages to be paid for any land so condemned shall be paid for by a special assessment, the said commissioners shall pay for the same, or tender the moneys to pay for the same, when sufficient of such assessment shall be collected to pay therefor. The commissioners of the board of public works are hereby authorized to receive the moneys from the city treasurer to make such tender, when the same is required to be made as herein provided.

SEC. 31. When the whole of any lot or parcel of land or other premises, under lease or other contract, shall be taken for any of the purposes aforesaid by virtue of this act, all the covenants, contracts and engagements between landlords and tenants, or any other contracting parties, touching the same, or any part thereof, shall, upon confirmation of such assessment, respectively cease and be absolutely discharged.

SEC. 32. If there should be any building standing, in whole or in part, upon the land to be taken for the purpose of any public improvement, the commissioners, before proceeding to make their assessment, shall first estimate and determine the whole value of such building to the owner, aside from the value of the land, and the injury to him in having such building taken from him, and, secondly, the value of such building to him to remove.

SEC. 33. At least five days personal notice shall be given to the owner, of such determination, when known and a resident of the city, or left at his usual place of abode; if not known or a non-resident, notice to all persons interested shall be given by publication for ten days in the corporation newspaper. Such notice shall be signed by the board of public works, and specify the lot upon which said building is situate, and the award of the commissioners. It shall also require parties interested to appear, by a day to be named therein, or give notice of their election to the board of public works, either to accept the award of the board of public works and allow such building to be taken with the land condemned or appropriated, or of their intention to remove such building at the value set thereon by the commissioners to remove. If the owner shall agree to remove the building, he shall have such time for this purpose as the board of public works may allow.

SEC. 34. If the owner refuse to take the building at the value to remove, or fail to give notice of his election as aforesaid, within the time prescribed, the board of public works shall have power to direct the sale of such building, at public auction, for cash, giving five days public notice of the sale. The proceeds of the sale shall be paid to the owner, or deposited to his use.

SEC. 35. Whenever a warrant shall have been issued for the collection of a special assessment, the same shall be delivered to the city collector, who shall give ten days notice by publication in the corporation newspaper, that he has received such warrant, describing the same by number and date, and time when received, the amount to be collected, the purpose for which collected, and the property assessed, by general description. Such assessments shall be a lien from the time of the confirmation of such assessment on the real estate assessed, and no transfer or sale shall affect such lien. The payment of such special assessment may be enforced by said city at the same time and in the same manner as is now provided by law for the collection of the general tax levied on said city.

SEC. 36. If the amount of such assessment shall not be paid within sixty days after the first publication of notice, by the city collector, that he has received such warrant for collection, said assessment shall be collected with damages at the rate of one per cent. for each and every month that the same remains unpaid; said damages to be collected from the expiration of said sixty days.

SEC. 37. Said board of public works shall, whenever ordered so to do by the common council of said city, make an assessment to pay for the expense, cost, benefit and damage of doing any work, or for the making of any public improvement which may have been heretofore, within the last five years, ordered by the common council of said city, and the assessment for which has been, for any cause, set aside or declared void, either in whole or in part, either by the courts of this State or the common council of said city, the making of which public improvement was authorized by any law in force at the time such public improvement was commenced. In all cases where payments have been made on former assessments, levied for or on account of the doing of such work, such payments shall be credited on such new assessment, when made, to the property for which such sums were paid, so that the assessment shall be equal and impartial in its results.

SEC. 38. Whenever any public improvement shall be ordered by the common council of said city to be made, and the assessment for the same (where the same is to be paid for by special assessment,) shall have been confirmed by the common council, and one-half of such special assessment shall have been paid into the city treasury, the said board of public works shall advertise for proposals for doing said work; a plan or profile of the work to be done, accompanied with specifications for the doing of the same, being first placed on file in the office of said board; which said plan, profile and specification shall at all times be open for public inspection; which advertisement shall be continued for at least ten days in the corporation newspaper; shall state the work to be done, and the estimate for the doing of the same, made by said board of public works. The bids for the doing of such work shall be sealed bids, directed to said board; and said bids shall be opened at the hour and place mentioned in said notice by said board of public works. When the expense of any work or public improvement shall exceed the sum of two hundred dollars, and the same is to be paid out of the general fund of said city, the doing of such work shall be let by contract, in the same manner as is provided in cases where the expense of the same is to be paid for by special assessment.

SEC. 39. All contracts entered into by said board of public works, and all bonds taken by them, shall be entered into and be made to the city of Chicago.

SEC. 40. All contracts shall be awarded by the said board to the lowest responsible bidder or bidders, who will sufficiently guarantee, to the satisfaction of said board, the performance of said work, under the superintendence and to the satisfaction of said board, copies of which contracts shall be filed in the office of the comptroller of said city.

SEC. 41. The board of public works shall reserve the right, in their said contracts, to finally decide all questions arising as to the proper performance of said work, and the sufficiency of the security offered for its performance; or, in case of improper construction, to suspend said work at any time, and new let the same; or to order the entire reconstruction of said work, if improperly done; or relet the same to some more capable and faithful contractor or contractors, with power hereby given to said board to adjust the difference of damages or price, (if any there be), which the contractor or contractors failing to properly construct such work, in such cases of default, should pay to the city, according to the just and reasonable interpretation of such contract, in their opinion; which difference or balance shall be recoverable at law in the name of said city, before any court having competent jurisdiction thereof, against such contractor or contractors. But in all cases where the said contractor or contractors shall properly perform and complete their said contracts, to the satisfaction of said board of public works, according to the plan and estimates aforesaid, and of the proper and required materials, the said board shall then certify the same to such contractor or contractors, granting him or them a certificate of the proper performance thereof, the nature and amount of the work done, and the particular piece or parcel of property chargeable therewith; which shall be countersigned by the comptroller, and entitle the holder or holders thereof to receive the amount that may be due thereon from the assessment for the doing of such work or making of such improvement, when the same is collected.

SEC. 42. No member of the board of public works, nor any person in the employ thereof, shall be interested, directly or indirectly, in any contract made and entered into with said board of public works, or in any contract for the materials to be furnished therefor; and all contracts made with said board in which any member or officer of said board shall be so interested, shall, at the option of the city, be declared utterly void and of no binding effect whatever; and any member or officer of said board interested in any contract shall thereby forfeit his office, and be removed therefrom on proof of such delinquency; and it is hereby made the duty of each member of said board of public works, and of the mayor, and of every officer of said city, to report to the common council any such delinquency when discovered.

SEC. 43. If the mayor of said city, or any member of the board of public works, or any officer of said city, shall have reason to suspect that any member of said board, or any officer of said board, or officer of said city, is interested in any contract made, or work done by said board, or that such member has been guilty of malfeasance in office, he shall forthwith report such fact to the common council, who shall, if they consider such charge probable, order a committee to be appointed by them from their body, to prefer allegations in writing against such member, before the judge of the circuit court for Cook county; and said judge shall, either in term time or in vacation, proceed to hear such allegations against such member of the board of public works, five days notice having been given to such member by service of a copy of such allegation, at which hearing witnesses may be produced both for and against such allegations; and if the judge shall deem said allegations sustained, such member shall, on the report of the finding by such judge to the common council, be dismissed from office, and the common council shall proceed to fill such vacancy, as is herein provided in cases of vacancy in such office. The judge of the circuit court, on the hearing of such allegations, may adjourn such hearing from time to time. No member of said board of public works shall perform any duties as a member of said board while such allegations are pending against him.

SEC. 44. All supplies of materials, or necessaries of any kind, exceeding in amount the sum of two hundred dollars, shall be purchased by said board of public works, by contract with the lowest responsible bidder, as is provided for the making of conracts for the doing of work.

SEC. 45. All proceedings had by said board of public works, in relation to the opening or closing of any street, alley, lane, highway, slip or canal, or for the widening of the Chicago river or any of its branches, shall be recorded by said board in a book or books kept for that purpose.

SEC. 46. Said commissioners of the board of public works in making an assessment, are hereby authorized to assess the property by them deemed benefited by such public improvement, to an amount sufficient to cover the expense of such improvement.

SEC. 47. All moneys received on any assessment made by the board of public works, shall be held by the treasurer of the city of Chicago as a special fund, to be applied to the payment of the improvement for which the assessment was made; and the certificate of the board of public works to the contractor doing such work, shall specify the work done, or improvement made, and the draft made by the city comptroller on the treasurer shall specify the same; and said money shall be used for no purpose whatsoever other than for the payment for such improvement.

HYDRAULIC AND SEWERAGE WORKS.

SEC. 48. That so much of the act entitled "An Act to incorporate the Chicago City Hydraulic Company," approved February 11th, A. D. 1851, and the several acts amendatory thereto, as provides in any manner for the election or appointment of the board of water commissioners for the city of Chicago, be and the same is hereby repealed.

SEC. 49. That so much of the act entitled "An Act to incorporate the board of sewerage commissioners for the city of Chicago," approved February 14th, A D. 1855, as provides for the appointment or election of a board of sewerage commissioners, be and the same is hereby repealed.

SEC. 50. Immediately upon the organization of the board of public works, as provided in this act, the respective offices of "water commissioners" and "sewerage commissioners" for the city of Chicago shall be totally abolished; and all powers of said two boards heretofore granted by law, (except as herein provided), are hereby vested in said board of public works, and which said board is hereby made respectively the board of water and the board of sewerage commissioners; the true intent and meaning of this act being to abolish the board of sewerage commissioners, and the Chicago city hydraulic company, as distinct corporations, and to vest all the powers conferred by said acts of incorporation, and the acts amendatory thereof, in the aforesaid board of public works, except as herein specified.

SEC. 51. All moneys now in the hands of said "water commissioners" and "sewerage commissioners," their respective treasurers, other officers or employees, belonging to the hydraulic works or sewerage funds, shall be forthwith paid over to the city treasurer, to the credit of the respective funds to which they belong, and receipts therefor shall be filed with the city comptroller and said board of public works; and all moneys hereafter collected, or arising from loans, taxes, assessments, sale of materials, or any source whatsoever for the use of said sewerage and hydraulic works, shall be in like manner paid into the city treasury. All moneys hereafter to be paid by said board of public works, on account of the sewerage or hydraulic works, shall be paid by the certificate of the board of public works to the city comptroller, and by his draft on the city treasurer.

SEC. 52. All accounts pertaining to the sewerage works of said city, and all accounts pertaining to the hydraulic works of said city, shall be kept in separate books of account; and all moneys deposited with the city treasurer on account of said works shall be by him kept separate and distinct from all other moneys, and shall only be applied for the uses and purposes for which the same were received; and such moneys shall be held by the treasurer of the city of Chicago as a special fund, separate and distinct from other funds; and he shall be deemed guilty of embezzlement, if he shall pay out such moneys for any account other than that to which such funds or moneys may belong, and shall be liable to indictment for so doing.

SEC. 53 Said board of public works shall receive and collect all water rents, water taxes or assessments, and sewerage permits and licenses, the same as is now done by said board of water commissioners and sewerage commissioners respectively, and they shall report to the city treasurer, once in each month, all moneys so received by them, and at the same time pay over to said city treasurer all such moneys, with a statement of the same; to which account the same belong, and shall receive his receipt for all moneys so paid over.

SEC. 54. All books, papers, instruments, tools, office fixtures, buildings, machinery, maps, charts, drawings and property, of what kind or nature soever, in the possession of the said boards of water and sewerage commissioners respectively, or either of them, their subordinates or employees, shall, at the time of the organization of the board of public works, as aforesaid, be immediately handed over to the said board; and it shall be the duty of said board to make correct inventories of all of said property, and file the same in the office of the city comptroller, and a duplicate thereof in the office of said board of public works.

SEC. 55. All bonds, contracts, agreements or obligations, of what kind or nature soever, heretofore authorized to be executed by said board of sewerage commissioners or water commissioners, and by them, or either of them, entered into, shall be carried out, and completed, and complied with by said board of public works. All contracts hereafter entered into by said board on account of the sewerage or water works of said city, shall specify that they are for such works, and are to be paid out of the funds pertaining to such works.

SEC. 56. The office expenses, and the expenses for clerks, engineers and assistants, and the salaries of said commissioners of the board of public works, shall be a charge, and shall be paid, share and share alike, out of the funds pertaining to the general fund of said city, and the funds pertaining to the water and sewerage works of said city; each of said funds to be charged one-third of said expense.

SEC. 57. Whenever the said board of public works shall deem it necessary for the interests of the city, and to protect the interests of the same from great loss and damage, they shall, on a report to the common council of such necessity, and of the reason for the same, have the right to ask from the council the power to enter into a contract (specifying such contract) without giving the notice in this act required to be given before letting a contract; and the common council are hereby authorized, on being satisfied of such necessity, may, by resolution, grant such power; but provided three-fourths of all the aldermen elect shall vote [in] favor of such resolution.

SEC. 58. The commissioners of said board of public works shall each receive an annual salary of twenty-five hundred dollars.

SEC. 59. The board of public works shall, at the first regular meeting of the common council holden in the month of May in each year, submit a statement, as near as may be, of the repairs and improvements to be paid for out of the general funds of the city, and necessary to be undertaken by said city during the current year commencing on the first day of June next following the making of such statement, and of the sums by said board of public works required to make such repairs and improvements, as near as the same can be estimated, which report shall be in detail, and such estimate having been revised by the common council, the aggregate amount of the sums required after such revision shall be provided for in the general tax levy, to be laid on said city, and no expenditure for an improvement to be paid for out of the general fund of said city, shall exceed in any one year the amount provided for such improvement in said general tax levy: *Provided, however*, Nothing herein contained shall prevent the common council from ordering any improvement, the necessity for which is caused by any casualty or accident happening after the making of such annual estimate herein provided for. The common council may authorize the mayor and comptroller to issue bonds to pay the expense incurred in the making of any improvement, the need for which has arisen as is last above mentioned, said bonds to run for a term not longer than one year, and the payment of which said bonds shall be specially provided for in the next succeeding general tax levy. The said city shall not issue bonds, or any other evidences of indebtedness for any purpose whatsoever, except as is herein provided: *Provided, however*, Nothing herein contained shall prevent the issue of any bonds now authorized to be issued by any law of this State, under the laws creating said boards of water commissioners and sewerage commissioners, or the acts amendatory thereto, or any acts relating to sewerage or supplying said city with water, but said board of public works are hereby expressly empowered to issue all such bonds as might have been issued by said board of water commissioners and said board of sewerage commissioners respectively, if this act had not been passed.

SEC. 60. In the assessment of damages and benefits for the opening of any street or alley, it shall be lawful for the commissioners in making such assessment, where part of the land to be laid out into such street or alley, has been theretofore donated by any person or persons for such street or alley, to appraise the value of the land so donated, and to apply the value of the land so donated, as far as the amount so appraised shall go, as an offset to the benefits assessed against the person or persons making such donation, or those claiming under him; nothing herein contained shall authorize any person or persons by whom such donation is made, to claim from the city the amount of such appraisal, except as an offset as herein provided.

SEC. 61. The board of public works shall elect from their number a president and a treasurer, who shall hold their offices for the term of two years, and until their successors are elected and qualified, and they shall establish by-laws for the regulation and conduct of their officers and employees.

SEC. 62. The common council of said city shall have power to require from any officer of said city, at any time, a report in detail of the transactions in his office, or of any other matter by said council deemed necessary, and the comptroller of said city shall hereafter make the report, now required to be made in the month of February, in each year, on or before the first day of April, in each year.

SEC. 63. Upon the petition of a majority of the owners of lots upon Michigan avenue, lying between Washington street and the north line of a short street running from Michigan avenue to lake Michigan, on the north line of block twenty-three (23) in fractional section fifteen (15) addition to Chicago, it shall be lawful for the common council to increase the width of said avenue thirty-six feet upon the east line thereof, from the north line of Randolph street to the north line of the short street running from Michigan avenue to lake Michigan, on the north line of block twenty-three (23) in fractional section fifteen (15) addition to Chicago, and secure the east line of the proposed increase of width by a substantial stone wall, so far as the same is necessary for this purpose. Said council shall grade the increased width aforesaid to a line of the present level of said street or avenue, and devote twenty feet of said width to the present road bed, graveling the same as the present road bed is graveled, and upon remaining sixteen feet of said increased width, construct and lay down a good and substantial stone sidewalk, and upon the wall aforesaid, so far as the same is constructed, and upon a proper stone foundation to be built, erect upon the same a good and substantial iron fence, along the whole line aforesaid. The said common council, to defray the expense of said improvement, are hereby authorized to appoint, in the manner as provided in the charter, two or more special assessors to assess the cost of said improvement, or have the same assessed by the board of public works, two-thirds of which shall be assessed upon the blocks of land fronting upon Michigan avenue, and lying between Washington street and Twelfth street, and the remaining one-third shall be paid out of the treasury of the city.

SEC. 64. No encroachment shall be made upon the land or water west of a line mentioned in the second section of an ordinance concerning the Illinois Central Railroad (which line is "not less than four hundred feet east from the west line of Michigan avenue, and parallel thereto,") by any railroad company, nor shall any cars, locomotives, engines, machines or other things belonging to any railroad or transportation company, be permitted to occupy the same, nor shall any cars or machinery be left standing upon said track fronting any part of Michigan avenue, nor shall the city council ever allow any encroachments west of the line above described. And any person, being the owner of or interested in any lot or part of a lot fronting on Michigan avenue, shall have the right to enjoin said company and all other persons and corporations from any violations of the provisions of this section, or of said ordinance, and by bill or petition in chancery in his or their own name, or otherwise, enforce the provisions of said ordinance, and of this section, and recover such damages for any such encroachment or violation, as the court shall deem just. The State of Illinois, by its canal commissioners, having declared that the public ground east of said lots should forever remain open and vacant, neither the common council of the city of Chicago, nor any other authority, shall ever have the power to permit encroachments thereon without the assent of all the persons owning lots or land on said street or avenue.

SEC. 65. It is hereby made the duty of the mayor and comptroller of said city, on or before the first day of April, 1861, or as soon thereafter as may be, to make a statement to the common council of said city, of the amount of scrip and floating debt outstanding against said city, and they shall proceed to issue and negotiate the bonds of said city, payable, principal and interest, in New York, and bearing interest at a rate not exceeding seven per cent. per annum, and becoming due and payable on the first day of April, 1881, to an amount sufficient to satisfy and retire the scrip and floating indebtedness outstanding against said city, and with the proceeds of said bonds, they shall proceed to pay and satisfy such scrip and floating indebtedness, which bonds shall be in the ordinary form of bonds of said city, and shall be issued in denominations of five hundred and a thousand dollars each, as the said mayor and comptroller may deem for the best interest of the city, and it is hereby made the duty of the common council of said city, at the time of the levying of the general tax in each year, to provide for the paying of the interest on the bonds issued under and in pursuance of this section, and they are hereby authorized to levy a tax sufficient to pay such interest semi-annnally, in addition to the amounts which they are now authorized by law to levy and collect.

SEC. 66. In addition to the amount of the bonds herein authorized to be issued by the said city, the common council of said city, on the first Monday of May, 1861, or as soon thereafter as may be, may provide by ordinance for the issuing of the bonds of said city, payable, principal and interest, in New York city, to an amount not exceeding the sum of one hundred thousand dollars, bearing interest at a rate not exceeding seven per cent. per annum, payable semi-annually, and payable in ten years from their date, and to negotiate and sell said bonds, and to use the proceeds of said bonds when sold, in paying the general expenses of said city, and the common council of said city shall, at the time of the levying of the annual tax levy on said city, provide for the paying of the interest on such bonds.

SEC. 66½. Digby V. Bell, Augustus H. Burley, and Samuel Myers, are hereby appointed three commissioners to examine into the condition of the finances of said city, who shall report the result of their investigation to the common council of said city. The said commissioners, when appointed, shall have power to examine into all claims outstanding against said city, the condition of the accounts of said city, and the accounts of said city heretofore audited and closed. The said commissioners shall have power to summon before them any and all officers of said city, or other persons, and shall also have power to require the production by any such officer, of the books and vouchers, or papers pertaining to his department. Said commissioners shall proceed to hear evidence in regard to any matter brought before them, and for this purpose they are hereby authorized to administer oaths to all persons appearing before them as witnesses, and they are hereby further authorized to commit to jail, as being in contempt, any person failing or refusing to appear before them to testify as to any matter when summoned so to do. All summons to be issued by said commissioners, shall be issued in the name of the People of the State of Illinois. No claim or indebtedness now outstanding against said city, shall be paid by said city out of the proceeds of the bonds by this act authorized to be issued, until the amount of such claim shall have been passed upon and reported to said council by said commissioners. At all hearings before said commissioners, the city attorney, or such other person as shall be appointed by said commissioners, shall appear on behalf of said city, and the parties presenting claims against said city shall have the right to be heard by counsel or in person. The commissioners shall, in addition to passing on all claims presented before them, investigate the accounts of said city, and the books of account of said city. The commissioners shall each receive five dollars per day for each and every day while engaged in such investigation. Any vacancy in said commission shall be filled by appointment of the governor; and in case said commissioners named in this act shall decline to accept the appointment, then said commissioners shall be appointed by the governor.

SEC. 66½. In addition to the other duties of the comptroller of said city, it is hereby made the duty of such comptroller, on or before the fifth day of each and every month, to make out a monthly statement, giving a full and detailed statement of all moneys received, and of whom and on what account received, and of all moneys ordered to be paid, or drawn for by warrant by him, (giving the name of the person in whose favor each order or warrant is drawn,) and on what account the same has been paid, for the month preceding the month in which such statement is made, and the said comptroller shall cause the said monthly statement to be published in the corporation newspaper of said city, before the seventh day of each month, and shall deliver a true copy of such statement to the said common council at the next meeting thereof, be the same a regular or special meeting, and on failure to comply with the provisions of this act, he shall be removed from office by the common council of said city at any meeting thereof, unless he show reasonable excuse for such failure.*

SEC. 92. This act shall take effect and be in force from and after its passage.

Approved February 18, 1861.

AN ACT to authorize the City of Chicago to make an Assessment to pay the Damages caused by the building of a Bridge at Van Buren Street in said City, and to pay certain Claims against the said City.

SECTION 1. *Be it enacted by the People of the State of Illinois, represented in the General Assembly,* The common council of the city of Chicago is hereby authorized and directed, on or before the making of the next general tax levy on said city, to appoint commissioners to make an assessment on the property by the assessors when appointed deemed benefited by the building of the bridge at Van Buren street in said city, in the year 1858, for an amount sufficient to pay and satisfy the claims against said city remaining unsatisfied for damages caused by reason of the building of said bridge, and widening of said river at that point, with the costs, expenses and disbursements, including amounts due Mahlon D. Ogden, Robert Shepard and Reuben Taylor, attending a former assessment of said damages, and such assessors shall, at the time of the making of such assessment, assess as well the damages and the benefits caused by the building of said bridge.

SEC. 2. This act shall be in force from and after its passage.

Approved February 20, 1861.

AN ACT to establish a Board of Police in and for the City of Chicago, and to prescribe their Powers and Duties.

SECTION 1. *Be it enacted by the People of the State of Illinois, represented in the General Assembly,* That after the passage of this act there shall be organized in said city of Chicago an executive department of the municipal government, to be known as the board of police of the city of Chicago. Said board shall consist of three commissioners, to be chosen, one from the south, one from the west, and one from the north division of said city, who shall constitute said board. That until election and qualification in the manner and at the time herein provided, the governor shall nominate, and by and with the advice and consent of the Senate, appoint the first commissioners of said board of police, who shall be and they are hereby declared the first commissioners of said board of police, and who shall respectively hold their offices for two, four and six years from and after the next general municipal election in said city, and until their successors are duly elected and qualified. Said board shall possess the powers and perform the duties authorized and enjoined by this act. A majority of said board shall constitute a quorum for the transaction of business.

SEC. 2. The said commissioners, when appointed, shall, within ten days after their appointment, or as soon thereafter as may be, proceed to organize said board and

---

* Sections 67 to 91 inclusive, were submitted to and rejected by the people, at an election held March 19, 1861.

decide by lot their respective terms of office; which decision shall be filed in the office of the city clerk. One of said commissioners shall go out of office at the end of each and every two years from and after the next general municipal election.

SEC. 3. At the general municipal election in said city in A. D. 1863, and biennially thereafter, there shall be elected at the general city election in said city, a commissioner of said board of police, to succeed the member whose term of office expires, so that one of said officers shall be successively elected every second year from the division of said city in which the commissioner resides whose term of office expires, and said commissioner when elected shall hold his office for six years. Should a vacancy occur, it shall be filled by appointment by the mayor, with the advice and consent of the common council of said city, until the next regular city election, when the qualified voters of said city may fill such vacancy by an election of a successor, who shall hold his office for the unexpired term. Said commissioners shall be elected in the same manner as is now provided by law for the election of other general city officers by general ticket, by the qualified voters of the whole city, and no person shall be elected a commissioner of said board of police, unless he has been a resident of said city for at least five years, and a resident in the division for which he is elected at least one year preceding his election; said commissioners, when appointed, and their successors in office, shall, before entering upon the duties of their office, take an oath to obey the constitution and laws of this State, and faithfully to perform the duties of their said office, the certificate of which oath shall be deposited in the office of the city clerk, to be by such clerk filed in his office. Any member of said board of police may at any time be removed from office for any misdemeanor, malfeasance or delinquency in office, by the judge of the circuit court for Cook county, on charges in writing, to be presented against him before such judge by the mayor of said city, on which hearing before such judge, witnesses may be produced and sworn both in support of the allegations and against them.

SEC. 4. The said commissioners, after the organization of said board, in pursuance of this act, shall assume control of the police force of said city, and shall proceed to organize the same in pursuance of the provisions of this act, and for this purpose they are hereby authorized to retain such officers of the present police force of said city as said board shall deem necessary for the more perfect reorganization of said police, which officers shall be discharged by said board, when, in their discretion, the service of the same can be dispensed with.

SEC. 5. The officers of said board of police shall be a president and a treasurer, who shall each be elected from among the said commissioners. The clerk of the police court of said city shall be *ex officio* clerk of said board of police.

SEC. 6. It shall be the duty of the board of police hereby constituted, at all times of the day and night, within the boundaries of the said city of Chicago, to preserve the public peace, to prevent crime and arrest offenders; to protect rights of persons and property; to guard the public health; to preserve order; to remove nuisances existing in public streets, roads, places and highways; to provide a proper police force at every fire, in order that thereby the firemen and property may be protected; to protect strangers and travelers at steamboat and ship landings, and railway stations; and to obey and enforce all ordinances of the common council, within the said city of Chicago, which are applicable to police or health. Whenever any crime shall be committed in said city of Chicago, or within the county of Cook, and the person or persons accused or suspected of being guilty, shall flee from justice, the said board of police may, in their discretion, authorize any person or persons to pursue and arrest such accused or suspected person or persons, and return them to the proper criminal court, having jurisdiction of the offense, for trial.

SEC. 7. The said duties of the police shall be more especially executed under the direction and control of said board, and according to rules and regulations which it is hereby authorized to pass from time to time, for the more proper government and discipline of its subordinate officers, and the police force of the said city of Chicago. The said police force shall consist of a general superintendent of police and one deputy superintendent of police, three captains of police, six sergeants of police, and sixty police patrolmen, and as many more police patrolmen as may be ordered by the common council of the said city of Chicago, on the application of the board of police; the said officers hereby created for the said police force, shall be severally filled by appointment from the police force after the first organization of said force, in the mode prescribed by this act, and each shall hold office only during such time as he shall faithfully observe and execute all the rules and regulations of the said board, the laws of the State and the ordinances existing within the city of Chicago.

SEC. 8. The qualifications, enumeration and distribution of duties, mode of trial and removal from office, of each officer of said police force, shall be particularly defined and prescribed by rules and regulations of the board of police: *Provided, however*, That no person shall be so appointed to office or hold office in the police force aforesaid, who is not a citizen of the United States, or who shall not have resided within the State of Illinois two years next preceding his appointment, or who shall ever have been convicted of crime: *Provided*, That no person shall be removed therefrom except upon written charges preferred against him to the board of police, and after an opportunity shall have been afforded him of being heard in his defense, the board of police shall have power to suspend any member of the police department of the city, pending the hearing of the charges preferred against him: *And provided*, That whenever any vacancy shall occur in the office of captain of police, the same shall be filled by an appointment from among the persons then in office, as sergeant of police, and a like vacancy in the office of sergeant of police shall be filled by appointment from among the persons then in office as police patrolmen.

SEC. 9. The members of the police force of the said city of Chicago shall possess, in every part of the county of Cook, all the common law and statutory powers of constables, except for the service of civil process, and any warrant for search or arrest by any magistrate of the State of Illinois may be executed in any part of the county of Cook by any member of the police force of the said city of Chicago, without any backing or indorsement of the said warrant, and according to the terms thereof. The general and deputy superintendents and captains of police having just cause to suspect that any felony has been, or is being, or is about to be committed within any building, or on board of any ship, boat or vessel within the said city of Chicago or county of Cook, may enter the same at all hours of the day or night to take all necessary measures for the effectual prevention or detection of all felonies, and may take then and there into custody all persons suspected of being concerned in such felonies, and also may take charge of all property which he or they shall have then and there just cause to suspect has been stolen.

SEC. 10. If the general superintendent of police shall report in writing to the board of police that there are good grounds for believing any house or room within the said city of Chicago is kept or used as a common gaming house or cock pit, and if two or more householders dwelling within the said district, and not belonging to the police force, shall make oath in writing, before any one of the commissioners of police and annexed to the said report, (which oath every commissioner of police is hereby empowered to administer, receive and subscribe,) that the premises complained of by the general superintendent of police are commonly reported, and are believed by the deponents to be kept as a common gaming house or cock pit, it shall be lawful for any commissioner of police, by order in writing, to authorize the general superintendent of police or the deputy superintendent of police to enter upon such premises, taking with him or them such members of the patrol force as shall be necessary, and if necessary, to use force for the purpose of effecting such entry, whether by breaking open doors or otherwise, and the said superintendent or deputy superintendent shall be authorized to take into custody all persons who shall be found therein, and to destroy all implements of gaming found therein, and shall forthwith convey the person or persons found therein before any magistrate in said city, who shall forthwith proceed to hear the proof, and if there be probable cause for believing that such person or persons have been guilty of any crime or misdemeanor, then the said magistrate shall forthwith order such person or persons to find good bail, with two householders of said city of Chicago as his or their sureties, conditioned for his or their appearance at the proper criminal court, to answer any indictment which may be found, and, in default thereof, such magistrate shall commit such person or persons to the county jail.

SEC. 11. It is hereby made the duty of the board of police, for more effectually distributing and enforcing its police government and discipline, to divide the said city of Chicago into precincts without regard to ward boundaries, and to assign captains of police and sergeants of police to each of said precincts, as they shall deem for the best interest of said city. The board may from time to time establish a station or sub-station in each precinct or division, for the accommodation of the police force on duty therein. It shall not suspend members of the police force from pay for more than thirty days. It shall promulgate all regulations and orders through the general superintendent of police, who shall take the place of the mayor of the city of Chicago as being at the head of the police department or force in the said city, but always subject to the orders and regulations of the board of police, and it shall be the duty of the police force to respect and obey the said general superintendent of police as the head and chief of the same, subject to the rules and regulations and general orders of the board of police.

SEC. 12. The board of police, whenever it shall see fit, shall, on the application of any person or persons, showing the necessity thereof, appoint and swear any number of additional patrolmen to do duty at any place within the city of Chicago, at the charge and expense of the person or persons by whom the application shall be made, and the patrolmen so appointed shall be subject to the orders of the board of police, and shall obey the rules and regulations of the board, and conform to its general discipline, and to such other special regulations as may be made, and shall wear such dress or emblem as the board may direct, and shall, during the term of their holding appointment, possess all the powers, privileges and duties of the patrol force herein prescribed. The persons so appointed may be removed at any time by the board of police, without assigning cause therefor, upon one month's notice of the intention so to do, given to the person or persons who applied for the appointment as aforesaid. The board of police may also, upon any emergency of riot, pestilence, invasion, or during any day of public election or celebration, appoint as many special patrolmen from among the citizens of Chicago as it may deem advisable, and for a specified time, and during the term of service of any such special patrolmen, he shall possess all the powers and privileges and perform all the duties of patrolmen of the standing police force of the city.

SEC. 13. No member of the police force, under penalty of forfeiting the pay which may be due to him, shall withdraw or resign from the police force, unless he shall have given one week's notice thereof in writing to the general superintendent of police; and no person who shall ever have been removed from the police force established by this act, for cause, shall be re-appointed by the board of police to any office in the said police force.

SEC. 14. All stolen property taken by members of the police force, shall be kept in a place and by a person to be designated by the board of police. Every such article of property shall be entered in a book kept for the purpose, together with the name of the owner, if ascertained, and the name of the place where found, and of the person from whom taken, with the general circumstances and the date of its receipt, and the name of the officer recording the same. The board of police shall also cause to be kept general complaint books, in which shall be entered every complaint preferred upon personal knowledge of the circumstances thereof, with the name and residence of the complainant. It shall also cause to be kept books for the registry of lost, missing or stolen property, for the general convenience of the public and of the police force of the city. It shall also cause to be kept books of records wherein shall be entered the name of every member of the police force, with his time and place of nativity, the time and place when he became a citizen (if he was born out of the United States,) his age, his former occupation, number of family and the residence thereof, the date of appointment or dismissal from office, with the cause of the latter, and in every such record sufficient space shall be left against all such entries wherein to make record of the number of arrests made by such members of the police force, or of any special services deemed meritorious by the captains of police. It shall also cause to be kept in proper books the accounts of the treasurer of the board, and number of the several meetings thereof, and all receipts for moneys or warrants or checks for moneys, shall be written in books kept for the purpose, and the said receipts signed by the person or persons in every case receiving money, warrants or checks from the treasurer. The board of police shall also cause to be kept and bound, all police returns and reports.

SEC. 15. It shall be the duty of the common council of the city of Chicago, in accordance with the practice and ordinances now existing therein, to provide at the expense of said city, all necessary accommodations, within such precincts, as shall be contained within the boundaries of the said city, for the station houses required by the board of police, for the accommodation of the police force of such precincts, for the lodging of vagrants and disorderly persons, and for the temporary detention of persons arrested for offenses. It shall also be the duty of the said common council to furnish the same suitably, and to warm and light the same by day and night, and so far as the detention of persons under arrest is concerned, the same shall be lawful in any part of said city, on direction to that effect by any captain of police; and in every case of arrest, the same shall be made known forthwith to the captain upon duty in the precinct wherein the arrest was made, by the person making the same, and it shall be the duty of the said captain, as soon as practicable after such notice, to make written return thereof according to the rules and regulations of the board of police, together with the name of the party arrested, the offense, the place of arrest, and the place of detention. The board of police shall provide suitable accommodations within said city of Chicago for the detention of witnesses who are unable to furnish security for their appearance in criminal proceedings, and such accommodations shall be in premises other than those employed for the confinement of persons charged with crime, fraud or disorderly conduct; and it shall be the duty of all magistrates, in committing witnesses, to have regard to the rules and regulations of the board of police in respect to their detention.

SEC. 16. All public police property, books, records, and accoutrements, now in the possession of the police department of Chicago, are hereby given for the use of the board of police herein authorized, but the ownership of the same, and the use thereof, as aforesaid, shall be according to the ordinances which the common council of the city of Chicago have enacted or may hereafter enact. The board of police shall have power to erect and maintain, under the general laws of the State relating to telegraph lines, all such lines of telegraph in such places within the said city, as for purposes of police the board shall deem necessary, whenever the common council shall authorize the establishment of such telegraph line or lines.

SEC. 17. The necessary expenses incurred in the execution of criminal process, and the maintenance of the police department hereby created within the said city of Chicago, shall be a city charge. The board of supervisors of Cook county assembled, may call upon the board of police to appoint for duty within the said county as many men as it shall enumerate and describe, upon appropriating to the police fund the necessary expenses and salaries to be incurred thereby. Any of the village or town authorities within the said county may also make such demand upon the board of police, upon making the like provisions of pay, and it shall be the duty of the board of police to appoint such officers, who shall thereafter become regular members of the police force of the city of Chicago, and subject to all the rules and regulations of the board, discharge the duties and possess powers and privileges as such members. The supervisors of the county of Cook are hereby authorized from time to time to levy and raise by tax upon the real and personal property taxable within said county, such sum or sums of money as may be required to carry into effect the provisions of this section or the police purposes of this act.

SEC. 18. No person holding office under this act shall be liable to military or jury duty while actually on duty.

SEC. 19. The board of police shall at all times cause the ordinances of the city of Chicago to be properly enforced; and it shall be the duty of the said board, at all times whenever consistent with the rules and regulations of the board, and with the requirements of this act, to furnish all information desired, and comply with all the requests made by the common council of said city, or by the mayor thereof, to quell riots, suppress insurrections, protect the property and preserve the public tranquility. The board of police shall have the power to issue subpœnas tested in the name of its president, to compel before it the attendance of witnesses upon any proceeding authorized by its rules and regulations. Each commissioner of police, the general superintendent of police, and each deputy superintendent of police, and the chief clerk of the board of police, are hereby given power to administer, take, receive and subscribe all affirmations and oaths to any witnesses summoned and appearing in any matter or proceeding authorized as aforesaid, or to any depositions necessary by the rules and regulations of the board of police. Any willful and corrupt false swearing by any witness or person making deposition before any of the officers last mentioned, to any material fact, in any necessary proceeding under the said rules and regulations, shall be deemed perjury, and punished in the manner now prescribed by law for such offense. The provisions of law now existing in respect to attachment of witnesses before justices of the peace, and to the compulsory attendance of the said witnesses, to appear and testify before them, are hereby applied to the case of witnesses subpœnaed before the board of police.

SEC. 20. It shall be a misdemeanor, punishable by imprisonment in the county jail, not less than one year nor exceeding two years, or by a fine not less than two hundred and fifty dollars, for any person, without justifiable or excusable cause, to use personal violence upon any elector in the said city of Chicago, or upon any member of the police force thereof, when in the discharge of his duty; or for any such member to neglect making any arrest for an offense against the law of the State, committed in his presence, or for any person not a member of the police force to falsely represent himself as being such member with a fraudulent design.

SEC. 21. The treasurer of the board of police and each commissioner shall receive such annual salaries as may be fixed upon and allowed by the common council of the city of Chicago; but no other compensation shall be paid or allowed to the members of the board. The general superintendent of police shall receive a salary of fifteen hundred dollars per annum. The deputy superintendent of police shall receive an annual salary of twelve hundred dollars. Each captain of police shall receive a like salary of seven hundred dollars per annum, and each sergeant of police a like salary of six hundred and fifty dollars. The pay of each police patrolman shall be at the rate of six hundred dollars per annum. The salaries shall be paid quarterly and the pay monthly to each person entitled thereto; the salary of each commissioner shall be paid to him by the comptroller of the said city of Chicago; each captain shall receive monthly from the treasurer of the board, the sums required for the pay of the patrolmen doing duty within his police precinct. No member of the board of police or of the police force shall receive or share in, for his own benefit, under any pretense whatsoever, any present, fee, gift or emolument for police service other than the regular salary and pay provided by this section, except by the unanimous consent of the board of police.

SEC. 22. All rewards, fees, proceeds of gifts and emoluments that may be allowed by the board of police to be paid and given for or on account of extraordinary services of any member of the police force, and all moneys arising from the sale of unclaimed goods, shall be paid into the bank wherein the treasurer of the board of police shall be required (as hereinafter provided) to keep his account. The payment so made shall constitute a fund to be called the "Police Life and Health Insurance Fund;" and the persons who shall from time to time fill the office of the said treasurer of the board of police and that of the comptroller of the city of Chicago, are hereby declared the trustees of the said fund, and may invest the same as they shall see fit, either in whole or part.

SEC. 23. Whenever any member of the police force, in actual performance of his duty, and in consequence of the performance of such duty, shall become bodily disabled, his necessary expenses during the time his disability as aforesaid continues, may become a charge upon the fund provided for in the preceding section, at the discretion of said board of police. The board of police shall inquire into the circumstances, and if satisfied the charge upon the said fund is correct, may order the same to be paid by the draft of the said trustees upon the said fund, each writing his signature thereto. But the provisions of this section shall not apply to special patrolmen appointed as hereinbefore provided for, at the request and expense of private parties.

SEC. 24. The common council of the city of Chicago shall annually raise and collect, by tax upon the real and personal property taxable within the city of Chicago, such sums of money as the board of police for the city of Chicago, before the time fixed by law for the comptroller of said city to present to the common council of said city his estimate for the expenses for the next fiscal year, in each year, shall report as requisite and needful to be raised by said city of Chicago, which sums of money shall be applied by the said board of police for the fiscal purposes of this act. Such sum of money provided for, when collected, shall be paid into the city treasury of the city of Chicago, and shall be styled the police fund, and shall be paid therein and therefrom under the fiscal regulations of law relating to the finances of said city and the provisions of this act.

SEC. 25. The treasurer of the board of police shall disburse all moneys required for the expenses of the said board, but always upon his said check or warrant upon the police fund drawn upon the city treasurer of said city of Chicago, which said police fund shall be deposited by the said city treasurer in such bank or banks within the said city of Chicago as shall be designated for that purpose by the comptroller of the said city of Chicago. No expenses other than salaries and pay herein provided shall ever be incurred by the board of police, except for rents, stationery, printing, advertising, fuel and light, unless the same shall be expressly authorized, and provision therefor made, as a separate county or city charge by the board of supervisors for the county of Cook or the common council of the city of Chicago, within which the expenditure becomes necessary.

SEC. 26. The treasurer of the board of police shall, before entering upon the duties of his office, execute a bond by himself, together with sufficient sureties not less than two, in the penalty of one hundred thousand dollars, to the city of Chicago, conditioned for the faithful performance of his duties; the sureties to justify before a judge of the superior court of Chicago in said Cook county, and to be approved by him. This bond shall be filed in the office of the comptroller of said city. Whenever any of its conditions shall be violated, the said bond may be sued upon by the city, and the proceeds of suit paid to the credit of the police fund.

SEC. 27. The board of police shall require and make suitable provisions respecting security to be entered into by the general and deputy superintendents of police, and by the captains of police, and for the taking, by members of the police force, of an oath of office, and the registry of the certificate of the same in a book to be kept for that purpose by the board of police, which oath of office may be taken before any commissioner of police, who is hereby empowered to administer and receive the same.

SEC. 28. From and after the first meeting of the board of police, under the provisions of this act, it shall possess all the power and authority heretofore conferred by law upon the mayor of the city of Chicago, at the head therein of the police department of said city, or upon the common council of said city of Chicago, which power and authority shall relate to or in any way be connected with the police government, police appointments or police discipline within said city; and from and after the said first meeting of the board of police of the city of Chicago, the duty and authority and power of each and all of the aforementioned officers, in relation to police government, appointment and discipline, shall wholly cease, and vest as aforesaid, in the said board of police constituted by this act.

SEC. 29. The general superintendent of police shall make to the board of police, quarterly reports in writing of the state of the police force, with such statistics and suggestions as he may deem advisable for the improvement of the police government and discipline of said force. The board of police shall, on or before the first Monday in May, in each year, report in writing the condition of the police within the said city, to the common council.

SEC. 30. All statutes, parts of statutes and provisions of law inconsistent with the provisions of this act, are hereby repealed, together with all modes and qualifications of appointment to office, as members of police departments, or of elections to office therein, inconsistent with the provisions of this act.

SEC. 31. This act shall be deemed a public act, and be in force from and after its passage.

Approved February 21, 1861.

AN ACT to amend an Act approved February 16th, A. D. 1857, entitled "An Act to amend an Act entitled 'An Act to reduce the Law incorporating the City of Chicago, and the several Acts amendatory thereof, into one Act, and to amend the same,'" approved February 14, 1851.

SECTION 1. *Be it enacted by the People of the State of Illinois, represented in the General Assembly*, Each and all of the police magistrates and justices of the peace, and the clerk of the police court, within and for the city of Chicago, are hereby authorized and empowered to amend all records by them, or either of them, made in all cases where males within the ages prescribed by law, have been brought before them, charged with an offense punishable by commitment to the reform school, and where such person or persons have been there committed; and all such orders, records and minutes of such police magistrates, justices of the peace or clerk, are hereby declared to be good, sufficient, valid and binding in law, and sufficient to warrant the commitment: *Provided*, Sufficient appear in the order, minutes or records, that it was the opinion and order of such court, that such person should be committed to the reform school.

SEC. 2. Certified copies of such orders or records shall be the only proper evidence in all courts where the existence or sufficiency of such records are called in question, whether original or amended.

SEC. 3. In all cases where the legality of any commitment to the reform school is called in question, such commitment shall be deemed legal and valid, provided the warrant of commitment shall, upon its face, show a legal cause of commitment, and in all cases, whether upon *habeas corpus* or otherwise, the court before which such cause is pending, shall only examine into the sufficiency of the warrant.

SEC. 4. In application for *habeas corpus* to take from the control of the guardians, superintendent or other officer of said reform school, any male within the ages prescribed by law, such person, or some one on his behalf, shall first pay to the court or judge to which application is made, the legal costs of such application.

SEC. 5. It shall be the duty of the mayor of the city of Chicago, each year, on the application of the board of guardians of said reform school, to appoint some proper and discreet person, to be named by said guardians, as commissioner, before whom all males within the ages prescribed by law shall be sent, before any police magistrate or justice of the peace shall sentence or order such male to be committed to the reform school. Such commissioner shall keep a true and perfect record of his doings in relation to all persons brought before him, and shall retain the same during his term of office, and at the expiration thereof, shall deliver the same, with all preceding records, to his successor, and shall be paid such sum from the reform school funds as the board of guardians shall, from time to time, direct, and which shall not in the aggregate amount to more than the sum of fifteen hundred dollars in any one year.

SEC. 6. Whenever any police magistrate or justice of the peace within the city of Chicago, shall have brought before him any male within the ages of six and seventeen years of age, which he has reason to believe is a vagrant, or destitute of proper parental care, wandering about the streets, or committing mischief, or growing up in mendicancy, ignorance, idleness and vice, he shall cause such person, together with the warrant on which he is arrested, and the list of witnesses which may be necessary to establish the situation and condition of such person, to be transmitted to said commissioner; and thereupon it shall be the duty of such commissioner before whom such person is brought, to issue a summons or order in writing, addressed to the father of such person, if he be living and resident within the city; and if not, then to his mother, if she be living and so resident; and if not, then addressed to his lawful guardian, if any there be resident within said city; or if not, to the person with whom such boy, according to the examination and testimony, if any, received by such commissioner, the said boy shall reside; and if there be no person with whom he steadily resides, the commissioner may, at his discretion, appoint some suitable person to act in his behalf, requiring him or her, as the case may be, to appear before him at such time and place as he shall in said summons or order appoint, and to show cause, if any there be, why the said boy shall not be committed to the reform school. And upon the appearance before him of the party named in said summons or order, or if, after due service had of the summons or order aforesaid, there shall be no such appearance, the said commissioner shall, upon the expiration of the time named in said summons or order for said appearance, proceed to examine said boy, and the party appearing in answer to said summons or order, if any such there be, and to take such testimony in relation to the case as may be produced before him; and in case it shall be proven to the satisfaction of the commissioner by such examination, or by competent testimony, that said boy is a suitable subject for the reform school, and that his moral welfare and the good of society require that he should be sent to said school for instruction, employment and reformation, he shall so decide, and shall thereupon certify his said opinion and decision to said magistrate or justice of the peace, as near as may be, in the following words:

To A. B., Esq., a Justice of the Peace:

I hereby certify that —— —— has been examined by me, and upon competent evidence, proved to be a suitable person for commitment to the reform school.

C. D., Commissioner.

And the finding said fact by said commissioner and his decision thereon, shall not thereafter in any case be reversed by any tribunal or court. And thereupon said magistrate or justice of the peace shall commit such person to the reform school; and such commitment shall be by warrant in substance as follows:

To any Sheriff, Constable or Police officer within the City of Chicago:

You are hereby commanded to take charge of —— ——, a boy above the age of six, and under the age of seventeen years, who has been found by competent evidence to be a suitable subject for commitment to the reform school within this city, and a proper object for its care, discipline and instruction, and to deliver said boy, with this warrant, without delay to the superintendent or other officer in charge of said school, at the place where the same is established; and for so doing this shall be your sufficient warrant.

Dated in the city of Chicago, in the county of Cook, this —— day of ——, A. D. 18—.

—— ——, J. P.

But no variance from the preceding form shall be deemed material, provided it sufficiently appear upon the face of the warrant that the said boy is committed in exercise of the powers given by this act, or the one to which it is an amendment. And in case said commissioner shall be of opinion, and shall decide that such boy is not a proper subject for commitment to the reform school, he shall order such boy, with the warrant, etc., to be transmitted back to such police magistrate or justice of the peace, who shall thereupon deal with him in the same manner he would have done had he not been transmitted to or examined by said commissioner. And said commissioner shall, in the performance of his duties under and by virtue of this act, be clothed with all the powers justices of the peace are, to compel the attendance of witnesses and all other persons whose attendance and presence may be necessary to enable him to fully investigate the situation of all persons who may be brought before him, and the police officers and constables of said city shall be subject to his direction, and shall serve, when called upon for that purpose, any summons, order or warrant he may be directed, and shall receive for such service the same compensation he is allowed for serving criminal process in justice courts.

SEC. 7. The board of guardians of said reform school are hereby authorized and empowered, in their discretion, to establish a branch reform school for girls under the age of sixteen and over the age of six years, and for that purpose to purchase such lands and erect such buildings as in their judgment are required. And such girls may for the same causes and by the same courts and in the same manner be sentenced and committed to said branch reform school, that boys may be to the reform school; and all ordinances of the city and statutes of this State relative to the power, management and control of said reform school, by the board of guardians, are hereby made applicable to said branch reform school, and the same powers are delegated to and vested in them in relation to the same, and all ordinances and statutes regulating the powers and duties of police magistrates, justices of the peace and other courts, and of the commissioner, shall in all respects be made applicable to girls under the age of sixteen years, and over the age of six years, where they are found to be vagrant, or destitute of parental care, wandering about the streets, committing mischief or leading a vicious life, or are found in the streets, highways or public places, in circumstances of want, or suffering, or neglect, or exposure.

SEC. 8. Neither this act nor the one to which it is an amendment shall be affected by the repeal or amendment of the act incorporating the city of Chicago, unless there is some clause expressly repealing or amending the same.

SEC. 9. This act shall be deemed a public act, and shall take effect from its passage.

Approved February 22, 1861.

DECISIONS OF THE SUPREME COURT.

A corporate body can act only in the manner prescribed by the act of incorporation, which gives it existence. *Betts* v. *Menard*, Breese, 395.

The Court of County Commissioners, established by an act passed March 22nd, 1819, had no jurisdiction in actions wherein bodies politic or corporate were parties. *County of Vermillion* v. *Knight*, 1 Scam. 97.

In the enactments of legislative bodies, where persons are spoken of, no other than natural persons will be intended, unless it be absolutely necessary to give effect to some powers already conferred on artificial persons, and which it is necessary should be exercised, to carry into effect the objects contemplated in their grant or charter. *Blair* v. *Worley*, 1 Scam. 178.

A summons from a justice of the peace to the defendants to answer "for a violation of an ordinance of the town of Jacksonville, relative to nuisances," is insufficient; the statute, under which the suit was brought, and which authorizes the president and trustees to impose fines for the breach of such ordinances, provides for the recovery of the fines by action of *debt;* and, in bringing suit under this statute, debt is most clearly the form of action. *Israel et al.* v. *The Town of Jacksonville*, 1 Scam. 290.

Under the act of 1837, incorporating the city of Chicago, the criminal jurisdiction of the municipal court of the city of Chicago was confined to the territorial limits of said city; hence, an indictment, purporting to be found by "grand jurors chosen, selected and sworn in and for the city of Chicago and county of Cook," was held to be bad, and should have been quashed on motion. *Bell* v. *The People*, 1 Scam. 397.

The "Act supplemental to an Act to incorporate the city of Chicago," also passed in 1837, had no application to criminal proceedings. *Idem.*

Where the capias, issued for the arrest of a person charged with an assault and battery, stated that the act complained of was "contrary to the law of the State of Illinois, and in violation of the ordinances of the town of Lynville," and the cause was placed on the justice's docket in the name of the "President and Trustees of Lynville, and the justice gave judgment in favor of the "President, etc.;" and on appeal, the Circuit Court directed the cause to be docketed in the name of the "People," and tried the cause as between the "People" and the defendant: *Held*, that there was no error, and that so much of the warrant as stated the offense to be against the corporate authorities was nothing more than surplusage, and did not vitiate it. *Shirtliff* v. *The People of Illinois*, 2 Scam. 7.

In suits by corporations, the same rules prevail as in suits by natural persons. Process in favor of a corporation can be sent out of the county, where the suit is commenced, only in such cases as it might be so sent in suits in favor of persons. *Holbrook* v. *The Peoria Bridge Company*, 2 Scam. 32.

The act of February 11th, 1835, "to change the corporate powers of the town of Chicago," declared that the individuals therein named, and their successors, should be a body politic and corporate, by the name of the "Trustees of the Town of Chicago," and that they should have a common seal. *Kinzie* v. *Chicago*, 2 Scam. 187.

A body corporate can act only in the mode prescribed by the law creating it. *Idem.*

A lease was executed by the "Trustees of the Town of Chicago," signed by the trustees, who affixed no seal to their name, but a single seal was attached to the left of the signatures of the trustees; the lease was void for the want of the corporate seal. *Idem.*

The mode of assenting to and authenticating the acts of a corporate body, which uses a seal, is to affix the seal, with a declaration that it is the seal of the corporation, and to verify the act by the signatures of the president and secretary. *Idem.*

Under the general incorporation law of 1831, and the amendments thereto, passed in 1835, a justice of the peace had jurisdiction of a suit against an individual for a breach of an ordinance of an incorporated town, prohibiting the sale of liquor in a less quantity than one gallon, and imposing a fine, not exceeding five dollars, for such breach; in such case, it is not necessary that the fine should be first imposed by such corporation and then the suit brought, but the fine, which is prescribed in the ordinance, may be originally sued for before the justice; such suit can be maintained in the name of the president and trustees of such town, and such an ordinance is not repugnant to the constitution of the United States or of this State. *King et al.* v. *Jacksonville*, 2 Scam. 305.

A penalty imposed by an ordinance of an incorporated town for selling liquor without license, is not a tax. *Idem.*

It is not necessary, in a declaration by a corporation, to aver the corporate existence, or to plead the act of incorporation. *Bank of Washtenaw* v. *Montgomery*, 2 Scam. 422.

Corporations may institute suits in the courts of other States and countries than those under whose laws they may have been established. *Idem.*

Section five, of "An Act to incorporate the inhabitants of such towns as may wish to be incorporated," conferred upon the president and trustees of incorporated towns the power "to provide for licensing public shows," and, by fair construction, suspended, within the limits of such towns, so much of the act of 1829 as required a license from the county treasurer. *Woodward* v. *Turnbull*, 3 Scam. 1.

The interest of an inhabitant of a municipal corporation, being a resident tax-payer, is too remote and contingent to render him incompetent as a witness, in behalf of the corporation, in a suit to recover a penalty imposed by the charter of the corporation. *Sawyer* v. *City of Alton*, 3 Scam. 127.

The tenth section of "An Act to incorporate the city of Alton," approved July 21st, 1837, which provided that the common council should be required to keep all the roads and bridges within the city in good order and repair, and, for that purpose, should have the exclusive right to call on all male persons between the ages of twenty-one and fifty years, residents of the city, to perform three days' labor on the roads and bridges annually, or to pay one dollar for each day such residents should refuse to labor, was held to be not in violation of the constitution of this State; under the constitution of Illinois, when property is to be taxed, the mode of levying the tax must be by valuation, and the tax must be uniform, but the legislature possesses the power to impose such other taxes as may be consonant with public justice, and as the circumstances of the country may require. *Idem.*

A poll or capitation tax, without regard to property, is constitutional. *Idem.*

The legislature has power to pass a general law, declaring the streets, in all towns surveyed and recorded, to be public highways. It also has the right to exercise this power in a special case. *Edwards* v. *Pope*, 3 Scam. 465.

To establish the incorporation of a town, the act of the legislature incorporating the town being read in evidence, an offer was made to introduce the original minutes of the board of trustees of the town, proved by the clerk of the board, showing the acceptance of the charter and their acts under it. The minutes had been transcribed into a book kept by the board of trustees, which, upon inquiry and search amongst the records and files of the corporation and its officers, could not be found: *Held*, that the minutes were admissible, and were good evidence to establish the fact. *Fitch et al.* v. *Pinckard et al.*, 4 Scam. 69.

The act of incorporation being produced, proof of acts by the corporation under it have been held sufficient evidence of the acceptance of the charter and organization of the corporation. *Idem.*

The minutes and entries, made by the officers of a corporation, if it appear that they have been kept in a proper place, and by a proper person, are admissible in evidence. *Idem.*

A town corporation has no power to declare that the collector's deed shall be evidence of a compliance with all the prerequisites of the ordinance providing for the sale of lots for taxes. *Idem.*

The legislature alone possesses the power to make or alter the rules of evidence. *Idem.*

A purchaser under a sale of town lots for taxes due to a corporation, and made by it, must prove every material allegation or fact necessary to show a right of recovery. He must show not only a power in the corporation to levy and collect a tax, but that the land was subject to that taxation; that the tax levied was authorized; that it was due and unpaid, and that the powers granted had been strictly complied with. *Idem.*

All fixed and permanent buildings and improvements upon land are a part of the land, and under a section in a town charter, which authorizes the corporation to levy and collect taxes upon all real estate within the town, not exceeding one-half of one per centum upon the assessed value thereof, it is necessary to estimate the whole value of the lot and buildings, in assessing the value of a town lot. *Idem.*

Under a clause in a town charter, authorizing the passage of such ordinances, from time to time, as might be necessary to carry into effect the power of the incorporation to levy and collect taxes upon all the real estate within the town, the board of trustees have no authority to exempt buildings upon the town lots from valuation, in assessing the value of said lots, or to discriminate as to what real estate shall be taxed; and an ordinance thus discriminating or changing the objects of taxation, is in violation of the town charter, and void. *Idem.*

A corporation must strictly pursue the power creating it or giving it power to act; a power to sell property for taxes is a naked power, and must be strictly pursued; everything required to be done must be done, and those claiming under a tax sale will be required to make strict proof that everything was done that is required by the statute. *Idem.*

Where a town ordinance required the collector to give notice that the taxes were due, and, if not paid by a certain day, that he would proceed to advertise and sell the property assessed, and also required him, if the taxes were not paid by the day fixed, to advertise and sell; and to prove the notice and advertisement, newspapers were introduced, published in 1837, containing the notice and advertisement, dated "1836:" *Held*, that parol proof was not admissible to show that the date was a mistake, and that it was intended for 1837. *Idem.*

The doctrine is undoubtedly correct, that the legislature has no power to direct, that any portion of the debts due a private corporation shall be received in anything but gold and silver coin, as the act of incorporation is regarded as a contract between the government and the corporators, which the legislature may not repeal or impair, so long as the latter keep within the limits of their charter. But it is equally well settled in respect to public corporations, created for public purposes, that the legislature has the exclusive right, as trustee of the public interest, to regulate, control and direct the corporation, and its funds and franchises, for the reason that the whole interest and franchises are given, by the act of incorporation, for the public use and advantage. *Bush* v. *Shipman et al.*, 4 Scam. 186.

The legislature has absolute control over municipal corporations, to create, change, modify or destroy them at pleasure. *The People* v. *Wren*, 4 Scam. 269.

The creation of a municipal corporation depends in no degree upon the assent or dissent of the inhabitants of the particular locality, unless such a condition be contained in the law of its creation. *Idem.*

Counties or other public corporations do not become dissolved by the neglect of the corporators to elect officers. *Idem.*

The legislature has the power to contract with a corporation to exempt its property from taxation; such contracts have frequently been made, and their validity has not been doubted. *State Bank of Illinois* v. *The People*, 4 Scam. 303.

A fiscal agent, whether of a government, a corporation or an individual, is held to the strictest accountability, and never permitted, at the expense of his principal, to speculate in the funds of that principal in his hands for management. *Hamilton et al.* v. *Cook County*, 4 Scam. 519.

An order, drawn by the mayor of a city on its treasurer, commonly called a city order, is a proper subject of set-off in a suit, brought by the city against the holder of the order, to recover a penalty accruing under an ordinance of the city. *City of Springfield* v. *Hickox*, 2 Gilm. 241.

A prior demand on the treasurer is not necessary to charge the city upon such order. *Idem.*

The word "may" means "must" or "shall" in cases where the public interest and rights are concerned, and where the public or third persons have a claim, *de jure*, that the power should be exercised. *Schuyler County* v. *Mercer County*, 4 Gilm, 20.

Ordinarily, a law which in general terms speaks of plaintiffs and defendants, applies to persons only; and States, counties and municipal corporations are not affected by its provisions, unless expressly named and brought within them. *Idem.*

In suits, brought by corporations, the defendant, by pleading the general issue admits the capacity of the plaintiff to sue. If he would deny the existence of the corporation, he must put in a plea for that purpose. *McIntyre* v. *Preston*, 5 Gilm. 48.

Where a party has shown the power of a corporation to take a note, it is incumbent on the opposite party to show that such power has been taken away. *Idem.*

If a corporation has the power to take a note, and hold and convey real or personal estate, it necessarily has the power to negotiate such note in the transaction of its ordinary business; and where such corporation has the power to take and transfer a note for any purpose, it will be inferred that it was taken and transferred in the ordinary course of business, until the contrary is shown. *Idem.*

Corporations may, in this State, assign notes, the word "person" being sometimes so construed as to include them. *Idem.*

Corporations may transact business through, and are bound by, the acts of their officers. *Idem.*

Where a bill in chancery was filed by certain companies or corporations, it was *held*, that no other allegation that they were incorporated, was necessary. *Frye* v. *The Bank of Illinois*, 5 Gilm. 332.

A defendant in a bill in chancery, brought by several companies as corporations, suffered the bill to be taken as confessed: *Held*, that he thereby admitted that they were incorporated, and had the capacity to sue. *Idem.*

The public are entitled to the use and enjoyment of the whole of a highway, and no individual can appropriate a portion of it to his own exclusive use, and shield himself from responsibility to the public, by saying that enough is still left for the accommodation of others; as where materials are temporarily placed in the street to be used in erecting a building, leaving sufficient room for the passage of the public on the other side. *People* v. *City of St. Louis et al.*, 5 Gilm. 351.

In prosecutions for nuisances, the defendant cannot set off equivalent or even greater benefits, resulting to the public by the erection of a real and substantial obstruction in a public road or river. *Idem.*

A private citizen may not take the public welfare into his own hands, and justify himself for a violation of some of its rights, under a plea of a general benefit. *Idem.*

To prove the due publication of a town ordinance, the records of the corporation, containing the original ordinances, were produced, and an offer made by the defendant to prove, by the clerk of the corporation, that he posted up copies of those ordinances. The plaintiff objected to this evidence, and the court excluded it, on the ground that the defendant must either produce the notices, or one of them, which were originally posted, or account for their absence: *Held*, that the testimony was improperly excluded, as the *publication* of the ordinances, and not their *contents*, was the main fact sought to be established by the clerk. *Teft* v. *Size*, 5 Gilm. 432.

Incorporated towns, under the statutes of Illinois, have the power to enforce their ordinances against nuisances by reasonable forfeitures, where the end cannot otherwise be attained. *Idem.*

The acknowledgment and recording of a town plat is a solemn dedication of the land embraced by streets, to the corporation, to be held in trust for the uses and purposes of the public. *Canal Trustees* v. *Havens*, 11 Ill. 554.

On the recording of the plat, the fee in the streets, *eo instanti*, passes to the corporation; and if the plat is recorded before the town has a corporate existence, the fee remains in abeyance, subject to vest in the corporation the moment it is created. *Idem.*

The purchaser of a town lot, designated upon a recorded plat, only acquires a title to the land included within the actual limits of the lot, as designated. He takes no interest in the street, except in common with the public, and is estopped by the solemn act of his grantor from claiming title to the centre of the street. *Idem.*

In a proceeding under the acts incorporating the city of Chicago, which authorize the common council to lay out streets, etc., and to make assessments, etc., in that behalf, it is erroneous to superadd the costs of such proceedings to the damages awarded to the owner of the ground appropriated. *Morris et al.* v. *The City of Chicago*, 11 Ill. 650.

Public or municipal corporations, which exist only for public purposes, and possess no powers except such as are bestowed upon them for public political purposes, are subject, at all times, to the control of the legislature, which may alter, modify or abolish them at pleasure. *County of Richland* v. *County of Lawrence*, 12 Ill. 1.

The State may make a contract with, or a grant to, a public municipal corporation, which it cannot subsequently impair or resume; but in such case the corporation is to be regarded as a private company. *Idem.*

A grant may be made to a public corporation for purposes of private advantage, and although the public may also derive a common benefit therefrom, yet the corporation stands on the same footing, as respects such grant, as would any body of persons upon whom like privileges are conferred. *Idem.*

The owner of a lot on the street of a city took up the sidewalk in front of his premises, and extended his coal cellar under it: *Held*, that the authority to make such cellars may be implied, in the absence of any action of the corporate authorities to the contrary, they having been aware of the progress of the work; but while a license thus to use a part of the public street is inferred, it is on condition that the person doing so shall use more than ordinary care and expedition in the prosecution of the work. *Nelson* v. *Godfrey*, 12 Ill. 20.

If the owners of land agree upon a plan, and make a survey into lots, and lay off ground for public use, as a street or landing, and make sales in reference thereto, this amounts to a dedication of such ground to the public. *Godfrey* v. *The City of Alton*, 12 Ill. 29.

A map of the survey is not essential to the validity of a dedication. *Idem.*

The statute of frauds does not apply to the dedication of ground to the public. *Idem.*

A dedication may be made by grant, or other written instrument, or it may be evidenced by acts and declarations, without writing. No particular form is required to the validity of a dedication; it is purely a question of intention. *Idem.*

A dedication may be made by survey and plat alone, without any declaration, either oral or on the plat, when it is evident from the face of the plat, that it was intended to set apart certain grounds for the use of the public. *Idem.*

A dedication must be understood and construed with reference to the objects and purposes for which it was made. This is peculiarly the case with a public landing upon a navigable water-course. That is necessarily inseparable from the margin of the water, however that may fluctuate. All accretions to a public landing must necessarily attach to and form a part of it. *Idem.*

When an easement is granted to the public upon the margin of a navigable stream, the right to use and treat it as a landing is undoubted. *Idem.*

If the banks of a navigable river are dedicated, the dedicator has no interest in the bed of the stream, which he can reserve to the prejudice of the public easement over it. *Idem.*

The rights of the public are not barred by our statute of limitations, which prescribes that certain real actions shall be brought within seven years after possession taken by a defendant. *City of Alton* v. *Illinois Transportation Company*, 12 Ill. 38.

Where certain blocks of lots in a city were dedicated to the city for certain purposes, specified in the deed, it was held, that for such purposes the city might improve and control them, and adopt all needful rules and regulations for their management, but that she could not alien or dispose of them for her own exclusive benefit, nor are they subject to the payment of her debts. She holds them in trust for the benefit of the public. *Idem.*

A corporation, which is a mere creature of the law, can only exercise such powers as are conferred upon it by the act of incorporation. *Trustees of Jacksonville* v. *McConnell*, 12 Ill. 138.

A power, conferred by the charter of a town upon its board of trustees, to assess and collect a tax upon all personal estate within the town, includes the power to tax money loaned. *Idem.*

The act of 1839, empowering the president and trustees of incorporated towns to grant licenses, and requiring them to pay all moneys, derived from this source, into the county treasury, does not repeal special laws previously passed, empowering particular corporations to grant licenses and to retain moneys, so obtained, for their own use. *The Town of Ottawa* v. *County of La Salle*, 12 Ill. 339.

Where two acts are seemingly repugnant, they should, if possible, be so construed that the latter may not operate as a repeal of the former by implication. The law does not favor a repeal by implication. *Idem.*

It is error, in a proceeding for opening a street in the city of Chicago, to include the costs of the proceeding in the assessment. *Canal Trustees et al.* v. *The City of Chicago*, 12 Ill. 403.

The real estate belonging to the trustees of the Illinois and Michigan Canal, is liable to assessments for opening streets and other improvements of a like character. *Idem.*

Assessments for improvements are not a charge upon an estate, which reduces its value; they have none of the distinctive features of a tax, being imposed for a special purpose, and not for a general or public object. *Idem.*

The grant of a franchise to a public corporation may, at any time, be resumed by the State; public corporations and their rights and effects are subject to the general superintendence and control of the State, so that their property is not diverted from the uses and objects for which it was given or purchased. *Trustees of Schools, etc.*, v. *Tatman*, 13 Ill. 27.

The acknowledgment and recording of a town plat vests the legal title to the streets in the corporation; therefore, the person making such plat and dedication, not having the legal title nor exclusive right of possession, cannot bring an action of trespass for an injury to the soil or freehold, as he could in the case of a highway. The corporation alone can seek redress for such injury. *Hunter* v. *Middleton*, 13 Ill. 50.

The title to the streets and alleys of a town may revert to the original proprietor, on the destruction of the corporation, or on abandonment of the ground appropriated to streets and alleys; but until such reversion, the fee is out of the original proprietor as completely as if he had made an absolute and unconditional conveyance. *Idem.*

The authority of a collector of taxes in a town, to distrain for taxes, depends entirely upon the ordinance, and he can only distrain at the time and in the manner which that authorizes; he acts under a special authority, and must show affirmatively the warrant for his proceeding. *Allen* v. *Scott*, 13 Ill. 80.

The acknowledgment and recording of a town plat vests the fee to the streets and alleys in the corporation; but the public have an interest in streets and alleys, although the ground has not been set apart for the purpose in the manner prescribed by the statute. *Manly et al.* v. *Gibson*, 13 Ill. 308.

A dedication of ground to public uses may be made in other ways than by the making and recording of a town plat. *Idem.*

In the case of a valid plat, the title to the ground, set apart for public purposes, is held by the corporation for the use and benefit of the public; in the case of a dedication by a different mode, the fee continues in the proprietor, burdened with the public easement. *Idem.*

An action of assumpsit may be sustained against a corporation upon an implied contract. *Seagraves* v. *The City of Alton*, 13 Ill. 366.

Where a city is liable, by the terms of its charter, to support the paupers within its limits, if, upon application to the authorities for that purpose, they refuse to do so, and an individual supply the pauper, there is an implied promise on the part of the corporation to pay the individual, which will support an action of assumpsit. *Idem.*

Except in extreme cases, a corporation cannot be made responsible to an individual for relief granted to a pauper, until an opportunity has been afforded the corporation to make the necessary provision; it is only when the corporation is clearly in default that she can be held liable on an implied contract. *Idem.*

Where the law imposes an obligation on a corporation, which it refuses to discharge, it may be held liable, civilly, at the suit of a party who sustains damage in consequence of its refusal; in legal contemplation, a corporation assumes to perform what its charter enjoins upon it. *Idem.*

A city has a right to become a stockholder in a railroad company, and give her proxy to whom she pleases. *Ryder* v. *Alton and Sangamon R. R. Co.*, 13 Ill. 516.

As a general rule, a corporator cannot be called to testify on behalf of the corporation in which he is interested, but there are exceptions. *Idem.*

A corporator may be called to prove that he was the depositary of the muniments of the corporation. *Idem.*

A corporator may produce and identify a paper in his custody. *Idem.*

The clerk of a corporation is a competent witness to identify its books and verify its records, although he is a member of the corporation, and interested in the suit in which the books and records are to be used as evidence. *Idem.*

The books of a corporation are admissible, for the purpose of showing its acts and proceedings, and the regularity and legality of the same. *Idem.*

It is the undoubted right of the legislature to repeal so much of an act incorporating a city, as gives authority to its officers to grant licenses for the sale of ardent spirits, whether the money to be derived from the sale of such licenses was especially appropriated to the support of paupers or otherwise. *Gutzweller* v. *The People*, 14 Ill. 142.

The valuation and assessment of a railroad and its property, for city purposes, must be governed by the same rules which govern counties. *Sangamon and Morgan R. R. Co.* v. *County of Morgan, etc.*, 14 Ill. 163.

The trustees of a town possess only such powers as are expressly conferred by their charter, or are necessary to carry into effect the powers granted; and if they transcend those powers, their acts are not binding, either on the town or on third persons. They have no power to give away the funds of the town, or appropriate them to purposes not warranted by the charter; but the power to sue and be sued includes authority to settle or adjust claims; and a settlement of an existing controversy by the trustees in good faith, binds the corporation. *Town of Petersburg* v. *Mappin et al.*, 14 Ill. 193.

Where a street has been opened by the trustees of a town, having the same powers in that respect as are given to the city of Springfield, the board of trustees of the town exercise the same functions as do the council of the city, and the president of the board the same functions as does the mayor of the city; and the question of the expediency of opening the street, is solely for the consideration of the trustees, and cannot be inquired into by the Circuit Court on appeal. *Dunlap* v. *Mt. Sterling*, 14 Ill. 251.

The original plan of making the south branch of the Chicago river a part of the Illinois and Michigan Canal having been abandoned, it was *held*, that it was not the duty of the trustees to condemn and appropriate blocks 14 and 15, in the city of Chicago, for the purpose of forming a basin at the confluence of the north and south branches of the river. *The People ex rel. Chicago* v. *Illinois and Michigan Canal*, 14 Ill. 292.

The mode of appropriating land for the purposes of a street, and assessing the cost of the improvement upon the property to be benefited thereby, as provided for in an amendment to the charter of the city of Chicago, passed in 1847, was essentially changed by the "Act to reduce the law incorporating the city of Chicago, and the several acts amendatory thereof, into one act, and amend the same," approved February 14th, 1851. By the act of 1851, the common council appoint commissioners to ascertain the compensation to be paid to the owners of the land taken, and assess the cost of opening the street upon the adjoining property; and the commissioners report their proceeding for the action of the common council. By the act of 1847, the court appointed the commissioners and reviewed their proceedings. The proceeding under the act of 1847 was before the court; under the act of 1851, it is before the common council. The first act vested the jurisdiction in the court; the last act vests it in the common council. In this respect, the two acts are plainly repugnant to each other; and the last, by necessary implication, operates as a repeal, *pro tanto*, of the former. *Illinois and Michigan Canal* v. *City of Chicago*, 14 Ill. 334.

The Illinois Central Railroad Company have the right, under their charter, to locate their road in the waters of Lake Michigan, the city of Chicago having assented. *Illinois Central R. R. Co.* v. *Rucker*, 14 Ill. 353.

The failure of the company to locate their road within the limits of the city by the first day of January, 1852, as required by their charter, does not work a forfeiture of their right to condemn lands for their use, where the assent of the city to such location was not given until after that day had elapsed. *Idem.*

A party will not be liable to the penalty, inflicted by an ordinance of an incorporated town, for selling liquor, unless it clearly appears, from the evidence, that the ordinance took effect before the act complained of was committed. *Newlan* v. *Aurora*, 14 Ill. 364.

The provisions of those city charters, which authorized the mayors to be commissioned as justices of the peace, and vested them with judicial powers, were abrogated by the new constitution. *State ex rel. City of Rockford* v. *Maynard*, 14 Ill. 419.

In an action for assault, battery and imprisonment, if the plea to it professes to answer the assault, etc., and imprisonment, the etc. will make the plea broad enough to answer the battery complained of. *Bryan* v. *Bates*, 15 Ill. 87.

The powers of the cities, and their ministerial officers, and their ministerial duties, continue, and were not changed by the new constitution. And the city marshal of the city of Springfield has the power to arrest, without warrant, any offender, for violations of certain ordinances committed in his presence. *Idem.*

The principle laid down in the case of *The People* v. *Maynard*, 14 Illinois Reports, does not affect the general police powers of cities, but has reference only to the judicial powers of mayors, acting as a court under city ordinances. *Idem.*

A suit should be brought against a corporation, and not against the individuals incorporated by a common appellation. *Insane Hospital* v. *Higgins*, 15 Ill. 185.

The public is an ever existing grantee, capable of taking dedications for public uses, and its interests are a sufficient consideration to support them. *Warren* v. *Town of Jacksonville*, 15 Ill. 236.

The mode of making dedications is immaterial. They are not within the statute of frauds, and are good by parol. *Idem.*

The intention of the party, manifested by express consent or acquiescence in the user, will govern in determining what is a dedication. *Idem.*

Privies in estate will be bound by the acts and deeds of their grantors, and they cannot resume a grant, after the public has entered upon its use, while the use continues. *Idem.*

A deed containing recitals of the dedication of land for the purposes of a street, cannot be delivered and accepted partially, for the purpose of conveying title to the grantee, and yet so as not to give effect to the conditions, recitals and limitations in it. *Idem.*

It will be presumed that deeds, duly acknowledged and recorded, have been delivered to and accepted by the vendee, and that parties and privies, as well as the public, are acquainted with their contents. Whoever questions these facts must assume the burden of disproving them. *Idem.*

No inference or conclusion will be drawn against the owner of land lying unenclosed, which is traveled over, to establish an easement in favor of the public; nor can a right by prescription be raised against the consent of the owner, though the use may be so long unobjected to, as to authorize the finding of an implied consent, and raise the presumption of a grant. *Idem.*

It is enough to sue in the name of a corporation, without showing, on the face of the declaration, how it came into existence; it requires a plea of *nul tiel* corporation to put in issue the fact of incorporation. *Morris* v. *Trustees of Schools*, 15 Ill. 266.

Where a corporation has the power to extend and open streets within the corporate limits, this powor applies to all lands within its boundaries, whether the same be laid out into town lots or not. *Curry* v. *Mt. Sterling*, 15 Ill. 320.

If a party, having had all the notice required by the statute in such cases, suffers a street to be opened through his land without objection, he cannot afterwards interpose a claim for compensation. He should insist upon his claim in due time, so that the corporation may vacate the ordinance, if it regards the assessment of damages as unreasonable. *Idem.*

Where a statute, which provides for the assessment of damages upon the opening of streets in an incorporated town, directs that injuries and benefits shall be alike considered, if the property will sell for as much with as without the street, the jury may well consider that no damage has been sustained. *Idem.*

Where an officer, who is present at the commission of an offense, or on hue and cry, is not able to make an arrest, and calls in other officers or the *posse*, the justification of those who aid him is as broad as his own. *Main* v. *McCarty et al.*, 15 Ill. 441.

An arrest may be made, for violating a city ordinance of the city of Chicago against keeping open a tippling house on the Sabbath. *Idem.*

An ordinance of the city of Chicago, which authorizes an arrest, without a warrant, for breaches of the peace or threats of breaches, is not invalid. *Idem.*

The policemen of the city of Chicago have the power to arrest, without warrant, for breaches of the city ordinances committed in their presence. *Idem.*

An arrest for a breach of the peace need not be made immediately, and may be made after peace is restored and the affray over, or upon the information of an officer who was present, witnessing it, after the affray was over. *Idem.*

Mandamus is a proper remedy against an ex-mayor to obtain possession of a seal, books, papers, muniments, etc., the property of the corporation; and a pretended intrusion into, or retention of the office of mayor, will not justify the withholding of such property, so as to drive the informant to resort to a quo warranto. *The People ex rel. Brewster et al.* v. *Kilduff*, 15 Ill. 492.

An ordinance which declares the selling of spirituous liquors a nuisance, and imposes a fine for the offense, is valid, if the corporate powers conferred upon the town are broad enough to authorize the ordinance. *Goddard* v. *Town of Jacksonville*, 15 Ill. 588.

A town, incorporated under the general law, may provide by ordinance against disposing of any vinous, spirituous or mixed liquors in a less quantity than one barrel, without first taking out a license, and such ordinance is not repugnant to the general law, prohibiting a sale without a license in a quantity less than one quart. *Byers et al.* v. *President and Trustees of Olney*, 16 Ill. 35.

Where a municipal corporation has been recognized by acts of the legislature, empowering it to act as a body corporate, in issuing and negotiating obligations of the town, and upon the faith of which individuals may have invested their money, all inquiry into the question of the original legal organization of the town is precluded. *Jameson* v. *People ex rel. Nettleton*, 16 Ill. 257.

Municipal corporations are created for the public good — are demanded by the wants of the community; and the law, after long continued use of corporate powers, and the public acquiescence, will indulge in presumptions in favor of their legal existence. *Idem.*

The mayor of a city has no judicial power under our constitution. *Busman* v. *The City of Peoria*, 16 Ill. 484.

The mayor of a city, having no power to enter a judgment of fine under our constitution, an appeal from his decision, can confer no jurisdiction of the offense upon the Circuit Court. *Idem.*

An action for damages, resulting from negligence in not repairing the streets, will lie against a municipal corporation, if the duty to repair is fully and completely enjoined upon the corporation, and adequate means to perform that duty are placed within its power. *Browning* v. *City of Springfield*, 17 Ill. 143.

It is competent for the legislature to designate any one or more of the justices of the peace in any town or city, who shall have exclusive jurisdiction of complaints for violating the ordinances of the town or city. *In the matter of James Welch*, 17 Ill. 161.

The act of the legislature of the 27th February, 1854, entitled "An Act for the better government of towns and cities, and to amend the charters thereof," was passed, not in the exercise of the power conferred upon the legislature to establish inferior local courts of civil and criminal jurisdiction in the cities of this State, but under the power conferred upon them to create justices of the peace, and it did not repeal by implication, or supersede the law establishing the Recorder's Court of the city of Chicago. *Idem.*

The Recorder's Court of the city of Chicago is a constitutional tribunal. *Idem.*

In this State, "police magistrates" and "police justices," are equally within the meaning of the constitution, and the intention of the law, passed for the better government of towns and cities, approved February 28th, 1854; and votes given for persons to fill those offices under either designation, should be counted and returned in favor of the persons for whom they may have been cast. *The People ex rel. Akin et al.* v. *Matteson et al.*, 17 Ill. 167.

Where a public road has been used for twenty years, the owner of the land over which it passes acquiescing therein, the law presumes a dedication. *Green et al.* v. *Oakes*, 17 Ill. 249.

Where, upon a proceeding by town authorities to condemn land for opening streets, they describe said land, in all their proceedings, as being the land of a certain individual, they cannot afterwards deny the right of that individual to be heard upon the question of damages, upon the ground of his want of title; their conduct amounts to an admission of his ownership of the land. *President and Trustees of Mt. Sterling* v. *Givens*, 17 Ill. 255.

A dedication may be manifested by express or implied consent, from acquiescence in the user, and the user does not depend upon any fixed period of time. *Alvord* v. *Ashley*, 17 Ill. 363.

The dedication, as also the extent or quantity of land embraced in it, is a mixed question of law and fact, to be submitted to the jury. *Idem.*

The actual use and repair of a highway by the public, is evidence of its acceptance for such purpose. *Idem.*

A party will be estopped from denying a dedication, by the acquiescence in it of his grantors. *Idem.*

In an action of debt for the violation of a town ordinance against selling liquor, in order to justify a recovery, it should be shown that the liquor had been sold after the ordinance took effect. *Newlan* v. *Aurora*, 17 Ill. 379.

If a corporation is made garnishee, it may answer by its proper officer, but the answer must be sworn to by such officer. *Oliver* v. *Chicago and Aurora R. R. Co.*, 17 Ill. 587.

Where a street has been ordered to be opened or extended; commissioners for the assessment of damages have been appointed, and made and reported an assessment, which has been accepted and confirmed; a warrant has been issued for the collection of the amounts assessed for payment of such damages, and such street has been ordered to be opened, the parties entitled to such damages for property taken, etc., are entitled to a mandamus to compel the city to proceed to collect and pay over the same. *Higgins* v. *City of Chicago*, 18 Ill. 276.

If an assessment for opening or extending a street in the city of Chicago has been confirmed by the common council, the city is concluded by its own confirmation from objecting to the assessment on account of any supposed irregularities in the proceedings of the commissioners, or for reasons alone applicable to parties interested. *Idem.*

Public taxes or special assessments for public improvements may be levied upon the public property of municipal corporations; it is a mere question of policy. *Idem.*

In assessing damages on property for benefits arising from the laying or extending of streets, the public square of the city may receive a due share of the benefit with any other realty on the same street; and the corporation of the city may, if not specially exempted, justly pay a part of the assessments, proportionate to the benefits conferred by the improvements. *Idem.*

Where there is a special assessment, for public improvements, upon a person's real estate, a lien is created upon his personalty, from the delivery of the warrant to the collector. *Idem.*

In a proceeding to open a street in the city of Peoria, under the acts incorporating that city, the owner of property offered to make certain proofs before the County Court, before which the report of the commissioners was pending for confirmation, that the commissioners had prejudged his case, and that proof before them, by him, would have been useless; which the County Court refused to receive: *Held*, that this was erroneous; and that affidavits, showing the value of the property, its condition, and the benefits and injuries, were also proper to be produced. *Cole* v. *City of Peoria*, 18 Ill. 301.

A child, four years of age, fell into a water tank, constructed by the city of Chicago, and was drowned: *Held*, that the father, as administrator, could maintain an action under the act, which gives a remedy, when the death of a person is caused by the wrongful act, default or neglect of another; the action under this statute is to be brought by the executor or administrator of the deceased, and is not limited to those cases, where he leaves a widow; any money recovered by such an action, is not to be treated as a part of the estate of the deceased, so that creditors can get any benefit from it, but is to be distributed among those to whom the personal estate would descend, in the absence of a will, according to the statute of descents. *City of Chicago* v. *Major*, 18 Ill. 349.

Orphans may have a redress under this statute, where both parents are killed, and a husband, also, has redress for the loss of his wife. *Idem.*

The damages, recovered in an action under the act, which gives a remedy when the death of a person is caused by the wrongful act, default or neglect of any person, company or corporation, can only be for the pecuniary loss, not for the bereavement; and the judgment of the jury, in determining the amount of damages, must be governed by their own knowledge and experience, applied to the proofs in the case. *Idem.*

A long and unreasonable delay, on the part of the city, in repairing the tank, would justify the jurors in presuming, that the city had been notified of its defects, and was guilty of negligence in omitting to repair it. It is not sufficient, that such a tank is so constructed as to be safe for all such persons as ordinarily use the streets of the city. *Idem.*

The jurors are to judge, whether the parents of the child, in such a case, were guilty of negligence, and the burden of proof is upon the plaintiff, to show negligence in the defendant, as well as to acquit himself of it. *Idem.*

The proviso to the first section of the fifth article of the constitution of this State, which reads as follows: "*Provided*, That inferior courts may be established by the general assembly in the cities of this State, but such courts shall have a uniform organization and jurisdiction," limits the territorial jurisdiction of the courts to be established under it, to the cities for which, and within which, they are established; consequently, an act of the legislature, which establishes a court within a city nominally, and requires its sessions to be held within the city limits, but extends its territorial jurisdiction beyond those limits, is unconstitutional. *The People* v. *Evans*, 18 Ill. 361.

If a town ordinance make it a penal offense to ride or drive a horse furiously in any street of the town, the motive of a person on trial for violating the ordinance is proper for the consideration of the jury in determining upon the appropriate penalty to be inflicted by way of punishment for the public wrong. *Morton* v. *President and Trustees of Princeton*, 18 Ill. 383.

Where the charter of a town requires its officers to keep a record of all their proceedings, by-laws, etc., in a book to be provided for that purpose, and declares that such book, purporting to be the records of the corporation, shall be received in all courts, without further proof, as evidence of all matters therein contained, no other proof of any of such matters than such book is necessary, and an honest correction of the record does not vitiate the by-laws. *The President and Trustees of the Town of St. Charles* v. *O'Mailley*, 18 Ill. 407.

Where a charter authorizes the recovery of several fines in one action, if the proof is clear as to four distinct offenses, a verdict for the penalty of but one is improper, as it would be a bar to a future prosecution for the other penalties. *Idem.*

In a suit for violation of a town ordinance forbidding sale of liquor, a witness is not to be discredited, from the simple fact that he may fill the character of informer or spy. *Idem.*

Where the act, authorizing the creation of a municipal corporation, directs that the government of the locality shall be vested in a president and four trustees, and that a justice of the peace, elected in a particular manner, shall be *ex officio* president—if that person shall not be commissioned and enter upon the duties of his office in the time required, the act becomes inoperative, and the inhabitants of the locality owe the same duties to the prior organization which they previously owed. *Haynes* v. *The County of Washington*, 19 Ill. 66.

A city, whose charter confers the power to levy and collect taxes upon all property within its corporate limits, has no power to tax property of residents of the city, having its actual *situs* without those limits. *Wilkey* v. *City of Pekin*, 19 Ill. 160.

In a suit for the breach of a city ordinance, relating to the sale of spirituous liquors, the fact that the liquor was owned by three, only two of whom are sued, is no objection to a recovery, such an action being in the nature of a tort, in which one or more of the offending parties may be sued. *President and Trustees of Jacksonville* v. *Holland et al.*, 19 Ill. 271.

The legislature has the constitutional right to authorize counties and cities to aid the construction of railroads, by lending their credit, or by taking stock. *Prettyman* v. *Supervisors of Tazewell County et al.*, 19 Ill. 406.

A mechanics' lien only extends to the appurtenances upon the premises sought to be subjected to it. Where the appurtenance is in the street, and not upon the lot, (as a vault under a sidewalk, adjacent to the building,) the lien does not reach it. *Parmelee et al.* v. *Hambleton et al.*, 19 Ill. 615.

Dedication of a highway may be proved in various ways, as by grant, by user, or by the acts and declarations of the owner. No particular length of time is necessary for evidence of dedication. *Morey* v. *Taylor*, 19 Ill. 634.

The acceptance of dedication of a highway by the public, may be shown by user, or by the acts of public officers, repairing and keeping it up, though the latter evidence of acceptance is not essential. *Idem.*

A copy of a city ordinance, certified in conformity with the charter, is proper evidence of the existence of such ordinance, in a suit where the city is a party. *Pendergrast* v. *City of Peru*, 20 Ill. 51.

In a suit for violating a city ordinance, by selling liquor without license, if the defendant stated that the city charged too much for license, and pleads guilty to the charge of violating the ordinance, it will be held that the fact is established, that he had not a license, that he sold liquor, and that his plea of guilty had reference to that offense, although the ordinance contained other provisions of prohibition, and other penalties. *Idem.*

To prove the existence of a corporation, it is sufficient to produce the charter, and prove acts done under it, and in conformity with it. Proof, and that, too, by written evidence, that all the preliminary steps, etc., were taken, is not necessary. *President and Trustees of Mendota* v. *Thompson*, 20 Ill. 197.

A corporation, acting as such, cannot be questioned collaterally, on the ground that it has not complied with its charter. *Idem.*

A municipal corporation is not dissolved, because, at its organization, persons not eligible were elected trustees; if their authority is questioned, it should be by *quo warranto*. *Idem.*

The city of Chicago has no authority to levy special assessments for deepening the Chicago river, although it has authority to levy such assessments for widening said river. *Wright et al.* v. *City of Chicago*, 20 Ill. 252.

Special authority, delegated by legislative enactment to particular persons, or summary proceedings, without personal service, to take away a man's property and estate, against his consent, must be strictly pursued, and it must so appear on the face of the proceedings. *City of Chicago* v. *Rock Island R. R. Co.*, 20 Ill. 286, (modified by *City of Chicago* v. *Colby*, 20 Ill. 614).

Prior to the passage of the amendatory act of 1857, orders for the sale of real estate, etc., to satisfy assessments, were entered by the common council, and applications for them made by the special collectors, but, after its passage, such an order could be made by no other authority than a court of general jurisdiction in the city, nor an application for it by any other person than the collector himself. *Idem.*

A special collector for one of the divisions of the city of Chicago, to whom a warrant had been issued before the passage of this amendatory act, directing him to collect an assessment for the extension of a street, out of the goods and chattels of the respective owners of the real estate assessed, had he levied upon the goods and chattels under the warrant, and while it was alive, could have completed the execution by their sale after the passage of the amendatory act, upon the general principle, that, when an officer commences to execute a *fi. fa.* by a levy, he may complete it, notwithstanding the writ may have died, or his office have expired, before its completion. *Idem.*

In a prosecution for selling spirituous liquors, in violation of a city ordinance, it is error to instruct the jury, that, before they can find the defendant guilty, they must believe the liquor was handed to a person, who asked for it, and was paid for or charged to some one; liquor may be sold in many other modes than by being handed to a person, nor is it necessary that it should be asked for, to make its sale complete. *Kimball* v. *The People*, 20 Ill. 348.

Where a statute directs that assessments for city improvements shall be made upon real estate in any natural division of the city benefited thereby, it is a limitation on the powers of the commissioners not to go out of a natural or obvious division to make assessments, but having selected the area, to assess such property in it for taxation, as will most likely be benefited. *City of Ottawa* v. *Macy et al.*, 20 Ill. 413.

A notice to parties interested in the property assessed, which conforms to the law under which the city is incorporated, and to the city ordinance in that regard, will be sufficient, although it is general to "all persons interested," to attend and make their objections to the confirmation of the assessment. *Idem.*

Where the city charter does not, but the ordinance passed under it does, direct that the collector shall make return of his warrant in thirty days, an omission to make the return within that time, will not make the proceedings void; such an ordinance is merely directory, and for the benefit of the city council. *Idem.*

If the collector shall make a return that he could not find goods and chattels whereon to levy and collect the amount assessed, that will be conclusive of the fact stated. If the return is false, the officer is responsible. *Idem.*

It is not a valid objection to a special assessment for improving the street of a city, that the city council did not finally dispose of the question of confirming the report of the commissioners, on the day it was made. Where the day fixed in the notice is for hearing objections, the city council is not bound to decide at once, but may take time for deliberation. *Idem.*

Church property in cities may be assessed for special purposes, though not liable for ordinary taxes. *Idem.*

Because an incorporated city is authorized to pass ordinances, in relation to the sale of spirituous liquors, declaring such sale a nuisance, the general law of the State on the same subject, is not thereby repealed. While a license from the city authorities will protect the holder of it from the penalty imposed by the general law of the State, yet, if those authorities fail or refuse to grant a license, the general law will be violated by a sale in the city limits, and the offender may be punished under it. *Gardner* v. *The People*, 20 Ill. 430.

By the charter of the city of Chicago, authority is conferred upon the city to remove obstructions from, and to widen, deepen and straighten the harbor of Chicago; and that harbor is declared to embrace the Chicago river, and its branches, to their source, and to extend one mile into the lake: *Held*, that this grant from the legislature did not create the obligation to do all these acts; and the city will not be liable to any party, in damages, for the non-performance of these permitted acts, unless it commences some of them, and does them in such an improper manner that injury results therefrom. *Goodrich* v. *City of Chicago*, 20 Ill. 445.

A party, who receives damages from a sunken hulk in the harbor of Chicago, cannot recover of the city, because the city has neglected to exercise the authority conferred upon it to clear out the harbor. *Idem.*

Where the school inspectors of a city are authorized to district the city, as to them may seem best, and to establish such rules for the admission of pupils as they think proper, these duties will not be interfered with except in extreme cases. *Grove* v. *School Inspectors of Peoria*, 20 Ill. 532.

The school inspectors of a city may refuse to admit a child, residing in one district, into a school established in another district, if the latter school be full; they may sustain a school in a house outside of the city limits, and keep the same in repairs for the use of children living within the city. If the board is guilty of injustice, or oppression, or partiality, the remedy lies with the electors of the city to change the board at the next election. *Idem.*

The second section of "An Act to amend the charters of the several towns and cities in this State," approved March 1st, 1854, repeals so much of the act of 1851, as empowers the common council of the city of Chicago to order a sale of real estate to enforce the payment of assessments. *City of Chicago* v. *Colby*, 20 Ill. 614.

Special assessments and taxes are different, and the same rule of construction, where the words are used in statutes, will not be indiscriminately applied to these terms. *Idem.*

The case of *The City of Chicago* v. *The Rock Island Railroad Company*, 20 Ill. 286, should be limited in so far as it holds that the common council of the city of Chicago had power to order a sale of real estate to enforce the payment of assessments, or the collector power to sell property under such an order, after the adoption of the act of March, 1854, and so far as it holds the act of 1851 in force after the adoption of the act of 1854. *Idem.*

The act of February 14th, 1857, amendatory of the charter of the city of Chicago, repeals the second section of the act approved March 1st, 1854, so far as it relates to the city of Chicago. *Idem.*

The Cook County Court of Common Pleas, and the Circuit Court of Cook county, have jurisdiction to render judgment for taxes and assessments; but the County Court has not. *Idem.*

Those powers of a corporation, which have been secured to it by contract, the legislature cannot deprive it of, without just compensation. *Bank of the Republic* v. *County of Hamilton*, 21 Ill. 53.

Those powers of a corporation, which are mere endowments of existence, are subject to legislative control. *Idem.*

A city, as an incorporation, can only bind itself for the payment of money for labor, done for its benefit, by ordinance or by resolution, or it might, by either of these modes, authorize its officers or agents to make such contracts. *City of Alton* v. *Mulledy et al.*, 21 Ill. 76.

Where a city contracted with a railroad company to construct a levee, and authorized it to take earth from certain streets for that purpose, and the railroad company employed the plaintiff to perform the labor, and the plaintiff removed earth from another and different street: *Held*, that no promise could be implied on the part of the city to pay the plaintiff for such labor, although the city surveyor had surveyed the latter street before the work had been commenced, and some of the committee on the improvement saw the plaintiff at work, and made no objection. *Idem.*

An insane person, having property adequate to his support, is not a pauper, and the county is not liable for the support of such person, nor is the city, in which he resides, liable for his support. *City of Alton* v. *County of Madison*, 21 Ill. 115.

Where a city voluntarily supported an insane person possessed of means adequate to that purpose: *Held*, that as no legal obligation rested on the city or county for the maintenance of such person, there could be no implied promise by the county to repay the city for such support. *Idem.*

The powers of all corporations are limited by the grants in their charters, and cannot be extended beyond them. *Town of Petersburg* v, *Metzker*, 21 Ill. 205.

The charter of a town authorized the board of trustees to inflict such punishment for any offense against the laws of the incorporation, as was or might be provided by law for like offenses against the laws of the State: *Held*, that this did not authorize the passage of an ordinance, imposing a fine of from five to fifty dollars for an assault and battery, the minimum fine for such an offense under the laws of the State being three dollars. *Idem.*

The answer of a corporation aggregate in a suit against it in equity, should be under seal, but not under oath. If a sworn answer is desired, some managing officer should be made a party, who can answer under oath. *Supervisors of Fulton County* v. *Miss. and Wabash R. R. Co.*, 21 Ill. 338.

The fact of dedication, upon a conflict of testimony, is left for the jury, and their finding will not usually be disturbed. *Daniels* v. *The People*, 21 Ill. 439.

The public may acquire the right to the use of land as a highway, by dedication, by use in the nature of prescription, or by condemnation; and the use of it, and the repairing of it by the public authorities, establish the existence of the road. *Idem.*

The use of land for a highway for the period of twenty years, is sufficient to establish the existence of the highway. *Idem.*

The constitutional prohibition against lending credit to aid in the construction of railroads, applies to the State, but not to counties and cities. *Robertson et al.* v. *City of Rockford et al.*, 21 Ill. 451.

Municipal corporations are under the control of the legislature, and their charters may be enlarged or diminished by an act incorporating a railroad company. *Idem.*

Where the legislature confers upon a city the power to lend its credit to each of two railroad companies, and, by the same act, empowers the companies to consolidate their roads, such power of the city may be exercised as effectually after, as before the consolidation. *Idem.*

The charter of a city, which authorizes the passage of ordinances to restrain or prohibit the sale of intoxicating drinks, supposes that the usual penalties by way of fine will be resorted to, to enforce the observance of those ordinances. *City of Pekin* v. *Smelzel*, 21 Ill. 464.

An ordinance prohibiting the sale of beer, is not repugnant to the general laws of the State; beer of some kinds being an intoxicating drink. *Idem.*

Cities may exercise powers by ordinance, regulating the sale of intoxicating drinks beyond those authorized by the general laws of the State; greater penalties may be inflicted. *Idem.*

Courts of general jurisdiction in the city of Chicago may examine into the proceedings of the common council, as to all matters connected with a tax or assessment, without resort to the common law writ of certiorari. *Pease* v. *City of Chicago*, 21 Ill. 500.

The common council of the city of Chicago has no authority to levy a tax or assessment for the purpose of collecting money to pay for improvements, voluntarily and previously made without the order of the council. *Idem.*

By its charter, a railroad company was authorized to bring its road to Chicago, and to acquire property within the city: *Held*, that by this it was intended to allow the road to run into the city. *Moses et al.* v. *Pittsburgh, Fort Wayne and Chicago R. R. Co.*, 21 Ill. 516.

Where, by a city charter, its local authorities are vested with exclusive control over the streets, as in the city of Chicago, and those authorities grant permission to locate railway tracks along a street, the owner or occupants of property fronting on such street, cannot enjoin the laying of such tracks, nor receive any damage or compensation for such use of a street. *Idem.*

The fee simple title to the streets of the city of Chicago, as of other cities, is vested in the municipal corporation. *Idem.*

Steam, as a motive power, may be used along the streets of a city, by proper permission. *Idem.*

The charter of a city, which confers upon the city authorities the power to erect, establish and keep in repair the bridges within the limits of the city, operates as a repeal of so much of the act to establish township organization, previously passed, as confers such power upon the commissioners of highways; the city, and not the township authorities, have the exclusive control of the streets and bridges within the corporate limits; nor can the township authorities levy a tax upon the citizens of the city, for the purpose of erecting a bridge within its limits. *Town of Ottawa et al.* v. *Walker et al.*, 21 Ill. 605.

A court of equity may stay the collection of a tax by injunction, where such tax is levied without authority of law, or for fraudulent purposes. *Idem.*

If the ordinance of a town declares, it shall not be lawful to "suffer" hogs to run at large, a plea by an officer in an action of trespass, which justifies the taking of them, on the ground that they were at large in violation of the ordinance, must aver that they were at large by the sufferance of the owner. *Case* v. *Hall*, 21 Ill. 632.

Though incorporated companies are not expressly named in the attachment act, yet the word "person" shall be deemed to extend to and include bodies politic and corporate, as well as individuals. *Mineral Point R. R. Co.* v. *Keep*, 22 Ill. 9.

A judgment for an assessment against lots or lands within a city, under the act of March 1st, 1854, should be special, and a precept should issue against the lots or lands assessed. A general judgment or execution would be wrong. *Brown* v. *City of Joliet*, 22 Ill. 123.

Before the court can render a judgment for an assessment, the amount assessed should appear in dollars and cents; but the return of the commissioners, appointed to make the assessment, may be amended under the statute of jeofails. *Idem.*

Municipal corporations are not bound to discharge indebtedness elsewhere than at their treasuries. *People ex rel. Peoria and Oquawka R. R. Co.* v. *Tazewell County*, 22 Ill. 147.

Counties and cities in this State have not the right to make bonds issued in aid of railroads payable in the city of New York. *Idem.*

Authorities, representing counties and cities, are not compelled, when the inhabitants thereof have voted in favor of issuing bonds to aid in constructing railroads, to issue the same, or to subscribe for the whole stock; there is a discretion resting with such authorities in that regard. *Idem.*

The common council of the city of Chicago had authority to appoint special collectors under the charter of 1851, and whether they had this power or not, the collector, elected by the people, was not justified in withholding moneys, upon the ground that the fees received by such special collectors, for the collection of special assessments, belonged to him. *Russell* v. *City of Chicago*, 22 Ill. 283.

The law raises a presumption in favor of the regularity of all proceedings levying special assessments in the city of Chicago, and if these proceedings are to be defeated, such presumption must be rebutted, by showing, affirmatively, that something was omitted or improperly done. *McAuley* v. *City of Chicago*, 22 Ill. 563.

In proceedings levying special assessments, in the city of Chicago, an additional notice to parties interested is not required, where an assessment is referred back to the commissioners, or postponed from one meeting of the common council to another. *Idem.*

In making assessments for public improvements in the city of Chicago, the costs of engineering and superintending the work, and collecting the assessment, may be included in the assessment. *Gibson et al.* v. *City of Chicago*, 22 Ill. 566.

The Cook County Court of Common Pleas can continue a case for assessments in the city of Chicago, and render a judgment at a subsequent term, the same as in any other case within its general jurisdiction. *Idem.*

In showing an assessment for public improvements in the city of Chicago, there must be something to indicate clearly what the figures used in the assessment roll stand for, or are intended to represent. It will not be conjectured that they are designed for dollars and cents, unless it is so indicated. *Idem.*

The charter of the city of Chicago does not permit any property to be specifically burthened to an amount greater than three per cent. in any one year, for improvements on streets, etc., whether the assessment be for one or many improvements. *Morrison et al.* v. *City of Chicago*, 22 Ill. 573.

In special assessments in the city of Chicago, after the report of the commissioners has been confirmed by the common council, the party has his remedy at law by an appeal to a court of record in Cook county, or by resort to the writ of certiorari; equity will not interfere to enjoin the collection of the assessment for mere irregularities in the proceedings. *McBride* v. *City of Chicago*, 22 Ill. 574.

If the assessment is vitiated by fraud, or the party assessed is likely to sustain an irreparable injury, equity may relieve. *Idem.*

Assessments by the city of Chicago, for improvements already made by parties, other than the city, are illegal. *Peck* v. *City of Chicago*, 22 Ill. 578.

In proceedings to subject land to the payment of special assessments, in the city of Chicago, the common council of the city formerly had the power to make an order directing the collector to sell the delinquent premises, but the amendment of the city charter, passed in 1857, required the judgment of a court of general jurisdiction, before the sale of the land; this judgment of the court takes the place of the order of the common council, and can only be made in a case where the common council could have passed such an order before the law of 1857. *Hamilton et al.* v. *City of Chicago*, 22 Ill. 580.

Prior to the passage of the act of 1857, the law limited not only the time within which the order of sale should be made by the common council, but actually the sale itself, to within two years of the date of the order, confirming the corrected assessment roll, unless the sale was delayed by injunction or other legal proceedings. *Idem.*

The court of law, in such proceedings, cannot render a judgment of condemnation against the land assessed, after two years from the order of confirmation of the assessment roll; the judgment is strictly *in rem*, and creates no personal liability against the owner of the land. *Idem.*

The collector for the city of Chicago is required to state, in his report asking for judgment against delinquent lots, etc., the amount of taxes and assessments which remain unpaid after the first Tuesday of January, but not the particular object for which the assessment was levied, nor the value of the property upon which it has been levied. *Bristol* v. *City of Chicago*, 22 Ill. 587.

The collector's report is *prima facie* evidence of the amount due, if the owner of the land is in default, and upon this, judgment may be rendered. The report does not prejudice any party by any statement in it, beyond what the law requires to be stated. A party may appeal, and rebut a presumption arising from the report of the collector. *Idem.*

No piece of property can be assessed to an amount exceeding three per cent. in one year for any improvement specified in the first section of the charter of the city of Chicago; and if it be shown that a greater sum has been levied, judgment should be refused. *Idem.*

Ten per cent. may be collected, in addition to the assessment and costs, in case the assessment is not paid before the collector's report is filed. *Idem.*

In proceedings to collect the payment of special assessments, in the city of Chicago, if it be stipulated that judgment shall be rendered as if by default, upon certain conditions, the judgment by default is based upon the collector's report, as the only legitimate evidence before the court, but it is good only as to so much of the report as the law authorizes and requires the collector to make; the court cannot act upon any unauthorized matter which the collector puts into his report. *Ogden et al.* v. *City of Chicago*, 22 Ill. 592.

Before a party can be convicted for violating a town ordinance, it must be shown to the court, by proper proof, that the ordinance has been adopted and published, as required by the charter. *Trustees of Elizabethtown* v. *Lefler*, 23 Ill. 90.

To procure a conviction for the violation of a town ordinance, it is not sufficient to show that the charter authorizes the town to adopt such an ordinance; the ordinance itself must be offered in evidence. *Idem.*

An action of trespass will lie against a municipal corporation. *Allen* v. *City of Decatur*, 23 Ill. 332.

Where the statute permits an acknowledgment to be made before the mayor of a city, such acknowledgment before the mayor of a town is not in compliance with the statute. *Dundy* v. *Chambers et al.*, 23 Ill. 369.

All the personal property of the tax payer is bound for the payment of his taxes, from the time the town collector receives his warrant until they are paid. *Hill et al.* v. *Higley*, 23 Ill. 418.

The delivery of the warrant to the collector creates a lien upon all the personal property, and not merely upon the property assessed. *Idem.*

Where the act, incorporating a town, indicates a particular day for the first election of officers, this is only directory, and an omission to elect on that day is not fatal. *Coles County* v. *Allison*, 23 Ill. 437.

Officers of a town, elected on the proper day, refusing to qualify, become officers *de facto*, and their acts are valid, as to third persons, and can only be inquired into directly, and not collaterally. *Idem.*

Cities and towns may acquire the title to streets and alleys by conveyance, by dedication, by prescription, or by the surveying and platting of a town or city, if acknowledged and recorded in the mode prescribed by the statute. *City of Belleville* v. *Stookey*, 23 Ill. 441.

A town plat, properly certified, acknowledged and recorded, has, by the statute, the force and effect of a deed to pass to the city the title to the streets and alleys,

42

provided it describes them with such certainty, by measurement and description, that they may be located and distinguished from the lots. *Idem.*

The fact of a dedication may be inferred from the intention of the parties, and such intention may be determined from all the circumstances which surround the transaction; if the owner of property within the limits of a city continue to pay taxes on it, as his own, no intention on his part to dedicate it for the purposes of a street will be presumed, and if the city continue to receive such taxes, and enforce their payment, no intention of accepting a dedication of such ground will be presumed on the part of the city. *Idem.*

The statute, requiring security for costs in penal actions, does not apply to actions for violation of city or town ordinances. *Town of Lewiston* v. *Proctor*, 23 Ill. 533.

If a person act as justice of the peace or police magistrate, whether he was irregularly elected, or for a proper period, cannot be inquired into collaterally; his decisions under color of office will be enforced. *Idem.*

A town, organized under the general law, may recover a penalty before a justice of the peace, exceeding five dollars, for an offense against an ordinance to prevent selling ardent spirits without a license. *Hamilton* v. *President and Trustees of Carthage*, 24 Ill. 22.

In a proceeding to collect a fine by a municipal corporation, its existence cannot be collaterally attacked. Evidence that the corporation has acted as such, is sufficient. *Idem.*

The North Chicago City Railway Company and the Chicago City Railway Company, two horse railways in the city of Chicago, created for the same purpose and operated by the same description of propelling power, have the power to connect with each other, make running arrangements, or lease their tracks to each other, under the act of February 17th, 1855; that act embraces horse as well as steam railways. *City of Chicago* v. *Evans et al.*, 24 Ill. 52.

Where one railway company leases its road to another, the lessee must, in operating it, be governed by the charter of the lessor. *Idem.*

Ordinances, passed by the common council of a city, which do not confer rights or authority, are harmless, unless steps are taken to make them available. *Idem.*

An ordinance of the common council of the city of Chicago cannot confer upon two railway companies the power to so extend their roads as to connect with each other; the companies must look to their charter for such power. *Idem.*

The legislature has the constitutional right to authorize counties and cities to become shareholders in railroad companies. *Johnson* v. *Stark County*, 24 Ill. 75.

The fact that a coupon is made payable in New York, or elsewhere than at the treasury of the county or city issuing it, will not invalidate it; the objectionable words will be regarded as surplusage. *Idem.*

City bonds and public securities of this character are negotiable by delivery only, without indorsement, in the same manner as bank bills, especially when they are payable to bearer. *Idem.*

An action may be maintained, upon the implied assumpsit of the city of Chicago to collect the assessment, and pay the amount awarded to property holders for opening a street. *Wheeler* v. *City of Chicago*, 24 Ill. 105.

The word "shall" in a statute may be held to be merely directory, when no advantage is lost, no right destroyed, and no benefit sacrificed, either to the public or to any individual, by giving it that construction. *Idem.*

The tenth section of the sixth chapter of the charter of the city of Chicago provides, in relation to proceedings for special assessments, that, when the assessment roll is completed, "the commissioners shall sign and return the same to the common council within forty days of their appointment;" the common council extended the time for the return of the assessment roll beyond the forty days, and within the extended time the return was made: *Held*, that the legislature did not intend to make the time specified for the return of the assessment roll indispensable to the validity of the proceedings. *Idem.*

The legislature may authorize cities to subscribe stock in railroads within or running through their jurisdiction. *Perkins et al.* v. *Lewis et al.*, 24 Ill. 208.

The streets and alleys of an unincorporated town or village, used and recognized by the public as such, are highways, and are to be protected from obstruction in the same manner as other public roads. *Leach* v. *Waugh*, 24 Ill. 228.

Otherwise, if the town is incorporated; then, the title to the streets and alleys is vested in the town, and they are subject to the control of the corporate authorities. *Idem.*

The owner of all the lots adjoining a street may so vacate the town plat as to abolish the street, unless the public, by user, has acquired the right to enjoy it as a highway, but the owner of lots abutting on only one side of a street, has no such power. *Idem.*

In this State, corporations, like individuals, are subject to the control of the legislature, so far as it relates to the enforcing of obligations. *Reapers' Bank* v. *Willard et al.*, 24 Ill. 433.

In a proceeding to collect an assessment under the charter of the city of Chicago, any defense is allowable which shows that the assessment ought not to be collected. *City of Chicago* v. *Burtice et al.*, 24 Ill. 489.

The honest judgment of the commissioners, for assessing property in the city of Chicago, will not be disturbed. But when the assessment is proved to be so far from the real value as to raise the presumption that the property was designedly over estimated, the court ought to set it aside; and, for this reason, proof of the value of the property assessed is allowable. The action of the common council in confirming the assessment is not conclusive. *Idem.*

In special proceedings by the city of Chicago to collect assessments for public improvements, the court is vested with the same discretion to set aside a default and admit a defense to be made, as it is authorized to exercise in other cases. The exercise of such discretion will rarely be interfered with by the Supreme Court. *City of Chicago* v. *Adams*, 24 Ill. 492.

The commissioners to make an assessment for a city improvement in the city of Chicago, having failed, in their assessment roll, to show what was the meaning of the column of figures headed "valuation," parol evidence is inadmissible to supply the deficiency. *City of Chicago* v. *Walker*, 24 Ill. 493.

The commissioners' return of the assessment roll, like the return of process, is amendable, and they should themselves have amended it, after having obtained leave of the common council so to do; but parol evidence cannot take the place and perform the office of an amended return. *Idem.*

Under the amended charter of the city of Chicago, all persons, whose interests would be affected by a sale of property in proceedings to collect special assessments, may appear and contest the assessment, whether they be the legal or equitable owners or mere incumbrancers. *City of Chicago* v. *Rosenfeld et al.*, 24 Ill. 495.

The only reason for sending to the Supreme Court a copy of the publication of the notice of the collector of a special assessment in the city of Chicago, that he will apply to the court for judgment, is, to show that the court had personal jurisdiction over the parties interested in the land. If the record shows that they appeared, such copy is needless. *Burnham* v. *City of Chicago*, 24 Ill. 496.

The charter of the city of Chicago gives the common council power to assess for graveling streets. *Idem.*

A pavement is not limited to uniformly arranged masses of solid material, as blocks of wood, brick or stone, but it may be as well formed of pebbles or gravel or other hard substance, which will make a compact, even, hard way or floor. *Idem.*

When the court below has found that an assessment was made fairly and in good faith, the Supreme Court will not disturb such finding without great reluctance, although the valuation might be so unjust and extravagant as to furnish good grounds for reversal. *Idem.*

An ordinance of the city of Chicago proposed to vacate a street in front of certain blocks, and lay out a new street, and convey to the owners of lots in those blocks what remained in the old street in front of their lots respectively, to a certain specified line on the margin of the Chicago river: *Held*, that the meaning of the word "front" must be determined from the intention and understanding of the parties; there is no reason why a different rule should be adopted for ascertaining what lies in front of or opposite to a lot, from that by which it must be determined what lies in front of a block. *Tracy et al.* v. *City of Chicago*, 24 Ill. 500.

A bond given to influence an alderman to a particular course, in the discharge of his duties, is illegal and void, and it makes no difference to whom it is executed. It is bribery. *Cook* v. *Shipman*, 24 Ill. 614.

Where a city charter gives opportunity to make objections to an assessment before the city council, in whom power over the subject is vested, and this opportunity is neglected, it will be held, that all objections are waived. *City of Ottawa et al.* v. *Chicago and Rock Island R. R. Co.*, 25 Ill. 43.

If proper notice of the proceedings in relation to the assessment is not given, the party aggrieved should bring the record before the Circuit Court by certiorari. *Idem.*

A complete remedy at law being within the power of an aggrieved party, a court of equity will not take jurisdiction, because there are irregularities, or even a want of compliance with some material requirements of the law, connected with the assessment of a city for public improvements. *Idem.*

A decree, enjoining the collection of an assessment, is not sufficient, when offered in evidence, as a bar to the recovery of a judgment of confirmation of such assessment. *Idem.*

Corporations possess only such powers as are specifically granted by their charters, or are necessary to carry into effect the granted powers. *Illinois Conference Female College* v. *Cooper*, 25 Ill. 148.

A corporation has no right to pass by-laws, which will impair the effect of contracts previously made with it. *Idem.*

Where a party fenced out a strip of land, which was designed for a road for the use of the public, and the dedication was accepted by the public before his retraction, he cannot subsequently change his purpose and resume the grant. *Proctor* v. *The Town of Lewiston*, 25 Ill. 153.

On a question of the dedication of the right of way, it is the right of the owner to have his declarations, made after such alleged dedication, as well as at the time, go to the jury, as evidence tending to rebut the intention of dedication, but it is for the jury to determine whether such declarations were the result of a change of purpose and a design to resume a dedication, which he had at the time intended to make to the public. *Idem.*

The omission, in an assessment roll, of some word or character to designate what the figures in the columns headed "valuation" were intended to represent, is one of the defects which are remedied by the 44th section of the Revenue Act of 1853. *Hill et al.* v. *Figley*, 25 Ill. 156.

A collector's warrant confers the same authority, and performs the same office, as a *fi. fa.*, and when regular and fair on its face, protects the officer and those acquiring rights under it, to the same extent as an execution. *Idem.*

Where a county in this State collects a revenue from taxes, levied on property in a city, situated in such county, and on property in the county outside of the city, an act of the legislature which declares that, after certain expenditures are allowed the county and city, the surplus of taxes shall be divided between the city and county, in proportion to the amount collected from each, and directs the county treasurer to pay to the city treasurer a certain proportion of the taxes, to which the city may be entitled, to be applied by the city in repairing streets and building and repairing bridges in the city, is constitutional. *People ex rel. City of Springfield* v. *Power, County Judge, etc.*, 25 Ill. 187.

In a suit by one corporation against another, it is erroneous to render a judgment against the members of the one corporation, as individuals, in favor of the members of the other. *Campbell et al.* v. *Brunk et al.*, 25 Ill. 225.

In the case of *Johnson* v. *Stark County*, 24 Ill. 75, the court recognized the doctrine that in exercising a power, all acts performed in excess of, or beyond the power delegated, must be rejected as unwarranted, but if, after the rejection of such acts, there has been enough done to show a proper execution of the power, the act will be sustained, irrespective of the act performed beyond the power delegated; in other words, so much of the act done as is within the power granted, shall be upheld, whilst all beyond shall be rejected, as an excess of power. *City of Quincy* v. *Warfield*, 25 Ill. 317.

Where a municipal corporation is authorized to issue bonds bearing eight per cent. interest, if issued bearing twelve, they will be valid, *pro tanto*, and the municipal corporation will be liable on the bonds for the principal and eight per cent. *Idem.*

Where the municipal authorities of a city are authorized to issue bonds, generally, though to a limited amount, each year, they may, without exceeding their authority, issue such bonds in payment of other bonds overdue — the city authorities being the proper judges of such action. *Idem.*

The *onus* of showing that bonds issued by a municipal corporation are illegal, is on the party seeking to impeach them, the law intending that they were properly issued. And where the recommendation of a financial committee is essential, in order to authorize the issue of the bonds, and nothing appearing in the record to the contrary, it will be intended that such recommendation was made before the bonds were issued. *Idem.*

An assessment made for the purpose of opening a street in a city, may be recovered from the city, if the street is not opened within a reasonable time, and any period of time, which would bar the recovery if the action should be delayed, would be considered reasonable. *Bradford* v. *City of Chicago*, 25 Ill. 411.

A party who has paid money upon an illegal assessment, may recover it back from the city. *Idem.*

The payment of an assessment is not voluntary, where the officer has a warrant by virtue of which he may levy and sell. *Idem.*

The law has imposed the duty upon the city of Chicago to keep the streets and sidewalks in a condition for the safe and convenient transit of all persons, and the city is primarily liable in an action for damages to a person who passes along one of said streets, and, while in the exercise of ordinary care, falls into an opening, used as an area for light and access to the basement of a building in process of erection, and carelessly left uncovered during the night and day. *Scammon et al.* v. *City of Chicago*, 25 Ill. 424.

But the owner of the fee of the land, in which such opening is dug, if he has contracted with a skillful party to erect the building thereon, and for that purpose has surrendered the premises for the use of the contractor, is not, during the erection of the building, answerable in damages to the sufferer from such accident, nor is he liable over to the city for the amount of damages recovered against the city on account of such accident. *Idem.*

The contractors are the parties liable in such case, and such contractors cannot be regarded as the servants of the owner of the premises. *Idem.*

In an action of assumpsit against the city of Chicago to recover damages awarded to parties, which they had severally sustained by the appropriation of their real estate to the extension of a street, the city is estopped from denying the validity of the assessment roll. *City of Chicago* v. *Wheeler*, 25 Ill. 478.

A city is estopped, after real estate has been condemned to public use and appropriated, and the owners wholly deprived of its use, from setting up that the commissioners who made the assessment were not disinterested freeholders of the city; it does not lie with the city to insist that it has not done its duty. *Idem*

The city authorities, by acting upon an assessment, will be held to have waived all objection to antecedent irregularities. *Idem.*

Although the dollar mark may be omitted in some parts of an assessment, made in reference to opening a street of a city; yet, if there are sufficient evidences on the roll to determine the amounts of damages or benefits, it will be sufficient. *Idem.*

If the city refuses to pay allowances made to the owners of property, which has been taken to open or extend a street, beyond a reasonable time, as for the space of two years, interest will be allowed on such claims. *Idem.*

In an action on the case against the city of Chicago, for negligence in the common council for failing to collect an assessment, levied to compensate the plaintiff for damages sustained by reason of opening a street over his lot, it was held, that corporations and incorporated companies may be sued in that character for damages arising from a breach, by them, of a duty imposed by law, and that the party injured has his election, whether he will sue in trespass or case, or will waive the tort, and proceed for the value of the property. *Clayburgh* v. *City of Chicago*, 25 Ill. 535.

A provision in the charter of a city in this State, which exempts its citizens from working on any road beyond the limits of the city, and from paying taxes to procure laborers to work upon the same, is unconstitutional, being in violation of the fifth section of the ninth article of the constitution, which provides that the corporate authorities of counties, townships, school districts, cities, towns and villages, may be vested with power to assess and collect taxes for corporate purposes, such tax to be uniform, with respect to persons and property, within the jurisdiction of the body imposing the same. *O'Kane* v. *Treat et al.*, 25 Ill. 557.

A city within a town in this State, is a part of the municipal corporation of the town, and the inhabitants thereof are subject to a road tax imposed by the town upon all the inhabitants of the town, under the law authorizing it; such a tax is a tax for corporate purposes. *Idem.*

An execution cannot be issued against a municipal corporation on a judgment for debt or damages recovered against it; mandamus can be issued to compel payment, or to compel a levy of taxes sufficient to discharge the judgment. *City of Chicago* v. *Hasley*, 25 Ill. 595.

The common council of the city of Chicago had power expressly given to them to appoint one or more collectors, in addition to the one to be elected by the people of the city. *Wilder et al.* v. *City of Chicago*, 26 Ill. 182.

Where an ordinance of the common council of the city of Chicago was in force concerning the assessment and collection of taxes, by which the collector was to pay into the city treasury all moneys collected by him as fast as collected, he has no right to retain a dollar for any purpose. *Idem.*

A city has the right to establish and change the grade of a street, and to compel the owners of lots to grade the street accordingly. *Roberts* v. *City of Chicago*, 26 Ill. 251.

When a city undertakes to do work, it must do it in good faith, and with reasonable care and diligence, and for damages resulting from want of these, it is undoubtedly responsible. *Idem.*

Where the owners of lots neglect to grade a street in pursuance of a city ordinance fixing a grade, and the city does it with reasonable care and diligence, it is not liable to owners of lots for the inconvenience occasioned by the necessary obstructions to the streets, while they are being graded, nor for the expense of raising the buildings to conform to the new grade. *Idem.*

Where a declaration charges that a city, by its agents and servants, maliciously, wrongfully and without reasonable cause, obstructed and filled up a street, it is sufficient; if the charge is sustained by proof, the city is liable. *Idem.*

The court will not inquire, when a grade has been fixed by the city authorities, whether it was the best grade that could have been established. *Idem.*

Where a city is authorized to construct a road in a particular manner, but does it in a different one, it will be answerable in damages to a party sustaining injury on such road, as much as though it had not exceeded or deviated from its authority. *City of Pekin* v. *Newell*, 26 Ill. 322.

A law, authorizing a city to levy an assessment to make compensation for damages sustained by opening a street, is not repugnant to the constitution. *City of Peoria* v. *Kidder*, 26 Ill. 351.

An assessment is not a tax within the purview of the constitution. *Idem.*

There can be no more just and reasonable mode of making compensation for public improvements in cities, than by assessing it on those who receive a direct benefit from the improvement, in the enhanced value of their real estate over and above any injury they may sustain. *Idem.*

Where the city has the right, under its charter, to extend streets and make assessments, a court of equity will not interfere to restrain the collection of an assessment, imposed for the purpose of extending a street upon property liable to the burthen. *Idem.*

A justice of the peace, who is not designated as a police magistrate, and who acts at the instance of the city of Chicago, may recover from the city, fees earned by him in his official capacity. Such fees, earned by a member of the common council, do not come within the prohibition of the charter, forbidding aldermen from receiving compensation for their services. *De Wolf* v. *The City of Chicago*, 26 Ill. 445.

A laborer, employed by the city of Chicago to work on its streets, can recover his wages from the city, although the officer whose business it was to superintend the work, disobeyed the orders of his superiors, by not suspending the work. The laborer is not chargeable with notice of the order of suspension. *City of Chicago* v. *Roth*, 26 Ill. 458.

The offense of keeping and maintaining a "calaboose" by an incorporated town, is not an offense against the statute, for which an indictment will lie. *Town of Paris* v. *People*, 27 Ill. 74.

The transposition of some of the words, composing the name of a corporation, may make no essential difference in their sense, and will not vitiate where it is evident what corporation was intended. *Chadsey* v. *McCreery*, 27 Ill. 254.

In an action to recover a penalty for obstructing a village street, after the ordinance establishing the offense and the penalty has been given in evidence without objection, evidence of a private act of the legislature, legalizing the ordinances, was properly excluded from the jury. The statute might have been proper preliminary evidence, but after the introduction of the ordinances it became irrelevant. *Town of Lewiston* v. *Proctor*, 27 Ill. 414.

Where the plea of *nul tiel corporation* is pleaded, it operates as a special traverse, that the plaintiff is a corporation, and is in bar of the action by a corporation. *Idem.*

In an action to recover a penalty for obstructing a highway, if the complainant gives a local description sufficient to fix the precise point obstructed, and also the *termini* of the road, the latter may be disregarded; but when the allegation is general, that a road, leading from one point to another, has been obstructed, the existence of the road, between the points named, must be proved, as a matter of essential description. *Idem.*

In a prosecution for obstructing a highway, every fact necessary to show the prosecution entitled to recover, must be established by a clear preponderance of evidence. But when the judgment necessarily involves the life or limb of the citizen, the benign rule, that the crime must be proved beyond a reasonable doubt, should prevail unimpaired. This doctrine is too firmly established to be shaken, by authority, if not on principle, in all proceedings by indictment. *Idem.*

The fact that a road has not been repaired by the public, is proper for the consideration of the jury, in determining whether it is regarded, by those having charge of the highways, as a public road. *Idem.*

A continuous and uninterrupted use of a highway by the public, for a period of twenty years, creates a prescriptive right, as well in the public as in private individuals. Such a right, once obtained, is valid, and may be enjoyed by the public to the same extent as if a grant existed, it being the legal intendment that its use was originally formed upon such a right, and it continues until it is clearly and unmistakeably abandoned. *Idem.*

It is sufficient to show the organization of a corporation in fact and user under it, when put in issue by the plea of *nul tiel corporation*, although there may have been irregularities or omissions in the organization. *Marsh* v. *Astoria Lodge No.* 112, *I. O. O. F.*, 27 Ill. 421.

A corporation can have no faculty, not given by the act creating it: if the right to sue is not expressly granted to a corporation, it may still exercise the faculty, if all the powers incident to corporations are conferred upon it. *Idem.*

A judgment in favor of a corporation, when properly assigned during the life of a corporation, may be enforced after the corporation has ceased to exist. *Leach* v. *Thomas*, 27 Ill. 457.

The legislature has the constitutional right to authorize counties, towns and cities to aid in the construction of railroads by lending credit, issuing bonds, or taking stock. Fraud in the election authorizing such action, must be set up in apt time, and before rights have accrued. *Butler et al.* v. *Dunham et al.*, 27 Ill. 474.

In towns incorporated under the provisions of the charters of Springfield and Quincy, ordinances prohibiting the sale of ardent spirits must be published, before a penalty can be enforced under them. *Barnet* v. *President, etc., of Newark*, 28 Ill. 62.

When a town is regularly laid out, platted, and the proper acknowledgment thereof made and recorded, the streets and alleys must preserve the width given them by the plat, not to be enlarged or contracted by any power. The gift of the streets is to the public, with the width the proprietor may choose to give them. *Waugh, suing, etc.*, v. *Leech*, 28 Ill. 488.

The dedication of streets is purely a question of intention, and that may be evidenced by a survey and plat alone, without any declaration, either oral or on the plat. *Idem.*

The law does not require, when a town plat is acknowledged, that the evidence of the title should be produced. The survey, plat and acknowledgment are acts and evidence of ownership. *Idem.*

Dedication is a mixed question of law and fact, and the court should instruct the jury that surveying the land, acknowledging and recording the plat, and selling lots with the streets as abuttals, amount, in law, to a dedication. *Idem.*

All assessments under the charter of the city of Chicago for paving streets, must be levied in proportion to the number of feet of each lot, adjoining the street; if made on any other property, or by any different rule, they cannot be sustained. *Lill* v. *City of Chicago*, 29 Ill. 37.

Where the valuation, in assessments under the charter of the city of Chicago, for paving streets, is made on the front feet of the lots adjoining the street to be improved, no matter how unjust it is, the order of the common council, confirming the report of the commissioners, is conclusive, unless upon an appeal prosecuted in the mode prescribed in the charter. *Idem.*

A notice by commissioners, appointed to open a street in a city, given to the owners of lots and land over which the street will run when it shall be opened, will not be a sufficient notice to a person whose lots or land do not adjoin or lie near the proposed street. *Kidder* v. *City of Peoria*, 29 Ill. 77.

The city of Chicago is not liable for damages, resulting from the proper exercise of authority in permitting railroad tracks to be laid in the streets, or in raising the grade of streets. Unless the authorities of a city exceed their power in this regard, there is no liability. *Murphy* v. *City of Chicago*, 29 Ill. 279.

The habendum clause of a deed, by which a party conveys a portion of a street to a city for the purposes of a street, and none other, restricts the use of the premises to that of a street alone. *Idem.*

A city has no right to use any of its streets for other purposes than those of streets. *Idem.*

It is the settled law of this State, that it is a legitimate use of a street or highway, to allow a railroad track to be laid down in it, and, for so doing, the city is not liable for any damage which may accrue to individuals. *Idem.*

The grade of the streets is within the exclusive control of the common council, and individuals discommoded thereby must submit, without compensation, to such improvements for the general good. *Idem.*

Where an action is brought, by a city, for a violation of a city ordinance, regulating the sale of fresh meat, it is erroneous to instruct the jury, that such an ordinance may be passed, yet, if unlawful, as being in restraint of trade, the ordinance is not binding; since, if the power exists, the trade in violation thereof could not be lawful. *City of Peoria* v. *Calhoun*, 29 Ill. 317.

It is the province of the court, and not the jury, to determine whether a city ordinance is valid or invalid. *Idem.*

An assessment imposed for the purpose of widening streets is not a tax, nor is an assessment of labor for the repair of roads and streets. *Town of Pleasant* v. *Kost*, 29 Ill. 317.

The law of 1845, exempting inhabitants of town and city corporations from road labor outside of their corporate limits, is constitutional, and the inhabitants are not bound to labor outside of their corporate limits, or under others than their corporate authorities. *Idem.*

A charter of a city in this State, which provides that its inhabitants shall be exempt from performing labor on the roads beyond the city limits, or taxes to procure labor for such purpose, and that the property within the city shall be exempt from taxes levied for county purposes, provided the city shall support the resident paupers thereof, and pay the expenses of the Circuit Court in all criminal cases for offenses committed by citizens, and all jail fees, etc., is constitutional. *Hunsaker et al.* v. *Wright et al.*, 30 Ill. 146.

The legislature has no power, under the constitution, to exempt any person or class of persons from the payment of taxes; but it may commute a tax for a payment of money or other equivalent, and is the sole judge of the value and propriety of such equivalent. *Idem.*

The plea of *nul tiel corporation* is a plea in bar, and should not be stricken from the files, because a plea to the merits has been interposed. *Hoereth* v. *The Franklin Mill Co.*, 30 Ill. 151.

Where a corporation sues by a wrong name, the defendant can only take advantage of it by a plea in abatement; but where there is no misnomer, the defendant can only plead *nul tiel corporation* in bar. *Idem.*

The law, requiring security for costs, in prosecutions under penal statutes, does not refer to prosecutions under city ordinances. *City of Quincy* v. *Ballance*, 30 Ill. 185.

Incorporated towns have the exclusive privilege of granting licenses to sell spirituous liquors, and of prescribing the terms on which they may be sold within the corporate limits, and no person need have any other license than the town ordinances. If he brings himself within their provisions, he is not liable to indictment under the State law. *Bennett* v. *People*, 30 Ill. 389.

The plea of *non-assumpsit*, in an action against a corporation, admits the existence of the corporation. *Gay, impl., etc.*, v. *Keys*, 30 Ill. 413.

The legislature has authority, under the constitution, to confer on an incorporated town the power to declare what shall be nuisances, and to provide for their abatement. *Roberts* v. *Ogle*, 30 Ill. 459.

Under this power, an ordinance, declaring that swine running at large are nuisances, and providing for the abatement thereof, is valid. *Idem.*

Under the act of February 10, 1851, incorporating the Illinois Central Railroad Company, no city or town authority can impose a tax for municipal purposes, on the property of that company, which may be within its limits. *Neustadt* v. *Illinois Central R. R. Co.*, 31 Ill. 484.

The city of Amboy has authority, under its charter, to pass ordinances to punish a party committing an assault and battery. *City of Amboy* v. *Sleeper*, 31 Ill. 499.

If a coupon given for interest, upon a bond executed by a city, could in any event draw interest, in the absence of an express agreement, it could only be after a proper demand of payment. *City of Pekin* v. *Reynolds*, 31 Ill. 529.

But there being no agreement on the subject, the city is not liable to pay interest on its coupons at all; whatever powers cities may possess to contract for the payment of interest, in the absence of express legislation on the subject, their indebtedness, without such agreement, does not bear interest. *Idem.*

At common law, interest was not allowed in any case. It is the creature of the statute alone. Hence, cities and towns, as has heretofore been held in regard to the State and counties, not being mentioned in the statute regulating interest, are not within its provisions. *Idem.*

Municipal corporations cannot bind themselves to pay their indebtedness at any other place than their treasury, unless specially authorized by legislative enactment. *Idem.*

The city of Ottawa has authority, under its charter, to pass an ordinance imposing a penalty upon commanders of canal boats, etc., for injuries done by them to bridges over the Illinois and Michigan canal, within the city limits, notwithstanding the same power was previously conferred by law upon the canal "Board of Trustees." *Korah* v. *The City of Ottawa*, 32 Ill. 121.

But in exercising its power to erect a bridge over the canal, the city must so construct it as not materially to obstruct the navigation, or to create unnecessary difficulty in passing it with boats, without striking the bridge; otherwise they cannot recover for injuries resulting therefrom. *Idem.*

The power to erect and keep bridges in repair, implies the authority to employ the means necessary and proper to the end; and the imposition of fines for a willful or negligent injury to such structures, would not be an improper means of aiding to keep them in repair. *Idem.*

There can scarcely be a doubt that, under the authority to regulate the police of the city, the city may impose fines and forfeitures for injury to public property within the city limits. *Idem.*

If the grant of the same power to the Illinois and Michigan canal trustees, and to the city of Ottawa, is repugnant, the last expressed will of the legislature must control. *Idem.*

It is a well-settled rule, that summary proceedings, such as an application for judgment against land or lots of ground upon a special assessment roll, by which a man's property may be taken from him without his consent, and where there is no personal service of process, must be strictly pursued, and this must be shown on the face of the proceedings. *City of Chicago* v. *Wright et al.*, 32 Ill. 192.

Where application was made for a judgment against land and lots, upon unpaid assessments for the grading, paving and macadamizing of certain streets in the city of Chicago, objection was made to the assessment roll, because it did not show damages as well as benefits to the property owners, resulting from the proposed improvements, and the objection was held to be fatal to the application. *Idem.*

The application, in this case, was made since the act of 1861, relating to that subject, and it was *held*, that while before that act the question of benefits and damages to property holders was limited to a certain description of improvements, different from those contemplated in this case, yet by the 28th section of the amendatory act of 1861, the question of damages, as well as of benefits, was to be regarded, whenever any public improvements should be originated and carried on to completion by means of assessments. This section embraces as well the taking of private property for public grounds, streets and alleys, as their improvement after they have been established. *Idem.*

The objection to the assessment roll, going to the origin of the proceedings, the property owners were not precluded from availing of it before the court, upon the application for a judgment, notwithstanding they failed to appear and make it before the common council. *Idem.*

All defects appearing on the face of the proceedings, which go to show the requirements of the law have not been observed, and, therefore, that the court had no legal right to render the judgment, can be urged on appeal or error. As in an ordinary suit at law, where a default is taken, the Supreme court cannot, on appeal or error, inquire into the facts of the case, but they can pronounce upon the legality of the proceedings, and on the right of the court below to render any judgment in the case. *Idem.*

INDEX.

ACCOUNTS against the city, how audited 36, 37, 57, 58, 108, 124, 126, 137, 199, 328

ACTING MAYOR, when and how appointed 15
powers and duties of 15, 297

ACTIONS by city in police court, how brought 114
against city only in courts of record 159

ADVERTISEMENT, several notices may be in one 179, 180

AFFIDAVIT OF MERITS, not required of city 159

ALARMS, false, how punished 288, 525

ALDERMEN, to compose, with the mayor, the common council, (see *Common Council*.) .. 5, 22
election of 6
to be divided into classes 7
vacancies, how created and filled 7
not to be taken as sureties, on obligations made to city 11
to receive no compensation, hold no lucrative office, or be interested in city contracts .. 22
ex officio fire-wardens and conservators of the peace 15
exempted from jury and military duty 15, 120, 121
first election of, under revised charter 160
powers under fire department ordinance 229, 231

ALLEYS. (See *Streets*.)

AMUSEMENTS, power to license, regulate and prohibit, (see *Shows*) 25, 27
dangerous, penalties 286, 287

ANIMALS, power to punish abuse of 26
penalty for cruelty to 282
obstructing and crossing sidewalks, etc. 339
fastening, to trees, etc. 348

ANNUAL ESTIMATES, of city expenses, to be made by comptroller 38
of expense of repairs and improvements, to be made by board of public works 57
of police expenses, to be made by police commissioners 107, 108
of expenses of reform school, to be made by board of guardians 137
of sums required to be raised for use of water works, to be made by board of public works 147
of sums required to be raised for sewerage works, to be made by board of public works 155
of sums required to be raised for fire department, to be made by board of police 198

ANNUAL REPORTS, to be made by comptroller 37, 38, 47
to be made by treasurer 40
to be made by collector 41, 42
to be made by board of public works 52, 147, 156
to be made by police commissioners 109, 199
to be made by board of education 127, 128
to be made by superintendent of schools 129
to be made by guardians of reform school 130, 131

APPEALS from assessments for condemnation of real estate 66, 67
from other assessments, not permitted 70
from police commissioners 100, 101
from police court 114
when taken by city to an appellate court, no bond required 159
from justices to recorder's court, when 513, 514
from recorder's court to circuit court 515

APPENDIX. Town charter, Feb. 11, 1835 .... 530—532
amendment of same, Jan. 15, 1836 532
Chicago Hydraulic Company charter, Jan. 18, 1836 .... 532, 533
city charter, March 4, 1837 .... 534—550
amendment of same, same date 550
repeal of so much of same as established municipal court, Feb. 15, 1839 .... 550, 551
repeal of so much as related to schools, and making new provisions, March 1, 1839 .. 551, 552
amendment of same charter, Feb. 27, 1841 .... 552, 553
legalizing plat of school section, and amending same charter, March 3, 1843 554
supplementary to same charter, Feb. 16, 1847 .... 554—560
organizing South Chicago school district, Feb. 23, 1847 .... 560, 561
exempting firemen from street tax, Feb. 10, 1849 561
city charter, Feb. 14, 1851 .... 561—583
Chicago City Hydraulic Company charter, Feb. 15, 1851 .... 583—587
fines to be paid into city treasury, Feb. 17, 1851 587
wards to elect supervisors, Feb. 17, 1851 588

APPENDIX—*continued.*
amendment of hydraulic company charter, June 15, 1852 588
amendment of city charter, as to sale of liquors, June 23, 1852 588
amendment, reinstating former provisions on same subject, Feb. 12, 1853 .... 588, 589
amendment, extending city limits, etc., Feb. 12, 1853 589
amendment, as to elections, Feb. 12, 1853 .... 589, 590
amendment, on various subjects, Feb. 28, 1854 .... 590, 591
incorporating sewerage commissioners, Feb. 14, 1855 .... 591—599
amendment of hydraulic company charter, Feb. 15, 1855 .... 599—603
reform school established, Feb. 14, 1857 .... 603—605
amendment of city charter on various subjects, Feb. 16, 1857 .... 606—618
fish inspector, Feb. 18, 1857 .... 619, 620
amendment as to sewerage commissioners, Feb. 14, 1859 .... 620, 621
amendment of act of Feb. 16, 1857, as to public parks, Feb. 19, 1859 621
amendatory of a great number of former acts relating to the city, Feb. 18, 1861 .... 621—638
Van Buren street bridge assessment, Feb. 20, 1861 638
establishing board of police, Feb. 21, 1861 .... 638—639
amendment as to reform school, Feb. 22, 1861 .... 639—641
DECISIONS OF SUPREME COURT .... 642—666

APPROPRIATIONS, by common council, when to be made 44
vote to be taken by yeas and nays 28
separate accounts with each, to be kept by treasurer 39

ARDENT SPIRITS, power to regulate sale of, (see *Spirituous Liquors*) 24

AREA WALLS, power to construct 60
mode of procedure 60, 61, 69, 70, 76, 178, 340

ARMORIES, superintendence of 52

ARMS AND MILITARY EQUIPMENTS, under control of board of police 196

ARREST, exemption from 13, 110

ASHES, power to regulate deposit of 119
regulation concerning 228
when may be placed in streets 348
removal of, by scavengers 321

ASSESSMENTS, special, provisions concerning .... 59—79, 177—179
to be made by commissioners of board of public works 53, 54
commissioners to be sworn in all cases 62, 70
commissioners not to serve when interested 76
mayor not to act as commissioner 14, 58
special commissioner, how appointed 76
for what to be levied 60
to be ordered only by a three-fourths vote in certain cases, to be taken by ayes and noes, 62
moneys collected on, to be held as special funds 40, 41
surplus moneys raised by, to be refunded 75
for condemnation of real estate .... 62—68
for widening river may include expense of excavation 62
application for confirmation of, how and when made 65, 66
confirmation of, when final and conclusive 66, 70
appeal from confirmation of 66, 67
when annulled or set aside, another to be made 66, 70
for deepening and dredging the river 69
for improvement of streets 69, 70, 177, 178
for sidewalks and drains 71, 72, 177, 178
for erection of lamp posts 73, 178, 179
for removal of nuisances 73, 74, 179
on railway companies, how levied and collected 69, 70, 178
to be borne and paid by owners of real estate 74
if paid by tenants, they may recover of owners 74
appointment of guardians for infant owners 74
when proceedings may be reviewed on *certiorari* 74, 75
formal defects not to invalidate 67, 89, 95
when first insufficient, a second may be levied 75
on failure to collect, new assessment may be made 75
a lien for five years, and the further time necessary to collect 75
for widening Michigan avenue 77, 78
COLLECTION OF .... 85—96
warrants, when and how issued 66, 85, 86
warrants to be delivered to collector 85, 86
proceedings by collector .... 86—88, 180
damages, when collectable 87, 88
application for judgment against delinquent property 88
proceedings thereon 89, 90
costs to be taxed 90
form of judgment 90
process of sale 90
sale of real estate, how conducted .... 90—92
when sales to be made 94, 95
certificates of sales .... 91—93
redemption from sales 92, 93, 95, 96
deeds, when and how issued 92, 93, 95
effect of deeds in evidence 93, 94
WATER ASSESSMENTS, (see *Water Works*) .... 142—146

ASSESSMENT ROLLS, in condemnation proceedings, how made and returned .... 63—65
revision and confirmation of 66
objections to, when to be filed 66
for deepening the river 69
for improving streets 69, 70
for construction and repair of sidewalks 71, 72
for erection of lamp posts 73
for removal of nuisances 73, 74

ASSESSORS, board of, how composed 9
how and when appointed 9, 188, 191
qualifications of 9
duties, powers and liabilities of 16
appraisal of property by, for taxation, when to be completed and filed 84
to give notice of time and place to hear objections 84
power to revise appraisal 84
to supervise preparation of tax lists 84, 85
penalty for neglect or violation of duty 95

ATTORNEY. (See *City Attorney*, *State's Attorney.*)
police not to receive gifts from, or interfere in retainer of, for persons arrested 100, 195
property taken from person arrested, not to be delivered to 105

AUCTIONEERS, power to tax, license and regulate 24
ordinances concerning .... 210—212, 338, 339

AUDITOR, power to provide for appointment of 48
general duties of, defined 48
how to be appointed and removed 48, 191

BALL, playing of, power to prevent and regulate 27
penalty for playing, in public parks and grounds 298

BALL ALLEYS, power to tax, license, regulate and suppress 24
penalties for keeping 288

BARNS, power to regulate and remove 25, 31
lights in, power to regulate the use of 26
lights and fires in, regulated 227

BATHING, power to regulate 26
where prohibited, and penalty 281

BEEF, power to regulate inspection of 28

BEGGARS, power to restrain and punish 27
punishment of 281, 288

BELLMEN, how appointed and removed 10
number of, to be determined by common council 5

BILLIARD TABLES, power to tax, license, regulate and suppress 24
penalties for keeping 288

BILLS OF MORTALITY, power to direct the keeping of 28
duties of board of police concerning 110

BIRDS, killing, etc., of, penalty 288

BIRTHS, power to regulate registration of 28

BOARD OF ASSESSORS. (See *Assessors.*)

BOARD OF CLAIMS COMMISSIONERS, abolished 160

BOARD OF EDUCATION. (See *Schools.*)

BOARD OF ENGINEERS, consulting, on plans for cleansing river 182

BOARD OF GUARDIANS. (See *Reform School.*)

BOARD OF HEALTH, (see *Police*) .... 110—112

BOARD OF POLICE, (see *Police*) .... 96—112

BOARD OF PUBLIC WORKS, (see *Public Works*) .... 49—59

BOARD OF SUPERVISORS 161, 169

BOATS AND VESSELS, in the harbor, power to regulate 30
sanitary provisions concerning .... 111, 112, 255—260
as to gunpowder and gun cotton 240, 246
regulations in harbor, and passing bridges .... 242—247

BONDS. (See *City Bonds*, also *Official Bonds.*)

BOOT BLACKS, ordinance concerning 212, 213

BOUNDARIES, of city, defined 2
of wards .... 2—4
of school districts .... 324—326

BREAD, power to regulate the weight and sale of 28

BREWERIES, power to direct location, regulate and license, (see *Nuisances*) 25

BREWERS, power to tax, license and regulate 24

BRIDEWELL, keeper of, how appointed and removed 10, 29, 191
power to establish 29
who may be confined in 29, 32, 114, 159

BRIDEWELL—*continued.*
prisoners may be kept at labor.... 29
power to release from 114
power to purchase grounds and erect buildings for.... 46
authority to issue bonds for.... 46
ordinance concerning.... 213—216

BRIDGES, (See *Harbor*, *Railroads.*)
power to require railroad companies to construct, at railroad crossings 29
power to erect.... 29
power to regulate passing of.... 30
board of public works to have special charge of.... 52
expense of constructing, how paid.... 76
may be constructed by private persons 76, 77
penalty for injuring 77, 245
ordinance concerning .... 216—218

BRIDGE TENDERS, how appointed and removed 10, 187, 188
number of, may be determined by common council 5

BUILDINGS, permits for raising and moving.... 53
materials for, not to be placed in streets without permit 53
not to be built of wood within fire limits.... 53, 118, 224—227
damages to, in opening streets 64, 65
regulations to prevent fires .... 224—230
encumbering streets with, penalties.... 317, 346

BURIAL OF THE DEAD, power to regulate 28
in unsold lots of cemetery prohibited 218, 219

BUTCHERS, power to license and regulate, (see *Markets*, *Slaughter Houses*, *Slaughtering*) 26

CABMEN, power to license and regulate, (see *Vehicles*).... 24

CANAL LANDS, power to tax improvements on.... 81

CANALS, powers as to .... 150, 180—184, 206—208
ordinance concerning 518, 519

CARAVANS, power to prohibit, license and regulate, (see *Shows*) 25

CARMEN, power to license and regulate, (see *Vehicles*) 24

CARTERS, power to license and regulate, (see *Vehicles*).... 24

CATTLE, running at large, power to restrain, (see *Pounds*) 27
power to distrain and impound 27
crossing bridges, not more than eight at once 216
indecent exhibition of bull, penalty 281
penalty for keeping, offensively.... 290

CELLARS, power to cleanse, (see *Nuisances*) 25
power to fill up and drain 31
penalty for leaving doors open.... 287

CEMETERIES, beyond city limits, power to establish and regulate 32, 33
placed under superintendence of board of public works 33
sale of lots.... 33
lots exempt from execution 33
grounds exempt from taxation.... 33, 159
act granting land to town for.... 32
never to be used for any other purpose 164
ordinance concerning 164
.... 218, 219

CERTIORARI, in special assessment proceedings, when writ may be issued.... 74, 75

CESS-POOLS, construction of, power to regulate 152
regulations concerning.... 331, 332

CHANCE GIFT distribution, punishment for 334

CIRCUS, power to prohibit, license and regulate, (see *Shows*) 25

CISTERNS, power to regulate 28

CITY ATTORNEY, election of, and term of office 6
duties of 15, 16, 191, 209

CITY BONDS, to pay floating debt, power to issue 45, 46
power to complete the issue of certain bonds heretofore authorized.... 46, 140, 152
for house of correction, power to issue.... 46
to meet those falling due, power to issue 46, 142, 154
power to issue water-loan bonds to amount of $500,000.... 140, 141
power to issue sewerage bonds to amount of $500,000 .... 152, 153
list of all bonds outstanding to be kept by comptroller 47, 142, 154
no bonds to be issued, unless specially authorized by city charter 48
interest on, how provided and paid.... 45, 46, 47, 142, 147, 154, 156
sinking fund provisions 80, 81, 155, 156, 157
power to purchase outstanding bonds 142, 146, 147, 154
board of public works to keep registers of bonds.... 142, 154
power to issue, for various purposes.... 181, 182, 185, 188, 189
registration and indorsements of 189, 372, 373

CITY CHARTER. (For former Charters, see *Appendix.*)
declared a public act ... 160
construction and effect of ... 158, 159, 160, 162
to take effect from its passage ... 163
CITY CLERK, how appointed ... 10, 191
term of office ... 10
duties of ... 15, 276
to publish notice of elections ... 6
to notify officers of their election or appointment ... 12
to have custody of official bonds and oaths ... 11, 14
power to administer oaths ... 15
to furnish schedules of taxable real estate to assessors ... 84
to prepare the tax lists ... 84, 85
to compute the taxes ... 85
to issue tax and assessment warrants ... 85, 86, 143, 144
to register the names of firemen ... 121
CITY ENGINEER, how appointed ... 50
powers and duties of ... 50
consulting board of engineers on plans for cleansing river ... 182
CITY GOVERNMENT, vested in common council ... 5, 23
officers of ... 5, 182
CITY LIMITS, defined ... 2
CITY OF CHICAGO, incorporated ... 1, 2
general corporate powers ... 2
limits and jurisdiction ... 2
three divisions established ... 2
division into wards ... 2—4
government of, in whom vested ... 5
inhabitants competent as judges, justices, jurors or witnesses in city actions ... 159
vested rights preserved ... 159
not liable for board of prisoners in county jail ... 159
not required to furnish appeal bond in any suit ... 159
not required to furnish affidavit of merits in any action ... 159
suits against, to be brought only in courts of record ... 159
execution not to be issued against ... 159, 160
CITY PHYSICIAN, how appointed ... 10, 191
duties of ... 19, 252—255
COAL, weighing and sale of, power to regulate ... 28
fraud in sale, penalty ... 366
COLLECTION OF TAXES AND ASSESSMENTS, (see *Taxes, Assessments*) ... 83—96
COLLECTOR, election of ... 6
term of office ... 6
to give bond ... 19, 20, 42
an officer of treasury department ... 34
duties of ... 41, 276
official books and papers subject to examination ... 41
to pay over daily all moneys collected ... 41, 42
treasurer's receipts to be filed with comptroller ... 41
weekly reports of moneys collected to be made to comptroller ... 41
annual statement to be made to common council ... 41, 42
removable for misconduct ... 42
settlement with comptroller, controversies, how decided ... 43
power to appoint clerks ... 43
provisions respecting the safe keeping of public moneys ... 43, 44
may be required to perform other duties ... 43
embezzlement by, how punished ... 43, 44
to give notice of all tax and assessment warrants issued for collection ... 86, 87, 180
special provisions respecting collection of personal property tax ... 86, 87
damages on unpaid taxes and assessments, when collectable ... 87, 88
power to levy on personal property ... 87
application for judgment against delinquent real estate, when and how made ... 88
power to sell real estate ... 90, 91
notice of sale, how given ... 90, 91
mode of conducting sale ... 91, 92
precept to be returned ... 92
to grant certificates to purchasers ... 91, 92
penalty for wrongful sale ... 42
penalty for willful neglect of duty ... 95
successor in office may complete unfinished proceedings ... 94
provisions respecting collection of warrants for water assessments ... 144, 145
fees and proceedings on sale of goods and chattels ... 180
COMBUSTIBLE SUBSTANCES, keeping and conveying of, power to regulate ... 26
regulations to prevent fires ... 227—230
petroleum and other dangerous liquids ... 303—306
gunpowder and gun cotton ... 239—241, 246
COMMISSIONS, to city officers, by whom issued ... 20

COMMON COUNCIL, general powers and duties of ... 22—33

- of whom composed ... 5, 22
- may divide wards into election districts ... 5, 6
- may establish new offices ... 5
- may order election of alderman to fill vacancy ... 7
- may increase number of assessors ... 9
- to appoint inspectors of election ... 10
- power to remove city officers ... 10, 11
- may fill vacancies in certain offices ... 11
- power to regulate elections ... 12
- to canvass election returns ... 12
- may appoint presiding officer in absence of mayor ... 22
- to appoint acting mayor in case of vacancy ... 15
- acts passed by, to be approved by mayor ... 15
- to reconsider acts vetoed by mayor ... 15
- members to be fire-wardens and conservators of the peace ... 15
- members exempt from military and jury duty ... 15, 120, 121
- proceedings to be recorded by clerk ... 15
- may define duties of officers ... 19
- may require officers to give bonds ... 19
- to approve certain official bonds ... 19
- to designate corporation newspaper ... 20, 200
- may establish officers' salaries ... 20, [illegible]
- may provide for removal of officers for taking illegal fees ... 20, 21
- may provide additional salary for recorder ... 21
- meetings, when to be held ... 22
- quorum, how constituted ... 22
- members to receive no compensation ... 22
- members not eligible to salaried office ... 22
- members not to be interested in contracts with city ... 22
- special meetings, how called ... 22
- shall establish its own rules ... 22
- to judge of the election of members ... 22, 23
- may compel the attendance of absent members ... 23
- ordinances and petitions to be referred to committees ... 23
- reports of committees to be deferred and published on request of two members ... 23
- power to rescind or reconsider measures at special meetings limited ... 23
- may require reports from city officers ... 23
- vote to raise or appropriate money, to be taken by yeas and nays ... 23
- general powers of ... 23—33
- power to establish and regulate cemetery grounds ... 32, 33
- mayor, with concurrence of, may remove treasurer for misconduct ... 40
- may establish place of deposit for city moneys ... 40
- power to authorize expenditures limited ... 44, 45
- may direct comptroller to borrow money for repairs, in case of necessity ... 45
- may authorize issue of bonds for certain purposes, 46, 140, 141, 152, 153, 181, 182, 185, 188, 189
- to raise annual tax for payment of interest on funded debt ... 45, 46, 80
- to levy tax for sinking fund ... 80, 81
- may provide for appointment of city auditor ... 48
- power to regulate employment of agents by board of public works ... 51, 52
- may assign additional duties to board of public works ... 52, 53
- power to regulate erection of frame buildings within fire limits ... 53, 118
- may prescribe fees for permits issued by board of public works ... 53
- power to regulate the moving of buildings through the streets ... 53
- power to authorize contracts by board of public works, without advertising for bids ... 56
- power to authorize river or harbor improvement, without contract ... 180
- to levy tax to pay for necessary repairs and improvements ... 57
- power to lay out, widen and discontinue streets and alleys ... 60
- power to purchase, lay out and improve parks and public grounds ... 60
- power to improve streets ... 60
- power to widen and deepen the river ... 60
- power to erect and construct sidewalks, area walls, lamp posts and drains ... 60
- power to make wharves and slips at ends of streets ... 60
- to refer petitions for public improvements to board of public works ... 61
- may direct improvements after reports from board of public works ... 61
- three-fourths vote required for improvements in certain cases ... 62
- ayes and noes to be taken ... 62
- power to revise and confirm assessments ... 66, 70, 71, 73
- may levy new assessments in certain cases ... 75, 76
- power to widen Michigan avenue ... 77, 78
- power to levy and collect taxes ... 79, 80, 185, 186, 188, 197
- when to be levied ... 85
- to levy tax for police expenses ... 108
- may require information respecting books and accounts of police commissioners ... 108
- power to make quarantine regulations ... 112
- power to assign additional duties to board of health ... 112
- power to remit penalties imposed by police court ... 114
- may authorize appointment of deputy clerks in police court ... 115, 191
- may provide for appointment of prosecuting attorney, in police court ... 117
- power to provide police court in each division of city ... 191
- power to establish fire limits ... 118
- general powers for prevention of fires ... 118, 119

COMMON COUNCIL—*continued.*
power in relation to school lands and fund 122, 123, 124
power to establish and maintain schools 123, 125
power to purchase land and erect buildings for reform school 130
shall establish penalties for violating regulations concerning use of water 146
to raise annual tax for support of water works 147
shall establish penalties for violating regulations concerning sewers 157
to raise annual tax for sewerage purposes 155
may fix pay of fish inspector 167
power as to vacating streets, etc 168, 193, 206
powers as to canals and tunnels .... 180—185, 206—208

COMMUNICATIONS to common council, to be referred to committees 23

COMPTROLLER, how appointed 35
removable at pleasure of mayor and common council 35
a member of board of guardians 9, 130
to give bond 19, 20, 35
may give directions respecting the law business of the city 15
to have charge of the sale of cemetery lots 33
chief of treasury department 35
books to be kept by 35
official books and papers subject to examination by mayor and common council 35
general powers and duties of 35, 36
to audit claims against city 36
may examine claimants under oath 36
to draw all warrants on treasurer 36, 39, 58, 108, 124, 137, 199
to charge receiving officers with moneys collected 37
to countersign tax and assessment warrants 37
power to require reports from revenue officers 37
to report defaulting officers to mayor for removal 37
to publish annual financial statement 37, 38, 47
to submit to common council an annual estimate of city expenses 38
to prepare and publish monthly statements of receipts and expenditures 38, 39
adjustment of accounts with treasurer and collector, controversies, how decided 43
power to appoint clerks 43
may be required to perform additional duties 43
power to sell and negotiate city bonds 45, 141, 153
shall keep a list of outstanding city bonds 47, 142, 154
duty respecting payment of interest on funded debt 36, 47, 142, 147, 154, 156
may be authorized to borrow from certain funds to meet demands on another 47, 48
to sign tax and special assessment warrants 85, 86
to deliver tax and special assessment warrants to collector 85, 86
to keep a record of tax and assessment sales 92
may cancel erroneous sales 93
to record redemptions from tax and assessment sales 92
to keep a memorandum of tax and assessment deeds issued 92, 93
to act in place of collector in case of vacancy 94
to pay witnesses for city in police court 116
to require police-court clerk to make reports and pay over moneys 117
power to purchase outstanding city bonds 80, 81, 142, 146, 154, 155
fee for tax and assessment deeds 93
fee for receiving auctioneers' return 211
fee for indorsing bonds and coupons 372
to regulate and have charge of market 279, 280

CONCERTS, power to prohibit, license and regulate, (see *Shows*) 25

CONDEMNATION OF REAL ESTATE, mode of procedure .... 60—68
assessments for, how made .... 62—68
when condemnation effectual 67, 68, 179
payment of damages 67, 68
proceedings to be recorded 68
possession, when to be taken by city 68, 179
contracts and leases discharged by 68
condemnation and sale of buildings 64, 65
appeal from confirmation of assessment 66, 67
for canals 184, 207, 208

CONSERVATORS OF THE PEACE, who constitute 15
powers of, defined 159

CONSTABLES, how chosen 6
power of appointing additional 5
to give bond 18, 19
not to serve process beyond city, except in specified cases 19
power to serve process beyond city for violation of cemetery regulations 33

CONTRACTS, with city, municipal officers not to be interested in 21, 22, 48, 56, 57
not to be made by city, unless appropriation has been made for expense 48
by board of public works, how made .... 54—57
copies of, for public work, to be filed with comptroller 55
payable from special assessments, how let 55
for supplies and materials, how made 56
for sewerage or water works, shall specify that they are for such works 57

CONTRACTORS, to give a guaranty to city 55
may receive estimates as work progresses 55
no claim on city, when payable from special assessments, unless assessment collected... 55
COOK COUNTY, seat established at Chicago.... 165
CORPORATE PROPERTY, to be transferred by retiring officers to their successors.... 20
penalty for willful injury to. 77, 148, 156, 157, 245, 247, 332
in whom vested 158
CORPORATION NEWSPAPER, how designated.... 20, 200
what to be published in..20, 23, 37, 38, 39, 54, 62, 64, 65, 68, 70, 71, 84, 86, 87, 88, 90, 91, 143, 158, 200
COUNSEL TO THE CORPORATION, how appointed.... 10
term of office 10
duties of 15, 16, 191
COUNTY SEAT, established at Chicago.... 165
COURTS. (See *Police Court*, *Recorder's Court*.)
CROSS-WALKS, power to construct.... 60
expense of, how paid.... 76, 178
penalty for obstructing.... 339
CRUELTY TO ANIMALS, power to punish.... 26
penalty for.... 282

DANGEROUS LIQUIDS, ordinance concerning.... 303—306
DANGEROUS SPORTS, penalties.... 286, 287
DEATHS, registration of, power to regulate.... 28
DECISIONS OF SUPREME COURT. (See *Appendix*.)
DEEDS for taxes and assessments, when and how issued.... 92
of what *prima facie* evidence 93
of what conclusive evidence.... 93
proof required to defeat 93, 94
not to be questioned, unless redemption money has been tendered.... 94
fee to comptroller for.... 93
DEFAULTERS, not eligible to office 12
to be reported to mayor for removal 37, 40, 42, 117
DISEASE, contagious, power to make regulations concerning, (see *Health*).... 27, 31
DISORDERLY ASSEMBLAGES, power to prevent 25
penalty for.... 287
DISORDERLY CONDUCT, penalties.... 282, 283, 287, 312, 357, 359
DISORDERLY HOUSES, power to restrain and suppress 25
how punished.... 282, 284
DISPENSARIES, power to establish, (see *Health*).... 31
DISTILLERIES, power to direct location of, (see *Nuisances*).... 25, 26
power to prohibit, license and regulate.... 25, 26
DISTILLERS, power to tax, license and regulate, (see *Nuisances*).... 24
DISTURBANCES, power to prevent 25
penalty for.... 287
DIVISIONS of city, defined.... 2
DOCKS, encumbering of, power to prevent, (see *Wharves*).... 26
superintendence of, by board of public works.... 52
DOGS, power to tax, restrain, and destroy.... 27
ordinance concerning.... 220—222
DRAINS, power to cleanse and regulate.... 31
power to construct.... 60, 152
mode of procedure 60, 61, 71, 72, 177, 178
regulations concerning.... 201, 293, 294
ordinance concerning sewers and.... 330—332
DRAYMEN, power to license and regulate, (see *Vehicles*).... 24
how to fasten dray when horse left.... 286, 287
DRUNKENNESS, penalty for 282, 283

ELECTION DISTRICTS, wards to be divided into 5, 6
ELECTIONS, municipal, when to be held.... 6, 162
notice of, how given.... 6
special, provisions concerning 6
determined by plurality vote 6
officers to be elected 6
of aldermen and constables.... 6, 7
in case of tie, how determined.... 7
of commissioners of public works.... 7, 8, 160, 161
of police commissioners 7, 8, 161, 193, 194
inspectors of, how appointed.... 10
manner of conducting 12, 13

ELECTIONS — *continued.*
manner of contesting ... 12
power to regulate ... 12
returns of ... 12

ELIGIBILITY TO OFFICE ... 12

EMBEZZLEMENT, by revenue officers, how punished ... 43, 44, 148
by commissioners of public works, how punished ... 58, 59

ENGINEERS, consulting board of, on plans for cleansing river ... 182

ENGINEERS OF FIRE DEPARTMENT, how elected ... 6
term of office ... 6
duties of ... 120
office abolished ... 199

ENGINE HOUSES, superintendence of ... 52, 197
common council to procure fit ... 199

EVIDENCE, of official papers and proceedings ... 15
of tax and assessment sales ... 92
of erroneous tax and assessment sales ... 93
tax lists conclusive, as to amount assessed ... 85
of publication of ordinances ... 158
ordinances, when to be received as ... 160, 200
tax and assessment deeds ... 93

EVIDENCES OF DEBT, not to be issued, unless expressly authorized by charter ... 48

EXECUTION, on judgments in police court, when and how issued ... 113, 114
not to be issued against city ... 159, 160

EXHIBITIONS, power to prohibit, license and regulate, (see *Shows*) ... 25

EXPENDITURES. (See *Receipts and Expenditures.*)
not to exceed amount provided in annual appropriation bill ... 44, 45
for improvements payable from general fund limited ... 45
by police commissioners limited ... 108
by board of education limited ... 189

FEES, of fish inspector ... 17, 167
for licenses ... 25, 222
of inspectors, weighers and gaugers, power to prescribe ... 28
for licensing land surveyors ... 50
for permits ... 53, 184, 347
received by salaried officers, to be paid into city treasury ... 21
of police justices, to be paid into city treasury ... 115
not to be received by members of police force ... 99, 100, 194, 195
of collector, for selling goods and chattels ... 180
ordinance concerning ... 222, 223
of scavengers ... 328
(See *Auctions, Comptroller, Hay, Inspectors, Weights and Measures, Vehicles, Wood.*)

FERRIES, power to regulate and license ... 29

FINANCE COMMITTEE, to examine and pass upon doubtful claims ... 36, 37
to examine annually all warrants paid by treasurer ... 40
to examine collector's books and vouchers ... 41
to examine and compare annual reports of comptroller, treasurer and collector ... 42, 43
to adjust accounts between officers of treasury department ... 43
power to authorize the borrowing of money ... 45
power to authorize issue of bonds ... 45, 46
power to authorize issue of drafts on treasurer ... 47
may authorize comptroller to borrow from one fund to meet demands on another ... 47
accounts of board of public works, subject to inspection of ... 59

FINANCES, of corporation, general control of ... 23
comptroller to have supervision over ... 35, 36
annual statement of, to be published ... 37, 38
temporary loans authorized in certain cases ... 45
how provided for ... 45, 80
bonds authorized to be issued ... 45, 46, 140—142, 152—154, 181, 182, 185, 188, 189
power to borrow money to pay interest on bonded debt ... 47, 147, 156
interest on bonded debt to be raised by annual tax ... 45, 46, 80
sinking fund for general bonded debt ... 80, 81
power to levy and collect taxes ... 79—83, 185, 186, 188, 197
sinking fund for sewerage debt ... 155—157

FINES, power to enforce ordinances by ... 32
imposed by police court, power to remit ... 114
in criminal cases in city to be paid into city treasury ... 518

FIRE DEPARTMENT ... 118—121, 197—200
engineers of, how elected ... 6
power to make regulations for prevention of fires ... 118, 119
power to purchase engines and apparatus ... 119, 199
power to appoint firemen ... 119, 197
duties of engineers ... 120
power to appoint fire marshal ... 120
firemen exempted from military and jury duty ... 120, 121

FIRE DEPARTMENT—*continued.*
firemen to be registered by city clerk 121
fire-insurance rates, how appropriated 82, 83
fund for relief of disabled firemen 121
fire-telegraph fund 121, 165, 166, 524, 525
power to construct hydrants to extinguish fires 138
under control of board of police 197
new organization of .... 197—200
offices of engineers abolished 199
fire marshals and fire police .... 197—200
bridges to be kept closed for, at alarms 218
ordinance concerning .... 228—233
duties as to gunpowder and gun cotton 240
firemen misusing wrenches of hydrants, penalty 360, 361

FIRE LIMITS, power to establish 118
permits to erect frame buildings within 58
established 223, 224
regulations concerning buildings in .... 224—227

FIRE MARSHAL, power to provide for appointment of 120
appointment of, under new organization .... 197—200
powers and duties of .... 120, 197—199, 231—233

FIREMEN'S BENEVOLENT ASSOCIATION 83, 165, 166

FIRE TELEGRAPH, provisions concerning .... 121, 165, 166, 523—526

FIRE WARDENS 15, 120, 198

FIRE WORKS, power to prevent 119
regulations concerning 285

FISCAL YEAR, when to commence 44

FISH, inspection of .... 16—18
power to regulate sale of 28
ordinance concerning 263, 264

FISH INSPECTOR, how appointed 10, 191
term of office 10, 191
duties, powers and liabilities of .... 16—18
fees of 17, 167
ordinance concerning 263, 264

FLOATING DEBT, power to issue bonds for 45

FLOUR, power to regulate inspection of 28
ordinance concerning .... 264—268

FORESTALLING, power to prevent and punish 24, 26

FRAUDULENT PRACTICES, power to restrain 24
penalties for .... 249, 281, 302, 305, 306, 311, 355—357, 366, 369

FUND, separate accounts of each, to be kept by treasurer 39
power to use moneys of one, to meet demands upon another 47, 48
what funds excepted from this rule 40, 41, 47, 124, 148

FUNDED DEBT, interest on, to be raised by annual tax 45, 46, 80
power to borrow money to pay interest on 47, 147, 156
sinking fund for 80, 81

GAMBLERS, punishment of 281, 284, 285, 384

GAMING, power to restrain and punish 24, 31, 32, 102, 103
power to destroy instruments used in 25, 103, 284
punishment for 282, 284, 285, 384

GAS COMPANIES, charters and ordinances concerning .... 373—379
to notify board of public works before laying pipes 330

GAS METERS, ordinance concerning inspection of 268, 269

GAS PIPES, power to regulate the laying of, in public streets 58
notice to be given before laying 330

GAUGERS, power to appoint, (see *Liquors*) 28
duties of, power to regulate 28
fees of, power to prescribe 28
how appointed, and term of office 10, 191

GEESE, power to restrain 27

GENERAL FUND, how raised 79
expenses chargeable to 52, 76, 79, 178

GERMAN NEWSPAPER, publication in 20, 200

GIFT DISTRIBUTION, chance, punishment for 384

GOATS, power to restrain 27

GRADES, power to establish and alter 30
ordinance concerning .... 233—238

GROCERIES, disorderly, power to suppress 25

GROCERS, power to license and regulate, (see *Spirituous Liquors*) 24

GROUNDS, power to fill up and drain, (see *Parks and Public Grounds*) 81
GUN COTTON. (See *Gunpowder.*)
GUNPOWDER, storing of, power to regulate 26
keeping and conveying of, power to regulate 26
ordinances concerning, and gun cotton .... 239—241, 246

HACKMEN, power to license and regulate, (see *Vehicles*) 24
HARBOR, power to preserve and regulate, (see *River*) 24, 29, 30
power to widen and deepen 24
what to include 30
marine insurance rates to be applied to improvement of 33
improvement without contract 180
ordinance concerning .... 241—247
regulations of vessels in harbor and passing bridges .... 242—247
HARBOR MASTER, how appointed 10, 187, 188
term of office 10, 188
duties of .... 16, 240—247
HAWKERS, power to license and regulate, (see *Peddlers*) 25
HAY, weighing and selling of, power to regulate 28
ordinance concerning .... 248—250
burning of, regulated 280
HEALTH, powers for the preservation of, (see *City Physician*) 27, 31
life insurance rates to be used for sanitary purposes 33
general powers and duties of board of .... 110—112, 201, 202
physicians to report infected patients .... 110—111, 253, 254
act concerning health regulations .... 201—205
duties of health officer 201, 202, 203, 204, 251, 252, 253
ordinance concerning .... 250—260
penalties for offenses against .... 253—260
HEALTH OFFICER, appointment, removal and salary 201, 202
duties of .... 201—204, 251—253
HOOPS, rolling of, power to prevent 27
ordinance concerning 287
HORSE RACING, power to prevent 26
on streets, etc 285
HORSE RAILWAYS, power to regulate running of cars 29
power to regulate laying of tracks 29
general ordinance concerning .... 260—263
gauge and rail of 260, 261
sprinkling of streets by 261
tracks not to obstruct streets 261, 391, 395, 403, 407, 415, 416, 418, 428
improvement and repair of streets by,
261, 262, 391, 395, 398, 403, 409, 415—417, 420, 421, 424, 428—431, 433, 435, 436, 438, 439, 441
not to stop cars on cross streets 262
teams and vehicles to give way to 262, 263, 381
charter of Chicago City Railway Company .... 379—382
charter of North Chicago Railway Company .... 379—382
charter of Chicago West Division Railway Company .... 383—385
penalty for obstructing either of said companies 384
charters of said companies extended and powers enlarged .... 387—389
charter of Chicago and Evanston Railroad Company 385, 386
ordinance, favor of Mason and Phillips .... 389—393
ordinance, favor of Fuller, Parmelee and Bigelow .... 393—399
ordinances, north division .... 389—393, 427—442
ordinances, south division .... 389—406, 408—413, 423—426, 432, 433, 436—442
ordinances, west division .... 393—408, 410—423
ordinance, favor of Chicago and Evanston Railroad Company .... 436—442
liability for baggage 380, 388
consent of property owners to construction of, when required .... 381—383, 420, 428
restrictions as to power to be used 382, 390, 394, 402, 421, 425
fare 388, 391, 392, 395, 403, 422, 425, 426, 428, 435, 439
purchase of, by city 392, 393, 397
control of, by common council 390, 391, 403, 414, 423, 434
for what purposes may be used 390, 394, 395, 402, 421, 425
liability for negligence 403, 429, 431
funeral facilities by 422, 425, 434, 435, 439, 440
contracts, covenants, releases, resolutions and stipulations by,
405, 406, 408, 412—414, 417, 422, 423, 436, 441, 442
HORSES, power to restrain, (see *Pounds*, *Teams*) 27
crossing bridges, not more than eight at once 216
indecent exhibition of stud horse, penalty 281
immoderate driving on streets 285
HOSPITALS, power to establish, (see *Health*) 31
superintendence of 52
keepers and assistants, power to appoint 5
HOUSE OF CORRECTION. (See *Bridewell.*)

HOUSE OF REFUGE, power to establish, (see *Reform School*) ... 31
HOUSES OF ILL FAME, power to suppress ... 25
punishment for ... 281, 282
HYDRANTS, public, power to regulate ... 28
power to construct ... 138
ordinance concerning ... 360—363

ICE, cutting and sale of, power to regulate ... 28
impure, power to restrain sale of ... 28
ordinances concerning ... 286, 442, 443
ILL FAME, keepers, inmates and frequenters, punishment of ... 281, 282
IMMODERATE DRIVING, power to restrain ... 26
penalty for ... 285
IMPOUNDING, power to authorize, (see *Pounds*) ... 27
IMPRISONMENT, power to enforce ordinances by ... 32, 288
IMPROVEMENTS. (See *Public Improvements.*)
INDECENT EXPOSURE, power to prevent ... 26, 27
penalties for ... 281, 282
INFANTS, guardians of, when necessary, how appointed ... 74
INFORMER, reward to ... 295, 319, 320
INSPECTION, of fish ... 16, 17, 18, 28, 263, 264
of lumber ... 28
of salt, flour and other provisions ... 28, 264—268
of gas meters ... 268, 269
of whisky and other liquors ... 28, 269—271
of petroleum, etc. ... 304, 305
of wood ... 367—370
INSPECTORS, power to appoint ... 5, 28
fees of, power to prescribe ... 28
how appointed ... 10, 191
fees of ... 17, 167, 263, 264, 267, 269, 271, 305, 367
INSPECTORS OF ELECTION, how appointed ... 10
number of ... 5
duties, powers and liabilities of ... 12
INSURANCE RATES, how collected and appropriated ... 81, 82, 83, 121
INTELLIGENCE OFFICES, ordinance concerning ... 271, 272
INTEREST, on funded debt, to be raised by annual tax ... 45, 46, 80
to be paid by comptroller ... 36, 142, 154
power to provide for, by temporary loans ... 47, 147, 156

JAIL, power to enforce ordinances by imprisonment in ... 32
board of prisoners, when city not liable for ... 159, 516
JOB PRINTING, how to be done ... 190
JUDGE, citizens competent in city actions ... 159
JUDGMENTS, against city, power to provide for, by temporary loans ... 45
JUNK SHOPS, power to tax, license and regulate ... 24, 25
ordinance concerning ... 272—274
JUROR, citizens competent in city actions ... 159
JURY DUTY, who exempted from ... 15, 110, 120, 121
JUSTICE, citizens competent in city actions ... 159

KITES, flying of, power to regulate ... 27
penalty for ... 286

LAKE. (See *Nuisances.*)
LAKE VIEW AVENUE COMPANY, charter and ordinance concerning ... 443—448
LAMP POSTS, power to erect ... 60
mode of procedure ... 60, 61, 62, 73, 178, 179
ordinance concerning ... 274, 275
LAMPS, lighting of, power to regulate ... 29
superintendence of ... 52
power to levy tax for ... 80
ordinance concerning ... 274, 275, 349
LAND SURVEYORS, power to license, (see *Surveyors of Land*) ... 50, 51
LANES. (See *Streets.*)
LARD, steaming and rendering of, power to license and regulate, (see *Nuisances*). ... 25, 26

LAW DEPARTMENT, officers of 15, 16
LAWS, former, governing the city. (See *Appendix.*)
LEGAL PROCEEDINGS, comptroller to have supervision over 36
LICENSES, power to issue 25
  not to be granted for more than one year 25
  fees for 25, 50
  ordinance concerning 275, 276
 (See *Auctions, Boot Blacks, Gunpowder, Intelligence Offices, Junk Dealers, Markets, Newsboys, Pawnbrokers, Peddlers, Porters and Runners, Sale by Sample, Scavengers, Shows, Spirituous Liquors, Vehicles.*)
LIEN, against vessels 30, 243, 246
  of special assessments 75, 76
  of taxes 87
  of water rents 143
LIGHTS, in stables and out-houses, power to regulate 26
  regulations concerning 227
  in streets, superintendence of 52
  power to levy taxes for 80
LIQUIDS, dangerous, ordinance concerning .... 303—306
LIQUORS, sale of, power to regulate, (see *Spirituous Liquors*) 24
  inspection of, power to regulate 28
  ordinance concerning inspection of .... 269—271
LOCOMOTIVE ENGINES, power to regulate use of, within city, (see *Railroads*) 29
  encumbering streets with, penalty 345, 346
LOTTERIES, punishment for 334
LUMBER, storing of, within fire limits, power to regulate 28
  measuring and inspecting of, power to regulate 28
LUMBER YARDS, power to prohibit, within fire limits 28
  regulation concerning 230

MARKETS, power to establish and regulate 26
  superintendence of 52, 279, 280
  ordinance concerning .... 277—280
MAYOR, election of 6
  term of office 6
  power of appointment to office 10
  power to fill vacancies 8, 11
  vacancy in office, how filled 11
  general duties of 14
  salary of 14
  to preside over common council 14, 22
  a member of boards of police and public works 14, 49, 97
  power to administer oaths 14
  veto, power of 15
  acting mayor, how appointed, and duties 15, 297
  may call special meetings of common council 22
  to countersign all warrants on the treasurer 36, 39, 58, 108, 124, 187, 199
  power to remove defaulters 37
  may remove treasurer and collector for misconduct 40, 42
  power to release prisoners from bridewell 114
  no longer member of boards of police and public works 196
MEAL, inspection of, power to regulate 28
MEATS, sale of, power to license and regulate, (see *Markets*) 26
MENDICANT CHILDREN, power to provide for, (see *Reform School*) 31
MENDICANTS, power to restrain and punish, (see *Beggars*) 27
MICHIGAN AVENUE, power to widen and improve 77, 78
  encroachments on public grounds east of, prohibited 78
MILITARY DUTY, who exempted from 110, 120, 121
MILK, selling impure, penalty 287
MISDEMEANORS, ordinance concerning .... 280—288
MULES, power to restrain 27
MUNICIPAL YEAR, when to commence 6
MUSICAL ENTERTAINMENTS, power to license and regulate, (see *Shows*) 25
MUSICIANS, bands crossing bridges 217, 218

NEWSBOYS, ordinance concerning 289, 448
NOISE AND DISTURBANCE, power to prevent 25, 27
  penalty for 287, 288

NUISANCES, power to define and abate, (see *Markets, Misdemeanors, Scavengers*)..... 27, 31
assessments for removal of........ 73, 74, 179
expense of removing, recoverable by suit........ 73, 74
board of health may abate........ 110
health act concerning........ 200—205
ordinance concerning........ 290—295

OATH, officers empowered to administer........ 14, 15, 36, 52, 100, 109
of voters........ 13
of city officers........ 14
of commissioners of public works........ 58
of police commissioners........ 97
required of all clerks in treasury department........ 43
to be taken by all police officers........ 109
accounts of treasury officers to be verified by........ 44

OFFICIAL BONDS, when to be filed........ 11, 12, 19, 20
may be required of all city officers........ 19
by whom to be approved........ 19, 97, 196
city officers not to be sureties on........ 11
may be required from persons licensed........ 25
of comptroller........ 35
of treasurer........ 41
of collector........ 42
of commissioners of public works........ 49, 50
of police commissioners........ 97, 196
of police court clerk........ 115
of superintendent of reform school........ 131
of land surveyors........ 50, 51
of fish inspector........ 18
of assistant fish inspector........ 18
of constables........ 18, 19
of school agent........ 123, 193
of officers of police........ 109

OFFICIAL BOOKS AND PAPERS, to be surrendered by retiring officers........ 20

OFFICERS, of city, enumerated........ 5, 182
to be elected by the people........ 6, 7, 8
to be appointed by mayor........ 10
to be appointed by common council........ 10
to be appointed by mayor and common council........ 9, 10, 35
to be appointed by board of public works........ 50
vacancies, how filled........ 8, 11
removal of........ 8, 10, 35, 37, 40, 42, 117
qualifications of........ 8, 9, 12, 99, 194, 195
bonds of, when to be filed........ 11, 12
not to be taken as sureties by city........ 11
to be notified of election or appointment........ 12
within what period to qualify........ 12
to be sworn........ 14
duties of, may be defined by common council........ 19
may be required to give bonds........ 19
to transfer official books and papers to their successors........ 20
how commissioned........ 20
may be removed for taking illegal fees........ 20, 21
paid by salary, to pay all fees into city treasury........ 21
may be required to make reports to common council........ 23
in receipt of city revenue, may be removed if delinquent........ 37, 40, 42
salaries, how paid........ 21, 194
when to be established........ 187

OMNIBUS DRIVERS, power to license and regulate, (see *Vehicles*)........ 24
not to stop on street crossings........ 262

ORDERS, to raise or appropriate money, how to be passed by council........ 23

ORDINANCES, to be approved by mayor........ 15
to take effect if not disapproved........ 15
publication of........ 20, 158, 160, 200
to be referred by common council to committees........ 23
to raise or appropriate money, how to be passed by council........ 23
power of common council to pass, amend and repeal........ 32
observance of, how enforced........ 32, 113, 114
imposing penalties, to be published before going into effect........ 158
former, continued in force........ 158, 200, 205
when to be received as evidence........ 160
ratification of various acts and........ 186, 187
ordinance concerning........ 295—298

PACKING HOUSES, power to license and regulate, (see *Nuisances*)........ 25

PARKS, superintendence of........ 52
power to purchase and lay out........ 60

PARKS — *continued.*
power to improve ... 60
expense, how paid ... 76
ordinance concerning ... 298, 299

PAWNBROKERS, power to tax, license and regulate ... 24
ordinance concerning ... 299—301
not affected by junk-dealers' ordinance ... 274

PEDDLERS, power to license and regulate, (see *Newsboys, Sale by Sample*) ... 25
ordinances concerning ... 301—303, 366
to have weights and measures sealed ... 366

PENALTIES, power to impose ... 32, 71, 72, 146, 157
power to remit ... 114
ordinances imposing, to be published before taking effect ... 158
commutation of ... 276, 283, 284
in criminal cases in city to be paid into city treasury ... 513

PERMANENT IMPROVEMENTS, power to levy taxes for, (see *Public Improvements*) 76, 80

PERMITS, for removing buildings ... 58
for depositing building materials in street ... 58
for raising buildings and sidewalks ... 58
for constructing vaults under sidewalks and streets ... 58
for erecting frame buildings within fire limits ... 59
for draining into river or canals ... 184
fees for ... 58, 347
regulations concerning ... 347

PEST HOUSE, power to establish, (see *Health*) ... 31

PETITIONS, to common council, to be referred to committees ... 28

PETROLEUM, ordinance concerning ... 303—306

PHYSICIANS, to report cases of infectious disease, (see *City Physician, Health*) ... 110, 253, 254
penalty for neglect ... 110, 111, 253, 254

PLATS, of subdivisions, to be approved by board of public works ... 51

POISON, sold, to be labeled ... 285

POLICE. (For former laws, see *Appendix.*)
BOARD OF ... 96—112
of whom composed ... 7, 14, 97, 196
mayor no longer member of ... 196
election of commissioners ... 7, 8, 160, 161, 193, 194
their term of office ... 7, 8, 193, 194
qualifications of commissioners ... 8, 194
vacancies, how filled ... 8, 196
removal of commissioners ... 8, 9
oath and bond of commissioners ... 97, 196
commissioners' salary ... 99, 194
to appoint president and secretary ... 97
secretary's salary ... 97
general powers and duties ... 97, 98, 195, 196
power to construct telegraph ... 97
power to establish rules and regulations ... 98, 99, 195
power to suspend members of police force ... 99, 196
power to establish precincts and stations ... 103, 106
power to appoint special policemen and patrolmen ... 103, 104
to keep general complaint books ... 105
to keep books for registry of lost and stolen property ... 105
to keep a record of police force ... 105, 106
to keep books of account ... 106
to keep a record of proceedings ... 106
to provide accommodations for detention of witnesses ... 107
to furnish annual estimate of police expenses ... 107, 108
to furnish annual estimate of expenses of fire department ... 198
power to incur expense, limited ... 108
books and accounts of, subject to inspection ... 108
to furnish information to common council, if required ... 108
to cause ordinances to be enforced ... 108
power to subpœna witnesses ... 100, 109
power to administer oaths ... 100, 109
to require security from officers of police ... 109
to require members of police force to take oath of office ... 100
to make annual reports as to police and fire departments ... 109, 199
to act as a board of health ... 110
power to abate nuisances ... 110
other sanitary powers ... 110—112, 201, 202, 250—260
as to job printing ... 190
fire-arms and military equipments, under control of ... 196
control of fire department ... 197
to appoint health officer ... 201, 202
POLICE FORCE, organization of ... 98, 195
appointments to, how made ... 97, 98, 99
who ineligible ... 99, 195

POLICE—POLICE FORCE—*continued.*
removals to be made only for cause........ 99, 195, 196
charges, how to be made and tried........ 100, 101
members removed, not to be re-appointed........ 104
not to retain attorney for persons arrested........ 100, 195
members to receive no fees or presents........ 99, 100, 194, 195
pay of officers and members........ 99, 185, 186, 194
appointment of superintendent and other officers........ 97, 98, 99
members not to become or furnish bail for persons arrested........ 107
members not to resign without giving previous notice........ 104
not to conduct prosecutions in police court........ 116
powers of policemen........ 102, 112, 306—308, 312, 357—359
may serve civil process issued by police court........ 102
superintendent to act as chief........ 108
superintendent to make reports quarterly........ 109
exempted from military and jury duty, and arrest on civil process........ 110
arrests made by, to be reported........ 106
persons arrested may give bail........ 107
detention and examination of arrested persons........ 106
provisions respecting seizure and custody of stolen property........ 104, 105, 106, 107
police life and health insurance fund........ 101
penalty for refusing to arrest criminals........ 110
penalty for assaulting policemen when on duty........ 110
penalty for fraudulently pretending to be a policeman........ 110, 308
POLICE EXPENSES, made a city charge........ 107
power to levy taxes for........ 79, 107, 186, 197
warrants on police fund, how drawn........ 108
power to appoint police officers for county and town authorities........ 107
ordinance concerning police department........ 306—308
MAYOR'S POLICE........ 308

POLICE COURT........ 113—118, 191
justices of, how designated........ 118, 161, 191
jurisdiction of........ 113
sessions to be held daily........ 113
powers and duties of justices........ 113
execution, when and how issued........ 113, 114
appeals and change of venue........ 114, 191
actions in, by city, how brought........ 114
sessions of, where to be held........ 106, 113, 118, 191
penalties imposed by, power to remit........ 114
clerk of, provisions concerning........ 115, 118, 191
power to appoint clerk *pro tem.*........ 115
witness fees, when to be taxed........ 116
witness fees to be paid into city treasury........ 116
witnesses for city, how paid........ 116
police officers not to conduct prosecutions........ 116
power to appoint prosecuting attorney........ 117
his salary and duties........ 117, 118

POLICE COURT CLERK, election of........ 6, 115
term of office........ 6, 115
oath and bond of........ 115
salary of........ 115
powers and duties of........ 115, 116, 117
may be removed for neglect of duty........ 117
power to appoint, *pro tem.*, by police court........ 115
deputies........ 115, 191

POLICE FUND, how raised and disbursed........ 79, 107, 108, 186, 197

POLICE JUSTICES, how designated........ 118, 161, 191
term of office........ 118
vacancies, how filled........ 118, 161
powers and duties of........ 113, 116
salary of........ 114, 115
to relinquish fees to city........ 115

POLLS, at elections, when to be opened and closed........ 12

POLL TAX, abolished........ 81

PORK, inspection of, power to regulate........ 28

PORTERS, power to license and regulate........ 24
ordinance concerning........ 309—312

POST OFFICE BOXES, on lamp posts........ 274, 275

POUNDS, power to establish, (see *Dogs*)........ 28
ordinances concerning........ 312—316, 370, 371

PRIVIES, power to cleanse and remove........ 25
power to regulate........ 81, 152
regulations concerning........ 201, 293, 323, 324, 331, 332

PROPERTY OF CITY, penalty for injury to........ 77, 148, 156, 157, 245, 247, 332

PROSTITUTES, power to restrain and punish........ 27
ordinance concerning........ 282

PROVISIONS, inspection of, power to regulate........ 28

PUBLICATION OF ORDINANCES, when and how to be made.... 20, 158, 160
in German language.... 20, 200

PUBLIC BUILDINGS, power to erect.... 26
superintendence of.... 52
repairs on, how paid.... 76
penalty for willful injury to.... 77

PUBLIC CONVEYANCES, sanitary regulations as to.... 255—260

PUBLIC GROUNDS, encumbering of, power to prevent.... 26
superintendence of.... 52
power to purchase and lay out.... 60
power to improve.... 60
expense of, how paid.... 76
penalty for willful injury to.... 77
east of Michigan avenue, special provisions concerning.... 77, 78
ordinance concerning.... 298, 299

PUBLIC IMPROVEMENTS.... 59—79
expenditures for, from general fund, limited.... 44, 45
power to borrow money for, in case of accidents.... 45
superintendence of.... 52
to be let by contract.... 54, 55
contracts for, when payable by special assessment.... 55
power to complete without contract in certain cases.... 55, 56
power to make, and assess expenses therefor.... 60
may be made before assessment.... 179
applications for, to be made or referred to board of public works.... 60, 61
when vote of common council must be by ayes and noes.... 62
when three-fourths vote required.... 62
proceedings for condemnation of real estate.... 62—68
improvement of streets.... 69, 70, 177, 178
construction and repair of sidewalks and drains.... 71—73, 177, 178
expense of river improvement may be defrayed by tax.... 76
river improvement, when payable from general fund.... 76
river improvement, when payable by assessment.... 60, 69
river or harbor improvement made without contract.... 180

PUBLIC SQUARES, power to lay out.... 60
power to improve.... 60
expense of, how paid.... 76
penalty for willful injury to.... 77
ordinance concerning.... 298, 299

PUBLIC WORKS. (For former laws, see *Appendix*.)
BOARD OF, of whom composed.... 7, 14, 49, 182, 196
mayor no longer member of.... 196
election of commissioners.... 7, 8, 160, 161
their term of office.... 7, 8
qualifications of commissioners.... 8
vacancies, how filled.... 8
removal of commissioners.... 8, 9, 56, 57
commissioners' salary.... 49, 182
bond of commissioners.... 49, 50
oath of commissioners.... 58
to appoint president and treasurer.... 50
to appoint secretary.... 50
to appoint a city engineer.... 50
power to license land surveyors.... 50, 51
to approve plats of subdivisions.... 51
power to employ assistants.... 51, 52
office expenses, how paid.... 52
quorum of.... 52
to keep record of proceedings.... 52
to preserve copies of plans and contracts.... 52
to make annual reports.... 52, 147, 156
power to administer oaths.... 52
general powers and duties of.... 33, 52, 53
to make special assessments.... 53, 54
contracts by, how to be made.... 54, 55
may grant estimates to contractors, as work progresses.... 55
power to employ workmen to complete improvements.... 55, 56
purchase of materials, how made.... 56
advertisement for bids dispensed with in certain cases.... 56
contracts and bonds to be in name of city.... 56
not to be interested in contracts.... 56
to have exclusive charge of water and sewerage works.... 57, 133, 149
to pay over weekly all public moneys to treasurer.... 57
to carry out contracts of water and sewerage commissioners.... 57
to furnish annual estimates of sums required for repairs and improvements.... 57
president to certify to all bills contracted.... 57, 58
president to countersign all treasury warrants for public work.... 58
not to profit from deposit of public funds.... 58
not to use public moneys.... 58
provisions concerning custody of public moneys.... 58

PUBLIC WORKS—*continued.*
embezzlement by, defined and punished ... 58, 59
liable on official bonds for loss of public moneys ... 59
to keep accounts of receipts and expenditures ... 59
accounts of, subject to inspection ... 59
to receive and report on all applications for public improvements ... 60, 61
power to recommend improvements ... 61
assessments by, for condemnation of real estate ... 62—68
to record condemnation proceedings ... 68
to pay over damages for land condemned ... 67
to publish notice of readiness to pay ... 68
assessments by, for dredging river ... 69
assessments by, for improving streets ... 69, 70, 177, 178
assessments by, for sidewalks and drains ... 71, 72, 177, 178
assessments by, for lamp posts ... 73, 178, 179
assessments by, for removal of nuisances ... 73, 74, 179
to make new assessment, when first annulled or insufficient ... 66, 70, 75, 76
not to serve as assessment commissioners when interested ... 76
duties of, in relation to water works ... 137—148
duties of, in relation to sewerage works ... 148—157
may make improvement before assessment ... 179
may improve river and harbor without contract ... 180
provisions for cleansing the river ... 180—184, 206—208
powers as to job printing ... 190
to regulate ... 28

QUALIFICATIONS, of city officers ... 12
of voters ... 13
of assessors ... 13
of police commissioners ... 9
of commissioners of public works ... 8, 194
of aldermen ... 8
of police officers ... 6
QUARANTINE, power to make laws of ... 98, 99, 195, 196
power to remove vessels to ... 27
ordinance concerning ... 111, 112
... 255—260
QUORUM, of common council ... 22
of board of public works ... 52
of board of police ... 97
of board of guardians ... 130

RAILROAD CARS, sanitary regulations as to ... 255—260
encumbering streets with ... 316, 317, 319, 345, 346
RAILROADS, location of tracks, power to direct ... 29
power to require building of bridges at crossings ... 29
power to regulate running of horse-railway cars ... 29
power to regulate laying of horse-railway tracks ... 29
to derive no additional rights from revised charter ... 162
provision concerning use of tracks in streets by different companies ... 162, 163
general ordinance concerning ... 816—820
speed, lights, whistle, bell, regulations concerning ... 816, 817
obstructing streets, with cars, buildings or materials ... 816, 817, 819
sign boards, "*Stop Speed*," "*Ring the Bell*," ... 817, 818
cylinder cocks not to be open to permit escape of steam ... 818
engineers and conductors to be furnished copy of ordinance ... 818
names of engineers and conductors to be furnished to officers of city, when, etc. ... 818
flagmen, where stationed, and duties ... 818, 819
penalties for violating ordinance ... 819
informers, reward to ... 819, 820
special ordinances concerning ... 449—512
Chicago, Alton and St. Louis railroad company ... 497—499
Chicago and Milwaukee railroad company ... 472, 473, 480—488
Chicago and Mississippi railroad company ... 465, 466
Chicago and Northwestern railway company ... 480—486, 488—491
Chicago and Rock Island railroad company ... 450—458, 466, 467, 480, 487, 488
Chicago, Burlington and Quincy railroad company ... 495—497, 506—509
Chicago, St. Charles and Mississippi air-line railroad company ... 460—463
Chicago, St. Paul and Fond du Lac railroad company ... 473—476
Fort Wayne and Chicago railroad company ... 463—465, 497—499
Galena and Chicago Union railroad company ... 449, 450, 491, 499—503
Illinois and Wisconsin railroad company ... 459, 460
Illinois Central railroad company ... 454—459, 467, 468, 493, 494
Joliet and Chicago railroad company ... 469—471, 492, 493
Michigan Southern and Northern Indiana railroad company ... 466, 467, 480, 487, 488
Pittsburgh, Fort Wayne and Chicago railway company, 468, 469, 473—480, 487, 488, 489, 492—495, 504, 505, 509—512
South Branch canal company ... 471, 472
protection of city front against lake, by Illinois Central railroad company, 454—459, 467, 468

RAILROADS—*continued.*
regulations concerning bridge to be erected by said company........ 493, 494
connecting blocks 87 and 88 in school section with railroads........ 480, 487, 488
connecting warehouse of L. Newberry & Co. with railroad........ 491
connecting elevator of Steele & Taylor with railroads........ 497—499
contract with Galena and Chicago Union railroad company as to State street bridge, etc........ 499—508
vacation of part of Adams street, and construction of tunnel at Washington street 509—512

RAILWAY COMPANY, how assessed for improvements........ 69, 70, 178

RECEIPTS AND EXPENDITURES. (See *Expenditures.*)
annual statement of, to be published........ 37, 38
annual estimate of, to be furnished by comptroller........ 38
monthly statements of, to be published........ 38, 39
treasurer to make report of, annually........ 40
accounts of, to be kept by board of public works........ 59

RECONSIDERATION, at special meetings of common council, power limited........ 23

RECORDER, compensation of........ 21
power to sentence criminals to city bridewell........ 159

RECORDER'S COURT, acts concerning........ 512—518

REDEMPTION, from tax and assessment sales........ 92, 95, 96

REFORM SCHOOL. (For former laws, see *Appendix*)........ 129—137
objects of........ 130, 135
power to purchase lands and erect buildings........ 130
government of, in whom vested........ 130
superintendent of, how appointed........ 130
duties of superintendent........ 131, 132
bond of superintendent........ 131
power to remove superintendent........ 132
commissioner of, how appointed........ 132
powers and duties of commissioner........ 132, 133, 134
compensation of commissioner........ 132
commitments to, by justices and police magistrates........ 132, 133, 134
commitments by courts of record........ 134, 135
period of detention........ 135
power to discharge from........ 135
power to bind out inmates........ 135, 136
for girls, power to establish........ 136, 137
power to levy taxes for........ 79, 80, 137
funds, how disbursed........ 137
BOARD OF GUARDIANS, how constituted........ 9, 130
appointment of guardians........ 9, 161
term of office........ 9
to receive no compensation........ 21
not to be interested in contracts........ 21
officers of board........ 130
duties of........ 130
to make annual reports........ 130, 131
to furnish annual estimate of expenses........ 137

REGISTRATION, of births and deaths, power to regulate........ 28

REGRATING, power to prevent and punish........ 24

RELIGIOUS WORSHIP, disturbance of, power to punish........ 32
punishment for disturbing........ 281, 287

REMOVAL FROM OFFICE........ 10, 11, 20, 21
of commissioners of police and public works........ 8, 9, 56, 57
of officers of treasury department........ 35, 37, 40, 42
of police court clerk........ 117
of police officers........ 98, 99, 100, 101, 195, 196
of school agent........ 198

RENDERING ESTABLISHMENTS, power to prohibit, license and regulate........ 25, 26
regulations concerning, (see *Nuisances*)........ 201—205, 290—298

REPORTS. (See *Annual Reports.*)
of committees in common council, when to be laid over and published........ 23
may be required by common council from city officers........ 28
of receipts and expenditures, to be made monthly by comptroller........ 38, 39
collector to make, weekly........ 41
to be made weekly by board of public works to treasurer........ 57
by school agent........ 127, 188, 198

RESERVOIRS, public, power to regulate........ 26
power to construct........ 188

RESOLUTIONS, to raise or appropriate money, how passed........ 23

RIOT, power to prevent........ 25
penalty for........ 287

RIVER, power to remove obstructions in, (see *Harbor*, *Nuisances*)........ 24
power to widen and deepen........ 24, 60
extent of city's jurisdiction........ 26

RIVER — *continued.*
improvements, under superintendence of board of public works 52
proceedings for widening .... 60—68
proceedings for deepening........ 60, 61, 69
expense of improving, may be defrayed by general tax........ 76, 80
improvement without contract........ 180
provisions for cleansing........ 180—184, 206—208
ordinance concerning........ 518, 519

RUNNERS, power to license and regulate 28
ordinance concerning........ 309—312

SALARIES, of mayor........ 14
of commissioners of public works........ 49, 182
of police officers........ 99, 185, 186, 194
of other officers, to be established by common council........ 20, 21
when payable........ 21, 194
when to be established........ 187
of fire department........ 199

SALE BY SAMPLE, ordinance concerning........ 320

SALES, for taxes and assessments, how conducted........ 91, 92
when to be made........ 94, 95
certificates of, assignable........ 93
redemption from 92, 95, 96
record of, to be kept by comptroller........ 92
erroneous, to be canceled 93

SALT, inspection of, power to regulate........ 28

SCAVENGERS, ordinance concerning........ 321—324

SCHOOL AGENT, how appointed........ 10, 192, 193
term of office........ 10, 192
to give bond........ 19, 20, 123, 193
powers of........ 123
compensation of........ 123, 193
to report quarterly to common council........ 127
to report monthly to board of education........ 188
to report when required........ 193

SCHOOL DISTRICTS, power to create........ 123
of South Chicago, abolished 124, 125, 162
boundaries of........ 324—326

SCHOOL FUND, management of........ 122, 123
principal not to be impaired........ 122
interest to be used only to pay teachers........ 122
to be kept loaned........ 123
mode of investment........ 123
when new securities may be required........ 124
debts due to, from deceased persons, to be paid first........ 124
loans overdue to bear 15 per cent. interest........ 124
judgments to bear 12 per cent. interest 124
power to purchase land for school fund on execution sales........ 124
judicial costs not to be charged to........ 124

SCHOOL LANDS, improvements on, subject to taxation........ 81
management of........ 122

SCHOOLS. (For former laws, see *Appendix*)........ 121—129
power to establish and support........ 123
power to create districts 123
to be established in each district. 125, 192
who may attend........ 125, 126, 192
children from adjoining towns, when........ 192
for negroes and mulattoes........ 125
disturbance of, power to punish........ 32
punishment for disturbing........ 281
power to levy taxes for........ 79, 188
teachers not to be interested in purchases, or work done for........ 21
management of school lands and fund........ 121—124
school-tax fund........ 124
ordinance concerning .... 324—329
BOARD OF EDUCATION, how constituted........ 9, 191, 192
members to receive no compensation........ 21
not to be interested in sale of school books........ 129
not to receive gifts, etc. 129
not to be agents of booksellers........ 129
powers as to job printing........ 190
employees not to be interested in purchases, or work done for schools........ 21
powers and duties of........ 125—128, 192
teachers to report monthly........ 126
officers of........ 127
to keep a record of proceedings........ 127
powers to be exercised only at formal meetings........ 127, 189

SCHOOLS—*continued.*
proceedings to be published..... 127
to make annual reports..... 127, 128
power to appoint superintendent..... 128
duties of superintendent..... 128, 129
superintendent not to be interested for bookseller, etc..... 129

SCHOOL-TAX FUND, how raised..... 79, 188
how used and disbursed..... 124
bills chargeable to..... 126, 328, 329

SEAL, ordinance concerning..... 329

SEALERS OF WEIGHTS AND MEASURES. (See *Weights and Measures.*)
power to appoint..... 5, 29
how appointed,..... 10, 191

SECOND-HAND GOODS, dealers in, power to tax, license and regulate..... 24, 25
ordinance concerning..... 272—274

SEWERAGE FUND, office expenses chargeable to..... 52
to be raised by annual tax..... 80, 155
to be used only for sewerage purposes..... 153, 156
power to invest surplus..... 154

SEWERAGE WORKS. (For former laws, see *Appendix*)..... 148—157
superintendence of..... 57, 149
contracts for, to specify they are for said works..... 57
moneys received for permits, to be paid over weekly to treasurer..... 57
contracts for, to be paid from sewerage fund..... 57
contracts made by sewerage commissioners to be performed by board of public works.. 57
power to levy taxes for..... 80, 155
power to make surveys..... 149
power to purchase books and charts..... 149
power to lay sewers..... 149, 150
power to construct canals..... 150
power to purchase real estate..... 150
power to enter upon lands and agree on compensation..... 150
power to condemn lands for..... 150, 151
power to change grade of streets..... 151
connections with private drains..... 151, 152
power to construct private drains..... 151, 152
power to regulate construction and drainage of privies and cess-pools..... 152
power to issue bonds..... 152, 153, 154
provisions concerning issue and sale of bonds..... 153, 154
principal and interest to be paid by comptroller..... 154
power to purchase outstanding bonds..... 154
board of public works to report annually amount required for sewerage purposes..... 155
treasurer to report monthly to board of public works amount of sewerage tax collected 155
facts to be stated in annual report..... 156
power to borrow money to pay interest on sewerage bonds..... 156
sewerage accounts to be kept separately..... 156
penalty for willful injury to sewers..... 156, 157, 332
power to make rules and regulations concerning sewers..... 157
sinking fund provisions..... 155, 157

SEWERS AND DRAINS, ordinance concerning..... 330—332

SHEEP, power to restrain..... 27

SHOOTING GALLERY, penalty for keeping..... 288

SHOWS, power to license and regulate..... 25
ordinance concerning..... 332—334

SIDEWALKS, encumbering of, power to prevent..... 26
power to compel removal of snow and ice from..... 27
power to control and regulate..... 30
superintendence of..... 52
permits for raising..... 58
construction of vaults under, how regulated..... 58
power to construct and repair..... 60
mode of procedure..... 60, 61, 62, 71, 72, 177, 178
owners of adjacent property responsible for safe condition of..... 72, 73
penalty for willful injury to..... 77
penalty for leaving, unsafe..... 287, 339
ordinance concerning..... 334—340, 371
obstructing and injuring, penalties for..... 339, 346—348

SINKING FUND, for general bonded debt..... 80, 81
for sewerage debt..... 155, 156, 157

SINKS, power to regulate..... 31
ordinance concerning..... 293, 294

SLAUGHTER HOUSES, power to direct location of, (see *Nuisances*)..... 25, 26
power to prohibit, license and regulate..... 25, 26
ordinance concerning..... 519—522

SLAUGHTERING, all to be done on premises of John Reid & Co..... 520, 521
rules and regulations concerning..... 520—522

SLIPS, power to fill up and regulate 31
power to construct 60
expense of, how paid 76

SNOW AND ICE, on sidewalks, power to compel removal of 27
ordinance concerning 339

SOAP FACTORIES, power to abate, (see *Nuisances*) 25

SPIRITUOUS LIQUORS, sale of, power to regulate and license, (see *Liquors*) 24
license for sale of .... 25, 190, 340—342
no concerts or exhibitions in or through place licensed 334

STABLES, power to regulate, (see *Nuisances*) 25
lights in, power to regulate 26
regulations concerning 227

STATE'S ATTORNEY, city to pay fees of, in recorder's court 167, 522, 523

STEAMING LARD AND TALLOW, power to prohibit, license, etc., (see *Nuisances*) 25, 26

STONES, throwing, how punished 286, 288

STREETS, encumbering, power to prevent 26, 30
obstructions in, power to remove 27
power to control and regulate 27, 30
to establish and alter grades of 30
superintendence of 52
use of, by whom regulated 58
removal of buildings through 58
construction of vaults under 58
use of, for building materials 58
laying of gas and water pipes in 58, 330
power to lay out and widen 30, 60
power to vacate 30, 60, 167, 168, 193, 206
power to improve 60
proceedings to open and widen .... 60—68
proceedings to improve 60, 61, 62, 69, 70, 177, 178
cleaning of, expense, how paid 76
ordinary repairs, expense, how paid 76
improvements at intersections of, how paid for 76, 178
penalty for willful injury to 77
obstructions of, by railroads 316, 317, 319
ordinance concerning .... 342—344
names and numbers 343, 348
obstructions and encroachments .... 344—348
injuring and repairing 347, 348

STREET TAX, abolished 81
power to levy 185

SUITS, by city, to recover penalties, how brought 114
against city only in court of record 159

SUPERINTENDENT OF PUBLIC SCHOOLS, how appointed 128
salary of 128
duties of 128, 129
not to be interested for, or receive gifts from, bookseller, etc 129

SUPERVISORS, election of, one from each ward 161, 169
board of, to fill vacancy in board of police 196
may require police in county, and levy taxes therefor 197

SUPREME COURT, decisions of. (See *Appendix*.)

SURETY, city officers not to be, on obligations made to city 11

SURVEYORS OF LAND, power to license 50
oath of 50
bond of 50, 51
license to be recorded 51
powers of 51
revocation of license 51

SWINE, power to restrain, (see *Pounds*) 27
penalty for keeping offensively 290
for suffering to be at large 294, 313

TALLOW, steaming and rendering of, power to prohibit, license, etc., (see *Nuisances*) 25, 26

TALLOW CHANDLER SHOPS, power to abate, (see *Nuisances*) 25

TANNERIES, power to abate, (see *Nuisances*) 25
power to license and regulate 25, 26

TAVERNS, power to license and regulate, (see *Spirituous Liquors*) 24

TAXATION, powers of .... 45, 46, 76, 79—88, 185, 186, 188, 197
of foreign insurance companies .... 81—83
property subject to, how appraised 84, 85
tax lists, when and how made 84, 85

TAXES, power to levy (see *Taxation*) 79, 80, 81, 185, 186, 188, 197
improvements on school and canal lands and wharfing privileges subject to 81
collection of .... 83—96

TAXES—*continued.*
when and how levied ... 85
warrants for, when and how issued ... 85
lien of, on personal property ... 87
lien of, on real estate ... 87
damages for non-payment ... 87, 88
application for judgment for ... 88
proceedings thereon ... 89, 90
form of judgment ... 90
process of sale ... 90
power to sell real estate for ... 90
notice of sale ... 90, 91
abbreviations may be used in describing real estate ... 91
sales for, when to be made ... 94, 95
sale for, how conducted ... 91, 92
certificates of purchase ... 91, 92, 93
redemption from sales ... 92, 95, 96
deeds for, when and how issued ... 92, 95, 96
effect of tax deeds in evidence ... 93, 94
formal defects in proceedings not to invalidate levy ... 89, 95
penalty for selling land on which taxes have been paid ... 42
may be levied in county for police ... 107
in certain towns ... 162, 197

TEAMS, power to compel owners to fasten ... 26
how to cross bridges ... 216, 217
penalty for not fastening ... 286, 287
injuring or obstructing sidewalks and streets ... 339, 348
to give way to horse cars ... 262, 263, 381

TELEGRAPHS, ordinances concerning ... 523—526

THEATRES, power to license and regulate, (see *Shows*) ... 25

TOWNS, several offices abolished in North, South and West Chicago ... 161, 162
taxes in said towns ... 162, 197

TREASURER, election of ... 6
term of office ... 6
bond of ... 41
duties of ... 39, 41
accounts of, subject to inspection ... 39
warrants on, how drawn ... 36, 37, 39, 58, 108, 124, 137, 199
to keep separate accounts with each fund and appropriation ... 39
duties of, in relation to custody of city funds ... 40, 43
not to use city moneys ... 40, 43, 44
may be removed for misconduct ... 40
to make annual reports ... 40
to keep a register of all warrants paid ... 40
to hold special assessment money as special funds ... 40, 41
power to appoint clerks ... 43
embezzlement by, how punished ... 43, 44, 148
to hold moneys received for water works as a special fund ... 147, 148
to report monthly to board of public works amount of sewerage tax collected ... 155
to hold sewerage moneys as a special fund ... 156

TREASURY DEPARTMENT ... 33—48
offices of ... 34
clerks in, how appointed ... 43
officers of, prohibited from using city funds ... 43, 44
all reports and accounts made by officers of, to be verified by oath ... 44
controversies between officers of, in adjustment of accounts, how determined ... 48

TREES, in streets and public grounds, powers concerning ... 30
ordinance concerning ... 349

TUNNELS, powers as to ... 29, 184, 185
ordinances concerning ... 509—512, 526—528

UNWHOLESOME BUSINESS, power to restrain, (see *Nuisances*) ... 25, 26
UNWHOLESOME HOUSES AND PLACES, power to cleanse and abate, (see *Nuisances*) 25, 26
UNWHOLESOME SUBSTANCES, power to remove and destroy, (see *Nuisances*) ... 31

VACANCIES, to be filled for unexpired term only ... 10
in office of mayor, how filled ... 11
in office of alderman, how filled ... 7
in boards of police and public works, how filled ... 8, 196
in other offices, how filled ... 11, 161

VAGRANTS, power to restrain ... 27
power to imprison ... 81, 82
who shall be deemed ... 81, 82, 281
punishment of ... 281

VAULTS, under streets and sidewalks, power to regulate ... 58
penalty for leaving, unsafe ... 287

VEGETABLES, sale of, power to restrain, license and regulate ... 26
VEHICLES. (See *Bridges*, *Fire Department*, *Misdemeanors*, *Police Department*, *Teams*.)
ordinance concerning ...
to give way to horse cars ... 850—859
VETO, when mayor may exercise ... 262, 263, 381
VOTERS, qualifications of ... 15
oath required from, when challenged ... 13
exempted from arrest on civil process on election day ... 13
penalty for illegal voting ... 13
penalty for assaulting voters at the polls ... 13
VOTING, how conducted ... 110
illegal, punishable ... 12
13

WARDS, boundaries of, defined ...
to be divided into election districts ... 2—4
how represented in common council ... 5, 6
how represented in board of supervisors ... 6, 7
161, 169
WARRANTS, on treasurer, how drawn ... 36, 37, 39, 58, 108, 124, 187, 199
to be canceled when paid ... 40
register of, to be kept by treasurer ... 40
to be examined annually by finance committee ... 40
for taxes and assessments, how issued ... 85, 86
for taxes and assessments, how collected ... 86—96
for water rents ... 143—146
WATER, waste of, power to prevent ... 28
penalty for wasting ... 360
WATER FUND, office expenses chargeable to ... 52
to be used only for water works ... 141, 147, 148
power to invest surplus ... 146, 147
WATER RENTS, how assessed and collected ... 142—146
WATER WORKS. (For former laws, see *Appendix*) ... 137—148
superintendence of ... 57, 138
contracts for, to specify they are for said works ... 57
moneys received for, to be paid over to treasurer weekly ... 57
contracts for, to be paid from water fund ... 57
contracts made by water commissioners, to be performed by board of public works ... 57
power to construct reservoirs and lay pipes ... 138
public hydrants to be provided ... 138
injuring hydrants, penalty ... 360
misusing wrenches of hydrants, penalty ... 360, 361
power to purchase real estate ... 138, 139
power to construct buildings and machinery ... 139
power to purchase books and charts ... 139
power to make surveys ... 139
power to enter upon lands and agree on compensation ... 139
power to condemn lands ... 139, 140
power to construct aqueducts and pumping works ... 140
power to extend inlet pipes into the lake and erect piers ... 140
power to issue bonds ... 140, 141, 142
provisions concerning issue and sale of bonds ... 141, 142
principal and interest to be paid by comptroller ... 142
power to purchase outstanding bonds ... 142, 146, 147
water rents, how assessed and collected ... 142—146
lien of assessments ... 143
record of assessments to be kept ... 143
power to make rules and regulations concerning use of water ... 146
regulations established ... 361, 362
facts to be stated in annual report ... 147
board of public works to report amount required to be raised by tax ... 147
power to levy taxes for ... 80, 147
power to borrow money to pay interest on water-loan bonds ... 147
accounts for said works to be kept separately ... 147, 148
moneys received for, to be used for no other purpose ... 148
penalty for willful injury to property of ... 148, 360
obstructing access to ... 362, 363
ordinance concerning ... 360—363
WEIGHERS, power to appoint, (see *Hay*) ... 5, 28
fees of, power to prescribe ... 28
how appointed ... 10, 191
WEIGHTS AND MEASURES, power to require sealing of ... 29
ordinances concerning ... 248, 363—366
WELLS, public, power to regulate ...
28
WHARFING PRIVILEGES, ends of streets may be leased as ... 23, 24
improvements on, subject to taxation ... 81
certain acts concerning, continued in force ... 160
said acts in full ... 169—176
ordinance concerning ... 528, 529

WHARFAGE, regulation concerning ... 174
WHARVES, encumbering of, power to prevent ... 26
superintendence of ... 52
power to make, at ends of streets ... 60
expense of making and repairing, how paid ... 76
authority to build ... 174, 175
penalty for incumbering ... 344, 345
penalty for building, without authority ... 528, 529
WHISKY, inspection of, power to regulate, (see *Liquors*) ... 28
WITNESSES, citizens declared competent, in city actions ... 159
fees of, in police court ... 116
WOOD, storing of, within fire limits, power to regulate ... 28
measuring of, power to regulate ... 28
sale of, power to regulate ... 28
ordinance concerning ... 367—370
penalty for fraud in sale of ... 366, 369
WOODEN BUILDINGS, power to prohibit within fire limits ... 118
permits for, within fire limits ... 53
ordinance concerning ... 224—227
YARDS, power to regulate and fill up ... 31
YEAS AND NAYS, to be taken on all orders to raise, borrow or appropriate money ... 23
when required on orders for public improvements ... 62
when required in board of education ... 189

www.ingramcontent.com/pod-product-compliance
Lightning Source LLC
LaVergne TN
LVHW021047110826
845150LV00001B/5

* 9 7 8 1 4 2 5 5 6 8 5 4 2 *